Java™ Programming with Microsoft® Visual J++® 6.0: Comprehensive

Java™ Programming with Microsoft® Visual J++® 6.0: Comprehensive

Joyce Farrell
McHenry County College

Don Gosselin

ONE MAIN STREET, CAMBRIDGE, MA 02142

an International Thomson Publishing company I(T)P®

Cambridge • Albany • Bonn • Boston • Cincinnati • London • Madrid • Melbourne • Mexico City
New York • Paris • San Francisco • Singapore • Tokyo • Toronto • Washington

Java™ Programming with Microsoft® Visual J++® 6.0: Comprehensive is published by Course Technology.

Associate Publisher	Kristen Duerr
Product Manager	Cheryl Ouellette
Associate Product Manager	Margarita Donovan
Developmental Editor	Marilyn Freedman
Production Editor	Melissa Panagos
Text Designer	Doug Goodman
Cover Designer	Efrat Reis

© 1999 by Course Technology— I(T)P®

For more information contact:

Course Technology, Inc.
One Main Street
Cambridge, MA 02142

International Thomson Editores
Seneca, 53
Colonia Polanco
11560 Mexico D.F. Mexico

ITP Europe
Berkshire House 168-173
High Holborn
London WCIV 7AA
England

ITP GmbH
Königswinterer Strasse 418
53227 Bonn
Germany

Nelson ITP, Australia
102 Dodds Street
South Melbourne, 3205
Victoria, Australia

ITP Asia
60 Albert Street, #15-01
Albert Complex
Singapore 189969

ITP Nelson Canada
1120 Birchmount Road
Scarborough, Ontario
Canada M1K 5G4

ITP Japan
Hirakawacho Kyowa Building, 3F
2-2-1 Hirakawacho
Chiyoda-ku, Tokyo 102
Japan

All rights reserved. This publication is protected by federal copyright law. No part of this publication may be reproduced, stored in a retrieval system, or transmitted in any form or by any means, electronic, mechanical, photocopying, recording, or otherwise, or be used to make derivative work (such as translation or adaptation), without prior permission in writing from Course Technology.

Trademarks
Course Technology and the Open Book logo are registered trademarks and CourseKits is a trademark of Course Technology. Custom Editions is a registered trademark of International Thomson Publishing.

I(T)P® The ITP logo is a registered trademark of International Thomson Publishing.
Microsoft and Windows are registered trademarks of Microsoft Corporation. Java is a trademark of Sun Microsystems.

Some of the product names and company names used in this book have been used for identification purposes only, and may be trademarks or registered trademarks of their respective manufacturers and sellers.

Disclaimer
Course Technology reserves the right to revise this publication and make changes from time to time in its content without notice.

ISBN 0-7600-1174-5

Printed in Canada

3 4 5 6 7 8 9 WC 03 02 01

Preface

Java Programming With Microsoft Visual J++ 6.0: Comprehensive is designed to provide a guide for the beginning programmer to develop applications and applets using the Java programming language and the Microsoft Visual J++ development environment. This textbook assumes that students have no programming language experience.

Organization and Coverage

Java Programming With Microsoft Visual J++ 6.0: Comprehensive introduces students to object-oriented programming concepts along with the Java syntax to implement them. The Microsoft Visual J++ development environment is introduced in Chapter 1. Advanced development environment tools are explained throughout the book. Object-oriented techniques are discussed in Chapter 1 and explored extensively in Chapters 2, 3, and 4, which is earlier than in many other texts. Chapters 5 and 6 teach students the fundamentals of structured logic using decisions, loops, and array manipulation. In Chapter 7, students write Java applets that use GUI components, and in Chapter 8 they gain extensive experience using Java graphics.

Chapters 9 and 10 provide students with a thorough grounding in inheritance concepts, which leads to a deeper understanding of the Abstract Windows Toolkit in Chapter 11. Students understand why the Toolkit components work—and not just *how* they work—so they will be able to use Java components that will be developed in the future.

Chapter 12 teaches students about layout managers and the Java event-handling model. Along with Chapter 13's coverage of exception handling, students learn important object-oriented design concepts that they will need not just for Java programming, but throughout their programming careers.

Chapters 14 and 15 present file handling techniques and multithreading. These topics often are ignored in introductory texts, or presented in too much detail. Here, the beginning student gains a thorough, understandable foundation in these important concepts.

Finally, Chapter 16 covers Windows applications and packaging, which teaches students to use the power of the Visual J++ 6.0 development environment to create Windows applications using Windows Foundation Classes.

Java Programming With Microsoft Visual J++ 6.0: Comprehensive combines text explanation with step-by-step exercises that illustrate the concepts being explained, reinforcing the reader's understanding and retention of the material presented. Java applications are introduced prior to applets, so the reader has a more thorough understanding of the programming process, and testing of a user's programs is simplified.

The reader using *Java Programming With Microsoft Visual J++ 6.0: Comprehensive* builds applications and applets from the bottom up, rather than using pre-written objects, and using features of the Microsoft Visual J++ development environment. This technique facilitates a deeper understanding of the concepts used in object-oriented programming. When readers complete this book, they will know how to create and modify simple Java language applications and applets, and they will have the tools to create more complex examples. Readers will also have a fundamental knowledge of object-oriented programming concepts that will be useful whether they continue to learn more about the Java language or go on to other object-oriented languages, such as C++ and Visual Basic.

Java Programming With Microsoft Visual J++ 6.0: Comprehensive distinguishes itself from other Java language books in the following ways:

- It is written and designed specifically for readers without previous programming experience.
- The code examples are short; one concept is featured in each code example.
- Object-oriented techniques are covered earlier than in many other texts.
- Text explanation is interspersed with step-by-step exercises.
- Java applications are introduced prior to applets, so a reader has a more thorough understanding of the programming process, and testing is simplified.
- Java applications are built from the bottom up; the user gains a clear picture of how complex programs are built.
- Important object-oriented design concepts are introduced at an introductory level.
- The Microsoft Visual J++ development environment and Java programming techniques are presented in easy-to-understand lessons.

After completing this textbook, you will be able to use Microsoft Visual J++ to write applications and applets with the Java programming language. You also will be familiar with the topics covered in the Sun Certified Programmer Examination. After practicing and applying those topics to writing professional business applications, you will be ready to take the certification exam.

Features

Java Programming With Microsoft Visual J++ 6.0: Comprehensive is a superior textbook because it also includes the following features:

- **"Read This Before You Begin" Page** This page is consistent with Course Technology's unequaled commitment to helping instructors introduce technology into the classroom. Technical considerations and assumptions about hardware, software, and default settings are listed in one place to help instructors save time and eliminate unnecessary aggravation.
- **Case Approach** Each chapter addresses programming-related problems that users could reasonably expect to encounter in business. Many of the cases are followed by a demonstration of an application that could be used to solve the problem. Showing users the completed application before they learn how to create it is motivational and instructionally sound. By allowing readers to see the type of application they will create after completing the chapter, this approach motivates readers to learn because they can see how the programming concepts that they are about to learn can be used and, therefore, why the concepts are important.
- **Step-by-Step Methodology** The unique Course Technology methodology keeps readers on track. They always write program code within the context of solving the problems posed in the chapter. The text constantly guides readers and lets them know where they are in the process of solving the problem. The numerous illustrations guide students to create useful, working programs.

- **HELP?** These paragraphs anticipate the problems readers are likely to encounter and help them resolve these problems on their own. This feature facilitates independent learning and frees the instructor to focus on substantive issues rather than on common procedural errors.
- **Tips** These notes provide additional information—for example, an alternative method of performing a procedure, background information on a technique, a commonly-made error to watch out for, or the name of a Web site the reader can visit to gather more information.
- **Summaries** Following each chapter is a Summary that recaps the programming concepts and commands covered in each section.
- **Review Questions** Each chapter concludes with meaningful, conceptual Review Questions that test readers' understanding of what they learned in the chapter.
- **Exercises** Programming Exercises provide users with additional practice of the skills and concepts they learned in the lesson. These exercises increase in difficulty and are designed to allow the student to explore the language and programming environment independently.
- **Debugging Exercises** Each chapter contains four programs that contain the types of errors that readers are likely to make in their own programs. By debugging these files, readers learn to recognize the source of errors and learn how to fix them. These exercises also expose readers to errors that they might never make, but that other programmers do make. The ability to modify existing programs is an important programming skill.

The Visual J++ Programming Environment

This book was written using Microsoft Visual J++ 6.0 Standard Edition installed on a computer running Windows NT 4.0. Visual J++ is also available in a Professional Edition and an Enterprise Edition. While the Professional Edition and Enterprise Edition include more advanced tools than the Standard Edition, all editions of Visual J++ contain the same core functionality.

The Supplements

All of the supplements for this text are found in the Instructor's Resource Kit, which is available on Course Technology's Web site or on a CD-ROM.

- **Instructor's Manual** The Instructor's Manual was quality assurance tested and is available through the Course Technology Faculty Online Companion on the World Wide Web at www.course.com. (Call your customer service representative for the specific URL and your password.) The Instructor's Manual contains the following items:
    - Complete instructions for downloading the Java Developers' Kit from the Sun Web site or installing it from the CD-ROM included with the book.
    - Answers to all of the Review Questions and solutions to all of the Programming Exercises in the book.
    - Teaching notes to help introduce and clarify the material presented in the chapters.
    - Technical notes that include troubleshooting tips.

- **Course Test Manager Version 1.2 Engine and Test Bank** Course Test Manager (CTM) is a cutting-edge Windows-based testing software program, developed exclusively for Course Technology, that helps instructors design and administer examinations and practice tests. This full-featured program allows students to generate practice tests randomly that provide immediate on-screen feedback and detailed study guides for incorrectly answered questions. Instructors can also use Course Test Manager to create printed and online tests over a network. You can create, preview, and administer a test on any or all chapters of this textbook entirely over a local area network. Course Test Manager can grade the tests students take automatically at the computer and can generate statistical information on individual as well as group performance. A CTM test bank has been written to accompany this textbook and is included on the CD-ROM. The test bank includes multiple-choice, true/false, short answer, and essay questions.
- **Solutions Files** Solutions Files contain a possible solution to every program students are asked to create or modify in the chapters and cases. (Due to the nature of programming, students' solutions might differ from these solutions and still be correct.)
- **Student Files** Student Files, containing all of the data that students will use for the chapters and exercises in this textbook, are provided through Course Technology's Online Companion, on the Instructor's Resource Kit CD-ROM, and on the Student Resource Kit CD-ROM. A Help file includes technical tips for lab management. See the inside covers of this textbook and the "Read This Before You Begin" page before Chapter 1 for more information on Student Files.

Acknowledgments

Thanks to my wonderful wife, Kathy, for her eternal patience; to my cat, Maybelline, for keeping me company; to my dog, Noah, for taking me for walks on those rare occasions when I unchain myself from the computer; and to all of my friends and family for understanding when I disappear for days on end. I would also like to thank Nan Fritz and her staff at nSight.; Kristen Duerr, Managing Editor; Cheryl Ouellette, Product Manager; Margarita Donovan, Associate Product Manager; Melissa Panagos, Production Editor; and Alex White and Nicole Ashton, Quality Assurance testers.

Many thanks to the reviewers for their invaluable comments and suggestions, including Chic Day, University of Tennessee, Chattanooga; Dennis Corry, Holy Family College; John Humphrey, Asheville Buncombe Technical CC; and Morgan Spriggs.

As always, thanks to my friend and colleague, George T. Lynch, for getting me started. Finally, a very special thanks to Marilyn Freedman, Developmental Editor, for her outstanding work and for making me a better writer.

Don Gosselin

Thanks to my husband Geoff, whose constant support makes everything I do possible, and whose presence makes it all fun. Thanks to my daughters, Andrea and Audrey, who are managing to age me as well as keep me young at the same time.

Finally, I would like to dedicate this book to my wonderful mother- and father-in-law, Linda and Geoff Farrell.

Joyce Farrell

Contents

PREFACE *v*

READ THIS BEFORE YOU BEGIN *xxiii*

chapter 1
PROGRAMMING, JAVA, AND MICROSOFT VISUAL J++ *1*

Section A: An Overview of Programming and Java *3*

   Programming *3*

   Object-Oriented Programming *4*

   The Java Programming Language *7*

   Microsoft Visual J++ *8*

   Summary *9*

   Questions *10*

   Exercises *13*

Section B: The Microsoft Visual J++ Development Environment *14*

   Creating a New Project in Visual J++ *14*

   Visual J++ IDE *17*

      Managing Windows *17*

      The Main Window *20*

      Project Explorer *23*

      Designers *25*

      The Toolbox *26*

      The Task List *27*

      The Properties Window *30*

   Visual J++ Help *33*

Adding Files to a Project 37

Adding Projects to a Solution 38

Renaming Solutions and Projects 40

Saving Solutions, Projects, and Files 41

Closing Solutions, Projects, and Files 42

Opening Existing Solutions and Projects 43

Creating and Opening Individual Files 44

Exiting Visual J++ 46

Summary 47

Questions 49

Exercises 51

chapter 2

A FIRST PROGRAM USING JAVA 53

Section A: Creating a Program 54

Java Programming Structure 54

The Text Editor Window 61

Writing Your First Java Program 65

Adding Comments to a Program 68

Running a Program 70

Modifying a Program 76

Summary 78

Questions 79

Exercises 81

Section B: Using Data 82

Variables and Constants 82

The int Data Type 84

Arithmetic Statements 87

The Boolean Data Type 90

Floating-Point Data Types 91

Numeric Type Conversion 93

The char Data Type 94

Summary 96

Questions 97

Exercises 100

chapter 3
USING METHODS, CLASSES, AND OBJECTS 103

Previewing the SetUpSite Program Using the EventSite Class 104

Section A: Programming Using Methods 105

Creating Methods with No Arguments 105

Methods That Require a Single Argument 112

Methods That Require Multiple Arguments 115

Methods That Return Values 117

Summary 119

Questions 120

Exercises 122

Section B: Using Classes 124

Classes 124

Class Outline 126

Creating a Class 129

Using Instance Methods 131

Declaring Objects 134

Organizing Classes 137

Using Constructors 145

Summary 148

Questions 149

Exercises 152

chapter 4

ADVANCED OBJECT CONCEPTS 155

Section A: Class Features 156

Blocks and Scope 156

Overloading 163

Ambiguity 166

Sending Arguments to Constructors 168

Overloading Contructors 172

Summary 174

Questions 174

Exercises 177

Section B: Using Methods 180

The this Reference 180

Working with Constants 183

Using Automatically Imported, Prewritten Constants and Methods 186

Using Prewritten Imported Methods 190

Object Browser 195

Summary 196

Questions 198

Exercises 200

chapter 5

INPUT, SELECTION, AND REPETITION 203

Previewing the ChooseManager Program Using the Event Class 204

Section A: Input and Decision Making 205

Simple Keyboard Input 205

Drawing Flowcharts 211

Making Decisions with the `if` Structure 212

The `if...else` Structure 215

Compound Statements *217*

Nested `if` and Nested `if...else` *222*

Summary *223*

Questions *223*

Exercises *226*

Section B: Special Operators, the `switch` Statement, and Precedence *229*

AND and OR Operators *229*

The `switch` Statement *234*

The Conditional Operator *237*

The NOT Operator *237*

Precedence *238*

Summary *240*

Questions *240*

Exercises *243*

Section C: Looping and Shortcut Arithmetic *245*

The `while` Loop *245*

Shortcut Arithmetic Operators *251*

The `for` Loop *254*

The `do...while` Loop *256*

Nested Loops *257*

Summary *261*

Questions *262*

Exercises *265*

chapter 6

ARRAYS AND STRINGS *267*

Previewing a Program That Uses Arrays and Strings *268*

Section A: Arrays *269*

Declaring an Array *269*

Initializing an Array *272*

Using Subscripts with an Array 273

Declaring an Array of Objects 274

Searching an Array for an Exact Match 278

Searching an Array for a Range Match 283

Passing Arrays to Methods 284

Using the Array Length 290

Summary 291

Questions 292

Exercises 295

Section B: Strings 297

Declaring Strings 297

Comparing Strings 299

Other String Methods 303

Converting Strings to Numbers 306

Summary 308

Questions 309

Exercises 312

Section C: Advanced Array Techniques 313

Sorting Primitive Array Elements 313

Sorting Arrays of Objects 319

Sorting Strings 322

Using Two-Dimensional Arrays 324

Understanding Multidimensional Arrays 327

Using StringBuffer 328

Summary 330

Questions 331

Exercises 333

chapter 7

APPLETS *335*

    Previewing the PartyPlanner Applet *336*

Section A: HTML and Applet Basics *337*

    Applets and HTML Documents *337*

    Creating an HTML Document with the HTML Editor *342*

    Writing a Simple Applet Using a Label *348*

    Changing a Label's Font *354*

    Adding TextField and Button Components to an Applet *356*

    Event-Driven Programming *359*

        Preparing Your Applet to Accept Event Messages *360*

        Telling Your Applet to Expect Events to Happen *360*

        Telling Your Applet How to Respond to Any Events That Happen *360*

    Adding Output to an Appet *363*

    Summary *365*

    Questions *367*

    Exercises *371*

Section B: The Applet Life Cycle and More Sophisticated Applets *373*

    The Applet Life Cycle *373*

    A Complete Interactive Applet *379*

    Using the setLocation() Method *384*

    Using the setEnabled() Method *387*

    Getting Help *387*

    Summary *388*

    Questions *389*

    Exercises *391*

chapter 8

GRAPHICS 393

Previewing the StopLight Applet 394

Section A: Graphics Basics 395

The paint() and repaint() Methods 395

The drawString() method 398

The setFont() and setColor() Graphics Object Methods 400

Setting the Background Color 404

Creating Your Own Graphics Object 404

Drawing Lines and Rectangles 407

Drawing Ovals 410

Summary 412

Questions 413

Exercises 416

Section B: More Graphics Methods 419

Drawing Arcs 419

Creating Three-Dimensional Rectangles 421

Creating Polygons 421

Copying an Area 423

Using Font Methods 425

Using Simple Animation 434

Summary 439

Questions 439

Exercises 442

chapter 9

INTRODUCTION TO INHERITANCE 443

Previewing an Example of Inheritance 444

Section A: Inheritance 447

The Inheritance Concept 447

Extending Classes 450

Overriding Superclass Methods 456

Summary 460

Questions 460

Exercises 462

Section B: Using Superclasses and Subclasses 464

Working with Superclasses That Have Constructors 464

Using Superclass Constructors That Require Arguments 467

Accessing Superclass Methods 470

Information Hiding 471

Using Methods That You Cannot Override 475

Summary 478

Questions 480

Exercises 482

chapter 10

ADVANCED INHERITANCE CONCEPTS 485

Previewing an Example of Using an Abstract Class 486

Section A: Abstract Classes and Dynamic Method Binding 487

Creating and Using Abstract Classes 487

Using Dynamic Method Binding 497

Creating Arrays of Subclass Objects 499

Summary 502

Questions 503

Exercises 505

Section B: Software Design and Interfaces 507

The Object Class and Its Methods 507

The toString() Method 507

The equals() Method 508

Using Inheritance to Achieve Good Software Design 513

Creating and Using Interfaces 514

Summary 517

Questions 518

Exercises 520

chapter 11

UNDERSTANDING THE ABSTRACT WINDOWS TOOLKIT (AWT) 523

Previewing the Party Planner Applet for Chapter 11 524

Section A: Applying Inheritance Concepts to the Frame Class 526

Using the Frame Class 526

Creating a Frame That Closes 530

Using an Adapter 533

Using Additional Frame Class Methods 536

Using Container Methods 539

Summary 544

Questions 546

Exercises 548

Section B: Using Components 550

Using Component Methods 550

Using a Checkbox 552

Using the CheckboxGroup Class 556

Using the Choice Class 559

Using a List 563

Summary 569

Questions 570

Exercises 572

chapter 12

USING LAYOUT MANAGERS AND THE EVENT MODEL 575

Previewing the Chap12Applet Project 576

Section A: Using Layout Managers 578

Using BorderLayout 578

Using FlowLayout 583

Using GridLayout 585

Using Panels 586

Advanced Layout Managers 591

Summary 591

Questions 593

Exercises 596

Section B: Using Events 597

Understanding Events and Event Handling 597

Using AWTEvent Class Methods 604

Using Event Methods from Higher in the Inheritance Hierarchy 607

Using Mouse Events 610

Summary 613

Questions 614

Exercises 616

chapter 13

EXCEPTION HANDLING AND DEBUGGING 619

Section A: Introduction to Exceptions 621

Understanding Exceptions 621

Trying Code and Catching Exceptions 625

Using the Exception getMessage() Method 627

Throwing and Catching Multiple Exceptions 629

Using the **finally** Block 632

Understanding the Limitations of Traditional Error Handling 634

Summary 636

Questions 637

Exercises 640

Section B: Advanced Exception Concepts and Debugging 641

Specifying the Exceptions a Method Can Throw 641

Handling Exceptions Uniquely with Each `catch` 647

Creating Your Own Exceptions 649

Understanding Debugging 652

Tracing Program Execution with the Visual J++ Debugger 654

Using Step Commands 655

Tracing Program Execution with Breakpoints 657

Tracing Variables and Expressions with Debug Windows 659

Using the Autos Window 660

Using the Locals Window 661

Using the Watch Window 661

Using the Immediate Window 662

Combining Debug Windows 663

Tracing Exceptions through the Call Stack 665

Summary 667

Questions 669

Exercises 671

chapter 14

FILE INPUT AND OUTPUT 673

Previewing a Program That Uses File Data 674

Section A: Introduction to the File Class 675

Using the File Class 675

Data File Organization and Streams 679

Using Streams 681

Writing to a File 685

Reading from a File 686

Summary 687

Questions 688

Exercises 690

Section B: Advanced File Techniques 691

Writing Formatted File Data 691

Reading Formatted File Data 698

Creating Random Access Files 702

Summary 705

Questions 706

Exercises 708

chapter 15

MULTI-THREADING AND ANIMATION 711

Previewing a Program That Displays Animation 712

Section A: Introduction to Multithreading 713

The Concept of Multithreading 713

Using the Thread Class 714

Understanding a Thread's Life Cycle 717

Using the sleep() Method 720

Thread Priority 721

Using the Runnable Interface 723

Summary 727

Questions 728

Exercises 731

Section B: Animation 732

Creating an Animated Figure 732

Reducing Flickering 738

Using Images 742

Garbage Collection 745

Putting Your Animation in a Browser Page 746

Summary 750

Questions 750

Exercises 752

chapter 16

WINDOWS APPLICATIONS AND PACKAGING 753

Previewing the Windows Party Planner Application 754

Section A: J/Direct and Windows Foundation Classes for Java 756

Windows Architecture and the Win32 API 756

Using J/Direct to Access the Win32 API 757

Native Applications versus Architecturally Neutral Applications 761

Windows Foundation Classes for Java 763

Using the Visual J++ Application Wizard 766

WFC Forms 770

WFC Controls 776

Summary 781

Questions 783

Exercises 786

Section B: WFC Events and Packaging 787

WFC Events 787

Creating and Using Packages 791

Using Visual J++ Packaging to Distribute Programs 793

Summary 797

Questions 797

Exercises 799

index 801

Read This Before You Begin

To the Student

Student Disks

To complete the chapters and exercises in this book, you need Student Disks. Your instructor will provide you with Student Disks or ask you to make your own.

If you are asked to make your own Student Disks, you will need three blank, formatted high-density disks. You will need to copy a set of folders from a file server or standalone computer onto your disks. Your instructor will tell you which computer, drive letter, and folders contain the files you need. The following table shows you which folders go on each of your disks, so that you will have enough disk space to complete all the chapters and exercises:

Student Disk	Write this on the disk label	Put these folders on the disk
1	Chapters 1, 2, 3, and 4	Chapter.01, Chapter.02, Chapter.03, Chapter.04
2	Chapters 5 ,6, 7, and 8	Chapter.05, Chapter.06, Chapter.07, Chapter.08
3	Chapters 9 , 10, 11, and 12	Chapter.09, Chapter.10, Chapter.11, Chapter.12
4	Chapters 13, 14, 15, and 16	Chapter.13, Chapter.14, Chapter.15, Chapter.16

When you begin each chapter, make sure you are using the correct Student Disk. See the inside front or inside back cover of this book for more information on Student Disk files, or ask your instructor or technical support person for assistance.

Using Your Own Computer

You can use your own computer to complete the chapters and exercises in this book. To use your own computer, you will need the following:

- Microsoft Visual J++. You can install Microsoft Visual J++ 6.0 from the CD-ROM that came with this book.
- PC with a Pentium-class processor; Pentium 90 or higher processor recommended
- Microsoft Windows 95 or later operating system or Microsoft Windows NT operating system version 4.0 with Service Pack 3 or later (service pack included with Visual J++)
- 24 MB of RAM for Windows 95 or later (48 MB recommended); 32 MB for Windows NT 4.0 (48 MB recommended)

- Microsoft Internet Explorer 4.01 Service Pack 1 (included with Visual J++)
- Hard-disk space required: typical installation: 107 MB; maximum installation: 157 MB
- Additional hard-disk space required for the following products: Internet Explorer: 43 MB typical, 59 MB maximum; MSDN™, Microsoft Developer Network, Library: 57 MB typical, 493 MB maximum; Windows NT 4.0 Option Pack: 20 MB for Windows 95 or later, 200 MB for Windows NT 4.0
- CD-ROM drive
- VGA or higher-resolution monitor; Super VGA recommended
- Microsoft Mouse or compatible pointing device
- Student Disks. You can get the Student Disk files from your instructor or from the CD-ROM that comes with this book. You will not be able to complete all of the chapters and exercises in this book using your own computer until you have Student Disks. The student files may also be obtained electronically through the Internet. See the inside front or back cover of this book for more details.

Visit Our World Wide Web Site

Additional materials designed especially for you might be available for your course on the World Wide Web. Go to **www.course.com**. Search for this book title periodically on the Course Technology Web site for more details.

To the Instructor

To complete all of the exercises and chapters in this book, your students must use a set of student files. These files are included in the Instructor's Resource Kit, as well as on the CD-ROM that accompanies this book. They may also be obtained electronically through the Internet. See the inside front cover of this book for more details. Follow the instructions in the Help file to copy the student files to your server or standalone computer. You can view the Help file using a text editor, such as WordPad or Notepad.

Once the files are copied, you can make Student Disks for the students yourself, or tell students where to find the files so they can make their own Student Disks. Make sure the files get copied correctly onto the Student Disks by following the instructions in the Student Disks section, which will ensure that students have enough disk space to complete all of the chapters and exercises in this book.

Course Technology Student Files

You are granted a license to copy the student files to any computer or computer network used by student who have purchased this book.

CHAPTER 1

Programming, Java, and Microsoft Visual J++

case ▶ As you read your e-mail, a sinking feeling descends on you. There's no denying the message: "Please see me in my office as soon as you are free—Lynn Greenbrier." Lynn Greenbrier is the head of programming for Event Handlers Incorporated, and you have worked for her as an intern for only two weeks. Event Handlers manages the details of private and corporate parties; every client has different needs, and the events are interesting and exciting.

"Did I do something wrong?" you ask as you enter her office. "Are you going to fire me?"

Lynn stands to greet you and says, "Please wipe that worried look off your face! I want to know if you are interested in a new challenge. Our programming department is going to create several new applications in the next few months. We've decided that Microsoft Visual J++ is the way to go. It's object-oriented and perfect for applications on the World Wide Web, which is where we want to expand our marketing efforts."

"I'm not sure what 'object-oriented' means," you say, "but I've always been interested in computers, and I'd love to learn more about programming. What do I need to do to get started?"

SECTION A
objectives

In this section you will learn about
- Programming tasks
- Procedural programming concepts
- Object-oriented programming concepts
- The Java programming language
- Visual J++

An Overview of Programming and Java

Programming

A computer **program** is simply a set of instructions that you write to tell a computer what to do. Computers are constructed from circuitry that consists of small on/off switches, so you *could* write a computer program by writing something along the following lines:

first switch—on
second switch—off
third switch—off
fourth switch—on

Your program could go on and on, for several thousand switches. A program written in this style is written in **machine language,** which is the most basic circuitry-level language. The problems with this approach lie in keeping track of the many switches involved in programming any worthwhile task and in discovering the errant switch or switches if the program does not operate as expected. Additionally, the number and location of switches vary from computer to computer, which means that you would need to customize a machine language program for every type of machine on which you want the program to run.

Fortunately, programming has evolved into an easier task because of the development of high-level programming languages. A **high-level programming language** allows you to use a vocabulary of reasonable terms like "read," "write," or "add" instead of the sequences of on/off switches that perform these tasks. High-level languages also allow you to assign intuitive names to areas of computer memory, like "hoursWorked" or "rateOfPay," rather than having to remember the memory locations (switch numbers) of those values.

Each high-level language has its own **syntax,** or rules of the language. For example, depending on the specific high-level language, you might use the verb "print" or "write" to produce output. All languages have a specific, limited vocabulary and a specific set of rules for using that vocabulary. Programmers use a computer program called a **compiler** (or **interpreter** or **assembler**) to translate their high-level language statements into machine code. The compiler issues an error message each time the programmer uses the programming language incorrectly; then the programmer can correct the error and attempt another translation by compiling the program again. When you are learning a computer programming language such as the Java programming language, C++, or COBOL, you really are learning the vocabulary and syntax rules for that language.

In addition to learning the correct syntax for a particular language, a programmer also must understand computer programming logic. The **logic** behind any program involves executing the various statements and procedures in the correct order to produce the desired results. For example, although you know how to drive a car well, you may not reach your destination if you do not follow the correct route. Similarly, you might be able to use a computer language's syntax correctly, but be unable to execute a logically constructed, workable program. Examples of logical errors include multiplying two values when you meant to divide them, or producing output prior to obtaining the appropriate input.

Object-Oriented Programming

There are two popular approaches to writing computer programs: procedural programming and object-oriented programming.

Procedural programming involves using your knowledge of a programming language to create computer memory locations that can hold values and writing a series of steps or operations that manipulate those values. The computer memory locations are called **variables** because they hold values that might vary. For example, a payroll program written for a company might contain a variable named `rateOfPay`. The memory location referenced by the name `rateOfPay` might contain different values (a different value for every employee of the company) at different times. During the execution of the payroll program, each value stored under the name `rateOfPay` might have many **operations** performed on it—for example, reading the value from an input device, multiplying the value by another variable representing hours worked, and printing the value on paper. For convenience, the individual operations used in a computer program often are grouped into logical units called **procedures**. For example, a series of four or five comparisons and calculations that together determine an individual's federal withholding tax value might be grouped as a procedure named `calculateFederalWithholding`. A procedural program defines the variable memory locations, and then **calls** or **invokes** a series of procedures to input, manipulate, and output the values stored in those locations. A single procedural program often contains hundreds of variables and thousands of procedure calls.

Object-oriented programming is an extension of procedural programming in which you take a slightly different approach to writing computer programs.

Thinking in an object-oriented manner involves envisioning program components as **objects** that are similar to concrete objects in the real world. Then you manipulate the objects to achieve a desired result. Writing object-oriented programs involves both creating objects and creating applications that use those objects.

Objects also are called components.

To illustrate the difference between procedural and object-oriented programs, consider the procedures for copying and moving files in a command-line environment, such as DOS, or a graphical user interface (GUI) system, such as Windows. In DOS, if you want to move several files from a floppy disk to a hard disk, you type a command at the command line. In Windows, you accomplish the same task by dragging the files with a mouse. The difference lies in whether you issue a series of commands, in sequence, to move the three files or you drag icons representing the files from one screen location to another, much as you would physically move paper files from one file cabinet to another in your office. You can move the same three files using either operating system, but Windows allows you to manipulate the files like their real-world paper counterparts. In other words, GUI systems allow you to treat files as objects.

Objects in both the real world and in object-oriented programming are made up of states. **States** describe the characteristics of an object and are also known as **attributes**. For example, a word processing document is an object. States of the word processing document include the font name, the point size, and the date it was last edited. Similarly, some of your automobile's attributes are its make, model, year, and purchase price. Other attributes include whether the automobile is currently running, its gear, its speed, and whether it is dirty. All automobiles possess the same attributes, but not, of course, the same values for those attributes.

A collection of attributes and other characteristics is referred to as a category or **class**. An object derived from an existing class is called an **instance** of the class. Your red Chevrolet with the dent is an instance of the class that is made up of all automobiles, and your Golden Retriever named Goldie is an instance of the class that is made up of all dogs. Particular instances of objects inherit their characteristics from a class. **Inheritance** refers to the ability of an object to take on the characteristics of the class on which it is based. For example, when you create a new word processing document, which is a type of an object, it usually inherits the properties of a template on which it is based; the template is a type of class. The document inherits characteristics of the template such as font size, line spacing, and boilerplate text. Thinking of items as instances of a class allows you to apply your general knowledge of the class to individual members of the class. If your friend purchases an automobile, you know it has a model name, and if your friend gets a dog, you know the dog has a breed. You might not know the exact contents or current state of your friend's automobile or her dog's shots, but you do know what attributes exist for the Automobile and Dog classes. In Windows operating systems, you expect each window to have specific, consistent attributes, such as a title bar and a close button, because each window inherits these attributes as a member of a class of window components.

> By convention, programmers using the Java programming language begin their class names with an uppercase letter. Thus the class that defines the attributes and methods of an automobile would probably be named `Automobile`, and the class for dogs would probably be named `Dog`. However, following this convention is not required to produce a workable program.

Besides having attributes, objects use methods to accomplish tasks. **Methods** are code segments used to perform a task or take some action. Automobiles, for example, can move forward and backward. Each movement, forward or backward, can be considered a method of the automobile. Methods are also used to change attributes. For example, filling an automobile with gas is a method that changes the automobile's fuel level. Minimizing and maximizing windows, changing font sizes, and printing are all examples of methods. To better understand the difference between attributes and methods, consider a word processing program. Boldfaced text in a document is an attribute. The act of *changing* text to boldface is a method.

The states or attributes of object-oriented programming are similar to the variables of procedural programs, and the methods of object-oriented programs are similar to the procedures of procedural programming. The key difference between object-oriented programming and procedural programming lies in the fact that attributes and methods are encapsulated into objects that are then used much like real-world objects. **Encapsulation** is the technique of assembling the attributes, methods, and other elements of an object into a single, self-contained unit. Programmers sometimes refer to encapsulation as using a "black box," or a device that you can use without regard to the internal mechanisms. Well-written encapsulated objects hide the low-level details of how attributes are set and methods are executed.

An encapsulated object's attributes and methods are executed through an interaction or **interface** between the method and the object. For example, if you can fill your automobile with gasoline, it is because you understand the interface between the gas pump nozzle and the automobile's gas tank opening. You don't need to understand how the pump works mechanically or where the gas tank is located inside your automobile. If you can read your speedometer, it does not matter how the display figure is calculated. As a matter of fact, if someone produces a superior, more accurate speed-determining device and inserts it in your automobile, you don't have to know or care how it operates, as long as your interface remains the same. An example of an object and its interface is a Windows word processing program. The word processing program itself is actually a type of object made up of numerous other objects. The program window is called the **user interface**. The items you see in the word processing window, such as the menu, toolbars, and other elements, are interface items used for executing methods. For example, if you click an icon to format text in bold, that icon is an interface element that executes a bold method. You do not need to know how the method works, only how to execute it. The same principles of encapsulation apply to programs that incorporate existing objects.

For example, if a programmer is writing a word processing application and wants to include an existing object that runs a spell check, the programmer simply needs to know the interface command to place in the code that starts the spell check—not how the spell check methods actually work.

The Java Programming Language

The **Java programming language** was developed by Sun Microsystems as an object-oriented language that is used both for general-purpose business programs and interactive World Wide Web-based Internet programs. Two advantages that have made the Java programming language very popular in recent years are its excellent security features and that it is **architecturally neutral**, which means that you can use the Java programming language to write a program that will run on any platform. A **platform** is an operating system and its hardware type. For example, MS-DOS and Windows 95/98/NT for PCs, Mac OS 8 for Macintosh computers, and Solaris for SPARC are considered to be platforms. Before the development of Java, programs were written for a single platform. To use the same program on another platform, you had to port the program to work with the new platform. Redesigning software to work on a different platform is called **porting**. Software vendors usually have to produce multiple versions of the same product (a DOS version, Windows 3.1 version, Windows 95 version, Windows 98 version, Macintosh version, and so on) so all users can use the program. A platform can be compared to an automobile whereas a program can be compared to an engine. All automobiles have engines, but to make an engine from one automobile work in another, it must usually be redesigned. Similarly, to ensure that a Japanese reader can understand a book written in English, you must translate the book's text into Japanese.

After a Java program is written, it is compiled into a format called **bytecode**. The bytecode can then be run on any platform that has a Java programming language interpreter. An **interpreter** is a program that translates code from one format to another. The language interpreter for the Java programming language is called the **Java Virtual Machine (Java VM)**. A Java VM creates a simulated processor on the platform for which it was designed. This simulated processor intercepts Java bytecode and translates it into a format that the platform can understand, eliminating the need to port the original Java code.

> Think of a Java VM as a universal translator. If the Java VM interpreted languages instead of bytecode, it would translate documents from one language to any other language. You could write a letter to anyone in the world in your language. After the Java VM translated the letter, the person to whom you wrote it would be able to read it in his or her native language.

Another advantage of Java is that it is simpler to use than many other object-oriented languages. The Java programming language is modeled after the C++ programming language. Although neither language qualifies as "simple" to read or understand on first exposure, the Java programming language eliminates some of the most difficult features to understand in C++.

For C++ programmers, pointers and multiple inheritance are two of the most difficult language features to master. These are among the troublesome C++ features that the Java programming language eliminates.

Microsoft Visual J++

Microsoft Visual J++ is a Windows-based development environment for creating Java applications. Microsoft Corporation created Visual J++ as a Java development environment based on the Java language specifications leased from Sun Microsystems. The original development environment for creating Java programs is Sun Microsystems' Java Development Kit, or JDK. Implementations of the JDK are available in several platforms including Windows NT/95/98, Solaris, and Macintosh. Since Java is architecturally neutral, programs created in any JDK implementation will run on any of the other platforms.

By leasing the Java programming language to other software vendors such as Microsoft, Sun Microsystems has enabled companies to create new Java development environments that are very similar to existing development environments. Because multiple Java development environments exist, programmers can create Java applications in development environments similar to ones with which they are familiar. For example, Microsoft Visual J++ and Microsoft Visual C++ share a common development environment. Since Visual J++ and Visual C++ share a common development environment and programming language structure, a Visual C++ programmer can learn Java programming much more easily with Visual J++. In comparison, the JDK is primarily a text and command-line development environment. To a programmer who has worked only in a visual development environment such as Visual C++, the transition to programming in a text and command-line environment such as the JDK can be confusing.

Although the interpreter and other components of each JDK implementation are designed for a specific platform, the programming syntax is identical. As a result, programmers can use the same Java programming skills in the exact same way on any platform for which a JDK is available. The core Java language syntax in Visual J++ is essentially the same as in the JDK. However, Visual J++ is not actually a programming language. It is a development environment used for creating programs with the Java language. The "visual" aspect of Visual J++ is used for designing the user interface of a program. The underlying code is still written in the Java language. Thus, programmers who have worked with the JDK can use the same core Java programming skills with Visual J++, and vice versa.

Like Java, Visual J++ is used for general-purpose business programs and interactive World Wide Web-based Internet programs. Unlike the different platform implementations that are available for the JDK, Visual J++ is designed exclusively for use with 32-bit Windows platforms such as Windows 95, Windows 98, and Windows NT. However, it produces the same compiled bytecode created with the JDK, and you can execute the code on any platform for which there is a Java VM.

SUMMARY

- A computer program is a set of instructions. To write a program in machine language, you must keep track of thousands of on/off switches.

- High-level programming languages allow you to use a vocabulary of English-like terms. Each high-level computer language has its own syntax, or rules of the language. A software program called an interpreter (or compiler or assembler) translates high-level language statements into machine code.

- To program correctly, you must learn the syntax of a language and programming logic.

- Procedural programming involves creating computer memory locations to hold values, and then writing a series of steps or operations that manipulate those values.

- Variables represent memory locations that hold values.

- Computer program operations often are grouped into logical units called procedures.

- Object-oriented programming involves creating program components as objects that are similar to concrete objects in the real world. You can then manipulate these objects to achieve a desired result.

- A collection of methods, attributes, and other characteristics is referred to as a category or class.

- An object derived from an existing class is called an instance of the class.

- Particular instances of objects inherit their characteristics from a class. Inheritance refers to the ability of an object to take on the characteristics of the class upon which it is based.

- Objects in both the real world and in object-oriented programming are made up of states. States describe the characteristics of an object and are also known as attributes.

- The states or attributes of object-oriented programming are similar to the variables of procedural programs.

- An object's methods are code segments used to perform a task or take some action and are similar to the procedures of procedural programming.

- To compare attributes to methods, consider a word processing program. Boldfaced text in a document is an attribute. The act of *changing* text to boldface is a method.

- Encapsulation is the technique of assembling the attributes, methods, and other elements of an object into a single, self-contained unit.

- An encapsulated object's attributes and methods are executed through an interaction or interface between the method and the object.

- The Java programming language is an object-oriented language that is used both for Web-based Internet and general-purpose programs. Key attributes of the Java programming language are its security features and the fact that it is architecturally neutral.

- Redesigning software to work on a different platform is called porting. Before the development of Java, programs were written for a single platform. To use the same program on another platform, you had to port the program to work with the new platform.

- After a Java program is written, it is compiled into a format called bytecode. The bytecode can then be run on any platform that has a Java programming language interpreter or Java Virtual Machine (VM).

- A Java VM creates a simulated processor on the platform for which it was designed. This simulated processor intercepts Java bytecode and translates it into a format that the platform can understand, eliminating the need to port the original Java code.

- Microsoft Visual J++ is a Windows-based development environment for creating Java applications. Microsoft Corporation created Visual J++ as a Java development environment based on the Java language specifications leased from Sun Microsystems.

- The "visual" aspect of Visual J++ is used for designing the user interface of a program. The underlying code is still written in the Java language.

- Visual J++ is designed exclusively for use with 32-bit Windows platforms such as Windows 95 and Windows NT. However, it produces compiled bytecode that can be executed on any platform for which there is a Java VM.

QUESTIONS

1. The most basic circuitry-level programming languages are called _____.
   a. high-level programming languages
   b. object-oriented programming languages
   c. machine languages
   d. basic programming languages

2. Languages that let you use a vocabulary of descriptive terms like "read," "write," or "add" are known as _____ languages.
   a. high-level
   b. machine
   c. procedural
   d. object-oriented

3. Programmer-named computer memory locations are called _____.
   a. compilers
   b. variables
   c. addresses
   d. appellations

4. High-level programming language rules and procedures are called _____.
   a. functions
   b. syntax
   c. subroutines
   d. methods

5. Programs used to translate high-level programming code into machine language are called _____ (choose three).
   a. compilers
   b. interpreters
   c. translators
   d. assemblers

6. Executing programming statements and procedures in the correct order to produce the desired results is called _____.
   a. methodology
   b. programming
   c. process
   d. logic

7. For convenience, the individual operations used in a computer program often are grouped into logical units called _____.
   a. procedures
   b. variables
   c. constants
   d. logistics

8. Writing a series of consecutive steps and creating computer memory locations to hold values is called _____ programming.
   a. high-level
   b. procedural
   c. object-oriented
   d. low-level

section A

9. Creating an instance of a class and modifying its attributes is an example of _____ programming.
   a. high-level
   b. procedural
   c. object-oriented
   d. low-level

10. Envisioning program components as objects that are similar to concrete objects in the real world is the hallmark of _____.
    a. command-line operating systems
    b. procedural programming
    c. object-oriented programming
    d. machine languages

11. An object's attributes also are known as its _____.
    a. states
    b. orientations
    c. methods
    d. procedures

12. An instance of a(n) _____ inherits its attributes from it.
    a. object
    b. procedure
    c. method
    d. class

13. Objects used to accomplish tasks in object-oriented programming are called _____.
    a. functions
    b. methods
    c. procedures
    d. routines

14. The combination of methods and attributes into a single object is called _____.
    a. encapsulation
    b. compiling
    c. compressing
    d. saving

15. An object's attributes and methods are accessed through a(n) _____.
    a. function
    b. procedure
    c. interface
    d. method

16. A program that must be redesigned for another platform must be _____.
    a. copied
    b. recompiled
    c. converted
    d. ported

17. Java programs are _____ (choose three).
    a. written for a single platform
    b. architecturally neutral
    c. based on the C++ programming language
    d. executed with a Java Virtual Machine
18. You must compile programs written in the Java programming language into _____.
    a. bytecode
    b. source code
    c. javadoc statements
    d. object code

EXERCISES

1. Name some attributes that might be appropriate for each of the following classes:
   a. a television set: _____
   b. an employee paycheck: _____
   c. patient medical records: _____
   d. tax returns: _____
   e. a house: _____
2. Create a list of objects in your everyday life that are instances of a class. Identify the class from which each object was instantiated. Which methods and attributes of the object are inherited from the class? Is the object an instance of more than one class? For example, a guitar is an instance of a general musical instrument class. As an instrument, it inherits the method to make sounds. As an instance of the more specific guitar class, an individual guitar inherits the attribute of strings.
3. Think of a set of common, related tasks that you can create as either a procedural program or an object-oriented program. One example might be cleaning your house. First, list the steps in the proper order that are required to run the program as a procedural program. Next, break the steps into "objects" that do not have to be performed in sequential order. What are the attributes and methods of these objects? Can you simplify the program by creating an instance of an existing class? What parts of the program must be run in a procedural fashion?
4. The Java programming language is architecturally neutral, meaning that it does not have to be rewritten or ported for different platforms. Create a list of objects in your everyday life and identify a situation where they would need to be ported to function properly. For example, you may receive a letter written in Russian. Unless you understand Russian, the letter would need to be translated (or ported) before you could read it.

SECTION B

objectives

In this section you will learn how to
- Start and exit Visual J++
- Identify the components of the Visual J++ Environment
- Understand projects and solutions
- Set the properties of an object
- Obtain help
- Create new projects and add files to a project
- Add projects to a solution
- Rename solutions and projects
- Save solutions, projects, and files
- Open and close solutions and projects
- Create and open individual files

The Microsoft Visual J++ Development Environment

Creating a New Project in Visual J++

Before creating a new project, you must start Visual J++.

To create a new project in Visual J++:

1. If necessary, start Windows, and then place your Student Disk in the appropriate disk drive. Click the **Start** button on the taskbar. The Start menu appears. Point to **Programs** on the Start menu. The Programs menu appears to the right of the Start menu. Point to **Microsoft Visual J++** on the Programs menu. The Visual J++ menu appears to the right of the Programs menu. Click **Microsoft Visual J++**. The Visual J++ copyright screen appears momentarily, and then the New Project dialog box appears as shown in Figure 1-1.

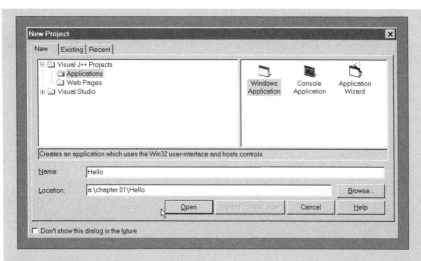

Figure 1-1: New Project dialog box

> If the New Project dialog box does not open automatically when you first start Visual J++, select New Project from the File menu or press Ctrl+N.

2   Click the **Applications** folder, then click **Windows Application**.

3   Click in the **Name** text box and replace the default project name with **Hello**, and then press the **Tab** key to move to the Location text box.

When you first open Visual J++, you start a session, which lasts until you exit. The first time you open the New Project dialog box in a Visual J++ session, Visual J++ suggests a default project name of Project1. Each subsequent time you open the New Project dialog box in a given session, Visual J++ increases the suggested project name by one (as in Project1, Project 2, Project3, and so on).

> Use the New tab in the New Project dialog box to open a new project, the Existing tab to open an existing project, and the Recent tab to open a recently opened project.

4   Type **A:\chapter.01\Hello** in the Location text box. If your Student Disk is not in drive A, enter the appropriate drive letter. For example, if your Student Disk is in drive B, type **B:\chapter.01**. If you do not know the drive letter of your Student Disk, click the **Browse** button to see the available drives and directories on your computer.

5   Click the **Open** button. Visual J++ creates a new project called Hello in the chapter.01\Hello directory on your Student Disk. The Integrated Development Environment appears.

Visual J++ is part of Microsoft's Visual Studio family of development products. Visual Basic, Visual C++, Visual FoxPro, Visual InterDev, Visual SourceSafe, and the MSDN Library are also members of Visual Studio. Visual J++ and Visual InterDev share a common workspace called the **Integrated Development Environment** (IDE). For each instance of the IDE, there is a single solution containing one or more projects. A **project** is the application you are creating. A **solution** is also an application, but composed of one or more projects. For example, you may have one project that handles accounts receivable and another project that handles accounts payable. Both projects function as separate applications, but can also be combined to create an accounting solution. Through the IDE, you can simultaneously open projects from Visual J++ and Visual InterDev in the same solution. Thus, you can create a single solution using both development tools. Microsoft's goal is for all members of Visual Studio eventually to share the same IDE. This common IDE will allow programmers to create solutions using any combination of Visual Studio development tools. An example of the Visual J++ IDE is shown in Figure 1-2.

Projects can be part of one or more solutions. They can be opened individually within a new solution or as part of an existing solution. Any changes to the project itself are reflected in all solutions that contain the project.

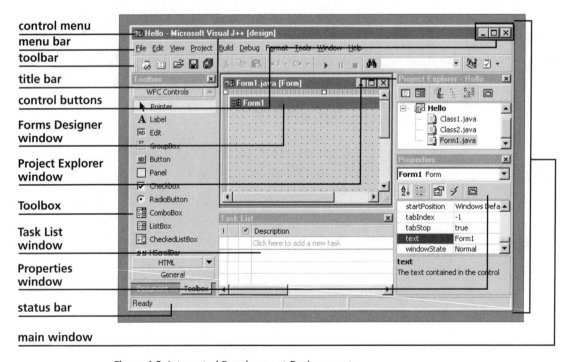

Figure 1-2: Integrated Development Environment

Your screen will not look identical to Figure 1-2. When you create a new project, none of its associated files, such as Java code pages, are actually opened. The project is added only to the IDE workspace. Several windows are visible only after you open an associated file. For example, the Designer window is visible only after you open a form or HTML file. Other components, such as the Properties window, do not display information unless you select an object. The visible elements in Figure 1-2 are for illustration purposes only.

Visual J++ IDE

Visual J++ contains a number of different types of windows and tools used for creating, editing, and managing the various pieces of a project. This section focuses on the elements shown in Figure 1-2: the main window, Project Explorer window, Designer window, Toolbox window, and Properties window.

To customize various aspects of the Visual J++ IDE, select Options from the Tools menu.

Managing Windows

With so many windows available in the IDE, it is easy for one window to hide another. As you work through this book, you will probably find it necessary to move and resize the windows on your screen. Windows in the IDE can be floating or dockable. You can drag a floating window to any part of the screen. A window set to dockable "snaps" to different positions on the screen. If you want to move a window, it is usually easier to manage with the dockable property turned off. Figure 1-3 shows examples of docked and floating windows.

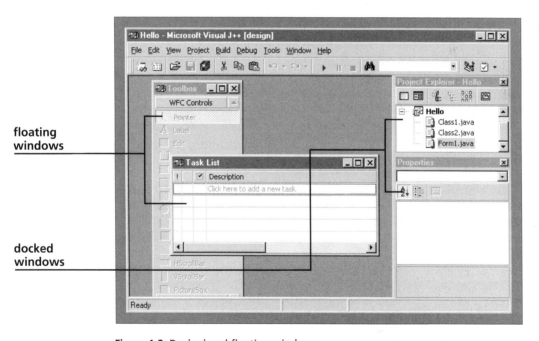

Figure 1-3: Docked and floating windows

You can arrange windows automatically using the Cascade, Tile Horizontally, and Tile Vertically commands in the Window menu.

section B

To turn the dockable property of a window on or off:

1 Activate a window whose dockable property you want to change, then select **Dockable** from the **Window** menu. A check mark (✓) next to the Dockable menu item indicates that the property is selected. If there is no check mark next to the Dockable menu item, then the window is floating. An example of how to set a window's dockable attribute is shown in Figure 1-4.

Figure 1-4: Setting a window's dockable attribute

You can also change a window's dockable property by clicking your right mouse button (right-clicking) on a window's title bar and selecting Dockable from the shortcut menu.

To move a window:

1 Point to a window's **title bar** and hold down your left mouse button, then drag to the desired position.

To resize a window:

1 Point to the side, corner, top, or bottom of a window, click and hold the left mouse button, and drag to the desired size. Pointing to a corner changes the mouse pointer to ↖ or ↗. Pointing to the top or bottom of a window changes the mouse pointer to ↕. Pointing to the side changes the mouse pointer to ↔. Dragging the top or bottom of a window resizes it vertically, dragging the left or right sides resizes it horizontally, and dragging a corner resizes horizontal and vertical dimensions simultaneously.

As you are working in Visual J++, you may find a specific window arrangement to be particularly useful. Or, you may find it more convenient to revert to a default window design. Use the **Define Window Layout** dialog box for saving and applying a new window layout scheme and for reverting to a default layout. You can select one of three default layout schemes: Default Debug, Default Design, and Default Full Screen. The **Default Debug** layout is useful when you are debugging Java code. The **Default Design** layout is what you see when you start Visual J++ for the first time before moving or resizing any of the windows. **Default Full Screen** removes all elements of the main window including the title bar, menu bar, toolbars, and status bar. If visible, the Windows Start menu is also hidden. This view allows the active document window (such as a form) to use the entire Visual J++ IDE, and is particularly useful if you have a small monitor and want to see the active window more clearly.

You can switch to Full Screen by selecting Full Screen from the View menu.

To save a window layout:

1. Arrange the windows in the Visual J++ IDE as desired.
2. Select **Define Window Layout** from the **View** menu. The Define Window Layout dialog box appears as shown in Figure 1-5.

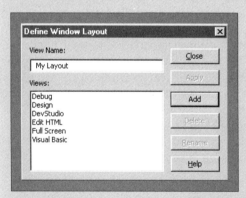

Figure 1-5: Define Window Layout dialog box

3. Type a **name** for the layout in the View Name text box, click the **Add** button, and then click the **Close** button.

To switch to an existing layout:

1. Select **Define Window Layout** from the **View** menu. The Define Window Layout dialog box appears.
2. Select a **layout** from the **Views** list, click the **Apply** button, and then click the **Close** button. The selected layout is applied to the Visual J++ IDE.

   Other layouts may appear in your Views list, such as the Visual Basic layout, which arranges the Visual J++ IDE to resemble the Visual Basic workspace.

You can also switch to an existing layout by clicking the Load/Save Window UI drop-down list box [Edit HTML] on the Standard toolbar.

You can delete or rename layouts by using the Delete and Rename buttons in the Define Layout Window dialog box. Note that you cannot delete or rename the Default Debug, Default Design, and Default Full Screen layouts.

The Main Window

The Visual J++ main window includes the title bar, control menu, control buttons, menu bar, toolbars, and status bar. The **title bar** displays the name of the current solution—in this case, Hello. It also indicates that Visual J++ is working in design time, which means that it is currently in a mode used for designing applications. The control menu and control buttons are used for managing the Visual J++ main window itself. The **control menu** displays a menu of commands for moving, sizing, minimizing, maximizing, and closing the Visual J++ window. Control buttons are the Minimize button, Maximize button, and the Close button. The **Minimize** button ▬ minimizes the Visual J++ main window; the **Maximize** button ▢ maximizes the Visual J++ main window, and the **Close** button ✕ exits Visual J++. The **status bar** displays various types of information about the Visual J++ environment or about the current operation.

Menu Bar At the top of the Visual J++ IDE is the menu bar. The **menu bar** is a standard Windows element containing menus of commands to perform various Visual J++ tasks. You can access a menu by clicking a menu name in the menu bar with your left mouse button or by holding the Alt key and the menu's underlined letter simultaneously (for example, pressing Alt+F opens the File menu). Menu commands followed by an arrow display a submenu of additional options. Menu commands followed by an ellipsis (...) display a dialog box that prompts for further information. For example, the New Project... command in the File menu opens the New Project dialog box. Menu commands not followed by an ellipsis immediately perform the specified task. For example, selecting Project Explorer from the View menu immediately displays the Project Explorer window. An example of the File menu is shown in Figure 1-6.

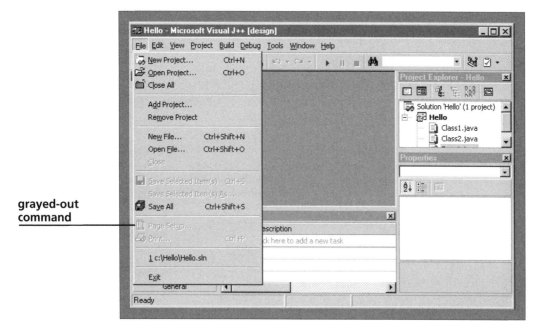

grayed-out command

Figure 1-6: File menu

help Menu commands that appear grayed out, such as the Print command in Figure 1-6, are not available in the current context. In this case, the object that was highlighted when the File menu was clicked is not printable.

Toolbars Toolbars contain buttons representing various Visual J++ commands. To execute a command from a toolbar button, click once on the desired button with your left mouse button. Certain buttons, such as the Load/Save Window UI button Edit HTML, display a drop-down list of items for you to choose. Visual J++ contains 14 built-in toolbars. Each toolbar appears automatically in the appropriate context. For example, the HTML toolbar appears when you open an HTML document. You can also manually display or hide each toolbar at any time, although the icons appear grayed out if they don't apply to the current task. The Standard toolbar is shown in Figure 1-7.

Figure 1-7: Standard toolbar

To display a description, or ToolTip, for a specific toolbar button, hold your pointer over the desired button.

To display or hide toolbars:

1 Point to **Toolbars** on the **View** menu, and then click the toolbar you want to display or hide. A check mark (✓) next to a toolbar name indicates that the toolbar is visible. Toolbar names that do not have a check mark next to them are not currently visible.

You can also display and hide toolbars by right-clicking an existing toolbar and selecting an item from the shortcut menu. To create, delete, or customize toolbars or to change various toolbar options, select Customize from the Toolbars submenu. An example of the Toolbars submenu is shown in Figure 1-8.

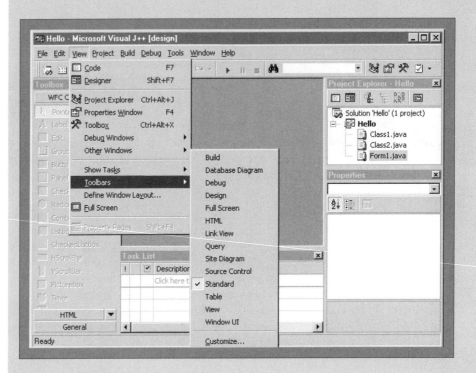

Figure 1-8: Toolbars submenu

> **tip**
>
> Like Visual J++ windows, toolbars can be floating or docked. To dock a floating toolbar, double-click the toolbar's title bar with your left mouse button. To move a floating toolbar, position your mouse cursor over the toolbar's title bar, then hold your left mouse button and drag to the desired position. To move a docked toolbar, position your mouse cursor over the move handle that appears on the left side of the toolbar, then hold your left mouse button and drag to the desired position.

Project Explorer

Visual J++ projects are normally composed of multiple files representing a specific type of resource or object. One of the most common file types you will use in Visual J++ is a Java file with an extension of .java. Other types of files used in a Visual J++ project include HTML files, form files, and graphic files. Projects in Visual J++ are directory-based, meaning that all files to be included with a project must reside in a project's root directory or in folders beneath the root directory. For example, if you have a project saved in a folder named myProject, all the files that are part of the project must also be in the myProject folder or within a folder beneath the myProject folder. You use the **Project Explorer** in the IDE to manage the various projects and associated files contained in a solution. Projects, folders, and files are displayed in a hierarchical list that may remind you of Windows Explorer.

Next you will use Project Explorer to display the contents of the Hello solution.

To display Project Explorer:

1. Select **Project Explorer** from the **View** menu. An example of the Project Explorer window is shown in Figure 1-9.

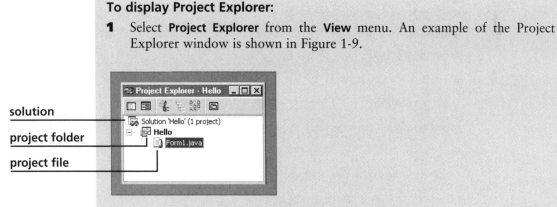

Figure 1-9: Project Explorer window

2. The first item in the Project Explorer list is the Solution icon. Click the **Hello** project folder located directly beneath the Solution icon.

Notice the Plus box ⊞ or Minus box ⊟ located to the left of the Hello project folder. You can use the Plus box and Minus box for expanding and collapsing folders. The Plus box indicates that an item contains other items that are not currently displayed. The Minus box indicates that all items beneath the associated item are currently visible. Clicking the Plus box displays all files and folders contained within a folder. Clicking the Minus box hides all files and folders that are contained within a folder. The Plus box and Minus box are also used in Windows Explorer for expanding and collapsing drives and folders.

3 If it is visible, click the **Plus** box next to the Hello project folder. A single file, the Form1.java file, should be visible beneath the Hello project folder.

This solution contains only one project, named Hello. If it contained additional projects, they would be located in an alphabetical list beneath the Solution icon.

You can also display Project Explorer by clicking the Project Explorer button on the Standard toolbar or pressing Ctrl+Alt+J.

Figure 1-10 displays a list of keyboard shortcuts that are available when working with Project Explorer.

Command	Press
Move to the beginning of the list	Home
Close Project Explorer	Shift+Esc
Collapse the list	Left arrow
Move to the end of the list	End
Expand the list	Right arrow
Expand/collapse the list or open the selected file	Enter
Move the insertion point to the beginning of the next line	Shift+Enter
Move to the next line	Down arrow
Move to the next project	Tab
Open Designer	Shift+F7
Open the editor for the selected file	F7

Figure 1-10: Project Explorer keyboard shortcuts

Command	Press
Move to the previous line	Up arrow
Move to the previous project	Shift+Tab
Display Project Explorer help	F1
Display the shortcut menu	Shift+F10

Figure 1-10: Project Explorer keyboard shortcuts (continued)

Notice the four buttons visible in the Project Explorer window: Package View, Directory View, Show All Files, and Properties. The **Package View button** displays project files according to Java packages, which are arranged as folders in the project directory. The **Directory View button** displays the default view, which consists of a hierarchical list of all subfolders contained in the project's directory structure. The **Show All Files button** displays all files contained in every project's directory structure. Icons representing files located within a project's directory structure that have not been added to the project appear grayed out. The **Properties button** opens the Properties window for an item selected in the Project Explorer window, such as a Java file.

You will learn about Java packages in Chapter 4.

Other buttons can appear in the Project Explorer window, depending on a selected file type. For example, a View Code button appears when a Java code file is selected.

Files can exist within a project's directory structure and *not* be part of the project.

Designers

Designers are used in Visual J++ for creating the visual aspects of forms and HTML files. A **form** is a standard element of most Windows applications. It contains a title bar, Minimize button, Maximize button, Close button, and control menu. You use forms to display information and receive input from the user. The default name of Form1 is assigned to the first form added to a project. This name appears as a caption in the form's title bar. **HTML files** are the Web pages with which you are probably familiar from the Internet. A default name of Page1 is assigned to the first HTML file added to a project.

Next you will open the Form1.java file in the Forms Designer window.

You will work with HTML files in Chapter 7.

To display the Forms Designer:

1 Highlight the **Form1.java** file in Project Explorer and select **Designer** from the **View** menu. The Forms Designer window appears as shown in Figure 1-11.

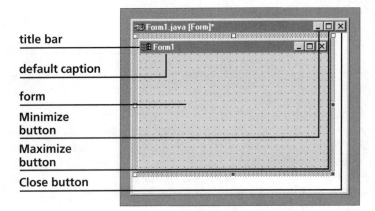

Figure 1-11: Forms Designer window

You also can display the Forms Designer window by pressing Shift+F7 or by right-clicking the name of a form in Project Explorer and selecting View Designer from the shortcut menu.

The Toolbox

The Toolbox contains tools used in designer windows for adding controls to forms and HTML pages. Controls are user interface items such as check boxes, command buttons, graphics, and other objects. Three control sets are available, depending on the active window: WFC Controls, HTML tools, and General tools. Windows Foundation Classes **(WFC) Controls** are available when designing Windows forms, **HTML tools** are available when designing Web pages, and **General tools** contain controls that are available at various places in Visual J++. WFC Controls are visible in Figure 1-12.

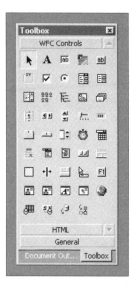

Figure 1-12: Toolbox

To display the Toolbox:

1 Select **Toolbox** from the **View** menu.

To display a description, or ToolTip, for a specific Toolbox button, hold your pointer over the desired button.

You can also display the Toolbox by clicking the Toolbox button on the Standard toolbar or by pressing Ctrl+Alt+X. Select Customize Toolbox from the Tools menu to change the tools available on your Toolbox.

The Task List

You use the Task List primarily in the Text Editor window when working with Java code. It lists warnings, compiler errors, specially marked code comments, and named shortcuts. You will work with most of these functions in Chapter 2. Although most of the tasks listed in the Task List are automatically generated by Visual J++, you can add your own tasks containing notes, items to be completed, and so on. An example of the Task List is shown in Figure 1-13.

priority
task type
completed
description
file containing a compiler error
location in the file containing the compiler error

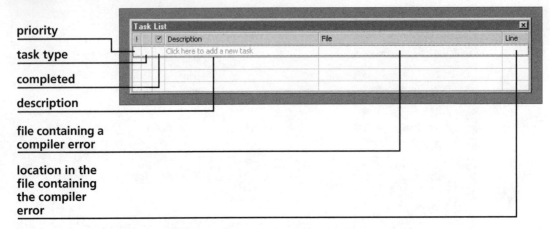

Figure 1-13: Task List

You will learn about the Text Editor window in Chapter 2.

As you can see in Figure 1-13, the Task List contains six columns. The first column indicates the priority level of the task: High, Nothing, or Low. The second column displays an icon indicating the type of task: SmartEditor Errors, Compiler Errors, Comments /*, Named Shortcuts, and User-Defined Tasks. Visual J++ automatically creates the icons. The third column contains a check box used for indicating when a task is complete. The fourth column contains a description of the task. If the task is a compiler error, the fifth column displays the name of the file containing the error, and the sixth column shows the location of the error in the file.

You cannot mark certain tasks, such as compiler errors, as complete using the Task List's check box column. In the case of a compiler error, you must first correct the code causing the error. Most compiler errors are automatically removed from the Task List once the code is corrected.

Next you will display the Task List and add a new task.

To display and add a task:

1 Select **Show Tasks** from the **View** menu, and then select **All**.

From the Show Tasks submenu on the View menu, you can select the types of tasks to display. You can select Previous, Comment, Compile/Build/Deploy, User, Shortcut, SmartEditor, Current File, Checked, or Unchecked.

2 Display the Task List by selecting **Other Windows** from the **View** menu, and then selecting **Task List**.

3. Click in the **Description** column where it reads "Click here to add a new task," then type **Change form's background color**.
4. Click the **first column** and select a priority level of **High**.

> You can also display the Task List by clicking the Task List button on the Standard toolbar or by pressing Ctrl+Alt+K.

Figure 1-14 displays a list of keyboard shortcuts that are available when working with the Task List.

Command	Press
Cancel an edit	Esc
Close the Task List	Shift+Esc
Close the edit mode or move to the associated window for a highlighted task in non-edit mode	Enter
Copy to the Clipboard	Ctrl+C or Ctrl+Ins
Cut to the Clipboard	Ctrl+X or Shift+Delete
Delete	Delete
Mark a task as complete	Space bar on a selected, editable task item
Move to the next displayed task	F12
Move to the next task column when in edit mode	Tab
Open/close the edit mode	F2
Paste to the Clipboard	Ctrl+V or Shift+Insert
Move to the previous displayed task	Shift+F12
Move to the previous task column when in edit mode	Shift+Tab
Display the shortcut menu	Shift+F10
Display Task item help	F1
Display Task List help	Ctrl+F1
Undo	Ctrl+Z or Alt+Backspace

Figure 1-14: Task List keyboard shortcuts

The Properties Window

Visual J++ contains many different types of objects. An object can be as simple as a check box control or as complex as a project or solution. Almost every type of Visual J++ element that you can treat as an individual component is an object. Note that certain types of objects, such as projects, are themselves composed of multiple objects. For example, a project object is composed of multiple file objects.

The **Properties window** in Visual J++ (and other Visual Studio tools) is used for managing the appearance and behavioral aspects of objects. For example, a form object has several types of properties including background color, border styles, and other attributes. Visual J++ assigns a default setting to the properties for each object.

The Properties window lists only the properties that can be set at design time; it does not list properties that can be set only through code. In subsequent chapters, you will learn how to set properties through code when a program executes.

Next you will display the properties of Form1 in the Properties window.

To display the Properties window of a form object:

1 Activate the **Form1** designer window by clicking with your mouse or by selecting the **Designer** window from the **Window** menu.

2 Select **Properties Window** from the **View** menu. An example of the Properties window listing the form's properties is shown in Figure 1-15.

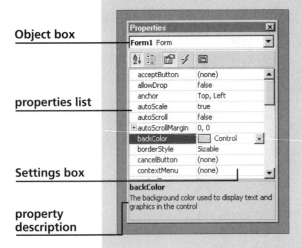

Figure 1-15: Properties window listing the form's properties

Different properties are displayed for different types of objects.

tip

You can also display the Properties window by clicking the Properties Window button on the Standard toolbar or by pressing F4. You can also right-click an object and select Properties from the shortcut menu.

To navigate through the properties in the list, use the Properties window scroll arrows or the shortcut keys listed in Figure 1-16.

| Keyboard Shortcuts in the Properties List | |
Command	Press
Move to the beginning of the list	Home
Close the Properties window	Shift+Esc
Collapse the solution or project	Left arrow or (-)
Move down one page	Page Down
Move to the end of the list	End
Expand the solution or project	Right arrow or (+)
Move to the next line	Down arrow
Move to the next property beginning with the *alpha* character	Ctrl+Shift+*alpha*
Move to the previous line	Up arrow
Display Properties window help	Ctrl+F1
Switch among a property, the properties settings box, and the Object box	Tab
Move up one page	Page Up

| Keyboard Shortcuts in the Settings Box | |
Command	Press
Cancel property changes	Esc
Copy to the Clipboard	Ctrl+C or Ctrl+Ins
Cut to the Clipboard	Ctrl+X or Shift+Delete
Delete	Delete
Move to the next property beginning with the *alpha* character	Ctrl+Shift+*alpha*

Figure 1-16: Properties window keyboard shortcuts

Keyboard Shortcuts in the Settings Box	
Command	Press
Paste from the Clipboard	Ctrl+V or Shift+Insert
Display the shortcut menu	Shift+F10
Switch among the property, the properties settings box, and the Object box	Tab
Switch between the Object box and the active Properties tab	Shift+Tab
Undo	Ctrl+Z or Alt+Backspace

Figure 1-16: Properties window keyboard shortcuts (continued)

The currently selected object is displayed in the **Object box** located directly beneath the Properties window title bar. You can use the Object box to select other objects contained *within* the active object. For example, you can select any controls available in an active form window directly from the Object box, rather than selecting them with your mouse on the form. The available properties for the selected object appear in the left column of the Properties window, whereas associated settings for each property appear in the right column, also called the **Settings box**. If multiple objects are selected, only properties that are common to all of the objects are available. A description for the selected property is displayed at the bottom of the Properties window. You can change the setting for some properties, such as the text property, by simply typing a new value in the property's Settings box. Other properties, such as the borderStyle property, allow you to select from a list of predefined settings. More complex properties use common dialog boxes and editors for selecting properties. For example, the font property displays a standard Windows font dialog box.

To view detailed help information on a specific property, select the property and press F1.

You can list properties alphabetically by clicking the **Alphabetic button** or by category by clicking the **Categorized button**. Two additional buttons, the Event View button and the Property View button, are also available, depending on the object. The **Event View button** displays only the event properties associated with an object, whereas the **Property View button** displays all properties (including event properties) for a selected object. The Property View button is the default view. It is always visible in the Properties window but is grayed out if the selected object does not contain event properties.

Next you will use the Properties window to change the background color of Form1.

> You will learn about events in Chapter 7.

To change the background color property of the current form:
1. Click **BackColor** in the Properties list of the Properties window. Notice the list arrow in the Settings box.
2. Click the **Settings** box list arrow, then click the **Palette** tab.
3. Select a color from the list of color choices. The background color of the form changes to the selected color.

Now that you have changed the form's background color, you will mark the Change form's background color task as complete.

To mark the Change form's background color task as complete:
1. Select **Show Tasks** from the **View** menu, and then select **User**.
2. Click the third column in the Change form's background color task. A checkmark appears and the task description is crossed out.

Visual J++ Help

As you work in Visual J++, you often will need to access help quickly on a particular subject. For example, you may not fully understand what a menu command does, may need help with the syntax of a code function, or would simply like to see an overview of a particular subject. At these times, it can be unproductive (and somewhat frustrating) to thumb through a book or reference guide to find the information that will help you. Luckily, Visual J++ (like most good Windows applications) provides several types of help resources. The main help resources available in Visual J++ are ToolTips, InfoView, context-sensitive help, and Internet help.

When you are working with toolbar buttons, it is easy to forget what command a particular button represents. **ToolTips** describe the function a button performs and can be momentarily displayed next to your mouse pointer for individual buttons. To display a ToolTip for a particular button, hold your mouse pointer over a button for a moment. The ToolTip pops up below and just to the right of your mouse pointer and stays visible until you move your mouse pointer off the button. Figure 1-17 displays an example of the ToolTip for the Open Project button on the Standard toolbar.

Figure 1-17: ToolTips

For advanced help and reference information, Visual J++ has an on-line help system called **InfoViewer**. All the development tools in Visual Studio share InfoViewer. As you recall, Visual Studio includes Visual Basic, Visual C++, Visual FoxPro, Visual InterDev, Visual SourceSafe, and the MSDN Library. The Visual Studio shared on-line help system can be quite useful if you work with several of these development tools simultaneously or if you are using combinations of the tools to create a single application. For example, you may be developing a Java application in Visual J++ that includes a project created in Visual InterDev. If you need help with both of these tools while creating your applications, it is much more convenient to use a consolidated help system.

The InfoViewer window contains two panes: the table of contents window and the topic window. The **table of contents window** contains four tabs: Contents, Index, Search, and Favorites. The **Contents tab** contains help topics in a table of contents format that is very similar to folders in Windows Explorer or Project Explorer. The **Index tab** is used for browsing a list of keywords and topics. The **Search tab** allows you to search for a particular word or phrase. The **Favorites tab** contains bookmarks to topics of particular interest. Help topics selected in any of the table of contents tabs are displayed in the **topic window**. Also available in the InfoViewer window is a menu bar and toolbar containing various navigation and topic manipulation tasks. Figure 1-18 shows the InfoViewer window opened to the Contents tab and a topic entitled "What's New in Visual J++."

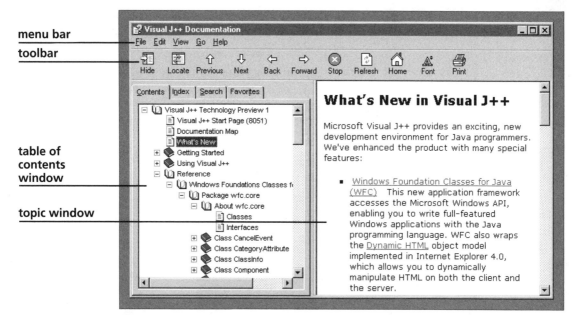

Figure 1-18: InfoViewer

In the following steps, you will open InfoViewer, locate a topic, and create a bookmark so you can quickly return to it later.

> **To locate and create a bookmark for a topic in InfoViewer:**
>
> **1** Select **Search** from the **Help** menu. The InfoViewer window appears, opened to the Search tab.
>
>
>
> You can also display the InfoViewer Contents tab by selecting Contents from the Help menu, and the InfoViewer Index tab by selecting Index from the Help menu.
>
> **2** Type **Toolbox** in the **Type in word(s) to search** box, select the **Match similar words** and **Search titles only** check boxes at the bottom of the Search tab, then click the **List Topics** button. A list of topics displays in the **Select topic** list. Select the **Toolbox** topic in the **Visual Studio Environment** location, and then click the **Display** button. The Toolbox topic displays in the topic window. In Figure 1-19, notice that the words on which you selected to search are highlighted.

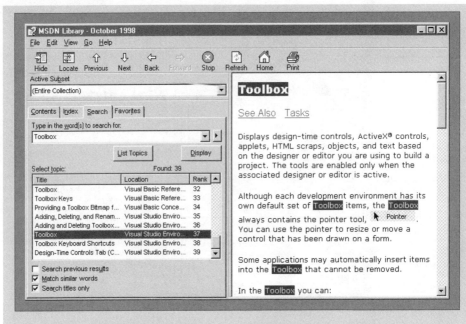

Figure 1-19: Search tab in InfoViewer

3   Click the **Favorites** tab. In the Current topic box at the bottom of the Favorites tab, replace Toolbox with **My Topic**. Then click the **Add** button. The My Topic entry appears in the Topics list.

In future InfoViewer sessions, use the Display button to show this topic. You can delete the topic by highlighting it and clicking the Remove button. Note that the Remove button does not delete the topic from the InfoViewer database—it deletes only the bookmark to the topic.

Words that are red and underlined are hyperlinks to other topics that are associated with the current topic. You can immediately "jump" to another topic by clicking its hyperlink.

InfoViewer also displays **context-sensitive help** for dialog boxes and programming terms. Rather than searching for a help topic yourself, you can have InfoViewer automatically display the help topic associated with a selected item. You display context-sensitive help by selecting a control in a dialog box, highlighting a property in the Properties window, or placing your cursor in a keyword or function in the Text Editor window and pressing the F1 key. Various windows such as Project Explorer also display context-sensitive help when you press the F1 key, and many dialog boxes contain a context-sensitive Help button. For example, if you press the F1 key or the Help button when the Existing tab of the New Project dialog box is open, InfoViewer opens and displays the Existing Tab topic. For certain items, InfoViewer displays a list of context-sensitive help topics from which you can choose. For example, if you press the F1 key in the Text Editor window when your cursor is located somewhere within the `import` keyword, InfoViewer opens and displays the Topics Found dialog box, as illustrated in Figure 1-20.

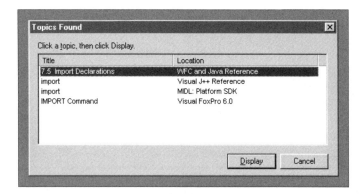

Figure 1-20: Topics Found dialog box

Visual J++ help is also available on the Internet. Select Microsoft on the Web from the Help menu to access links to several useful Microsoft Web sites including Online Support and Microsoft Developer Network Online. For a list of support options available from Microsoft, select Technical Support from the Help menu.

Do not rely too heavily on any single help option. They are all designed for specific purposes. For example, you could look in on-line help for a description of a particular toolbar button—although doing so would be difficult if you did not know the function of the button in the first place. Instead, it is easier to hold your mouse over a button until the ToolTip appears.

Adding Files to a Project

The various resources that make up projects and solutions are contained in disk files. These include Java files, HTML pages, controls, and other elements. In this section, you will add a new Java file to the project.

To add a new file to the project:
1. Click the **Hello** project folder in Project Explorer.
2. Select **Add Item** from the **Project** menu. The Add Item dialog box appears, as shown in Figure 1-21.

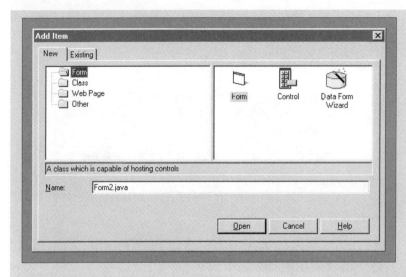

Figure 1-21: Add Item dialog box

3 Click the **Form** folder, and then click the **Form** icon. The name in the Name text box should be Form2.java. Click the **Open** button. The new file appears in the Hello project folder in Project Explorer.

You also can add a new item by clicking the Add Item button on the Standard toolbar or by right-clicking a project folder in Project Explorer and selecting Add Item from the shortcut menu.

To remove a file from a project, highlight the file in Project Explorer, then select Remove from Project from the Project menu.

Adding Projects to a Solution

Solutions are composed of one or more projects. You can add new or existing projects to a solution. For example, you may have created a project that organizes your album collection. Now you are creating a more general music collection solution that organizes all your albums, CDs, and cassettes. Since the album project already exists, you can add it to the music collection solution, along with the CD and cassette projects you will create. You then combine all three projects to create a single music collection solution. This solution is a good example of an object-oriented program. Each project is an object, and you are combining them to create a larger object—the solution.

Next you will add a new project to the current solution:

To add a new project to the current solution:

1 Click on the **Solution** icon in the Project Explorer window.

2 Select **Add Project** from the **File** menu. The Add Project dialog box appears, opened to the New tab, as shown in Figure 1-22.

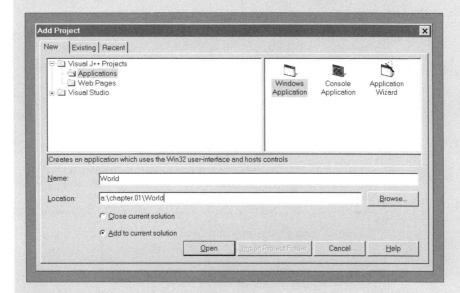

Figure 1-22: Add Project dialog box

> To add an already existing project to the solution, you would click the Existing tab or Recent tab.

3 Click the **Applications** folder, then click **Windows Application**.

4 Click in the **Name** text box and replace the default project name with **World**, and then press **Tab** to move to the Location text box. Type **A:\chapter.01\World** in the Location text box. If your Student Disk is not in drive A, enter the appropriate drive letter.

5 Click **Add to current solution**, and then click the **Open** button. The new project appears in Project Explorer.

> You can also add a new project by right-clicking the solution icon in Project Explorer and selecting Add Project from the shortcut menu.

Renaming Solutions and Projects

When you first created the current solution, Visual J++ automatically named the solution Hello, based on the name of the Hello project you created. This naming scheme works fine if there is only one project in a solution. Since there are now two projects in your solution, you will change the solution name to something more logical.

▶ **help**

When you rename solutions, projects, and other files, you are really renaming the disk files that they represent.

> **To rename the Hello solution:**
> **1** Click the **Solution 'Hello'** icon in Project Explorer, then select **Rename** from the **File** menu. The highlighted name becomes an active text box in the Project Explorer window. Type **Hello_World** and press **Enter**.

▶ **tip**

....
Renaming projects requires the same procedure as renaming solutions. Renaming Java files (with an extension of .java) requires additional steps, which you will learn about in Chapter 2.
....

Your Project Explorer window should be similar to Figure 1-23.

Figure 1-23: Project Explorer window

▶ **help**

You must expand the solution and project folders for your Project Explorer window to match Figure 1-23.

Saving Solutions, Projects, and Files

As you are developing a project and solution, you need to compile and execute them to make sure they perform as you would like. Unfortunately, even the most well-thought-out code can cause your computer to freeze or even crash. If your computer crashes—and it probably will—you will lose any unsaved changes to your solution. Therefore, it is a good practice to save your solution at regular intervals and especially before compiling and executing a program.

> You will learn more about compiling, testing, and executing solutions in subsequent chapters.

Recall that a solution consists of one or more projects, whereas a project consists of one or more files. If you make changes to a file contained in a project, you must save the file to ensure that the changes are available the next time you access the file. For example, you must save any changes you make to the text in a Java code file. Properties and other settings for solutions and projects are also contained in physical files on your computer. Therefore, you must also save projects and solutions if you made any changes to their properties and settings. Solution files have an extension of .sln and project files have an extension of .vjp.

To save the Hello_World solution:

1 Select **Save All** from the **File** menu.

> You can also save solutions by clicking the Save All button on the Standard toolbar.

To save individual files:

1 Activate the window containing the file you want to save or highlight the filename in Project Explorer.

2 Select **Save <filename>** from the **File** menu.

> You can also save individual files by clicking the Save icon on the Standard toolbar or by pressing Ctrl+S.

You can save just the properties and files within an individual project by highlighting the project name and clicking the Save icon or by selecting Save <project name> from the File menu. Highlighting the name of a solution and selecting Save <solution name> from the File menu performs the same task as selecting Save All from the File menu; all files and projects that are part of the solution are saved.

> You can create a new file or project by selecting Save *<filename>* As from the File menu. Selecting Save As creates a new copy of the file or project and adds it to your solution. The original file or project is still available in your solution.

Closing Solutions, Projects, and Files

As you work with solutions and projects, you may want to close the current solution or project before opening new ones. For practice, you will now close the Hello_World solution.

To close the Hello_World solution:

1. Select **Close All** from the **File** menu.
2. Before closing the solution, Microsoft Visual Studio displays a dialog box prompting you to save any unsaved files, as shown in Figure 1-24. Click **Yes** if you want to save your changes.

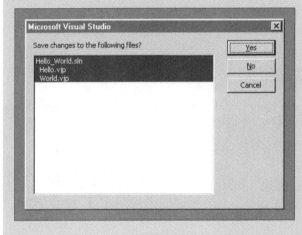

Figure 1-24: Microsoft Visual Studio Save dialog box

> If you have multiple projects and files open, the Visual J++ IDE can become difficult to work with since the screen may become too crowded. Therefore, you may find it necessary to close individual projects and files when you are through working with them.

To close individual projects or files:

1 Activate the window containing the project file you want to close or highlight the project or filename in Project Explorer.

2 Select **Close** from the **File** menu.

Opening Existing Solutions and Projects

When you open a saved solution, you also open all of the projects it contains. You also can open a project independently of any solutions in which it is contained. When you open a project without opening its solution, you open the project in a blank, empty solution. Since the Hello_World solution you are working on is composed of two projects, you are going to open the solution instead of the individual project files.

To open the Hello_World solution:

1 Select **Open Project** from the **File** menu. The Open Project dialog box appears, as shown in Figure 1-25.

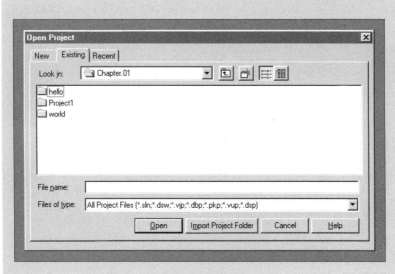

Figure 1-25: Open Project dialog box

2 Click the **Recent** tab, select the **Hello_World** file, and click the **Open** button. If the Hello_World.sln file is not visible in the Recent tab, click the **Existing** tab and locate the file in the Chapter.01 folder on your Student Disk.

> Before opening the new solution or project, Microsoft Visual Studio displays a dialog box prompting you to save any unsaved files in the currently open solution.

> You also can open existing solutions and projects by pressing Ctrl+O. You also can select recently opened solutions and projects from the list of recently opened files available from the File menu.

Creating and Opening Individual Files

As you recall, Visual J++ programs are created using solutions and projects. Solutions contain one or more projects, which in turn contain one or more files. The solution and project structure makes it much easier to manage the many files that can compose a program. However, you may find that you need to create only one file, not an entire solution or project. For example, you may need to create only an HTML document. Visual J++ allows you to create and open individual files that are not part of a project. Since files in Visual J++ must exist in a project within a solution, a temporary project named Miscellaneous Files is created whenever you create or open individual files.

> You will work with HTML documents in Chapter 7.

To create an individual file:

1 Select **New File** from the **File** menu. The New File dialog box appears, as shown in Figure 1-26.

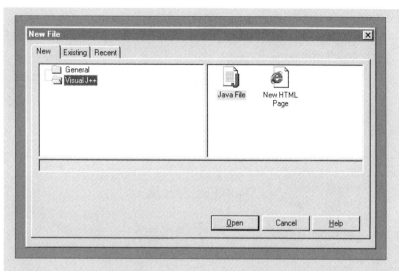

Figure 1-26: New File dialog box

2. Click the **Visual J++** folder, click **Java File**, and then click the **Open** button. The new file opens and appears in the Miscellaneous Files project in Project Explorer.

> The file has only been created, not saved. You must save the file before closing it or exiting Visual J++.

3. Select **Save Java file** from the File menu, change to the **Chapter.01** folder on your Student Disk, and save the file as **TestFile.java**.
4. Close TestFile.java by selecting **Close** from the **File** menu.

> You also can create a new file by pressing Ctrl+Shift+N.

To open TestFile.java as an individual file:

1. Select **Open File** from the **File** menu. The Open File dialog box appears, as shown in Figure 1-27.

section B

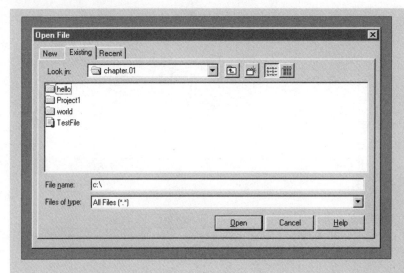

Figure 1-27: Open File dialog box

2 Locate **TestFile** in the Chapter.01 folder on your Student Disk, click the filename once, and then click the **Open** button. TestFile opens and appears in the Miscellaneous Files project in Project Explorer.

You also can open an individual file by pressing Ctrl+Shift+O.

Exiting Visual J++

Exiting the Visual J++ IDE is the same as exiting most other Windows applications.

To exit Visual J++:
1 Select **Exit** from the **File** menu.
2 Before exiting the IDE, Microsoft Visual Studio displays a dialog box prompting you to save any unsaved files in your solution. Click **Yes** if you want to save your changes.

You also can exit the Visual J++ IDE by clicking the Close button ⊠ in the title bar or by pressing Alt+F4.

SUMMARY

- Visual J++ is part of Microsoft's Visual Studio family of development products.

- When you first open Visual J++, you start an instance, which lasts until you exit.

- For each instance of the IDE, there is a single solution containing one or more projects. A project is the application you are creating. A solution is also an application, but is composed of one or more projects.

- Projects can be part of one or more solutions. You can open them individually within a new solution or as part of an existing solution. Any changes to the project itself are reflected in all solutions in which it is contained.

- Windows in the IDE can be floating or dockable. To change a window's dockable property, point at the window, click your right mouse button, and then select Dockable from the Shortcut menu.

- To move a window, point to a window's title bar, hold down your left mouse button, then drag to the desired position.

- To resize a window, point to the side, corner, top, or bottom of the window, click and hold the left mouse button, then drag to the desired size.

- The Define Window Layout dialog box is used for saving and applying a new window layout scheme and for reverting back to a default layout. To access the Define Window Layout dialog box, select Define Window Layout from the View menu.

- The Visual J++ main window includes the title bar, the control menu, control buttons, the menu bar, toolbars, and the status bar.

- The menu bar is a standard Windows element containing menus of commands to perform various Visual J++ tasks. You can access a menu by clicking a menu name in the menu bar with your left mouse button or by holding the Alt key and the menu's underlined letter simultaneously (for example, pressing Alt+F opens the File menu).

- Toolbars contain buttons representing various Visual J++ commands. To execute a command from a toolbar button, click once on the desired button with your left mouse button.

- Projects in Visual J++ are directory-based, meaning that all files to be included with a project must reside in a project's root directory or in folders beneath the root directory.

- Project Explorer is used in the IDE to manage the various projects and associated files contained in a solution. Projects, folders, and files are displayed in a hierarchical list similar to Windows Explorer. To display Project Explorer, select Project Explorer from the View menu.

- Designers are used in Visual J++ for creating the visual aspects of forms and HTML files. To display the form designer, select a form in Project Explorer and then select Designer from the View menu.

- The Toolbox contains tools used in Designer windows for adding controls to forms and HTML pages. Controls are user interface items, such as check boxes, command buttons, graphics, and other elements. To display the Toolbox, click the Toolbox button on the Standard toolbar.

- You use the Task List primarily in the Text Editor window when working with Java code. It lists warnings, compiler errors, specially marked code comments, and named shortcuts. You can add your own tasks containing notes, items to be completed, and so on. To display the Task List, select Other Windows from the View menu, then select Task List.

- The Properties window in Visual J++ (and other Visual Studio tools) is used for managing the various types of appearance and behavioral aspects of objects. Different properties are displayed for different types of objects. To display the properties of an object, select the object, then select Properties Window from the View menu.

- Descriptions, or ToolTips, of individual toolbar buttons can be displayed momentarily next to your mouse pointer. To display a ToolTip for a particular button, hold your mouse over a button for a moment.

- Visual J++ has an on-line help system called InfoViewer, which all the development tools in Visual Studio share.

- InfoViewer displays context-sensitive help for dialog boxes and programming terms. Display context-sensitive help by selecting a control in a dialog box or by placing your cursor in a keyword or function in the Text Editor window and pressing the F1 key. Many dialog boxes also contain a context-sensitive Help button.

- Visual J++ help is available on the Internet. Select Microsoft on the Web from the Help menu to access links to several useful Microsoft Web sites including Online Support and Microsoft Developer Network Online.

- Select Technical Support from the Help menu for a list of Microsoft support options.

- The various resources that make up projects and solutions are contained in disk files. These include Java files, HTML pages, controls, and other elements.

- To add a new file to a project, select the project folder in Project Explorer, then select Add Item from the Project menu.

- To add a new project to the current solution, click the Solution icon in the Project Explorer window, then select Add Project from the File menu.

- To rename files, select the file you want to rename in Project Explorer, then select Rename from the File menu. Renaming Java files (with an extension of .java) requires additional steps, which you will learn about in Chapter 2.

- To save the current solution, select Save All from the File menu.

- To save an individual file, activate the window containing the file you want to save or highlight the filename in Project Explorer, then select Save *<filename>* from the File menu.

- To close a solution, select Close All from the File menu.

- To close individual projects or files, activate the window containing the project file you want to close or highlight the project or filename in Project Explorer, then select Close from the File menu.
- To open a project or solution, select Open Project from the File menu.
- To create an individual file, select New File from the File menu.
- To open an individual file, select Open file from the File menu.
- To exit Visual J++, select Exit from the File menu.

QUESTIONS

1. Visual J++ is part of _____.
   a. Windows NT
   b. Microsoft Office Professional
   c. Microsoft Visual Studio
   d. the Java Development Kit

2. The Visual J++ user interface shared with Visual InterDev is called _____.
   a. Project Explorer
   b. Application Programming Interface (API)
   c. Microsoft Visual Studio
   d. Integrated Development Environment (IDE)

3. Visual J++ projects are contained within a single _____.
   a. solution
   b. window
   c. Visual J++ session
   d. project folder

4. Which layout scheme(s) cannot be deleted? (Choose all that apply.)
   a. Default Debug
   b. Visual Basic
   c. Default Design
   d. Default Full Screen

5. User interface controls are selected from the _____.
   a. Standard toolbar
   b. Toolbox
   c. menu bar
   d. Task List

6. For what are designers used? (Choose two.)
   a. creating Windows forms
   b. designing code pages
   c. customizing Visual J++
   d. creating HTML pages

section B

7. Files that are part of a project must be contained _____.
   a. within the project directory or in folders beneath the project directory
   b. in any directory that is accessible from your computer
   c. in a series of directories beneath the Visual J++ program directory, where each directory contains a single Java file
   d. on floppy disks

8. Which of the following messages are *not* automatically created in the Task List?
   a. compiler errors
   b. SmartEditor errors
   c. named shortcuts
   d. save reminders

9. The _____ is used for modifying the attributes of an object.
   a. Project Explorer
   b. Properties window
   c. Task List
   d. menu commands

10. _____ is used for managing the various projects and associated files in a solution.
    a. The Properties window
    b. Windows Explorer
    c. The Toolbox
    d. Project Explorer

11. When multiple objects are selected, the Properties window displays _____.
    a. nothing
    b. all properties for each of the selected objects
    c. properties that are unique to each individual object
    d. properties that are common to all of the selected objects

12. ToolTips are displayed for _____.
    a. object properties
    b. toolbar buttons
    c. menu commands
    d. Toolbox controls

13. Words and phrases in InfoViewer that are red and underlined are called _____.
    a. syntax descriptions
    b. keywords
    c. comments
    d. hyperlinks

14. Which of the following items have context-sensitive help? (Choose two.)
    a. menu commands
    b. dialog boxes
    c. Text Editor window
    d. toolbar buttons

15. When should you save your files?
    a. Only when you are finished
    b. After your computer crashes
    c. At regular intervals
    d. It is unnecessary to save your files
16. If you make changes to files and exit without saving them, Visual J++ _____.
    a. saves them for you
    b. prompts you to save your work
    c. discards your changes
    d. creates new copies of the files that include the changes
17. The Visual J++ on-line help system, InfoViewer, is shared with _____.
    a. the Java Development Kit
    b. Microsoft Visual Studio
    c. Microsoft Office
    d. all applications in Windows NT
18. When you attempt to open a file that is not contained within a project, Visual J++ _____.
    a. creates a new project based on the name of the file you are opening
    b. adds the file to the currently open project
    c. opens the file in a project named Miscellaneous Files
    d. does not allow you to open the file

EXERCISES

1. Explain the difference between solutions and projects.
2. Identify the parts of the Visual J++ IDE that are covered in this chapter. Explain what each element is used for and how it is displayed. Also identify the elements that can be customized.
3. Explain what will happen when you select the following types of menu commands:
    a. A menu command followed by an ellipsis (...)
    b. Menu commands followed by an arrow
    c. Menu commands not followed by an ellipsis (...) or arrow
    d. Grayed out menu commands
4. Create a custom toolbar named Chapter1Commands. Add buttons to the toolbar for the commands you have learned in this chapter.
5. Identify the different types of Visual J++ help resources and how they are accessed. Describe situations in which each type of help is most appropriate.
6. Display the elements in the Visual J++ IDE you feel you will use most often and hide the elements you will not use frequently. Now modify the size and placement of elements to your liking. You may find it convenient to make some windows dockable and some windows floating. Save the layout as My FavoriteLayout.

7. Create a new Windows application project named FormPractice and save the FormPractice project in the Chapter.01 folder on your Student Disk. Add a new task that reads "Update form properties." Open the Form1.java file in the Form Designer window and use the Properties window to change the background to your favorite color. Then resize the form using your mouse. Which property in the Properties window displays the form's dimensions? Are they updated automatically as you resize the form with your mouse? Try changing other properties such as the text property, which changes the text displayed in the form's title bar. When you are through changing the form's properties, mark the "Update form properties" task as complete.

8. Create a new Windows application project named Basketball and save the Basketball project in the Chapter.01 folder on your Student Disk. Rename the Basketball solution as Sports. Add new Windows application projects to the solution named Football, Baseball, Hockey, and Cricket. Save each project in the solution in the Chapter.01 folder on your Student Disk. Now rename the Sports solution as American Sports and save it as SportsProgram.sln. Since the program is for American sports, delete the project named Cricket. Save and close the solution, and then open each of the projects individually. Within each project, add a new form named SportsForm.java.

9. Create a new Java file that is not associated with a project. Save the file as NoProject.java in the Chapter.01 folder on your Student Disk. Close the NoProject file and then open it as an individual file that is displayed in the Miscellaneous Files project in Project Explorer.

10. Search for the topic "Project Explorer" in InfoViewer. Before you start your search, select Search titles only. From the list of topics you receive, locate the topic "Project Explorer (Visual J++)" located in the Visual J++ Reference. Add a bookmark named "Visual J++ Project Explorer" to the topic.

CHAPTER 2

A First Program Using Java

case ▶ "Well, we've covered a lot of ground," says Lynn Greenbrier, head of computer programming for Event Handlers Incorporated. "You now understand the basics of object-oriented programming and how Java relates to Visual J++. You've also had a chance to see how the Visual J++ IDE works. Are you ready to write your first program?"

"I think so," you reply. "I know how to start Visual J++, create new projects, and add new files. But how do these files become programs? Where do you actually write Java code? What if you make a mistake? When do you..."

"Okay! Okay!" Lynn says with a laugh. "We'll cover those tasks next!"

SECTION A
objectives

In this section you will learn how to
- Write a Java program
- Use the Text Editor window and its features
- Add comments to a Java program
- Run a Java program
- Modify a Java program

Creating a Program

Java Programming Structure

In this section, you will learn the elements of a simple Java program and begin to learn Java syntax. You will also create your own objects and endow them with your own methods.

At first glance, even the simplest Java program involves a fair amount of confusing syntax. Consider the following simple program. This program consists of seven lines, and its only task is to print "First Java program" on the screen.

```java
public class First
{
     public static void main(String[] args)
     {
          System.out.println("First Java program");
     }
}
```

The statement that accomplishes the actual work in this program is `System.out.println("First Java program");`. One of the most important things to notice about this statement is that it ends with a semicolon. All Java programming language statements must end with a semicolon.

The text "First Java program" is a literal string of characters. A **literal string** of characters is a series of characters that will appear exactly as entered. Any literal string in Java must appear between double quotation marks.

The literal string "First Java program" appears within parentheses because the string is an argument to a method. Arguments to methods must always appear within parentheses. **Arguments** consist of information that a method requires to perform its task. For example, you might place a catalog order with a company that sells sporting goods. Processing a catalog order is a method that consists of a set of standard procedures. Each catalog order requires information—which item number you are ordering, the quantity of the item being ordered, and the payment method. This information can be considered the order's argument. If you order two of item 5432 from a catalog, you expect different results than if you order 1,000 of item 9008. Likewise, if you pass the argument "Happy Holidays" to a method, you expect different results than if you pass the argument "First Java program."

> **When you send something, such as a literal string, to a method, you are passing an argument.** For example, think of a wide receiver on a football team as a method and a football as an argument. When the quarterback throws the football to the wide receiver, he is passing an argument to a method. The wide receiver then takes the argument and performs a task with it (a touchdown it is hoped).

Within the statement `System.out.println("First Java program");`, the method to which you are passing "First Java program" is named println(). The println() method prints a line of output on the screen, positions the cursor on the next line, and stands ready for additional output.

> **Method names usually are referenced by their following parentheses, as in** `println()`, **so you can distinguish method names from variable names.**

Within the statement `System.out.println("First Java program");`, `out` is an object. The `out` object represents the screen. Several methods, including println(), are available with the `out` object. Of course, not all objects have a println() method (for instance, you can't print to a keyboard, your automobile, or your dog), but the creators of the Java platform assumed you frequently would want to display output on a screen. Therefore, the `out` object was created and endowed with the method named println().

> **The print() method is very similar to the println() method.** With println(), after the message prints, the insertion point appears on the following line. With print(), the insertion point does not advance to a new line; it remains on the same line as the output.

Within the statement `System.out.println("First Java program");`, *System* is a class. System defines the attributes of a collection of similar "System" objects, just as the Dog class defines the attributes of a collection of similar Dog objects. One of the System objects is `out`. (You can probably guess that another System object is `in` and that it represents an input device.)

> **The Java programming language is case sensitive—the class named System is a completely different class from one named system, SYSTEM, or even sYsTeM.**

The dots (periods) in the statement `System.out.println("First Java program");` are used to separate the names of the class, object, and method. You will use this same class-dot-object-dot-method format repeatedly in Java programs.

The statement that prints the string "First Java program" is embedded in the program shown in Figure 2-1.

```
public class First
{
    public static void main(String[] args)
    {
        System.out.println("First Java program");
    }
}
```

Figure 2-1: Printing a string

Everything that you use within a Java program must be part of a **class**. When you write `public class First`, you are defining a class named First. You can define a Java class using any name or identifier you need, as long as it meets the following requirements:

- A class name must begin with a letter of the alphabet (which includes any non-English letter, such as α or π), an underscore, or a dollar sign.
- A class name can contain only letters or digits.
- A class name cannot be a Java programming language reserved keyword, such as `public` or `class` (see Figure 2-2 for a list of reserved keywords).
- A class name cannot be one of the following values: `true`, `false`, or `null`.

The Java programming language is based on Unicode, which is an international system of character representation. The term *letter* indicates English-language letters, as well as characters from Arabic, Greek, and other alphabets. See Section B of this chapter for more information on Unicode.

Abstract	Final	protected
Boolean	Finally	public
Break	Float	return
Byte	For	short
Case	Goto	static
Catch	If	super
Char	Implements	switch
Class	Import	synchronized
Const	Instanceof	this

Figure 2-2: Java programming language reserved keywords

Continue	Int	throw
Default	Interface	throws
Delegate	Long	transient
Do	Native	true
Double	New	try
Else	null	void
Extends	Package	volatile
false	Private	while

Figure 2-2: Java programming language reserved keywords (continued)

It is a Java programming language standard to begin class names with an uppercase letter and use other uppercase letters as needed to improve readability. Figure 2-3 lists some valid and conventional class names for the Java programming language.

Class Name	Description
Employee	Begins with an uppercase letter
UnderGradStudent	Begins with an uppercase letter, contains no spaces, and emphasizes each new word with an initial uppercase letter
InventoryItem	Begins with an uppercase letter, contains no spaces, and emphasizes the second word with an initial uppercase letter
Budget2001	Begins with an uppercase letter and contains no spaces

Figure 2-3: Some valid class names in the Java programming language

Figure 2-4 lists some class names that are valid, but unconventional.

> You should follow established conventions for the Java programming language so your programs will be easy for other programmers to interpret and follow. This book uses established Java programming conventions.

Class Name	Description
employee	Begins with a lowercase letter
Undergradstudent	Does not indicate new words with initial uppercase letters, and thus is difficult to read
Inventory_Item	Uses the underscore to indicate new words, which is unconventional in Java
BUDGET2001	Appears as all uppercase letters

Figure 2-4: Some unconventional class names in the Java programming language

Figure 2-5 lists some illegal class names.

Class Name	Description
An employee	The space character is illegal
Inventory Item	The space character is illegal
class	`class` is a reserved word
2001Budget	Class names cannot begin with a digit
Phone#	The # symbol is not allowed

Figure 2-5: Some illegal class names in the Java programming language

In Figure 2-1, the line `public class First` contains the keyword `class`, which identifies First as a class. The reserved word `public` is an access modifier. An **access modifier** defines the circumstances under which a class can be accessed. Public access is the most liberal type of access; you will learn about public and other types of access in Chapter 3.

You enclose the contents of all classes within curly brackets ({ and }). A class can contain any number of data items and methods. In Figure 2-1, the class First contains only one method within its curly brackets. The name of the method is main(), and the main() method contains its own set of brackets and only one statement—the println() statement.

> Use whitespace to organize your program code and make it easier to read. Whitespace is any combination of spaces, tabs, and carriage returns (blank lines). In general, whitespace is optional in the Java programming language. You can insert whitespace between words or lines in your program code by typing spaces, tabs, or blank lines, because the compiler will ignore these extra spaces. However, you cannot use whitespace within any identifier or keyword.

For every opening curly bracket ({) in a Java program, there must be a corresponding closing curly bracket (}). The placement of the opening and closing curly brackets is not important to the compiler. For example, the following method is executed exactly the same as the one shown in Figure 2-1. The only difference is that the method is organized differently. Usually, code in which you vertically align each pair of opening and closing curly brackets is easier to read. You should strive to type your code so it is easy to read.

```
public static void main(String[] args) {
System.out.println("First Java program"); }
```

The statement `public static void main(String[] args)` is the method header for the main() method. All Java applications must include a method named main(), and most Java applications have additional methods. When you execute a Java application, the compiler always executes the main() method first. The **method header** is the first line of a method. You can see that it is quite complex. The meaning and purpose of each of the terms used in the method header will become clearer as you complete this textbook; a brief explanation will suffice for now.

> Unlike Java applications, Java *applets* do not require a method named main(). You will learn about applets in Chapter 7.

In the method header `public static void main(String[] args)`, the word `public` is an access modifier, just as it is when you define the First class. In the English language, the word *static* means showing little change, or stationary. In the Java programming language, the reserved keyword `static` also means unchanging, and it indicates that every member created for the First class will have an identical, unchanging main() method. Within the Java programming language, `static` also implies uniqueness. Only one main() method for the First class will ever be stored in the memory of the computer. Of course, other classes eventually might have their own, different main() methods.

> When you refer to the String class in the main() method header, the square brackets indicate an array of String objects. You will learn more about arrays and the String class in Chapter 6.

In English, the word *void* means empty. When the keyword `void` is used in the main() method header, it does not indicate that the main() method is empty, but rather that the main() method does not return any value when it is called. This keyword's presence doesn't mean that main() doesn't produce output—in fact, the method does. Rather, `void` means the main() method does not send any value back to any other method that might use it. You will learn more about returning values from a method in Chapter 3.

In the method header `public static void main(String[] args)`, you already might recognize that the contents between the parentheses, (`String[] args`), must represent an argument passed to the main() method, just as the string "First Java program" in `System.out.println("First Java program");` is an argument passed to the println() method. String represents a Java class that can be used to represent character strings. The identifier `args` is used to hold any Strings that might be sent to the main() method. The main() method *could* do something with those arguments, such as print them. But in Figure 2-1, the main() method does not actually use the `args` identifier. Nevertheless, you must place an identifier within the main() method's parentheses. The identifier does not need to be named `args`—it could be any legal Java identifier—but the name `args` is traditional.

The simple program shown in Figure 2-1 has many pieces to remember. However, for now, you can use the program shown in Figure 2-6 as a shell, where you replace the line `/******/` with any statements that you want to execute.

A First Program Using Java

```
public class First
{
     public static void main(String[] args)
     {
          /******/
     }
}
```

Figure 2-6: Shell output program

The Text Editor Window

When you create programs in the Sun Java Development Kit (JDK), you write the Java code in a text editor such as Notepad, WordPad, or any word processing program capable of creating simple text files. In contrast, Microsoft Visual J++ has its own built-in text editor called the Text Editor window. The Text Editor window has the same text editing capabilities as other Windows text editors: you can cut and paste, drag and drop, and search for specific text strings. These and other text editing options are available on the Edit menu.

The various types of code elements in the Text Editor window are distinguished by syntax coloring. This color coding makes it easier to understand the structure and code in a Java program. For example, the default syntax coloring for keywords such as `public` is blue. If you need to locate a statement containing the keyword `public`, you can start by looking at just the blue text. Of course, if you know the specific text contained in the statement, it can be much easier to use the Find and Replace command on the Edit menu. If you do not know the specific text, the syntax coloring can help you greatly limit the lines that you need to examine. Consider a large word processing document in which you need to locate a piece of text. If you can't remember the exact text string for which to search, then the Find and Replace command is useless; you would need to examine each line of text in the document manually. However, manually searching for text is simpler if the specific type of text is indicated by color.

> You can change Text Editor options, including syntax color choices, by selecting Options from the Tools menu, then selecting a category under the Text Editor node.

As you are writing Java code, you may find it difficult to remember which methods and properties (or **members**) are available in a specific class or what arguments need to be passed to a particular method or object. For example, the System class alone contains 22 members. The Text Editor window uses a feature that is part of IntelliSense technology called **Statement Completion** to aid in the creation of Java code. As you are writing Java code, member lists and parameter information display automatically according to the current object. For example, if you type `System.`, making sure to include the period at the end, a list of the 22 members available in the System class displays. An example of Statement Completion for System is shown in Figure 2-7.

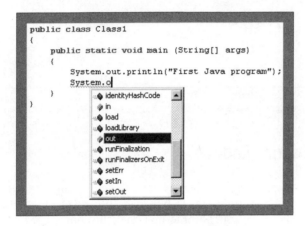

Figure 2-7: Example of Statement Completion

Another tool for writing Java code is **Word Completion**, which is used to complete class names and other elements automatically that IntelliSense recognizes by the first few characters you type. For example, if you type the letter *S*, then press Ctrl+space bar, a list containing all elements beginning with the letter *S* displays. If the letter or letters you type are unique to a specific element, IntelliSense automatically inserts that element name into your code. For example, if you type *Sy*, then press Ctrl+space bar, the keyword System is inserted into your code because this is the only element that begins with the letters *Sy*. You can also use Word Completion by selecting Complete Word from the Edit menu.

> To display list members for a class or object manually, place your insertion point anywhere in the class or object name and select List Members from the Edit menu or press Ctrl+J. To display parameter information manually, place your insertion point anywhere in a statement and select Parameter Info from the Edit menu or press Ctrl+Shift+I.

In addition to providing Statement Completion and Word Completion, IntelliSense also provides **dynamic syntax checking** as you are writing code in the Text Editor window. Dynamic syntax checking is visible in the form of red squiggly lines that appear beneath various Java code elements. These lines represent syntax errors in your code. They appear as you first start typing code and usually disappear after you complete an error-free statement. If a red squiggly line does not disappear after you complete a statement, a description of the error, called a **SmartEditor error**, appears in the Task List. You can also hold your mouse over a red squiggly line to receive an ErrorTip describing the syntax error. For on-line help on a particular syntax error, hold your mouse over a red squiggly line, click your right mouse button, and select Error Help from the shortcut menu.

help
If you do not receive Statement Completion, Word Completion, or dynamic syntax checking when you are working in the Text Editor window, select Options from the Tools menu. In the Options dialog box, expand the Text Editor node and click the Java Tasks category. Make sure all of the check boxes are selected, then click the OK button.

Figure 2-8 displays a list of keyboard shortcuts that are available when working in the Text Editor window.

Command	Press
Move to the beginning of the member list	Ctrl+Home
Enter box selection/stream selection mode	Ctrl+R+S
Invoke the Word Completion tool	Ctrl+space bar
Display context-sensitive help	F1
Copy to the Clipboard	Ctrl+C or Ctrl+Ins
Cut selected lines to the Clipboard	Ctrl+M
Cut to the Clipboard	Ctrl+X or Shift+Delete
Delete	Delete
Delete the selection to the left of the insertion point	Backspace
Delete the word to the left of the insertion point	Ctrl+Backspace
Delete the word to the right of the insertion point	Ctrl+Delete
Display and hide spaces and tab marks	Ctrl+R+W
Display a list of members	Ctrl+J
Display or hide a shortcut	Ctrl+K+H
Move to the end of the member list	Ctrl+End
Highlight one word to the left	Ctrl+Shift+left arrow
Highlight one word to the right	Ctrl+Shift+right arrow
Highlight one line below	Shift+down arrow
Highlight one page below	Shift+Page Down
Highlight one character to the left	Shift+left arrow

Figure 2-8: Text Editor window keyboard shortcuts

Command	Press
Highlight one character to the right	Shift+right arrow
Highlight to the end of the current line	Shift+End
Highlight to the start of the current line	Shift+Home
Highlight one line above	Shift+up arrow
Highlight one page above	Shift+Page Up
Highlight to the end of the document	Ctrl+Shift+End
Highlight to the matching brace	Ctrl+Shift+]
Highlight to the start of the document	Ctrl+Shift+Home
Find	Ctrl+F
Find the matching brace	Ctrl+]
Find the next occurrence of the current word or selection	Ctrl+F3
Find the previous occurrence of text in the Find window	Shift+F3
Find the next occurrence of text in the Find window	F3
Find the previous occurrence of the current word or selection	Ctrl+Shift+F3
Display help	Ctrl+F1
Indent one tab stop left	Shift+Tab
Indent one tab stop right	Tab
Indent selected lines of code based on the surrounding lines of code	Alt+F8
Change to lowercase letters	Ctrl+U
Enter overtype mode	Insert
Display Parameter Info	Ctrl+Shift+I
Paste from the Clipboard	Ctrl+V or Shift+Insert
Display Quick Info	Ctrl+I
Redo	Ctrl+Y or Ctrl+Shift+Z or Alt+Shift+Backspace

Figure 2-8: Text Editor window keyboard shortcuts (continued)

A First Program Using Java

Command	Press
Replace	Ctrl+H
Scroll up one line	Ctrl+Up Arrow
Select the current word	Ctrl+Shift+W
Transpose the characters around the insertion point	Ctrl+T
Transpose the current and previous lines	Alt+Shift+T
Transpose the current and next words or operators	Ctrl+Shift+T
Undo	Ctrl+Z or Alt+Backspace
Change to uppercase letters	Ctrl+Shift+U

Figure 2-8: Text Editor window keyboard shortcuts (continued)

Writing Your First Java Program

Now that you understand the basic framework of a program written in the Java programming language and how to use the Text Editor window, you are ready to write your first Java program. It is a tradition among programmers that the first program you write in any language produces "Hello, world!" as its output. You will create such a program now.

To write your first Java program:

1 If necessary, start Visual J++. Otherwise select **New Project** from the **File** menu. The New Project dialog box appears.

> You also can open a new project by clicking the New Project button on the Standard toolbar or by pressing Ctrl+N.

2 Click the **Applications** folder on the **New** tab, then click **Console Application**. Replace the suggested project name in the Name text box with **Hello**, change the location of the Hello project to the Chapter.02 folder on your Student Disk, and then click the **Open** button. The new project is created in the Visual J++ IDE.

3 Click the **Plus** box icon next to the Hello project icon in Project Explorer. A file named Class1.java appears beneath the Hello project folder.

4 Rename the Class1.java file as **Hello.java**. While the Hello.java file is highlighted in Project Explorer, press **Enter** to open it in the Text Editor window as shown in Figure 2-9.

> You can also open a file by double-clicking the filename in Project Explorer.

> Visual J++ automatically assigns a filename extension of .java to Java code files. This filename extension is necessary for the file to be recognized by a Java language compiler. When you rename a Java file, be sure to include the .java extension.

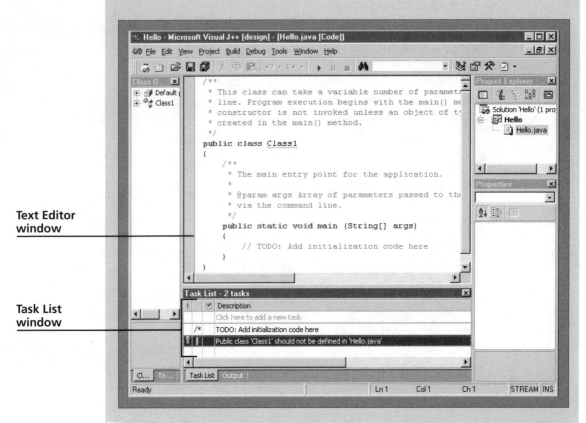

Text Editor window

Task List window

Figure 2-9: Hello.java file in the Text Editor window

After opening the Hello.java file in the Text Editor window, you should see two tasks in the Task List window. One of the tasks should read `Public class 'Class1' should not be defined in 'Hello.java'`. The Text Editor's dynamic syntax checking automatically creates this task. Class1 is the name that Visual J++ automatically assigned the Java file and its class name in this project.

A First Program Using Java

A class name in Java programming must be the same as the class's filename. Because you renamed the Class1.java file as Hello.java, you must also rename the Class1 class as Hello. Remember that the Java programming language is case sensitive. The case of the class name must match the case of the filename. For example, if you renamed the Java file as HELLO (all uppercase) instead of Hello (initial uppercase), the class name must also be HELLO (all uppercase). The case of the Java filename extension .java is ignored.

5 Locate the line `public class Class1` and rename Class1 to **Hello**. After you change the class name to Hello, the `Public class 'Class1' should not be defined in 'Hello.java'` task in the Task List window is automatically removed.

   The other task in the Task List window should read `// TODO: Add initialization code here`. This comment is added to the Task List automatically when you first create a Java file and points you to the location in the Java file where you should start inputting your code. You will learn about comments in the next section.

6 In the Text Editor window, locate the line `// TODO: Add initialization code here`. Replace it with **`System.out.println ("Hello, world!");`**. As you type, notice the Statement Completion lists that appear. Double-click an item in a Statement Completion list to insert it into your code, or highlight an item and press the **Tab** key. You also can continue to type the statement manually. When the line is complete, the `// TODO: Add initialization code here` line is automatically removed. Your finished file should be the same as Figure 2-10.

```
/**
 * This class can take a variable number of parameters on the command
 * line. Program execution begins with the main() method. The class
 * constructor is not invoked unless an object of type 'Class1'
 * created in the main() method.
 */
public class Class1
{
    /**
     * The main entry point for the application.
     *
     * @param args Array of parameters passed to the application
     * via the command line.
     */
    public static void main (String[] args)
    {
        System.out.println("Hello, world!");
    }
}
```

Figure 2-10: Complete main() method for the Hello class

> Visual J++ automatically places each curly bracket on its own line. Any curly brackets that you enter manually should also be placed on their own lines. Although placing curly brackets on their own line is not required in Java programming, it is good practice because it makes your code easier to read.

Adding Comments to a Program

As you can see, even the simplest Java program takes several lines of code, and contains somewhat perplexing syntax. Large programs that perform many tasks include much more code, and as you write longer programs, it becomes increasingly difficult to remember why you included steps or how you intended to use particular variables. **Program comments** are nonexecuting statements that you add to a program to document the purpose of various lines of code. Programmers use comments to leave notes for themselves and for others who might read their programs in the future. At the very least, your programs should include comments indicating the program's author, the date, and the program's name or function.

> As you work through this book, add comments as the first three lines of every program. The comments should contain the program name, your name, and the date. Your instructor might ask you to include additional comments.

Comments can serve a useful purpose when you are developing a program. If a program is not performing as expected, you can comment out various statements and run the program to observe the effect. When you **comment out** a statement, you turn it into a comment so the compiler will not execute it as a command. Commenting out statements helps you pinpoint the location of errors in malfunctioning programs.

There are four types of comments in the Java programming language:

- **Line comments** start with two forward slashes (//) and continue to the end of the current line. Line comments can appear on a line by themselves or at the end of a line following executable code.
- **Task List comments** also start with two forward slashes (//) and continue to the end of the current line. They can appear on a line by themselves or at the end of a line following executable code. If the text immediately following the two forward slashes (//) is the words TODO, UNDONE, or HACK, then the comments also will appear in the Task List window. These words are indicators, or **comment tokens**. You can add your own comment tokens or change each comment token's Task List priority level. You also can rename and delete the UNDONE and HACK comment tokens. To do so, you use the Task List category of the Options dialog box, which you can display by selecting Options from the Tools menu. You cannot delete or remove the TODO comment token because Visual J++ uses it when creating new projects and performing other tasks.

- **Block comments** start with a forward slash and an asterisk (/*) and end with an asterisk and a forward slash (*/). Block comments can appear on a line by themselves, on a line before executable code, or after executable code. Block comments also can extend across as many lines as needed.
- **Javadoc** comments are a special case of block comments. They begin with a forward slash and two asterisks (/**) and end with an asterisk and a forward slash (*/). Javadoc comments are displayed in the Class Outline window for a selected class. You will learn about Class Outline in Chapter 3.

It is easy to confuse the forward slash (/) and the backslash (\) characters, but they are two distinct characters. You cannot use them interchangeably.

You can use javadoc comments to generate documentation for your code with a program called javadoc that is part of the Java Development Kit (JDK).

You might recognize some of the comment types from the Hello program you just created. Visual J++ automatically includes sample Task List and javadoc comments in Java files when you create certain types of projects, such as console applications. As you become comfortable with Java programming, you might find it more convenient to delete the automatically created Task List and javadoc comments.

Figure 2-11 shows an example of how comments are used in code.

```
System.out.println("Hello");
// Demonstrating comments
/* This shows
        that these comments
              don't matter   */
System.out.println("World");  // This line executes
        //  up to where the comment started
/**  Everything but the println() line
     is a comment. */
```

Figure 2-11: Using comments in a program

Next you will add comments to your Hello.java program.

To add comments to your program:

1. Delete the following javadoc comments from the top of the file starting with the /** and ending with the */. These are default comments that Visual J++ automatically inserts into new Java files.

   ```
   /**
    * This class can take a variable number of parameters on
   the command...
    * created in the main() method.
    */
   ```

2. After deleting these comments, position your insertion point at the top of the file and press the **Enter** key to insert a new line. Press the **up arrow** key to go to the new line and type the following comments. Press the **Enter** key after typing each line. Insert your name and today's date where indicated.

   ```
   // Filename Hello.java
   // Written by <your name>
   // Written on <today's date>
   ```

3. Delete the following default javadoc comments (starting with the /** and ending with the */) that immediately follow the line that reads public class Hello:

   ```
   /**
    * The main entry point for the application...
    * via the command line.
    */
   ```

4. After deleting these comments, position your insertion point at the end of the public class Hello line, press the **Enter** key, and then type the following block comment in the program:

   ```
   /* This program demonstrates the use of the println()
   method to print the message Hello, world!   */
   ```

Running a Program

After you write and save your program, you must perform two steps before you can view the program output.

- You must set the project properties and determine which interpreter you will use to run the program. Visual J++ contains two Java interpreters for running Java applications: JVIEW and WJVIEW. **JVIEW** is used for starting Java applications from a console window. A **console window** is a command-line environment, such as MS-DOS. **WJVIEW** contains the same functionality as JVIEW except it can run a window-based Java application in a separate graphical user interface (GUI).

A First Program Using Java

- You must build the project to compile the program you wrote (called the **source** code) into bytecode. If you receive no error messages after building the project containing the file named Hello.java, then the program compiled successfully, and a file named Hello.class was created and saved in the project folder. After a successful build, you can run the class file on any computer that has a Java language interpreter.

To run your Hello.java program with JVIEW:

1 Select **Hello Properties** from the **Project** menu. The Launch tab of the Hello Properties dialog box appears as shown in Figure 2-12.

> The name of the Properties command changes to reflect the name of the current project. For example, your project name is Hello. If you opened a project named My Project, then the Properties command on the Project menu would read My Project Properties.

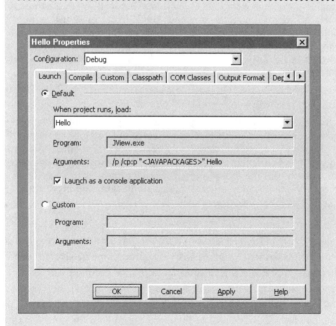

Figure 2-12: Hello Properties dialog box

2 The Launch tab of the Properties dialog box contains two radio buttons: Default and Custom. The Default button automatically selects default arguments for running JVIEW or WJVIEW, whereas the Custom button allows you to select your own arguments. If necessary, select the **Default** button. The Hello file should be visible in the When project runs, load drop-down list box. The Launch as a console application check box should be selected.

section A

Note the grayed-out Program text box. The program should read JView.exe. When you are finished, click the **OK** button.

> **help**
>
> When you rename a class file, you must select the Properties command before running the Build command or you will receive a compiler error in the Task List that reads `Specified main class '<filename>' not found`. This error occurs because the Properties dialog box is still looking for the previous filename in the When project runs, load drop-down list box. When using JVIEW from the command line to run a Java program, as you will in this exercise and most others in this text, setting properties in the Project dialog box is necessary only to remove the compiler error.

3 Select **Build** from the **Build** menu or press **Ctrl+Shift+B** to compile the program.

> **tip**
>
> The Build command is used in Visual J++ projects to compile Java code into class files as well as perform other functions for completing window-based Java programs. You can also compile individual Java files (*.java) into bytecode with a command-line program called the Microsoft Compiler for Java (JVC). You could use a text editor such as Notepad to create Java programs, use JVC to compile them, and use JVIEW or WJVIEW to run them, without ever using the Visual J++ environment. However, you would not be able to take advantage of the features of Visual J++ that make Java programming easier. In this text, you will use the Build command to compile your programs.

> **tip**
>
> Select the Build command only if it is the first time a project is being compiled. To recompile an already compiled project, select the Rebuild command from the Build menu. The Build command completely recompiles the entire project, whereas the Rebuild command compiles only changes since the last compilation. Compiling only the changes speeds up the programming process since compiling large projects from scratch with the Build command can take a significant amount of time.

> **help**
>
> If you receive a compiler error in the Task List, then the source code includes one or more syntax errors. A syntax error is a programming error that occurs when you introduce typing or structural errors into your program. For example, if your class name is hello (with a lowercase *h*) in the source code, but you saved the file as Hello.java, you will get an error message, such as `public class hello should not be defined in Hello.java`, after compiling the program because *hello* and *Hello* are not the same in a case-sensitive language. If this error occurs, make the necessary corrections in your Java code and select Rebuild from the Build menu.

A First Program Using Java

4 Go to a command-line prompt, such as a DOS prompt, and change to the drive, folder, and subdirectory where you saved the Hello project.

5 Execute your program in a console window by typing **jview Hello** at the command line. The output should appear on the next line, as shown in Figure 2-13.

> ▶ **tip**
>
> You can also execute your program using JVIEW from inside Visual J++ by selecting Start from the Debug menu or by pressing F5. For Java programs that simply create system output, such as the Hello program, JVIEW opens a command-line window, outputs information to the screen ("Hello World!") and then immediately closes the command-line window. The command-line window is closed immediately when output is complete because JVIEW views the program as being finished, as the program's only purpose is system output. For programs that provide a single line of output such as the Hello program, the command-line window opens and closes so quickly that it is difficult to read what is on the screen. To provide more time to view your work, you will start JVIEW directly from the command line for most system output exercises in this text.

> ▶ **help**
>
> Remember that Java is case sensitive. When you type `jview Hello` at the command line, the case of the file **Hello** must match the name of the file exactly.

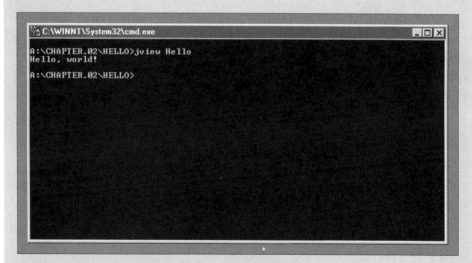

Figure 2-13: Output of the Hello program with JVIEW

> ▶ **help**
>
> Your console window might appear differently from Figure 2-13.

section A

To run your Hello.java program with WJVIEW:

1. Select **Hello Properties** from the **Project** menu. The Launch tab of the Hello Properties dialog box appears as shown in Figure 2-12.
2. Deselect the **Launch as a console application** check box. Note the grayed-out Program text box. The program should read WJView.exe. When you are finished, click the **OK** button.
3. Select **Rebuild** from the **Build** menu.
4. Point to **Other Windows** on the **View** menu, then select **Output**. For programs that create system output, such as your Hello project, WJVIEW displays output in the Output window. Adjust the window so that it is clearly visible on the screen.
5. Select **Start** from the **Debug** menu. The output from your program should appear in the Output window, as shown in Figure 2-14.

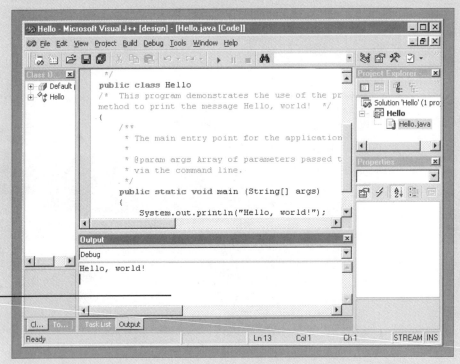

Output window

Figure 2-14: Output of the Hello program with WJVIEW

You also can select the Start command on the Debug menu by pressing F5.

A First Program Using Java

You can display the Output window by pressing Ctrl+Alt+O.

When you run a program using WJVIEW, you might notice that your project is saved automatically. You can turn this feature on or off and select other saving options by selecting Options from the Tools menu. The Options dialog box appears. In the Options dialog box, click the Saving option under the Environment node. Figure 2-15 shows the available saving options in the Options dialog box.

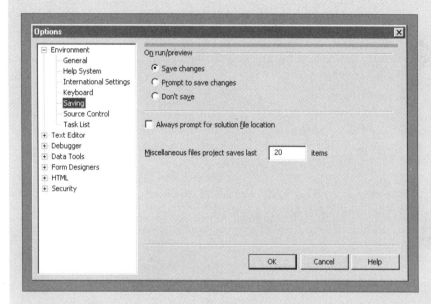

Figure 2-15: Saving options in the Options dialog box

Generally, you should not use WJVIEW for programs that create system output or that require user input from the command line. You will use JVIEW to run the majority of programs in this text, since many of the exercises create system output or require user input.

Modifying a Program

After viewing the program output, you might decide to modify your program to get a different result. For example, you might decide to change the output from the First program (near the beginning of the chapter) from `First Java program` to the following:

`My new and improved`
`Java program`

To produce the new output, first you must modify the Java file that contains the existing program. You want to change the literal string that currently prints "First Java program" and add an additional text string. Figure 2-16 shows the modifications to change the output.

```
public class First
{
    /**
    * The main entry point for the application.
    *
    * @param args Array of parameters passed to the application
    * via the command line.
    */
    public static void main (String[] args)
    {
        System.out.println("My new and improved");
        System.out.println("Java program");
    }
}
```

Figure 2-16: Changing a program's output

The addition of the statement `System.out.println("My new and improved");` and the removal of the word "First" from the string in the statement `System.out.println("Java program");` are the two changes that have been made. If you were to run the program right now, you would not see the new output—you would see the old output. Before the new source code will execute, you must do the following:

A First Program Using Java

- Rebuild the First class.
- Interpret the First.class bytecode with the `jview` command.

Next modify your Hello class and rerun the program.

To change the Hello class and rerun the program:

1. Add the following statement below the statement that prints "Hello, world!": `System.out.println("I'm ready for Java programming!");`. Make sure to type the semicolon at the end of the statement and use the correct case.

2. Select **Rebuild** from the **Build** menu to recompile the program.

   > help
   >
   > If you receive compiler errors in the Task List, fix the errors, and then repeat Step 2 until the program compiles successfully.

3. Execute the program as a console application by typing the command **jview Hello** at the command line. Your output should look like Figure 2-17.

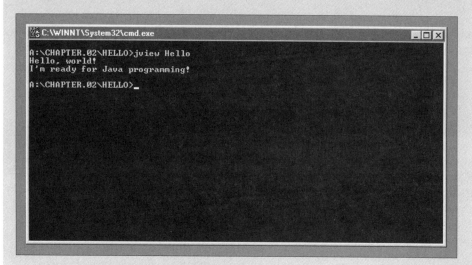

Figure 2-17: Output of the revised Hello program

SUMMARY

- All Java programming language statements end with a semicolon.

- A series of characters that appears between double quotation marks is a literal string.

- Java programming language methods might require arguments or messages to perform the appropriate task.

- When you send something, such as a literal string, to a method, you are said to be passing an argument.

- Periods (called dots) are used to separate classes, objects, and methods in program code.

- Everything that you use within a Java program must be part of a class. A Java programming language class might take any name or identifier that begins with either an uppercase or lowercase letter of the alphabet and contains only uppercase and lowercase letters, digits, and underscores. A class name cannot be a reserved keyword of the Java programming language.

- The reserved word `public` is an access modifier. An access modifier defines the circumstances under which a class can be accessed.

- The contents of all classes are contained within opening and closing curly brackets.

- The keyword `static` in a method header indicates that every member of a class will have an identical, unchanging method.

- The keyword `void` in a method header indicates that the method does not return any value when it is called.

- All Java application programs must have a method named main(). Most Java applications have additional methods.

- Visual J++ has its own built-in text editor called the Text Editor window, which is used for creating Java files and other text documents.

- The Text Editor window uses syntax coloring to distinguish among various types of Java code elements.

- The Text Editor window has a feature called Statement Completion that helps you create Java code. As you are writing Java code, member lists and parameter information appear automatically according to the current object.

- Another Text Editor tool for writing Java code is Word Completion, which automatically completes class names and other elements according to the first few characters you type.

- Dynamic syntax checking also helps you write code in the Text Editor window. This feature uses red squiggly lines, which appear beneath Java code elements, to indicate syntax errors in your code.

- Program comments are nonexecuting statements that you add to a program for documentation. There are four types of comments in the Java programming language: line comments, Task List comments, block comments, and javadoc comments.

- To compile your project, select Build from the Build menu. When you build a project, the compiler creates a file with a .class extension. You can run the .class file on any computer that has a Java language interpreter by entering the `jview` command followed by the name of the class file. Do not type the .class extension with the filename.

- Java code files can also be compiled using a command-line program called the Microsoft Compiler for Java (`jvc`).

- JVIEW is used for starting Java applications from a command line or console window. WJVIEW runs a window-based Java application in a separate graphical user interface (GUI) and contains the same functionality as JVIEW. For programs that create system output, WJVIEW displays the output in a separate window that runs within the Visual J++ IDE called the Output window.

- If you modify a program's source code file, you must rebuild the project before executing it again.

- The Build command completely recompiles the entire project whereas the Rebuild command compiles only changes since the last compilation. Compiling only the changes speeds up the programming process because compiling large projects from scratch with the Build command can take a significant amount of time.

- A syntax error is a programming error that occurs when you introduce typing or structural errors into your program.

QUESTIONS

1. All Java programming language statements must end with a _____.
    a. period
    b. comma
    c. semicolon
    d. closing parenthesis

2. Arguments to methods always appear within _____.
    a. parentheses
    b. double quotation marks
    c. single quotation marks
    d. curly brackets

3. In a Java program, you must use _____ to separate classes, objects, and methods.
    a. commas
    b. semicolons
    c. periods
    d. forward slashes

section A

4. All Java applications must have a method named _____.
   a. method()
   b. main()
   c. java()
   d. Hello()

5. Nonexecuting program statements that provide documentation are called _____.
   a. classes
   b. notes
   c. comments
   d. commands

6. The Java programming language supports four types of comments: _____, _____, _____, and javadoc.
   a. line, Task List, block
   b. string, literal, line
   c. constant, variable, block
   d. single, multiple, list

7. After you create a project, you _____ it.
   a. interpret and then build
   b. interpret and then resave
   c. build and then execute
   d. build and then interpret

8. Visual J++ uses _____ to display member lists and parameter information.
   a. JVIEW
   b. Statement Completion
   c. on-line help
   d. spell checking

9. Errors in Java code are displayed using _____.
   a. the Properties window
   b. dialog boxes
   c. dynamic syntax checking
   d. Project Explorer

10. The command to execute a console program is _____.
    a. `run`
    b. `execute`
    c. `javac`
    d. `jview`

11. You save text files containing Java language source code using the file extension _____.
    a. .java
    b. .class
    c. .txt
    d. .src

E X E R C I S E S

1. Note whether each of the following Java programming language identifiers are legal or illegal:
   a. weeklySales _____
   b. last character _____
   c. class _____
   d. MathClass _____
   e. myfirstinitial _____
   f. phone# _____
   g. abcdefghijklmnop _____
   h. 23jordan _____
   i. my_code _____
   j. 90210 _____
   k. year2000problem _____
   l. αβφfraternity _____

2. Name some attributes that might be appropriate for each of the following classes:
   a. TelevisionSet: _____
   b. EmployeePaycheck: _____
   c. PatientMedicalRecord: _____

3. Write, build, and test a program that prints your first name on the screen. Save the project as Name in the Chapter.02 folder on your Student Disk.

4. Write, build, and test a program that prints your full name, street address, city, state, and zip code on three separate lines on the screen. Save the project as Address in the Chapter.02 folder on your Student Disk.

5. Write, build, and test a program that displays the following pattern on the screen:

   ```
         X
        XXX
       XXXXX
      XXXXXXX
         X
   ```

   Save the project as Tree in the Chapter.02 folder on your Student Disk.

6. Write, build, and test a program that prints your initials on the screen. Compose each initial with six lines of the initials themselves, as in the following example:

   ```
           J     FFFFFF
           J     F
           J     FFFF
       J   J     F
       JJJJJJ    F
   ```

   Save the project as Initial in the Chapter.02 folder on your Student Disk.

SECTION B
objectives

In this section you will learn
- How to use variables and constants
- About the int data type
- How to write arithmetic statements
- About the boolean data type
- About floating-point data types
- About numeric type conversion
- About the char data type

Using Data

Variables and Constants

You can categorize data as variable or constant. Data is **constant** when it cannot be changed after a program is compiled; data is **variable** when it might change. For example, in the Java statement `System.out.println(459);`, the number 459 is a constant. Every time a program containing the statement is executed, the value 459 will print. You can call the number 459 a **literal constant** because its value is taken literally at each use.

> Besides using literal constants, you can use symbolic constants, which you will learn about in Chapter 4.

On the other hand, you can create a variable named ovenTemperature, and include the statement `System.out.println(ovenTemperature);` within a Java program. In this case, different values might appear when the program is executed multiple times, depending on what value is stored in ovenTemperature during each run of the program.

Variables are named memory locations that your program can use to store values. The Java programming language provides for eight **primitive types** of data:

- boolean
- byte
- char
- double
- float
- int
- long
- short

> The eight primitive data types are called primitive types because they are simple and uncomplicated. Primitive types also serve as the building blocks for more complex data types, called reference types. In Chapter 3, you will begin to create objects that are examples of reference types.

You name variables using the same naming rules for legal class identifiers described in Section A. Basically, variable names must start with a letter and cannot be any reserved keyword.

Variable names usually begin with lowercase letters to distinguish variable names from class names. However, variable names can begin with either an uppercase or a lowercase letter.

You must declare all variables you want to use in a program. A **variable declaration** includes the following:

- A data type that identifies the type of data that the variable will store
- An identifier that is the variable's name
- An optional assigned value, when you want a variable to contain an initial value
- An ending semicolon

For example, the variable declaration `int myAge = 25;` declares a variable of type int named myAge and assigns it an initial value of 25. This is a complete statement that ends in a semicolon. The equal sign (=) is the **assignment operator**. Any value to the right of the equal sign is assigned to the variable on the left of the equal sign. An assignment made when you declare a variable is an **initialization**; an assignment made later is simply an **assignment**. Thus, `int myAge = 25;` initializes myAge to 25, and a subsequent statement `myAge = 42;` might assign a new value to the variable. You should note that the expression `25 = myAge;` is illegal.

The variable declaration `int myAge;` also declares a variable of type int named myAge, but no value is assigned at the time of creation.

You can declare multiple variables of the same type in separate statements on different lines. For example, the following statements declare two variables—the first variable is named myAge and its value is 25. The second variable is named yourAge and its value is 19.

```
int myAge = 25;
int yourAge = 19;
```

You also can declare two variables of the same type in a single statement by separating the variable declarations with a comma, as shown in the following statement:

```
int myAge = 25, yourAge = 19;
```

If you want to declare variables of different types, you must use a separate statement for each type. The following statements declare two variables of type int (myAge and yourAge) and two variables of type double (mySalary and yourSalary):

```
int myAge, yourAge;
double mySalary, yourSalary;
```

The int Data Type

In the Java programming language, you use variables of type int to store (or hold) **integers**, or whole numbers. An integer can hold any whole number value from -2,147,483,648 to 2,147,483,647. When you assign a value to an int variable, you do not type any commas; you type only digits and an optional plus or minus sign to indicate a positive or negative integer.

> The legal integer values are -2^{31} through $2^{31}-1$. These are the highest and lowest values that you can store in four bytes of memory, which is the size of an int.

The types **byte**, **short**, and **long** are all variations of the integer type. You use byte or short if you know a variable will need to hold only small values so you can save space in memory. You use long if you know you will be working with very large values. Figure 2-18 shows the upper and lower value limits for each of these types.

Type	Minimum Value	Maximum Value	Size in Bytes
byte	-128	127	1
short	-32,768	32,767	2
int	-2,147,483,648	2,147,483,647	4
long	-9,223,372,036,854,775,808	9,223,372,036,854,775,807	8

Figure 2-18: Limits on integer values by type

It is important to choose appropriate types for the variables you will use in a program. If you attempt to assign a value that is too large for the data type of the variable, the compiler will issue an error message and the program will not execute. If you choose a data type that is larger than you need, you waste memory. For example, a personnel program might use a byte variable for number of dependents (because a limit of 127 is more than enough). It might use a short variable for hours worked in a month (because 127 isn't enough). It might use an integer for an annual salary (because even though a limit of 32,000 might be large enough for your salary, it isn't enough for the CEO).

> If your program uses a literal constant integer, such as 932, the integer is an int by default. If you need to use a constant higher than 2,147,483,647, you must follow the number with the letter *L* to indicate long. For example, `long    mosquitosInTheNorthWoods = 2444555888L;` stores a number that is greater than the maximum limit for the int type. You can type either an uppercase or lowercase *L* to indicate the long type, but the uppercase *L* is preferred to avoid confusion with the number one.

Next, you will write a program to declare and display numeric values.

A First Program Using Java

To declare and display values in a program:

1. Create a new console application project and name it **DemoVariables**. Save the **Demo Variables** project folder in the Chapter.02 folder on your Student Disk.
2. Rename the Class1.java file as **DemoVariables.java**, then open the file in the Text Editor window.
3. Replace the Class1 class name in the `public class Class1` line with **DemoVariables**.
4. Replace the `// TODO: Add initialization code here` comment with `int oneInt = 315;` to declare a variable of type int named oneInt with a value of 315.

> You can declare variables at any point within a method prior to their first use. However, it is common practice to declare variables first and place method calls second.

5. Press the **Enter** key at the end of the oneInt declaration statement, and then type the following two output statements. The first statement uses the print() method to output "The int is " and leaves the insertion point on the same output line. The second statement uses the println() method to output the value of oneInt and advances the cursor to a new line.

```
System.out.print("The int is ");
System.out.println(oneInt);
```

> When your output contains a literal string such as "The int is ", you should type a space before the closing quotation mark so there is a space between the end of the literal string and the value that prints.

6. Select **DemoVariables Properties** from the **Project** menu. Select the **DemoVariables** file in the When project runs, load drop-down list box and set the project to run as a console application. When you are finished, click the **OK** button.
7. Compile the file by selecting **Build** from the **Build** menu. If necessary, correct any errors and select **Rebuild** from the **Build** menu.
8. Execute the program as a console application by typing `jview DemoVariables` at the command line. The output should be "The int is 315".

Even though you plan to add additional statements to the DemoVariables program, by compiling and executing the program at this point, you are assured that it is working exactly as you intend. Sometimes it is a good idea to write and compile your programs in steps, so you can identify any syntax or logical errors as you go instead of waiting until you finish writing the entire program.

Next, you will declare two more variables in your program.

To declare two more variables in the program:

1 Return to the **DemoVariables.java** file in the Text Editor window.

2 Position the cursor at the end of the line that contains the oneInt declaration, press the **Enter** key, and then type the following variable declarations on separate lines:

```
short oneShort = 23;
long oneLong = 123456789876543L;
```

3 Position the cursor at the end of the line that contains the println() method that displays the oneInt value, press the **Enter** key, and then type the following statements to display the values of the two new variables:

```
System.out.print("The short is ");
System.out.println(oneShort);
System.out.print("The long is ");
System.out.println(oneLong);
```

4 Recompile the program by selecting **Rebuild** from the **Build** menu.

5 Execute the program as a console application by typing `jview DemoVariables` at the command line. Your output should match Figure 2-19.

Figure 2-19: Output of the DemoVariables program

In the previous program, you used two print methods to print a compound phrase with the following code:

```
System.out.print("The long is ");
System.out.println(oneLong);
```

To reduce the amount of typing, you can use one method and combine the arguments with a plus sign using the following statement: `System.out.println("The long is " + oneLong);`. It doesn't matter which format you use—the result is the same, as you will see next.

To change the two print methods into a single statement:

1 Return to the **DemoVariables.java** file in the Text Editor window.

2 Use the mouse to select the two statements that print "The int is" and the value of oneInt, and then press the **Delete** key to delete them. In place of the deleted statements, type the following println() statement: `System.out.println("The int is " + oneInt);` .

3 Select the two statements that produce output for the short variable, press the **Delete** key to delete them, and then type the statement `System.out.println("The short is " + oneShort);`.

4 Select the two statements that produce output for the long variables, delete them, and replace them with `System.out.println("The long is " + oneLong);`.

5 Rebuild and execute the program as a console application. The output should be the same as that shown in Figure 2-19.

Arithmetic Statements

Figure 2-20 describes the five standard arithmetic operators for integers. You use the arithmetic operators to manipulate values in your programs.

You will learn about shortcut arithmetic operators for the Java programming language in Chapter 5.

Operator	Description	Example
+	Addition	45 + 2, the result is 47
–	Subtraction	45 – 2, the result is 43
*	Multiplication	45 * 2, the result is 90
/	Division	45 / 2, the result is 22 (not 22.5)
%	Modulus (remainder)	45 % 2, the result is 1 (that is, 45 / 2 = 22 with a remainder of 1)

Figure 2-20: Integer arithmetic operators

> You do not need to perform a division operation before you can perform a modulus operation. A modulus operation can stand alone.

The operators / and % deserve special consideration. When you divide two integers, whether they are integer constants or integer variables, the result is an *integer*. Any fractional part of the result is lost. For example, the result of 45 / 2 is 22, even though the result is 22.5 in a mathematical expression. When you use the modulus operator with two integers, the result is an integer with the value of the remainder after division takes place—so the result of 45 % 2 is 1 because 2 "goes into" 45 twenty-two times with a remainder of 1.

> You can use modulus (%) only with integers. You can use the other four operators with floating-point data.

Next you will add some arithmetic statements to the DemoVariables.java program.

To use arithmetic statements in a program:

1 Return to the **DemoVariables.java** file in the Text Editor window.
2 Position the insertion point on the last line of the current variable declarations, press the **Enter** key, and then type the following declarations:

```
int value1 = 43, value2 = 10, sum, difference,
product, quotient, modulus;
```

3. Position the cursor after the statement that prints the oneLong variable, press the **Enter** key, and then type the following statements on separate lines:

```
sum = value1 + value2;
difference = value1 - value2;
product = value1 * value2;
quotient = value1 / value2;
modulus = value1 % value2;
```

4. Press the **Enter** key, and then type the following output statements:

```
System.out.println("Sum is " + sum);
System.out.println("Difference is " + difference);
System.out.println("Product is " + product);
System.out.println("Quotient is " + quotient);
System.out.println("Modulus is " + modulus);
```

5. Rebuild and execute the program as a console application. Your output should look like Figure 2-21. Analyze the output and confirm that the arithmetic is correct.

```
A:\CHAPTER.02\DemoVariables>jview DemoVariables
The int is 315
The short is 23
The long is 123456789876543
Sum is 53
Difference is 33
Product is 430
Quotient is 4
Modulus is 3

A:\CHAPTER.02\DemoVariables>
```

Figure 2-21: Output of the revised DemoVariables program

When you combine mathematical operations in a single statement, you must understand **operator precedence**, or the order in which Java evaluates parts of a mathematical expression. Multiplication, division, and modulus always take place prior to addition or subtraction in an expression. For example, the expression `int result = 2 + 3 * 4;` results in 14, because the multiplication (3 * 4) occurs before adding 2. You can override normal operator precedence by putting the first operation to perform in parentheses. The statement `int result = (2 + 3) * 4;` results in 20, because the addition within the parentheses takes place first, and then that result (5) is multiplied by 4.

> **tip**
> You will learn more about operator precedence in Chapter 4.

The Boolean Data Type

Boolean logic is based on true-or-false comparisons. Whereas an int variable can hold millions of different values (at different times), a **boolean variable** can hold only one of two values—true or false. The following statements declare and assign appropriate values to boolean variables:

```
boolean isItPayday = false;
boolean areYouBroke = true;
```

You also can assign values based on the result of comparisons to boolean variables. The Java programming language supports six comparison operators. A **comparison operator** compares two items, and an expression containing a comparison operator has a boolean value. Figure 2-22 describes the comparison operators.

> **tip**
> You will learn about other boolean operators in Chapter 5.

Operator	Description	true Example	false Example
<	Less than	3 < 8	8 < 3
>	Greater than	4 > 2	2 > 4
==	Equal to	7 == 7	3 == 9
<=	Less than or equal to	5 <= 5	8 <= 6
>=	Greater than or equal to	7 >= 3	1 >= 2
!=	Not equal to	5 != 6	3 != 3

Figure 2-22: Comparison operators

When you use any of the operators that have two symbols (==, <=, >=, or !=), you cannot place any whitespace between the two symbols.

Legal, but somewhat useless, declaration statements might include the following, which compare two values directly:

```
boolean isSixBigger = (6 > 5);
    // Value stored would be true
boolean isSevenSmallerOrEqual = (7 <= 4);
    // Value stored would be false
```

A First Program Using Java

> **tip**
>
> You can easily identify variable names as boolean if you use a form of "to be" (such as "is" or "are") as part of the variable name.

Boolean expressions are more meaningful when variables (that have been assigned values) are used in the comparisons, as in the following examples. The first statement compares the hours variable to a constant value of 40. If the hours variable is greater than 40, then the expression evaluates to `true`. In the second statement, the income variable must be greater than 100000 for the expression to evaluate to `true`.

```
boolean overtime = (hours > 40);
boolean highTaxBracket = (income > 100000);
```

Next, you will add two boolean variables to the DemoVariables.java file.

To add boolean variables to a program:

1. Return to the **DemoVariables.java** file in the Text Editor window.
2. Position the insertion point at the end of the line with the integer variable declarations, press the **Enter** key, and then type `boolean isProgrammingFun = true, isProgrammingHard = false;` to add two new boolean variables to the program.

Next add some print statements to display the values.

3. Press the **Enter** key, and then type the following statements:

   ```
   System.out.println("The value of isProgrammingFun is "
       + isProgrammingFun);
   System.out.println("The value of isProgrammingHard is "
       + isProgrammingHard);
   ```

4. Rebuild and test the program.

Floating-Point Data Types

A **floating-point** number contains decimal positions. The Java programming language supports two floating-point data types: float and double. A **float** data type can hold up to seven significant digits of accuracy. A **double** data type can hold 15 significant digits of accuracy. The term **significant digits** refers to the mathematical accuracy of a value. For example, a float given the value 0.324616777 will display as 0.246168 because the value is accurate only to the seventh decimal position. Figure 2-23 shows the minimum and maximum values for each data type.

> **tip**
>
> A float given the value 324616777 will display as 3.24617e+008, which means approximately 3.24617 times 10 to the 8th power, or 324617000. The e stands for *exponent*; the format is called scientific notation. The large value contains only six significant digits.

Type	Minimum	Maximum	Size in Bytes
float	$-1.4 * 10^{-45}$	$3.4 * 10^{38}$	4
double	$-1.7 * 10^{-308}$	$1.7 * 10^{308}$	8

Figure 2-23: Limits on floating-point values

A value written as $-1.4 * 10^{-45}$ indicates that the value is -1.4 multiplied by 10 to the negative 45th power, or 10 with 45 trailing zeros—a very large number.

Just as an integer constant, such as 178, is an int by default, a floating-point number constant such as 18.23 is a double by default. To store a value explicitly as a float, you can type the letter *F* after the number, as in `float pocketChange = 4.87F;`. You can type either a lowercase or an uppercase *F*. You also can type *D* (or *d*) after a floating-point value to indicate it is a double, but even without the *D*, the value will be stored as a double by default.

As with int, you can perform the mathematical operations of addition, subtraction, multiplication, and division with floating-point numbers. However, you cannot perform modulus operations using floating-point values. (Floating-point division yields a floating-point result, so there is no remainder.)

Next, you will add some floating-point variables to the DemoVariables.java file and perform arithmetic with them.

To add floating-point variables to the program:

1. Return to the **DemoVariables.java** file in the Text Editor window.
2. Position the insertion point after the line that declares the boolean variables, press the **Enter** key, and then type `double doubNum1 = 2.3, doubNum2 = 14.8, doubResult;` to add some new floating-point variables.
3. Press the **Enter** key, and then type the following statements to perform arithmetic and produce output:

```
doubResult = doubNum1 + doubNum2;
System.out.println("The sum of the doubles is "
   + doubResult);
doubResult = doubNum1 * doubNum2;
System.out.println("The product of the doubles is "
   + doubResult);
```

4. Rebuild and run the program.

Numeric Type Conversion

When you are performing arithmetic with variables or constants of the same type, the result of the arithmetic retains the same type. For example, when you divide two integers, the result is an integer, and when you subtract two doubles, the result is a double. Often, you might want to perform mathematical operations on unlike types. For example, in the following example, you multiply an integer by a double:

```
int hoursWorked = 37;
double payRate = 6.73;
grossPay = hoursWorked * payRate;
```

When you perform arithmetic operations with operands of unlike types, the Java programming language chooses a unifying type for the result. The Java programming language then **implicitly** (or automatically) converts nonconforming operands to the unifying type. The **unifying type** is the type of the involved operand that appears first in the following list:

1. double
2. float
3. long
4. int
5. short
6. byte

An operand is simply any value used in an arithmetic or logical operation.

In other words, grossPay is the result of multiplication of an int and a double, so grossPay itself must be a double. Similarly, the addition of a short and an int results in an int.

You can **explicitly** (or purposely) override the unifying type imposed by the Java programming language by performing a type cast. **Type casting** involves placing the desired result type in parentheses followed by the variable or constant to be cast. For example, two casts are performed in the following code:

```
double bankBalance = 189.66;
float weeklyBudget = (float) bankBalance / 4;
    // weeklyBudget is 47.40, one-fourth of bankBalance
int dollars = (int) weeklyBudget;
    // dollars is 47, the integer part of weeklyBudget
```

> **tip**
>
> It is easy to lose data when performing a cast. For example, the largest byte value is 127 and the largest int value is 2,147,483,647, so the following statements produce distorted results:
> `int anOkayInt = 200;`
> `byte aBadByte = (byte)anOkayInt;`
> A byte is constructed from eight 1s and 0s, or binary digits. The first binary digit, or bit, holds a 0 or 1 to represent positive or negative. The remaining seven bits store the actual value. When the integer value 200 is stored in the byte variable, its large value consumes the eighth bit, turning it to a 1, and forcing the aBadByte variable to appear to hold the value -56, which is inaccurate and misleading.

The double value `bankBalance / 4` is converted to a float before it is stored in weeklyBudget, and the float value weeklyBudget is converted to an int before it is stored in dollars. When the float value is converted to an int, the decimal place values are lost.

The char Data Type

You use the **char** data type to hold any single character. You place constant character values within single quotation marks because the computer stores characters and integers differently. For example, the statements `char aCharValue = '9';` and `int aNumValue = 9;` are legal. The statements `char aCharValue = 9;` and `int aNumValue = '9';` are illegal. A number can be a character, in which case it must be enclosed in single quotation marks and declared as a char type. However, you cannot store an alphabetic letter in a numeric type. The following code shows how you can store any character string using the char data type:

```
char myInitial = 'J';
char percentSign = '%';
char numThatIsAChar = '9';
```

A variable of type char can hold only one character. To store a string of characters, such as a person's name, you must use a data structure called a **String**. Unlike single characters, which use single quotation marks, String constants are written between double quotation marks. For example, the expression that stores the name Audrey as a String in a variable named firstName is `firstName = "Audrey";`.

> **tip**
>
> You will learn more about Strings in Chapter 6.

You can store any character—including nonprinting characters such as a backspace or a tab—in a char variable. To store nonprinting characters, you must use an **escape sequence**, which always begins with a backslash. For example, the following code stores a backspace character and a tab character in the char variables aBackspaceChar and aTabChar:

```
char aBackspaceChar = '\b';
char aTabChar = '\t';
```

In the preceding code, the escape sequence indicates a unique value for the character, instead of the letters *b* or *t*. Figure 2-24 describes some common escape sequences that are used in the Java programming language.

Escape Sequence	Description
\b	Backspace
\t	Tab
\n	Newline or line feed
\f	Form feed
\r	Carriage return
\"	Double quotation mark
\'	Single quotation mark
\\	Backslash

Figure 2-24: Common escape sequences

The characters used in the Java programming language are represented in **Unicode**, which is a 16-bit coding scheme for characters. For example, the letter *A* actually is stored in computer memory as a set of 16 zeros and ones as 0000 0000 0100 0001 (the spaces inserted after every set of four digits are for readability). Because 16-digit numbers are difficult to read, programmers often use a shorthand notation called **hexadecimal**, or **base 16**. In hexadecimal shorthand, 0000 becomes 0, 0100 becomes 4, and 0001 becomes 1, so the letter *A* is represented in hexadecimal as 0041. You tell the compiler to treat the four-digit hexadecimal 0041 as a single character by preceding it with the \u escape sequence. Therefore, there are two ways to store the character *A*:

```
char letter = 'A';
char letter = '\u0041';
```

For more information about Unicode, go to http://www.unicode.org.

The second option using hexadecimal obviously is more difficult and confusing than the first method, so it is not recommended that you store letters of the alphabet using the hexadecimal method. Nevertheless, it is important that you know how to use Unicode characters. You can produce some interesting values using the Unicode format. For example, the sequence \u0007 is a bell that produces a noise if you send it to output. In addition, letters from foreign alphabets (Greek, Hebrew, Chinese, and so on) that use characters instead of letters and other special symbols (foreign currency symbols, mathematical symbols, geometric shapes, and so on) are available using Unicode, but not on a standard keyboard.

Next you will add statements to your DemoVariables.java file to use the \n and \t escape sequences.

To use escape sequences in a program:

1. Return to the **DemoVariables.java** file in the Text Editor window.

2. Position the cursor after the last method line in the program, press the **Enter** key, and then type the following:

   ```
   System.out.println("\nThis is on one line\nThis on another");
   System.out.println("This shows\thow\ttabs\twork");
   ```

3. Rebuild and run the program. Your output should look like Figure 2-25.

```
A:\CHAPTER.02\DemoVariables>jview DemoVariables
The sum of the doubles is 17.1
The product of the doubles is 34.04
The value of isProgrammingFun is true
The value of isProgrammingHard is false
The int is 315
The short is 23
The long is 123456789876543
Sum is 53
Difference is 33
Product is 430
Quotient is 4
Modulus is 3

This is on one line
This on another
This shows      how     tabs    work

A:\CHAPTER.02\DemoVariables>
```

Figure 2-25: Output of the DemoVariables program demonstrating escape sequences

SUMMARY

- Data is constant when it cannot be changed after a program is compiled; data is variable when it might change.

- Variables are named memory locations that your program can use to store values. You can name a variable using any legal identifier. A variable name must start with a letter and cannot be any reserved keyword. You must declare all variables you want to use in a program. A variable declaration requires a type and a name; it also can include an assigned value.

- The Java programming language provides for eight primitive types of data: boolean, byte, char, double, float, int, long, and short.

- A variable declaration includes: a data type that identifies the type of data that the variable will store; an identifier that is the variable's name; an optional assigned value, when you want a variable to contain an initial value; and an ending semicolon.

- The equal sign (=) is the assignment operator. Any value to the right of an equal sign is assigned to the variable on the left of the equal sign.

- You can declare multiple variables of the same type in separate statements or in a single statement, separated by commas.

- Variables of type int are used to hold integers, or whole numbers. An integer can hold any whole number value from -2,147,483,648 to 2,147,483,647. The types byte, short, and long are all variations of the integer type.

- There are five standard arithmetic operators for integers: + - * / and %.

- Operator precedence is the order in which parts of a mathematical expression are evaluated. Multiplication, division, and modulus always take place prior to addition or subtraction in an expression.

- A boolean type variable can hold `true` or `false`.

- There are six comparison operators: > < == >= <= and !=.

- A floating-point number contains decimal positions. The Java programming language supports two floating-point data types: float and double.

- When you perform mathematical operations on unlike types, the Java programming language implicitly converts the variables to a unifying type. You can explicitly override the unifying type imposed by the Java programming language by performing a type cast.

- You use the char data type to hold any single character. You type constant character values in single quotation marks. You type String constants that store more than one character between double quotation marks.

- You can store some characters using an escape sequence, which always begins with a backslash.

- The characters used in Java programming are represented in the 16-bit Unicode scheme.

QUESTIONS

1. When data cannot be changed after a program is compiled, the data is _____.
   a. constant
   b. variable
   c. volatile
   d. mutable

section B

2. Which of the following is *not* a primitive data type in the Java programming language?
   a. boolean
   b. byte
   c. int
   d. sector

3. Which of the following elements is *not* required in a variable declaration?
   a. a type
   b. an identifier
   c. an assigned value
   d. a semicolon

4. The assignment operator in the Java programming language is _____.
   a. =
   b. ==
   c. :=
   d. ::

5. Which of the following values can you assign to a variable of type int?
   a. 0
   b. 98.6
   c. 'S'
   d. 5,000,000,000,000

6. Which of these data types can store a value in the least amount of memory?
   a. short
   b. long
   c. int
   d. byte

7. The modulus operator _____.
   a. is represented by a forward slash
   b. provides the remainder of integer division
   c. provides the remainder of floating-point division
   d. Two of the preceding answers are correct.

8. According to the rules of operator precedence, division always takes place prior to _____.
   a. multiplication
   b. modulus
   c. subtraction
   d. Two of the preceding answers are correct.

9. A boolean variable can hold _____.
   a. any character
   b. any whole number
   c. any decimal number
   d. the values `true` or `false`

10. The "equal to" comparison operator is _____.
    a. =
    b. ==
    c. !=
    d. !!

11. The value 137.68 can be held by a variable of type _____.
    a. int
    b. float
    c. double
    d. Two of the preceding answers are correct.

12. When you perform arithmetic with values of diverse types, the Java programming language _____.
    a. issues an error message
    b. implicitly converts the values to a unifying type
    c. requires you to convert the values explicitly to a unifying type
    d. requires you to perform a cast

13. If you attempt to add a float, an int, and a byte, the result will be a(n) _____.
    a. float
    b. int
    c. byte
    d. error message

14. Explicitly overriding an implicit type is a _____.
    a. mistake
    b. type cast
    c. format
    d. type set

15. Which assignment is correct?
    a. `char aChar = 5;`
    b. `char aChar = "W";`
    c. `char aChar = '*';`
    d. Two of the preceding answers are correct.

16. An escape sequence always begins with a(n) _____.
    a. 'e'
    b. forward slash
    c. backslash
    d. equal sign

17. The 16-bit coding scheme employed by the Java programming language is _____.
    a. Unicode
    b. ASCII
    c. EBCDIC
    d. hexadecimal

section B

EXERCISES

1. What is the numeric value of each of the following expressions as evaluated by the Java programming language?
   a. 4 + 6 * 3
   b. 6 / 3 * 7
   c. 18 / 2 + 14 / 2
   d. 16 / 2
   e. 17 / 2
   f. 28 / 5
   g. 16 % 2
   h. 17 % 2
   i. 28 % 5
   j. 28 % 5 * 3 + 1
   k. (2 + 3) * 4
   l. 20 / (4 + 1)

2. What is the value of each of the following boolean expressions?
   a. 4 > 1
   b. 5 <= 18
   c. 43 >= 43
   d. 2 == 3
   e. 2 + 5 == 7
   f. 3 + 8 <= 10
   g. 3 != 9
   h. 13 != 13
   i. -4 != 4
   j. 2 + 5 * 3 == 21

3. Which of the following expressions are illegal? For the legal expressions, what is the numeric value of each of the following statements as evaluated by the Java programming language?
   a. 2.3 * 1.2
   b. 5.67 - 2
   c. 25.0 / 5.0
   d. 7.0 % 3.0
   e. 8 % 2.0

4. Choose the best data type for each of the following, so that no memory storage is wasted. Give an example of a typical value that would be held by the variable and explain why you chose the type you did.
   a. your age
   b. the U.S. national debt
   c. your shoe size
   d. your middle initial

5. Create a Java program that declares variables to represent the length and width of a room in feet. Name the project Room and save it in the Chapter.02 folder on your Student Disk. Assign appropriate values to the variables—for example, length = 15 and width = 25. Compute and display the floor space of the room in square feet (area = length * width). Do not display only a value as output; display explanatory text with the value—for example, "The floor space is 375 square feet."

6. Create a Java program that declares variables to represent the length and width of a room in feet, and the price of carpeting per *square foot* in dollars and cents. Name the project Carpet and save it in the Chapter.02 folder on your Student Disk. Assign appropriate values to the variables. Compute and display, with explanatory text, the cost of carpeting the room.

7. Create a Java program that declares variables to represent the length and width of a room in feet, and the price of carpeting per *square yard* in dollars and cents. Name the project Yards and save it in the Chapter.02 folder on your Student Disk. Assign the value 25 to the length variable and the value 42 to the width variable. Compute and display the cost of carpeting the room. There are nine square feet in one square yard.

8. Create a Java program that declares a minutes variable that represents minutes worked on a job and assign a value. Name the project Time and save it in the Chapter.02 folder on your Student Disk. Display the value in hours and minutes. For example, 197 minutes becomes 3 hours and 17 minutes.

9. Open the FixDebug project located in the FixDebug folder in the Chapter.02 folder on your Student Disk. Each of the following files in the FixDebug project has syntax and/or logical errors. In each case, fix the problem and run each file as a console application using JVIEW.
   a. DebugTwo1.java
   b. DebugTwo2.java
   c. DebugTwo3.java
   d. DebugTwo4.java

10. Create a Java program that declares variables to hold your three initials. Name the project Initials and save it in the Chapter.02 folder on your Student Disk. Display the three initials with a period following each one, as in "J.M.F."

11. Create a Java program that contains variables that hold your tuition fee and your book fee. Name the project Fees and save it in the Chapter.02 folder on your Student Disk. Display the sum of the variables.

12. Create a Java program that contains variables that hold your hourly rate and number of hours that you worked. Name the project Payroll and save it in the Chapter.02 folder on your Student Disk. Display your gross pay, your withholding tax (which is 15 percent of your gross pay), and your net pay.

CHAPTER 3

Using Methods, Classes, and Objects

case ▶ "How do you feel about programming so far?" asks Lynn Greenbrier, head of computer programming for Event Handlers Incorporated, and your new-found mentor.

"It's fun!" you reply. "It's great to see something actually work, but I still don't have much of an idea what the other programmers are talking about when they mention 'object-oriented programming.' I think everything is an object, and objects have methods, but I'm not really clear on this whole thing at all."

"Well then," Lynn says, "let me explain about methods, classes, and objects."

Previewing the SetUpSite Program Using the EventSite Class

In this chapter, you will create a program called SetUpSite that assigns values to the data in an event site that Event Handlers Incorporated uses to manage events, and then displays that data on the screen. Before you start working, you will preview the SetUpSite program that is saved on your Student Disk. You will create a similar program in this chapter.

To preview the SetUpSite program on your Student Disk:

1 Start Visual J++, open the **Chap3Events.vjp** project from the Chap3Events folder in the Chapter.03 folder on your Student Disk, then open the **Chap3EventSite.java** file and examine the code. This file contains a class definition for a class that stores information about event sites that Event Handlers Incorporated uses to host events that it plans.

2 Open the **Chap3SetupSite.java** file and examine the code.

3 Select **Chap3Events Properties** from the **Project** menu. The Properties dialog box appears. Select the **Chap3SetUpSite** file in the When project runs, load drop-down list box and make sure the **Launch as a console application** check box is selected, then click the **OK** button. Compile the project by selecting **Build** from the **Build** menu.

> **help**
>
> As you recall from Chapter 2, the Build command is used in Visual J++ projects to compile Java code into class files.

4 Type **jview Chap3SetUpSite** at the command line to execute the program as a console application. Information about an event site used by Event Handlers Incorporated will appear on the screen as shown in Figure 3-1.

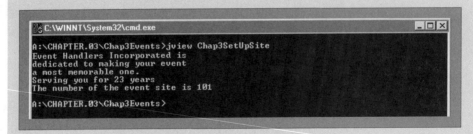

Figure 3-1: Output of the Chap3SetUpSite program

Although the output shown in Figure 3-1 is modest, you have just witnessed several important programming concepts in action. The Chap3EventSite file contains a class definition that represents a real-life object: a site at which Event Handlers can hold an event. The class includes methods to assign values to and get values from data fields that pertain to event sites. The Chap3SetUpSite file creates an actual site with data representing a site number, a fee, and a manager's name. You will create similar files in this chapter.

SECTION A
objectives

In this section you will learn how to create

- Methods with no arguments
- Methods that require a single argument
- Methods that require multiple arguments

Programming Using Methods

Creating Methods with No Arguments

A **method** is a series of statements that carry out some task. Any class can contain an unlimited number of methods. Within a class, the simplest methods you can invoke don't require any arguments or return any values. For example, consider the First Java program's First class that you saw in Chapter 2 and that appears in Figure 3-2. The methods in First class do not require any arguments or return any values.

```
public class First
{
        public static void main(String[] args)
        {
                System.out.println("First Java program");
        }
}
```

Figure 3-2: First class

Suppose you want to add three additional lines of output to this program to display your company's name and address. Of course, you can simply add three new println() statements, but you might choose instead to create a method to display the three lines.

> **Although there are differences, if you have programmed using other programming languages, you can think of methods as being similar to procedures, functions, or subroutines.**

There are two major reasons to create a method to display the three new lines. First, the main() method will remain short and easy to follow because main() will contain just one statement to call a method rather than three separate println() statements to perform the work of the method. Second, and more importantly, a method is easily *reusable*. After you create the name and address method, you can reuse it in any program that needs the company's name and address. In other words, you do the work once, and then you can use the method many times. A method must include the following:

- A declaration (or header or definition)
- An opening curly bracket
- A body
- A closing curly bracket

The method declaration contains the following:

- Optional access modifiers
- The return type for the method
- The method name
- An opening parenthesis
- An optional list of method arguments (you separate the arguments with commas if there are more than one)
- A closing parenthesis

You first learned about access modifiers in Chapter 2. The access modifier for a method can be any of the following modifiers: `public`, `protected`, `private`, `abstract`, `static`, `final`, `synchronized`, or `native`. Most often, you give methods public access. Endowing a method with public access means any class can use it. Additionally, like main(), any method that can be used from anywhere within the class (that is, any class-wide method) requires the keyword modifier `static`. Therefore, you can write the nameAndAddress() method shown in Figure 3-3. According to its declaration, the method is public and static. It returns nothing, so its return type is `void`. The method receives nothing, so its parentheses are empty. Its body, consisting of three println() statements, appears within curly brackets.

You will learn about the use of most of the non-public modifiers throughout this text.

```
public static void nameAndAddress()
{
        System.out.println("Event Handlers Incorporated");
        System.out.println("8900 U.S. Hwy 14");
        System.out.println("Crystal Lake, IL 60014");
}
```

Figure 3-3: The nameAndAddress() method

You place the entire method within the program that will use it, but not within any other method. Figure 3-4 shows where you can place a method in the First program.

```
public class First
{
        public static void main(String[] args)
        {
                System.out.println("First Java program");
        }
// You can place additional methods here,
// outside the main() method
}
```

Figure 3-4: Placement of methods

If the main() method calls the nameAndAddress() method, then you simply use the nameAndAddress() method's name as a statement within the body of main(). Figure 3-5 shows the complete program.

```
public class First
{
        public static void main(String[] args)
        {
                nameAndAddress();
                System.out.println("First Java program");
        }
        public static void nameAndAddress()
        {
                System.out.println("Event Handlers Incorporated");
                System.out.println("8900 U.S. Hwy 14");
                System.out.println("Crystal Lake, IL 60014");
        }
}
```

Figure 3-5: First class calling the nameAndAddress() method

The output from the program shown in Figure 3-5 appears in Figure 3-6. Because the main() method calls the nameAndAddress() method before it prints the phrase "First Java program," the name and address appear first in the output.

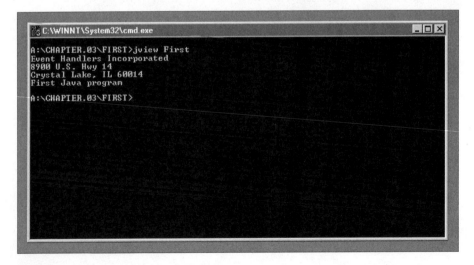

Figure 3-6: Output of the First program with the nameAndAddress() method

Using Methods, Classes, and Objects 109

If you want to use the nameAndAddress() method in another program, one additional step is required. In the Java programming language, the new program, with its own main() method, is a different class. If you place the method named nameAndAddress() within the new class, the compiler will not recognize it unless you write it as `First.nameAndAddress();` to notify the new class that the method is located in the First class. Notice the use of the class name, followed by a dot, and then followed by the method. You already used similar syntax for the System.out.println() method.

tip

If you want one class to call another class's method, both classes should reside in the same folder. If they are not saved in the same place, your compiler will issue the error message, "undefined variable or class name."

tip

Two different classes each can have their own method named nameAndAddress(). Such a method in the second class would be entirely distinct from the identically named method in the first class.

Next, you will create an Events project with a new class named SetUpSite that you eventually will use to set up one EventSite object. For now, the class will contain a main() method and a statementOfPhilosophy() method for Event Handlers Incorporated.

To create the SetUpSite class:

1 Create a new console application project and name it **Events**. Save the **Events** project folder in the Chapter.03 folder on your Student Disk.
2 Rename the default Class1.java file as **SetUpSite.java**, then open the file in the Text Editor window.
3 Replace the Class1 class name in the `public class Class1` line with **SetUpSite**.
4 Replace the `// TODO: Add initialization code here` comment with **statementOfPhilosophy();**
5 Type the following code for the statementOfPhilosophy() method just before the closing curly bracket for the SetUpSite class code:

```
public static void statementOfPhilosophy()
{
     System.out.prinln("Event Handlers Incorporated is");
     System.out.println("dedicated to making your event");
     System.out.println("a most memorable one.");
}
```

6 Select **Events Properties** from the **Project** menu. Select the **SetUpSite** file in the When project runs, load drop-down list box and set the project to run as a console application. Click the **OK** button after selecting project properties.

7 Build the project. If necessary, correct any syntax errors and rebuild the project again. Figure 3-7 shows the error that appears in the Task List when the first println() statement is spelled incorrectly as prinln(). Notice that the error refers you to the file and line number where it occurred.

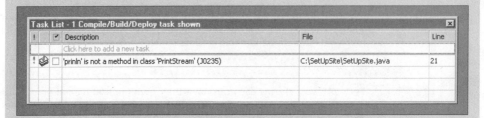

Figure 3-7: Task List displaying a syntax error in the SetUpSite program

8 Execute the program as a console application by typing `jview SetUpSite` at the command line. Your output should look like Figure 3-8.

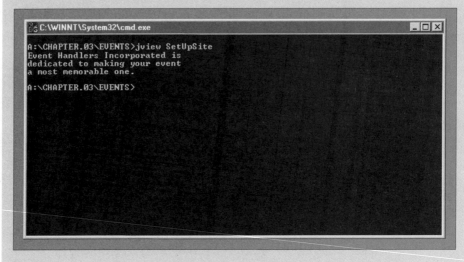

Figure 3-8: Output of the SetUpSite program

Next, you will see how to call the statementOfPhilosophy() method from another class.

Using Methods, Classes, and Objects

To call a method from another class:

1. First, add a new class file to your project by selecting **Add Class** from the **Project** menu. The Add Item dialog box appears. In the Add Item dialog box, select **ClassMain** from the Class folder, then change the suggested filename to **TestStatement.java** and click the **Open** button. The new class opens in the Text Editor window.

   > **help**
   >
   > Selecting the ClassMain option from the Class folder of the Add Item dialog box creates a new class file containing a main() method. Selecting just the Class option simply creates a new class file with no methods. Java applications must contain at least one main() method.

2. Modify the code in the TestStatement.java file so that it matches the program that appears in Figure 3-9.

```java
public class TestStatement
{
    public static void main(String[] args)
    {
        System.out.println
            ("Calling method from another class:");
        SetUpSite.statementOfPhilosophy();
    }
}
```

Figure 3-9: TestStatement program

3. Rebuild the project. If necessary, correct any syntax errors and rebuild the project again.
4. Execute the program as a console application by typing **jview TestStatement** at the command line. Your output should look like Figure 3-10.

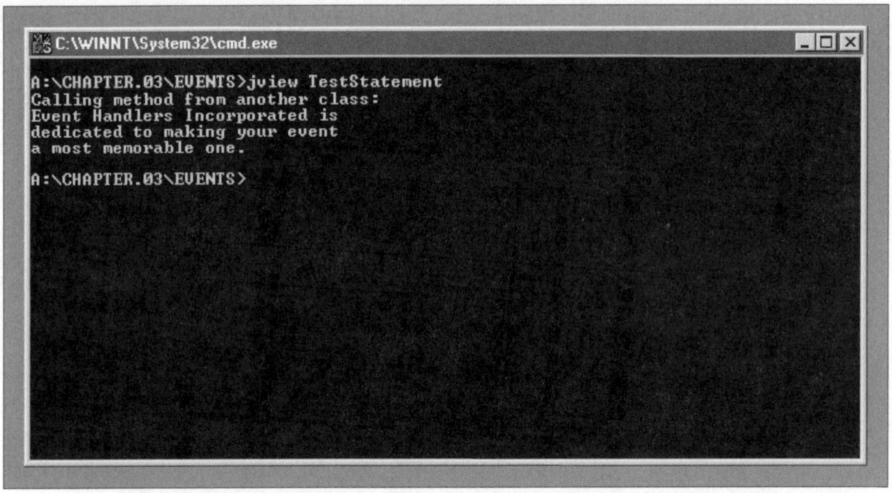

```
C:\WINNT\System32\cmd.exe                                    _ □ ×

A:\CHAPTER.03\EVENTS>jview TestStatement
Calling method from another class:
Event Handlers Incorporated is
dedicated to making your event
a most memorable one.

A:\CHAPTER.03\EVENTS>
```

Figure 3-10: Output of the TestStatement program

Methods That Require a Single Argument

Some methods require additional information. If a method could not receive communications from you, called **arguments**, then you would have to write an infinite number of methods to cover every possible situation. For example, when you make a restaurant reservation, you do not need to use a different method for every date of the year at every possible time of day. Rather, you supply the date and time as information to the method, which then is carried out in the same manner no matter what date and time are involved. If you design a method to square numeric values, it makes sense to design a square() method that you can supply with an argument that represents the value to be squared, rather than having to develop a square1() method, a square2() method, and so on.

An important principle of object-oriented programming is the notion of implementation hiding. **Implementation hiding** conceals the code that actually performs a task. When you make a request to a method, you don't know the details of how the method is executed. For example, when you make a reservation, you do not need to know how the restaurant actually makes the reservation—perhaps the headwaiter writes it in a book, marks it on a large chalkboard, or enters it into a computerized database. The implementation details are of no concern to you as a client, and if the restaurant changes its methods from one year to the next, the *change* does not affect your use of the reservation method.

With well-written object-oriented programming methods, the invoking program must know the name of the method and what type of information to send it (and what type of return to expect), but the program does not need to know how the method works. Additionally, you can substitute a new, improved method and, as long as the interface to the method does not change, you won't need to make any changes in programs invoking the method.

> **tip**
> At any call, the println() method can receive any one of an infinite number of arguments. No matter what message is sent to println(), the message displays correctly.

> **tip**
> Hidden implementation methods often are referred to as existing in a black box.

When you write the method declaration for a method that can receive an argument, you need to include the following items within the method declaration parentheses:

- The type of argument
- A local name for the argument

For example, the declaration for a public method named predictRaise() that displays a person's salary plus a 10 percent raise could have the declaration `public void predictRaise(double moneyAmount)`. You can think of the parentheses in a method declaration as a funnel into the method—data arguments listed there are "dropping in" to the method.

The argument double moneyAmount within the parentheses indicates that the predictRaise() method will receive a number of type double. Within the method, the number (or salary amount) will be known as moneyAmount. Figure 3-11 shows a complete method.

```
public void predictRaise(double moneyAmount)
{
        double newAmount;
        newAmount = moneyAmount * 1.10;
        System.out.println("With raise salary is "
          + newAmount);
}
```

Figure 3-11: The predictRaise() method

The predictRaise() method is a void method because it does not need to return any value to any class that uses it—its only function is to receive the moneyAmount value, multiply it by 1.10 (resulting in a 10 percent salary increase), and then display the result.

Within a program, you can call the predictRaise() method by using either a constant value or a variable as an argument. Thus, both `predictRaise(472.25);`

and `predictRaise(mySalary);` would invoke the predictRaise() method correctly, assuming that mySalary was declared as a double value and assigned an appropriate value. You can call the predictRaise() method any number of times, with a different constant or variable argument each time. Each of these arguments becomes known as moneyAmount within the method. The identifier moneyAmount holds any double value passed into the method. Interestingly, if the value in the method call is a variable, it might possess the same identifier as moneyAmount or a different one, like mySalary. The identifier moneyAmount is simply the name the value "goes by" while it is being used within the method, no matter what name it "goes by" in the calling program.

The variable moneyAmount is a local variable to the predictRaise() method.

If a programmer changes the way in which the 10 percent raise is calculated—for example, by coding `newAmount = moneyAmount + (moneyAmount * .10);`—no program that uses the predictRaise() method will ever know the difference. The program will pass a value into predictRaise() and then a calculated result will appear on the screen.

Figure 3-12 shows a complete program that uses the predictRaise() method twice. The program's output appears in Figure 3-13.

```
public class DemoRaise
{
    public static void main(String[] args)
    {
        double mySalary = 200.00;
        System.out.println("Demonstrating some raises");
        predictRaise(400.00);
        predictRaise(mySalary);
    }
    public static void predictRaise(double moneyAmount)
    {
        double newAmount;
        newAmount = moneyAmount * 1.10;
        System.out.println("With raise salary is " + newAmount);
    }
}
```

Figure 3-12: Complete program using the predictRaise() method twice

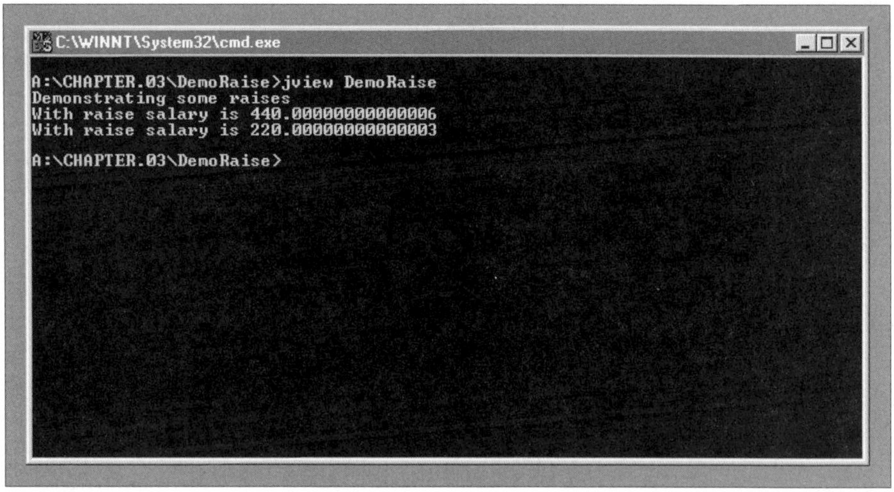

Figure 3-13: Output of the DemoRaise program

Notice the output in Figure 3-13. Floating-point arithmetic is always somewhat imprecise.

Methods That Require Multiple Arguments

A method can require more than one argument. You can pass multiple arguments to a method by listing the arguments within the call to the method and separating them with commas. For example, rather than creating a predictRaise() method that adds a 10 percent raise to every person's salary, you might prefer to create a method to which you can pass two values—the salary to be raised as well as a percentage figure by which to raise it. Figure 3-14 shows a method that uses two such arguments.

```
public static void predictRaiseGivenIncrease
       (double moneyAmount, double percentRate)
{
       double newAmount;
       newAmount = moneyAmount * (1 + percentRate);
       System.out.println("With raise salary is "
          + newAmount);
}
```

Figure 3-14: The predictRaiseGivenIncrease() method

Notice that a declaration for a method that receives two or more arguments must list the type for each argument separately, even if the arguments have the *same* type.

In the header of the predictRaiseGivenIncrease() method, the arguments in parentheses are shown on separate lines to fit in this book's text space. You also could place the parentheses and arguments on the same line as the function header.

It is very important that arguments passed to a method with multiple arguments be passed in the correct order. In Figure 3-14, two arguments (`double moneyAmount` and `double percentRate`) appear within the parentheses in the method header. The arguments are separated by a comma, and each argument requires its own named type (in this case, both are double) as well as an identifier. When values are passed to the method in a statement like `predictRaiseGivenIncrease(mySalary,promisedRate);`, the first value passed will be referenced as moneyAmount within the method, and the second value passed will be referenced as percentRate. The call `predictRaiseGivenIncrease(200.00, .10);` results in output that represents a 10 percent raise based on a $200 salary amount (or $220). But `predictRaiseGivenIncrease(.10, 200.00);` results in output representing a 200 percent raise based on a salary of 10 cents (or $20.10).

If two method arguments are the same type—for example, two doubles—passing them to a method in the wrong order results in a logical error. If an argument expects arguments of diverse types, then passing arguments in the wrong order results in a syntax error.

You can write a method so that it takes any number of arguments in any order. However, when you call a method, the arguments you send to a method must match, in both number and type, the arguments listed in the method declaration. Thus, a method to compute an automobile salesperson's commission amount might require arguments such as an integer value of a car sold, a double percentage commission rate, and a character code for the vehicle type. The correct method will execute only when three arguments of the correct types are sent in the correct order.

The arguments in a method call often are referred to as actual parameters. The variables in the method declaration that accept the values from the actual parameters are the formal parameters.

Methods That Return Values

The return type for a method can be any type used in the Java programming language, which includes the primitive (or scalar) types int, double, char, and so on, as well as class types (including class types you create). Of course, a method also can return nothing, in which case the return type is void.

A method's return type is known more succinctly as a method's type. For example, the declaration for the nameAndAddress() method is written `public static void nameAndAddress()`. This method is public and it returns no value, so it is type void. A method that returns `true` or `false` depending on whether or not an employee worked overtime hours might be `public boolean overtime()`. This method is public and it returns a boolean value, so it is type boolean.

> In addition to returning the primitive types, a method can return a class type. If a class named BankLoan exists, a method might return an instance of a BankLoan as in `public BankLoan approvalProcess()`. In other words, a method can return anything from a simple int to a complicated BankLoan with 20 data fields.

The header for a method that displays a raise amount is `public static void predictRaise(double moneyAmount)`. If you want to create a method to return the new, calculated salary value rather than display the raised salary, the header would be `public static double calculateRaise(double moneyAmount)`. Figure 3-15 shows this method.

```
public static double calculateRaise(double moneyAmount)
{
     double newAmount;
     newAmount = moneyAmount * 1.10;
     return newAmount;
}
```

Figure 3-15: The calculateRaise() method

Notice the return type double in the method header. Also notice the return statement that is the last statement within the method. The **return** statement causes the value stored in newAmount to be sent back to any method that calls the calculateRaise() method.

If a method returns a value, then when you call the method, you usually will want to use the returned value, although you are not required to do so. For example, when you invoke the calculateRaise() method, you might want to assign the value to a double variable named myNewSalary, as in `myNewSalary =`

calculateRaise(mySalary);. The calculateRaise() method returns a double, so it is appropriate to assign the returned value to a double variable.

Alternatively, you can choose to display a method's returned value directly without storing it in any variable, as in System.out.println("New salary is " + calculateRaise(mySalary));. In this last statement, the call to the calculateRaise() method is made from within the println() method call. Because calculateRaise() returns a double, you can use the method call calculateRaise() in the same way that you would use any simple double value. Besides printing the value of calculateRaise(), you can perform math with the value, assign it, and so on.

Next, you will add a method to the SetUpSite class that both receives an argument and returns a value. The purpose of the method is to take the current year and calculate how long Event Handlers Incorporated has been in business.

To add a method that receives an argument and returns a value:

1 Open the **Events** project, then open the **SetUpSite.java** file in the Text Editor window.

2 Position the insertion point to the right of the opening curly bracket of the main() method of the class, and then press the **Enter** key to start a new line.

3 Type `int currentYear = 2000;` to declare a variable to hold the current year, and then press the **Enter** key.

4 Type `int age;` to declare another variable to hold the age of Event Handlers Incorporated.

5 Position the insertion point at the end of the call to the statementOfPhilosophy() method in the main() method of the class, and then press the **Enter** key to start a new line. You will add a call to receive the current year and calculate how long Event Handlers Incorporated has been in business by subtracting the year of its inception, which is 1977.

6 Type `age = calculateAge(currentYear);` in a call to a calculateAge() method.

7 Press the **Enter** key, and then type `System.out.println("Serving you for " + age + " years");` to print the number of years the company has been in business. Now you will write the calculateAge() method.

8 Position the insertion point after the closing bracket of the statementOfPhilosophy() method and before the closing bracket of the program, press the **Enter** key to start a new line, and then enter the method shown in Figure 3-16. The method will receive an integer value. Within the calculateAge() method, the value will be known as currDate. Note that the name currDate does not possess the same identifier as currentValue, which is the variable being passed in, although it could. Notice also that the method declaration indicates an int value will be returned.

```
public static int calculateAge(int currDate)
{
     int yrs;
     yrs = currDate - 1977;
     return yrs;
}
```

Figure 3-16: The calculateAge() method

9. Rebuild, save, and execute the program as a console application. The results should be the same as those shown in Figure 3-17.

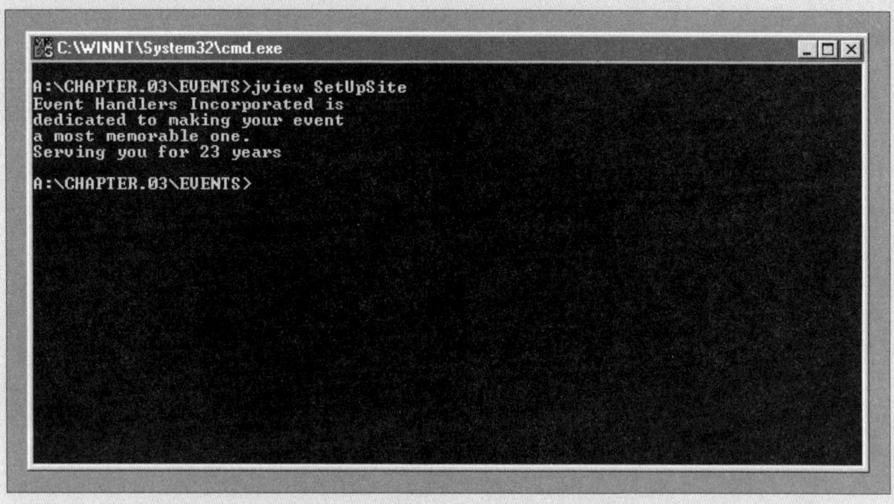

```
A:\CHAPTER.03\EVENTS>jview SetUpSite
Event Handlers Incorporated is
dedicated to making your event
a most memorable one.
Serving you for 23 years

A:\CHAPTER.03\EVENTS>
```

Figure 3-17: Output of the SetUpSite program with the CalculateAge() method

SUMMARY

- A method is a series of statements that carry out some task. Using a method makes programs easier to follow. Methods are easily reusable.
- Any class can contain any number of methods.
- Methods must include a declaration (or header or definition), an opening curly bracket, a body, and a closing curly bracket. A method declaration contains optional access modifiers, the return type for the method, the method name, an opening parenthesis, an optional list of method arguments, and a closing parenthesis.

- The access modifier for a method can be any of the modifiers `public`, `protected`, `private`, `abstract`, `static`, `final`, `synchronized`, or `native`. Most often, methods are given public access.

- Any method that is a classwide method requires the keyword modifier `static`.

- You place a method within the program that will use it, but not within any other method. If you place a method call within a class that does not contain the method, to call the method you must use the class name, followed by a dot, followed by the method.

- Some methods require a message or argument.

- An important principle of object-oriented programming is the notion of implementation hiding, or concealing the details of how the method is executed.

- When you write the method declaration for a method that can receive an argument, you need to include the type of the argument and a local name for the argument within the method declaration parentheses.

- You can call a method within a program using either a constant value or a variable as an argument.

- You can pass multiple arguments to methods by listing the arguments and separating them by commas within the call to the method.

- The arguments you send to the method must match in both number and type the parameters listed in the method declaration.

- The return type for a method (the method's type) can be any Java type, including `void`.

- You use a return statement to send a value back to a program that calls a method.

QUESTIONS

1. The Java platform's term for a series of statements that carry out some task is a _____.
   a. procedure
   b. method
   c. subroutine
   d. function

2. A Java class _____.
   a. cannot contain methods
   b. must contain at least one method
   c. cannot contain more than eight methods
   d. can contain any number of methods

3. Methods must include all of the following except _____.
   a. a declaration
   b. a call to another method
   c. curly brackets
   d. a body

4. All method declarations contain _____.
   a. the keyword `static`
   b. one or more access modifiers
   c. arguments
   d. parentheses

5. Which of the following is not a method access modifier?
   a. `general`
   b. `private`
   c. `native`
   d. `protected`

6. A method named printStatistics() is void and takes no arguments. Which of the following is a correct call to printStatistics()?
   a. `printStatistics();`
   b. `void printStatistics();`
   c. `void printStatistics(void);`
   d. `void printStatistics(73.4);`

7. A public method named computeSum() is located in classA. To call the method from within classB, use the statement _____.
   a. `computeSum(classB);`
   b. `classB(computeSum());`
   c. `classA.computeSum();`
   d. You cannot call computeSum() from within classB.

8. Which of the following method declarations is correct for a method named displayFacts() if the method receives an int argument?
   a. `public void int displayFacts()`
   b. `public void displayFacts(int)`
   c. `public void displayFacts(int data)`
   d. `public void displayFacts()`

9. The method with the declaration `public int aMethod(double d)` has a method type _____.
   a. `int`
   b. `double`
   c. `void`
   d. You cannot determine the method type.

10. Which of the following is a correct call to a method declared as `double aMethod(char code)`?
    a. `double aMethod();`
    b. `double aMethod('V');`
    c. `aMethod(int 'M');`
    d. `aMethod('Q');`

11. A method named max() that requires two integer arguments is declared as _____.
    a. `public void max()`
    b. `public void max(int a,b)`
    c. `public void max(int a, int b)`
    d. `public void max (a,b)`

12. A method is declared as `public void showResults(double d, int i)`. Which of the following is a correct method call?
    a. `showResults(double d, int i);`
    b. `showResults(12.2, 67);`
    c. `showResults(4, 99.7);`
    d. Two of these answers are correct.

13. The method with the declaration `public char procedure(double d)` has a method type of _____.
    a. `public`
    b. `char`
    c. `procedure`
    d. `double`

14. The method `public boolean testValue(int response)` returns _____.
    a. a boolean value
    b. an integer value
    c. no value
    d. You cannot determine what is returned.

15. Which of the following could be the last legally coded line of a method declared as `public int getVal(double sum)`?
    a. `return;`
    b. `return 77;`
    c. `return 2.3;`
    d. Any of these could be the last coded line of the method.

EXERCISES

1. Name any device you use every day. Discuss how implementation hiding is demonstrated in the way this device works. Is it a benefit or a drawback to you that implementation hiding exists for methods associated with this object?

2. a. Create a project named Numbers in the Chapter.03 folder on your Student Disk. In the main() method of the Numbers class, create two integer variables. Assign values to the variables. Create two additional methods in the Numbers class, sum() and difference(), that compute the sum of and difference between the values of the two variables, respectively. Each method should perform the computation and display the results. In turn, call each of the two methods from main(), passing the values of the two integer variables.

   b. Add a method named product() to the Numbers class. The product() method should compute the multiplication product of two integers, but not display the answer. Instead, it should return the answer to the calling main() program, which displays the answer.

3. Create a project named Eggs in the Chapter.03 folder on your Student Disk. In the main() method of the Eggs class, create an integer variable named numberOfEggs to which you will assign a value. Create a method in the Eggs class to which you pass numberOfEggs. The method displays the eggs in dozens; for example, 50 eggs is 4 full dozen (and 2 left over).

4. Create a project named Monogram in the Chapter.03 folder on your Student Disk. In the main() method of the Monogram class, create three character variables that hold your first, middle, and last initials, respectively. Create a method in the Monogram class to which you pass the three initials and that displays the initials twice—once in the order *first, middle, last*, and a second time in traditional monogram style (*first, last, middle*).

5. Create a project named Exponent in the Chapter.03 folder on your Student Disk. Its main() method holds an integer value, and in turn passes the value to a method that squares the number and a method that cubes the number. The main() method prints the results. Create the two methods that respectively square and cube an integer that is passed to them, returning the calculated value.

6. Create a project named Cube in the Chapter.03 folder on your Student Disk that displays the result of cubing a number. Pass a number from one method to another method that cubes a number and returns the result. The display should execute within the method that calls the cube method.

7. Create a program named Calculator in the Chapter.03 folder on your Student Disk that displays the result of a sales transaction. The calculation requires three numbers. The first number represents the product price. The second number is the salesperson commission. These two numbers should be added together. The third number represents a customer discount; subtract this third number from the result of the addition. Create two classes. The first class contains the method to do the calculation. The three numbers are passed to this method by a statement in the other class. The display is performed in the class that calls the calculation method.

8. Write a program named Divide that displays the result of dividing two numbers and displays the remainder. Create the calculation and display in the same method, which is a separate method from the main() method.

SECTION B
objectives

In this section you will learn
- Class concepts
- What the Class outline window is and how to use it
- How to create classes
- How to use instance methods
- How to declare objects
- How to organize classes
- How to use constructors

Using Classes

Classes

When you think in an object-oriented manner, everything is an object and every object is a member of a class. You can think of any inanimate physical item as an object—your desk, your computer, and the building in which you live are all called objects in everyday conversation. You also can think of living things as objects—your houseplant, your pet fish, and your sister are objects. Events also are objects—the stock purchase you made, the mortgage closing you attended, or a graduation party that was held in your honor are all objects.

tip

In the Java programming language, a program you write to use other classes is a class itself.

Everything is an object, and every object is a member of a more general class. Your desk is a member of the class that includes all desks, and your pet fish is a member of the class that contains all fish. An object-oriented programmer would say that your desk is an instance of the Desk class and your fish is an instance of the Fish class. These statements represent **is-a relationships** because you can say, "My oak desk with the scratch on top *is a* Desk and my goldfish named Moby *is a* Fish."

The difference between a class and an object parallels the difference between abstract and concrete. An object is an **instantiation** of a class; an object is one tangible example of a class. Your goldfish, my guppy, and the zoo's shark each constitute one instantiation of the Fish class.

Objects **inherit** attributes from classes. Inheritance makes the concept of a class useful because of its reusability. For example, if you are invited to a graduation party, you automatically know many things about the object's (the party's) attributes. You assume there will be a starting time, a number of guests, some quantity of food, and some kind of gift. You understand what a party entails because of your previous knowledge of the Party class, of which all parties are members. You don't know the number of guests or the date or the time of this particular party, but you understand that because all parties have a date and a time, then this one must too. Similarly, even though every stock market purchase is unique, each stock purchase must have a dollar amount and a number of shares. All objects have predictable attributes because they are members of certain classes.

> **tip**
>
> The data components of a class often are referred to as the **instance variables** or **member variables** of that class. Also, class object attributes often are called **fields** to help distinguish them from other variables you might use.

In addition to their attributes, class objects have methods associated with them, and every object that is an instance of a class is assumed to possess the same methods. For example, for all parties, at some point you must set the date and time. You might name these methods setDate() and setTime(). Party guests need to know the date and time, and might use methods named getDate() and getTime() to find out the date and time of the party.

Your graduation party, then, might possess the identifier myGraduationParty. As a member of the Party class, myGraduationParty, like all parties, might have data members for the date and time and methods setDate() and setTime(). When you use them, the setDate() and setTime() methods require arguments, or information passed to them. For example, `myGraduationParty.setDate("May 12")` and `myGraduationParty.setTime("6 P.M.")` invoke methods that are available for myGraduationParty and send it arguments. When you use an object and its methods, think of being able to send a message to the object to direct it to accomplish some task—you can tell the party object named myGraduationParty to set the time and date you request. Even though yourAnniversaryParty also is a member of the Party class, and even though it also has setDate() and setTime() methods, you will want to send different arguments to yourAnniversaryParty than I want to send to myGraduationParty. Within any object-oriented program, you are continuously making requests to objects' methods, and often including arguments as part of those requests.

Additionally, some methods used in a program must return a message or value. If one of your party guests uses the getDate() method, it is in the hope that the method will respond to the guest with the desired information. Similarly, within object-oriented programs, methods often are called upon to return a piece of information to the source of the request. For example, a method within a Payroll class that calculates federal withholding tax might return a tax figure in dollars and cents. A method within an Inventory class might return `true` or `false` depending on the method's determination of whether an item is at the reorder point.

There are two parts to object-oriented programming. First, you must create the classes of objects from which objects will be instantiated. Second, you must write other classes to use the objects (and their data and their methods). The same programmer does not need to accomplish these two tasks. Often, you will write programs that use classes created by others; similarly, you might create a class that others will use to instantiate objects within their own programs. A program or class that instantiates objects of another prewritten class is a **class client** or **class user**.

section B

tip

> The System class that you used in Chapter 2 is an example of using a class that was written by someone else. You did not have to create it or its println() method; both were created for you by Java's creators.

Class Outline

While you have been working with the files in your project, you may have noticed the Document Outline window. When a Java file is open in the Text Editor window, Class Outline is visible in the Document Outline window. The Visual J++ IDE uses **Class Outline** to manage the various classes and class members contained in a package. **Packages**, also called **libraries**, are related groups of classes and class members that make up your entire Java program. These groups of classes and class members include classes you write, instance variables, and base classes (or superclasses) from which your classes are extended. Classes and class members in a package are displayed in a hierarchical list that is very similar to Project Explorer.

help

> Do not confuse Visual J++ solutions with packages. A solution *contains* all the files in the application you are developing, such as graphic files, Java files, HTML files, and so on. In contrast, a package *organizes* classes such as Java files or other types of class files that may be required by the program you are writing.

Class Outline has a number of useful features that make working with classes and class members easy. As your Java files grow, scrolling through the Text Editor window to find a particular method or instance variable becomes time consuming. Class Outline makes it possible to navigate quickly to a specific class or class member by double-clicking the desired object, similar to the way you open a file from Project Explorer by double-clicking a filename. In addition, Class Outline is automatically updated to reflect any changes you make to the names of classes or class members. Class Outline also has a Javadoc pane. If the open Java file contains javadoc comments, Class Outline displays the first line of the first javadoc comment in the Javadoc pane.

To display the Class Outline and navigate to a method:

1. Open the **Events** project from the Chapter.03 folder on your Student Disk, then open the **SetUpSite.java** file in the Text Editor window.
2. Display Class Outline by selecting **Other Windows** from the **View** menu, then selecting **Document Outline**.

tip

> You can also open Class Outline by pressing Ctrl+Alt+T.

Using Methods, Classes, and Objects

3 Click the **SetUpSite** class object in Class Outline. If you have not deleted them, the default javadoc comments that are automatically created with a new project appear in the Javadoc pane at the bottom of the Class Outline window.

4 Click the **Plus** box icon to the left of the SetUpSite class. The class members appear beneath SetUpSiteClass. Your Class Outline window should look similar to Figure 3-18. Right-click the **statementOfPhilosophy()** method to show a shortcut menu and select **Go To Definition**. Your cursor moves to the first line of the statementOfPhilosophy() method in SetUpSiteClass.

> **tip**
>
> You can also double-click a class member name to move to its associated definition in the Text Editor window.

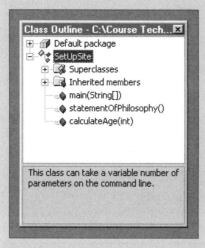

Figure 3-18: Class Outline window

5 Close the **SetUpSite.java** file.

Packages, classes, and class members are represented in Class Outline by their names and one or more icons. For example, Class Outline designates a method with the private modifier by the Method icon and the Private Access icon. These icons make it easy to identify parts of a Java class and their associated modifiers. Class Outline icons and their descriptions are shown in Figure 3-19.

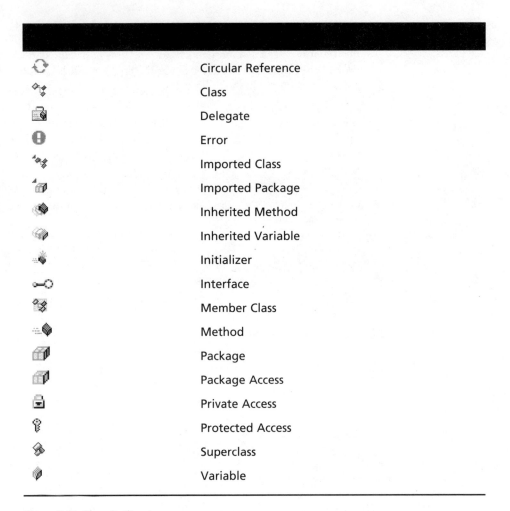

Figure 3-19: Class Outline icons

Class Outline contains several commands that use dialog boxes to automate the task of adding classes, methods, and member variables to a package. You can also cut, copy, paste, and delete classes and class members, and change individual class properties. You access Class Outline commands by right-clicking a class or member name to display the shortcut menu.

As you work with Class Outline, keep in mind that you can perform most of the available commands, such as adding new methods, by manually editing a Java class file, as you have done up to this point in the exercises. Class Outline simply automates some of the process for you. When entering code such as a simple method containing a single statement, it is often easier to type the code manually than to go through the extra steps of using a Class Outline command and opening a dialog box.

> Although the majority of the exercises in this text instruct you to enter Java code in the Text Editor window manually so that you can become familiar with basic code input, you should experiment on your own with the Class Outline commands.

Creating a Class

When you create a class, first you must assign a name to the class, and then you must determine what data and methods will be part of the class. Suppose you decide to create a class named Employee. One instance variable of Employee might be an employee number, and two necessary methods might be a method to set (or provide a value for) the employee number and another method might be to get (or retrieve) that employee number. To begin, you create a class header with three parts:

- An optional access modifier
- The keyword `class`
- Any legal identifier you choose for the name of your class

For example, a header for an Employee class is `public class Employee`. The keyword `public` is a class access modifier. You can use the following class access modifiers when defining a class: `public`, `final`, or `abstract`.

Public classes are accessible by all objects, which means that public classes can be **extended**, or used as a basis for any other class. Extended is the most liberal form of access. Public access means that if you develop a good Employee class, and someday you want to develop two more specific classes, SalariedEmployee and HourlyEmployee, then you will not have to start from scratch. Each new class can become an extension of the original Employee class, inheriting its data and methods.

The other access modifiers (or the omission of any access modifier) impose at least some limitations on extensibility. (You use the other access modifiers only under special circumstances.) You will use the public access modifier for most of your classes. If you do not specify an access modifier, access becomes **friendly**, which means that it can be extended only by other classes within the same project.

After writing the class header `public class Employee`, you write the body of the Employee class, containing its data and methods, between a set of curly brackets. Figure 3-20 shows the shell for the Employee class.

```
public class Employee
{
        // Instance variables and methods go here
}
```

Figure 3-20: Employee class shell

You place the instance variables, or fields, for the Employee class as statements within the curly brackets. For example, you can declare an employee number that will be stored as an integer simply as `int empNum;`. However, programmers frequently include an access modifier for each of the class fields and declare empNum as `private int empNum;`. The allowable field modifiers are `private, public, protected, final, static, transient,` and `volatile`.

Most class fields are private, which provides the highest level of security. Private access means that no other classes can access a field's values, and only methods of the same class are allowed to set, get, or otherwise use private variables. Private access is sometimes called **information hiding**, and is an important component of object-oriented programs. A class's private data can be changed or manipulated only by a class's own methods, and not by methods that belong to other classes.

In contrast, most class methods are not usually private. The resulting private data/public method arrangement provides a means for you to control outside access to your data—only a class's nonprivate methods can be used to access a class's private data. The situation is similar to hiring a public receptionist to sit in front of your private office controlling the messages passed in to you (perhaps deflecting trivial or hostile ones) and the messages you pass out (perhaps checking your spelling, grammar, and any legal implications). The way in which the nonprivate methods are written controls how you use the private data.

If you do not provide an access modifier for a class field, its access is friendly, which is more liberal access than private.

The entire class so far appears in Figure 3-21. It defines a public class named Employee, with one field, which is a private integer named empNum.

```
public class Employee
{
        private int empNum;
}
```

Figure 3-21: Employee class with one data field

Next, you will create a class to store information about event sites for Event Handlers Incorporated.

To create the class:

1 Open the **Events** project from the Chapter.03 folder on your Student Disk.

2. Add a new class file to your project by selecting **Add Class** from the **Project** menu. The Add Item dialog box appears. In the Add Item dialog box, select **Class** from the class folder, then change the suggested filename to **EventSite.java** and click the **Open** button. The new class opens in the Text Editor window.

3. Type `private int siteNumber;` between the curly brackets to insert the private data field that will hold an integer site number for each event site used by the company.

4. Rebuild the project. If necessary, correct any syntax errors and rebuild the project again. Do not execute the program yet.

Using Instance Methods

Besides data, classes contain methods. For example, one method you need for an Employee class that contains an empNum is the method to retrieve (or return) any Employee's empNum for use by another class. A reasonable name for this method is getEmpNum() and its declaration is `public int getEmpNum()` because it will have public access, return an integer (the employee number), and possess the identifier getEmpNum(). Figure 3-22 shows the complete getEmpNum() method.

```
public int getEmpNum()
{
      return empNum;
}
```

Figure 3-22: The getEmpNum() method

The getEmpNum() method contains just one statement: the statement that accesses the value of the private empNum field.

Notice that, unlike the class methods you created in Section A of this chapter, the getEmpNum() method does not employ the `static` modifier. The keyword `static` is used for classwide methods, but not for methods that "belong" to objects. If you are creating a program with a main() method that you will execute to perform some task, then many of your methods will be static so you can call them from within main(). However, if you are creating a class from which objects will be instantiated (called **instance methods**), most methods will probably be non-static as you will be associating the methods with individual objects.

section B

 tip

> You can call class methods without creating an instance of the class. Instance methods require an instantiated object.

Next, you will add an instance method to the EventSite class using Class Outline. The new instance method will retrieve the value of an event site's number.

To add an instance method to the EventSite class using Class Outline:

1 Return to the **EventSite.java** file in the Text Editor window.

2 Right-click the **EventSite** class in Class Outline, then select **Add Method** from the shortcut menu. The Add Method dialog box appears as shown in Figure 3-23.

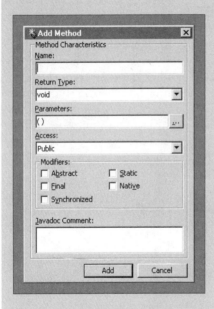

Figure 3-23: Add Method dialog box

3 Type **getSiteNumber** as the method name and select **int** from the **Return Type** drop-down list box. The other dialog box options allow you to select parameters and access modifiers. You can also enter any javadoc comments you want to include with the new method. Click the **Add** button to create the new method. The new getSiteNumber() method appears beneath the **Inherited members** folder of the EventSite class node in Class Outline. You might need to expand the EventSite class node and/or the Inherited members folder to see the getSiteNumber() method.

Using Methods, Classes, and Objects

4. Double-click the **getSiteNumber** method in Class Outline to place the insertion point in the getSiteNumber() method in the Text Editor window. The getSiteNumber() method appears as follows:

   ```
   public int getSiteNumber()
   {
           // To Do:  Add your own implementation.
           int returnValue;
           returnValue = 0;
           return returnValue;
   }
   ```

5. The three lines between the method's curly brackets are automatically added when you use the Add Method dialog box to create a method with a return type. You can use these lines as a basis for a method that returns a value or replace them with your own statements. For this exercise, replace these lines with **return siteNumber;**.

> This exercise is a good example of when it is probably easier to type the new method into your Java file rather than use the Add Method command in Class Outline.

When a class contains data fields, you want a means to assign values to the data fields. For an Employee class with an empNum field, you need a method with which to set empNum. Figure 3-24 shows a method that sets empNum. The method is a void method because there is no need to return any value to a calling program. The method receives an integer, locally called emp, to be assigned to empNum.

```
public static void setEmpNum(int emp)
{
        empNum = emp;
}
```

Figure 3-24: The setEmpNum() method

Next, you will add a setSiteNumber() method to the EventSite class. This method takes an integer argument and assigns it to the siteNumber of an EventSite object.

To add a method to the EventSite class using Class Outline:

1. Right-click the **EventSite** class in Class Outline, then select **Add Method** from the shortcut menu. The Add Method dialog box appears.

section B

2 Type **setSiteNumber** as the method name and select **void** from the **Return Type** drop-down list box. Click the **Ellipsis** button to the right of the Parameters text box. The Edit Parameter List dialog box appears as shown in Figure 3-25.

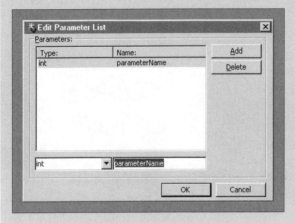

Figure 3-25: Edit Parameter List dialog box

3 Select **int** in the Type list box. In the Name text box, change the suggested parameterName to **n**, then click the **OK** button.

The Edit Parameter List dialog box is useful for adding and deleting parameters, especially for methods with multiple arguments.

4 Select **Public** from the **Access** drop-down list box, then click the **Add** button in the Add Method dialog box to create the new method. The new setSiteNumber() method appears beneath the Inherited members folder of the EventSite class node in Class Outline.

5 Double-click the **setSiteNumber()** method in Class Outline to place the insertion point in the setSiteNumber() method in the Text Editor window.

6 Replace the `// TODO: Add your own implementation.` comment with **siteNumber = n;**. The argument *n* represents any number sent to this method.

7 Rebuild the project. If necessary, correct any syntax errors and rebuild the project again. (You cannot run this file as a program.)

Declaring Objects

Declaring a class does not create any actual objects. A class is just an abstract description of what an object will be like if any objects are ever actually instantiated. Just as you might understand all the characteristics of an item you intend to manufacture long before the first item rolls off the assembly line, you can create a class with fields and methods long before you instantiate any objects that are members of that class.

A two-step process creates an object that is an instance of a class. First, you supply a type and an identifier, just as when you declare any variable. Second, you allocate computer memory for that object. For example, you might define an integer as `int someValue;` and you might define an Employee as `Employee someEmployee;`, where someEmployee stands for any legal identifier you choose to represent an Employee.

When you declare an integer as `int someValue;`, you notify the compiler that an integer named someValue will exist, and you reserve computer memory for it at the same time. When you declare the someEmployee instance of the Employee class, you are notifying the compiler that you will use the identifier someEmployee. However, you are not yet setting aside computer memory in which the Employee named someEmployee might be stored—that is done automatically only for primitive type variables. To allocate the needed memory, you must use the **new** operator. After you define someEmployee with the `Employee someEmployee;` statement, the statement that actually sets aside enough memory to hold an Employee is `someEmployee = new Employee();`. You also can define and reserve memory for someEmployee in one statement, as in `Employee someEmployee = new Employee();`. In this statement, Employee is the object's type (as well as its class), and someEmployee is the name of the object. The equal sign is the assignment operator, so a value is being assigned to someEmployee. The **new** operator is allocating a new, unused portion of computer memory for someEmployee. The value that the statement is assigning to someEmployee is a memory address at which it is to be located. You do not need to be concerned with what the actual memory address is—when you refer to someEmployee, the compiler will locate it at the appropriate address for you—but someEmployee does need to know its own address.

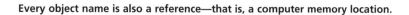

Every object name is also a reference—that is, a computer memory location.

The last portion of the statement, `Employee()`, with its parentheses, looks suspiciously like a method name. In fact, it is the name of a method that constructs an Employee object. Employee() is a **constructor method**. You will write your own constructor methods later in this section, but when you don't write a constructor method for a class object, Java writes one for you, and the name of the constructor method is always the same as the name of the class whose objects it constructs.

Next, you will instantiate an EventSite object.

To instantiate an object:
1. Open the **SetUpSite.java** file in the Text Editor window.
2. Place the insertion point at the end of the opening curly bracket within the main() method of the SetUpSite class, press the **Enter** key to start a new line, and then type `EventSite oneSite = new EventSite();` to allocate memory for a new EventSite object named oneSite.
3. Rebuild the project. If necessary, correct any syntax errors and rebuild the project again.

After an object has been instantiated, you can access its methods using the object's identifier, a dot, and a method call. For example, if an Employee class method to change a salary is written using the code in Figure 3-26, and an Employee was declared with `Employee clerk = new Employee();`, then the clerk's salary can be changed to 350.00 with the call `clerk.changeSalary(350.00);`. The method changeSalary() is applied to the object clerk, and the argument 350.00 (a double type value) is passed to the method.

```
public void changeSalary(double newAmount)
{
      salary = newAmount;
}
```

Figure 3-26: The changeSalary() method

Within the same program, the statements `Employee secretary = new Employee();` and `secretary.changeSalary(420.00);` would apply the same changeSalary() method, but using a different argument value, to different objects that belong to the same class.

Next, you will add calls to the getSiteNumber() and setSiteNumber() methods for the oneSite object member of the EventSite class.

To add the calls to the methods for the oneSite object member:

1. Return to the **SetUpSite.java** file in the Text Editor window.
2. Just below the declaration for oneSite, provide the SetUpSite() method with a variable to hold any site number returned from the getSiteNumber() method by typing `int number;` and then pressing the **Enter** key.
3. Next, call the method setSiteNumber() to set the site number for oneSite. Type `oneSite.setSiteNumber(101);`. The number in parentheses could be any integer number.
4. After the statement that prints the age of the company (`System.out.println("Serving you for " + age + " years");`), call the getSiteNumber() method and assign its return value to the number variable by typing `number = oneSite.getSiteNumber();` and then pressing the **Enter** key.
5. Add a call to the println() method to display the value stored in number by typing `System.out.println("The number of the event site is " + number);`
6. Rebuild the project. If necessary, correct any syntax errors and rebuild the project again.
7. Execute the program as a console application by typing **jview SetUpSite**. Your output should look like Figure 3-27.

Using Methods, Classes, and Objects   137

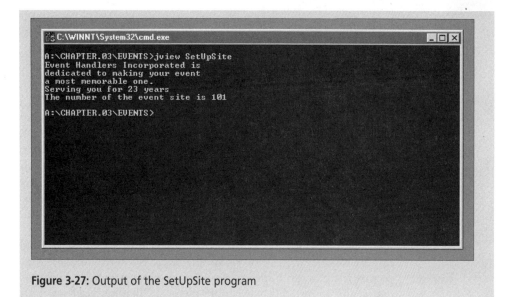

Figure 3-27: Output of the SetUpSite program

Organizing Classes

Most classes you create will have more than one data field and more than two methods. For example, in addition to requiring an employee number, an Employee needs a last name, a first name, and a salary, as well as methods to set and get those fields. Figure 3-28 shows how you could code the data fields for Employee.

```
public class Employee
{
        private int empNum;
        private String empLastName;
        private String empFirstName;
        private double empSalary;
// Methods will go here
}
```

Figure 3-28: Employee class with data fields

Although there is no requirement to do so, most programmers place data fields in some logical order at the beginning of a class. For example, empNum is most likely used as a unique identifier for each employee (what database users often call a

primary key), so it makes sense to list the employee number first in the class. An employee's last name and first name "go together," so it makes sense to store these two Employee components adjacently. Despite these common-sense rules, there is a lot of flexibility in how you position your data fields within any class.

> A unique identifier is one that should have no duplicates within an application. In other words, although an organization might have many employees with the last name Johnson or a salary of $400.00, there will only be one employee with employee number 128.

Because there are two String components in the current Employee class, they might be declared within the same statement, such as `private String empLastName, empFirstName;`. However, it usually is easier to identify each Employee field at a glance if the fields are listed vertically.

Even if the only methods created for the Employee class include one set method and one get method for each instance variable, eight methods are required. Most organizations usually require many more fields for an Employee record (such as an address, a phone number, a hire date, the number of dependents, and so on) and many more methods. Finding your way through the list can become a formidable task. For ease in locating class methods, many programmers prefer to store them in alphabetical order. If you name all methods that get values so they begin with "get" and name all methods that set values so they being with "set," alphabetical order also results in functional groupings. Figure 3-29 shows how the complete class definition for an Employee might appear.

> Another reasonable course of action is to pair the get and set methods for a particular field. In other words, you can choose to place the getEmpNum() and setEmpNum() methods adjacently.

```
public class Employee
{
        private int empNum;
        private String empLastName;
        private String empFirstName;
        private double empSalary;
        public int getEmpNum()
        {
                return empNum;
        }
```

Figure 3-29: Employee class with data fields and methods

```java
        public String getFirstName()
        {
                return empFirstName;
        }
        public String getLastName()
        {
                return empLastName;
        }
        public double getSalary()
        {
                return empSalary;
        }
        public void setEmpNum(int e)
        {
                empNum = e;
        }
        public void setFirstName(String first)
        {
                empFirstName = first;
        }
        public void setLastName(String last)
        {
                empLastName = last;
        }
        public void setSalary(double sal)
        {
                empSalary = sal;
        }
}
```

Figure 3-29: Employee class with data fields and methods (continued)

The Employee class still is not a particularly large class, and each of its methods is very short, but it is already becoming quite difficult to manage. It certainly can use some well-placed comments, as shown in Figure 3-30.

```java
// Programmer: Joyce Farrell
// Date: February 13, 2000
// Employee.java to hold employee data
public class Employee
{
        // private data members
        private int empNum;
        private String empLastName;
        private String empFirstName;
        private double empSalary;
        // getEmpNum method returns employee number
        public int getEmpNum()
        {
                return empNum;
        }
        // getFirstName method returns employee first name
        public String getFirstName()
        {
                return empFirstName;
        }
        // … and so on
}
```

Figure 3-30: Employee class with data fields, methods, and comments

Although good program comments are crucial to creating understandable code, you will leave them out of many examples in this book to save space.

You may have noticed that member variables and methods appear in Class Outline in the same order in which they appear in a Java file—not in alphabetic order. However, when you use Class Outline commands to add a new variable or method, the variable or method is inserted into your program in alphabetic order. Inserting new variables and methods in alphabetical order makes it much easier to organize your classes while you build them. You cannot, however, use Class Outline to reorder existing classes—you must reorder them manually using cut and paste commands.

> **tip**
>
> Because Class Outline commands insert new variables and methods in alphabetical order, you may find it more convenient to use Class Outline commands instead of manually entering new code.

Next you will add data fields and methods to the EventSite class alphabetically using Class Outline commands.

To expand the EventSite class to contain data fields and methods:

1 Return to the **EventSite.java** file in the Text Editor window. Your program should resemble Figure 3-31.

```
public class EventSite
{
    private int siteNumber;
    public int getSiteNumber()
    {
        return siteNumber;
    }
    public void setSiteNumber(int n)
    {
        siteNumber = n;
    }
}
```

Figure 3-31: EventSite.java program

You will add two new data fields to the EventSite class: a double to hold a usage fee for the site, and a String to hold the site manager's last name.

2 Right-click the **EventSite** class in Class Outline, then select **Add Member Variable** from the shortcut menu. The Add Member Variable dialog box displays as shown in Figure 3-32.

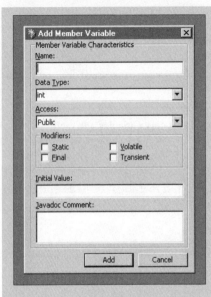

Figure 3-32: Add Member Variable dialog box

3 Type **usageFee** as the variable name, select **double** from the **Data Type** drop-down list box, then select `private` from the **Access** drop-down list box. The other dialog box options allow you to select access modifiers and an initial value. You can also enter any javadoc comments you want to include with the new variable. Click the **Add** button to create the new variable. The new usageFee variable appears beneath the Inherited members folder of the EventSite class node in Class Outline.

4 Repeat Steps 2 and 3 to add `private String managerName;` as an EventSite data field.

> **help**
>
> The String data type is listed in the Data Type drop-down list box as `java.lang.String`.

You also will enter four new methods to set and get data from each of the two new fields. To ensure that the methods are easy to locate later, you will place them in alphabetical order within the class.

5 Right-click the **EventSite** class in Class Outline, then select **Add Method** from the shortcut menu. The Add Method dialog box appears.

6 Type **getUsageFee** as the method name, select a return type of **double**, and select access of **public**. Do not set any parameters or modifiers. Add a descriptive comment to the Javadoc Comments text box and click the **Add** button.

Using Methods, Classes, and Objects

7 Double-click the **getUsageFee()** method in Class Outline to place the insertion point in the getUsageFee() method in the Text Editor window and replace the `// TODO: Add your own implementation.` comment with `return usageFee;` Also delete the three default statements that follow the comment.

8 Now add the following methods using the Add Method command in Class Outline. Add descriptive comments to each method using the Javadoc Comments text box in the Add Method dialog box.

```
public String getManagerName()
{
        return managerName;
}
public void setUsageFee(double amt)
{
        usageFee = amt;
}
public void setManagerName(String name)
{
        managerName = name;
}
```

9 Rebuild the project. If necessary, correct any syntax errors and rebuild the project again.

You have created an EventSite class that contains both data and methods. However, no actual event sites exist yet. You must write a program that instantiates one or more EventSite objects to give actual values to the data fields for that object and to manipulate the data in the fields using the class methods. Next, you will create a program to test the new expanded EventSite class.

To create the test program:

1 Add a new class file to your project by selecting **Add Class** from the **Project** menu. The Add Item dialog box appears. In the Add Item dialog box, select **Class** from the class folder, then change the suggested filename to **TestExpandedClass.java** and click the **Open** button. The new class opens in the Text Editor window.

2 Enter the class that tests the new expanded EventSite class. The class should look like Figure 3-33.

```
// Programmer: <your name>
// Date: <current date>
// Program: TestExpandedClass
// Tests the expanded EventSite class
public class TestExpandedClass
{
    public static void main(String[] args)
    {
        EventSite oneSite = new EventSite();
        oneSite.setSiteNumber(101);
        oneSite.setUsageFee(32508.65);
        oneSite.setManagerName("Jefferson");
        System.out.print("The number of the event site is ");
        System.out.println(oneSite.getSiteNumber());
        System.out.println("Usage fee "
           + oneSite.getUsageFee());
        System.out.println("Manager is "
           + oneSite.getManagerName());
    }
}
```

Figure 3-33: TestExpandedClass class

tip

You should get into the habit of documenting your programs with your name, today's date, and a brief explanation of the program. Your instructor might ask you to insert additional information as comment text, as well.

3 Rebuild the project. If necessary, correct any syntax errors and rebuild the project again.

4 Execute the program as a console application by typing **jview TestExpandedClass**. Your output should look like Figure 3-34.

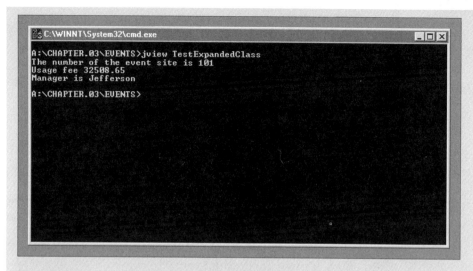

Figure 3-34: Output of the TestExpandedClass program

Using Constructors

When you create a class, such as Employee, and instantiate an object with a statement like `Employee chauffeur = new Employee();`, you are actually calling a constructor method named Employee() that is provided by the Java compiler. A **constructor method** is a method that establishes an object. The constructor method named Employee() establishes one Employee with the identifer chauffeur, and provides the following specific initial values to the Employee's data fields:

- Numeric fields are set to 0 (zero).
- Character fields are set to Unicode \u0000.
- The boolean fields are set to `false`.
- The object type fields are set to `null` (or empty).

If you do not want an Employee's fields to hold these default values, or if you want to perform additional tasks when you create an Employee, then you can write your own constructor. Any constructor method you write must have the same name as the class it constructs, and constructor methods cannot have a return type. For example, if every Employee has a starting salary of 300.00, then you could write the constructor method for the Employee class that appears in Figure 3-35. Any Employee instantiated will have a default empSal figure of 300.00.

section B

```
Employee()
{
      empSal = 300.00;
}
```

Figure 3-35: Employee class constructor

You can write any statement in a constructor. Although you usually would have no reason to do so, you could print a message from within a constructor or perform any other task. Next, you will add a constructor to the EventSite class and demonstrate that it is called when an EventSite object is instantiated.

To add a constructor to the EventSite class:

1. Return to the **EventSite.java** file in the Text Editor window.
2. Place the insertion point at the end of the line containing the last field declaration (`private double usageFee`), and then press the **Enter** key to start a new line.
3. Add the following constructor function that sets any EventSite siteNumber to 999 and any manager's name to "ZZZ" upon construction:

```
EventSite()
{
      siteNumber = 999;
      managerName = "ZZZ";
}
```

4. Rebuild the project. If necessary, correct any syntax errors and rebuild the project again.
5. Add a new class file to your project by selecting **Add Class** from the **Project** menu. The Add Item dialog box appears. In the Add Item dialog box, select **Class** from the class folder, then change the suggested filename to **TestConstructor.java** and click the **Open** button. The new class opens in the Text Editor window.
6. Enter the code as shown in Figure 3-36.

Using Methods, Classes, and Objects

```
public class TestConstructor
{
    public static void main(String[] args)
    {
        EventSite oneSite = new EventSite();
        System.out.print
           ("The number of the event site is ");
        System.out.println
           (oneSite.getSiteNumber());
        System.out.print("The manager is ");
        System.out.println(oneSite.getManagerName ());
    }
}
```

Figure 3-36: TestConstructor class

7 Rebuild, save, and execute the program as a console application. Confirm that it declares a oneSite object of type EventSite, calls the constructor, and assigns the indicated initial values, as shown in Figure 3-37.

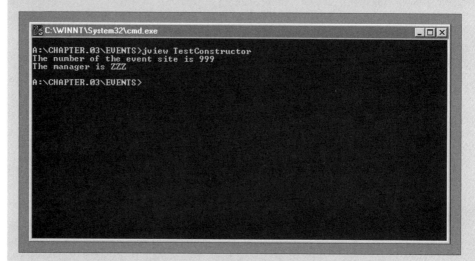

Figure 3-37: Output of the TestConstructor program

SUMMARY

- When you think in an object-oriented manner, everything is an object and every object is a member (an instance, or an instantiation) of a class. This concept is known as an is-a relationship.

- Objects inherit attributes from classes. Class objects have attributes and methods associated with them. Class instance methods that will be used with objects usually are not static.

- You can send messages to objects. Additionally, some methods used in a program must return a message or value.

- There are two parts to object-oriented programming: creating the classes of objects from which objects will be instantiated and writing other classes to use the objects.

- A class header contains an optional access modifier, the keyword `class`, and any legal identifier you choose for the name of your class.

- The class access modifiers are `public`, `final`, and `abstract`. You can also choose to specify no modifier. Public classes are accessible by all objects, which is the most liberal form of access, and can be extended, or used as a basis for any other class.

- The instance variables, or fields, of a class are placed as statements within the class's curly brackets.

- Allowable field modifiers are `private`, `public`, `protected`, `final`, `static`, `transient`, and `volatile`. Most class fields are private, which provides the highest level of security.

- Information hiding is an important component of object-oriented programs; a class's private data can be changed or manipulated only by a class's own methods.

- Declaring a class does not create any actual objects; you must instantiate any objects that are members of a class.

- To create an object that is an instance of a class, you supply a type and an identifier, and then allocate computer memory for that object using the `new` operator.

- Most programmers place data fields in some logical order at the beginning of a class. Many programmers prefer to store data fields in alphabetical order.

- You use the Class Outline feature in the Visual J++ IDE to manage the various classes and class members contained in a package. Class Outline displays classes and class members in a package in a hierarchical list that is very similar to Project Explorer. Packages, also called libraries, are related groups of classes and class members that make up your entire Java program.

- A solution contains all the files in the application you are developing, such as graphic files, in addition to Java files. A package only organizes classes such as Java files or other types of class files that might be required by the program you are writing.

- Class Outline contains several commands that use dialog boxes to automate the task of adding classes, methods, and member variables to a package. You can also cut, copy, paste, and delete classes and class members and change individual class properties. You access Class Outline commands by right-clicking a class or member name to display the shortcut menu.

- As you work with Class Outline, keep in mind that you can always perform most of the available commands, such as adding new methods, by manually editing a Java class file. Class Outline simply automates some of the process for you.

- Class Outline commands insert new variables and methods into a class alphabetically, making it much easier to organize your classes while you build them.

- A constructor method establishes an object and provides specific initial values for the object's data fields. A constructor method always has the same name as the class of which it is a member. The Java compiler will supply default constructor methods or you can write your own. Constructor methods might not have a return type.

- In constructor methods, numeric fields are set to 0 (zero), character fields are set to Unicode \u0000, boolean fields are set to `false` and object type fields are set to `null` by default.

QUESTIONS

1. Every object is a member or instance of a more general _____.
   a. class
   b. program
   c. method
   d. syntax

2. The data components of a class often are referred to as the _____ of that class.
   a. access types
   b. instance variables
   c. methods
   d. objects

3. Class objects have both attributes and _____.
   a. fields
   b. data
   c. methods
   d. instances

4. You send messages to an object through its _____.
   a. fields
   b. methods
   c. classes
   d. data

section B

5. You create classes, from which _____ are instantiated.
   a. fields
   b. data
   c. other classes
   d. objects

6. A program or class that instantiates objects of another prewritten class is a(n) _____.
   a. class client
   b. superclass
   c. object
   d. patron

7. A class header must contain _____.
   a. an access modifier
   b. the keyword `class`
   c. the keyword `static`
   d. the keyword `public`

8. Which of the following access modifiers can you use to define a class?
   a. `open`
   b. `static`
   c. `abstract`
   d. `concrete`

9. Most classes are created with the access modifier _____.
   a. `private`
   b. `public`
   c. `liberal`
   d. `open`

10. The body of a class is written _____.
    a. as a single statement
    b. within parentheses
    c. between curly brackets
    d. as a method call

11. Allowable field modifiers include _____.
    a. `private`
    b. `final`
    c. both of these
    d. neither of these

12. Which of the following is not a field modifier?
    a. `public`
    b. `preserved`
    c. `protected`
    d. `private`

13. Most class fields are _____.
    a. private
    b. public
    c. static
    d. final

14. The concept of allowing a class's private data to be changed only by a class's own methods is known as _____.
    a. structured logic
    b. object orientation
    c. information hiding
    d. data masking

15. At the time you declare a class, you _____.
    a. declare one object of the class
    b. instantiate one object of the class
    c. declare multiple objects of the class
    d. instantiate no actual objects

16. When you declare a variable as in `double salary;`, you _____.
    a. also must explicitly allocate memory for it
    b. need not explicitly allocate memory for it
    c. must explicitly allocate memory for it only if it is stored in a class
    d. can declare it to use no memory

17. When you declare an object that is an instance of a class, you _____.
    a. also must explicitly allocate memory for it
    b. need not explicitly allocate memory for it
    c. must explicitly allocate memory for it only if it is stored in a class
    d. can declare it to use no memory

18. To allocate memory, you must use the _____ operator.
    a. `alloc`
    b. `malloc`
    c. `create`
    d. `new`

19. You can allocate memory for an object _____.
    a. with an assignment statement
    b. in the same statement as the object declaration
    c. either of these
    d. neither of these

20. If an object someThing has a method someMethod(), then you can call the method using the statement _____.
    a. `someThing/someMethod();`
    b. `someThing.someMethod();`
    c. `someMethod/someThing();`
    d. `someMethod.someThing();`

section B

21. If a class is named Student(), then the class constructor name is _____.
   a. any legal Java identifier
   b. any legal Java identifier that begins with S
   c. StudentConstructor
   d. Student()

22. If you use the default constructor, _____.
   a. numeric fields are set to 0 (zero)
   b. character fields are set to blank
   c. boolean fields are set to true
   d. object type fields are set to 0 (zero)

23. A constructor can contain _____.
   a. assignment statements
   b. println() statements
   c. either of these
   d. neither of these

EXERCISES

1. a. Create a project named Pizza in the Chapter.03 folder on your Student Disk. Add data fields to the Pizza class representing toppings (such as "pepperoni"), an integer for diameter in inches (such as 12), and a double for price (such as 13.99). Include methods to get and set values for each of these fields.

   b. Add a class named TestPizza to the Pizza project that instantiates one Pizza object and demonstrates the use of the Pizza set and get methods.

2. a. Create a project named Student in the Chapter.03 folder on your Student Disk. Add fields to the Student class for an ID number, number of credit hours earned, and number of points earned. (For example, many schools compute grade point averages based on a scale of 4, so a three-credit-hour class in which a student earns an A is worth 12 points.) Include methods to assign values to all fields. The Student class also has a field for grade point average. Include a method to compute the grade point average field by dividing points by credit hours earned. Write methods to display the values in each Student field.

   b. Add a class named ShowStudent to the Student project that instantiates a Student object from the class you created. Compute the Student grade point average, and then display all the values associated with the Student.

   c. Create a constructor method for the Student class you created. The constructor should initialize each Student's ID number to 9999 and his or her grade point average to 4.0. Write a program that demonstrates that the constructor works by instantiating an object and displaying the initial values.

3. a. Create a project named Circle in the Chapter.03 folder on your Student Disk. Add fields to the Circle class named radius, area, and diameter. Include a constructor that sets the radius to 1. Also include methods named setRadius(), getRadius(), computeDiameter(), which computes a circle's diameter, and computeArea(), which computes a circle's area. (The diameter of a circle is twice its radius, and the area is 3.14 multiplied by the square of the radius.)

b. Add a class named TestCircle to the Circle project whose main() method declares three Circle objects. Using the setRadius() method, assign one circle a small radius value and assign another a larger radius value. Do not assign a value to the radius of the third circle; instead, retain the value assigned at construction. Call computeDiameter() and computeArea() for each circle and display the results.

4. a. Create a project named Checkup in the Chapter.03 folder on your Student Disk with fields that hold a patient number, two blood pressure figures (systolic and diastolic), and two cholesterol figures (LDL and HDL). Include methods to get and set each of the fields. Include a method named computeRatio() that divides LDL cholesterol by HDL cholesterol and displays the result. Include an additional method named ExplainRatio() that explains that LDL is known as "good cholesterol" and that a ratio of 3.5 or lower is considered optimum.

    b. Add a class named TestCheckup to the Checkup project whose main() method declares four Checkup objects. Provide values for each field for each patient, and then display the values. Blood pressure numbers are usually displayed with a slash between the systolic and diastolic values. (Typical numbers are values like 110/78 or 130/90.) With the cholesterol figures, display the explanation of the cholesterol ratio calculation. (Typical numbers are values like 100 and 40 or 180 and 70.)

5. Create a project named Employee in the Chapter.03 folder on your Student Disk that displays employee IDs and first and last names of employees. Use two classes. The first class contains the employee data and separate methods to set the IDs and names. The other class creates objects for the employees and uses the objects to call the set methods.

6. Create a project named Invoice in the Chapter.03 folder on your Student Disk that displays an invoice of several items. It should contain the item name, quantity, price, and total cost on each line for the quantity and item cost. Use two classes. The first class contains the item data and methods to get and set the item name, quantity, and price. The other class creates objects for the items and uses the objects to call the set and get methods.

7. Create a project named RoomSchedule in the Chapter.03 folder on your Student Disk that schedules several meetings for a meeting room. It should contain the day of the week, starting time, and ending time for each meeting. Use two classes. The first class contains the meeting data and methods to get and set the day of the week and times. The other class creates objects for the meetings and uses the objects to call the set and get methods.

8. Each of the following files in the Chapter.03 folder on your Student Disk has syntax and/or logical errors. Add the files to a new project called FixDebug. Save the FixDebug project under the Chapter.03 folder on your Student Disk. In each case, fix the problem and run each file as a console application using JVIEW.
    a. DebugThree1.java
    b. DebugThree2.java
    c. DebugThree3.java
    d. DebugThree4.java

CHAPTER 4

Advanced Object Concepts

case ▶ Lynn Greenbrier, your mentor at Event Handlers Incorporated, pops her head into your cubicle on Monday morning. "How's the programming going?" she asks.

"I'm getting the hang of using objects," you tell her, "but I want to create lots of objects, and it seems like I am going to need so many methods for the classes that I create that it's going to be very hard to keep track of them." You pause a moment and add, "And all these set methods are driving me crazy—I wish an object could just start with values."

"Anything else bothering you?" Lynn asks.

"Well," you reply, "I don't mean to complain, but shouldn't some objects and methods that are used by all kinds of programmers already be created for me? I can't be the first person who ever thought about taking a square root of a number or calculating a billing date for 10 days after service."

"You are in luck!" Lynn smiles. "Java's creators already thought about these things. Let me tell you about some of the more advanced things you can do with your classes."

SECTION A
objectives

In this lesson you will learn
- About blocks and scope
- How to overload a method
- About the concept of ambiguity
- How to send an argument to a constructor
- How to overload a constructor

Class Features

Blocks and Scope

Within any class or method, the code between a pair of curly brackets is called a **block**. For example, the program shown in Figure 4-1 contains two blocks. The first block, or **outside block**, begins immediately after the method declaration and ends at the end of the method. The second block, or **inside block**, is contained within the second set of curly brackets and contains three statements: the declaration of anotherNumber and two println() statements. The inside block is **nested** within the outside block.

tip

Although you can create as many blocks as you need within any program, it is not wise to do so without a reason, and it is considered to be poor programming style if you do.

```
public static void methodWithTwoBlocks()
{
     int aNumber = 22;
       // aNumber comes into existence
     System.out.println("aNumber is " + aNumber);
     {
          int anotherNumber = 99;
            // anotherNumber comes into existence
          System.out.println("aNumber is " + aNumber);
          System.out.println("anotherNumber is " +
          anotherNumber);
```

Figure 4-1: The methodWithTwoBlocks() method

```
        }        // End of block — anotherNumber ceases to exist
        System.out.println("aNumber is " + aNumber);
}        // End of outer block — aNumber ceases to exist
```

Figure 4-1: The methodWithTwoBlocks() method (continued)

A block can exist entirely within another block or entirely outside and separate from another block, but blocks can never overlap.

If you declare a variable in one program that you write, you cannot use that variable in another program. Similarly, when you declare a variable within a block, you cannot reference that variable outside the block. The portion of a program within which you can reference a variable is the variable's **scope**. A variable comes into existence, and **comes into scope**, when you declare it. A variable ceases to exist, and **goes out of scope**, at the end of the block in which it is declared.

In the methodWithTwoBlocks() method shown in Figure 4-1, the variable aNumber exists from the point of its declaration until the end of the method. This means aNumber exists both in the outer block and within the inner block and can be used anywhere in the method. The variable anotherNumber comes into existence within the inner block, ceases to exist when the inner block ends, and cannot be used beyond its block.

Figure 4-2 shows some invalid statements. The first assignment `aNumber = 75;` is invalid because aNumber has not been declared yet. Similarly, Invalid statement 2, `anotherNumber = 489;`, is invalid because it has not been declared yet. Invalid statement 3 is also invalid because anotherNumber still has not been declared. After you declare anotherNumber, you can use it for the remainder of the block, but Invalid statement 4 is outside the block—anotherNumber has gone out of scope. The last statement in Figure 4-2, `aNumber = 29;`, will not work because it falls outside the block in which aNumber was declared; it actually falls outside the methodWithTwoBlocks() method.

```
public static void methodWithTwoBlocks()
{
        aNumber = 75; // Invalid statement 1
        int aNumber = 22;
        System.out.println("aNumber is " + aNumber);
        anotherNumber = 489;   // Invalid statement 2
        {
```

Figure 4-2: The methodWithTwoBlocks() method with some invalid statements

```
                anotherNumber = 165; // Invalid statement 3
                int anotherNumber = 99;
                System.out.println("aNumber is " + aNumber);
                System.out.println("anotherNumber is " +
                        anotherNumber);
        }
        System.out.println("aNumber is " + aNumber);
        System.out.println("anotherNumber is " +
                anotherNumber); // Invalid statement 4
}
aNumber = 29; // Invalid statement 5
```

Figure 4-2: The methodWithTwoBlocks() method with some invalid statements (continued)

There is no requirement that you vertically align the opening and closing brackets for a block, but your programs are much easier to read if you do.

Within a method, you can declare a variable with the same name multiple times, as long as each declaration is in its own, nonoverlapping block. For example, the two declarations of variables named someVar in Figure 4-3 are valid because each variable is contained within its own block. The first instance of someVar has gone out of scope before the second instance comes into scope.

```
public static twoDeclarations()
{
        { // Begin first block
                int someVar = 7;
                System.out.println(someVar);
        } // End first block
        { // Begin second block
                int someVar = 845;
                System.out.println(someVar);
        } // End second block
}
```

Figure 4-3: The twoDeclarations() method

You cannot declare the same variable name more than once within nested blocks. For example, in Figure 4-4, the second declaration of aValue causes an error because you cannot declare the same variable twice within the outer block of the method. By the same reasoning, the third declaration of aValue is also invalid, even though it appears within a new block. The block that contains the third declaration is entirely within the outside block, so the first declaration of aValue has not gone out of scope.

```
public static methodWithRedeclarations()
{
        int aValue = 35;
        System.out.println(aValue);
        int aValue = 99;   // Invalid — second declaration
        {
                int anotherValue = 58; // Valid
                int aValue = 99; // Invalid — third declaration
        // This block is inside the outer block
        }
}
```

Figure 4-4: Invalid methodWithRedeclarations()

Although you cannot declare a variable twice within the same method, you can reassign the value it holds. For example, the statement `int aValue = 35;` declares the aValue variable as an integer and assigns an initial value of 35. If you repeat the variable declaration within an inner block, as in the third declaration of Figure 4-4, it is invalid. However, the reassignment statement `aValue = 35;` is valid because it only assigns a new value to the variable and does not attempt to declare it.

> **help**
> You will receive a compiler error if you attempt to assign a value to a variable that has not been declared.

If you declare a variable within a class, and use the same variable name within a method of the class, then the variable used inside the method takes precedence, or **overrides**, the first variable. For example, consider a class that holds Employee information including two integer fields, aNum and aDept, as shown in Figure 4-5.

```
public class Employee
{
        private int aNum = 44;
        private int aDept = 55;
        public void empMethod()
        {
                int aNum = 88;
                        // aNum overrides the class variable aNum
                System.out.println("aNum is " + aNum);
                System.out.println("aDept is " + aDept);
        }
        public void anotherEmpMethod()
        {
                System.out.println("aNum is " + aNum);
                System.out.println("aDept is " + aDept);
        }
}
```

Figure 4-5: Employee class with an overriding variable

Figure 4-5 shows an Employee class with two integers and two void methods. If a program instantiates an Employee object with a statement such as `Employee adminAssistant = new Employee();`, then either empMethod() or anotherEmpMethod() can be called using the adminAssistant object and the dot operator.

When the method call is `adminAssistant.empMethod();`, the output will indicate that aNum is 88 and aDept is 55. The empMethod() will use the local aNum valued at 88, but use the class aDept valued at 55. When the method call is `adminAssistant.anotherEmpMethod();`, the output will show that aNum is 44 and aDept is 55; in both cases, the class variables are used because they have not been overridden within anotherEmpMethod(). When you write programs, it is best to avoid confusing situations that arise when you give the same name to a class variable and a method variable. However, if you do use the same name, you need to be aware that the method variable will override the class variable.

Next, you will create a method with several blocks to demonstrate block scope.

Advanced Object Concepts

To demonstrate block scope:

1. Start Visual J++ and create a new console application project named **DemoBlock**. Save the **DemoBlock** project folder in the Chapter.04 folder on your Student Disk.

2. Rename the default Class1.java file as **DemoBlock.java**, then open the file in the Text Editor window.

3. Replace the Class1 class name in the `public class Class1` line with **DemoBlock**.

4. Replace the `// TODO: Add initialization code here` comment with `int x = 1111;`

5. On new lines, type the following two println() statements:

   ```
   System.out.println("Demonstrating block scope");
   System.out.println("In first block x is " + x);
   ```

6. Begin a new block by typing an opening curly bracket ({) on the next line. Within the new block, declare another integer by typing `int y = 2222;` Within this new block, type the following two statements to display the values of *x* and *y*:

   ```
   System.out.println("In second block x is " + x);
   System.out.println("In second block y is " + y);
   ```

7. End the block by typing a closing curly bracket (}). On the next line, begin a new block with an opening curly bracket. Within this new block, declare a new integer with the same name as the integer declared in the previous block by typing `int y = 3333;`

8. Enter two println() statements, a method call, and two more println() statements, as follows:

   ```
   System.out.println("In third block x is " + x);
   System.out.println("In third block y is " + y);
   demoMethod();
   System.out.println("After method x is " + x);
   System.out.println("After method block y is " + y);
   ```

9. Close this block by typing a closing curly bracket.

10. Type `System.out.println("At the end x is " + x);` This last statement in the program displays the value of *x*.

11 Finally, enter the following demoMethod() just before the closing curly bracket for the DemoBlock class. This method creates its own x and y, assigns different values, and then displays them.

```
public static void demoMethod()
{
int x = 8888, y = 9999;
System.out.println("In demoMethod x is " + x);
System.out.println("In demoMethod block y is " + y);
}
```

12 Select **DemoBlock Properties** from the **Project** menu. Select the **DemoBlock** file in the When project runs, load drop-down list box and set the project to run as a console application. When you are finished, click the **OK** button.

13 Build the project. If necessary, correct any syntax errors and rebuild the project.

14 Execute the program as a console application by typing **jview DemoBlock** at the command line.

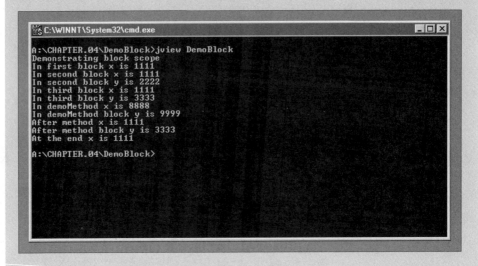

Figure 4-6: Output of the DemoBlock program

It is important to understand the impact that blocks have on your variables. Once you understand the scope of variables, you can locate the source of many errors within your programs more easily.

To gain a more complete understanding of blocks and scope:

1 Change the values of x and y in the program and then rebuild the project. Try to predict the exact output before rerunning the program.

Overloading

Overloading involves using one term to indicate diverse meanings. When you use the English language, you overload words all the time. When you say "open the door," "open your eyes," and "open a computer file," you are talking about three very different actions using very different methods and producing very different results. However, anyone who speaks English fluently has no trouble understanding your meaning because the verb *open* is understood in the context of the noun that follows it.

When you overload a Java method, you write multiple methods with a shared name. The compiler understands your meaning based on the arguments you use with the method. For example, suppose you create a class method to apply a simple interest rate to a bank balance. The method receives two double arguments—the balance and the interest rate—and displays the multiplied result. Figure 4-7 shows the method.

```
public static void simpleInterest
       (double bal, double rate)
{
       double interest;
       interest = bal * rate;
       System.out.println("Interest on " + bal + " at " +
          rate + " interest rate is " + interest);
}
```

Figure 4-7: The simpleInterest() method with two double arguments

The simpleInterest() method can receive integer arguments even though it is defined as needing double arguments because integers will be promoted or cast automatically to doubles, as you learned in Chapter 2.

When a program calls the simpleInterest() method and passes double values, as in `simpleInterest(1000.00, 0.04)`, the simple interest will be calculated correctly as four percent of 1000.00. Assume, however, that the interest rate passed to the simpleInterest() method comes from inconsistent user input. Some users who want to indicate an interest rate of four percent might type .04, and others might type 4 assuming that they are typing four percent. When the simpleInterest() method is called with arguments 10000.00 and .04, the interest is calculated correctly as 40.00. When the method is called using 1000.00 and 4, the interest is calculated incorrectly as 4000.00.

Beginning programmers often confuse overloading with overriding. You will learn to override methods in Chapter 7.

A solution to this problem is to overload the simpleInterest() method. **Overloading** involves writing multiple methods with the same name, but with different arguments. For example, in addition to providing the simpleInterest() method shown in Figure 4-7, you could add the method shown in Figure 4-8.

```
public static void simpleInterest
      (double bal, int rate)
      // Notice rate type
{
      double interest, rateAsPercent;
      rateAsPercent = rate/100.0;
      // Converts whole number rate to decimal equivalent
      interest = bal * rateAsPercent;
      System.out.println("Interest on " + bal + " at " +
         rate + " interest rate is " + interest);
}
```

Figure 4-8: The simpleInterest() method with a double and an integer argument

Note that this program calculates the rateAsPercent figure by dividing by 100.0, and not by 100. If two integers are divided, the result is a truncated integer; dividing by a double 100.0 causes the result to be a double. Alternatively, you could use a cast.

If you call the method simpleInterest() using two double arguments, as in `simpleInterest(1000.00, .04)`, the first simpleInterest() method shown in Figure 4-7 will execute. However, if you use an integer as the second parameter in the call to simpleInterest(), as in `simpleInterest(1000.00, 4)`, then the method shown in Figure 4-8 will execute and the whole number rate figure will be divided by 100.0 correctly before it is used to determine the interest earned.

Of course, you could use methods with different names to solve the dilemma of producing an accurate simple interest figure—for example, simpleInterestRateUsingDouble() and simpleInterestRateUsingInt(). Using this approach would require that you place a decision within your program to determine which of the two methods to call. It is more convenient to use one method name and then let the compiler determine which method to use. Also, it

Advanced Object Concepts

is easier to remember one reasonable name for tasks that are functionally identical except for argument types.

You will learn about placing a decision within your program in Chapter 5.

Next, you will overload methods to display event dates for Event Handlers Incorporated. The methods will take one, two, or three integer arguments. If there is one argument, it is the month, and the event is scheduled for the first of the given month in the year 2001. If there are two arguments, they are the month and the day in the year 2000. Three arguments represent the month, day, and year.

In addition to creating your own class to store dates, you can use a built-in Java class to handle dates. You will learn about this class in Section B.

To overload an overloadDate() method to take one, two, or three arguments:

1 Create a new console application project named **DemoOverload**. Save the **DemoOverload** project folder in the Chapter.04 folder on your Student Disk.

2 Rename the default Class1.java file as **DemoOverload.java**, then open the file in the Text Editor window.

3 Replace the Class1 class name in the `public class Class1` line with **DemoOverload**.

4. Replace the `// TODO: Add initialization code here` comment with the following statements:

```
int month = 6, day = 24, year = 2003;
overloadDate(month);
overloadDate(month,day);
overloadDate(month,day,year);
```

5 After the closing bracket of the main () methods, create the following overloadDate() method that requires one argument:

```
public static void overloadDate(int mm)
{
System.out.println("Event date " + mm + "/1/2001");
}
```

6 Create the following overloadDate() method that requires two arguments:

```
public static void overloadDate(int mm, int dd)
{
   System.out.println("Event date " + mm + "/" +
      dd + "/2001");
}
```

7 Create the following overloadDate() method that requires three arguments:

```
public static void overloadDate(int mm, int dd, int yy)
{
System.out.println("Event date " + mm + "/" +
  dd + "/" + yy);
}
```

8 Select **DemoOverload Properties** from the **Project** menu. Select the **DemoOverload** file in the When project runs, load drop-down list box and set the project to run as a console application. When you are finished, click the **OK** button.

9 Build the project and execute the program as a console application by typing **jview DemoOverload** at the command line. Figure 4-9 shows the output. Notice that whether you call the overloadDate() method using one, two, or three arguments, the date prints correctly because you have successfully overloaded the overloadDate() method.

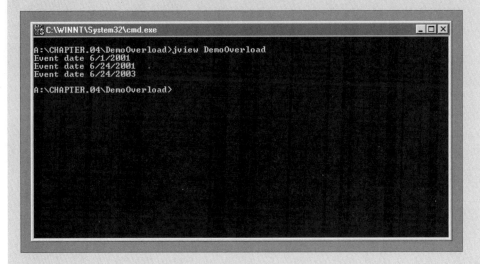

Figure 4-9: Output of the DemoOverload program

Ambiguity

When you overload a method, you run the risk of creating an **ambiguous** situation—one in which the compiler cannot determine which method to use. For example, consider the simple method shown in Figure 4-10.

```
void simpMeth(double d)
{
     System.out.println("Method receives double parameter");
}
```

Figure 4-10: The simpMeth() method with a double argument

Passing the argument as either a double variable or an int variable causes the method to work as expected. For example, if you declare a double variable named doubleValue or an int variable named intValue, then either method call (`simpMeth(doubleValue);` or `simpMeth(intValue);`) will result in the output "Method receives double parameter". When you call the method with the integer argument, then the integer is cast as (or promoted to) a double, and the method works as well.

> **Note** that if the method with the declaration `void simpMeth(double d)` did not exist (but the declaration `void simpMeth(int i)` did exist), then the method call `simpMeth(doubleValue);` would fail. Although an integer can be promoted to a double, a double cannot be demoted to an integer. This convention makes sense if you consider the potential loss of information when a double value is reduced to an integer.

If you add a second overloaded simpMeth() method within a program that takes an integer parameter (as shown in Figure 4-11), then the output changes when you call `simpMeth(intValue);`. Instead of promoting an integer argument to a double, the compiler recognizes a more exact match for the method call that uses the integer argument, so it calls the version of the method that produces the output "Method receives integer parameter".

```
void simpMeth(int i)
{
     System.out.println("Method receives integer parameter");
}
```

Figure 4-11: The simpMeth() method with an integer argument

A more complicated and potentially ambiguous situation arises when the compiler cannot make a determination as to which of several versions of a method to use. Consider the following overloaded simpleInterest() method declarations:

```
public static void simpleInterest(double bal, double rate)
public static void simpleInterest(double bal, int rate)
                    //Notice rate type
```

A call to simpleInterest() with two double arguments executes the first version of the method, and a call to simpleInterest() with a double and an integer argument executes the second version of the method. With each of these calls, the compiler can find an exact match for the arguments you are sending. However, if you call simpleInterest() using two integer arguments, as in `simpleInterest(300,6);`, an ambiguous situation arises because there is no exact match for the method call. Because two integers can be promoted to two doubles (thus matching the first version of the overloaded method), or just one integer can be promoted to a double (thus matching the second version), the compiler does not know which version of the simpleInterest() method to use and the program will not execute. You could argue that *int, int* is "closer" to *double, int* than it is to *double, double*, but the compiler does not presume to make such decisions for you.

An overloaded method is not ambiguous on its own—it becomes ambiguous only if you create an ambiguous situation. A program with potentially ambiguous methods will run problem-free if you do not make any ambiguous method calls.

It is important to note that you can overload methods correctly by providing different argument lists for methods with the same name. Methods with identical names that have identical argument lists but different return types are not overloaded—they are illegal. For example, `int aMethod(int x)` and `void aMethod(int x)` cannot coexist within a program. The compiler determines which of several versions of a method to call based on argument lists. When the method call `aMethod(17);` is made, the compiler will not know which method to execute because both methods take an integer argument.

Sending Arguments to Constructors

In Chapter 3, you learned that Java automatically provides a constructor method when you create a class. You also learned that you can write your own constructor method, and that you often do so when you want to ensure that fields within classes are initialized to some appropriate default value. Additionally, you can write constructor methods that receive arguments. Such arguments often are used for initialization purposes when the values that you want to assign to objects upon creation might vary.

For example, consider the Employee class with two data fields shown in Figure 4-12. Its constructor method assigns 999 to each potentially instantiated Employee's empNum. Any time an Employee object is created using a statement such as `Employee partTimeWorker = new Employee();`, even if no other data-assigning methods ever are used, you are ensured that the partTimeWorker Employee, like all Employees, will have an initial empNum of 999.

Advanced Object Concepts

```
public class Employee
{
        private int empNum;
        private double empSalary;
                // Constructor method
        Employee()
        {
                empNum = 999;
        }
        // Other methods go here
}
```

Figure 4-12: Employee class data fields

You can use a setEmpNum() method to assign values to individual Employee objects after construction, but a constructor method assigns the values at the time of creation.

Alternatively, you might choose to create Employees with initial empNums that differ for each Employee. To accomplish this within a constructor, you need to pass an employee number to the constructor. Figure 4-13 shows an Employee constructor that receives an argument. With this constructor, you pass an argument using a statement such as `Employee partTimeWorker = new Employee(881);`. When the constructor executes, the integer within the method call is passed to Employee() and assigned to the empNum.

```
Employee(int num)
{
        empNum = num;
}
```

Figure 4-13: Employee constructor method with an argument

To demonstrate a constructor with an argument, you will use a new version of the EventSite class you created in Chapter 3.

To alter a constructor:

1. Create a new console application project named **EventSite**. Save the **EventSite** project folder in the Chapter.04 folder on your Student Disk.
2. Rename the default Class1.java file as **EventSite.java**, then open the file in the Text Editor window.
3. Replace the default code and comments with the EventSite class shown in Figure 4-14. This file is similar to the EventSite.java text file you created in Chapter 3, but comments have been added for clarity.

```
public class EventSite
{
        private int siteNumber;
        private double usageFee;
        private String managerName;
        // Constructor
        EventSite()
        {
                siteNumber = 999;
                managerName = "ZZZ";
        }
        // getManagerName() gets managerName
        public String getManagerName()
        {
                return managerName;
        }
        // getSiteNumber() gets the siteNumber
        public int getSiteNumber()
        {
                return siteNumber;
        }
```

Figure 4-14: EventSite.java class

```
        // getUsageFee() gets the usageFee
        public double getUsageFee()
        {
              return usageFee;
        }
        // setManagerName() assigns a name to the manager
        public void setManagerName(String name)
        {
              managerName = name;
        }
        // setSiteNumber() assigns a site number
        public void setSiteNumber(int n)
        {
              siteNumber = n;
        }
        // setUsageFee() assigns a value to the usage fee
        public void setUsageFee(double amt)
        {
              usageFee = amt;
        }
}
```

Figure 4-14: EventSite.java class (continued)

4. Modify the existing constructor by typing the following code so the constructor takes an argument for the site number and then assigns the argument value to the siteNumber field:

```
EventSite(int siteNum)
{
  siteNumber = siteNum;
  managerName = "ZZZ";
}
```

> 5 Add a new main class file to your project by selecting **Add Class** from the **Project** menu. The Add Item dialog box appears. In the Add Item dialog box, select **ClassMain** from the Class folder, then change the suggested filename to **DemoConstruct.java** and click the **Open** button. The new class opens in the Text Editor window.
>
> 6 Add the following statements between the main() method's curly brackets:
>
> ```
> EventSite aSite = new EventSite(678);
> System.out.println("Site number is " +
> aSite.getSiteNumber());
> ```
>
> 7 Select **EventSite Properties** from the **Project** menu. Select the **DemoConstruct** file in the When project runs, load drop-down list box and set the project to run as a console application. When you are finished, click the **OK** button.
>
> 8 Build the project and execute the program as a console application by typing **jview DemoConstruct** at the command line. The site number (678) should be assigned to the aSite object.

Overloading Constructors

If you create a class from which you instantiate objects, Java automatically provides you with a constructor. Unfortunately, if you create your own constructor, the automatically created constructor no longer exists. Therefore, once you create a constructor that takes an argument, you no longer have the option of using the automatic constructor that requires no arguments.

Fortunately, as with any other method, you can overload constructors. Overloading constructors provides you with a way to create objects with or without initial arguments, as needed. For example, in addition to using the constructor method shown in Figure 4-14, you can create the second constructor method for the Employee class shown in Figure 4-15. When both constructors reside within the Employee class, you have the option of creating an Employee object either with or without an initial empNum value. When you create an Employee object with `Employee aWorker = new Employee();`, the constructor with no arguments is called and the Employee object receives an initial empNum value of 999. When you create an Employee object with `Employee anotherWorker = new Employee(7677);`, the constructor that requires an integer is used, and the anotherWorker Employee receives an initial empNum of 7677.

Advanced Object Concepts

```
Employee()
{
      empNum = 999;
}
```

Figure 4-15: Employee constructor method with no argument

Similarly, you could create constructors that require two, three, or more arguments. You can use the arguments to initialize field values, but you also can use arguments for any other purpose. For example, you could use the presence or absence of an argument simply to determine which of two possible constructors to call, yet not make use of the argument within the constructor method. As long as the constructor argument lists differ, there is no ambiguity in which constructor method to call.

Next, you will overload the EventSite constructor to take either no arguments, in which case the site number is 999, or an argument that is the site number.

To overload the EventSite constructor:

1. Return to the **EventSite.java** file in the Text Editor window.
2. Position the insertion point at the end of the comment `// Constructor`, type **s** to make the word *Constructor* plural, and then press the **Enter** key to start a new line.
3. Above the existing constructor that requires an argument, add the new overloaded constructor that requires no argument by typing the following:

   ```
   EventSite()
   {
     siteNumber = 999;
     managerName = "ZZZ";
   }
   ```

4. Return to the **DemoConstruct.java** file in the Text Editor window.
5. Position the insertion point at the end of the statement `EventSite aSite = new EventSite(678);`, and then press the **Enter** key to start a new line.
6. Create a new EventSite with no constructor argument by typing `EventSite anotherSite = new EventSite();`.

7. Position the insertion point after the println() statement that displays the site number of aSite, `System.out.println("Site number is " + aSite.getSiteNumber());`, and then press the **Enter** key to start a new line. Type the following statement to print the site number of anotherSite:

   `System.out.println("Another site number is " + anotherSite.getSiteNumber());`

8. Rebuild the project and execute the program as a console application by typing **jview DemoConstruct** at the command line. The two site numbers should print as 678 and 999.

SUMMARY

- A block is the code between a pair of curly brackets. You can nest blocks within other blocks.

- A variable's scope is the portion of a program within which you can reference the variable. A variable comes into existence, and comes into scope, when you declare it, and it ceases to exist, and goes out of scope, at the end of the block in which it is declared.

- Within a method, you can declare a variable with the same name multiple times as long as each declaration is in its own, nonoverlapping block. Within nested blocks, you cannot declare the same variable name more than once.

- If you declare a variable within a class and use the same variable name within a method of the class, then the variable used inside the method takes precedence, or overrides, the first variable.

- Overloading involves writing multiple methods with the same name but different argument lists. Methods that have identical argument lists but different return types are not overloaded; they are illegal.

- Constructor methods can receive arguments and be overloaded. If you explicitly create a constructor for a class, the automatically created constructor no longer exists.

QUESTIONS

1. The code between a pair of curly brackets in a method is a _____.
   a. function
   b. block
   c. brick
   d. sector

2. When a block exists within another block, the blocks are _____.
   a. structured
   b. nested
   c. sheltered
   d. illegal

3. The portion of a program within which you can reference a variable is the variable's _____.
   a. range
   b. space
   c. domain
   d. scope

4. A variable ceases to exist at the end of the _____ in which it is declared.
   a. statement
   b. block
   c. class
   d. program

5. You can declare a variable with the same name multiple times _____.
   a. within a statement
   b. within a block
   c. within a method
   d. never

6. You can declare two variables with the same name as long as _____.
   a. they appear within the same block
   b. they are assigned different values
   c. they are of different types
   d. their scopes do not overlap

7. If you declare a variable within a class and declare and use the same variable name within a method of the class, _____.
   a. the variable used inside the method takes precedence
   b. the class variable takes precedence
   c. they become the same variable with the same memory address
   d. an error will occur

8. A method variable will _____ a class variable with the same name.
   a. acquiesce to
   b. destroy
   c. override
   d. alter

9. Using a single method name to execute diverse tasks is known as _____.
   a. overriding
   b. overexecuting
   c. overloading
   d. overcompensating

10. Overloaded methods must have the same _____.
    a. name
    b. number of arguments
    c. argument names
    d. type of argument

11. Overloaded methods cannot have the same _____.
    a. name
    b. number of arguments
    c. number and type of arguments
    d. return type

12. A situation in which the compiler cannot determine which method to use is said to be _____.
    a. dubious
    b. suspicious
    c. unreconciled
    d. ambiguous

13. If a method is written to receive a double argument, and you pass an integer to the method, then the method will _____.
    a. work correctly; the integer will be promoted to a double
    b. work correctly; the integer will remain an integer
    c. execute, but any output will be incorrect
    d. not work; an error message will be issued

14. Methods with the same name that have identical argument lists but different return types are _____.
    a. legal
    b. overloaded
    c. unstructured
    d. illegal

15. A constructor _____ arguments.
    a. can receive
    b. cannot receive
    c. must receive
    d. can receive a maximum of 10

16. A constructor _____ overloaded.
    a. can be
    b. cannot be
    c. must be
    d. is always automatically

17. If you do not create a constructor for a class, _____.
    a. you cannot instantiate objects
    b. Java automatically creates one
    c. the class will not compile
    d. the class will simply exist without a constructor

18. If you create one constructor method for a class, and the constructor requires a double argument, you _____ when you instantiate a member of the class.
    a. must provide an argument
    b. must not provide an argument
    c. can provide any number of arguments
    d. can provide one or no arguments as needed

EXERCISES

1. a. Create a console application project named Commission in the Chapter.04 folder on your Student Disk, then create a class that includes three variables: a double sales figure, a double commission rate, and an integer commission rate. Create two overloaded methods named computeCommission(). The first method takes two double arguments representing sales and rate, multiplies them, and then displays the results. The second method takes two arguments: a double sales figure and an integer commission rate. This method must divide the commission rate figure by 100.0 before multiplying by the sales figure and displaying the commission. Supply appropriate values for the variables and write a main() method that tests each overloaded method.
   b. Add a third overloaded method to the Commission project you created in Exercise 1a. The third overloaded method takes a single argument representing sales. When this method is called, the commission rate is assumed to be 7.5 percent and the results are displayed. To test this method, add an appropriate call in the Commission program's main() method.

2. Create a console application project named Pay in the Chapter.04 folder on your Student Disk, then create a class that includes five double variables that hold hours worked, rate of pay per hour, withholding rate, gross pay, and net pay. Create three overloaded computeNetPay() methods. Gross pay is computed as hours worked multiplied by pay per hour. When computeNetPay() receives values for hours, pay rate, and withholding rate, it computes the gross pay and reduces it by the appropriate withholding amount to produce the net pay. When computeNetPay() receives two arguments, the withholding rate is assumed to be 15 percent. When computeNetPay() receives one argument, the withholding is assumed to be 15 percent and the hourly rate is assumed to be 4.65. Write a main() method that tests all three overloaded methods.

3. a. Create a console application project named Household in the Chapter.04 folder on your Student Disk, then create a class that includes data fields for the number of occupants and the annual income, as well as methods named setOccupants(), setIncome(), getOccupants(), and getIncome() that set and return those values, respectively. Additionally, create a constructor that requires no arguments and automatically sets the occupants field to 1 and the income field to 0. In the Household project, create a program named TestHousehold that demonstrates that each of the methods works correctly.
   b. Create an additional overloaded constructor for the Household project you created in Exercise 3a. This constructor receives an integer argument and assigns the value to the occupants field. Add any needed statements to TestHousehold to ensure that the overloaded constructor works correctly.

c. Create a third overloaded constructor for the Household project you created in Exercises 3a and 3b. This constructor receives two arguments, the values of which are assigned to the occupants and income fields, respectively. Alter the TestHousehold program to demonstrate that each version of the constructor works properly.

4. Create a console application project named Box in the Chapter.04 folder on your Student Disk, then create a class that includes integer data fields for length, width, and height. Create three constructors that require one, two, and three arguments, respectively. When one argument is used, assign it to length, assign zeros to height and width, and print "Line created". When two arguments are used, assign them to length and width, assign zero to height, and print "Rectangle created". When three arguments are used, assign them to the three variables and print "Box created". Create a program named TestBox that demonstrates that each of the methods works correctly.

5. What is the result when you compile and run the following code? Why?

```java
class Scope
{
   int scopeInt = 1;
   void scopeDisplay()
   {
      int scopeInt = 10;
      System.out.println("scopeInt = " + scopeInt);
   }
   public static void main(String[] args)
   {
      Scope scopeExercise = new Scope();
      scopeExercise.scopeDisplay();
   }
}
```

6. a. What is the result when you compile and run the following code? Why?

```java
class Overload
{
   public static void main(String[] args)
   {
      Overload overloadExercise = new Overload();
      overloadExercise.methodOv();
      overloadExercise.methodOv(6.1, 3);
   }
   void methodOv()
   {
      System.out.println("no arguments");
   }
   void methodOv(double dblArg, int intArg)
   {
      System.out.println("dblArg = " + dblArg +
      "intArg = " + intArg);
   }
}
```

b. What happens when you build and run the program shown in Exercise 6a if you replace the line `overloadExercise.methodOv(6.1, 3);` with `overloadExercise.methodOv(6, 3);`, and why?
c. What happens if you change the program shown in Exercise 6a as follows, and why?

```
class Overload
{
   public static void main(String[] args)
   {
      Overload overloadExercise = new Overload();
      overloadExercise.methodOv(6.1, 3.2);
   }
   void methodOv(double dblArg, float fltArg)
   {
      System.out.println("dblArg = " + dblArg +
      "fltArg = " + fltArg);
   }
   void methodOv(float fltArg, double dblArg)
   {
      System.out.println("dblArg = " + dblArg +
      "fltArg = " + fltArg);
   }
}
```

d. If the program shown in Exercise 6c results in a compiler error, how would you fix the program so it compiles and runs successfully?

SECTION B
objectives

Using Methods

In this lesson you will learn
- About the `this` reference
- How to use constants
- How to use prewritten classes and methods that are automatically imported
- How to use prewritten methods that you import
- How to use the Object Browser

The this Reference

When you start creating classes from which you will instantiate objects, the classes can become large very quickly. Besides possessing data fields, each class can have many methods, including several overloaded versions. If you instantiate many objects of a class, the computer memory requirements can become substantial. Fortunately, it is not necessary to store a separate copy of each variable and method for each instantiation of a class.

Usually, you want each instantiation of a class to have its own data fields. For example, if an Employee class contains fields for employee number, name, and salary, every individually instantiated Employee object needs its own unique number, name, and salary values. However, when you create a method for the Employee class, any Employee object can share the same method. Whether the method performs a calculation, sets a field value, or constructs an object, each instantiated object shares the same instructions. Therefore, you store just one copy of a method that all instantiated objects use.

In Chapter 3, you learned that most methods you create within a class are instance methods. Instance methods do not contain the keyword `static` and are duplicated with each object. In other words, instantiated objects contain their own copy of instance methods. You also created static methods by including the keyword `static` in method declarations. For example, the main() method in a program and the methods main() calls without an object reference are static. Static methods, or **class methods**, are not duplicated with instantiated objects; they are shared by each instantiated object.

When you use an object method, you use the object name, a dot, and the method name—for example, `aWorker.getEmpNum();`. When you refer to the aWorker.getEmpNum() method, you are referring to the general, shared Employee class getEmpNum() method; the aWorker object has access to the method because aWorker is an instantiated member of the Employee class. However, within the getEmpNum() method, when you access the empNum *field,* you are referring to aWorker's private, individual copy of the empNum field. Because many

Employees might exist, but just one copy of the method exists no matter how many Employees there are, when you call `aWorker.getEmpNum();`, the compiler needs to determine *whose* copy of empNum should be returned by the single getEmpNum() method. The compiler accesses the correct object's field because you implicitly pass to the getEmpNum() method a reference to aWorker. This reference is called the **this** reference. For example, the two getEmpNum() methods shown in Figure 4-16 perform identically. The first method simply uses the this reference without you being aware of it; the second method uses the this reference explicitly.

The keyword `this` is a reserved word in Java.

When you pass a reference, you pass a memory address.

```
public void getEmpNum()
{
        return empNum;
}
public void getEmpNum()
{
        return this.empNum;
}
```

Figure 4-16: The getEmpNum() methods with implicit and explicit `this` references

Usually, you do not want or need to refer to the `this` reference within the methods you write, but the `this` reference is always there, working behind the scenes, so the data field for the correct object can be accessed.

Class methods do not have a `this` reference because they have no object associated with them.

In addition to creating class methods, you also can create class variables using the static keyword. **Class variables** are variables that are shared by every instantiation of a class. For example, you might have a company ID number that is the same for all Employee objects. You can add a static class variable to the class definition, as shown in Figure 4-17. The figure also shows a simple method to display the employee number along with the employee's COMPANY_ID.

```
public class Employee
    {
    static private int COMPANY_ID = 12345;
    private int empNum;
    private double empSalary;
    Employee(int num)
    // Constructor requiring employee number
    {
    empNum = num;
    }
    public void showCompanyID()
    {
    System.out.println("Worker " + empNum
       + " has company ID " + COMPANY_ID);
    }
    // Other class methods can go here
}
```

Figure 4-17: Employee class with a static ID number field

No matter how many Employee objects are eventually instantiated, each will refer to the single COMPANY_ID field. For example, if two Employees are created with `Employee firstWorker = new Employee(444);` and `Employee secondWorker = new Employee(777);`, when you write the statement `firstWorker.showCompanyID()`, its resulting output is Worker 444 has COMPANY_ID 12345, and when you write the statement `secondWorker.showCompanyID();`, the statement's resulting output is Worker 777 has COMPANY_ID 12345. The different workers have individual IDs, but the same company ID.

Additionally, if you change the value of COMPANY_ID in the Employee class, the value changes for all class instantiations. Therefore, besides values such as a company ID, good candidates for static class variables are fields such as a legal minimum wage or a maximum number of hours that an employee is allowed to work in a single week. When such values change for one employee, they change uniformly for all employees.

As with classes and methods, you can set the access level of class variables with access modifiers. The access modifier for a class variable can be any of the following modifiers: `public`, `private`, `protected`, and `default`. Public access allows a class variable to be accessed by any class. Private access allows a class variable to be accessed only by the class in which it is contained. Protected access makes the variable accessible from within its class or by classes inherited from its class. Default access makes the variable available to any class within the same package.

> Packages are related groups of classes and class members that make up a program. You will learn about packages later in this chapter.

> Access modifiers can be used only on class variables; you will receive a compiler error if you attempt to use them on a variable contained within a method.

Working with Constants

In Chapter 2, you learned to create literal constants within a program. A literal constant is a fixed value, such as the literal string "First Java program". A literal constant also can be a number, such as 7 or 5.68, or a character such as R. After a program is compiled, these constants are reduced to binary machine language, and they will never change. Variables, on the other hand, *do* change. When you declare `int empNum;`, you expect that the value stored in empNum will be different at different times or for different employees.

Sometimes, however, a variable or data field should be **constant**; that is, it should not be changed during the execution of a program. The concept of a *constant variable* is somewhat of an oxymoron. For example, the value for a company ID is fixed, so you do not want any methods to alter the company ID value while a program is running. To prevent alteration, insert the keyword `final` in the company ID variable declaration so the name COMPANY_ID becomes a **symbolic constant**, which indicates that when you compile any program that uses an object that contains the COMPANY_ID, the field has a final, unalterable value. By convention, constant fields are written using all uppercase letters. The compiler does not require using uppercase identifiers for constants, but using uppercase identifiers helps you distinguish symbolic constants from variables. For readability, you can insert underscores between words in symbolic constants.

> Mathematical constants are good candidates for receiving `final` status. For example, when PI is defined as `static final double PI = 3.14159;`, it appropriately becomes a constant that should never take on any other value. A fixed sales tax rate `static final double SALES_TAX = 0.075;` remains fixed for every use within a program.

tip

You can also use the keyword `final` with methods or classes. When used in this manner, `final` indicates limitations placed on inheritance. You will learn more about inheritance as you become more proficient at object-oriented programming.

You cannot change the value of a symbolic constant after declaring it; any attempt to do so will result in a compiler error. You must initialize a constant with a value, which makes sense when you consider that a constant cannot be changed later. If a constant does not receive a value upon creation, it can never receive a value at all. Figure 4-18 shows a typical declaration of a constant.

```
public class Employee
{
      static final private int COMPANY_ID = 12345;
      // Rest of class goes here
```

Figure 4-18: Employee class with the symbolic constant COMPANY_ID

A constant always has the same value within a program, so you probably are wondering why you cannot use the actual literal value. For example, why not code `12345` when you need the company ID rather than going to the trouble of creating the COMPANY_ID symbolic constant? There are at least three good reasons to use the symbolic constant rather than the literal one:

- The number 12345 is more easily recognized as the company ID if it is associated with an identifier like COMPANY_ID.
- If the company ID changes, you would change the value of COMPANY_ID at one location within your program—where the constant is defined—rather than searching for every use of 12345 to change it to a different number.
- Even if you are willing to search for every instance of 12345 in a program to change it to a new company ID value, you might inadvertently change the value 12345 that is being used differently for something else, like an employee's employee number or salary.

Next, you will create a class variable to hold the location of the company headquarters for Event Handlers Incorporated. The location of the company headquarters for Event Handlers is an ideal candidate for a class variable. Because the location of the headquarters is the same for every event no matter where the actual event is held, the value for the headquarters should be stored just once, but every EventSite object should have access to the information.

Advanced Object Concepts

To create a class variable for the EventSite class:

1. Open the **EventSite** project from the Chapter.04 folder on your Student Disk, then open the **EventSite.java** file in the Text Editor window.
2. Position the insertion point after the opening bracket of the class, and then press the **Enter** key to start a new line.
3. Type the class variable `static final public String HEADQUARTERS = "Crystal Lake, IL";`
4. Add a new class file to your project by selecting **Add Class** from the **Project** menu. The Add Item dialog box appears. In the Add Item dialog box, select **ClassMain** from the class folder, then change the suggested filename to **DemoClassVar.java** and click the **Open** button. The new class opens in the Text Editor window. Modify the class so that it matches the demonstration program shown in Figure 4-19. This program shows the headquarters is the same for all EventSites.

```
public class DemoClassVar
{
   public static void main(String[] args)
   {
        EventSite oneSite = new EventSite();
        EventSite anotherSite = new EventSite();
        oneSite.setSiteNumber(101);
        anotherSite.setSiteNumber(202);
        System.out.print("The number of one site is ");
        System.out.println(oneSite.getSiteNumber());
        System.out.print("Headquarters located at ");
        System.out.println(oneSite.HEADQUARTERS);
        System.out.print("The number of another site is ");
        System.out.println(anotherSite.getSiteNumber());
        System.out.print("Headquarters located at ");
        System.out.println(anotherSite.HEADQUARTERS);
   }
}
```

Figure 4-19: DemoClassVar program

5 Rebuild the project and execute the program as a console application by typing **jview DemoClassVar** at the command line. Figure 4-20 shows the program's output.

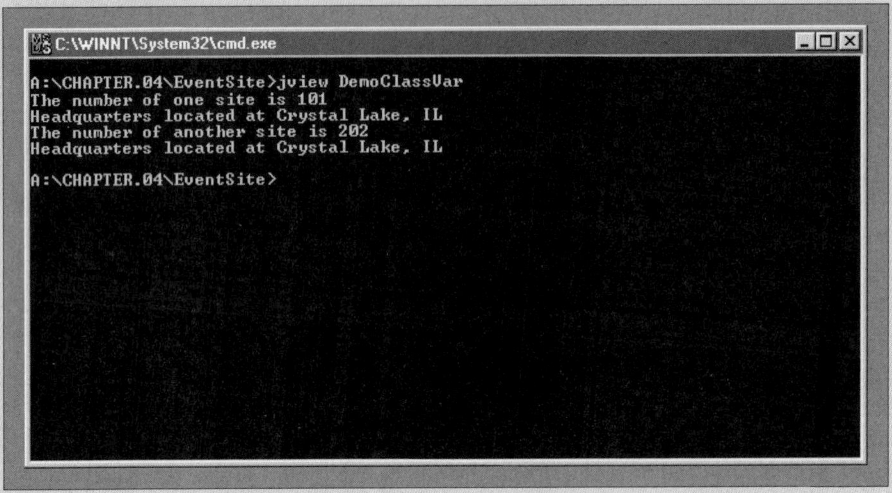

```
A:\CHAPTER.04\EventSite>jview DemoClassVar
The number of one site is 101
Headquarters located at Crystal Lake, IL
The number of another site is 202
Headquarters located at Crystal Lake, IL

A:\CHAPTER.04\EventSite>
```

Figure 4-20: Output of the DemoClassVar program

Using Automatically Imported, Prewritten Constants and Methods

There are many times when you need to create classes from which you will instantiate objects. You can create an Employee class with fields appropriate for describing employees and their functions, and an Inventory class with fields appropriate for whatever type of item it is that you manufacture. There are, however, many classes that a wide variety of programmers need. Rather than having each Java programmer "reinvent the wheel," the creators of Java created nearly 500 classes for you to use in your programs.

You have already used several prewritten classes without being aware of it. System, Character, Boolean, Byte, Short, Integer, Long, Float, and Double actually are classes from which you can create objects. These classes are stored in a **package**—a folder that provides a convenient grouping for classes—which is sometimes called a **library of classes**. Many Java packages contain classes that are available only if you explicitly name them within your program. However, the group of classes that contains the previously listed classes is used so frequently that it is available automatically to every program you write. The package that is implicitly **imported** into every Java program is named java.lang. The classes it contains are **fundamental classes**, or basic classes, as opposed to **optional classes** that must be explicitly named.

> You will begin to import optional classes explicitly later in this chapter.

The class java.lang.Math contains constants and methods that you can use to perform common mathematical functions. A commonly used constant is PI. Within the Math class, the declaration for PI is `public final static double PI = 3.14159265358979323846;`. Notice that PI is:

- `public`, so any program can access it directly
- `final`, so it cannot be changed
- `static`, so only one copy exists
- `double`, so it holds a large floating-point value

> In geometry, PI is an approximation of the value of the ratio of the circumference of a circle to its diameter.

All of the constants and methods in the Math class are static, which means they are class variables and class methods.

> Another useful constant is E, which represents the base of natural logarithms. Its definition is `public final static double E = 2.7182818284590452354;`.

You can use the value of PI within any program that you write by referencing the full package path in which the constant PI is defined—for example `areaOfCircle = java.lang.Math.PI * radius * radius;`. However, the Math class is imported automatically into your programs, so if you simply reference `Math.PI`, Java will recognize this code as a shortcut to the full package path. Therefore, the preferred (and simpler) statement is `areaOfCircle = Math.PI * radius * radius;`.

In addition to constants, there are many useful methods available within the Math class. For example, the Math.max() method returns the larger of two values, and the method Math.abs() returns the absolute value of a number. The statement `largerValue = Math.max(32, 75);` results in largerValue assuming the value 75. The statement `posVal = Math.abs(-245);` results in posVal assuming the value 245. Figure 4-21 lists some common Math class methods.

Method	Return Value
Abs(x)	Absolute value of x
Acos(x)	Arccosine of x
Asin(x)	Arcsine of x
Atan(x)	Arctangent of x
Atan2(x,y)	Theta component of the polar coordinate (r,theta) that corresponds to the Cartesian coordinate x,y
Ceil(x)	Smallest integral value not less than x (ceiling)
Cos(x)	Cosine of x
Exp(x)	Exponent, where e is the base of the natural logarithms
Floor(x)	Largest integral value not greater than x
Log(x)	Natural logarithm of x
Max(x,y)	Larger of x and y
Min(x,y)	Smaller of x and y
Pow(x,y)	x raised to the y power
Random()	Random double number between 0.0 and 1.0
Rint(x)	Closest integer to x (x is a double, and the return value is expressed as a double)
Round(x)	Closest integer to x (where x is a float or double, and the return value is an integer or long)
Sin(x)	Sine of x
Sqrt(x)	Square root of x
Tan(x)	Tangent of x

Figure 4-21: Common Math class methods

tip

Because all constants and methods in the Math class are public, there is no need to create an instance. You cannot instantiate objects of type Math because the constructor for the Math class is private and your programs cannot access the constructor. If you want to prohibit someone from creating an instance of a class you create, you can use the same technique.

Unless you are a mathematician, you won't use many of these Math class methods, and it is unwise to do so unless you understand their purposes. For example, because it is illegal to take the square root of a negative number, the method call `imaginaryNumber = Math.sqrt(-12);` causes a compiler error and does not execute.

Next, you will use the Math class to perform some basic calculations.

To write a program that uses some Math class methods:

1. Create a new console application project named **DemoMath**. Save the **DemoMath** project folder in the Chapter.04 folder on your Student Disk.
2. Rename the default Class1.java file as **DemoMath.java**, then open the file in the Text Editor window.
3. Replace the Class1 class name in the `public class Class1` line with **DemoMath**.
4. Replace the `// TODO: Add initialization code here` comment with a double variable named val by typing **double val = 26.9;**, then press the **Enter** key.
5. Type the following statement to display the value on the screen: **System.out.println("The value is " + val);**.
6. On separate lines, type the following statements to demonstrate the Math class methods:

   ```
   System.out.print("Absolute value of val is ");
   System.out.println(Math.abs(val));
   System.out.print("Absolute value of -val is ");
   System.out.println(Math.abs(-val));
   System.out.print("The square root of val is ");
   System.out.println(Math.sqrt(val));
   System.out.print("Val rounded is ");
   System.out.println(Math.round(val));
   ```

> The expression `-val` means that the value of the variable val is negative. The minus sign (–) used in this manner is a unary or single-argument operator. You will learn more about unary operators in Chapter 5.

7. Select **DemoMath Properties** from the **Project** menu. Select the **DemoMath** file in the When project runs, load drop-down list box and set the project to run as a console application. When you are finished, click the **OK** button.

8   Build the project and execute the program as a console application by typing **jview DemoMath** at the command line, then compare your results to Figure 4-22.

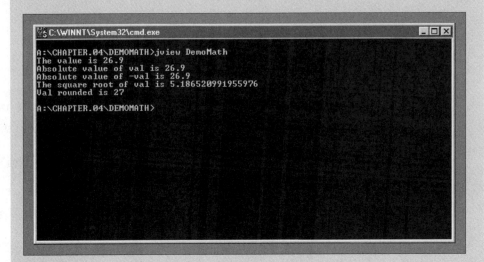

Figure 4-22: Output of the DemoMath program

9   Add additional statements that demonstrate any of the other Math methods that you might use in your programs. Rebuild the project and test the program again.

Using Prewritten Imported Methods

Java contains hundreds of classes, only a few of which—such as java.lang—are included automatically in the programs you write. To use any of the other prewritten classes, you must use one of three methods:

- Use the entire path with the class name.
- Import the class.
- Import the package of which the class you are using is a part.

For example, the java.util class package contains useful methods that deal with dates and times. Within this package, a class named Date is defined. You can instantiate an object of type Date from this class by using the full class path, as in **java.util.Date myAnniversary=new java.util.Date();**. You can also shorten the declaration to **Date myAnniversary = new Date();** by including **import java.util.Date;** as the first line in your program. An import statement allows you to abbreviate the lengthy class names by notifying the

Java program that when you use *Date*, you mean the java.util.Date class. You must place any import statement you use before any executing statement in your program. That is, you can have a blank line or a comment line—but nothing else—prior to an import statement.

> **tip**
> Notice that the import statement ends with a semicolon.

> **tip**
> *Date* is not a reserved word; it is a class you are importing. If you do not want to import java.util's Date class, you are free to write your own Date class.

An alternative to importing a class is to import an entire package of classes. You can use the asterisk (*) as a **wildcard symbol** to represent all the classes in a package. Therefore, the import statement `import java.util.*;` imports the Date class and any other java.util classes as well. There is no disadvantage to importing the extra classes, and you will most commonly see the wildcard method in professionally written Java programs.

> **tip**
> If you are familiar with DOS or UNIX wildcards, it may seem easier simply to import all Java language classes by typing `import java.*;`. Unfortunately, the wildcard works only with specific packages, as in `import java.util.*;` or `import java.lang.*;`.

> **tip**
> The import statement does not move the entire imported class or package into your program as its name implies. Rather, it simply notifies the program that you will be using the data and method names that are part of the imported class or package.

The Date class has several constructors. For example, if you construct a Date object with five integer arguments, they become the year, month, date, hours, and minutes. A Date object constructed with three integer arguments assumes the arguments to be the year, month, and date, and the time is set to midnight. A Date object constructed with no arguments assigns the current day, month, date, year, hour, minute, and second. Date objects are based on the number of milliseconds before or after midnight, January 1, 1970. You can retrieve this number with a method that is named getTime(). This statement `System.out.println ("Milliseconds since 1/1/70 are " + myAnniversary.getTime());` results in the output `Milliseconds since 1/1/70 are 1003122000000` when the program is run at midnight on October 15, 2001.

> **tip**
> If you set the hours in a Date object, a 24-hour clock is assumed—for example, 13 is 1 p.m.

Although it is interesting, the number of milliseconds elapsed since 1970 is not a useful piece of information for most people. Fortunately, the Date class contains a variety of other useful methods such as setMonth(), getMonth(), setDay(), getDay(), setYear(), and getYear() that supply more useful information. The program shown in Figure 4-23 shows the values of two dates being set and retrieved.

```java
import java.util.*;
public class DemoDate
{
        public static void main(String[] args)
        {
                Date toDay = new Date();
                Date birthDay = new Date(82,6,14);
                System.out.println(toDay);
                System.out.print("Current month is ");
                System.out.println(toDay.getMonth());
                System.out.print("Current day is ");
                System.out.println(toDay.getDate());
                System.out.print("Current year is ");
                System.out.println(toDay.getYear());
                System.out.print("Birth month is ");
                System.out.println( birthDay.getMonth());
                System.out.print("Birthday is ");
                System.out.println( birthDay.getDate());
                System.out.print("Birth year is ");
                System.out.println( birthDay.getYear());
        }
}
```

Figure 4-23: DemoDate program

You can perform arithmetic using dates. For example, if toDay is declared to hold today's date with `Date toDay = new Date();`, then you can use the following code to find the availability date of a bank certificate that matures in 180 days by adding 180 to the date part of the Date object:

```
toDay.setDate(toDay.getDate() + 180);
System.out.println("In 180 days it will be " + toDay);
```

The compiler will interpret an incorrect date, such as March 32, as being April 1, which makes many calculations with dates easier. For example, if you bill a customer on August 30 and allow 10 days for payment, you can add 10 to the billing day, and the compiler will understand August 40 to be September 9.

For information about time, including how leap years and leap seconds are calculated, go to the U.S. Naval Observatory Web site at http://tycho.usno.navy.mil.

Any year that you use with these Date class methods is a value that is 1900 less than the actual year. For example, 82 means 1982, and 105 means 2005. The month is a value from 0 through 11; January is 0, February is 1, and so on. Although these conventions take some getting used to, you need to be familiar with them when working with dates.

Next, you will use the Date class by declaring some Date variables and keeping track of the length of time it takes for the program to run.

To write a program that uses the Date class:

1 Create a new console application project named **DemoDate**. Save the **DemoDate** project folder in the Chapter.04 folder on your Student Disk.

2 Rename the default Class1.java file as **DemoDate.java**, then open the file in the Text Editor window.

3 Replace the Class1 class name in the `public class Class1` line with **DemoDate**.

4 Add `import java.util.*;` to the first line of the file.

5 Declare a variable named startTime and assign it the current time by replacing the `// TODO: Add initialization code here` comment with `Date startTime = new Date();`

6 Declare another variable to hold the day your Java programming class began—for example, `Date classStart = new Date(100,7,25);` (where 100,7,25 in this example is August 25, 2000). Don't forget that the current year is 1900 less than the actual year and that the months are numbered 0 through 11.

section B

7 Display the current date and the class start date by typing the following:

```
System.out.println("The current date is " + startTime);
System.out.println("The class started on " + classStart);
```

Now enter a statement to print the time it takes to run this program. You will create a new endTime object that will hold the current date and time as of its creation. Depending on the speed of the computer processor you are using, this time should be a few hundred milliseconds later than it was when the program started. The calculation involves using the getTime() method for the endTime and startTime objects and displaying the difference between the two values.

To use the getTime() method:

1 Press the **Enter** key and then type the following code to include the getTime() method:

```
Date endTime = new Date();
System.out.print("Time elapsed is ");
System.out.print(endTime.getTime() -
startTime.getTime());
System.out.println("milliseconds");
```

2 Select **DemoDate Properties** from the **Project** menu. Select the **DemoDate** file in the When project runs, load drop-down list box and set the project to run as a console application. When you are finished, click the **OK** button.

3 Build the project and execute the program as a console application by typing **jview DemoDate** at the command line.

> **help**
>
> When you build the DemoDate.java program, you might receive the following error from the compiler: 'Date(int, int, int)' has been deprecated by the author of 'java.Util.date'(J5014'). A deprecation error simply indicates that your program uses something that has been improved in subsequent versions of Java. Your program still compiles properly.

4 Add some extra println() statements to the program, then rebuild and run the program again. Does the program take longer to execute?

Object Browser

You can view the available Java packages and their contents, as well as Component Object Model (COM) components, with **Object Browser**. Object Browser displays classes, properties, methods, constants, and other members in a hierarchical list that is very similar to the display in other IDE components, such as the Class Outline and Properties windows. The Object Browser window contains two lists for viewing package members: the primary list and the dependent list. The **primary list** displays classes and/or members, whereas the **dependent list** displays either the members of a class selected in the primary list or the classes to which a selected member belongs. You can find information about a selected item in the description pane at the bottom of the Object Browser window, along with hyperlinks to other classes and packages associated with the selected item. You select sorting, grouping, and display options from the shortcut menu or Object Browser toolbar. An example of the Object Browser window is shown in Figure 4-24.

The Component Object Model (COM) is an industry standard protocol for cross-platform development of object-oriented technology.

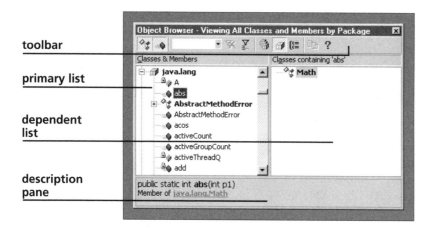

Figure 4-24: Object Browser window

Next you will practice using Object Browser by locating the PI constant in the java.lang package.

To display Object Browser:

1 Point to **Other Windows** on the **View** menu, then select **Object Browser**. The Object Browser window appears.

section B

> **You can also display Object Browser by pressing F2.**

2   Locate java.lang in the primary list and click the **Plus** box ⊞ to expand the package.

3   Locate and click the **Math** class beneath the java.lang node in the primary list. Members of the Math class display in the dependent list.

4   Click the **PI** constant in the dependent list. Notice the modifiers for the PI constant are displayed in the description pane along with the java.lang.Math class of which it is a member as shown in Figure 4-25.

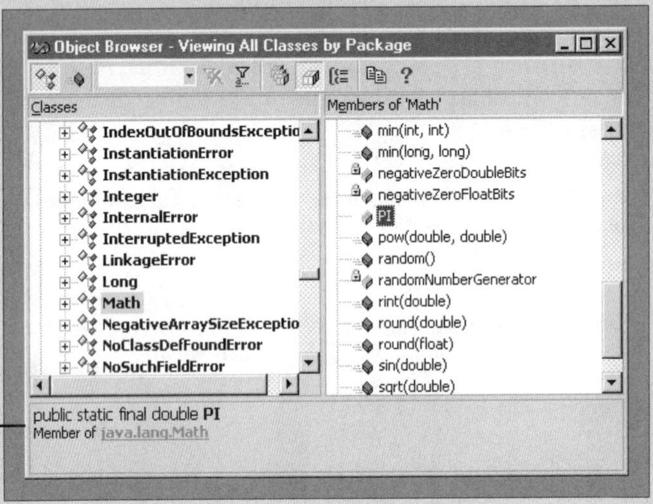

description of PI constant

Figure 4-25: PI constant in the Object Browser window

SUMMARY

- Instance methods do not contain the keyword `static` and are duplicated with each object.

- Static methods, or class methods, are not duplicated with instantiated objects; they are shared by each instantiated object.

- The compiler accesses the correct object's data fields because you implicitly pass a `this` reference to class methods.

- Class methods do not have a `this` reference because they have no object associated with them.

- Class variables are declared with the `static` keyword and are shared by every instantiation of a class.

- The access modifier for a class variable can be any of the following modifiers: `public`, `private`, `protected`, and `default`. Public access allows a class variable to be accessed by any class. Private access restricts access of the variable to the class in which it is contained. Protected access makes the variable accessible from within its class or from classes inherited from its class. Default access makes the variable available to any class within the same package.

- After a program is compiled, literal constants never change.

- The values stored in symbolic constants never change. You create a symbolic constant by inserting the keyword `final` before a variable name. By convention, constant fields are written using all uppercase letters. A constant must be initialized with a value.

- Java contains nearly 500 prewritten classes.

- Classes are stored in libraries of classes called packages, which are simply folders that provide a convenient grouping for classes.

- The java.lang package is implicitly imported into every Java program. This package contains fundamental classes, as opposed to optional classes that must be explicitly named.

- The class java.lang.Math contains constants and methods that you can use to perform common mathematical functions. All of the constants and methods in the Math class are static, which means that they are class variables and class methods. Common useful Math class methods include those used for finding an absolute value, taking a square root, and rounding.

- To use a prewritten class other than java.lang, you must use its entire path with the class name, import the class, or import the package that contains the class.

- An import statement allows you to abbreviate lengthy class names by notifying the Java program that when you use class names you are referring to those within the imported class. Any import statement you use must be placed before any executing statement in your program.

- An alternative to importing a class is to import an entire package of classes. To do so, you use the asterisk (*) as a wildcard symbol to represent all the classes in a package.

- The Date class has several constructors: one that takes no argument and assigns the current day, month, year, hour, minute, and second to a Date object, and others that take the date or the date and time.

- Date objects are based on the number of milliseconds before or after midnight, January 1, 1970. You can retrieve this number with a method named getTime().

- The Date class contains a variety of other useful methods such as setMonth(), getMonth(), setDay(), getDay(), setYear(), and getYear().

- You can perform arithmetic using Date class objects.

- You can view the available Java packages and their contents with Object Browser.

section B

QUESTIONS

1. Usually, you want each instantiation of a class to have its own copy of _____.
   a. the data fields
   b. the class methods
   c. both of these
   d. neither of these

2. If you create a class and instantiate two objects, you usually store _____ for use with the objects.
   a. one copy of each method
   b. two copies of the same method
   c. two different methods
   d. data only, not methods,

3. When you create multiple class objects and use a class method, the compiler accesses the correct object's data because you _____.
   a. explicitly pass the object
   b. explicitly pass a copy of the object
   c. explicitly pass a reference to the object
   d. implicitly pass a reference to the object

4. The `this` reference _____.
   a. can be used implicitly
   b. must be used implicitly
   c. must not be used implicitly
   d. must not be used

5. The `this` reference specifies which _____ you are referencing.
   a. method
   b. object
   c. class
   d. program

6. Methods that you associate with individual objects are _____.
   a. `private`
   b. `public`
   c. `static`
   d. `nonstatic`

7. Static methods also are called _____ methods.
   a. `this`
   b. `private`
   c. `class`
   d. `nonreferenced`

8. Static methods do not have a(n) _____.
   a. return type
   b. argument list
   c. header
   d. `this` reference

9. Variables that are shared by every instantiation of a class are _____.
   a. class variables
   b. `private` variables
   c. `public` variables
   d. illegal

10. The word closest in meaning to *static* as used by the Java programming language is _____.
    a. *hidden*
    b. *difficult*
    c. *single*
    d. *multiple*

11. If you change the value of a static variable in a class, it is changed for _____.
    a. only new objects instantiated after the change
    b. only objects already in existence before the change
    c. all objects of the class
    d. no objects of the class

12. The keyword `final` in a variable declaration indicates _____.
    a. the end of the program
    b. a static field
    c. a symbolic constant
    d. that no more variables will be declared in the program

13. A symbolic constant _____.
    a. must be initialized
    b. cannot be changed during program execution
    c. both of these
    d. neither of these

14. Java classes are stored in a folder or _____.
    a. packet
    b. package
    c. bundle
    d. gaggle

15. The classes in java.lang _____ into every program you write.
    a. are implicitly imported
    b. are implicitly copied
    c. must be explicitly imported
    d. must not be explicitly imported

16. Which of the following statements determines the square root of **number** and assigns it to the variable **s**?
    a. s = sqrt(number);
    b. s = Math.sqrt(number);
    c. number = sqrt(s);
    d. number = Math.sqrt(s);

17. To use any of the prewritten classes besides those in the java.lang package, you must _____.
    a. use the entire path with the class name
    b. import the class
    c. import the package of which the class you are using is a part
    d. use any of these methods

18. The wildcard symbol used with the import statement is the _____.
    a. ampersand
    b. plus sign
    c. exclamation point
    d. asterisk

19. The date constructed with `Date oneDay = new Date(103,1,2);` is _____.
    a. January 1, 2003
    b. January 2, 2003
    c. February 1, 2003
    d. February 2, 2003

20. The date stored in a Date object is stored in _____.
    a. milliseconds
    b. seconds
    c. minutes
    d. years

EXERCISES

1. Create a console application project named Shirt in the Chapter.04 folder on your Student Disk, then create a class with data fields for collar size and sleeve length. Include a constructor method that takes arguments for each field. Also include a String class variable named material and initialize it to "cotton." Write a program named TestShirt to instantiate three Shirt objects with different collar sizes and sleeve lengths, and then display all the data, including material, for each shirt.

2. Create a console application project named CheckingAccount in the Chapter.04 folder on your Student Disk, then create a class with data fields for an account number and a balance. Include a constructor method that takes arguments for each field. Include a double class variable that holds a value for the minimum balance required before a monthly fee is applied to the account, and set the minimum balance to 200.00. Write

a program named TestAccount in which you instantiate two CheckingAccount objects and display the account number, balance, and minimum balance without fee for both accounts.

3. Write a program to determine the answers for each of the following:
   a. The square root of 30
   b. The sine and cosine of 100
   c. The value of the floor, ceiling, and round of 44.7
   d. The larger and the smaller of the character K and the integer 70

4. Write a program to calculate how many milliseconds it is from today until the first day of summer (assume that this date is next June 21).

5. Write a program to calculate how many days it is from today until the end of the current year.

6. What is the result when you compile and run the following code, and why?

```
public class MathEx6
{
        public static void main(String[] args)
        {
                System.out.println(Math.round(1.49));
                System.out.println(Math.round(1.50));
                System.out.println(Math.round(-1.49));
                System.out.println(Math.round(-1.50));
        }
}
```

7. What is the result when you compile and run the following code, and why?

```
public class MathEx7
{
        public static void main(String[] args)
        {
                System.out.println(Math.ceil(1.49));
                System.out.println(Math.ceil(1.50));
                System.out.println(Math.ceil(-1.49));
                System.out.println(Math.ceil(-1.50));
        }
}
```

8. What is the result when you compile and run the following code, and why?

```
public class MathEx8
{
        public static void main(String[] args)
        {
                System.out.println(Math.floor(1.49));
                System.out.println(Math.floor(1.50));
                System.out.println(Math.floor(-1.49));
                System.out.println(Math.floor(-1.50));
        }
}
```

section B

9. Create a console application project named EmployeeWithDate in the Chapter.04 folder on your Student Disk and modify the Employee class shown in Figure 4-17 by changing the class name to EmployeeWithDate. Then change the showCompanyID() method so it shows the current date in addition to the employee number and company ID. Then write a program that creates two or more EmployeeWithDate objects.

10. Each of the following files in the Chapter.04 folder on your Student Disk has syntax and/or logical errors. Add the files to a new project called FixDebug. Save the FixDebug project under the Chapter.04 folder on your Student Disk. In each case, fix the problem and run each file as a console application using JVIEW.
    a. DebugFour1.java
    b. DebugFour2.java
    c. DebugFour3.java
    d. DebugFour4.java

CHAPTER 5

Input, Selection, and Repetition

case ▶ "Why are you frowning?" asks Lynn Greenbrier, your mentor at Event Handlers Incorporated.

"It's fun writing programs," you tell her, "but I don't think my programs can do much yet. When I use programs written by other people, I'm allowed to respond to questions and make choices. In addition, other people's programs keep running for a while—the programs I write finish as soon as they start."

"You're disappointed because the programs you've written so far simply carry out a sequence of steps," Lynn says. "You need to make your programs interactive by accepting user input. Then you need to learn about the two powerful structures—decision making and looping."

Previewing the ChooseManager Program Using the Event Class

To preview the ChooseManager program using the Event class:

1 If necessary, start Visual J++. Open the **Chap5Event.vjp** project from the Chap5Event folder in the Chapter.05 folder on your Student Disk, then open the **Chap5Event.java** file in the Text Editor window and examine the code. This file contains a class definition for a class that stores information about events that Event Handlers Incorporated will handle. You will create a similar class file in this chapter.

2 Open the **Chap5ChooseManager.java** file in the Text Editor window and examine the code. This file contains a program that will demonstrate prompting the user for input and creating objects based on the input.

3 Set the project properties to run the **Chap5ChooseManager** file as a console application, then build the project.

4 Execute the program as a console application by typing **jview Chap5ChooseManager** at the command line. At the prompt to enter C, P, or N, ignore the directions and enter an *invalid* letter. Do this as many times as you like—the program will prompt you again until you enter a valid letter. Then enter C, P, or N to see the name of the manager and the minimum charge assigned to your event. You will create a similar program in this chapter.

SECTION A
objectives

In this section you will learn
- How to accept keyboard input
- About the decision structure
- How to use an `if` statement
- How to use an `if...else` statement
- How to use compound statements in an `if` or `if...else` structure
- How to nest `if` statements

Input and Decision Making

Simple Keyboard Input

In Chapters 2 through 4 of this text, you wrote programs that created objects, performed mathematical calculations, and produced output. A shortcoming of these programs is that you must know the values with which you want to work at the time you write the program. It would be far more useful to provide a program with values at **run time**, that is, while the program is executing. A program that accepts values at run time is **interactive** because it exchanges communications or interacts with the user. Providing values during the execution of a program requires input, and the simplest form of input to use is keyboard entry from the program's user.

You already have used the System class and its `out` object and println() method to produce output. A similar object is `in`. The `in` object has access to a method named read() that retrieves data from the keyboard. Figure 5-1 shows a program that accepts simple user input.

```
public class DemoInput
{
 public static void main(String[] args)   throws Exception
 {
   char userInput;
   System.out.println("Please enter a character ");
   userInput = (char)System.in.read();
   System.out.println("You entered " + userInput);
 }
}
```

Figure 5-1: DemoInput program

The DemoInput class shown in Figure 5-1 has just one method—a main() method. At the end of the line containing the main() method header is the phrase `throws Exception`. The main() methods you have written that use `System.out.println();` have not required this phrase, but programs you write using `System.in.read();` do. An **exception** is an error situation. Because errors should be infrequent, they are the "exception to the rule." When a program user provides input, all sorts of error situations can arise. For example, the keyboard might be disconnected or the user might enter the wrong type of data. As you become a better Java programmer, you will learn to handle these exceptional situations by writing code to take appropriate action, such as issuing detailed messages that explain the problem to the user. For now, however, you can let the compiler handle the problem by **throwing the exception**, or passing the error to the operating system. The code `throws Exception` after the main() header passes the error to the operating system. A program that reads keyboard input will not compile without this phrase.

You write `Exception` with an uppercase *E* because it is a class name. Classes, by convention, begin with uppercase letters.

In Figure 5-1, a character named userInput is declared inside the main() method of the DemoInput program. The string "Please enter a character" prints on the screen. A message requesting user input commonly is called a **prompt** because it prompts or coaches the user to enter an appropriate response.

You are not required to supply a prompt every time there is user input, but you almost always will want to do so. Unless you supply a prompt, your user will see a blank screen and have little idea of how to proceed.

The statement `userInput = (char)System.in.read();` in the DemoInput program accomplishes three separate tasks:

- The method call `System.in.read();` gets the input from the keyboard. The read() method accepts a byte and returns an integer.
- The cast `(char)` converts the returned integer into a character.
- The assignment `userInput =` assigns the converted character to the variable userInput.

At first, it might not seem to make sense that `System.in.read();` returns an integer value. However, there are two reasons that Java's creators chose to have `System.in.read();` behave in this way:

- To the computer, all values are actually integers because computers store input (as well as everything else) as a series of 0s and 1s. The character *A*, for example, is stored in Unicode as 0000 0000 0100 0001, which also can be expressed as \u0041 or decimal 65.

- The `System.in.read()` method needs to return a value to indicate that no input is available. For example, when you use `System.in.read()` to read records from a disk file, at some point the end of the file is reached and no more input is available. Java's creators decided that the `System.in.read()` method should return the value –1 when the end of a file has been reached. To accomplish this, the read() method must have a return type of int.

tip

See Section B of Chapter 2 for more information about Unicode.

The final statement in the DemoInput program shown in Figure 5-1, `System.out.println("You entered " + userInput);`, **echoes**, or repeats, the userInput character. When you write interactive programs, it is often a good idea to echo the input so the user can visually confirm that the correct data was input.

When you run the DemoInput program, the prompt appears on the screen. The program will not proceed any further until you type a character and press the Enter key. A typed character is represented as an integer ranging from –127 to +127. The read() method accepts precisely one byte of input. Therefore, you cannot enter a floating-point number or a string of characters.

Next, you will write a simple program that accepts three bytes of user input and echoes them.

To write a program that accepts and echoes user input:

1. Create a new console application project named **UserInitials**. Save the **UserInitials** project folder in the Chapter.05 folder on your Student Disk.
2. Rename the default Class1.java file as **UserInitials.java**, then open the file in the Text Editor window.
3. Replace the Class1 class name in the `public class Class1` line with **UserInitials**.
4. Add `throws Exception` to the end of the main() method so that it reads `public static void main (String[] args) throws Exception`.
5. Replace the `// TODO: Add initialization code here` comment with `char firstInit, middleInit, lastInit;`
6. On new lines, prompt the user for three initials by typing the following:

   ```
   System.out.println("Please enter your three initials.");
   System.out.println
     ("Do not use periods between initials.");
   System.out.println("Press Enter when you're done.");
   ```

The instruction "Do not use periods between initials" is important because you will write the program to accept only three characters from the keyboard. If users enter *A.B.C.*, then they enter six characters—three letters and three periods. The first letter would become firstInit, the first period would become secondInit, and the second letter would become thirdInit. There would be no room to store the second period, the third letter, or the last period.

7 On new lines, type the following code to read each of the three initials into the appropriate variables:

```
firstInit = (char)System.in.read();
 middleInit = (char)System.in.read();
lastInit = (char)System.in.read();
```

8 On a new line, type the following code to write the statements that will echo the three initials to the screen:

```
System.out.println("Your initials are " + firstInit +
   middleInit + lastInit);
```

9 Select **UserInitials Properties** from the **Project** menu. Select the **UserInitials** file in the When project runs, load drop-down list box and set the project to run as a console application. When you are finished, click the **OK** button.

10 Build the project and execute the program as a console application by typing `jview UserInitials` at the command line. When you are prompted for three initials, enter any three characters and confirm that they are echoed to the screen correctly. Your output should look like Figure 5-2.

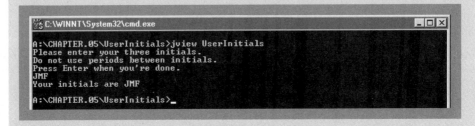

Figure 5-2: Output of the UserInitials program

The UserInitials program works correctly as long as the user follows directions and enters three initials and presses the Enter key only *once* after typing all three initials. However, just as the user cannot type periods between initials, a problem also arises if the user presses the Enter key after typing each initial, as you will see next.

To demonstrate that the user should not press the Enter key after typing each initial:

1 Run the UserInitials program again at the command prompt. When you see the prompt to enter your initials, type an initial and then press the **Enter** key. The program will terminate before you can type the second initial. The output will display only one initial, as shown in Figure 5-3.

```
A:\CHAPTER.05\UserInitials>jview UserInitials
Please enter your three initials.
Do not use periods between initials.
Press Enter when you're done.
J
Your initials are J

A:\CHAPTER.05\UserInitials>
```

Figure 5-3: Output of the UserInitials program after the user presses the Enter key between initials

The problem occurs because when you use read() to accept a character from the keyboard, every key you press—including the Enter key—is accepted, one at a time. When you type your first initial, it is correctly stored in the firstInit variable. When you press the Enter key after entering the first initial, the value for the Enter key is stored in two bytes—the middleInit and the lastInit variables. When all three variables display on the screen, you see the first initial and the cursor on a new line below the initial. The cursor advances a line because the middleInit and lastInit together hold the Enter key value.

The values for the two bytes occupied by the Enter key are \u000D and \u000A, or decimal 13 and 10. When you store the Enter key, you do not need to be concerned with these values any more than you need be concerned that the letter E is stored as \u0046. It is important to know, however, that every character is stored using a code.

Currently, you can deal with this input problem by being very specific in your instructions to the user and insisting that the user type all three initials before pressing the Enter key. Alternatively, you can ask the user for one initial at a time, and take care of the Enter key yourself. You can absorb the extra Enter key after each initial by reading it in with two read() method calls, and then not storing the bytes anywhere, as you will see next.

To eliminate the Enter key problem in the User Initials program:

1. In the User Initials.java text file, delete the following three lines of code that prompt the user for initials:

   ```
   System.out.println("Please enter your three initials.");
   System.out.println
     ("Do not use periods between initials.");
   System.out.println("Press Enter when you're done.");
   ```

2. Replace the deleted lines with the following single statement:

   ```
   System.out.print("Enter your first initial and press Enter. ");
   ```

3. Position the insertion point at the end of the read() statement that reads the firstInit variable, and then press the **Enter** key to start a new line. Then type the following statements to read in the two Enter key bytes without storing them: `System.in.read(); System.in.read();`

4. Press the **Enter** key, and then type the following prompt for the second initial on the new line: `System.out.print("Enter your second initial and press Enter. ");`

> You might choose to place a final `System.in.read(); System.in.read();` statement after the statement that reads the third initial, to discard the Enter key. Because the program doesn't accept any more input after reading the third initial, these extra read() statements will not affect program execution. However, if you add extra read() statements to absorb the last Enter, the Enter key following the third initial already will be discarded if you decide to add additional input steps to this program later.

5. Position the cursor at the end of the statement that reads the middleInit variable, and then press the **Enter** key to start a new line. Then type the following statements to read the Enter key pressed after the second initial, and to prompt for the third initial:

   ```
   System.in.read(); System.in.read();
   System.out.print
     ("Enter your third initial and press Enter. ");
   ```

6. Rebuild and run the program. Respond to each prompt by typing your initial and then pressing the **Enter** key. Your output should display your three initials correctly.

Drawing Flowcharts

> This section is not intended to be a thorough discussion of flowcharting. Instead, it is a brief introduction to the topic so you can use flowcharts as a visual aid in the next sections.

When writing programs, computer programmers seldom simply sit down at a keyboard and begin typing. Programmers must plan the complex portions of programs using paper and pencil tools. Programmers often use pseudocode or flowcharts to help them plan a program's logic. Using **pseudocode** requires you to write down the steps required to accomplish a given task. You write pseudocode in English; you concentrate on the logic required, and not the syntax used in any programming language. As a matter of fact, a task you pseudocode does not have to be a computerized task. If you have ever written a list of things you must accomplish during a day (1. Wash car, 2. Study for test, 3. Buy birthday gift for Mom), then you have written pseudocode. A **flowchart** is similar to pseudocode, but you write the steps you need in diagram form, as a series of shapes connected by arrows.

> You learned the difference between a program's logic and its syntax in Chapter 2.

Some programmers use a wide variety of shapes to represent different tasks in their flowcharts, but you can draw simple flowcharts that express very complex situations using just rectangles and diamonds. You use a rectangle to represent any unconditional step, and a diamond to represent any decision. For example, Figure 5-4 shows a flowchart of a day's tasks.

Figure 5-4: Flowchart of a day's tasks

Sometimes your days don't consist of a series of unconditional tasks—some of the tasks may or may not occur based on decisions you make. Flowchart creators place decisions within diamond shapes and draw paths to alternative courses of action emanating from sides of the diamonds. Figure 5-5 shows a flowchart of a day's tasks in which some of the tasks are based on decisions.

section A

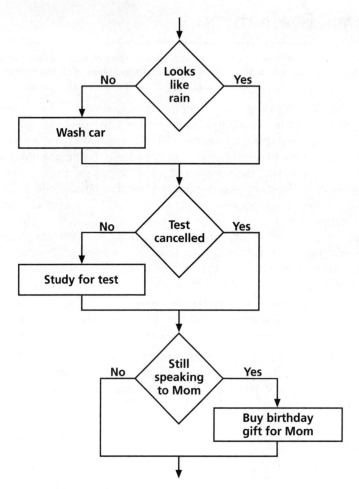

Figure 5-5: Flowchart of a day's tasks with decisions

Making Decisions with the `if` Structure

You already can write a program that produces different output based on input; for example, a user who types *JFK* into the UserInitials program receives different output than a user who types *FDR*. Additionally, after you learn to write programs that can accept input, you gain a powerful new capability—you are able to alter the events that occur within a program based on user input. Now you can make decisions.

Making a **decision** involves choosing between two alternative courses of action based on some value within a program. For example, the program that produces your paycheck can make decisions about the proper amount to withhold for taxes; the program that guides a missile can alter its course; and a program that monitors your blood pressure during surgery can determine when to sound an alarm. Making decisions is what makes computer programs seem "smart."

The value upon which a decision is made is always a boolean value, which is always one of two values—true or false. Figure 5-6 shows the logic of the decision structure.

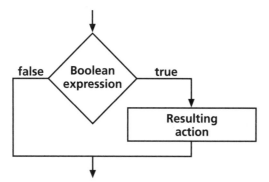

Figure 5-6: Decision structure

One statement you can use to make a decision is the **if** statement. For example, you can store a value in an integer variable named someVariable, and then print the value of someVariable when the user wants to see it. As you can see in Figure 5-7, you can prompt the user to enter Y or N (for "Yes" or "No") and store the response in a character variable.

```
char userResponse;
int someVariable = 512;
System.out.println
  ("Do you want to see the value of someVariable?");
System.out.println("Enter Y for yes or N for no");
char userResponse = (char)System.in.read();
```

Figure 5-7: Storing a user's response

You can use the entered character as part of a boolean expression that will be evaluated as true or false. Figure 5-8 shows the six comparison operators that result in boolean values, as you learned in Chapter 2.

Operator	Description	true Example	false Example
<	Less than	3 < 8	8 < 3
>	Greater than	4 > 2	2 > 4
==	Equal to	7 == 7	3 == 9
<=	Less than or equal to	5 <=5	8 <= 6
>=	Greater than or equal to	7 >= 3	1 >= 2
!=	Not equal to	5 != 6	3 != 3

Figure 5-8: Comparison operators

The double equal sign (==) is used to determine equality; the following is the if statement that makes the decision to print:

```
if(userResponse == 'Y')
  System.out.println
    ("The value of someVariable is " + someVariable);
```

Remember that you reference character values using single quotation marks.

If the userResponse variable holds the value 'Y', then the boolean value of the expression userResponse == 'Y' is true and the subsequent println() statement will execute. If the value of the expression userResponse == 'Y' is false, then the println() statement will not execute. The userResponse == 'Y' expression will be false if userResponse holds anything other than 'Y', including 'y', 'N', 'n', 'A', or any other value.

The boolean expression (userResponse == 'Y') must appear within parentheses. You are not required to leave a space between the keyword if and the opening parentheses, but if you do, the statement is easier to read and is less likely to be confused with a method call. There is no semicolon at the end of the first line of the if statement if(userResponse == 'Y') because the statement does not end there. The statement ends after the println() call, so that is where you type the semicolon. You also could type the same statement on one line and execute it in the same manner. However, the two-line format is more conventional and easier to read, so you usually will type if and the boolean expression on one line, press the Enter key, and then indent a few spaces before coding the action that will occur if the boolean expression evaluates as true. Be careful, though—when you use the two-line format, do not type a semicolon at the end of the first line, as in the following example:

```
if(userResponse == 'Y');
// Notice the incorrect semicolon here
  System.out.println("The value of someVariable is "
    + someVariable);
```

Input, Selection, and Repetition

When this incorrectly coded `if` expression is evaluated, the statement ends if it evaluates as `true`. Whether the expression evaluates as `true` or `false`, execution continues with the next independent statement that prints someVariable. In this case, the `if` statement accomplishes nothing.

Another very common programming error occurs when a programmer uses a single equal sign rather than the double equal sign when attempting to determine equivalency. The expression `userResponse = 'Y'` does not compare userResponse to 'Y'. Instead, it attempts to assign the value 'Y' to the userResponse variable. When the expression is part of an `if` statement, this assignment is illegal. The confusion arises in part because the single equal sign is used within boolean expressions in `if` statements in many other programming languages such as COBOL, Pascal, and BASIC. Adding to the confusion, Java programmers use the word *equals* when speaking of equivalencies. For example, you might say, "If userResponse equals 'Y'..." rather than "If userResponse is equivalent to 'Y'..."

An alternative to using a boolean expression, such as `userResponse == 'Y'`, is to store the boolean expression's value in a boolean variable. For example, if userSaidYes is a boolean variable, then `userSaidYes = (userResponse == 'Y');` compares userResponse to 'Y' and stores `true` or `false` in userSaidYes. Then you can write the `if` as `if(userSaidYes)....` This alternative adds an extra step to the program, but makes the `if` statement more similar to an English statement.

The `if...else` Structure

Consider the following statement:

```
if(userResponse == 'Y')
  System.out.println("The value of someVariable is "
    + someVariable);
```

Such a statement is sometimes called a **single-alternative `if`** because you only perform an action based on one alternative, which is the case when userResponse is 'Y'. Often, you require two options for the next course of action, or a **dual-alternative `if`**. For example, if the user does not respond 'Y' to a prompt, you might want to print a message that at least acknowledges that the response was received. The **`if...else` statement** provides the mechanism to perform one action when a boolean expression evaluates as `true` and perform a different action when a boolean expression evaluates as `false`. Figure 5-9 shows the logic for the `if...else` structure. Figure 5-10 shows an example `if...else` structure coded in Java. In Figure 5-10, the value of someVariable is printed when userResponse is equivalent to 'Y'. When userResponse is any other value, the program prints the message "Too bad."

You can code an `if` without an `else`, but it is illegal to code an `else` without an `if`.

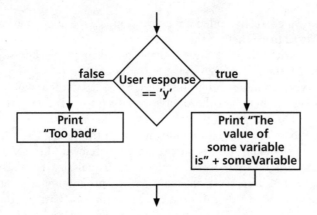

Figure 5-9: The if...else structure

```
if(userResponse == 'Y')
   System.out.println("The value of someVariable is "
       + someVariable);
else
   System.out.println("Too bad.");
```

Figure 5-10: Dual-alternative if

The indentation shown in the if...else example in Figure 5-10 is not required, but is standard usage. You vertically align the keyword if with the keyword else, and then indent the action statements that depend on the evaluation.

When you execute the code shown in Figure 5-10, only one of the println() statements will execute; the one that executes depends upon the evaluation of (userResponse == 'Y'). Each println() statement is a complete statement, so each statement ends with a semicolon.

Next, start writing a program for Event Handlers Incorporated that determines which of several employees will be assigned to manage a client's scheduled event. To begin, you will prompt the user to answer a question about the event type, and then the program will display the name of the manager who handles such events. There are two event types: Corporate events are handled by Dustin Britt, and private events are handled by Carmen Lindsey.

To write a program that chooses between two managers:

1. Create a new console application project named **ChooseManager**. Save the **ChooseManager** project folder in the Chapter.05 folder on your Student Disk.
2. Rename the default Class1.java file as **ChooseManager.java**, then open the file in the Text Editor window.
3. Replace the Class1 class name in the `public class Class1` line with **ChooseManager**.
4. Add `throws Exception` to the end of the main() method so that it reads `public static void main (String[] args) throws Exception`.
5. Replace the `// TODO: Add initialization code here` comment with `char eventType;`
6. On a new line, type the following three-line prompt that explains what is expected of the user:

   ```
   System.out.println
     ("Enter type of event you are scheduling");
   System.out.println("C for a corporate event");
   System.out.println("P for a private event");
   ```

7. On a new line, type the following statement that reads in the type of event:
   `eventType=(char)System.in.read();`
8. On a new line, type the following print() statement that explains the output:
   `System.out.print("The manager for this event will be ");`
9. Code the following `if...else` structure to determine which of two managers will be assigned to the event:

   ```
   if(eventType == 'C')
     System.out.println("Dustin Britt");
   else
     System.out.println("Carmen Lindsey");
   ```

10. Select **ChooseManager Properties** from the **Project** menu. Select the **ChooseManager** file in the When project runs, load drop-down list box and set the project to run as a console application. When you are finished, click the **OK** button.
11. Build the project and execute the program as a console application by typing `jview ChooseManager` at the command line. Confirm that the program selects the correct manager when you choose C for a corporate event or P for a private event.

Compound Statements

Often there is more than one action to take following the evaluation of a boolean expression within an `if` statement. For example, you might want to print several separate lines of output or perform several mathematical calculations. To execute more than one statement that depends on the evaluation of a boolean expression, you use a pair of curly brackets to place the dependent statements within a block. For example, the program segment shown in Figure 5-11 determines whether an employee has worked more than 40 hours in a single week, and if so, the program computes regular and overtime salary and prints the results.

```
if(hoursWorked > 40)

{

 regularPay = 40 * rate;

 overTimePay = (hours - 40) * 1.5 * rate;

   // Time and a half for hours over 40

 System.out.println("Regular pay is " + regularPay);

 System.out.println("Overtime pay is " + overTimePay);

}   // The if structure ends here
```

Figure 5-11: An if statement with multiple dependent statements

When you create a block, you do not have to place multiple statements within it. It is perfectly legal to block a single statement.

If you compare Figures 5-11 and 5-12, you will see that in Figure 5-11, the regularPay calculation, the overTimePay calculation, and the println() statement are executed only when hours > 40 is true. In Figure 5-12, the curly brackets are omitted. Within this program, when hours > 40 is true, regularPay is calculated and the if expression ends. The next three statements that compute overTimePay and print the results always execute every time the program runs, no matter what value is stored in hours. These last three statements are *not* dependent on the if statement; they are independent, stand-alone statements. The indentation might be deceiving; it looks as though four statements depend on the if statement, but it is not indentation that causes statements following an if statement to be dependent. Rather, curly brackets are required if the four statements must be treated as a block.

```
if(hoursWorked > 40)

 regularPay = 40 * rate;   // The if structure ends here

 overTimePay = (hours - 40) * 1.5 * rate;

 System.out.println("Regular pay is " + regularPay);

 System.out.println("Overtime pay is " + overTimePay);
```

Figure 5-12: An if statement with a single dependent statement

The code shown in Figure 5-12 might not compile if regularPay was not assigned a value—the compiler will recognize that you are attempting to print the value of regularPay without calculating it. However, if you have assigned a value to regularPay, you can compile the program but the output still will not be what you intended. Within the code segment shown in Figure 5-12, if hoursWorked is greater than 40, then the program properly calculates both regular and overtime pay. Because `hoursWorked > 40` is `true`, the regularPay calculation is made. The overTimePay calculation and the println() statements will execute as well because they are statements that always execute and do not depend on the `if` statement.

However, in Figure 5-12, if the hoursWorked value is 40 or less—30 hours, for example—then the regularPay calculation will not execute (it executes only `if(hours > 40)`), but the next three independent statements will execute. The variable regularPay will hold whatever value you have previously assigned to it—0.0, for example—and the program will calculate the value of overTimePay as a negative number (because 30 - 40 results in -10). Therefore, the output will be incorrect.

Just as you can block statements to depend on an `if`, you also can block statements to depend on an `else`. Figure 5-13 shows an `if` structure with two dependent statements and an `else` with two dependent statements. The program executes the final two println() statements without regard to the hoursWorked variable's value; the println() statements are not part of the `if` structure.

```
if(hoursWorked > 40)
{
  regularPay = 40 * rate;
  overTimePay = (hours - 40) * 1.5 * rate;
    // Time and a half for hours over 40
}
else
{
  regularPay = hours * rate;
  overTimePay = 0.0;
}
System.out.println("Regular pay is " + regularPay);
System.out.println("Overtime pay is " + overTimePay);
```

Figure 5-13: An `if...else` statement with multiple dependent statements

Next, you will create an Event class. Each Event object includes two data fields: the type of event and the base price Event Handlers charges per hour for the event type. The Event class also contains a constructor method and get methods for the two fields. Later, you will construct different objects based on `if` statements.

To create the Event class:

1. Add a new class file to the project by selecting **Add Class** from the **Project** menu. The Add Item dialog box appears. In the Add Item dialog box, select **Class** from the **Class** folder, then change the suggested filename to **Event.java** and click the **Open** button. The new class opens in the Text Editor window and appears as follows:

   ```
   public class Event
   {
   }
   ```

2. On a new line between the curly brackets, type the following declarations for two data fields to hold the type of event and the minimum hourly rate that Event Handlers charges:

   ```
   private char eventType;
   private double eventMinRate;
   ```

3. On a new line, type the following constructor for the Event class. The constructor will require two arguments with which you will fill the two data fields.

   ```
   public Event(char event, double rate)
   {
    eventType = event;
    eventMinRate = rate;
   }
   ```

4. On new lines, type the following two get methods that return the field values:

   ```
   public char getEventType()
   {
    return eventType;
   }
   public double getEventMinRate()
   {
    return eventMinRate;
   }
   ```

5. Rebuild the project and correct any errors.

Now that you have created an Event class, you can now modify the ChooseManager program to perform multiple tasks based on user input. Not only will you display a message to indicate which manager is assigned to the event, but you also will instantiate a unique Event object, with different minimum rates to charge based on the type of event.

To modify the ChooseManager program:

1 Return to the **ChooseManager.java** file in the Text Editor window. You will declare two constants to hold the corporate hourly rate and the private hourly rate. If these hourly rates change in the future, they will be easy to locate at the top of the file, where you can change their values.

2 Position the insertion point just after the opening curly bracket for the ChooseManager class, press the **Enter** key to start a new line, and then type the following two constants:

```
static final double CORP_RATE = 75.99;
static final double PRI_RATE = 47.99;
```

Within the main() method of the ChooseManager class, you will define an Event object named anEvent. You do not want to construct the Event object until you discover whether it will be a corporate or private event; you simply want to declare it now.

3 Position the insertion point to the right of the statement that declares the eventType character variable, press the **Enter** key to start a new line, and then type the event declaration as **Event anEvent;**

4 Next type the following lines to modify the if...else structure that currently prints a manager's name so that the if and else are each controlling a block of two statements. The first statement in each block still prints the manager's name. The second statement constructs an appropriate Event object.

```
if(eventType == 'C')
{
 System.out.println("Dustin Britt");
 anEvent = new Event(eventType, CORP_RATE);
}
else
{
 System.out.println("Carmen Lindsey");
 anEvent = new Event(eventType, PRI_RATE);
}
```

5 To confirm that the event was constructed properly, type the following two println() statements immediately after the closing bracket for the if...else structure:

```
System.out.println("Event type is " +
 anEvent.getEventType());
System.out.println("Minimum rate charged is $" +
 anEvent.getEventMinRate());
```

6 Rebuild and run the program several times with different input at the prompt. Confirm that the output shows that the event has the correct manager, type, and rate based on how you respond to the prompt (with C or P). Note the way the program is structured; if you input anything other than C at the prompt, the program output is Carmen Lindsey.

Nested `if` and Nested `if...else`

Within an `if` or an `else` statement, you can code as many dependent statements as you need, including other `if` and `else` statements. Just as spoons are nested inside each other in a drawer, such statements with an `if` inside another `if` commonly are called **nested if statements**. Nested `if` statements are particularly useful when two conditions must be met before some action is taken.

For example, suppose you want to pay a $50 bonus to a salesperson only if the salesperson sells more than three items that total more than $1,000 in value during a specified time. Figure 5-14 shows the logic for this situation. Figure 5-15 shows the code to solve the problem.

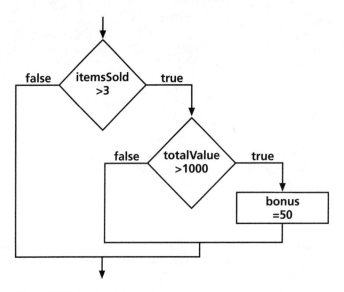

Figure 5-14: Nested `if` structure

Notice there are no semicolons in the code shown in Figure 5-15 until after the `bonus = 50;` statement. The expression `itemsSold > 3` is evaluated. If this expression is `true`, then the program evaluates the second boolean expression (`totalValue > 1000`). If that expression is also `true`, then the bonus assignment executes and the `if` structure ends.

```
if(itemsSold > 3)
  if(totalValue > 1000)
    bonus = 50;
```

Figure 5-15: Nested `if` statements

SUMMARY

- An interactive program accepts values at run time.
- The System.in.read() method accepts input from the keyboard.
- An exception is an error situation. You can let the compiler handle the problem by throwing the exception, which passes the error to the operating system.
- A message that requests user input commonly is called a prompt.
- The method System.in.read() accepts a byte from the keyboard and returns an integer value.
- When you write interactive programs, it often is a good idea to echo the input so the user can confirm visually that the data entered is correct.
- Every key typed at the keyboard must be accounted for—even the Enter key.
- Making a decision involves choosing between two alternative courses of action based on some value within a program.
- You can use the `if` statement to make a decision based on a boolean expression that evaluates as `true` or `false`. If the boolean expression enclosed in parentheses within an `if` statement is `true`, then the subsequent statement or block will execute.
- An `if` statement ends with a semicolon.
- A single-alternative `if` performs an action based on one alternative; a dual-alternative `if`, or `if...else`, provides the mechanism for performing one action when a boolean expression evaluates as `true`. When a boolean expression evaluates as `false`, a different action occurs.
- To execute more than one statement that depends on the evaluation of a boolean expression, you use a pair of curly brackets to place the dependent statements within a block.
- Within an `if` or an `else` statement, you can code as many dependent statements as you need, including other `if` and `else` statements. Nested `if` statements are particularly useful when two conditions must be met before some action occurs.

QUESTIONS

1. A program that accepts values at run time is _____.
   a. compiled
   b. interactive
   c. reciprocal
   d. object-oriented

section A

2. The `in` object is a member of the _____ class.
   a. Read
   b. IO
   c. System
   d. IN

3. An error situation is an _____.
   a. exclusion
   b. anomaly
   c. exemption
   d. exception

4. A program that uses System.in.read() requires the phrase _____ after the method header that contains the read() method.
   a. `import io`
   b. `throws Exception`
   c. `include System`
   d. `in.read() included`

5. A message that requests user input commonly is called a _____.
   a. coach
   b. prompt
   c. hint
   d. port

6. The read() method's return type is _____.
   a. integer
   b. character
   c. double
   d. byte

7. The process of repeating input characters is called a(n) _____.
   a. prompt
   b. rehash
   c. echo
   d. iteration

8. When you use read() to accept characters from the keyboard, _____.
   a. only alphabetic letters are accepted
   b. only letters and numbers are accepted
   c. only printable characters are accepted
   d. any character, including an Enter, can be accepted

9. A decision is based on a(n) _____ value.
   a. boolean
   b. absolute
   c. definitive
   d. convoluted

10. The value of (4 > 7) is _____.
    a. 4
    b. 7
    c. true
    d. false

11. The value of 3 != 13 is _____.
    a. 3
    b. 13
    c. true
    d. false

12. Assuming the variable q has been assigned the value 3, which of the following statements prints XXX?
    a. if(q != 3) System.out.println("XXX");
    b. if(q=3) System.out.println("XXX");
    c. Both of these statements print XXX.
    d. Neither of these statements prints XXX.

13. Assuming the variable q has been assigned the value 3, which of the following statements prints XXX?
    a. if(q > 0) System.out.println("XXX");
    b. if(q > 7); System.out.println("XXX");
    c. Both of these statements print XXX.
    d. Neither of these statements prints XXX.

14. Assuming the variable r has been assigned the value 8, which of the following statements prints ZZZ?
    a. if(r > 1) System.out.println("YYY"); else
       System.out.println("ZZZ");
    b. if(r < 1) System.out.println("YYY"); else
       System.out.println("ZZZ");
    c. if(r != 1) System.out.println("YYY"); else
       System.out.println("ZZZ");
    d. All of these statements print ZZZ.

15. What is the output of the following code segment?

    ```
    s = 20;
    if(s > 30)
      System.out.println("AAA");
      System.out.println("BBB");
    ```

    a. AAA
    b. BBB
    c. AAA
       BBB
    d. Nothing

16. What is the output of the following code segment?

    ```
    t = 10;
    if(t > 7)
    {
     System.out.println("AAA");
     System.out.println("BBB");
    }
    ```

    a. AAA
    b. BBB
    c. AAA
       BBB
    d. Nothing

17. When you code an if statement within another if statement, as in if(a > b) if(c > d) x = 0;, then the if statements are _____.
    a. notched
    b. nestled
    c. nested
    d. sheltered

18. When you code an if statement within another if statement, as in if(a > b) if(c > d) x = 0;, then _____.
    a. both a > b and c > d must be true for x to be set to 0
    b. either a > b and c > d must be true for x to be set to 0
    c. neither a > b nor c > d must be false for x to be set to 0
    d. under no conditions will x be set to 0

EXERCISES

In the following exercises, save each project that you create in the Chapter.05 folder on your Student Disk.

1. a. Create a console application project named Password that prompts the user for a four-character password, accepts four characters, and then echoes the characters to the screen.

   b. Create a console application project named Password2 that prompts the user for a four-character password, accepts four characters, and then echoes the characters to the screen. Test the first character. If it is B, issue a message that the password is valid; otherwise issue a message that the password is not valid.

   c. Create a console application project named Password3 that prompts the user for a four-character password, accepts four characters, and then echoes the characters to the screen. Test all four characters. If the characters spell B O L T, then issue a message that the password is valid; otherwise issue a message that the password is not valid.

2. a. Create a console application project named Furniture for a furniture company. Ask the user to choose *P* for pine, *O* for oak, or *M* for mahogany. Show the price of a table manufactured with the chosen wood. Pine tables cost $100, oak tables cost $225, and mahogany tables cost $310.

   b. Add to the program you wrote in Exercise 2a a prompt that asks the user to specify a large (*L*) or a small (*S*) table. Add $35 to the price of any large table.

3. Create a console application project named Admission for a college's admissions office. Create variables to store a student's numeric high school grade point average (for example, 3.2) and an admission test score. Print the message "Accept" if the student has any of the following:

   ■ A grade point average of 3.0 or above and an admission score test of at least 60
   ■ A grade point average below 3.0 and an admission score test of at least 80

   If the student does not meet either of the qualification criteria, print "Reject".

4. Create a console application project named Payroll that stores an hourly pay rate and hours worked. Compute gross pay (hours times rate), withholding tax, and net pay (gross pay minus withholding tax). Withholding tax is computed as a percentage of gross pay based on the following:

Gross Pay	Withholding Percentage
Up to and including 300.00	10
300.01 and up	12

5. a. Create a console application project named Calculate that stores two integers and allows the user to enter a character. If the character is *A*, add the two integers. If it is *S*, subtract the second integer from the first; if it is *M*, multiply the integers. Display the results of the arithmetic.

   b. Modify the Calculate program so the user also can enter a *D* for divide. If the second number is zero, then display an error message; otherwise divide the first number by the second and display the results.

6. a. Create a console application project named Lawn for a lawn-mowing service. The lawn-mowing season lasts 20 weeks. The weekly fee for mowing a lot under 400 square feet is $25. The fee for a lot 400 square feet or more but under 600 square feet is $35 per week. The fee for a lot 600 square feet or over is $50 per week. Store the values in the length and width variables and then print the weekly mowing fee, as well as the seasonal fee.

   b. To the Lawn program created in 6a, add a prompt that asks the user whether the customer wants to pay A) once, B) twice, or C) 20 times per year. If the user enters A for once, the fee for the season is simply the seasonal total. If the customer requests two payments, each payment is half the seasonal fee plus a $5 service charge. If the user requests 20 separate payments, add a $3 service charge per week. Print the payment amount.

7. a. Create a console application program named Balance that compares your checking account balance with your savings account balance (two doubles). Assign values to both variables and compare them, and then display either "Checking is higher" or "Checking is not higher".

   b. Change the Balance program so that it compares your checking account balance to your savings account balance to less than zero. If both statements are `true`, then display the message "Both accounts in the red". If the first balance is less than the second balance, and the first balance is greater than or equal to zero, then display the message "Both accounts in the black".

8. Create a console application project named Employee using the following code. Modify the code so that the constructor requires the user to enter the employee number from the keyboard. The employee number should be three digits. Next, write a program named InteractiveEmployee that instantiates an Employee object and uses the showCompanyID() method. Build the project and test this program.

```
public class Employee
{
        static private int COMPANY_ID = 12345;
        private int empNum;
        private double empSalary;
        Employee(int num)
        //Constructor requiring employee number
        {
                empNum = num;
        }
        public void showCompanyID()
        {
                System.out.println("Worker" + empNum)
                        + "has company ID " + COMPANY_ID);
        }
}
```

SECTION B
objectives

In this section you will learn
- How to use AND and OR operators
- How to use the `switch` statement
- How to use the conditional operator
- How to use the NOT operator
- More about operator precedence

Special Operators, the `switch` Statement, and Precedence

AND and OR Operators

For an alternative to nested `if` statements, you can use the **AND operator** within a boolean expression to determine whether two expressions are both `true`. The AND operator is written as two ampersands (&&). For example, the code shown in Figure 5-16 works exactly the same as the code shown in Figure 5-15. The itemsSold variable is tested, and if it is greater than 3, then the totalValue is tested. If totalValue is greater than 1,000, then the bonus is set to 50.

```
if(itemsSold > 3 && totalValue > 1000)
   bonus = 50;
```

Figure 5-16: Using the AND operator

You are never required to use the AND operator because using nested `if` statements always achieves the same result, but using the AND operator often makes your code more concise, less error-prone, and easier to understand.

It is important to note that when you use the AND operator, you must include a complete boolean expression on each side of the && operator. If you want to set a bonus to $400 if saleAmount is both over $1,000 and under $5,000, the correct statement is `if(saleAmount > 1000 && saleAmount < 5000) bonus = 400;`. Even though the saleAmount variable is used on both sides of the AND expression, the statement `if(saleAmount > 1000 && < 5000)...` is incorrect and will not compile.

With the AND operator, both boolean expressions must be `true` before the action in the statement can occur. You can use the **OR operator**, which is written as ||, when you want some action to occur even if only one of two conditions is `true`. For example, if you want to give a bonus of $200 if a salesperson satisfies at least one of two conditions—selling more than 100 items or selling any number of items that total more than $3,000 in value—then you can write the code using either one of the ways shown in Figure 5-17. Figure 5-18 shows the program logic.

A common use of the OR operator is to decide to take action whether a character variable is uppercase or lowercase, as in `if(selection == 'A' || selection == 'a') ....` The subsequent action occurs whether the selection variable holds an uppercase or lowercase A.

```
// Using two ifs
if(itemsSold > 100)
  bonus = 200;
else if(totalValue > 3000)
  bonus = 200;
// Using the OR operator
if(itemsSold > 100 || totalValue > 3000)
  bonus = 200;
```

Figure 5-17: OR code using two `if` statements and the OR operator

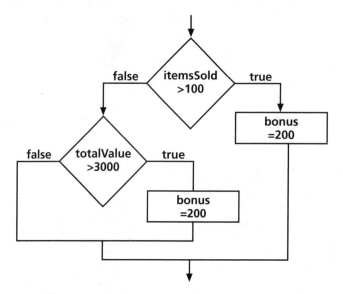

Figure 5-18: Diagram of OR logic

Sometimes situations arise in which there are more than two possible courses of action to take. Consider a situation in which salespeople can receive one of three possible commission rates based on their sales. For example, a sale totaling $1,001 or more earns the salesperson an eight percent commission, a sale totaling $500 to $1,000 earns six percent of the sale amount, and any sale totaling $499 or less earns five percent. Using three separate `if` statements to test single boolean expressions results in some incorrect commissions. Examine the code shown in Figure 5-19.

```
if(saleAmount > 1000)
  commRate = .08;
if(saleAmount > 500)
  commRate = .06;
if(saleAmount <= 500)
  commRate = .05;
System.out.println("Commission rate is " + commRate);
```

Figure 5-19: Incorrect assignment of three commissions

> **tip**
>
> As long as you are dealing with whole dollar amounts, the expression `if(saleAmount > 1000)` **can be expressed just as well as** `if(saleAmount >= 1001)`. **Additionally,** `if(1000 < saleAmount)` **and** `if(1001 <= saleAmount)` **have the same meaning. Use whichever has the clearest meaning for you.**

Using the code shown in Figure 5-19, if saleAmount is $5,000, the first `if` statement executes. The boolean expression `saleAmount > 1000` evaluates as `true` and .08 is correctly assigned to commRate. However, when saleAmount is $5,000, the next `if` expression (`saleAmount > 500`) also evaluates as `true`, so commRate, which was .08, is incorrectly reset to .06.

A partial solution to this problem is to use an `else` following the `if(saleAmount > 1000)` expression, as shown in Figure 5-20.

```
if(saleAmount > 1000)
  commRate = .08;
else if(saleAmount > 500)   // Notice the else
  commRate = .06;
if(saleAmount <= 500)
  commRate = .05;
System.out.println("Commission rate is " + commRate);
```

Figure 5-20: Inefficient assignment of three commissions

> You can place and indent the `if` following an `else`, but a program with many nested `if...else` combinations soon grows very long and "deep," and with indentations, later statements in the nest would move farther and farther to the right on the page. For easier-to-read code, Java programmers commonly place each `else` and its subsequent `if` on the same line.

With the new code in Figure 5-20, when saleAmount is $5,000, the expression `saleAmount > 1000` is `true` and the commRate becomes .08. When commRate is not greater than $1,000, the `else` statement executes and correctly sets commRate to .06.

The code shown in Figure 5-20 works correctly, but it is somewhat inefficient. When saleAmount is any amount over $500, either the first `if` sets commRate to .08 for amounts over $500, or its `else` sets commRate to .06 for amounts over $500. The boolean value that is tested in the next statement, `if(saleAmount <= 500)`, is always `false`. Rather than unconditionally asking `if(saleAmount <= 500)`, it's easier to use an `else`. If saleAmount is not over $1,000 and it is also not over $500, it must, by default, be less than or equal to $500. Figure 5-21 shows this improved logic, and Figure 5-22 shows its code.

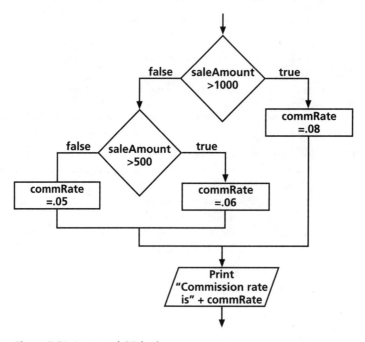

Figure 5-21: Improved OR logic

> Within a nested `if...else`, it is most efficient to ask the most likely question first. In other words, if you know that most saleAmount values are over $1,000, compare saleAmount to that value first. If, however, you know that most saleAmounts are small, you should ask `if(saleAmount <= 500)` first.

```
if(saleAmount >= 1000)
 commRate = .08;
else if(saleAmount > 500)
 commRate = .06;
else commRate = .05;
System.out.println("Commission rate is " + commRate);
```

Figure 5-22: Correct assignment of three commissions

Currently, the ChooseManager program identifies an event as a corporate event and assigns an appropriate manager and rate when the user enters C at the event-type prompt. When the user enters any other character, the event is considered to be private. Next you will improve the ChooseManager program so that if the user does not enter either C or P, an Event object with an "invalid" X type is instantiated.

To improve the ChooseManager program:

1 Open the **ChooseManager** project from the Chapter.05 folder on your Student Disk, then open the **ChooseManager.java** file in the Text Editor window.

2 In the ChooseManager.java text file, change the `if...else` structure that tests eventType so that it becomes a nested `if...else` with three possibilities. When the user inputs anything other than C or P, display an error message and create an Event object with a code 'X' for eventType and a rate of 0.0 for minEventRate:

Remember that the Event constructor that you created earlier in this chapter requires both a character and a double argument.

```
if(eventType == 'C')
{
 System.out.println("Dustin Britt");
 anEvent = new Event(eventType, CORP_RATE);
}
else if(eventType == 'P')
{
 System.out.println("Carmen Lindsey");
 anEvent = new Event(eventType, PRI_RATE);
}
else
{
```

```
   System.out.println("Invalid entry!");
   anEvent = new Event('X',0.0);
}
```

3 Rebuild and run the program several times to confirm that user responses of C or P result in valid Event objects, and that other responses result in an error message and an event of type X.

The switch Statement

By nesting a series of if and else statements, you can choose from any number of alternatives. For example, suppose you want to print a student's class year based on a stored number. Figure 5-23 shows the program.

```
if(year == 1)
   System.out.println("Freshman");
else if(year == 2)
   System.out.println("Sophomore");
else if(year == 3)
   System.out.println("Junior");
else if(year == 4)
   System.out.println("Senior");
else System.out.println("Invalid year");
```

Figure 5-23: Multiple alternatives

An alternative to the series of nested if statements is to use the **switch statement.** The switch statement is useful when you need to test a single variable against a series of exact integer or character values. The switch structure uses four new keywords:

- The keyword switch starts the structure and is followed immediately by a test expression enclosed in parentheses.
- The keyword case is followed by one of the possible values for the test expression, then a colon.
- The keyword break optionally terminates a switch structure at the end of each case.
- The keyword default optionally is used prior to any action that should occur if the test variable does not match any case.

You are not required to list the case values in ascending order as shown here. It is most efficient to list the most common case first, instead of the case with the lowest value.

For example, Figure 5-24 shows the `case` structure used to print the four school years.

```
switch(year)
{
 case 1:
  System.out.println("Freshman");
  break;
 case 2:
  System.out.println("Sophomore");
  break;
 case 3:
  System.out.println("Junior");
  break;
 case 4:
  System.out.println("Senior");
  break;
 default:
  System.out.println("Invalid year");
}
```

Figure 5-24: Sample case structure

The `switch` structure shown in Figure 5-24 begins by evaluating the year variable shown in the `switch` statement. If the year is equal to the first `case` value, which is 1, then the statement that prints "Freshman" will execute. The `break` statement bypasses the rest of the `switch` structure, and execution continues with any statement after the closing curly bracket of the `switch` structure.

If the year variable is not equivalent to the first `case` value of 1, then the next `case` value is compared, and so on. If the year variable does not contain the same value as any of the `case` statements, then the `default` statement or statements execute.

You can leave out the `break` statements in a `switch` structure. However, when you omit the `break`, if the program finds a match for the test variable, then all the statements within the `switch` statement from that point forward will execute. For example, in the code shown in Figure 5-24, when year is 3, the first two cases will be bypassed, but "Junior", "Senior", and "Invalid year" all will print. You should omit the `break` statements intentionally if you want all subsequent cases to execute once the test variable is matched.

You are never required to use a `switch` structure; you can always achieve the same results with nested `if` statements. The `switch` structure is simply a convenience that you can use when there are several alternative courses of action depending on a single integer or character variable. Additionally, it makes sense to use `switch` only when there are a reasonable number of specific matching values to be tested. For example, if every sale amount from 1 to 500 requires a five percent commission, it is not reasonable to test every possible dollar amount using the following code:

```
switch(saleAmount)
{
 case 1:
  commRate = .05;
  break;
 case 2:
  commRate = .05;
  break;
 case 3:
  commRate = .05;
  break;
 // ...and so on for several hundred more cases
```

With 500 different dollar values resulting in the same commission, running one test—`if(saleAmount <= 500)`—is far more reasonable than listing 500 separate cases.

Next you will modify the ChooseManager program to account for a new type of event. Besides corporate and private events, there will be special rates for nonprofit organizations. The entered code for nonprofit events will be N, and Robin Armanetti will be the manager assigned to these events. You will convert your nested `if` statements to a `switch` structure.

To convert the ChooseManager decision-making process to a `switch` structure:

1 In the **ChooseManager.java** file, position the insertion point at the end of the statement that declares the constant for PRI_RATE, press the **Enter** key to start a new line, and then type the following constant for NON_PROF_RATE:
`static final double NON_PROF_RATE = 40.99;`

2 To the list of current prompts, add the following prompt to tell the user to enter N for nonprofit organization events: `System.out.println ("N for nonprofit event");`

3 Delete the `if...else` statements that presently are used to determine whether the user entered C or P, and then replace them with the following `switch` structure:

```
switch(eventType)
{
  case 'C':
```

```
      System.out.println("Dustin Britt");
      anEvent = new Event(eventType, CORP_RATE);
      break;
    case 'P':
      System.out.println("Carmen Lindsey");
      anEvent = new Event(eventType, PRI_RATE);
      break;
    case 'N':
      System.out.println("Robin Armanetti");
      anEvent = new Event(eventType, NON_PROF_RATE);
      break;
    default:
      System.out.println("Invalid entry!");
      anEvent = new Event('X',0.0);
  }
```

▶ **tip**

Remember from Chapter 2 that characters are actually stored as integers.

4. Rebuild and test the program. Make sure the correct output appears when you enter C, P, N, or some other value as keyboard input.

The Conditional Operator

Java provides one more way to make decisions. The **conditional operator** requires three expressions separated by a question mark and a colon, and it is used as an abbreviated version of the `if...else` structure. As with the `switch` structure, you never are required to use the conditional operator; it is simply a convenient shortcut. The syntax of the conditional operator is `test Expression ? true Result: false Result;`.

The first expression, testExpression, is a boolean expression that is evaluated as `true` or `false`. If it is `true`, then the entire conditional expression takes on the value of the expression following the question mark (trueResult). If the value of the testExpression is `false`, then the entire expression takes on the value of falseResult. For example, `biggerNum = (a > b) ? a : b;` evaluates the expression a > b. If a is greater than b, then the entire conditional expression takes the value of a, which then is assigned to biggerNum. If a is not greater than b, then the expression assumes the value of b, and b is assigned to biggerNum.

The NOT Operator

You use the **NOT operator**, which is written as the exclamation point (!), to negate the result of any boolean expression. Any expression that evaluates as `true` becomes `false` when preceded by the NOT operator, and any `false` expression preceded by the NOT operator becomes `true`.

For example, suppose a monthly car insurance premium is $200 if the driver is age 25 or younger, and $125 if the driver is age 26 or older. Each of the following `if` statements correctly assigns the premium values:

```
if(age <= 25)   premium = 200;
        else premium = 125;
if(!(age <= 25)) premium = 125;
        else premium = 200;
if(age >= 26) premium = 125;
        else premium = 200;
if(!(age >= 26)) premium = 200;
        else premium = 125;
```

The statements with the NOT operator are somewhat harder to read, particularly because they require the double set of parentheses, but the result of the decision-making process is the same in each case. Using the NOT operator is clearer when the value of a boolean variable is tested. For example, a variable initialized as `boolean oldEnough = (age >= 25);` can become part of the relatively easy-to-read expression `if(!oldEnough)`....

Precedence

You learned in Chapter 2 that operations have higher and lower precedences. For example, within an arithmetic expression, multiplication and division are always performed prior to addition or subtraction. Figure 5-25 shows the precedence of the operators you have used.

Precedence	Operator(s)	Symbol(s)
Highest	Multiplication, division	* / %
	Addition, subtraction	+ -
	Relational	> < >= <=
	Equality	== !=
	Logical AND	&&
	Logical OR	||
	Conditional	?:
Lowest	Assignment	=

Figure 5-25: Operator precedence for operators used so far

In general, the order of precedence agrees with common algebraic usage. For example, in any mathematical expression such as x = a + b, the arithmetic is done first and the assignment is done last, as you would expect. The relationship of && and || might not be as obvious. Consider the program segment shown in Figure 5-26 and try to predict its output.

```
int tickets = 4;
int age = 40;
char gender = 'F';
if(tickets > 3 || age < 25 && gender == 'M')
  System.out.println("Do not insure");
if((tickets > 3 || age < 25) && gender == 'M')
  System.out.println("Bad risk");
```

Figure 5-26: Demonstrating && and || precedence

With the first if statement, the && takes precedence over the ||, so age < 25 && gender == 'M' is evaluated first. The value is false because age is not less than 25 and gender is not 'M'. So the expression is reduced to "tickets > 3 or false." Because the value of the tickets variable is greater than 3, the entire expression is true, and "Do not insure" is printed.

Even though the && is evaluated first in the expression age < 25 && gender == 'M' || tickets > 3, **there is no harm in adding extra parentheses as in** (age < 25 && gender == 'M') || tickets > 3. **The outcome is the same, but the intent is clearer to someone reading your code.**

In the second if statement shown in Figure 5-26, parentheses have been added so the || is evaluated first. The expression tickets > 3 || age < 25 is true because tickets is greater than 3. So the expression evolves to true && gender == 'M'. Because gender is not 'M', the value of the entire expression is false, and the "bad risk" statement does not print. The following are two important lessons:

- The order in which you use operators makes a difference.
- You always can use parentheses to change precedence or make your intentions clearer.

SUMMARY

- You can use the AND operator (&&) within a boolean expression to determine whether two expressions are both `true`.

- You can use the OR operator (||) when you want to carry out some action even if only one of two conditions is `true`.

- By nesting a series of `if` and `else` statements, you can choose from any number of alternatives.

- You use the `switch` statement to test a single variable against a series of exact integer or character values.

- The conditional operator requires three expressions separated by a question mark and a colon, and it is used as an abbreviated version of the `if...else` statement.

- You use the NOT operator (!) to negate the result of any boolean expression.

- Operator precedence makes a difference. You can always use parentheses to change precedence or make your intentions clearer.

QUESTIONS

1. The operator that combines two conditions into a single boolean value that is `true` when both of the conditions are `true` is _____.
   a. $$
   b. !!
   c. ||
   d. &&

2. The operator that combines two conditions into a single boolean value that is `true` when at least one of the conditions is `true` is _____.
   a. $$
   b. !!
   c. ||
   d. &&

3. Assuming a variable k has been initialized to 12, which of the following statements sets m to 0?
   a. if(k > 3 && k > 6) m = 0;
   b. if(k < 3 && k < 20) m = 0;
   c. if(k > 3 && k < 0) m = 0;
   d. All of these statements set m to 0.

4. Assuming a variable n has been initialized to 2, which of the following statements sets p to 0?
   a. if(n > 3 && n > 6) p = 0;
   b. if(n > 0 && > 1) p = 0;

c. `if(n < 7 && n == 2) p = 0;`
d. All of these statements set p to 0.

5. Assuming a variable f has been initialized to 5, which of the following statements sets g to 0?
   a. `if(f > 6 || f == 5) g = 0;`
   b. `if(f < 3 || f > 4) g = 0;`
   c. `if(f >= 0 || f < 2) g = 0;`
   d. All of these statements set g to 0.

6. If you write a program that prompts a user for a response, and you want to accept the letter A whether it is uppercase or lowercase, the correct `if` statement is _____.
   a. `if(ans == 'A' || ans == 'a') System.out.println("Good response");`
   b. `if(ans == 'A' && ans == 'a') System.out.println("Good response");`
   c. Both of these statements will work properly.
   d. Neither of these statements will work properly.

7. If you write a program that prompts a user for a response, and the response should be between 1 and 4 inclusive, then the proper `if` statement is _____.
   a. `if(ans >= '1' || ans <= '4') System.out.println("Good response");`
   b. `if(ans >= '1' && ans <= '4') System.out.println("Good response");`
   c. Both of these statements will work properly.
   d. Neither of these statements will work properly.

8. The `switch` statement tests a variable against _____.
   a. a single boolean value
   b. several possible boolean values
   c. several possible integer or character values
   d. several possible values of any type

9. Within a `switch` structure, each possible test value is immediately followed by a(n) _____.
   a. opening curly bracket
   b. colon
   c. semicolon
   d. comma

10. You can use the _____ statement to terminate a case in a `switch` structure.
    a. `switch`
    b. `end`
    c. `case`
    d. `break`

11. The `default case` _____ within a `switch` structure.
    a. must appear
    b. must not appear
    c. can be placed last
    d. can be placed anywhere

12. You _____ use a break statement after each case in a switch structure.
    a. must
    b. can, and usually do,
    c. must not
    d. can, but usually do not,

13. The conditional operator requires _____.
    a. two ampersands
    b. two pipes
    c. a question mark and a colon
    d. an exclamation point and an asterisk

14. Assuming a variable w has been assigned the value 15, then the statement
    w == 15 ? x = 2 : x = 0; assigns _____.
    a. 15 to w
    b. 2 to x
    c. 0 to x
    d. nothing

15. Assuming a variable y has been assigned the value 6, then the value of !(y < 7) is _____.
    a. 6
    b. 7
    c. true
    d. false

16. Assuming the variable z has been assigned the value 0, then the value of the expression !(z == 0) is _____.
    a. 0
    b. true
    c. false
    d. illegal

17. Assuming a = 5 and b = 9, then the value of a > 0 && b < 10 || b > 1 is _____.
    a. 5
    b. 9
    c. true
    d. false

18. Assuming a = 5 and b = 9, then the value of a > 0 || b < 10 && b > 1 is _____.
    a. 5
    b. 9
    c. true
    d. false

19. Assuming c = 4 and d = 14, then which of the following statements is true?
    a. c > 7 && d < 5 || d > 20
    b. c > 0 && d < 5 || d > 50
    c. c > 1 && d < 6 || d > 0
    d. c < 0 && d > 0 || d < 0

EXERCISES

In the following exercises, save each project that you create in the Chapter.05 folder on your Student Disk.

1. Create a console application project named PickEmployee that asks a user to input an initial. Display the full name of an employee who matches the initial: *A* is Armando, *B* is Bruno, and *Z* is Zachary. All other entries should cause a "No such employee" message to display.

2. Create a console application project named GetVowel that asks the user to type a vowel from the keyboard. If the character entered is not a vowel, display an error message.

3. Create a console application project named IQ that asks the user to enter his or her IQ score. If the user enters a number less than 0 or greater than 200, issue an error message; otherwise, issue an "above average", "average", or "below average" message for scores over, at, or under 100, respectively.

4. Create a console application project named Admissions2 for a college's admissions office. The user enters a numeric high school grade point average (for example, 3.2) and an admission test score. Print the message "Accept" if the student has any of the following:

   ■ A grade point average of 3.6 or above and an admission test score of at least 60
   ■ A grade point average of 3.0 or above and an admission test score of at least 70
   ■ A grade point average of 2.6 or above and an admission test score of at least 80
   ■ A grade point average of 2.0 or above and an admission test score of at least 90

   If the student does not meet any of the qualifications, print "Reject".

5. Create a console application project named Payroll2 that stores an employee's hourly pay rate and hours worked. Compute gross pay (hours times rate), withholding tax, and net pay (gross pay minus withholding tax). Withholding tax is computed as a percentage of gross pay based on the following:

Gross Pay	Withholding Percentage
0 to 300.00	10
300.01 to 400.00	12
400.01 to 500.00	15
500.01 and over	20

6. Create a console application project named PetAdvice that recommends a pet for a user based on the user's lifestyle. Prompt the user to enter whether he or she lives in an apartment, house, or dormitory (A, H, or D) and the number of hours the user is home during the average day. The user will select an hour category from a menu: A) 18 or more; B) 10 to 17; C) 8 to 9; D) 6 to 7; or E) 0 to 5. Print your recommendation based on the following:

Residence	Hours Home	Recommendation
House	18 or more	Pot bellied pig
House	8 through 17	Dog
House	Less than 8	Snake
Apartment	10 or more	Cat
Apartment	Fewer than 10	Hamster
Dormitory	6 or more	Fish
Dormitory	Fewer than 6	Ant farm

7. Create a console application project named Siblings that declares two ints named myNumberOfSiblings and yourNumberOfSiblings. Display an appropriate message to indicate whether your friend has more, fewer, or the same number of siblings as you. Display the number of siblings whether the `if` statement is `true` or not.

8. Create a console application project named Credits that compares the number of college credits you have earned with the number of college credits earned by a classmate or friend. Display an appropriate message to indicate whether your classmate has earned more, fewer, or the same number of credits as you. Display the number of college credits whether the `if` statement is `true` or not.

9. Create a console application project named Store that displays a menu of items in a store, with a price for each item. Include characters a, b, and c so the user can select a menu item. Prompt the user to choose an item using the character that corresponds to the item. After the user makes the first selection, show a prompt to ask whether another selection will be made. The user should respond Y or N to this prompt (for yes or no). If the user types N, display the cost of the item. If the user types Y, allow the user to select another item and then display the total cost of the two items. Use the `switch` statement to check the menu selection.

SECTION C
objectives

In this section you will learn
- About the loop structure
- How to use a `while` loop
- How to use shortcut arithmetic operators
- How to use a `for` loop
- How and when to use a `do...while` loop
- About nested loops

Looping and Shortcut Arithmetic

The `while` Loop

Making decisions is what makes programs seem smart; looping is what makes programs powerful. A **loop** is a structure that allows repeated execution of a block of statements. Within a looping structure, a boolean expression is evaluated. If it is `true`, then a block of statements, called the **loop body,** executes and then the boolean expression is evaluated again. As long as the expression is `true`, the statements in the loop body continue to execute. When the boolean evaluation is `false`, the loop ends. Figure 5-27 shows a diagram of the logic of a loop.

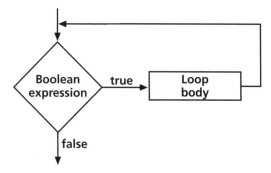

Figure 5-27: Logic of a loop

One execution of any loop is called an iteration.

You can use a **while loop** to execute a body of statements continuously while some condition continues to be `true`. A `while` loop consists of the keyword `while` followed by a boolean expression within parentheses, followed by the body of the loop, which can be a single statement or a block of statements surrounded by curly brackets.

For example, the code shown in Figure 5-28 causes the message "Hello" to display (theoretically) forever because there is no code to end the loop. Such a loop that never ends is called an **infinite loop**.

> An infinite loop might not actually execute infinitely. Eventually the computer memory will be exhausted (literally and figuratively!) and execution will stop. Depending on your system, however, this could take some time.

```
while (4 > 2)
  System.out.println("Hello");
```

Figure 5-28: Infinite loop example

In Figure 5-28, the expression 4 > 2 evaluates to true. You obviously never need to make such an evaluation, but if you do so in this while loop, the body of the loop is entered and "Hello" displays. Next, the expression is evaluated again. The expression 4 > 2 is still true, so the body is entered again. "Hello" displays repeatedly; the loop never finishes because 4 > 2 is never false.

It is always a bad idea to write an infinite loop. However, even experienced programmers write them by accident. So, before you start writing any loops at all, it is good to know how to break out of an infinite loop in case you accidentally find yourself in the midst of one. If you think your program is in a loop, you can press and hold down the Ctrl key and then press the C key or the Break key, which is located on the Pause key.

To prevent a while loop from executing infinitely, three separate actions need to occur:

- Some variable, the **loop control variable**, is initialized.
- The loop control variable is tested in the while statement.
- The body of the while statement must take some action that alters the value of the loop control variable.

For example, the code in Figure 5-29 shows a variable named loopCount being set to a value of 1. The while loop tests loopCount, and if it is less than 3, then the loop body is executed. The loop body shown in Figure 5-29 consists of two statements made into a block by their surrounding curly brackets. The first statement prints "Hello", and then the second statement adds one to loopCount. The next time loopCount is evaluated, it is 2. It is still less than 3, so the loop body executes again. "Hello" prints a second time and loopCount becomes 3. Now when the expression loopCount < 3 is evaluated, it is false, so the loop ends. Program execution would continue with any subsequent statements.

tip

To an algebra student, a statement like `loopCount = loopCount + 1` looks wrong—a value can never be one more than itself. In programming, however, `loopCount = loopCount + 1;` takes the value of loopCount, adds one to it, and then assigns the new value back into loopCount.

```
loopCount = 1;
while (loopCount < 3)
{
  System.out.println("Hello");
  loopCount = loopCount + 1;
}
```

Figure 5-29: Simple loop that executes twice

Notice that if the curly brackets are omitted from the code shown in Figure 5-29, the `while` loop ends at the end of the "Hello" statement. Adding one to loopCount is no longer part of the loop, so an infinite situation is created.

Also notice that if a semicolon mistakenly is placed at the end of the partial statement `while (loopCount < 3);`, the loop is also infinite. This loop has an **empty body**, or a body with no statements in it, so the boolean expression is evaluated, and because it is `true`, the loop body is entered. Because the loop body is empty, no action is taken, and the boolean expression is evaluated again. It is still `true` (nothing has changed), so the empty body is entered and the infinite loop continues.

It is very common to alter the value of a loop control variable by adding one to it, or **incrementing** the variable. However, not all loops are controlled by adding one. The loop shown in Figure 5-30 prints "Hello" twice, just as the loop in Figure 5-29 does, but its loop is controlled by subtracting 1 from a loop control variable, or **decrementing** it.

```
loopCount = 10;
while (loopCount > 8)
{
  System.out.println("Hello");
  loopCount = loopCount - 1;
}
```

Figure 5-30: Another simple loop that executes twice

section C

In the program segment shown in Figure 5-30, the variable loopCount begins with a value of 10. The loopCount is greater than 8, so the loop body prints "Hello" and decrements loopCount so it becomes 9. The boolean expression in the `while` loop is tested again. Because 9 is more than 8, "Hello" prints and loopCount becomes 8. Now loopCount is not greater than 8, so the loop ends.

The possibilities are endless. Figure 5-31 shows the loopCount being increased by 5, and the results are still the same—the loop prints "Hello" twice. You should not use such unusual methods because they simply make a program confusing. The clearest and best method is to start loopCount at 0 or 1, and continue while it is less than 2 or 3, incrementing by one each time through the loop.

```
loopCount = 30;
while (loopCount < 40)
{
 System.out.println("Hello");
 loopCount = loopCount + 5;
}
```

Figure 5-31: Third simple loop that executes twice

Within a loop, you are not required to alter the loop control variable by adding to it or subtracting from it. To write a loop that depends on arithmetic, you need to know as you are writing your program how many times you want a loop to execute. Often, the value of a loop control variable is not altered by arithmetic, but instead is altered by user input. For example, perhaps you want to continue performing some task while the user indicates a desire to continue. In that case, you do not know as you are writing the program whether the loop will be executed two times, 200 times, or no times at all.

Unlike a loop that you program to execute a fixed number of times, a loop that is controlled by the user is a type of indefinite loop because you are not sure how many times it will eventually loop.

Consider a simple program in which you display a bank balance and ask the user whether he or she wants to see what the balance will be after one year of interest has accumulated. Each time the user indicates a desire to continue, an increased balance appears. When the user finally indicates a desire to exit, the program ends. The program appears in Figure 5-32.

```
public class LoopingBankBal
{
 public static void main(String[] args)   throws Exception
 {
  double bankBal = 1000;
  double intRate = 0.04;
  char response;
  System.out.println("Do you want to see
    your balance? Y or N");
  response = (char)System.in.read();
  System.in.read(); System.in.read();
  // Absorbs Enter key
  while (response == 'Y')
  {
  System.out.println("Bank balance is " + bankBal);
  bankBal = bankBal + bankBal * intRate;
  System.out.println("Do you want to see
    next year's balance? Y or N");
  response = (char)System.in.read();
  System.in.read(); System.in.read();
    // Absorbs Enter key
  }
  System.out.println("Have a nice day!");
 }
}
```

Figure 5-32: LoopingBankBal program

tip

The program shown in Figure 5-32 continues to display bank balances while the response is Y. It could also be written to display while the response is not N, as in `while (response != 'N')`.... A value that a user must supply to stop a loop is called a sentinel value.

The program shown in Figure 5-32 contains three variables: a bank balance, an interest rate, and a response. The program asks the user, "Do you want to see your balance?" and reads the response. Recall that the second and third read() statements are required to accept the Enter key that is typed after the Y or N entry. The loop in the program begins with `while (response == 'Y')`. If the user types any response other than Y, then the loop body never executes; instead, the next statement to execute is the "Have a nice day!" statement at the bottom of the program. However, if the user enters Y, then all five statements within the loop body will execute. The current balance will display, and then the program increases the balance by the interest rate value. The program then prompts the user to type Y or N, and two characters are entered—the response and the Enter key. The loop ends with a closing curly bracket, and program control returns to the top of the loop, where the boolean expression in the `while` loop is tested again. If the user typed Y, then the loop is entered and the increased bankBal value that was calculated is finally displayed.

Next, you will improve the ChooseManager program so the user cannot make an invalid choice for the type of event.

To improve the ChooseManager program:

1. Open the **ChooseManager** project from the Chapter.05 folder on your Student Disk, then open the **ChooseManager.java** file in the Text Editor window.

2. Position the insertion point to the right of the statement that reads in the character for the event type, `eventType=(char)System.in.read();`. Press the **Enter** key to start a new line, and then type the beginning of the while loop that will continue to execute while the user's entry is not one of the three allowed event types:

   ```
   while (eventType != 'C' && eventType != 'P'
      && eventType != 'N')
   ```

3. On a new line, type the opening curly bracket for the `while` loop, press the **Enter** key, and then type the two statements that will absorb the Enter key remaining from the user's data entry:

   ```
   System.in.read(); System.in.read();
   ```

4. On a new line, display the following message so the user knows the data entry was invalid:

   ```
   System.out.println("Entry must be C or P or N!");
   ```

5 On another new line, read in the eventType value again by typing the following:

`eventType = (char)System.in.read();`

6 On a new line, type the closing curly bracket for the `while` loop. After making it through the `while` loop you just added, the program is guaranteed that the eventType is C, P, or N, so you can make the nonprofit event the default case.

7 Change the statement `case 'N':` to `default:`, and then delete the three lines that represent the current default case: the existing `default` keyword and the two statements that follow it.

8 Rebuild and test the program. No matter how many invalid entries you make, the program will continue to prompt you until you enter C, P, or N.

Shortcut Arithmetic Operators

It is common to increase the value of a variable in a program. As you saw in the last section, many loops are controlled by continuously adding one to some variable, or **counting**, as in `count = count + 1;`. Similarly, in the looping bank balance program, the program increased a bank balance by an interest amount with the statement `bankBal = bankBal + bankBal * intRate;`. In other words, the bank balance became its old value plus a new interest amount using a process known as **accumulating**.

Because increasing a variable is so common, Java provides you with several shortcuts for counting and accumulating. The statement `count += 1;` is identical in meaning to `count = count + 1;`. The `+=` adds and assigns in one operation. Similarly, `bankBal += bankBal * intRate;` increases bankBal by a calculated interest amount.

When you want to increase a variable's value by exactly one, you can use two other shortcut operators—the **prefix ++** and the **postfix ++**. To use a prefix ++, you type two plus signs before the variable name. The statement `someValue = 6;` followed by `++someValue;` results in someValue holding 7, or one more than it held before you applied the ++. To use a postfix ++, you type two plus signs just after a variable name. The statements `anotherValue = 56; anotherValue++;` result in anotherValue containing 57.

> You can use the prefix ++ and postfix ++ with variables, but not with constants. An expression such as `++84;` is illegal because an 84 must always remain as 84. However, you can create a variable as `int val = 84;` and then write `++val;` or `val++;` to increase the variable's value.

The prefix and postfix increment operators are **unary** operators because you use them with one value. Most arithmetic operators, such as those used for addition and multiplication, are **binary** operators that operate on two values.

When you simply want to increase a variable's value by one, there is no difference between using the prefix and postfix increment operators. Each operator results in increasing the variable by one. However, these operators function differently. When you use the prefix ++, the result is calculated and stored, and then the variable is used. For example, if b = 4;, then c = ++b; results in both b and c holding the value 5. When you use the postfix ++, the variable is used and then the result is calculated and stored. For example, if b = 4; and then c = b++;, 4 will be assigned to c, and then after the assignment, b is increased and takes the value 5. In other words, if b = 4, then the value of b++ is also 4, but after the statement is completed, the value of b will be 5. If d = 8 and e = 8, both ++d == 9 and e++ == 8 are true expressions.

To demonstrate the effect of the prefix and postfix increment operators:

1 Create a new console application project named **DemoIncrement**. Save the **DemoIncrement** project folder in the Chapter.05 folder on your Student Disk.

2 Rename the default Class1.java file as **DemoIncrement.java**, then open the file in the Text Editor window.

3 Replace the Class1 class name in the `public class Class1` line with **DemoIncrement**.

4 Add `throws Exception` to the end of the main() method so that it reads `public static void main (String[] args) throws Exception`.

5 Replace the `// TODO: Add initialization code here` comment with a variable v and assign it a value of 4. Then declare a variable named plusPlusV and assign it a value of ++v by typing the following:

```
int v = 4;
int plusPlusV = ++v;
```

6 The last statement, `int plusPlusV = ++v;`, will increase v to 5, so reset v to 4 before declaring a vPlusPlus variable to which you assign v++ by typing the following:

```
v = 4;
int vPlusPlus = v++;
```

7 Add the following statements to print the three values:

```
System.out.println("v is " + v);
System.out.println("++v is " + plusPlusV);
System.out.println("v++ is " + vPlusPlus);
```

8 Select **DemoIncrement Properties** from the **Project** menu. Select the **DemoIncrement** file in the When project runs, load drop-down list box and set the project to run as a console application. When you are finished, click the **OK** button.

9. Build the project and execute the program as a console application by typing **jview DemoIncrement** at the command line. Your output should look like Figure 5-33. Make sure you understand why the values display as they do.

```
C:\WINNT\System32\cmd.exe

A:\CHAPTER.05\DemoIncrement>jview DemoIncrement
v is 5
++v is 5
v++ is 4

A:\CHAPTER.05\DemoIncrement>_
```

Figure 5-33: Output of the DemoIncrement program

To illustrate how comparisons are made, add a few more variables to the DemoIncrement program.

10. Position the cursor to the right of the last println() statement, and then press the **Enter** key to start a new line.
11. Add three new integer variables and two new boolean variables: The first boolean variable compares ++w to y; the second boolean variable compares x++ to y:

```
int w = 17, x = 17, y = 18;
boolean compare1 = (++w == y);
boolean compare2 = (x++ == y);
```

12. Add the following statements to display the values stored in the compare variables:

```
System.out.println("First compare is " + compare1);
System.out.println("Second compare is " + compare2);
```

13. Rebuild and run the program. Make sure you understand why compare1's value is `true` and compare2's value is `false`.

Besides using the shortcut operator +=, you can use -= *= and /=. Each of these operators is used to perform the operation and assign the result in one step. For example, `balanceDue -= payment;` subtracts payment from balanceDue and assigns the result to balanceDue.

Besides using the prefix and postfix increment operators, you can use a prefix or postfix **decrement operator** (--) that reduces a variable's value by one. For example, if s and t are each assigned the value 34, then --s has the value 33 and t-- has the value 34, but t becomes 33.

The for Loop

You can use a `while` loop when you need to perform a task some predetermined number of times. A loop that executes a specific number of times is a **definite loop** or a **counted loop**. To write a definite loop, you initialize a loop control variable, and while the loop control variable does not pass a limit, you continue to execute the body of the `while` statement. To avoid an infinite loop, you must include in the body of the `while` loop a statement that alters the loop control variable. For example, the program segment shown in Figure 5-34 prints the series of integers 1 through 10. The variable val starts the loop holding a value of 1, and while the value remains under 11, the val continues to print and be incremented.

```
int val = 1;
while (val < 11)
{
  System.out.println(val);
  ++val;
}
```

Figure 5-34: Printing integers 1 through 10 with a `while` loop

Because you need similar definite loops so frequently when you write programs, Java provides you with a shorthand notation that you can use to create a loop. When you use a **for loop**, you can indicate the starting value for the loop control variable, the test condition that controls loop entry, and the expression that alters the loop control variable, all in one convenient place.

You begin a `for` loop with the keyword `for` followed by a set of parentheses. Within the parentheses, there are three sections separated by exactly two semicolons. The three sections are usually used for the following:

- Initializing the loop control variable
- Testing the loop control variable
- Updating the loop control variable

The body of the `for` statement follows the parentheses. As with an `if` statement or a `while` loop, you can use a single statement as the body of a `for` loop, or you can use a block of statements enclosed in curly brackets. The `for` statement shown in Figure 5-35 produces the same output as the `while` statement shown in Figure 5-34—the integers 1 through 10.

```
for(int val = 1; val < 11; ++val)
{
  System.out.println(val);
}
```

Figure 5-35: Printing integers 1 through 10 with a for loop

You did not have to declare the variable val within the `for` **statement. If you declared val earlier in the program block, then the** `for` **statement would be** `for(val = 1; val < 11; ++val)`. **In other words, the** `for` **statement does not need to declare a variable; it can simply give a starting value to a previously declared variable.**

Within the parentheses of the `for` statement shown in Figure 5-35, the first section prior to the first semicolon declares a variable named val and initializes it to 1. The program will execute this statement once, no matter how many times the body of the `for` loop executes.

After the initialization expression executes, program control passes to the middle, or test section, of the `for` statement. If the boolean expression found there evaluates to `true`, then the body of the `for` loop is entered. In the program segment shown in Figure 5-35, val is set to 1, so when `val < 11` is tested, it evaluates to `true`. The loop body prints the val.

After the loop body executes, the final one-third of the `for` loop executes, and val is increased to 2. Following the third section, program control returns to the second section, where val is compared to 11 a second time. Because val is still less than 11, the body executes: val (now 2) prints, and then the third, altering portion of the `for` loop executes again. The variable val increases to 3, and the `for` loop continues.

Eventually, when val is *not* less than 11 (after 1 through 10 have printed), the `for` loop ends, and the program continues with any statements that follow the `for` loop.

Although the three sections of the `for` loop are most commonly used for initializing, testing, and incrementing, you can also perform the following tasks:

- You can initialize more than one variable by placing commas between the separate statements, as in `for(g = 0, h = 1; g < 6; ++g)`.
- You can perform more than one test, as in `for(g = 0; g < 3 && h > 1; ++g)`.
- You can decrement or perform some other task, as in `for(g = 5; g >= 1; --g)`.
- You can even leave one or more portions of the `for` loop empty, although the two semicolons are still required as placeholders.

Usually you should use the `for` loop for its intended purpose, which is a shorthand way of programming a definite loop.

Occasionally, you will encounter a `for` loop that contains no body, such as `for(x = 0; x < 100000; ++x);`. This kind of loop exists simply to take time—for instance, when a brief pause is desired during the execution of a program.

> Java also contains a built-in method to pause program execution. The sleep() method is part of the Thread class in the java.lang package.

The do...while Loop

With all the loops you have written so far, the loop body might execute many times, but it is also possible that the loop will not execute at all. For example, recall the bank balance program that displays compound interest, part of which is shown in Figure 5-36.

```
System.out.println("Do you want to see your balance? Y or N");
response = (char)System.in.read();
System.in.read(); System.in.read(); // Absorbs Enter key
while (response == 'Y')
{
 System.out.println("Bank balance is " + bankBal);
 bankBal = bankBal + bankBal * intRate;
 System.out.println("Do you want to see
   next year's balance? Y or N");
 response = (char)System.in.read();
 System.in.read();   // Absorbs Enter key
}
```

Figure 5-36: Part of the bank balance program with a `while` loop

The program segment begins with the user prompt, "Do you want to see your balance? Y or N". If the user does not reply by typing Y, the loop body never executes. The `while` loop checks a value at the "top" of the loop before the body has a chance to execute. Sometimes you might need a loop body to execute at least one time. If so, you want to write a loop that checks at the "bottom" of the loop after the first iteration. The **do...while loop** is a loop that checks the bottom of the loop after one repetition has occurred.

Figure 5-37 shows a `do...while` loop for the bank balance program. The loop starts with the keyword `do`. The body of the loop follows and is contained within curly brackets. The bankBal variable is output before the user has any option of responding. At the end of the loop, the user is prompted, "Do you want to see next year's balance? Y or N". Now the user has the option of seeing more balances, but the first prompt was unavoidable. The userResponse is checked at the bottom of the loop. If it is Y, then the loop repeats.

```
do {
  System.out.println("Bank balance is " + bankBal);
  bankBal = bankBal + bankBal * intRate;
  System.out.println("Do you want to see
    next year's balance? Y or N");
  response = (char)System.in.read();
  System.in.read(); System.in.read(); // Absorbs Enter key
```

Figure 5-37: Part of the bank balance program with a `do...while` loop

In any situation where you want to loop, you never are required to use a `do...while` loop. Within the bank balance example, you could simply unconditionally display the bank balance once, prompt the user, and then start a `while` loop that might not be entered. However, when you know you want to perform some task at least one time, the `do...while` loop is convenient.

Nested Loops

Just as `if` statements can be nested, so can loops. You can place a `while` loop within a `while` loop, a `for` loop within a `for` loop, a `while` loop within a `for` loop, or any other combination you can think of.

For example, suppose you want to find all the numbers that divide evenly into 100. You can write a `for` loop that sets a variable to 1 and increments it to 100. For each of the 99 times through the loop, if 100 is evenly divisible by the number (that is, if 100 can be divided by a number without any remainder), then the program prints the number. Next, you will write a program that determines all the integers that divide evenly into 100.

section C

> **tip**
>
> To find all the numbers that divide evenly into 100, you actually have to test divisors only through 50. You cannot divide any number that is more than half of another number evenly into itself.

To write a program that finds the values that divide evenly into 100:

1. Create a new console application project named **EvenInt**. Save the **EvenInt** project folder in the Chapter.05 folder on your Student Disk.
2. Rename the default Class1.java file as **EvenInt.java**, then open the file in the Text Editor window.
3. Replace the Class1 class name in the `public class Class1` line with **EvenInt**.

> **help**
>
> You do not have to add `throws Exception` to the main() header since the program you are writing does not accept input.

4. Replace the `// TODO: Add initialization code here` comment with `int num;`.
5. Type a statement that explains the purpose of the program:

   `System.out.print("100 is evenly divisible by ");`.

6. Write the `for` loop that varies num from 1 to 99. With each iteration of the loop, test whether `100%num` is 0. As you recall from Chapter 2, the modulus operator (`%`) divides one integer by another and only returns the remainder. If you divide 100 by a number and there is no remainder, then the number goes into 100 evenly.

   ```
   for(num = 1; num < 100; ++num)
     if(100%num == 0)
       System.out.print(num + "  ");
       // Print the number and two spaces
   ```

7. Add an empty println() statement to advance the cursor to the next line by typing `System.out.println();`.
8. Select **EvenInt Properties** from the **Project** menu. Select the **EvenInt** file in the When project runs, load drop-down list box and set the project to run as a console application. When you are finished, click the **OK** button.
9. Build the project and execute the program as a console application by typing `jview EvenInt` at the command line. The program prints 100 is evenly divisible by 1 2 4 5 10 20 25 50.

What if you want to know what number goes evenly into 100, but also what every number *up to* 100 can be divided evenly by? You can write 99 more loops, or you can place the current loop inside a different, outer loop, as you will do next.

Input, Selection, and Repetition

When you use a loop within a loop, you should always think of the outer loop as the more all-encompassing loop. When you describe the task at hand, you often use the word "each" when referring to the inner loop. If you want to print three mailing labels *each* for 20 customers, the label variable would control the inner loop:

```
for(customer = 1; customer <= 20; ++customer)
  for(label = 1; label <=3; ++ label)
    printLabelMethod();
```

If you want to print divisors for *each* number from 1 to 100, then the loop that varies the number to be divided is the outside loop. You need to perform 100 mathematical calculations on each of the numbers, so that constitutes the "smaller" or inside loop.

To create a nested loop to print even divisors for every number up to 100:

1 In the file **EvenInt.java** in the Text Editor, create an outer loop that uses the variable testNum to test every number from 1 to 100. Position the insertion point after the declaration of num but before the semicolon that ends the declaration, and then type a comma and **testNum**.

2 Position the cursor to the right of the line with the variable declarations, press the **Enter** key to start a new line, and then type the other for loop:

```
for(testNum = 1; testNum <= 100; ++testNum)
```

3 Press the **Enter** key, and then type the opening curly bracket for this loop on the next line.

4 Change the statement that prints "100 is evenly divisible by" to the following:

```
System.out.print(testNum + " is evenly divisible by ");
```

5 Change the for statement that varies num from 1 to 100 so it varies num only from 1 to testNum. For example, during each iteration, if testNum is 46, you want to divide it only by numbers that are 45 or less. The code to make this change is as follows:

```
for(num = 1; num < testNum; ++num)
```

6 Change the statement that tests 100% num to **if(testNum%num == 0)**.

7 Following the empty println() statement, add the closing curly bracket for the outer for loop.

8 Rebuild and run the program. The output will scroll on the screen. When it stops, it should look similar to Figure 5-38.

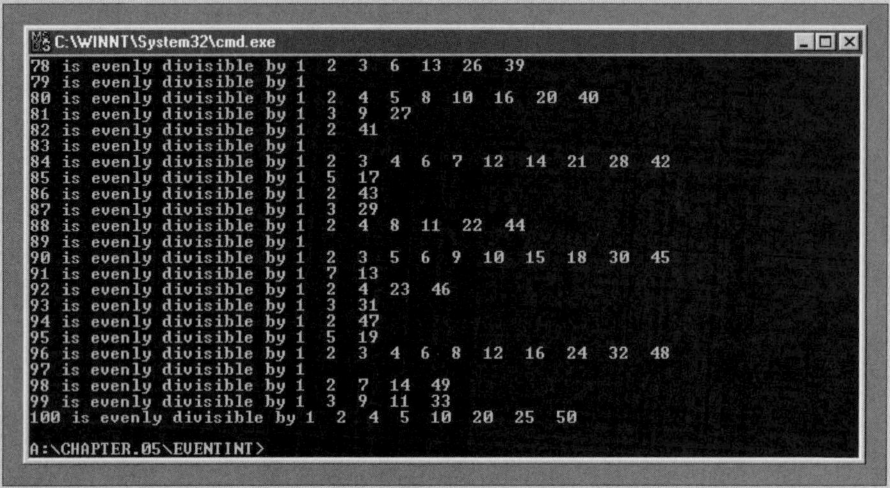

section C

![Figure 5-38 screenshot of cmd.exe output showing numbers 78-100 and their divisors]

Figure 5-38: Output of the EvenInt program

> Depending on your monitor resolution, you may see more or fewer lines than shown in Figure 5-38.

When the program shown in Figure 5-37 executes, 100 lines of output appear on the screen. But, as Figure 5-38 shows, the first 77 (or so) lines scroll by so rapidly that you can't read them. It would be helpful if you could stop the output after every 20 lines or so, because then you would have time to read the messages. You can put the modulus operator to use for this task. If you want to stop output when testNum is 20, 40, 60, and 80, then you can test testNum to see if it is evenly divisible by 20. When it is, you can pause program execution by asking the user to press the Enter key and accept keyboard input.

To pause your program after every 20 lines of output:

1 At the end of the EvenInt file and just prior to the closing bracket for the for loop, type the following code to test testNum. If 20 divides into it evenly, then tell the user to press the Enter key and accept an Enter key from the keyboard. There is no need to store the entered key in a variable.

```
if(testNum % 20 == 0)
{
 System.out.println("Press Enter to continue");
 System.in.read(); System.in.read();
}
```

> **2** Because the program now uses the System.in.read() method, you must position the insertion point at the end of the main() method header line and add **throws Exception**.
>
> **3** Rebuild and test the program. It will pause after every 20 lines of output and wait until you press the Enter key before continuing until the program ends.

SUMMARY

- A loop is a structure that allows repeated execution of a block of statements. A loop that never ends is called an infinite loop.

- Within a looping structure, a boolean expression is evaluated and if it is `true`, a block of statements, called the loop body, executes; then the boolean expression is evaluated again.

- You can use a `while` loop to execute a body of statements continuously while some condition continues to be `true`.

- You can break out of an infinite loop by pressing Ctrl+C or Ctrl+Break.

- To execute a `while` loop, you initialize a loop control variable, test it in a `while` statement, and then alter the loop control variable in the body of the `while` structure.

- To add one to a variable is to increment the variable. To subtract one is to decrement the variable.

- The += operator adds and assigns in one operation.

- The prefix ++ and the postfix ++ increase a variable's value by one.

- Unary operators are used with one value. Most arithmetic operators are binary operators that operate on two values.

- When you use the prefix ++, the result is calculated and stored, and then the variable is used. When you use the postfix ++, the variable is used, and then the result is calculated and stored.

- The shortcut operators += -= *= and /= perform operations and assign the result in one step.

- The prefix -- and postfix -- decrement operators reduce a variable's value by one.

- A loop that executes a specific number of times is a definite loop or counted loop.

- A `for` loop initializes, tests, and increments in one statement. There are three sections within the parentheses of a `for` loop that are separated by exactly two semicolons.

section C

- The do...while loop tests a boolean expression after one repetition has taken place, at the bottom of the loop.
- You can nest loops.

QUESTIONS

1. A structure that allows repeated execution of a block of statements is a(n) _____.
   a. cycle
   b. loop
   c. ring
   d. iteration

2. A loop that never ends is a(n) _____ loop.
   a. iterative
   b. infinite
   c. structured
   d. illegal

3. To construct a loop that works correctly, you should initialize a loop control _____.
   a. variable
   b. constant
   c. structure
   d. condition

4. What is the output of the following code?

   ```
   b = 1;
   while (b < 4)
   System.out.println(b + "   ");
   ```

   a. 1
   b. 1   2   3
   c. 1   2   3   4
   d. 1   1   1   1   1   1...

5. What is the output of the following code?

   ```
   b = 1;
   while (b < 4)
   {
     System.out.println(b + "   ");
      b = b + 1;
   }
   ```

   a. 1
   b. 1   2   3
   c. 1   2   3   4
   d. 1   1   1   1   1...

6. What is the output of the following code?

   ```
   e = 1;
   while (e < 4);
   System.out.println(e + " ");
   ```

   a. 1
   b. 1   1   1   1   1   1...
   c. 1   2   3   4
   d. 4   4   4   4   4   4...

7. If total = 100 and amt = 200, then after the statement total += amt, _____.

   a. total is equal to 200
   b. total is equal to 300
   c. amt is equal to 100
   d. amt is equal to 300

8. The modulus operator % is a _____ operator.
   a. unary
   b. binary
   c. tertiary
   d. postfix

9. The prefix ++ is a _____ operator.
   a. unary
   b. binary
   c. tertiary
   d. postfix

10. If g = 5, then the value of the expression ++g is _____.
    a. 4
    b. 5
    c. 6
    d. 7

11. If h = 9, then the value of the expression h++ is _____.
    a. 8
    b. 9
    c. 10
    d. 11

12. If j = 5 and k = 6, then the value of j++ == k is _____.
    a. 5
    b. 6
    c. true
    d. false

section C

13. You must always include _____ in a for loop's parentheses.
    a. two semicolons
    b. three semicolons
    c. two commas
    d. three commas

14. The statement for(a = 0; a < 5; ++a) System.out.print(a + " ");
    prints _____.
    a. 0 0 0 0 0
    b. 0 1 2 3 4
    c. 0 1 2 3 4 5
    d. nothing

15. The statement for(b = 1; b > 3; ++b) System.out.print(b + " ");
    prints _____.
    a. 1 1 1
    b. 1 2 3
    c. 1 2 3 4
    d. nothing

16. What does the following statement print?

    ```
    for(f = 1, g = 4; f < g; ++f,--g)
    System.out.print(f + " " + g + " ");
    ```

    a. 1 4 2 5 3 6 4 7...
    b. 1 4 2 3 3 2
    c. 1 4 2 3
    d. nothing

17. The loop that performs its conditional check at the bottom of the loop is a _____ loop.
    a. while
    b. do...while
    c. for
    d. for...while

18. What does this program segment print?

    ```
    d = 0;
    do
    {
     System.out.print(d + " ");
     d++;
    } while d < 2;
    ```

    a. 0
    b. 0 1
    c. 0 1 2
    d. nothing

19. What does this program segment print?

```
for(f = 0; f < 3; ++f)
  for(g = 0; g < 2; ++g)
    System.out.print(f + " " + g + " " );
```

a. 0 0 0 1 1 0 1 2 0 2 1
b. 0 1 0 2 0 3 1 1 1 2 1 3
c. 0 1 0 2 1 1 1 2
d. 0 0 0 1 0 2 1 0 1 1 1 2 2 0 2 1 2 2

20. What does this program segment print?

```
for(m = 0; m < 4; ++m);
  for(n = 0; n < 2; ++n);
    System.out.print(m + " " + n + " ");
```

a. 0 0 0 1 1 0 1 1 2 0 2 1 3 0 3 1
b. 0 1 0 2 1 1 1 2 2 1 2 2
c. 4 2
d. 3 1

EXERCISES

Each of the following exercises describes a program that you *could* write without using a loop—for example, you could alternatively write each program with a series of print statements. However, the purpose of these exercises is for you to practice the looping concepts learned in the chapter. For the following exercises, save each project that you create in the Chapter.05 folder on your Student Disk.

1. Create a console application project named EvenNums that prints all even numbers from 2 to 100 inclusive.

2. Create a console application project named ABCInput that asks a user to type A, B, C, or Q. When the user types Q, the program ends. When the user types A, B, or C, the program displays the message "Good job!" and then asks for another input. When the user types anything else, issue an error message and then ask for another input.

3. Create a console application project named TableOfSquares that prints every integer value from 1 to 20 along with its squared value.

4. Create a console application project named Sum50 that sums the integers from 1 to 50.

5. Create a console application project named EverySum that shows the sum of 1 to *n* for every *n* from 1 to 50. That is, the program prints 1, 3 (the sum of 1 and 2), 6 (the sum of 1, 2, and 3), and so on.

section C

6. Create a console application project named Perfect that prints every perfect number from 1 through 1,000. A number is perfect if it equals the sum of all the numbers that divide evenly into it. For example, 6 is perfect because 1, 2, and 3 divide evenly into it and their sum is 6.

7. Create a console application project named Investment that calculates the amount of money earned on an investment that earns 12 percent interest. Prompt the user to choose the investment amount from one menu and the number of years for the investment from a second menu. Display the total amount (balance) for each year of the investment. Use a loop instruction to calculate the balance for each year. Use the formula amount = investment * (1 + interest) raised to a power equal to the year (year 1, year 2, and so on) to calculate the balance.

8. Create a console application project named Quiz that creates a quiz that contains questions about a hobby, popular music, astronomy, or any other personal interest. After the user selects a topic, display a series of questions. The user should answer the questions with one character for multiple choice, true/false, or yes/no. If the user responds to a question correctly, display an appropriate message. If the user responds to a question incorrectly, display an appropriate response and the correct answer. At the end of the quiz, display the number of correct answers.

9. Create a console application project named Survey that displays a series of survey questions, with one-character answers. At the end of the survey, ask the user whether he or she wants to enter another set of responses. If the user responds no, then display the results of the survey for each question. Enter several sets of responses to test the program.

10. Each of the following files in the Chapter.05 folder on your Student Disk has syntax and/or logical errors. Add the files to a new project called FixDebug. Save the FixDebug project under the Chapter.05 folder on your Student Disk. In each case, fix the problem and run each file as a console application using JVIEW.

    a. DebugFive1.java
    b. DebugFive2.java
    c. DebugFive3.java
    d. DebugFive4.java

CHAPTER 6

Arrays and Strings

case ▶ "I've learned how to create objects and how to use decisions and loops to perform a variety of tasks with those objects," you say as you meet with Lynn Greenbrier, your mentor at Event Handlers Incorporated. "Still, it seems as though I'm doing a lot of work. If I need to check a variable's value against 20 possibilities, it takes me 20 `if` statements or a long `switch` statement to get the job done. And it would be great if I could alphabetize or sort the data in variables."

"I think what you're looking for," Lynn says, "is how to use the power of arrays. Do you have any other concerns?"

"Well, I can write interactive programs that accept a character, but I'd really like to let users enter words or numbers into programs."

"You need to learn about the array's close cousin, the String," Lynn says. "The wide variety of String methods provided with the Java programming language will help you use words and phrases efficiently. You'll even be able to let your users input numbers."

Previewing a Program That Uses Arrays and Strings

The Chap6Events program demonstrates a variety of procedures that rely on arrays or Strings for efficient execution. You will answer questions when prompted, and even play a game.

> ### To preview the Chap6Events program:
> **1** If necessary, start Visual J++. Open the **Chap6Events** project from the Chap6Events folder in the Chapter.06 folder on your Student Disk, then open the **Chap6Event.java** file in the Text Editor window and examine the code. This program is a simple Event class similar to one you created in Chapter 5.
>
> **2** Open the **Chap6Events.java** file in the Text Editor window and examine the code. This program is divided into three parts to demonstrate three of the major concepts you will learn about in this chapter. In the first part of the program, you enter codes for five upcoming events to be handled by Event Handlers Incorporated. The program stores all five events and displays them for you. The program will prompt you for Event types. The program prompts you to enter a C, P, or N for each of the five events. You can enter any other character, but you must enter five valid characters (C, P, or N) before the program will proceed. After you enter five valid characters, you will see a summary of the five events you selected. The second part of the program will prompt you for the number of guests at your event. If you enter a value over 100, you will see a message regarding a surcharge. The third part of the program will invite you to play a game similar to Hangman, in which you guess the motto of Event Handlers Incorporated.
>
> **3** Set the project properties to run the **Chap6Events** file as a console application, build the project, and then execute the program by typing `jview Chap6Events` at the command line. Test the program by following the on-screen directions; you can press Ctrl+C to stop the program at any time.

In this chapter, you will write programs that are similar to the three parts of this program.

SECTION A
objectives

In this section you will learn how to
- Declare an array
- Initialize an array
- Use subscripts with an array
- Declare an array of objects
- Search an array
- Pass an array to a method
- Use the length field

Arrays

Declaring an Array

While completing the first five chapters in this text, you stored values in variables. In the early sections, you simply stored a value and used it. In Chapter 5, you created loops that allowed you to "recycle" variables; that is, after creating a variable, you can assign a value, use the value, and then in successive cycles through the loop, reuse the variable as it holds different values.

There are times, however, when storing just one value in memory at a time does not fill your needs. For example, a sales manager who supervises 20 employees might want to determine whether each employee has produced sales above or below the average amount. When you enter the first employee's sales figure into a program, you can't determine whether it is above or below average, because you don't know what the average is until you have all 20 figures. Unfortunately, if you assign 20 sales figures to the same variable, when you assign the figure for the second employee, it replaces the figure for the first employee.

A possible solution is to create 20 separate employee sales variables, each with a unique name, so you can store all the sales until you can determine an average. A drawback to this method is that if you have 20 different variable names to be assigned values, then you need 20 separate assignment statements. If you have 20 different variable names, then the statement that calculates total sales is going to be something unwieldy like `total = firstAmt + secondAmt + thirdAmt + ...` and so on. This method might work for 20 salespeople, but what if you have 10,000 salespeople?

The best solution is to create an array. An **array** is a list of data items that all have the same type and the same name. You declare an array variable in the same way you declare any scalar variable, but you insert a pair of square brackets after the type. For example, to declare an array of double values to hold sales figures for salespeople, you write `double[] salesFigure;`.

> **tip**
>
> You also can declare an array variable by placing the square brackets after the array name, as in `double salesFigure[];`. This format is familiar to C and C++ programmers, but the preferred format among Java programmers is to place the brackets following the variable type and before the variable name, as in `double[] salesFigure;`.

After you create an array variable, you still need to create the actual array. You use the same procedure to create an array as you use to create an object. Recall that when you create a class named Employee, you can declare an Employee object with a declaration such as `Employee oneWorker;`, but that declaration does not actually create the oneWorker object. You create the oneWorker object when you use the keyword new and the constructor method, as in `oneWorker = new Employee();`. Similarly, declaring an array and actually reserving memory space for it are two distinct processes. To reserve memory locations for 20 salesFigure objects, you declare the array variable with `double[] salesFigure;`, and then you create the array with `salesFigure = new double[20];`. Just as with objects, you also can declare and create an array in one statement with `double[] salesFigure = new double[20];`.

> **tip**
>
> Some other languages, such as COBOL, BASIC, and Visual Basic, use parentheses rather than brackets to refer to individual array elements. By using brackets, the creators of Java made it easier for you to distinguish arrays from methods.

The statement `double[] salesFigure = new double[20];` reserves 20 memory locations for 20 salesFigures. You can distinguish each salesFigure from the others with a subscript. A **subscript** is an integer contained within square brackets that indicates one of an array's variables, or **elements**. In the Java programming language, any array's elements are numbered beginning with zero, so you can legally use any subscript from zero through 19 when working with an array that has 20 elements. In other words, the first salesFigure array element is `salesFigure[0]` and the last salesFigure element is `salesFigure[19]`.

It is a common mistake to forget that the first element in an array is element zero, especially if you know another programming language in which the first array element is element one. Making this mistake means you will be "off by one" in your use of any array.

> **tip**
>
> To remember that array elements begin with element zero, it might be helpful to think of the first array element as being "zero elements away from" the beginning of the array, the second element as being "one element away from" the beginning of the array, and so on.

When you work with any individual array element, you treat it no differently than you would treat a single variable of the same type. For example, to assign a value to the first salesFigure in an array, you use a simple assignment statement, such as `salesFigure[0] = 2100.00;`. To print the last salesFigure in an array of 20, you write `System.out.println(salesFigure[19]);`.

Next, you will create a small array to see how arrays are used. The array will hold salaries for four categories of employees.

To create a program that uses an array:

1. Create a new console application project named **DemoArray**. Save the **DemoArray** project folder in the Chapter.06 folder on your Student Disk.
2. Rename the default Class1.java file as **DemoArray.java**, then open the file in the Text Editor window.
3. Replace the Class1 class name in the `public class Class1` line with **DemoArray**.
4. Replace the `// TODO: Add initialization code here` comment with `double[] salary = new double[4];`
5. One by one, assign four values to the four salary array elements by typing the following:

```
salary[0] = 5.25;
salary[1] = 6.55;
salary[2] = 10.25;
salary[3] = 16.85;
```

6. To confirm that the four values have been assigned, print the salaries, one by one, using the following code:

```
System.out.println("Salaries one by one are:");
System.out.println(salary[0]);
System.out.println(salary[1]);
System.out.println(salary[2]);
System.out.println(salary[3]);
```

7. Set the project properties to run the DemoArray file as a console application, then build the project. If necessary, correct any syntax errors and rebuild. Execute the program by typing **jview DemoArray** at the command line. The program's output appears in Figure 6-1.

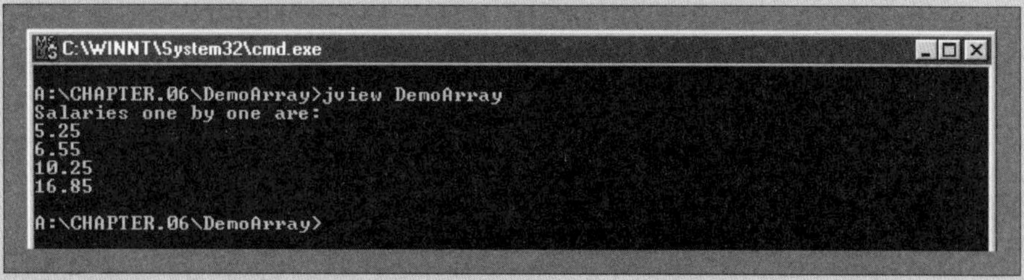

```
C:\WINNT\System32\cmd.exe
A:\CHAPTER.06\DemoArray>jview DemoArray
Salaries one by one are:
5.25
6.55
10.25
16.85
A:\CHAPTER.06\DemoArray>
```

Figure 6-1: Output of the DemoArray program

Initializing an Array

A variable that has a primitive type, such as int, holds a value. A variable with a reference type, such as an array, holds a memory address where a value is stored. Recall from Chapters 2 and 3 that primitive types, such as int, are named memory locations that you access directly. In contrast, reference types, such as an array, *represent* memory locations that the compiler accesses.

Array names actually represent computer memory addresses; that is, they are references, as are all Java objects. When you declare an array name, no computer memory address is assigned to it. Instead, the array variable name has the special value **null**, or Unicode value \u0000. When you declare `int[] someNums;`, the variable someNums has a value of `null`.

When you define someNums as `int someNums = new int[10];`, then someNums has an actual memory address value. Each element of someNums has a value of zero because someNums is a numeric array. By default, character array elements are assigned \u0000. Boolean array elements are automatically assigned `false`.

You already know how to assign a different value to a single element of an array, as in `someNums[0] = 46;`. You also can assign nondefault values to array elements upon creation. To **initialize** an array, you use a list of values, separated by commas and enclosed within curly brackets. For example, if you want to create an array named tenMult and store the first six multiples of 10 within the array, you can declare `int tenMult[] = {10, 20, 30, 40, 50, 60};`. When you initialize an array by giving it values upon creation, you do not give the array a size—the size will be assigned based on the number of values you place in the initializing list. Also, when you initialize an array, you do not need to use the keyword `new`; instead, new memory is assigned based on the length of the list of provided values.

> In Java, you usually do not use a semicolon after a closing curly bracket, for example, at the end of a method body. However, every statement in Java requires a semicolon, and an array initialization is a statement. Do not forget to type the semicolon after the closing bracket at the end of an array's initialization list.

Next you will alter your DemoArray program to initialize the array of doubles, rather than declaring it and assigning values later.

To initialize an array of doubles:

1   Return to the DemoArray.java file in the Text Editor window, delete the statement that declares the array of four doubles named salary (`double[] salary = new double[4];`), and then replace it with the following initialization statement: `double[] salary = {5.25, 6.55, 10.25, 16.85};`

2 Delete the four statements that individually assign the values to the array (`salary[0] = 5.25; salary[1] = 6.55; salary[2] = 10.25; salary[3] = 16.85;`).

3 Rebuild and test the program. The output is the same as Figure 6-1.

Using Subscripts with an Array

If you treat each array element as an individual entity, then there isn't much of an advantage to declaring an array over declaring individual scalar variables. The power of arrays becomes apparent when you begin to use subscripts that are variables rather than subscripts that are constant values.

For example, when you declare an array of five integers, such as `int[] valArray = {2, 14, 35, 67, 85};`, you often want to perform the same operation on each array element. To increase each array element by three, for example, you can write the following:

```
valArray[0] += 3;
valArray[1] += 3;
valArray[2] += 3;
valArray[3] += 3;
valArray[4] += 3;
```

With five array elements, this task is manageable. However, you can shorten the task by using a variable as the subscript. Then you can use a loop to perform arithmetic on each array element in the array. For example:

```
for(sub = 0; sub < 5; ++sub)
        valArray[sub] += 3;
```

The variable sub is set to zero, and then it is compared to five. Because it is less than five, the loop executes and three is added to valArray[0]. Then the variable sub is incremented and it becomes one, which is still less than five, so when the loop executes again, valArray[1] is increased by three, and so on. A process that took five statements now takes only one. Additionally, if the array had 100 elements, the first method of increasing the array values by three would result in 95 additional statements. The only change required in the `for` loop would be to compare sub to 100 instead of to five.

Next you will modify the DemoArray program to use a `for` loop with the array.

To use a `for` loop with the array in DemoArray:

1. Return to the DemoArray.java file in the Text Editor window, and then delete the four println() statements that print the four array values and replace them with the following `for` loop:

```
for(int x = 0; x < 4; ++x)
        System.out.println(salary[x]);
```

2. Rebuild and run the program. Again, the output is the same as Figure 6-1.

Declaring an Array of Objects

Just as you can declare arrays of integers or doubles, you can declare arrays that hold elements of any type, including objects. For example, assume you created the Employee class shown in Figure 6-2. This class has two data fields (empNum and empSalary), a constructor, and a get method for each field.

```
public class Employee
{
        private int empNum;
        private double empSalary;
        Employee(int num, double sal)
        {
                empNum = num;
                empSalary = sal;
        }
        public int getEmpNum()
        {
                return empNum;
        }
        public double getSalary()
        {
                return empSalary;
        }
}
```

Figure 6-2: Simple Employee class

Of course, you can create separate Employee objects with unique names, such as `Employee painter, electrician, plumber;`, but for many programs it is far more convenient to create an array of Employees. An array named emp that holds seven Employees is defined as `Employee[] emp = new Employee[7];`. This statement reserves enough computer memory for seven Employee objects named emp[0] through emp[6]. However, it does not actually construct those Employees; instead, you must call the seven individual constructors. According to the class definition shown in Figure 6-2, the Employee constructor requires two arguments: an employee number and a salary. If you want to number your Employees 101, 102, 103, and so on, and start each Employee at a salary of $5.35, then the loop that constructs seven Employee objects is as follows:

```
for(x = 0; x < 7; ++x)
      emp[x] = new Employee(101 + x, 5.35);
```

As x varies from 0 through 6, each of the seven emp objects is constructed with an employee number that is 101 more than x, and each of the seven emp objects holds the same salary of 5.35.

To use a method that belongs to an object that is part of an array, you insert the appropriate subscript notation after the array name and before the dot that precedes the method name. For example, to print data for seven Employees stored in the emp array, you can write the following:

```
for(x = 0; x < 7; ++x)
      System.out.println
         (emp[x].getEmpNum()+ " " + emp[x].getSalary());
```

Pay attention to the syntax of the Employee objects' method calls, such as `emp[x].getEmpNum()`. Although you might be tempted to place the subscript at the end of the expression after the method name as in `emp.getEmpNum[x]`, you cannot do so—the values in x (0 through 6) refer to a particular emp, and each emp has access to a single getEmpNum() method. The placement of the bracketed subscript following emp means the method "belongs" to a particular emp.

Next you will create an array of Event objects for Event Handlers Incorporated.

To create an array of Event objects:

1 Create a new console application project named **EventArray**. Save the **EventArray** project folder in the Chapter.06 folder on your Student Disk.

2 Add the **Event.java** file, contained in the Chapter.06 folder on your Student Disk, to the EventArray project by selecting **Add Item** from the **Project** menu. This is the same file that you created in Chapter 5. Examine the code so that you recall that the class contains two data fields: a character representing the type of event, and a double representing the minimum that is charged for the event. The constructor requires values for the two data fields. The class also contains methods to get the field values.

3 Rename the default Class1.java file as **EventArray.java**, then open the file in the Text Editor window.

4 Replace the Class1 class name in the `public class Class1` line with **EventArray**.

5 Replace the `// TODO: Add initialization code here` comment with the following code to declare an array of five Event objects. You also will declare an integer that can be used as a subscript.

```
Event[] someEvents = new Event[5];
int x;
```

6 Enter the following for loop that calls the Event constructor five times, making each Event type 'X' with a minimum charge of 0.0:

```
for(x = 0; x < 5; ++x)
      someEvents[x] = new Event('X',0.0);
```

7 To confirm that the Event objects have been created, print their values by typing the following:

```
for(x = 0; x < 5; ++x)
    System.out.println(someEvents[x].getEventType() +
       "  " + someEvents[x].getEventMinRate());
```

8 Set the project properties to run the **EventArray** file as a console application, build the project, and then execute the program by typing `jview EventArray` at the command line. Figure 6-3 shows the program's output.

Figure 6-3: Output of the EventArray program

An array of five Event objects—each of which has the same event type and fee—is not very interesting or useful. Next you will modify the EventArray program so that it creates five events interactively, with each event possessing unique properties.

Arrays and Strings

To create an interactive EventArray program:

1 Return to the **EventArray.java** file in the Text Editor window, position the insertion point to the right of the opening curly bracket of the EventArray class, press the **Enter** key, and then type the following statements to declare three constants for the corporate, private, and nonprofit event rates:

```
static final double CORP_RATE = 75.99;
static final double PRI_RATE = 47.99;
static final double NON_PROF_RATE = 40.99;
```

2 The program will accept keyboard input, so position the insertion point to the right of the main() method header, and then type **throws Exception**.

3 Just before the `for` statement that constructs five events, add the following two new variables that will hold an event type and rate and initialize them with dummy values:

```
char event = 'Z';
double rate = 0;
```

4 Within the `for` loop, remove the line that constructs events with type 'X' and fee 0.0 (someEvents[x] = new Event('X',0.0);), and then replace it with the following block that prompts the user for one of three event types and constructs an appropriate event based on the value entered:

```
{
    System.out.println
        ("Enter event type for Event " + (x + 1));
    System.out.println("C for corporate");
    System.out.println("P for private");
    System.out.println("N for nonprofit");
    event = (char)System.in.read();
    System.in.read(); System.in.read();
        // Absorbs Enter key
    if(event == 'C')
        rate = CORP_RATE;
    else if(event == 'P')
        rate = PRI_RATE;
    else rate = NON_PROF_RATE;
    someEvents[x] = new Event(event, rate);
}
```

5 Change the body of the last `for` loop as follows so it prints an event number along with the event information:

```
System.out.println("Event " + (x + 1) + " " +
        someEvents[x].getEventType()+ " " +
        someEvents[x].getEventMinRate());
```

> **tip**
> At this point, when you run the program, if you enter an event type that is not C or P, the program will assume that the rate is the nonprofit rate by default.

6 Rebuild and run the program several times. Confirm that no matter what combination of C, P, and N you use for data entry, the list of events is stored and displayed correctly.

Searching an Array for an Exact Match

When you want to determine whether some variable holds one of many valid values, one option is to use a series of `if` statements to compare the variable to a series of valid values. For example, suppose that a company manufactures 10 items. When a customer places an order for an item, you need to determine whether the item number on the order form is valid. If valid item numbers are sequential, such as 101 through 110, then the following simple `if` statement that uses a logical AND can verify the order number and set a boolean field to `true`: `if(itemOrdered >= 101 && itemOrdered < = 110) validItem = true;`. If the valid item numbers are nonsequential, however—for example, 101, 108, 201, 213, 266, 304, and so on—you must code the following deeply nested `if` statement or a lengthy OR comparison to determine the validity of an item number:

```
if(itemOrdered == 101)
      validItem = true;
else if(itemOrdered == 108)
      validItem = true;
else if(itemOrdered == 201)
      validItem = true;
// and so on
```

Instead of entering a long series of `if` statements, a more efficient solution is to compare the itemOrdered variable to a list of values in an array. You can initialize the array with the valid values with the following statement:

```
int[] validValues = {101, 108, 201, 213, 266,
                304, 311, 409, 411, 412};
```

Then, you can use a `for` statement to loop through the array, and set a boolean variable to `true` when a match is found:

```
for(int x = 0; x < 10; ++x)
{
      if(itemOrdered == validValues[x])
            validItem=true;
}
```

This simple `for` loop replaces the long series of `if` statements. What's more, if a company carries 1,000 items instead of 10, then the only part of the `for` statement that changes is the comparison in the middle. As an added bonus, if you set up another parallel array with the same number of elements and corresponding data, you can use the same subscript to access additional information. For example, if the 10 items your company carries have 10 different prices, then you can set up any array to hold those prices: `double[] prices = {0.89, 1.23, 3.50, 0.69...};` and so on. The prices must appear in the same order as their corresponding item numbers in the validValues array. Now the same `for` loop that finds the valid item number also finds the price, as shown in Figure 6-4. In other words, if the item number is found in the second position in the validValues array, then you can find the correct price in the second position in the prices array.

tip

If you initialize parallel arrays, it is convenient to use spacing so that the values that correspond to each other align visually on the screen or printed page.

```
int[] validValues = {101,  108,  201,  213,  266,
                     304,  311,  409,  411,  412};
     double[] prices = {0.89, 1.23, 3.50, 0.69, 5.79,
                        3.19, 0.99, 0.89, 1.26, 8.00};
     for(int x = 0; x < 10; ++x)
{
     if(itemOrdered == validValues[x])
     {
          validItem = true;
          itemPrice = prices[x];
     }
```

Figure 6-4: Accessing information in parallel arrays

tip

In an array with many possible matches, it is most efficient to place the more common items first, so they are matched right away. For example, if item 311 is the most often ordered item, place 311 first in the validValues array, and its price ($0.99) first in the prices array.

Within the code shown in Figure 6-4, you compare every itemOrdered with each of the 10 validValues. Even when an itemOrdered is equivalent to the first value in the validValues array (101), you always make nine additional cycles through the array. On each of these nine additional cycles, the comparison between itemOrdered and validValues[x] is always `false`. As soon as a match for an itemOrdered is found, it is most efficient to break out of the `for` loop early. An easy way to accomplish this is to set x to a high value within the block of statements executed when there is a match. Then, after a match, the `for` loop will not execute again because the limiting comparison (x < 10) will have been surpassed. Figure 6-5 shows this program.

```
for(x = 0; x < 10; ++x)
{
        if(itemOrdered == validValues[x])
    {
        validItem = true;
        itemPrice = prices[x];
        x = 10;    // Break out of loop when you find a match
    }
}
```

Figure 6-5: Breaking out of a `for` loop early

Instead of using the statement that sets *x* to 10 when a match is found, you could place a `break;` statement within the loop in the statement's place.

Some programmers disapprove of breaking out of a `for` loop early, whether you do it by setting a variable's value or by using a `break;` statement. If you (or your instructor) agree with this philosophy, then use a method that uses a `while` statement as described next.

As an alternative, you can choose to forgo the `for` loop entirely, and use a `while` loop to search for a match. Using this approach, you set a subscript to zero, and while itemOrdered is not equal to a value in the array, you increase the subscript and keep looking. You search only while the subscript remains lower than the number of elements in the array. If the subscript increases to 10, then you never found a match in the 10-element array. If the loop ends before the subscript reaches 10, then you found a match and can assign the correct price to the itemPrice variable. Figure 6-6 shows this programming approach.

Arrays and Strings

```
x = 0;
while(x < 10 && itemOrdered != validValues[x])
      ++x;
if(x != 10)
{
      validItem = true;
      itemPrice = prices[x];
}
```

Figure 6-6: Searching with a `while` loop

Next, you will delete the `if` statements that determine a price for each event at Event Handlers Incorporated and replace them with an array search.

To determine event pricing using parallel arrays:

1 Return to the **EventArray.java** file in the Text Editor window, position the insertion point to the right of the statement that declares the rate variable (`double rate = 0;`), and then press the **Enter** key to start a new line of text. Then type the following character array to hold the codes for the three allowed event types:
`char[] eventCode ={'C', 'P', 'N'};`

> Notice that you can use symbolic constants as well as literal constants as array elements. If you had reason to, you could even combine the two types of constants within the same array. You can even use variable names as array elements. Don't forget, however, that all elements within a single array must have the same type.

2 Press the **Enter** key, and then on the next line, add the following code to create a double array to hold the rates charged for the three event types:
`double[] eventRate = {CORP_RATE, PRI_RATE, NON_PROF_RATE};`

3 Remove the five lines of code (beginning with `if(event == 'C')`...) that constitute the `if...else` structure that determines the event rate. This `if` structure is no longer needed. Replace it with the following `for` loop that searches through the eventCode array, and, upon finding a match, selects a price from the eventRate array:

```
for(int i = 0; i < 3; ++i)
{
      if(event == eventCode[i])
            rate = eventRate[i];
}
```

4   Rebuild and run the program. Confirm that, just as before, no matter what combination of C, P, and N you use for data entry, the list of events is stored and displayed correctly.

When you run the program, if you enter an invalid event code, an Event object is created and an incorrect rate is assigned to the Event object. Now that you have an array of valid event codes, it is a simple matter to disallow any invalid event codes (those other than C, P, or N).

To force all five Event objects to contain valid codes and rates:

1   Within the EventArray.java program, position the insertion point to the right of the `double rate = 0;` variable declaration, press the **Enter** key to start a new line, and then enter the following code to create a boolean variable named codeIsValid: `boolean codeIsValid;`.

2   Position the insertion point at the beginning of the `for` statement that begins the search through the eventCode array (`for(int i = 0; ...`), and then press the **Enter** key to start a new line. Just before the `for` loop, you need to ensure that the codeIsValid variable is set to `false` by typing `codeIsValid = false;`.

3   Within the `for` loop, change the `if` statement that checks the eventCode array as follows so that if event is equivalent to one of the eventCodes, then a block of two statements will execute—besides setting the rate, the codeIsValid variable is set to `true`:

```
if(event == eventCode[i])
{
    rate = eventRate[i];
    codeIsValid = true;
}
```

You can make the program more efficient by breaking out of the `for` loop early when an event matches an eventCode array element. Set the loop control variable i to a high value when a match is found.

4   Place the insertion point to the right of `codeIsValid = true;`, and then press the **Enter** key to start a new line. Type `i = 3;` on the new line.

5   Position the insertion point at the beginning of the statement that constructs one of the five someEvents objects (`someEvents[x] = new Event(event, rate);`). Press the **Enter** key to start a new line and insert the following condition so the object is created only if the code is valid: `if(codeIsValid)`. To show clearly that it depends on the `if`, indent the line containing `someEvents[x] = new Event(event, rate);`.

6 Position the insertion point just after `someEvents[x] = new Event(event, rate);`, and then press the **Enter** key to start a new line. Enter the following `else` clause that reduces x:

```
else
   --x;
```

Now, for example, if a code is not valid on the third pass through the loop when x is 2, x will be decremented to 1. At the top of the `for` loop (in the third section within the parentheses), x is increased to 2 again for the next pass through the `for` loop. So if the user enters a valid code during this fourth execution of the loop, x still will be 2, and an object will be created correctly at someEvent[2].

7 Rebuild and run the program. Enter as many valid and invalid codes as you like. After five of the codes you enter are identified as valid, the five constructed objects will display.

Searching an Array for a Range Match

Searching an array for an exact match is not always practical. For example, suppose your company gives customer discounts based on quantity of items ordered. Perhaps no discount is given for any order of fewer than a dozen items, but there are increasing discounts available for orders of increasing quantities, as shown in Figure 6-7.

1 to 12	none
13 to 49	10%
50 to 99	14%
100 to 199	18%
200 or more	20%

Figure 6-7: Discount table for an imaginary company

One awkward option is to create a single array to store the discount rates. You could use a variable named numOfItems as a subscript to the array, but the array would need hundreds of entries—for example, `double[] discount = {0, 0, 0, 0, 0, 0, 0, 0, 0, 0, 0, 0, 0, .10, .10, .10 ...};`, and so on. When numOfItems is 3, for example, then discount[numOfItems] or discount[3] is 0. When numOfItems is 14, then discount[numOfItems] or discount[14] is .10. Because a customer might order thousands of items, the array would need to be ridiculously large.

tip

Notice that there are 13 zeros listed in discount array in the preceding example. The first array element has a zero subscript (and a zero discount for zero items). The next 12 discounts (1 through 12 items) are also discounts of zero.

A better option is to create parallel arrays. One array will hold the five discount rates, and the other array will hold five discount range limits. The Total Quantity Ordered column in Figure 6-7 shows five ranges. If you use only the first figure in each range, you can create an array that holds five low limits: `int[ ] discountRangeLimit = {1, 13, 50, 100, 200};`. A parallel array will hold the five discount rates: `double[ ] discount = {0, .10, .14, .18, .20};`. Then, starting at the last discountRangeLimit array element, for any numOfItems greater than or equal to discountRangeLimit[4], the appropriate discount is discount[4]. In other words, for any numOfItems less than discountRangeLimit[4], you should decrement the subscript and look in a lower range. Figure 6-8 shows the code.

```
int[ ] discountRangeLimit = {1, 13, 50, 100, 200};
double[ ] discount =        {0, .10, .14, .18, .20};
double customerDiscount;
int sub = 4;
while(sub >= 0 && numOfItems < discountRangeLimit[sub])
     --sub;
customerDiscount = discount[sub];
```

Figure 6-8: Searching an array of ranges

tip

Making sure that the subscript does not fall below zero in the statement `while(sub >= 0 && numOfItems < discountRangeLimit[sub])` is a good programming practice. Although this would happen only if numOfItems held a negative value, such a check will prevent a program error.

Passing Arrays to Methods

You already have seen that you can use any individual array element in the same manner as you would use any single variable of the same type. That is, if you declare an integer array as `int[ ] someNums = new int[12];`, then you can subsequently print someNums[0] or add one to someNums[1], just as you would for any integer. Similarly, you can pass a single array element to a method in exactly the same manner as you would pass a variable.

Examine the program shown in Figure 6-9. The program creates an array of four integers and prints them. Then the program calls a method, methodGetsOneInt(), four times, passing each element in turn. The method prints the number, changes the number to 999, and then prints the number again. Finally, back in main(), the four numbers are printed again.

```java
public class PassArrayElement
{
    public static void main(String[] args)
    {
        int[] someNums = {5, 10, 15, 20};
        int x;
        for(x = 0; x < 4; ++x)
           System.out.println("In main " + someNums[x]);
        for(x = 0; x < 4; ++x)
           methodGetsOneInt(someNums[x]);
        for(x = 0; x < 4; ++x)
           System.out.println("At end of main " + someNums[x]);
    }
    public static void methodGetsOneInt(int one)
    {
        System.out.println("In methodGetsOneInt " + one);
        one = 999;
        System.out.println("After change " + one);
    }
}
```

Figure 6-9: PassArrayElement program

Figure 6-10 shows the program output.

```
A:\CHAPTER.06\PassArrayElement>jview PassArrayElement
In main 5
In main 10
In main 15
In main 20
In methodGetsOneInt 5
After change 999
In methodGetsOneInt 10
After change 999
In methodGetsOneInt 15
After change 999
In methodGetsOneInt 20
After change 999
At end of main 5
At end of main 10
At end of main 15
At end of main 20

A:\CHAPTER.06\PassArrayElement>
```

Figure 6-10: Output of the PassArrayElement program

As you can see from Figure 6-10, the four numbers that were changed in the methodGetsOneInt() method remain unchanged back in main(). The variable named one is local to the methodGetsOneInt() method, and any changes to variables passed into the method are not permanent and are not reflected in the array in the main() program. Each variable named one in the methodGetsOneInt() method holds only a copy of the array element passed into the method.

The outcome is quite different when you pass an entire array to a method. Arrays, like all objects, are passed by reference, which as you will recall from Chapter 4, means that the method receives the actual memory address of the array and has access to the actual values in the array elements. The program shown in Figure 6-11 creates an array of four integers. After the integers print, the entire array is passed to a method named methodGetsArray(). Within the method, the numbers print, which shows that they retain their values from main(), but then the value 888 is assigned to each number. Even though the methodGetsArray() method is a void method (meaning nothing is returned to the main() method), when the program prints the array for the second time within main(), all of the values have been changed to 888, as you can see in Figure 6-12. Because arrays are passed by reference, the methodGetsArray() method "knows" the address of the array declared in main(), and makes its changes directly to the original array that was declared in the main() method.

```
public class PassArray
{
public static void main(String[] args) throws Exception
        {
        int[] someNums = {5, 10, 15, 20};
                int x;
                for(x = 0; x < 4; ++x)
                System.out.println("In main " +
                                someNums[x]);
                methodGetsArray(someNums);
                for(x = 0; x < 4; ++x)
                System.out.println("At end of main " +
                                someNums[x]);
}
        public static void methodGetsArray(int[] arr)
        {
        for(int y = 0; y < 4; ++y)
                {
                System.out.println("In methodGetsArray " +
                                arr[y]);
                        arr[y] = 888;
                }
        }
}
```

Figure 6-11: PassArray program

```
C:\WINNT\System32\cmd.exe                                    _ □ ×

A:\CHAPTER.06\PassArray>jview PassArray
In main 5
In main 10
In main 15
In main 20
In methodGetsArray 5
In methodGetsArray 10
In methodGetsArray 15
In methodGetsArray 20
At end of main 888
At end of main 888
At end of main 888
At end of main 888

A:\CHAPTER.06\PassArray>_
```

Figure 6-12: Output of the PassArray program

Next you will add a new method to the Event object class type. Then you will add steps to the EventArray program so you can pass an array of Event objects to a method. This program will demonstrate that changes made within the method affect values in the array permanently.

To add a new method to the Event class:

1 In the EventArray project, open the **Event.java** file in the Text Editor window. This text file contains the class definition for Event objects.

2 Add a new setEventMinRate() method that you can use to alter an Event object's eventMinRate. Position the cursor to the left of the final closing curly bracket for the Event class, and then press the **Enter** key to start a new line before the closing bracket. Then enter the following setEventMinRate() method:

```
public void setEventMinRate(double rate)
{
    eventMinRate = rate;
}
```

3 Rebuild the project.

Next you will add a method call and a method to the EventArray file. The method will receive an array of Event objects and increase the rate for each event by $5.00.

To add a method call and a method to the EventArray program:

1 Return to the EventArray.java file in the Text Editor window, position the insertion point to the left of the closing curly bracket for the main() method in the EventArray class, and then press the **Enter** key to insert a new blank line just before the closing curly bracket.

2. Enter the following method call to a raiseRates() method, which will receive the someEvents array and raise each event's rate by $5.00:

   `raiseRates(someEvents);`

3. Press the **Enter** key. To demonstrate that the rates changed as a result of the raiseRates() method, add the following print loop on the new line:

   > If you do not want to type this statement, you simply can use the Text Editor window's copy and paste functions to copy the identical statement that already exists within the program.

   ```
   for(x = 0; x < 5; ++x)
       System.out.println("Event " + (x + 1) + " " +
           someEvents[x].getEventType()+"    " +
           someEvents[x].getEventMinRate());
   ```

4. Place the insertion point to the right of the main() method's closing curly bracket, and then press the **Enter** key to start a new blank line before the closing bracket for the EventArray program. Then enter the following raiseRates() method. The method loops through the array five times. With each iteration, it gets the array element's current rate, stores it in a temporary double variable, and adds $5.00 to the temporary variable. Then the temporary variable value is assigned back into the array object's rate with the setEventMinRate() method.

   ```
   private static void raiseRates(Event[ ] evnt)
   {
       double temp;
       for(int q = 0; q < 5; ++q)
       {
               temp = evnt[q].getEventMinRate();
               temp += 5;
               evnt[q].setEventMinRate(temp);
       }
   }
   ```

   > You can replace the three statements `temp = evnt[q].getEventMinRate();`, `temp += 5;`, and `evnt[q].setEventMinRate(temp);` with one statement: `evnt[q].setEventMinRate(evnt[q].getEventMinRate() + 5);`. If this method call within a method call is clear to you, feel free to use it.

5. Rebuild and run the program. After you answer the prompts to create five events, their old rates and the new increased rates should appear on-screen. Figure 6-13 shows a sample run.

```
C:\WINNT\System32\cmd.exe
P for private
N for non-profit
N
Enter event type for Event 4
C for corporate
P for private
N for non-profit
C
Enter event type for Event 5
C for corporate
P for private
N for non-profit
P
Event 1  C  75.99
Event 2  P  47.99
Event 3  N  40.99
Event 4  C  75.99
Event 5  P  47.99
Event 1  C  80.99
Event 2  P  52.99
Event 3  N  45.99
Event 4  C  80.99
Event 5  P  52.99
A:\CHAPTER.06\EventArray>
```

Figure 6-13: Sample output of the EventArray program with the raiseRates() method

Using the Array Length

Every array object that you create is automatically assigned a data field named length. The **length field** contains the number of elements in the array. For example, when you declare double[] salaries = new double[8];, the value 8 is assigned to the field salaries.length.

When you work with array elements, you have to ensure that the subscript you use remains in the range zero through length -1. To access all eight elements of a salaries array, for example, you can code the number 8 explicitly as in for(x = 0; x < 8; ++x)... If you modify your program to hold more or fewer array elements, you must remember to change every appropriate reference to the array size within the program. The Text Editor window has a Find and Replace command on the Edit menu that lets you change all the 8s, but you must be careful not to change any 8s that have nothing to do with the array. A better technique is to use salaries.length, as in for(x = 0; x < salaries.length; ++x)... That way, if you change the size of the salaries array, then the array always will use the correct maximum length.

Next, you will remove the explicit 5 you have used in each for loop within the EventArray program, and replace each with a reference to the length field.

To use the array length field:

1. Locate the first `for` statement in the main() method of the EventArray file. This loop constructs five Event objects. Delete the 5 in the `for` expression and then replace it with **someEvents.length**.
2. Locate the next `for` loop in the EventArray program, which checks the event codes entered by a user. Delete the 3 from the `for` loop and replace it with **eventCode.length**.
3. Locate the next `for` loop, which prints array values. Delete the 5 in the `for` loop and replace it with **someEvents.length**.
4. The last `for` loop in the main() method of the EventArray program prints the objects. Replace the 5 in this loop with **someEvents.length**.
5. Within the raiseRates() method, locate the `for` loop that raises the rate of each array element. Within the raiseRates() method, the array name is evnt. Replace the 5 in this `for` loop with **evnt.length**.
6. Rebuild and run the program. The execution of the program should be the same as it was before—five objects are created and three valid event codes are checked. This version also adds five dollars to each rate.

SUMMARY

- An array is a list of variables that all have the same type and same name. You declare an array variable by inserting a pair of square brackets after the type.

- Declaring an array and actually reserving memory space for it are two distinct processes. You use the keyword new to actually reserve memory locations for the array elements.

- A subscript is an integer contained within square brackets that indicates one of an array's variables, or elements. An array's elements are numbered beginning with zero.

- When you work with any individual array element, you treat it no differently than you would a single variable. Array names actually represent computer memory addresses—they are references, as are all Java objects.

- When you declare an array name it has the value null, or Unicode value \u0000.

- When you define an array using new, the array name takes on a memory address value.

- Each element of a numeric array is automatically set to zero, character array elements are assigned \u0000, and boolean array elements are automatically assigned the value false.

- To initialize an array, you can use a list of values that are separated by commas and enclosed within curly brackets. When you initialize an array by giving it values upon creation, you do not give the array a size; the size will be assigned based on the number of values you place in the initializing list.

section A

- The power of arrays becomes apparent when you begin to use subscripts that are variables rather than subscripts that are constant values.

- Just as you can declare arrays of integers or doubles, you can declare arrays of any type, including objects.

- You must explicitly call individual constructors for array objects.

- To use a method that belongs to an object that is part of an array, you insert the appropriate subscript notation after the array name and prior to the dot that precedes the method name.

- You can find exact matches or range matches for a variable by looping through an array. It is efficient to break out of the loop as soon as a match is found.

- You can pass a single array element to a method in exactly the same manner you would pass a variable. The array element is passed by value; that is, a copy is made.

- You can pass an array to a method. Arrays, like all objects, are passed by reference; the method has access to the actual values in the array elements.

- You can use an array's length field to determine the number of elements in an array.

QUESTIONS

1. A list of variables that all have the same type and same name is a(n) _____.
   a. register
   b. array
   c. list
   d. index

2. When you declare an array variable, you must insert _____ after the type.
   a. a pair of square brackets
   b. a pair of parentheses
   c. a pair of curly brackets
   d. the keyword `array`

3. You reserve memory locations for an array when you _____.
   a. declare the array name
   b. use the keyword `new`
   c. use the keyword `mem`
   d. explicitly store values within the array elements

4. The statement `int[] value = new int[34];` reserves memory for _____ integers.
   a. 0
   b. 33
   c. 34
   d. 35

5. An integer contained within square brackets that indicates one of an array's variables is a(n) _____.
   a. pointer
   b. parameter
   c. argument
   d. subscript

6. If you declare an array as `int[] num = new int[6];`, the first element of the array is _____.
   a. num[0]
   b. num[1]
   c. num[]
   d. impossible to tell

7. If you declare an array as `int[] num = new int[6];`, the last element of the array is _____.
   a. num[5]
   b. num[6]
   c. num[7]
   d. impossible to tell

8. Array names are _____.
   a. values
   b. functions
   c. references
   d. allusions

9. Unicode value \u0000 also is known as _____.
   a. nill
   b. void
   c. nada
   d. null

10. When you initialize an array by giving it values upon creation, you _____.
    a. do not give the array a size
    b. also must give the array a size
    c. must make all the values zero, blank, or `false`
    d. must make sure each value is different from the others

11. Assume an array is declared as `int[] num = new int[4];`. Which of the following statements correctly assigns the value 100 to each of the four array elements?
    a. `for(x = 0; x < 3; ++x) num[x] = 100;`
    b. `for(x = 0; x < 4; ++x) num[x] = 100;`
    c. `for(x = 1; x < 4; ++x) num[x] = 100;`
    d. `for(x = 1; x < 5; ++x) num[x] = 100;`

12. If a class named Student contains a method setID() that takes an integer argument, and you create an array of 20 Student objects named scholar, which of the following statements correctly assigns an ID number to the first Student scholar?
    a. `Student[0].setID(1234);`
    b. `scholar[0].setID(1234);`
    c. `Student.setID[0](1234);`
    d. `scholar.setID[0](1234);`

13. Assuming `char[] goodResponses = {'Y','y','N','n'};`, which of the following statements tests userEntry and sets the boolean variable goodChoice to true if userEntry is in the goodResponses list?
    a. `for(x = 0; x < 4; ++x) if(userEntry = goodResponses)`
       `goodChoice == true;`
    b. `for(x = 0; x < 4; ++x) if(userEntry[x] = goodResponses)`
       `goodChoice = true;`
    c. `for(x = 0; x < 4; ++x) if(userEntry = goodResponses[x])`
       `goodChoice == true;`
    d. `for(x = 0; x < 4; ++x) if(userEntry == goodResponses[x])`
       `goodChoice = true;`

14. Two arrays with the same number of elements and corresponding data are _____.
    a. competitive
    b. illegal
    c. identical
    d. parallel

15. If a test is graded so that a score of 90 or above is an A, 80 to 89 is a B, and so on, you can create a gradeLimit array: `int[] gradeLimit = {90, 80, 70, 60, 0};` and a grade array: `char[] grade = {'A', 'B', 'C', 'D', 'F'};`. Which of the following statements assigns the correct grade to a letterGrade variable based on the variable score?
    a. `for(x = 0; x < 4; ++x)`
       `if(score >= gradeLimit[x]) letterGrade = grade[x];`
    b. `for(x = 4; x >= 0; --x)`
       `if(score >= gradeLimit[x]) letterGrade = grade[x];`
    c. `for(x = 0; x < 4; ++x)`
       `if(score >= grade[x]) letterGrade = grade[x];`
    d. `for(x = 4; x >= 0; --x)`
       `if(score <= gradeLimit[x]) letterGrade = grade[x];`

16. When you pass an array element to a method, the method receives _____.
    a. a copy of the array
    b. the address of the array
    c. a copy of the value in the element
    d. the address of the element

17. Arrays are passed by _____.
    a. reference
    b. value
    c. referral
    d. copying

18. When you pass an array to a method, the method receives _____.
    a. a copy of the array
    b. a copy of the first element in the array
    c. the address of the array
    d. nothing

19. If you pass an array from a main() method to a method named changeIt(), and the method changes a value in the array, then _____.
    a. you receive an error message
    b. the original array element in main() changes
    c. the original element in main() remains unchanged
    d. the original element in main() changes only if you return a value from the method

EXERCISES

1. Write a program that can hold five integers in an array. Display the integers from first to last, and then display the integers from last to first.

2. Write a program that prompts the user to make a choice for a pizza size—S, M, L, or X—and then displays the price as $6.99, $8.99, $12.50, or $15.00 accordingly.

3. a. Create a console application project named Taxpayer. Data fields for the Taxpayer class include Social Security number (use an int for the type, and do not use dashes within the Social Security number) and yearly gross income. Methods include a constructor that requires values for both data fields, and two get methods that return each of the data field values. Write a program that declares an array of 10 Taxpayer objects. Set each Social Security number to 999999999 and each gross income to zero. Display the 10 Taxpayer objects.
   b. Modify your program so each Taxpayer has a successive Social Security number from 1 through 10, and gross incomes that range from $10,000 to $100,000, increasing by $10,000 for each successive Taxpayer.

4. Create an array that stores 20 prices, such as 2.34, 7.89, 1.34, and so on. Display the sum of all the prices. Display all values less than 5.00. Calculate the average of the prices, and display all values higher than the calculated average value.

5. a. Create a console application project named GradePoint that prompts a professor to input grades for five different courses for 10 students. Prompt the professor to enter one grade at a time using the prompts "Enter grades for student #1" and "Enter grade #1". Verify that the professor enters only A, B, C, D, or F. Use variables for student numbers (1 through 10) and grade numbers (1 through 5).
   b. Modify the GradePoint program so that it calculates the grade point average (GPA) for each student. A student receives four grade points for an A, three grade points for a B, two grade points for a C, one grade point for a D, and zero grade points for an F. Store the grades and points in parallel arrays. Search the arrays to determine the points for the grade. Store the GPA for each student in another array. (Hint: *Copy* the GPA for each student to a different array by initializing the new array with GPAs from the other array).
   c. Display the GPA scores from each of the two GPA arrays to verify that the GPAs were copied correctly. Identify which array the scores are from.

6. a. Create a console application project named Quiz that displays a multiple choice quiz of 10 questions with topics related to your favorite hobby. Each question has one correct answer and three possible answers. Verify that the user enters only A, B, or C as the answer. Store the correct answers in an array. Store the user's answers in a second array. If the user responds to a question correctly, display "Correct!"; otherwise display "The correct answer is" and the letter of the correct answer.
   b. Modify the Quiz class so that it displays the number of correct answers after the user answers 10 questions. Determine the score by comparing the two arrays.

7. a. Create a console application project named EnterNumbers that lets the user enter numbers (1 through 9) one at a time, and then prints the numbers that the user entered. Allow the user to enter up to 10 numbers. If the user tries to enter an 11th number, display a message that no more numbers can be entered.
   b. Change the EnterNumbers program so that it lets the user delete or modify a number. Include a menu that shows the options to enter, remove, modify, or display a number, or quit the program. Verify that a correct option is entered. When the user chooses the remove option, prompt the user to specify which number to remove. Verify that the user enters a valid number (1 through 9), and then change that number in the array to 0.
   c. Change the EnterNumbers number program so that when the user chooses the modify option, the program prompts the user to specify which number to modify. Verify that the user enters a valid number (1 through 9), ask for the new number, verify that the user enters a valid number, and then change the number in the array.

SECTION B
objectives

In this section you will learn how to
- Declare a String object
- Compare String values
- Use other String methods
- Convert Strings to numbers

Strings

Declaring Strings

You learned in Chapter 2 that a sequence of characters enclosed within double quotation marks is a literal string. You have used many literal strings, such as "First Java program," within println() statements. You also can create objects that hold a series of characters and have the type **String**.

> **tip**
>
> You also used String in main() method headers.

The class String is defined in java.lang.String, which automatically is imported into every program you write. You create a String object by using the keyword new and the String constructor method, just as you would create an object of any other type. For example, `String aGreeting = new String("Hello");` is a statement that defines an object named aGreeting, declares it to be of type String, and assigns an initial value of "Hello" to the String. Alternatively, you can declare a String containing "Hello" with `String aGreeting = "Hello";`.

After declaring a String, you can display it in a print() or println() statement, just as you would for any other variable, as in `System.out.println("The greeting is " + aGreeting);`.

Also, as with any other object, you can create an array of Strings. For example, you can store three company department names as `String[] deptName = {"Accounting", "Human Resources", "Sales"};`. You can access these department names like any other array object. For example, to print them, you can use the following code:

```
for(int a = 0; a < deptName.length; ++a)
        System.out.println(deptName[a]);
```

> **tip**
>
> Notice that `deptName.length` refers to the length of the array deptName (three elements), and not to the length of any of the String objects stored in the deptName array. Each String object has access to a length() method that returns the length of a String. For example, if deptName[0] is "Accounting", then `deptName[0].length()` is 10.

section B

Next, you will create two arrays to hold event types and manager names for Event Handlers Incorporated. Then, when a user enters an event type, the appropriate event type and manager name will display on the screen.

To add event types and manager names to the EventArray program:

1 Open the **EventArray** project from the Event Array folder in the Chapter.06 folder on your Student Disk, then open the **EventArray.java** file in the Text Editor window.

2 Position the insertion point after the opening curly bracket of the main() method, press the **Enter** key to start a new line, then add the array of event types by entering the following:

```
String[] eventType =
     {"Corporate", "Private", "Non-Profit"};
```

3 Press the **Enter** key to start a new line, and then add the following array of manager names:

```
String[] managerName =
     {"Dustin Britt", "Carmen Lindsey", "Robin Armenetti"};
```

4 Locate the `for` loop that determines whether the user entered a valid code. Place the insertion point after the statement `codeIsValid = true;` that appears within the `for` statement, and then press the **Enter** key to start a new line.

At this point in the program, the variable i indicates the position of a correct event type in the eventCode array. The correct event type is in the same relative position in the eventType array as the correct manager's name is within the managerName array. In other words, managerName[i] "goes with" eventCode[i].

5 Type the following statement that prints the event type and manager's name on the new line:

```
System.out.println("The manager for " + eventType[i]
     + " events is " + managerName[i]);
```

6 To simplify screen output, comment out the call to raiseRate() as well as the lines that print the raised rates. Type **//** at the beginning of each of these lines.

7 Rebuild and test the program. Your output should look like Figure 6-14.

```
Enter event type for Event 3
C for corporate
P for private
N for non-profit
N
The manager for Non-Profit events is Robin Armenetti
Enter event type for Event 4
C for corporate
P for private
N for non-profit
C
The manager for Corporate events is Dustin Britt
Enter event type for Event 5
C for corporate
P for private
N for non-profit
P
The manager for Private events is Carmen Lindsey
Event 1   C   75.99
Event 2   P   47.99
Event 3   N   40.99
Event 4   C   75.99
Event 5   P   47.99

A:\CHAPTER.06\EventArray>
```

Figure 6-14: Output of the EventArray program with event types and manager names

Comparing Strings

A String is an object, like an array. In many programming languages, you create a string by creating an array of characters. In the Java programming language, however, String is a class, and each created String is a class object. Like an array object, or any other object, a String variable name is actually a reference; that is, a String variable name actually refers to a location in memory rather than to a particular value.

The distinction is subtle, but when you declare a variable of a basic, primitive type, such as `int x = 10;`, the memory address where x is located holds the value 10. If you later assign a new value to x—for example, `x = 45;`—then the value 45 replaces the 10 at the assigned memory address. When you declare a String as `String aGreeting = "Hello";`, aGreeting holds a memory address where the characters "Hello" are stored. If you subsequently assign a new value to aGreeting, such as `aGreeting = "Bonjour";`, then the address held by aGreeting is altered; now aGreeting holds a new address where the characters "Bonjour" are stored. "Bonjour" is an entirely newly created object with its own location. The "Hello" String is actually still in memory; it's just that aGreeting isn't holding its address anymore. Eventually, a part of the Java system called the **garbage collector** will discard the "Hello" characters. Strings, therefore, are never actually changed; instead, new Strings are created and String variables hold the new addresses. Strings and other objects that can't be changed are known as **immutable**.

Because String variables hold memory addresses, you cannot make a simple comparison to determine whether two String objects are equivalent. For example, if you declare two Strings as `String aGreeting = "Hello";` and `String anotherGreeting = "Hello";`, Java will evaluate a comparison such as `if(aGreeting == anotherGreeting)`... as `false`. When you compare aGreeting to anotherGreeting with the == operator, you are comparing their memory addresses, and not their values.

Fortunately, the String class provides you with a number of useful methods. The **equals()** method evaluates the contents of two String objects to determine whether they are equivalent. The method returns `true` if the objects have identical contents. For example, Figure 6-15 shows two String objects and several comparisons. Each of the comparisons in Figure 6-15 is `true`; each comparison results in printing the line "Name's the same".

```
String aName = "Roger";
String anotherName = "Roger";
if(aName.equals(anotherName))
      System.out.println("Name's the same");
if(anotherName.equals(aName))
      System.out.println("Name's the same");
if(aName.equals("Roger");
      System.out.println("Name's the same");
```

Figure 6-15: String comparisons

The equals() method returns `true` only if two Strings are identical in content. Thus a String holding "Roger " (with a space after the *r*) is *not* equivalent to a String holding "Roger" (with no space after the *r*).

Each String shown in Figure 6-15—aName and anotherName—is an object of type String, so each String has access to the equals() method. The aName object can call equals() with `aName.equals()`, or the anotherName object can call equals() with `anotherName.equals()`. The equals() method can take either a variable String object or a literal String as its argument.

The **equalsIgnoreCase() method** is very similar to the equals() method. As its name implies, it ignores case when determining whether two Strings are equivalent. Thus, `aName.equals("roGER")` is `false`, but `aName.equalsIgnoreCase("roGER")` is `true`. This method is very useful when users type responses to prompts in your program. You never can predict when a user might use the Shift key or the Caps Lock key during data entry. The equalsIgnoreCase() method allows you to test entered data without regard to capitalization.

The **compareTo() method** provides additional information. When you use compareTo() to compare two String objects, it returns zero only if the two Strings hold the same value. If there is any difference between the Strings, a negative number is returned if the calling object is "less than" the argument, and a positive number is returned if the calling object is "more than" the argument. Strings are considered to be "less than" or "more than" each other based on their Unicode values; thus, "a" is less than "b", and "b" is less than "c".

For example, if aName holds "Roger", then the method call `aName.compareTo("Robert")` returns a 5. The number is positive, indicating the "Roger" is more than "Robert". This does not mean that "Roger" has more characters than "Robert"; it means that "Roger" is alphabetically "more" than "Robert". The comparison proceeds as follows:

- The *R* in "Roger" and the *R* in "Robert" are compared, and found to be equal.
- The *o* in "Roger" and the *o* in "Robert" are compared, and found to be equal.
- The *g* in "Roger" and the *b* in "Robert" are compared—they are different. The numeric value of *g* minus the numeric value of *b* is 5 (because *g* is five letters after *b* in the alphabet), so the compareTo() method returns the value 5.

Often, you don't care what the return value of compareTo() is specifically; you simply want to determine whether it is positive or negative when, for example, you attempt to place two Strings in alphabetical order. For example, you can use a test such as `if(aWord.compareTo(anotherWord)<0)...` to determine whether aWord is alphabetically less than anotherWord. If aWord is a String variable that holds the value "hamster", and anotherWord is a String variable that holds the value "iguana", then the comparison `if(aWord.compareTo(anotherWord)<0)` yields `true`.

Next, you will compare two state names to each element in an array of Strings to determine whether each state name occurs within the array.

To compare a String to each element in an array:

1 Create a new console application project named **FindState**. Save the **FindState** project folder in the Chapter.06 folder on your Student Disk.

2 Rename the default Class1.java file as **FindState.java**, then open the file in the Text Editor window.

3 Replace the Class1 class name in the `public class Class1` line with **FindState**.

4 Replace the `// TODO: Add initialization code here` comment with the following array of String objects that holds the state names where Event Handlers Incorporated has offices:

```
String[] states = {"Alaska", "California", "Illinois",
     "Oregon", "Texas", "Wisconsin", "Wyoming"};
```

5. For testing purposes, assign the following two state names to two String objects named firstState and secondState:

```
String firstState = "Illinois";
  // This state will be found in the list
String secondState = "Ohio";
  // This state will not be found in the list
```

6. Next, declare the following integer variable that you will use as a subscript, and a boolean variable that you will set to true when a state name is found in the array:

```
int x;
boolean found = false;
```

7. Enter the following for loop that compares firstState to each state in the array. When a match is found, set the boolean found variable to true.

```
for(x = 0; x < states.length; ++x)
    if(firstState.equals(states[x]))
         found = true;
```

8. At the end of the loop, enter the following statements to print a statement indicating whether firstState was found:

```
if(found)
    System.out.println(firstState + " is in the list");
else
    System.out.println(firstState + " is not in the list");
```

9. Now enter the following statements to reset the variable found to false and then repeat the search process for the secondState variable:

```
found = false;
for(x = 0; x < states.length; ++x)
    if(secondState.equals(states[x]))
         found = true;
if(found)
    System.out.println(secondState + " is in the list");
else
    System.out.println(secondState + " is not in the list");
```

10. Set the project properties to run the **FindState** file as a console application, build the project, and then execute the program by typing **jview FindState** at the command line. The program's output appears in Figure 6-16.

```
C:\WINNT\System32\cmd.exe
A:\CHAPTER.06\FindState>jview FindState
Illinois is in the list
Ohio is not in the list
A:\CHAPTER.06\FindState>
```

Figure 6-16: Output of the FindState program

Other String Methods

A wide variety of additional String methods is available with the String class. The methods toUpperCase() and toLowerCase() convert any String to its uppercase or lowercase equivalent. For example, if you declare a String as `String aWord ="something";`, then `aWord = aWord.toUpperCase` assigns "SOMETHING" to aWord.

The method indexOf() determines whether a specific character occurs within a String. If it does, the method returns the position of the character. String positions, like array positions, begin with zero. The return value is -1 if the character does not exist in the String. For example, for `String myName = "Stacy";`, the value of `myName.indexOf('a')` is 2, and the value of `myName.indexOf('q')` is -1.

The method charAt() requires an integer argument which indicates the position of the character the method returns. For example, if myName is a String holding "Stacy", then the value of myName.charAt(0) is 'S' and myName.charAt(1) is 't'.

The methods endsWith() and startsWith() each take a String argument and return `true` or `false` if a String object does or does not end with or start with the specified argument. For example, if `String myName = "Stacy";`, then `myName.startsWith("Sta")` is `true` and `myName.endsWith("z")` is `false`.

The replace() method allows you to replace all occurrences of some character within a String. For example, if `String yourName = "Annette";`, then `String goofyName = yourName.replace('n', 'X');` assigns "AXXette" to goofyName.

The **toString() method** converts any primitive type to a String. So, if you declare a String as `theString` and an integer as `int someInt = 4;`, then `theString = toString(someInt);` results in the String "4" being assigned to theString. The toString() method is not part of the String class; it is a method included in Java that you can use with any type object. You actually have been using toString() throughout this book without knowing it. When you use print() and println(), their arguments are converted to Strings automatically if necessary.

> You don't need import statements to use toString() because it is part of java.lang, which is imported automatically.

tip

Because the toString() method takes arguments of any primitive type, including int, char, double, and so on, you know that it is an overloaded method.

You already know that you can join Strings with other Strings or values by using a plus sign (+); you have been using this approach in println() statements since Chapter 2. For example, you can print a firstName, a space, and a lastName with `System.out.println(firstName + " " + lastName);`. Joining Strings is called **concatenation**. Additionally, you can extract part of a String with the substring() method, and use it alone or concatenate it with another String. The substring method takes two arguments—a start position and an end position—that are both based on the fact that a String's first position is position zero. For example, the program segment shown in Figure 6-17 produces the output shown in Figure 6-18.

```
String[] dayOfWeek = {"Monday", "Tuesday",
     "Wednesday", "Thursday", "Friday"};
String sentence;
int x;
for(x = 0; x < dayOfWeek.length; ++ x)
    {
      sentence = "The abbreviation for " + dayOfWeek[x] +
      " is " + dayOfWeek[x].substring(0,3);
      System.out.println(sentence);
    }
```

Figure 6-17: Program segment demonstrating String concatenation

```
A:\CHAPTER.06\StringConcantenation>jview StringConcantenation
The abbreviation for Monday is Mon
The abbreviation for Tuesday is Tue
The abbreviation for Wednesday is Wed
The abbreviation for Thursday is Thu
The abbreviation for Friday is Fri

A:\CHAPTER.06\StringConcantenation>
```

Figure 6-18: Output of the String concatenation code segment

To demonstrate the use of the String methods, you will create a simple guessing game, similar to Hangman. The user will guess letters and attempt to guess the motto of Event Handlers Incorporated.

To create the guessing game:

1. Create a new console application project named **SecretPhrase**. Save the **SecretPhrase** project folder in the Chapter.06 folder on your Student Disk. The program will contain the target phrase that the user will try to guess ("Plan With Us") as well as a display phrase that is mostly asterisks (with a few hints).

2. Rename the default Class1.java file as **SecretPhrase.java**, then open the file in the Text Editor window.

3. Replace the Class1 class name in the `public class Class1` line with **SecretPhrase**.

4. The program will accept keyboard input, so position the cursor to the right of the main() method header, and then type **throws Exception**.

5. Replace the `// TODO: Add initialization code here` comment with the following:

   ```
   String targetPhrase = "Plan With Us";
   String displayPhrase = "P*** W*** U*";
   ```

6. Add the following variables that will hold the user's guess and the position of a guess that is found within the phrase:

   ```
   char guess;
   int position;
   ```

7. Next, add the following brief instruction:

   ```
   System.out.println("Play our game - guess our motto");
   ```

8. Then enter the statement to display the hint phrase:

   ```
   System.out.println(displayPhrase);
   ```

9. Add the following loop that continues while asterisks remain in the displayPhrase. The user will enter a letter. You will use the indexOf() method to determine whether the guessed letter appears in the targetPhrase. If it does not, then ask the user to guess again. If the guessed letter appears in the phrase, you reconstruct the display phrase with the following:

   - The substring of characters in the display phrase that come before the correct guess
   - The correct guess

- The substring of characters in the display phrase that appear after the correct guess; in other words, the appropriate asterisk is replaced with the correct letter

```
while(displayPhrase.indexOf('*') != -1)
{
  System.out.println("Enter a letter");
  guess = (char)System.in.read();
  System.in.read(); System.in.read();
      // Absorbs Enter key
  position = targetPhrase.indexOf(guess);
      // Determines position of guess
  if(position == -1) // If guess is not in target phrase
      System.out.println("Sorry - guess again");
  else  // If guess is in target phrase
  {
    displayPhrase = displayPhrase.substring(0,position)
      + guess + displayPhrase.substring
      (position+1,displayPhrase.length());
    System.out.println(displayPhrase);
  }
}
```

10 The `while` loop will continue until all the asterisks in the targetPhrase are replaced by correct letters. Therefore, after the closing curly bracket for the `while` loop, it is appropriate to code `System.out.println ("Congratulations!");`.

11 Set the project properties to run the **SecretPhrase** file as a console application, build the project, and then execute the program by typing `jview SecretPhrase` at the command line. Make sure you understand how all the String methods contribute to the success of this program.

Converting Strings to Numbers

If a String contains all numbers—for example, "649"—you can convert it from a String to a number so you can use it for arithmetic or use it like any other number. To convert a String to an integer, you use the **Integer** class, which is part of java.lang, and therefore automatically is imported into programs you write. A method of the Integer class is parseInt(), which takes a String argument and returns its integer value. For example, `int anInt = Integer.parseInt("649");` stores the numeric value 649 in the variable anInt. You can then use the integer value just as you would any other integer.

> **tip**
> The word *parse* in English means to resolve into component parts, as when you parse a sentence. In Java, to parse a String means to break its separate characters into a numeric format.

It is only slightly more difficult to convert a String object to a double value. You must use the **Double** class, which, like the Integer class, is imported into your programs automatically. Conversion to a double variable is a two-step process:

- You use the Double.valueOf() method to convert a String into a Double (with an uppercase *D*) object.
- You use the doubleValue() method to convert the Double object to a double (with a lowercase *d*) variable.

For example, to convert a String containing "147.82" to a double, you can use the following code:

```
String stringValue = new String("147.82");
Double tempValue = Double.valueOf(stringValue);
double doubleValue = tempValue.doubleValue();
```

The stringValue is passed to the Double.valueOf() method, which returns a Double object. The Double object, tempValue, is passed to the doubleValue() method, which returns a double variable.

> **tip**
> The Double and Integer classes are examples of wrappers. A wrapper is a class or object that is "wrapped around" a simpler thing. You use the Double (uppercase *D*) class to make it convenient to work with primitive double (lowercase *d*) variables.

When planning an event, Event Handlers Incorporated needs to know how many guests to expect. Next, you will prompt the user for the number of guests, read characters from the keyboard, store the characters in a String, and then convert the String to an integer.

To create a program that accepts integer input:

1. Create a new console application project named **NumInput**. Save the **NumInput** project folder in the Chapter.06 folder on your Student Disk.
2. Rename the default Class1.java file as **NumInput.java**, then open the file in the Text Editor window.
3. Replace the Class1 class name in the `public class Class1` line with **NumInput**.
4. The program will accept keyboard input, so position the cursor to the right of the main() method header, and then type `throws Exception`.
5. Replace the `// TODO: Add initialization code here` comment with the following variables to hold the input String, each character of input, and the resulting integer:

```
String inputString = new String();
char newChar;
int inputNumber;
```

6. Prompt the user for the number of guests and read in the first character by entering the following lines:

```
System.out.println("Enter the number of guests at your event");
newChar = (char)System.in.read();
```

7. Enter the following while loop that continues while you continue to enter digits. Within the loop, you will take the current input String and concatenate each new character to it. Then read another new character before looping back to check whether the next character is a digit.

```
while(newChar >= '0' && newChar <= '9')
{
        inputString = inputString + newChar;
        newChar = (char)System.in.read();
}
```

8. Use the following Integer.parseInt() method to convert the input String to an integer. Then use the integer in a numeric decision.

```
inputNumber = Integer.parseInt(inputString);
if(inputNumber > 100)
        System.out.println("A surcharge will apply!");
```

9. Set the project properties to run the **NumInput** file as a console application, build the project, and then execute the program by typing **jview NumInput** at the command line.

SUMMARY

- A sequence of characters enclosed within double quotation marks is a literal string.

- You create a String object by using the keyword new and the String constructor method.

- Each String is a class object, and a String variable name is actually a reference. Strings, therefore, are never actually changed; they are immutable.

- The equals() method evaluates the contents of two String objects to determine whether they are equivalent and then returns a boolean value.

- The equalsIgnoreCase() method determines whether two Strings are equivalent without considering case.

- The compareTo() method returns zero if two String objects hold the same value. It returns a negative number if the calling object is "less than" the argument and returns a positive number if the calling object is "more than" the argument.

- The methods toUpperCase() and toLowerCase() convert any String to its uppercase or lowercase equivalent.

- The method indexOf() determines whether a specific character occurs within a String. If it does, the method returns the position of the character. The return value is -1 if the character does not exist in the String.

- The methods endsWith() and startsWith() each take a String argument and return `true` or `false` if a String object does or does not end with or start with the specified argument.

- The replace() method allows you to replace all occurrences of some character within a String.

- The toString() method converts any primitive type to a String.

- You can join Strings with other Strings or values by using a plus sign (+); this process is called concatenation.

- You can extract part of a String with the substring() method, which takes two arguments—a start position and an end position—that are both based on the fact that a String's first position is position zero.

- If a String contains all numbers, you can convert it to a number.

- The method parseInt() takes a String argument and returns its integer value.

- The method Double.valueOf() converts a String to a Double object; the doubleValue() method converts a Double object to a double variable.

QUESTIONS

1. A sequence of characters enclosed within double quotation marks is a _____.
   a. symbolic string
   b. literal string
   c. prompt
   d. command

2. To create a String object, you can use the keyword _____.
   a. `object`
   b. `create`
   c. `char`
   d. `new`

section B

3. A String variable name is a _____.
   a. reference
   b. value
   c. constant
   d. literal

4. Objects that cannot be changed are _____.
   a. irrevocable
   b. nonvolatile
   c. immutable
   d. stable

5. If you declare two String objects as String word1 = new String("happy"); and String word2 = new String("happy");, then the value of word1 == word2 is _____.
   a. true
   b. false
   c. illegal
   d. unknown

6. If you declare two String objects as String word1 = new String("happy"); and String word2 = new String("happy");, then the value of word1.equals(word2) is _____.
   a. true
   b. false
   c. illegal
   d. unknown

7. The method that determines whether two objects are equivalent without regard to case is _____.
   a. equalsNoCase()
   b. toUpperCase()
   c. equalsIgnoreCase()
   d. equals()

8. If a String is declared as String aStr = new String("lima bean");, then aStr.equals("Lima Bean"); is _____.
   a. true
   b. false
   c. illegal
   d. unknown

9. If you create two String objects using String name1 = new String("Jordan"); and String name2 = new String("Jore");, then name1.compareTo(name2) has a value of _____.
   a. true
   b. false
   c. -1
   d. 1

10. If `String myFriend = new String("Ginny");`, then which of the following has the value 1?
    a. `myFriend.compareTo("Gabby");`
    b. `myFriend.compareTo("Gabriella");`
    c. `myFriend.compareTo("Ghazala");`
    d. `myFriend.compareTo("Hammie");`

11. If `String movie = new String("West Side Story");`, then the value of `movie.indexOf('s')` is _____.
    a. `true`
    b. `false`
    c. 2
    d. 3

12. The replace() method replaces _____.
    a. a String with a character
    b. one String with another String
    c. one character in a String with another character
    d. every occurrence of a character in a String with another character

13. The toString() method converts any _____ to a String.
    a. character
    b. integer
    c. float
    d. All of the preceding answers are correct.

14. Joining Strings is called _____.
    a. chaining
    b. joining
    c. linking
    d. concatenation

15. The first position in a String _____.
    a. must be alphabetic
    b. must be uppercase
    c. is position zero
    d. is ignored by the compareTo() method

16. The substring() method requires _____ arguments.
    a. no
    b. one
    c. two
    d. three

17. The method parseInt() converts a(n) _____.
    a. integer to a String
    b. integer to a Double
    c. Double to a String
    d. String to an integer

18. The difference between int and Integer is _____.
    a. int is a primitive type; Integer is a class
    b. int is a class; Integer is a primitive type
    c. nonexistent; they both are primitive types
    d. nonexistent; both are classes

EXERCISES

1. Write a program that stores vowels (*a, e, i, o,* and *u*) in an array. Ask the user to enter a character. Then the program should indicate whether the entered character is a vowel.

2. Store 40 characters in an array, such as `1234%$#@UHGF...` Write a program that produces a count of how many of the characters are letters in the English alphabet and how many of the characters are not letters.

3. Write a program that prompts the user for a first name. Print a greeting to the person using the name, such as "Hello Kimberly!"

4. Store 20 integer employee ID numbers in an integer array and 20 corresponding employee last names in a String array. When a user inputs an ID number, print the appropriate last name.

5. Create an array of Strings containing the days of the week ("Sunday" through "Saturday"). Review the use of the Date class in Chapter 4. The Date class contains a method getDay() that returns an integer value zero through six that represents Sunday through Saturday. Write a program in which you create a Date object, assign it a value, and then print a day that corresponds to the Date.

6. Create an array of Strings, each containing one of the top 10 reasons that you like Visual J++. Prompt a user to enter a number, convert the number to an integer, and then use the integer to print one of the reasons for the user.

7. Create an array of five Strings, each containing the first names of people in your family. Write a program that counts and shows the number of vowels in the Strings that you entered, without regard to case (uppercase versus lowercase letters).

8. Create a console application project named StudentId that lets the user enter a student ID number with nine numbers and then shows the student's first name and grade point average.

9. Create a console application project named PhoneNumber that changes the phone number for a person in a phone directory based on the person's ID number. The user should be able to enter an ID number (with nine digits) and then change the phone number for that person. To verify that the change was made correctly, show the person's name and new phone number.

SECTION C
objectives

In this section you will learn
- How to sort primitive array elements
- How to sort object array elements
- How to sort String array elements
- How to use two-dimensional arrays
- About multidimensional arrays
- About the StringBuffer class

Advanced Array Techniques

tip

This section presents additional array and String methods and techniques. Your instructor might omit this section; however, you will not suffer any loss in continuity.

Sorting Primitive Array Elements

Sorting is the process of arranging a series of objects in some logical order. When you place objects in order beginning with the object with the lowest value, you are sorting in **ascending** order; conversely, when you start with the object that has the largest value, you are sorting in **descending** order.

The simplest possible sort involves two values that are out of order. To place the values in order, you must swap the two values. For example, suppose you have two variables—valA and valB—and further suppose `valA = 16` and `valB = 2`. To exchange the values of the two variables, you cannot simply use the following code:

```
valA = valB; // 2 goes to valA
valB = valA; // 2 goes to valB
```

If valB is 2, then after you execute `valA = valB;`, both variables hold the value 2. The value 16 that was held in valA is lost. When you execute the second assignment statement, `valB = valA;`, each variable still holds the value 2.

The solution that allows you to retain both values is to employ a variable to hold valA's value temporarily during the swap:

```
temp = valA; // 16 goes to temp
valA = valB; // 2 goes to valA
valB = temp; // 16 goes to valB
```

Using this technique, valA's value (16) is assigned to the temp variable. The value of valB (2) is then assigned to valA, so valA and valB are equivalent. Then the temp value (16) is assigned to valB, so the values of the two variables finally are swapped.

If you want to sort any two values, valA and valB, in ascending order so that valA is always the lower value, then you use the following `if` statement to make the decision whether to swap. If valA is more than valB, you want to switch the values. If valA is not more than valB, you do not want the values to switch.

```
if(valA > valB)
{
      temp = valA;
      valA = valB;
      valB = temp;
}
```

Sorting two values is a fairly simple task; sorting more values (valC, valD, valE, and so on) is more complicated. Without using an array, sorting a series of numbers would be a daunting task; the task becomes manageable when you know how to use an array.

As an example, you might have a list of five numbers that you want to place in ascending numeric order. One approach is to use a method popularly known as a **bubble sort**. To use a bubble sort, you place the original, unsorted values in an array such as `int[] someNums = {88, 33, 99, 22, 54};`. After a series of comparisons and swaps, the numbers eventually will be placed in order within the array. You compare the first two numbers; if they are not in ascending order, you swap them. You compare the second and third numbers; if they are not in ascending order, you swap them. You continue down the list. If any someNums[x] is larger than someNums[x + 1], then you want to swap the two values.

With the numbers 88, 33, 99, 22, and 54, the process proceeds as follows:

- Compare 88 and 33. They are out of order. Swap them. The list becomes 33, 88, 99, 22, 54.
- Compare the second and third numbers in the list—88 and 99. They are in order. Do nothing.
- Compare the third and fourth numbers in the list—99 and 22. They are out of order. Swap them. The list becomes 33, 88, 22, 99, 54.
- Compare the fourth and fifth numbers—99 and 54. They are out of order. Swap them. The list becomes 33, 88, 22, 54, 99.

When you reach the bottom of the list, the numbers are not in ascending order, but the largest number, 99, has moved to the bottom of the list. It is because of this feature that the bubble sort gets its name—the "heaviest" value has sunk to the bottom of the list as the "lighter" values have bubbled up to the top.

Assuming b and temp both have been declared as integer variables, the code so far is as follows:

```
for(b = 0; b < 4; ++b)
     if(someNums[b] > someNums[b + 1])
     {
          temp = someNums[b];
          someNums[b] = someNums[b + 1];
          someNums[b + 1] = temp;
     }
```

Notice that the `for` statement tests every value of b from zero through three. The array someNums contains five integers. The subscripts in the array range in value from zero through four. Within the `for` loop, each someNums[b] is compared with someNums[b + 1], so the highest legal value for b is three when array element b (3) is compared to array element b + 1 (4). For a sort on any size array, the value of b must remain less than the array's length minus one.

The list of numbers that began as 88, 33, 99, 22, 54 is currently 33, 88, 22, 54, 99. Although the largest value is at the end of the list now, the list is still not in order. You must perform the entire comparison-swap procedure again.

- Compare the first two values—33 and 88. They are in order; do nothing.
- Compare the second and third values—88 and 22. They are out of order. Swap them so the list becomes 33, 22, 88, 54, 99.
- Compare the third and fourth values—88 and 54. They are out of order. Swap them so the list becomes 33, 22, 54, 88, 99.
- Compare the fourth and fifth values—88 and 99. They are in order; do nothing.

After this second pass through the list, the numbers are 33, 22, 54, 88, and 99—close to ascending order, but not quite. You can see that with one more pass through the list, the values 22 and 33 would swap, and the list finally would be placed in order. With the worst case list, one in which the original numbers were descending (as "out of ascending order" as they could possibly be), you would need to go through the list four times making comparisons and swaps. You always, at most, need to pass through the list its length minus one time. Figure 6-19 shows the entire procedure.

```
for(a = 0; a < (someNums.length -1); ++a)
     for(b = 0; b < (someNums.length - 1); ++b)
          if(someNums[b] > someNums[b + 1])
          {
               temp = someNums[b];
               someNums[b] = someNums[b + 1];
               someNums[b + 1] = temp;
          }
```

Figure 6-19: Ascending sort of the someNums arra

section C

To place the list in descending order, you need to make only one change to the method in Figure 6-19: You change the greater-than sign (>) in `if(someNums[b] > someNums[b + 1])` to a less-than sign (<).

Next you will write a program that includes a method that sorts characters that you enter from the keyboard.

To write a program that sorts characters:

1 Create a new console application project named **SortCharArray**. Save the **SortCharArray** project folder in the Chapter.06 folder on your Student Disk.

2 Rename the default Class1.java file as **SortCharArray.java**, then open the file in the Text Editor window.

3 Replace the Class1 class name in the `public class Class1` line with **SortCharArray**.

4 The program will accept keyboard input, so position the insertion point to the right of the main() method header, and then type **throws Exception**.

5 Replace the `// TODO: Add initialization code here` comment with the following code to declare a character array that can hold 10 characters and an integer x to use as a subscript with the array:

```
char[] someChars = new char[10];
int x;
```

6 Enter the following for loop that allows the user to enter 10 characters from the keyboard:

```
for(x = 0; x < 10; ++x)
{
    System.out.print("Enter a character ");
    someChars[x] = (char)System.in.read();
    System.in.read(); System.in.read();
}
```

7 Enter the following for loop that displays the characters as originally entered:

```
System.out.println("Before sort");
for(x = 0; x < 10; ++x)
        System.out.print(someChars[x] + " ");
```

8 Call a method named bubbleSort(). You will pass two arguments to bubbleSort(): the array and the length of the array.

```
bubbleSort(someChars, someChars.length);
```

9 Add a loop that prints the characters after the sort has executed:

```
System.out.println("\nAfter sort");
for(x = 0; x < someChars.length; ++x)
      System.out.print(someChars[x] + "  ");
```

> When you sort a series of numbers, you place them in arithmetic order. You sort characters by their numeric Unicode value.

10 Add a final println() statement to the program:

```
System.out.println();
```

You cannot build the project yet because you have not written the bubbleSort() method.

Next, you will add the bubbleSort() method to the SortCharArray program. An advantage of creating the sort as a method that is separate from the main() method is that you might want to use this method with other programs. The bubbleSort() method will sort any size array of characters; you might be able to use it in any application in which you have a number of characters to sort.

To write the bubbleSort() method:

1 Below the main() method's closing curly bracket in the existing SortCharArray program, write the header for a bubbleSort() method that takes a character array and an integer length as arguments, and then press the **Enter** key and type the method's opening curly bracket:

```
public static void bubbleSort(char[] array, int len)
{
```

2 Type the following code to declare two integers, a and b, to use in the method's `for` loops. Additionally, declare a temporary character variable.

```
int a,b;
char temp;
```

3 The two `for` loops you need to sort the array each must execute len minus one times. If you place the subtraction calculation within each `for` statement, as in `for(a = 0; a < (len - 1); ++a)`, then the subtraction is performed on each cycle through the loop. It is more efficient to calculate `len - 1` once, store the value in a variable, and use the new variable in the `for` loops. Figure 6-20 shows this process. Add this code to your program.

section C

```
int highSubscript = len - 1;
for(a = 0; a < highSubscript; ++a)
    {
        for(b = 0; b < highSubscript; ++b)
            if(array[b] > array[b + 1])
            {
                temp = array[b];
                array[b] = array[b+1];
                array[b + 1] = temp;
            }
    }
```

Figure 6-20: Portion of the sort process

4   Add the closing curly bracket for the bubbleSort() method.

5   Set the project properties to run the **SortCharArray** file as a console application, build the project, and then execute the program as a console application by typing `jview SortCharArray` at the command line. Figure 6-21 shows a typical program run.

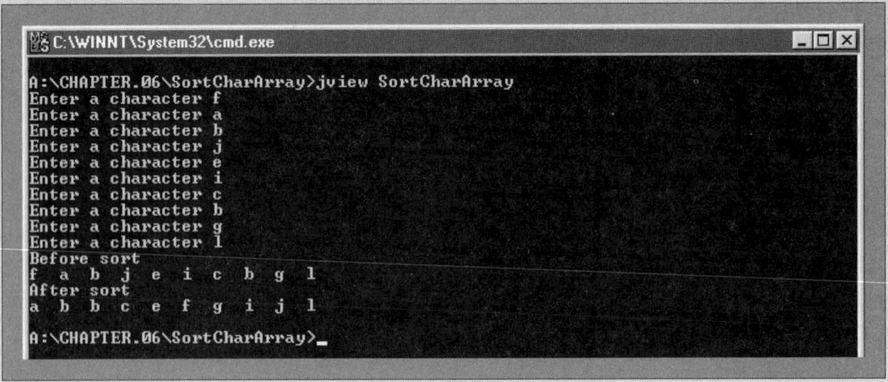

```
A:\CHAPTER.06\SortCharArray>jview SortCharArray
Enter a character f
Enter a character a
Enter a character b
Enter a character j
Enter a character e
Enter a character i
Enter a character c
Enter a character b
Enter a character g
Enter a character l
Before sort
f  a  b  j  e  i  c  b  g  l
After sort
a  b  b  c  e  f  g  i  j  l
A:\CHAPTER.06\SortCharArray>
```

Figure 6-21: Output of the SortCharArray program

When you use a bubble sort to sort any array into ascending order, the largest value "falls" to the bottom of the array after you have compared each pair of values in the array one time. The second time you go through the array making comparisons, there really is no need to check the last pair of values. The largest value is guaranteed to be at the bottom of the array already. You can make the sort process even more efficient by using a new variable for the inner `for` loop, and reducing it by one on each cycle through the array.

> **To make the array more efficient:**
> 1. Within the bubbleSort() method in the SortCharArray.java file, position the insertion point after the statement `int highSubscript = len - 1;`, and then press the **Enter** key to start a new line.
> 2. Declare a variable that holds the number of comparisons to make by typing the following:
>
>   `int compsToMake = len - 1;`
> 3. Replace the inner, b-loop statement, `for(b = 0; b < highSubscript; ++b)`, with `for(b = 0; b < compsToMake; ++b)`
> 4. Position the cursor after the closing curly bracket in the `if` block, and then press the **Enter** key to start a new line.
> 5. Type the statement that reduces compsToMake by one on each cycle through the array by typing `--compsToMake;`
> 6. Rebuild and run the program. The program executes exactly as before; however, it is more efficient. When you sort an array with 10 or 20 elements, you will not notice any improved efficiency. However, if you need to sort an array with thousands of elements, the program will run much faster if you employ this technique to reduce unnecessary comparisons.

Sorting Arrays of Objects

You can sort arrays of objects in much the same way that you sort arrays of primitive types. The major difference occurs when you make the comparison that determines whether you want to swap two array elements. When you construct an array of the primitive element type, you compare the two array elements to determine whether they are out of order. When array elements are objects, you usually want to sort based on a particular field of the object.

For example, assume you have created a simple Employee class as shown in Figure 6-22. The class holds two data fields, a constructor, and get and set methods for the fields.

```
public class Employee
{
        private int empNum;
        private double empSal;
        public Employee(int e, double s)
        {
                empNum = e;
                empSal = s;
        }
        public int getEmpNum()
        {
                return empNum;
        }
        public double getEmpSal()
        {
                return empSal;
        }
        public void setEmpSal(double r)
        {
                empSal = r;
        }
}
```

Figure 6-22: Employee class

You can write a program that contains an array of Employee objects using the statement `Employee[] someEmps = new Employee[5];`. After you assign employee numbers and salaries to the Employee objects, you want to sort the Employees in empSal order. You can pass the array and its length to a bubbleSort() method that is prepared to receive Employee objects. Figure 6-23 shows the method.

```
public static void bubbleSort(Employee[] array, int len)
{
        int a,b;
        Employee temp;
        int highSubscript = len - 1;
        for(a = 0; a < highSubscript; ++a)
                for(b = 0; b < highSubscript; ++b)
                        if(array[b].getEmpSal() >
                           array[b+1].getEmpSal())
                        {
                                temp = array[b];
                                array[b] = array[b + 1];
                                array[b + 1] = temp;
                        }
}
```

Figure 6-23: The bubbleSort() method for Employee objects

If you examine Figure 6-23 carefully, you might notice that it is very similar to a sort method you use for an array of any primitive type, but with three major differences:

- The bubbleSort() method header shows it receives an array of type Employee.
- The temp variable created for swapping is type Employee.
- The comparison for swapping uses the method call getEmpSal() to compare the salary for each Employee object in the array to the salary of the adjacent Employee object.

It is important to note that even though only Employee salaries are compared, you do not swap Employee salaries. You do not want to substitute one Employee's salary for another's. Instead, you swap the entire Employee so that each Employee's empNum and empSal are swapped as a unit.

section C

Sorting Strings

When you sort an array of Strings, you must remember that String names are addresses. Therefore, you cannot determine whether two String objects require swapping by comparing their names. Instead, you must use the compareTo() method. Next, you will sort a list of Strings.

To sort an array of String objects:

1. Create a new console application project named **SortStrings**. Save the **SortStrings** project folder in the Chapter.06 folder on your Student Disk.

2. Rename the default Class1.java file as **SortStrings.java**, then open the file in the Text Editor window.

3. Replace the Class1 class name in the `public class Class1` line with **SortStrings**.

4. Replace the `// TODO: Add initialization code here` comment with the following code to declare an array of student names and an integer variable to use as a subscript:

```
String[] students =
        {"Kim", "Ken", "Tom", "Kathy", "Brad"};
int x;
```

5. Write the code that prints the list of Strings, passes the list to a sortStrings() method, and prints the list again:

```
System.out.println("Before sort");
for(x = 0; x < 5; ++x)
        System.out.println(students[x]);
sortStrings(students, students.length);
System.out.println("\nAfter sort");
for(x = 0; x < 5; ++x)
System.out.println(students[x]);
```

6. Enter the SortStrings() method shown in Figure 6-24 after the main() method's closing curly bracket. The method uses the compareTo() method to determine whether two Strings should be swapped. Recall that when compareTo() returns a value greater than zero, then the first String is larger than (that is, out of order with) the second String.

Arrays and Strings

```
public static void sortStrings(String[] array, int len)
{
        int a,b;
        String temp;
        int highSubscript = len - 1;
        for(a = 0; a < highSubscript; ++a)
            for(b = 0; b < highSubscript; ++b)
                if(array[b].compareTo(array[b + 1]) > 0
)
                {
                    temp= array[b];
                    array[b] = array[b + 1];
                    array[b + 1] = temp;
                }
```

Figure 6-24: The sortStrings() method

7 Set the project properties to run the **SortStrings** file as a console application, build the project, and then execute the program as a console application by typing **jview SortStrings** at the command line. When you run the program, the output appears similar to Figure 6-25.

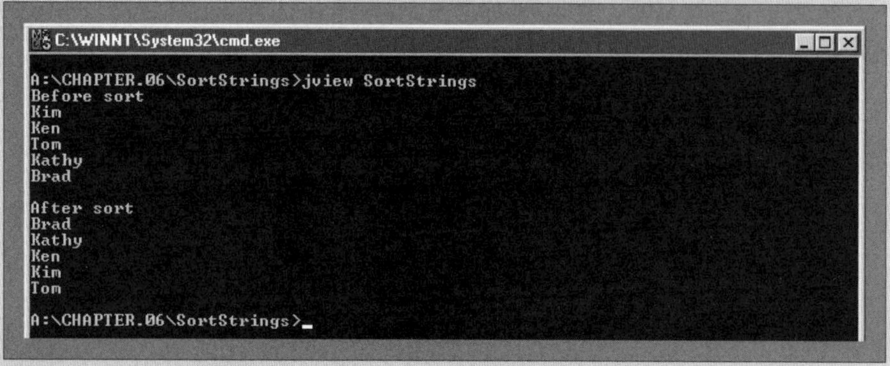

```
C:\WINNT\System32\cmd.exe
A:\CHAPTER.06\SortStrings>jview SortStrings
Before sort
Kim
Ken
Tom
Kathy
Brad
After sort
Brad
Kathy
Ken
Kim
Tom
A:\CHAPTER.06\SortStrings>
```

Figure 6-25: Output of the SortStrings program

Using Two-Dimensional Arrays

When you declare an array such as int[] numbers = new int[5];, you can envision the five declared integers as a column of numbers in memory, as shown in Figure 6-26. In other words, you can picture the five declared numbers stacked one on top of the next. An array that you can picture as a column of values is a **one-dimensional** or **single-dimensional** array.

| someNumbers[0] |
| someNumbers[1] |
| someNumbers[2] |

Figure 6-26: Single-dimensional array

> You can think of the single dimension of a single-dimensional array as the height of the array.

The Java programming language also supports two-dimensional arrays. **Two-dimensional arrays** have more than one column of values, as shown in Figure 6-27. It is easiest to picture two-dimensional arrays as having both rows and columns. When mathematicians use a two-dimensional array, they often call it a table or **matrix**; you might have used a two-dimensional array called a spreadsheet.

someNumbers[0][0]	SomeNumbers[0][1]	someNumbers[0][2]	someNumbers[0][3]
someNumbers[1][0]	SomeNumbers[1][1]	someNumbers[1][2]	someNumbers[1][3]
someNumbers[2][0]	someNumbers[2][1]	someNumbers[2][2]	someNumbers[2][3]

Figure 6-27: Two-dimensional array

> You can think of the two dimensions of a two-dimensional array as height and width.

When you declare a one-dimensional array, you type a set of square brackets after the array type. To declare a two-dimensional array, you type two sets of brackets after the array type. For example, int [][] someNumbers = new int [3][4]; declares an array named someNumbers that holds three rows and four columns.

Just as with a one-dimensional array, if you do not provide values for the elements in a two-dimensional numeric array, the values default to zero. You can assign values to the array elements later. For example, someNumbers[0][0] = 14; assigns the value 14 to the element of the someNumbers array that is in the first column of the first row. Alternatively, you can initialize a two-dimensional array with values when it is created. For example, the following code assigns values to someNumbers when it is created:

```
int [][] someNumbers =
        {       {8, 9, 10, 11},
                {1, 3, 12, 15},
                {5, 9, 44, 99}  };
```

The someNumbers array contains three rows and four columns. You contain the entire set of values within a pair of curly brackets. The first row of the array holds the four integers 8, 9, 10, and 11. Notice that these four integers are placed within their own set of curly brackets to indicate that they constitute one row, or the first row, which is row zero. Similarly, 1, 3, 12, and 15 make up the second row, which you reference with the subscript 1, and 5, 9, 44, and 99 are the values in the third row, which you reference with the subscript 2. The value of someNumbers[0][0] is 8. The value of someNumbers[0][1] is 9. The value of someNumbers [2][3] is 99. The value within the first bracket following the array name always refers to the row; the value within the second bracket refers to the column.

As an example, assume you own an apartment building with four floors—a basement which you refer to as floor zero, and three other floors numbered one, two, and three. Additionally, each of the floors has studio (no bedroom) and one- and two-bedroom apartments. The monthly rent for each type of apartment is different—the higher the floor, the higher the rent (the view is better), and with more bedrooms, the rent is higher. Figure 6-28 shows the rental amounts.

Floor	Zero Bedrooms	One Bedroom	Two Bedrooms
0	400	450	510
1	500	560	630
2	625	676	740
3	1,000	1,250	1,600

Figure 6-28: Rents charged

To determine a tenant's rent, you need to know two pieces of information: the floor on which the tenant rents an apartment, and the number of bedrooms in the apartment. Within a Java program, you can declare an array of rents using the following code:

```
int[][] rents =
    {       {400, 450, 510},
            {500, 560, 630},
            {625, 676, 740},
            {1000, 1250, 1600}   };
```

Assuming that you declare two integers to hold the floor number and bedroom count as `int floor, bedrooms;`, then any tenant's rent is `rents[floor][bedrooms]`.

To demonstrate the use of a two-dimensional array, you can create a short demonstration program. You will create a teacher's classroom seating chart that holds four rows and three columns. Then you will search for a particular student's location.

To write a program that uses a two-dimensional array to create a student seating chart:

1 Create a new console application project named **FindStudent**. Save the **FindStudent** project folder in the Chapter.06 folder on your Student Disk.

2 Rename the default Class1.java file as **FindStudent.java**, then open the file in the Text Editor window.

3 Replace the Class1 class name in the `public class Class1` line with **FindStudent**.

4 The program will accept keyboard input, so position the cursor to the right of the main() method header, and then type **throws Exception**.

5 Replace the `// TODO: add initialization code` comment with the following code to create a two-dimensional String array that holds the names of 12 students who sit in four rows. For convenience, assign each student a name with a unique initial. That way, you can search for a student's position using an initial.

```
String[][] students =
    {       {"Dave", "Bonnie", "Hannah"},
            {"Iris", "Keith", "Carl"},
            {"Amy", "Jessica", "Francis"},
            {"Ellen", "George", "Lydia"}   };
```

6 You will use a character variable to hold an initial input from the keyboard, and two integer variables to hold the row and column position of the student whose initial matches the input initial:

```
char stu;
int r, c;
```

7. Add the following statements to prompt the user for an initial and read the character from the keyboard:

   ```
   System.out.print("Enter student initial ");
   stu = (char)System.in.read();
   ```

8. You will use two nested `for` loops to test each combination of row and column position. When the character input at the keyboard matches the character in the first position of any of the Strings in the two-dimensional array, print the row and column position. Enter the following `for` loops:

   ```
   for(r = 0; r < 4; ++r)
       for(c = 0; c < 3; ++c)
           if(stu == students[r][c].charAt(0))
               System.out.println
                   ("Student is in row " + r + " and column " + c);
   ```

9. Set the project properties to run the **FindStudent** file as a console application, build the project, and then execute the program several times. Confirm that with each initial you type, the correct row and column positions are located. Figure 6-29 shows a sample program run.

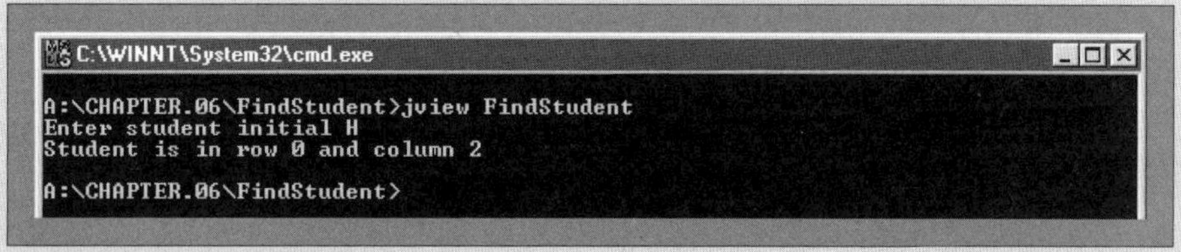

Figure 6-29: Output of the FindStudent program

Understanding Multidimensional Arrays

The Java programming language supports **multidimensional arrays**, or arrays of more than two dimensions. For example, if you own an apartment building with a number of floors and different numbers of bedrooms available in apartments on each floor, you can use a two-dimensional array to store the rental fees. If you own several apartment buildings, you might want to employ a third dimension to store the building number. An expression such as `rents[building][floor][bedrooms]` refers to a specific rent figure for a building whose building number is stored in the building variable and whose floor and bedroom numbers are stored in the floor and bedrooms variables. Specifically, `rents[5][1][2]` refers to a two-bedroom apartment on the first floor of building 5.

When you are programming in Java, you can use four, five, or more dimensions in an array. As long as you can keep track of the order of the variables needed as subscripts, and as long as you don't exhaust your computer's memory, Java will let you create arrays of any size.

Using StringBuffer

A limitation of the String class is that the value of a String is fixed after the String is created; that is, Strings are immutable. When you write `someString = "Hello";` and follow it with `SomeString = "Goodbye"`, you have not actually changed the contents of computer memory at someString, nor have you eliminated the characters "Hello". Instead, you have stored "Goodbye" at a new computer memory location and stored the new address in the someString variable. If you want to modify someString from "Goodbye" to "Goodbye Everybody", you cannot actually add a space and "Everybody" to the someString that contains "Goodbye". Instead, you must create an entirely new String, "Goodbye Everybody", and assign it to the someString address.

To circumvent these limitations, you can use the StringBuffer class. **StringBuffer** is an alternative to the String class, and can usually be used anywhere you would use a String. StringBuffer is more flexible than String in that you can insert or append new contents into a StringBuffer. The StringBuffer class provides you with three constructors:

- `public StringBuffer()`, which constructs a StringBuffer with no characters in it and a default size of 16 characters.
- `public StringBuffer(int length)`, which constructs a StringBuffer with no characters, and a capacity specified by length.
- `public StringBuffer(String s)`, which contains the same characters as are stored in the String object s. The capacity of the StringBuffer is the length of the String argument you provide, plus 16 additional characters.

Every StringBuffer object has a maximum capacity or size, but if you add additional characters to a StringBuffer so as to exceed the capacity, Java automatically provides a larger capacity.

The **append() method** lets you add characters to the end of a StringBuffer object. For example, if a StringBuffer is declared as `StringBuffer someBuffer = new StringBuffer("Happy ");`, then the statement `someBuffer.append("birthday")` alters someBuffer to hold "Happy birthday".

The **insert() method** lets you add characters at a specific location within a StringBuffer object. For example, if someBuffer holds "Happy birthday", then `someBuffer.insert(6, "30th ");` alters the StringBuffer to contain "Happy 30th birthday". The first character in the StringBuffer object occupies position zero.

To alter just one character in a StringBuffer, you can use the setCharAt() method. This method requires two arguments, an integer position, and a character. If someBuffer holds "Happy 30th birthday", then `someBuffer.setCharAt(6,'4');` changes the someBuffer value into a 40th birthday greeting.

Next, you will use StringBuffer methods.

To use StringBuffer methods:

1. Create a new console application project named **DemoStringBuffer**. Save the **DemoStringBuffer** project folder in the Chapter.06 folder on your Student Disk.
2. Rename the default Class1.java file as **DemoStringBuffer.java**, then open the file in the Text Editor window.
3. Replace the Class1 class name in the `public class Class1` line with **DemoStringBuffer**.
4. Replace the `// TODO: Add initialization code here` comment with the following code to create a StringBuffer variable, and then call a print() method (that you will create in Step 8) to print the StringBuffer:

```
StringBuffer str = new StringBuffer("singing");
print(str);
```

5. Enter the following append() method to add characters to the existing StringBuffer, and print again:

```
str.append(" in the dead of ");
print(str);
```

6. Enter the following insert() method to insert characters, print, insert additional characters, and print again:

```
str.insert(0, "Black");
print(str);
str.insert(5,"bird ");
print(str);
```

7. Add one more append() and print() combination:

```
str.append("night");
print(str);
```

8. After the main method's closing curly bracket, enter the following print() method that prints StringBuffer objects:

```
public static void print(StringBuffer s)
{
        System.out.println(s);
}
```

9 Set the project properties to run the **DemoStringBuffer** file as a console application, build the project, and then execute the program. Compare your output to Figure 6-30 and make sure you understand the effect of each program statement.

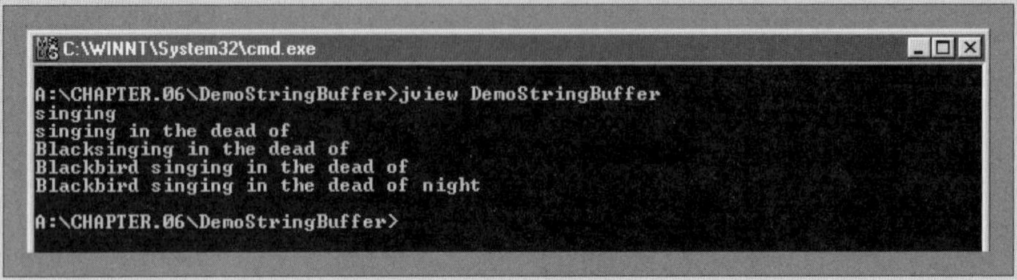

Figure 6-30: Output of the DemoStringBuffer program

SUMMARY

- Sorting is the process of arranging a series of objects in some logical order. When you place objects in order beginning with the object with the lowest value, you are sorting in ascending order; when you start with the object that has the largest value, you are sorting in descending order.

- To sort any two values in ascending order, you use an `if` statement to make the decision whether to swap the positions of the two values.

- To use a bubble sort, you place the original, unsorted values in an array, compare pairs of values, and, if they are not in ascending order, swap them. To use a bubble sort, you always, at most, need to pass through a list as many times as its length minus one time.

- You can sort arrays of objects you usually want to sort based on a particular field of the object.

- You must use the compareTo() method when sorting Strings.

- An array that you can picture as a column of values is a one-dimensional or single-dimensional array.

- The Java programming language supports multidimensional arrays, or arrays of more than two dimensions.

- To circumvent some limitations of the String class, you can use the StringBuffer class. You can insert or append new contents into a StringBuffer.

QUESTIONS

1. When you place objects in order beginning with the object with the lowest value, you are sorting in _____ order.
   a. acquiescing
   b. ascending
   c. demeaning
   d. descending

2. Which of the following lists is in descending order?
   a. 19, 14, 8, 3, 1
   b. 4, 6, 8, 99
   c. 2, 7, 1, 9
   d. 4, 4, 3, 4

3. Using a bubble sort involves _____.
   a. comparing parallel arrays
   b. comparing each array element to the average
   c. comparing each array element to the adjacent array element
   d. swapping every array element with its adjacent element

4. When you use a bubble sort to sort numbers in ascending order, at the end of the first pass through the array, the _____ number is at the bottom of the array.
   a. smallest
   b. largest
   c. originally first
   d. originally last

5. Which array types cannot be sorted?
   a. Arrays of characters
   b. Arrays of Strings
   c. Arrays of objects
   d. You can sort all of these array types.

6. Which list is in ascending order?
   a. d, f, m, y
   b. Z, T, S, F
   c. a, A, b, B
   d. z, y, x, Z

7. When array elements are objects, you usually want to sort based on a particular _____ of the object.
   a. field
   b. method
   c. name
   d. type

8. When you compare two Strings for sorting, you use the _____.
   a. String() method
   b. equal sign
   c. compareTo() method
   d. SortString() method

9. The array int[] values = new int[10]; is a _____ array.
   a. one-dimensional
   b. two-dimensional
   c. multidimensional
   d. nondimensional

10. If you declare an array as int[][] values = new int[6][3];, the array has _____ rows.
    a. two
    b. three
    c. five
    d. six

11. If you declare an array as int[][] values = new int[6][3];, then the array has _____ columns.
    a. two
    b. three
    c. five
    d. six

12. If you declare an array as double [][] money = new double[10][5];, then the last value in the first row is _____.
    a. money[0][4]
    b. money[0][5]
    c. money[9][0]
    d. money[10][0]

13. If you declare an array as char [][] codes[5][6];, which of the following statements is invalid?
    a. codes[3][3]
    b. codes[4][5]
    c. codes[0][0]
    d. codes[5][4]

14. Using Java, you can create an array with a maximum of _____ dimensions.
    a. two
    b. three
    c. four
    d. virtually unlimited

15. As an alternative to the String class, you can use
    a. char
    b. StringHolder
    c. StringBuffer
    d. StringMerger

16. The default capacity for a StringBuffer object is _____ characters.
    a. 0
    b. 2
    c. 16
    d. 32

17. The StringBuffer method you use to add characters at the end of a StringBuffer is _____.
    a. add()
    b. adjust()
    c. append()
    d. attach()

18. If aStringBufObject holds "abcdefg", then aStringBufObject.insert(2,"XXX") results in aStringBufObject holding _____.
    a. "XXX"
    b. "aXXXbcdefg"
    c. "abXXXcdefg"
    d. "aXXXefg"

EXERCISES

Save each of the following programs in the Chapter.06 folder of your Student Disk.

1. a. Create a console application project named SortDouble containing an array of 15 double values. Include a method to sort the values in ascending order. Display the results.
   b. Add a method to SortDouble to sort in descending order. Display the results.

2. a. Create a console application project named HairSalon for services offered by a hair styling salon. Data fields include a String to hold the service description (for example, "Cut", "Shampoo", "Manicure"), a double to hold the price, and an integer to hold the average minutes it takes to perform the service. Include a constructor that requires arguments for all three data fields and three get methods that each return one of the data field's values.
   b. Write a program named SortSalon that contains an array to hold six HairSalon objects and fill it with data. Include a method to sort the array in ascending order by price of service. Call the method and display the results.
   c. Add a method to the SortSalon program that sorts the HairSalon objects in descending order by time to perform the service. Call the method and display the results.
   d. Add a method to the SortSalon program that sorts the HairSalon objects in alphabetical order by service description. Call the method and display the results.
   e. Add a prompt to the SortSalon program giving the user three choices—sort by description, price, or time. Based on the user's input, call one of the three sort methods and display the results.

3. Create a class that holds three initialized StringBuffer objects: your first name, middle name, and last name. Create three new StringBuffer objects as follows:

   - An object named EntireName that holds your three names, separated by spaces
   - An object named LastFirst that holds your last name, a comma, a space, and your first name, in that order
   - An object named Signature that holds your first name, a space, your middle initial (not the entire name), a period, a space, and your last name

   Display all three objects.

4. Create a console application project named Schedule that allows the user to enter a course ID number and then displays the course name (such as "CIS 110") and the day of the week and time that the course is held (such as "Th 3:30"). Store the course name and day/time in a two-dimensional array.

5. Create a console application project named Video that stores an array of video titles (such as "True Grit") and their corresponding ID numbers in inventory (such as "145"). Display the list before it is sorted, and then display a list sorted by inventory ID number. Use two single-dimensional arrays—one for the titles and one for the scores.

6. Create a console application project named Rate that stores the name, title, and hourly wage of people employed by a grocery store. The data are: Ollie Regan, manager, $18/hour; William Sherman, assistant manager, $16/hour; Maureen Mooney, produce manager, $15/hour; Marty Sharik, bakery manager, $15.25/hour; and Marcella Riley, cashier manager, $13/hour. List the employee name and job title for employees who earn more than $15 per hour. Store the names and titles for each employee in a two-dimensional array, and store the rate in a single-dimensional array.

7. Each of the following files in the Chapter.06 folder on your Student Disk has syntax and/or logical errors. Add the files to a new project called FixDebug. Save the FixDebug project under the Chapter.06 folder on your Student Disk. In each case, fix the problem and run each file as a console application using JVIEW.
   a. DebugSix1.java
   b. DebugSix2.java
   c. DebugSix3.java
   d. DebugSix4.java

Applets

CHAPTER 7

case ▶ "It seems like I've learned a lot," you tell Lynn Greenbrier during a coffee break at Event Handlers Incorporated. "I can use variables, make decisions, write loops, and use arrays."

"You've come a long way," Lynn agrees.

"But," you continue, "it also seems like I know nothing! When I visit the simplest Web site, it looks far more sophisticated than my most advanced application. There is color and movement. There are buttons to click and boxes into which I can type responses to questions. Nothing I've done even approaches that."

"But you have a good foundation in Java programming," Lynn says. "Now you can put all that knowledge to work. By adding a few new objects to your repertoire, and by learning a little about applets, you can comfortably enter the world of interactive Web programming."

Previewing the PartyPlanner Applet

The PartyPlanner applet lets potential Event Handlers Incorporated customers calculate the cost of a planned event based on the number of guests they intend to invite. You can use a completed version of the applet that is saved in the Chapter.07 folder on your Student Disk now.

To run the PartyPlanner applet:

1 Go to the command prompt for the Chapter.07 folder on your Student Disk, type `jview /a partyplan.htm`, and then press the **Enter** key. It might take a few minutes for the AppletViewer window to open. See Figure 7-1.

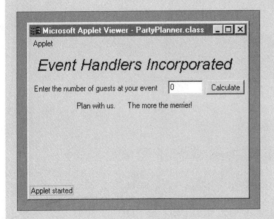

Figure 7-1: PartyPlanner applet

2 Use the applet as if you were a customer of Event Handlers Incorporated. Use the text box to enter any number of guests you want to invite to a hypothetical event. Then, either press the Enter key or click the Calculate button to view the results. The applet will quote you a per-person price as well as a price for the entire event. Enter a new number of guests, then press the Enter key or click the Calculate button. Then the applet will recalculate the rates.

3 Close the AppletViewer by clicking the **Close** button ⊠ in the upper-right corner of the AppletViewer window.

SECTION A
objectives

In this section you will learn
- How to write an HTML document to host an applet
- How to use the HTML Editor
- How to use AppletViewer
- How to write a simple applet using a Label
- How to change a Label's font
- How to add TextFields and Buttons to applets
- About event-driven programming
- How to add output to an applet

HTML and Applet Basics

Applets and HTML Documents

You have written many Java console applications. When you write a Java console application, you do the following:

- Create a console application project and write Java programming code in files with extensions of .java.
- Build the project to compile the .java files into bytecode. The bytecode is stored in files with extensions of .class.
- Use `jview` to interpret and execute the .class files.

Applications are stand-alone programs. In contrast, **applets** are programs that are designed to be called from within Web pages. An applet must be called from within a document written in HTML, or HyperText Markup Language. **HTML** is a simple language used to create Web pages for the Internet. You can also run applets within a program called **AppletViewer** using the `jview` command.

tip

HTML documents can have a file extension of .html or .htm. Visual J++ assigns a file extension of .htm to the HTML documents it creates.

When you create an applet, you do the following:

- Create a project and write Java programming code in files with extensions of .java, just like when you write an application.
- Design an HTML document that includes a statement to call your compiled Java class.
- Build the project to compile the applet's .java files into bytecode with extensions of .class, just like when you write an application.
- Open the HTML document in a Web browser such as Netscape Navigator or Microsoft Internet Explorer or in AppletViewer.

> **tip**
>
> The terms *HTML documents* and *Web pages* are used interchangeably in this text.

Java, in general, and applets, in particular, are popular topics among programmers, mostly because users can execute applets using a Web browser on the Internet. A **Web browser** is a program that allows you to display HTML documents on your computer screen. Web pages often contain Java applets.

HTML documents are text documents containing formatting instructions, called **tags**, along with the text that is to be displayed on a Web page. HTML tags range from formatting commands that boldface and italicize text to controls that allow user input, such as command buttons and check boxes. Other HTML tags allow you to display graphic images and other objects in a document or Web page. When you open an HTML document in a Web browser, the document is assembled and formatted according to the instructions contained in its tags. Tags are enclosed in brackets (< >) and consist of a starting tag and an ending tag that surround the text or other items they are formatting or controlling. For example, the starting tag to boldface a line of text is <B> and the ending tag is </B>. Any text contained between the pair of tags appears in bold when you open the HTML document in a Web browser. The following line is an example of how to boldface text in an HTML document:

`<B>this text will be boldfaced in a Web browser</B>`

> **tip**
>
> Although you need to understand basic HTML tags to create applets, this section provides only a brief overview of HTML since the primary purpose of this text is to teach Java programming. You can find a brief overview of the HTML tools available in Visual J++ later in this chapter. Refer to the Visual Studio on-line documentation for more information on HTML programming and the HTML tools, such as HTML Wizards and Toolbox controls, that are available in Visual J++.

> **tip**
>
> Unlike the Java programming language, HTML is not case-sensitive, so you can use <b> in place of <B>. However, using uppercase letters for HTML tags is conventional.

Although there is some overlap, creating Web pages using HTML is a distinctly different skill from Java programming. Although there are some programmatic aspects to the HTML language, its primary purpose is managing the display of HTML documents. Creators of HTML documents often have extensive graphic design and layout skills since the final product they create is a "visual document." Although Java programming requires some design skills for the creation of user interfaces and other elements, it is used primarily for creating applications. Even if you create only Java applications, you still need to know how to implement basic HTML tags.

All HTML documents begin with <HTML> and end with </HTML>. These tags inform a Web browser that the instructions between them are to be assembled into an HTML document. The opening and closing <HTML>...</HTML> tags contain all the text and other tags that compose the HTML document. The HTML language contains many tags for creating HTML documents. Some of the more common tags are listed in Figure 7-2.

Tag	Description
`<B></B>`	Formats enclosed text in a bold typeface.
`<BODY></BODY>`	Encloses the body of the HTML document.
` `	Inserts a line break.
`<CENTER></CENTER>`	Centers text according to the width of the page.
`<HEAD></HEAD>`	Encloses the page header.
`<Hn></Hn>`	Establishes heading levels, where *n* represents a number from 1 to 6.
`<HR>`	Inserts a horizontal rule.
`<HTML></HTML>`	Starts and ends an HTML document; this tag is required for all HTML documents.
`<I></I>`	Formats enclosed text in an italic typeface.
`<IMG src="...">`	Inserts an image file.
`<P>`	Inserts a new paragraph.
`<STRONG></STRONG>`	Formats enclosed text in a strong typeface, similar to bold.
`<TABLE></TABLE>`	Creates a table. Each table row is defined by `<TR>` and each table cell is defined by `<TD>`.
`<TITLE></TITLE>`	Encloses the page title. This tag must appear within the `<HEAD>` tags.
`<U></U>`	Underlines enclosed text.

Figure 7-2: Common HTML tags

When a Web browser assembles an HTML document, it ignores any whitespace in the code; only recognized HTML tags and text are included in the final, assembled document displayed in the Web browser. For example, you cannot use carriage returns in the body of an HTML document to insert spaces before and after a paragraph; the browser recognizes only paragraph `<P>` and line break `<BR>` tags for this purpose. If you use paragraph `<P>` tags to create blank lines in an HTML document, remember that certain Web browsers, such as Internet Explorer, ignore tags that do not contain any content. For example, if you use the tag `<P>` to create an empty line in an HTML document, it may be completely ignored. To prevent this from happening, include a **nonbreaking space** code (` `) and an ending tag so that the line reads `<P> </P>`. Figure 7-3 shows an HTML document, whereas Figure 7-4 shows how it appears in a Web browser.

```
<HTML>
<HEAD>
<TITLE>Hello World</TITLE>
</HEAD>
<BODY>
<H1>Hello World (this is the H1 tag)</H1>
<H2>This line is formatted with the H2 tag</H2>
<P>This body text line contains several character
formatting tags including
<I>italics</I>, <B>bold</B>, <U>underline</U>, and
<STRIKE>strikethrough</STRIKE>. The following code line
creates a line break followed by a horizontal rule:<BR>
<HR>
<IMG src="Checkmrk.jpg">This line contains an image.
</BODY>
</HTML>
```

Figure 7-3: HTML document

Some HTML tags, such as the paragraph tag `<P>`, do not necessarily require ending tags.

Although the tags you have seen so far are useful, the one tag you must use when creating Java applets is the `<APPLET>` tag, which you use to call a Java applet from a Web page. You can further configure the `<APPLET>` tag (and other HTML tags) using various parameters, called **attributes**, that you place within the closing bracket of the starting tag. For example, the following code calls an applet named myApplet using the `CODE`, `WIDTH`, and `HEIGHT` attributes:

```
<APPLET   CODE = "myApplet.class" WIDTH = 300 HEIGHT =
200></APPLET>
```

Figure 7-4: HTML document in a Web browser

Note that the `<APPLET>` tag consists of three parts:

- `CODE =` and the name of the compiled applet you are calling
- `WIDTH =` and the width of the applet on the screen
- `HEIGHT =` and the height of the applet on the screen

The applet you call must be a compiled Java applet (with a .class file extension). The width and height represent the area in which an applet is drawn on a Web page, measured in pixels. **Pixels** are the *pic*ture *el*ements, or tiny dots of light that make up the image on your video monitor. Many monitors display 640 pixels horizontally and 480 pixels vertically, so a statement such as `WIDTH = 300 HEIGHT = 200` will create an applet that occupies a little less than a quarter of most screens (half the height and half the width).

A VGA monitor displays 640 × 480 pixels. A Super VGA monitor displays up to 1280 × 1024 pixels. In general, the maximum size of your applets should be approximately 600 × 400 pixels to make sure that most people can see the entire applet. Keep in mind that the browser's menu bar and screen elements (such as the toolbar and the scrollbars) will take up some of the screen viewing area for an applet.

Creating an HTML Document with the HTML Editor

Since HTML documents are text files, just as Java files are, you can create them in any text editor such as Notepad, WordPad, or any word processing program capable of creating simple text files. If you use a text editor to create an HTML document, you cannot view the final result until you open the document in a Web browser. However, many applications (called HTML editors) are designed specifically for creating HTML documents. Some popular HTML editors, such as Microsoft FrontPage and Adobe PageMill, have graphical interfaces that allow you to create Web pages and immediately view the results, similar to the WYSIWYG (what-you-see-is-what-you-get) feature in word processing programs. In addition, many current word processing applications, including Microsoft Word and WordPerfect, allow you to save files as HTML documents. All these HTML editors still create simple text files, but they automate the process of applying tags. For example, if you create a document in Word that contains boldface text, then save it as an HTML document, the bold <B> tag is automatically added to the text in the HTML text file that is created.

Visual Studio has a built-in HTML editor called the **HTML Editor window**, which is similar to the Text Editor window used for creating Java code files. The HTML Editor window contains three views for working with HTML documents: Design view, Source view, and Quick View. **Design view** is used for graphically creating an HTML document, similar to the way you create a word processing document. **Source view** allows you to edit the raw HTML code and is similar to the Text Editor window. It contains many of the features found in the Text Editor, such as the text editing commands on the Edit menu, IntelliSense statement completion, and syntax coloring. **Quick View** displays an HTML document as it would appear in Microsoft Internet Explorer. An example of the HTML Editor window is shown in Figure 7-5.

Be aware that different Web browsers render HTML documents in different ways. For example, an HTML document displayed in Microsoft Internet Explorer can display differently in Netscape Navigator.

To change HTML Editor options, select Options from the Tools menu, then select a category under the HTML node in the Options dialog box. You can change HTML syntax color options under the Text Editor node in the Options dialog box.

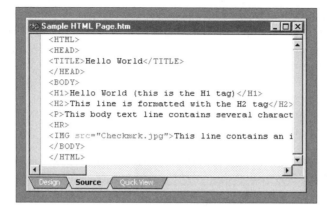

Figure 7-5: HTML Editor window

When the HTML Editor window is active, the Design and HTML toolbars appear and the HTML tools on the Toolbox are activated. The **Design toolbar** is used in Design view to adjust how an HTML document appears and how objects are positioned. The **HTML toolbar** is similar to a formatting toolbar in programs such as Word and Excel; you use it to apply HTML formatting tags to text. For example, if you highlight text in Design view and click the underline icon on the HTML toolbar, the highlighted text appears underlined. If you click the Source view tab, you will see that the <U>...</U> tag pair has been applied to the highlighted text. The **Toolbox** allows you to drag HTML objects onto an HTML page. HTML objects include items such as text boxes, buttons, and other graphic elements that appear on a Web page. As with all HTML elements, you create HTML objects with HTML tags. In Design view, you can see how these objects will look immediately; in Source view, you can see the actual code. The HTML toolbar and the HTML tools on the Toolbox are available in both Design view and Source view; they partially automate the process of creating and applying tags so you don't have to remember which tags perform what function.

If the Design or HTML toolbars are not visible, click Toolbars on the View menu, then click the toolbar you want to display. A check mark (✓) next to a toolbar name indicates that the toolbar is visible. You may also find it necessary to display the Toolbox window by selecting Toolbox from the View menu.

You can customize the Toolbox. For example, if you have HTML code pieces, known as *fragments*, that you use repeatedly, you can highlight them in Source view and drag them onto the Toolbox. Whenever you need to use them, you can then drag them from the Toolbox to your HTML document. Note that dragging a fragment to an HTML document does not remove it from the Toolbox. To delete, rename, or customize Toolbox items, right-click the Toolbox to display the shortcut menu.

section A

In addition to the Design toolbar, HTML toolbar, and the HTML tools on the Toolbox, HTML commands are also available on the HTML, Table, and Format menus that appear on the menu bar when the HTML Editor window is active. The **HTML menu** contains additional commands for inserting HTML tags. You use the **Table menu** to insert and format tables in an HTML document. The **Format menu** contains various commands that are also available on the Design toolbar and HTML toolbar. You can also insert HTML commands with keyboard shortcuts, as shown in Figure 7-6.

Command	Press
Toggle boldface for the current selection.	Ctrl+B
Toggle italics for the current selection.	Ctrl+I
Toggle underline for the current selection.	Ctrl+U
Display a dialog box to insert an HTML bookmark.	Ctrl+Shift+L
Display a dialog box to insert an HTML link.	Ctrl+L
Display a dialog box to insert an HTML image tag.	Ctrl+Shift+W
Toggle absolute positioning for the selected element.	Ctrl+K
Toggle absolute mode.	Ctrl+G
Lock or unlock the selected element (if absolutely positioned).	Ctrl+Shift+K
Toggle snap to grid.	Ctrl+Shift+G
Put the selected elements into a division.	Ctrl+J
Toggle details for the selected element.	Ctrl+Shift+Q
Toggle visible borders.	Ctrl+Q

Figure 7-6: HTML keyboard shortcuts

Remember that the primary purpose of all the tools available for creating HTML documents is to insert HTML tags. You can always insert tags manually, although the tags for some elements can become quite complex. For example, the following simple table uses more than 30 tags:

January	February	March
April	May	June
July	August	September
October	November	December

The following tags are required to create this table in HTML:

```
<TABLE>
    <TR>
        <TD>January</TD>
        <TD>February</TD>
        <TD>March</TD></TR>
    <TR>
        <TD>April</TD>
        <TD>May</TD>
        <TD>June</TD></TR>
    <TR>
        <TD>July</TD>
        <TD>August</TD>
        <TD>September</TD></TR>
    <TR>
        <TD>October</TD>
        <TD>November</TD>
        <TD>December</TD></TR>
</TABLE>
```

You can write this code manually—provided you know which tags to include. However, the easiest way to create this table is to use the Visual J++ Table tool. To use the Table tool, select Insert Table from the Table menu to display the Insert Table dialog box, just as you would when using a program such as Word. The Insert Table dialog box allows you to select several options, including the number of rows and columns to insert, border styles, and colors.

tip

A helpful feature of the Visual J++ HTML Editor—and of most good HTML editors—is that it automatically creates a basic HTML template when you add a new HTML document to a project.

As you work with HTML documents, you may notice the HTML Outline window. The HTML Outline window is used in Design view and Source view to navigate through the elements of an HTML document. HTML elements are displayed in a hierarchical list that is very similar to Project Explorer. To navigate to an HTML element displayed in the HTML Outline window, click the element once with your left mouse button.

tip

If the HTML Outline window is not visible, highlight Other Windows on the View menu, then select Document Outline.

tip

Another window you may see while working with an HTML document is the Script Outline window, which is used in Visual Studio for creating scripting language commands. You use scripting languages, such as JavaScript and VBScript, to add automated tasks and other programmatic features to a Web page.

You can use attributes to configure many HTML tags. For example, you already configured the <APPLET> tag with attributes that specify information about the applet to be started. The <BODY> tag that contains the body of an HTML document can be configured with many different parameters, including background color and margins. An HTML tag's attributes are also called its **properties**, much the same way an object has properties. To specify a tag's attributes, you can manually enter or modify them in the raw HTML code—if you know what the attributes are and how to use them correctly. Visual J++ makes working with attributes easy: You can specify them with the Properties window. An example of the Properties window displaying the <BODY> tag's attributes is shown in Figure 7-7.

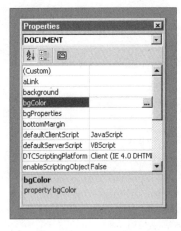

Figure 7-7: Properties window displaying an HTML tag's attributes

tip

If the Properties window is not visible, select Properties Window from the View menu.

tip

As you may recall from Chapter 1, an object's properties are displayed in the Properties window when the object is selected. To select an HTML "object," you click an element in Design view or place your insertion point within a tag in Source view.

Next you will use the HTML Editor to create a simple HTML document that will display the applet you will create in the next section. You will name the applet Greet, and it will occupy a screen area of 450 × 200 pixels.

To create a simple HTML document:

1 If necessary, start Visual J++. Otherwise, select **New Project** from the **File** menu. The New Project dialog box appears. Click the **Visual J++ Projects** folder on the New tab, then click **Empty Project**. Replace the suggested project name in the Name text box with **Greet,** change the location of the project folder to the Chapter.07 folder on your Student Disk, and then click the **Open** button.

2 Add a new HTML document to the project by selecting **Add Web Page** from the **Project** menu. The Add Item dialog box appears. Select **Page** from the **Web Page** folder, then change the suggested filename to **Test.htm** and click the **Open** button. The new HTML document opens in the HTML Editor window.

3 Click the **Source** tab located at the bottom of the HTML Editor window to display the HTML source code.

4 Place your cursor in the blank line following the tag that reads `<P> </P>` and type the opening `<APPLET>` tag that contains the applet's name and dimensions: `<APPLET CODE = "Greet.class" WIDTH = 450 HEIGHT = 200>`.

5 Press the **Enter** key to start a new line and type the applet's closing tag: `</APPLET>`.

6 Select **Refresh** from the **View** menu. The `<APPLET CODE>` changes to a solid rectangular box. The dimensions of the box represent the width and height in pixels that you entered in Step 4. If you click once on the applet, its attributes display in the Properties window. If the Properties window is not visible, select **Properties Window** from the **View** menu.

> You can use your mouse to adjust the height and width of applet when it is displayed graphically by clicking it once, and then dragging one of the sizing handles at the corners or sides of the rectangle. You can also drag the applet to a new position within the HTML document by holding your mouse over the rectangle and dragging when the mouse pointer appears as ✥.

> To display an applet control as raw HTML text in an active HTML document, select View Controls as Text from the View menu. To display the HTML text of an applet control as a graphic, select View Controls as Graphically from the View menu.

Writing a Simple Applet Using a Label

Writing an applet involves learning only a few additions and changes to writing a Java application. To write an applet, you must do the following:

- Add some import statements.
- Learn to use some Windows components and applet methods.
- Learn to use the keyword `extends`.

In Chapter 3, you used an `import` statement to access classes such as java.util.Date within your application. The purpose of importing the Date class was so you would not have to write common date-handling routines that already exist in Java. Similarly, Java's creators created a variety of classes to handle common applet needs. Most applets contain at least two import statements: `import java.applet.*;` and `import java.awt.*;`. The java.applet package contains a class named Applet—every applet you create is based on this class. The java.awt package is the **Abstract Windows Toolkit**, or **AWT**. It contains commonly used Windows **components** such as labels, menus, and buttons. You import java.awt so you don't have to "reinvent the wheel" by creating these components yourself. A Java applet isn't required to contain Windows components, but it almost always does.

For example, one of the simplest Window components is a label. **Label** is a built-in class that holds text that you can display within an applet. The Label class also contains fields that indicate appearance information, such as font and alignment. As with other objects, you can declare a Label without allocating memory, as in `Label greeting;`, or you can call the Label constructor without any arguments, as in `Label greeting = new Label();`. You can assign some text to the Label with the **setText() method**, as in `greeting.setText("Hi there");`. Alternatively, you can call the Label constructor and pass it a String argument so the Label is initialized upon construction, as in `Label greeting = new Label("Hello. Who are you?");`.

The method you use to add a component to an applet window is **add()**. For example, if you defined a Label as `Label greeting = new Label ("Hello. Who are you?");`, then you can place greeting within an applet using the command `add(greeting);`.

The object of the add() method is the applet itself, so when you add a component to a window, you could write `this.add();` in place of `add()`. You learned about the `this` reference in Chapter 4.

When you create an application, you follow any needed import statements with a class header such as `public class aClass`. Applets begin the same way as Java applications, but they also must include the words `extends Applet`. The keyword **extends** indicates that your applet will build upon, or **inherit**, the traits of the Applet class defined in the java.applet package.

The Applet class provides a general outline used by any Web browser when it runs an applet. In an application, the main() method calls other methods that you write. With an applet, the browser calls many methods automatically. Every applet includes the following four methods:

- `public void init()`
- `public void start()`
- `public void stop()`
- `public void destroy()`

If you fail to write one or more of these methods, Java creates them for you. The methods Java creates have opening and closing curly brackets only—in other words, they are empty. To create a Java program that does anything useful, you must code at least one of these methods.

The init() method is the first method called in any applet. You use it to perform initialization tasks, such as setting variables to initial values or placing applet components on the screen. You must code its header as `public void init()`.

Figure 7-8 shows the program to create an applet that displays "Hello. Who are you?" on the screen.

```java
import java.applet.*;
import java.awt.*;
public class Greet extends Applet
{
   Label greeting = new Label("Hello. Who are you?");
   public void init()
   {
       add(greeting);
   }
}
```

Figure 7-8: Greet applet

Next, you will create and run the Greet applet.

To create and run the Greet applet in a Web browser window:

1 Add a new class file to the project by selecting **Add Class** from the **Project** menu. The Add Item dialog box appears. In the Add Item dialog box, select **Class** from the **Class** folder, then change the suggested filename to **Greet.java**

and click the **Open** button. The new class opens in the Text Editor window and appears as follows:

```
public class Greet
{
}
```

2 Modify the class so that it matches the code shown in Figure 7-8.

> **help**
>
> If you forget to add extends Applet to the right of the class header, the applet may not compile correctly or may not execute correctly because of logical errors.

3 Select **Greet Properties** from the **Project** menu to display the Greet Properties dialog box, then select the **Test.htm** file to load when the project runs. Notice that IExplore.exe, the file that starts Internet Explorer, becomes the program that will load when the project is started. If you do not have Internet Explorer installed, or would like to use a different Web browser, click the **Custom** button, and then enter the program's path and filename in the **Program** text box. Click the **OK** button after selecting the project properties.

4 Build the project, then select **Start** from the **Debug** menu or press the **F5** key. The Test.htm file opens in a Web browser window as shown in Figure 7-9.

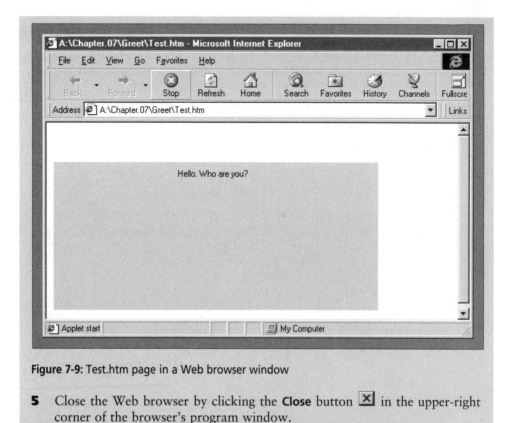

Figure 7-9: Test.htm page in a Web browser window

5 Close the Web browser by clicking the **Close** button ⊠ in the upper-right corner of the browser's program window.

In this chapter, you create an applet on a Web page by adding an HTML file and a Java file to an empty project. You can also automatically create an applet on a Web page by selecting the Applet on HTML option from the New Project dialog box. The Java file in an Applet on HTML project contains a sample applet that reads parameter information from the automatically created HTML file. Although the exercises in this text instruct you to create applets from an empty project, you should experiment on your own with an Applet on HTML project.

You can also view your applet using Quick View, or from the command line using `jview`, as you will see next.

section A

> Some applets will not work correctly using your browser. Java was designed with a number of security features, so that when an applet displays on the Internet, the applet cannot perform malicious tasks, such as deleting a file from your hard drive. If an applet does nothing to compromise security, then testing it using the Web browser, Quick View, or AppletViewer will achieve the same results.

To run the applet using Quick View:

1 Return to the **Test.htm** file in the HTML Editor window and click the **Quick View** tab. Quick View displays the applet, as shown in Figure 7-10.

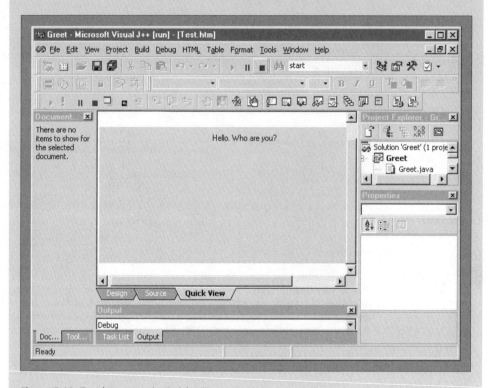

Figure 7-10: Test.htm page in Quick View

Applets

> If you change any parts of the HTML document or Java applet while Quick View is displayed, then you must select Refresh from the View menu to update and display the changes.

To run the applet using AppletViewer:

1 Save the **Test.htm** file.

> You must save the current changes to an HTML document before attempting to open it outside of Visual J++.

2 At the command line, type **jview /a Test.htm**. The /a option tells jview to run in **AppletViewer** mode. After a few moments, the AppletViewer window opens and displays the applet, as shown in Figure 7-11.

> The /a option is not used with Java applications—only with Java applets.

> Although Java filenames are case-sensitive, the case of the HTML filename that you open with jview is ignored. For example, jview /a test.htm will function correctly. However, be sure to include the .htm extension, or jview will search for a Java class file instead of an HTML file.

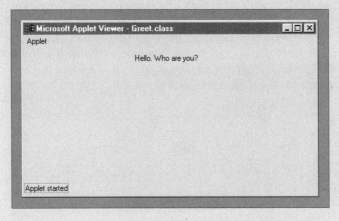

Figure 7-11: Test.htm page in AppletViewer

3. Use the mouse pointer to drag any corner of the AppletViewer window to resize it. Notice that if you widen the window by dragging its right border to the right, the window is redrawn on the screen and the Label is automatically repositioned to remain centered within the window.
4. Close the AppletViewer window by clicking the **Close** button ⊠.

The main purpose of the Test.htm file you created is to provide HEIGHT and WIDTH parameters to the Greet.class file and to demonstrate how an applet functions with an HTML document. You can also run just the Greet.class file without the Test.htm file, but since it is an applet, you must include HEIGHT and WIDTH parameters so that it sizes properly on the screen.

To run the Greet.class file without the Test.htm file:
1. At the command line, type `jview /a width=450 height=200 Greet`. After a few moments, the AppletViewer window opens and displays the applet, which should appear the same as Figure 7-11.
2. Close the AppletViewer window by clicking the **Close** button ⊠.

Changing a Label's Font

If you use the Internet and a Web browser to visit Web sites, you probably are not very impressed with your Greet.java applet. You might think that the string "Hello. Who are you?" is pretty plain and lackluster. Fortunately, Java provides you with a **Font** object that holds typeface and size information. The **setFont() method** requires a Font object argument. To construct a Font object, you need three arguments: typeface, style, and point size.

The **typeface** is a String representing a font. Common fonts are Arial, Helvetica, Courier, and Times Roman. The typeface is only a request; the system on which your applet runs might not have access to the requested font and therefore might substitute a default font. The **style** applies an attribute to displayed text and is one of three arguments, Font.PLAIN, Font.BOLD, or Font.ITALIC. The **point size** is an integer that represents 1/72 of an inch. Normal printed text is usually about 12 points; a headline might be 30 points.

To give a Label object a new font, you create the Font object, as in `Font headlineFont = new Font("Helvetica", Font.BOLD,36);`, and then you use the setFont() method to assign the Font object to a Label with the statement `greeting.setFont(headlineFont);`.

> The typeface name is a String, so you must enclose it in double quotation marks when you use it to declare the Font object.

Next, you will change the font of the text in your Greet applet.

To change the appearance of the greeting in the Greet applet:

1 Return to the **Greet.java** file in the Text Editor window.

2 Position the insertion point at the end of the line that declares the greeting Label, and then press the **Enter** key to start a new line of text.

3 Declare a Font object named bigFont by typing the following:
`Font bigFont = new Font("TimesRoman", Font.ITALIC,24);`

4 Place the insertion point to the right of the opening curly bracket of the init() method, and then press the **Enter** key to start a new line.

5 Set the greeting font to bigFont by typing `greeting.setFont(bigFont);`.

6 Rebuild the project, then return to the **Test.htm** file displayed in the **Quick View** tab in the HTML Editor window and select **Refresh** from the **View** menu. Figure 7-12 shows the output.

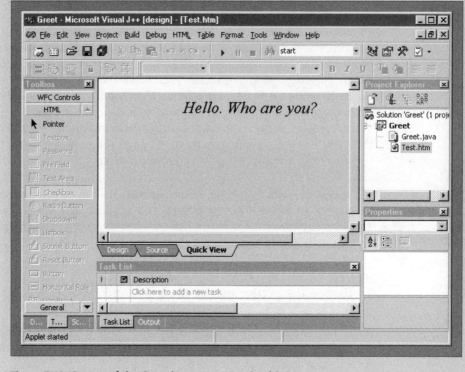

Figure 7-12: Output of the Greet.java program using bigFont

Adding TextField and Button Components to an Applet

In addition to including Labels, applets often contain other window features such as TextFields and Buttons. A **TextField** is a Windows component into which a user can type a single line of text data. (Text data includes any characters you can enter from the keyboard, including numbers and punctuation.) Typically, a user types a line into a TextField and then presses the Enter key on the keyboard or clicks a Button with a mouse to enter the data. You can construct a TextField object using one of several constructors:

- `public TextField()`, which creates an empty TextField with an unspecified length.
- `public TextField(int numColumns)`, where numColumns specifies a width for the field.
- `public TextField(String initialText)`, where initialText provides some initial text within the TextField.
- `public TextField(String initialText, int numColumns)`, where both initial text and width are specified.

For example, to provide a TextField for a user to answer the "Who are you?" question, you can code `TextField answer = new TextField(10);`. This statement provides a TextField that is empty and displays approximately 10 characters. To add the TextField named answer to an applet, you write `add(answer);`.

> **tip**
>
> The number of characters a TextField can actually display depends on the font being used and the actual characters typed. For example, in most fonts, *w* is wider than *i*, so a TextField of size 10 using the Arial font can display 24 *i* characters but only eight *w* characters.

> **tip**
>
> Try to anticipate how many characters your users will enter when you create a TextField. Even though the user can enter more characters than the number that display, the characters scroll out of view. It can be disconcerting to try to enter data into a field that is not large enough.

Several other methods are available for use with TextFields. The **setText() method** allows you to change the text in a TextField that already has been created, as in `answer.setText("Thank you");`. The **getText() method** allows you to retrieve the String of text in a TextField, as in `String whatDidTheySay = answer.getText();`.

When a user encounters a TextField you have placed within an applet, the user must position the mouse pointer in the TextField and click to get an insertion point. When the user clicks within the TextField, the TextField has **keyboard focus**, which means that the next entries from the keyboard will be entered at that location. When you want the insertion point to appear automatically within the TextField without requiring the user to click in it first, you can use the **requestFocus() method**. For example, if you have added a TextField named answer to an applet, then `answer.requestFocus()` causes the insertion point to appear within the TextField, and the user can begin typing immediately without moving the mouse. In addition to saving the user some time and effort, requestFocus() is useful when you have several TextFields and you want to direct the user's attention to a specific one. At any time, only one component within a window can have the keyboard focus.

When a TextField has the capability of accepting keystrokes, the TextField is **editable**. If you do not want the user to be able to enter data in a TextField, you can use the **setEditable() method** to change the editable status of a TextField. For example, if you want to give a user only one chance to answer a question correctly, then you can prevent the user from replacing or editing the characters in the TextField by using the code `answer.setEditable(false);`. If conditions change, and you want the user to be able to edit the TextField, use the code `answer.setEditable(true);`.

section A

A Button is even easier to create than a TextField. There are only two Button constructors:

- `public Button()`, which you use to create an unlabeled Button.
- `public Button(String label)`, which you use to create a labeled Button.

For example, to create a Button with the label "Press when ready", you write `Button readyButton = new Button("Press when ready");`. To add the Button to an applet, you write `add(readyButton);`. You can change a Button's label with the **setLabel() method**, as in `readyButton.setLabel("Don't press me again!");` or get the label and assign it to a String object with the **getLabel() method**, as in `String whatsOnButton = readyButton.getLabel();`.

Make sure that the label on your Button describes its function for the user.

As with TextField components, you can use the requestFocus() method with Button components. The surface of the Button that has the keyboard focus appears with an outline so it stands out from the other Buttons.

Next, you will add a TextField and a Button to your applet.

To add a TextField and a Button to the Greet.java applet:

1 Return to the **Greet.java** file in the Text Editor window.

2 Position the insertion point at the end of the line that defines the Font bigFont object, and then press the **Enter** key to start a new line of text.

3 Declare a Button that says "Press Me" and an empty TextField by typing the following:

```
Button pressMe = new Button("Press Me");
TextField answer = new TextField("",10);
```

4 Position the insertion point at the end of the add() statement that adds the greeting to the applet, and then press the **Enter** key to start a new line.

5 Add the TextField and the Button to the applet by typing the following:

```
add(answer);
add(pressMe);
```

6 On the following line, request focus for the answer by typing `answer.requestFocus();`.

7 Rebuild the project, then return to the **Test.htm** file displayed in the **Quick View** tab in the HTML Editor window and select **Refresh** from the **View** menu. Confirm that you can type characters into the TextField and that you can click the Button using the mouse. You haven't coded any action to take place as a result of a Button click yet, but the components should be functional.

Event-Driven Programming

An **event** occurs when someone using your applet takes action on a component, such as clicking the mouse on a Button object. The programs you have written so far in this text have been **procedural**—in other words, you dictated the order in which events occurred. You retrieved user input, wrote decisions and loops, and created output. When you retrieved user input, you had no control over how much time the user took to enter a response to a prompt, but you did control the fact that processing went no further until the input was completed. In contrast, with **event-driven programs**, the user might initiate any number of events in any order. For example, if you use a word processing program, you have dozens of choices at your disposal at any moment in time. You can type words, select text with the mouse, click a button to change text to bold, click a button to change text to italics, choose a menu item, and so on. With each word processing document you create, you choose options in any order that seems appropriate at the time. The word processing program must be ready to respond to any event you initiate.

Within an event-driven program, a component on which an event is generated is the **source** of the event. A Button that a user can click is an example of a source; a TextField that a user can use to enter text is another source. An object that is interested in an event is a **listener**. Not all objects can receive all events—you probably have used programs in which clicking many areas of the screen has no effect at all. If you want an object, such as your applet, to be a listener for an event, you must register the object as a listener for the source.

Newspapers around the world register with news services, such as the Associated Press or Reuters. The news service maintains a list of subscribers, and sends each one a story when important international events occur. Similarly, a Java component source object (such as a Button) maintains a list of registered listeners and notifies all registered listeners (such as an applet) when any event occurs, such as a mouse click. When the listener "receives the news," an event-handling method that is part of the listener object responds to the event.

tip

A source object and a listener object could be the same object. For example, a Button can change its label when a user clicks it.

To respond to user events within any applet you create, you must do the following:

- Prepare your applet to accept event messages.
- Tell your applet to expect events to happen.
- Tell your applet how to respond to any events that happen.

Preparing Your Applet to Accept Event Messages

You prepare your applet to accept mouse events by importing the java.awt.event package into your program and then adding the phrase `implements ActionListener` to the class header. The java.awt.event package includes event classes with names such as ActionEvent, ComponentEvent, and TextEvent. ActionListener is an **interface**, or a set of specifications for methods that you can use with Event objects. Implementing ActionListener provides you with standard event method specifications that allow your applet to work with ActionEvents, which are the types of events that occur when a user clicks a button.

> You can identify interfaces such as ActionListener by the fact that they are "implemented," and not "imported" (by writing `import java.applet.*)` or "extended" (by writing `extends Applet`).

Telling Your Applet to Expect Events to Happen

You tell your applet to expect ActionEvents with the **addActionListener() method**. If you have declared a Button named aButton, and you want to perform an action when a user clicks aButton, then aButton is the source of a message, and you can think of your applet as a **target** to which to send a message. You learned in Chapter 3 that the `this` reference is used to mean "this current method," so `aButton.addActionListener(this);` causes any ActionEvent messages (Button clicks) that come from aButton to be sent to "this current applet."

> Not all events are ActionEvents with an addActionListener() method. For example, TextEvents have an addTextListener() method.

Telling Your Applet How to Respond to Any Events That Happen

The ActionListener interface contains the **actionPerformed(ActionEvent e) method** specification. When an applet has registered as a listener with a Button, and a user clicks the Button, the actionPerformed() method will execute. You must write the actionPerformed() method, which like all methods contains a header and a body. You use the header `public void actionPerformed(ActionEvent e)`, where `e` is any name you choose for the event (the Button click) that initiated the notification of the ActionListener (the applet). The body of the method contains any statements that you want to execute when the action occurs. You might want to perform some mathematical calculations, construct new objects, produce output, or execute any other operation. For example, Figure 7-13 shows an actionPerformed() method that produces a line of output at the operating system prompt.

```
public void actionPerformed(ActionEvent someEvent)
{
        System.out.println
        ("I'm inside the actionPerformed() method!");
}
```

Figure 7-13: The actionPerformed() method that produces a line of output

Next, you will make your applet an event-driven program by adding functionality to your applet's Button and TextField. When the user enters a name and clicks the Button, the applet will display a new greeting using the setText method.

To add functionality to your applet:

1. Return to the **Greet.java** file in the Text Editor window.
2. For the third import statement in your program, add **import java.awt.event.*;**.
3. Position the insertion point at the end of the class header (`public class Greet extends Applet`), press the **space bar**, and then type **implements ActionListener**.
4. Position the insertion point at the end of the statement in the init() method that adds the pressMe button to the applet, and then press the **Enter** key. Prepare your applet for Button-source events by typing the statement **pressMe.addActionListener(this);**.

5 Position the cursor to the right of the closing curly bracket for the init() method, and then press the **Enter** key. Add the following actionPerformed() method after the init() method but before the closing bracket for the Greet class. This method declares a String that will hold the user's name, uses the getText() method on the answer TextField to retrieve the String, and changes the greeting label to display a new message.

```
public void actionPerformed(ActionEvent thisEvent)
{
    String name = answer.getText();
    greeting.setText("Hi there " + name + ".");
}
```

6 Rebuild the project, then return to the **Test.htm** file displayed in the **Quick View** tab in the HTML Editor window and select **Refresh** from the **View** menu.

7 Type your name in the TextField, and then click the **Press Me** button. Examine the greeting label. The personalized message "Hi there" and your name should display.

8 Use your mouse to highlight the name in the TextField in the AppletViewer window, and then type a new name. Click the **Press Me** button again. A new greeting appears in the greeting label.

In most applets that contain a TextField, there are two ways to get the applet to accept user input. Usually, you can enter text and click a Button, or you can enter text and press the Enter key. If your applet needs to receive an event message from a TextField, then you need to make your applet a registered Event listener with the TextField.

To add the ability to press the Enter key from within the TextField for input:

1 In the **Greet.java** file, position the insertion point at the end of the statement `pressMe.addActionListener(this);`, and then press the **Enter** key.

2 Make the answer field accept input by typing the following:
`answer.addActionListener(this);`

3 Rebuild the project, then return to the **Test.htm** file displayed in the **Quick View** tab in the HTML Editor window and select **Refresh** from the **View** menu. Confirm that you can input a name in the TextField by either clicking the Press Me button or by pressing the Enter key.

Adding Output to an Applet

An applet that changes the text in a Label is not very exciting. It would be more interesting to create a new Label that gets added to the applet with the add() method after the user enters a name. You can declare a new, empty Label with the statement `Label personalGreeting = new Label("");`. After the name is retrieved, you can use the setText() method to set the Label text for personalGreeting to `"Hi there " + name`.

> **To add a personalGreeting Label to the applet:**
>
> **1** Within the **Greet.java** file, remove the `greeting.setText ("Hi there " + name + ".");` statement from the actionPerformed() method.
>
> **2** Add the following statements to the actionPerformed() method to declare a new Label named personalGreeting, to set the text of the personalGreeting, and then to add personalGreeting to the applet:
>
> ```
> Label personalGreeting = new Label("");
> personalGreeting.setText("Hi " + name);
> add(personalGreeting);
> ```
>
> **3** Rebuild the project. This time, execute the applet using AppletViewer by typing **jview /a Test.htm** at the command line. Try typing a name in the TextField and then press the Enter key or click the Press Me button. When you type a name in the TextField and then press the Enter key, nothing happens. When you enter a name in the TextField and click the Press Me button, nothing happens.
>
> **4** Now use the mouse to resize the AppletViewer window by dragging one of its borders. The personalGreeting Label appears.
>
> **5** Close the AppletViewer window.

Your applet does not display personalGreeting, because it is added to the applet too late. The init() method lays out all the applet components when the applet starts, and the `add(personalGreeting);` statement is not part of the init() method. The AppletViewer screen is drawn only when it is created or when the applet is out of date. When you resize the AppletViewer window, it "knows" it must be redrawn to accommodate the new size. However, when you use add() to place a new component on the screen, the applet does not "realize" it is out of date.

help

In the preceding steps, you used the AppletViewer rather than Quick View to start the applet, to demonstrate how the AppletViewer window automatically knows when to redraw itself. The Quick View tab of the HTML Editor does not automatically redraw itself since it is not a separate window. Selecting the Refresh command from the View menu does not simply redraw the Quick View window; it also restarts the applet.

You can cause the applet to know it is out of date by using the **invalidate() method**, which marks the window so it knows that it is not up to date with recent changes. Then, you can cause the changes to take effect by using the **validate() method**, which redraws any invalid window.

To redraw your AppletViewer window after adding personalGreeting:

1 Within the actionPerformed() method of the Greet.java file, position the insertion point at the end of the `add(personalGreeting);` statement, and then press the **Enter** key. Then add the following statements:

```
invalidate();
validate();
```

2 Rebuild the project and execute the applet using AppletViewer. The greeting now displays immediately after you type a name and press the Enter key or click the Press Me button.

3 Close the AppletViewer window.

If you can add components to an applet, you should also be able to remove them; you do so with the **remove() method**. For example, after a user enters a name into the TextField, you might not want the user to use the TextField or its Button again, so you can remove them from the applet. You use the remove() method by placing the component's name within the parentheses. As with add(), you must redraw the applet after remove() to see the effects.

To remove the TextField and Button from the Greet applet:

1 Place the cursor at the end of the `add(personalGreeting);` statement in the actionPerformed() method of the Greet.java file, and then press the **Enter** key. Then enter the following statements:

```
remove(answer);
remove(pressMe);
```

2. Rebuild the project and execute the applet using AppletViewer. When you enter a name and either press the Enter key or click the Press Me button, the TextField and the Button disappear from the screen.
3. Close the AppletViewer window.

SUMMARY

- Applets are programs that are called from within another application. You run applets within a Web page or within a special type of console application called AppletViewer using `jview /a`.

- An applet must be called from within an HTML, or HyperText Markup Language, document.

- A Web browser is a program that allows you to display HTML documents on your computer screen; such documents often contain Java applets.

- HTML documents are text files containing formatting instructions, called tags, along with the text that is to be displayed on a Web page. Tags usually come in pairs. The tag that begins every HTML document is `<HTML>`, and the tag that ends every HTML document is `</HTML>`.

- HTML is not case-sensitive.

- To run an applet from within an HTML document, you add the `<APPLET>` and `</APPLET>` tags to your HTML document.

- You can place three attributes within the `<APPLET>` tag: `CODE`, `WIDTH`, and `HEIGHT`.

- Visual J++ has a built-in HTML editor called the HTML Editor window, which is similar to the Text Editor window used for creating Java code files. The HTML Editor window contains three views for working with HTML documents: Design view, Source view, and Quick View.

- If you have HTML code pieces, known as *fragments*, that you use repeatedly, you can highlight them in Source view and drag them onto the Toolbox.

- An HTML tag has attributes, also called *properties*, much the same way an object has properties. To specify a tag's attributes, you can manually enter or modify them in the raw HTML code, or you can modify them using the Properties window.

- Most applets contain at least two import statements: `import java.applet.*;` and `import java.awt.*;`. The java.awt package is the Abstract Windows Toolkit, or AWT. It contains commonly used Windows components such as labels, menus, and buttons.

- Label is a built-in class that holds text that can be displayed within an applet. The setText() method assigns text to a Label or any other component.

- You use the add() method to add a component to an AppletViewer window.

- Applet class headers include the words `extends Applet`.

- Four methods that are included in every applet are `public void init()`, `public void start()`, `public void stop()`, and `public void destroy()`.

- The init() method is the first method called in any applet. You use it to perform initialization tasks, such as setting variables to initial values or placing applet components on the screen.

- A Font object holds typeface and size information. To construct a Font object, you need three arguments: typeface, style, and point size. The typeface is a String representing a font. Common fonts are Arial, Helvetica, Courier, and Times Roman. The style applies an attribute to displayed text and is one of three arguments: Font.PLAIN, Font.BOLD, or Font.ITALIC. The point size is an integer that represents 1/72 of an inch.

- To give a Label object a new font, you create the Font object and then use the setFont() method to assign the Font object to a Label.

- A TextField is a Windows component into which a user can type a single line of text data. Typically, a user types a line into a TextField and then inputs the data by pressing the Enter key on the keyboard or clicking a Button with the mouse.

- You can create a TextField with or without initial text and with or without a specified size.

- The setText() method allows you to change the text in a TextField that has already been created. The getText() method allows you to retrieve the String of text in a TextField.

- You can create a Button with or without a label. You can change a Button's label with the setLabel() method, or get the label and assign it to a String object with the getLabel() method.

- An event occurs when your applet's user takes action on a component, such as using the mouse to click a Button object. In event-driven programs, the user might initiate any number of events in any order.

- Within an event-driven program, a component on which an event is generated is the source of the event. An object that is interested in an event is a listener.

- To respond to user events within any applet you create, you must prepare your applet to accept event messages, tell your applet to expect events to happen, and then tell your applet how to respond to any events that happen.

- Adding `implements ActionListener` to an applet's class header prepares an applet to receive event messages.

- An interface is a set of specifications for methods that you can use with events.

- An ActionEvent is the type of event that occurs when a user clicks a Button. You tell your applet to expect ActionEvents with the addActionListener() method. The ActionListener interface contains the `actionPerformed(ActionEvent e)` method specification. In the body of the method, you write any statements that you want to execute when an action takes place.

- You can alert the applet when it is out of date by using the invalidate() method, which marks the window as not up to date with recent changes. Using the validate() method redraws any out-of-date window.

QUESTIONS

1. Applets are _____.
   a. stand-alone programs
   b. Web pages
   c. called from within another application
   d. written in HTML

2. Which of the following is true about AppletViewer?
   a. It is a method.
   b. You must code it yourself.
   c. You execute it using `jview /a`
   d. You must call it from within an HTML document.

3. HTML stands for _____.
   a. HyperText Markup Language
   b. Hash Table Management Language
   c. Heap Task Monitoring List
   d. Help Topic Maintenance List

4. When you write a Java applet, you save the code with the _____ file extension.
   1. .app
   2. .htm
   3. .java
   4. .class

5. Java applications and Java applets are similar because both _____.
   a. can be started using AppletViewer
   b. can be executed as a console application
   c. are executed from within an HTML document
   d. have a main() method

6. To use an applet within an HTML document, you include the name of the _____.
   a. .java source code file
   b. .class compiled file
   c. .exe executable file
   d. Web site from which the applet will be run

7. A program that allows you to display HTML documents on your computer screen is a _____.
   a. search engine
   b. compiler
   c. browser
   d. server

8. HTML commands also are called _____.
   a. instructions
   b. regulations
   c. tips
   d. tags

9. All HTML commands are surrounded by _____.
   a. parentheses
   b. curly brackets
   c. dots
   d. angle brackets

10. Every HTML document begins and ends with _____.
   a. `<BODY>...</BODY>`
   b. `<HTML>...</HTML>`
   c. `<APPLET>...</APPLET>`
   d. `<TITLE>...</TITLE>`

11. To prevent certain Web browsers, such as Internet Explorer, from ignoring empty lines, add _____ between the paragraph tag pair `<P>` ... `</P>`.
   a. `#linebreak`
   b. `System.out`
   c. `break`
   d. ` `

12. The ending half of any HTML tag pair is preceded by a _____.
    a. dot
    b. forward slash
    c. backslash
    d. colon

13. The _____ tag is used for adding a Java applet to a Web page.
    a. `<HTML>`
    b. `<JAVA>`
    c. `<APPLET>`
    d. `<CODE>`

14. HTML code pieces that can be dragged onto the Toolbox and reused are called _____.
    a. blocks
    b. pieces
    c. snippets
    d. fragments

15. The name of any applet called using `CODE` within an HTML program must use the _____ extension.
    a. .exe
    b. .code
    c. .java
    d. .class

16. Usually, you should create your applets to run on a monitor that measures _____ pixels so most users can see the entire applet.
    a. 100 × 100
    b. 220 × 360
    c. 640 × 480
    d. 2200 × 100

17. Labels and Buttons are _____.
    a. components
    b. containers
    c. applets
    d. constituents

18. The method that places a value within a previously constructed Label is _____.
    a. getValue()
    b. setText()
    c. fillLabel()
    d. setValue()

section A

19. The add() method _____.
    a. adds two integers
    b. adds two numbers of any data type
    c. places a component within an AppletViewer window
    d. places a text value within an applet component

20. Which of the following methods is *not* included in every applet?
    a. init()
    b. add()
    c. stop()
    d. destroy()

21. The first method called in any applet is _____.
    a. main()
    b. start()
    c. init()
    d. whatever method appears first within the applet

22. A Font object contains all of the following arguments except _____.
    a. language
    b. typeface
    c. style
    d. point size

23. A Windows component into which a user can type a single line of text data is a(n) _____.
    a. InputArea
    b. DataField
    c. TextField
    d. Label

24. The constructor `public Button("4")` creates _____.
    a. an unlabeled Button
    b. a Button four pixels wide
    c. a Button four characters wide
    d. a Button with a "4" on it

25. You can change a Button's label using the _____ method.
    a. setText()
    b. getText()
    c. setLabel()
    d. getLabel()

26. A user might initiate any number of events in any order in _____ program.
    a. an event-driven
    b. a procedural
    c. a random
    d. any Java

27. ActionListener is an example of a(n) _____.
    a. import
    b. applet
    c. interface
    d. component

28. When an applet is registered as a listener with a Button, if a user clicks the Button, the method that executes is _____.
    a. buttonPressed()
    b. addActionListener()
    c. start()
    d. actionPerformed()

29. You let an applet know it is out of date by using the _____ method.
    a. date()
    b. change()
    c. invalidate()
    d. validate()

EXERCISES

For the following exercises, save each program that you create in the Chapter.07 folder on your Student Disk.

1. Create an applet with a Button labeled "Who's the greatest?" When the user clicks the Button, display your name in a large font.

2. a. Create an applet that asks a user to enter a password into a TextField and then press the Enter key. Compare the password to "Rosebud". If it matches, display "Access Granted"; if not, display "Access Denied".
   b. Modify the password applet in Exercise 2a to ignore differences in case between the typed password and "Rosebud".
   c. Modify the password applet in Exercise 2b to compare the password to a list of five valid passwords: "Rosebud", "Redrum", "Jason", "Surrender", or "Dorothy".

3. Create an applet with a Button. Display your name in an 8-point font. Every time the user clicks the Button, increase the font size for the displayed name by 4 points. Remove the Button when the font size exceeds 24 points.

4. Create an applet that displays the date and time in a TextField with the Label "Today is" when the user clicks a Button.

5. Create an applet that displays an employee's title in a TextField when the user types an employee's first and last names (separated by a space) in another TextField. Include Labels for each TextField. You can use arrays to store the employees' names and titles.

6. Create an applet that displays an employee's title in a TextField when the user types an employee's first and last names (separated by a space) in another TextField, or displays an employee's name in a TextField when the user types an employee's title in a TextField. Include a Label for each of the TextFields. Add a Label at the top of the applet with the text "Enter a name or a title". You can use arrays to store the employees' names and titles.

SECTION B
objectives

In this section you will learn
- About the applet life cycle
- How to create a more sophisticated interactive applet
- How to use the setLocation() method
- How to disable a component
- How to get help

The Applet Life Cycle and More Sophisticated Applets

The Applet Life Cycle

Applets are popular because they are easy to use in a Web page. Because applets execute in a browser, the Applet class contains methods that automatically are called by the browser. In Section A, you learned the names of four of these methods: init(), start(), stop(), and destroy().

You already have written your own init() methods. When you write a method that has the same method header as an automatically provided method, you replace or **override** the original version. Every time a Web page containing an applet is loaded in the browser, or when you run the jview /a command with an HTML document that calls an applet, if you have written an init() method for the applet, that method executes; otherwise the automatically provided init() method executes. You should write your own init() method when you have any initialization tasks to perform, such as setting up user interface components.

> Overriding a method means creating your own version that Java will use instead of using the automatically supplied version with the same name. It is not the same as *overloading* a method, which means writing several methods that have the same name but take different arguments. You learned about overloading methods in Chapter 4.

The start() method executes after the init() method, and it executes again every time the applet becomes active after it has been inactive. For example, on the Internet, users can leave a Web page, visit another page, and then return to the first site. The applet becomes inactive, and then active. You write your own start() method if there are any actions you want to take when a user revisits an applet;

for example, you might want to resume some animation that you suspended when the user left the applet.

When a user leaves a Web page, perhaps by minimizing a window or traveling to a different Web page, the stop() method is invoked. You override the existing empty stop() method only if you want to take some action when an applet is no longer visible. You usually do not need to write your own stop() methods.

The destroy() method is called when the user closes the browser or AppletViewer. Closing the browser or AppletViewer releases any resources the applet might have allocated. As with stop(), you usually do not have to write your own destroy() methods.

In summary, every applet has the same life cycle outline, as shown in Figure 7-14. When any applet executes, the init() method runs, followed by start(). If the user leaves the applet's page, stop() executes. When the user returns, start() executes again. The stop()-and-start() sequence might continue any number of times, until the user closes the browser (or AppletViewer) and the destroy() method is invoked.

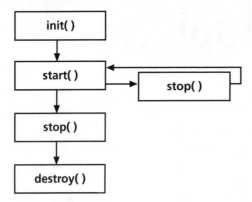

Figure 7-14: Applet life cycle outline

To demonstrate an applet's life cycle methods in action, you can write an applet that overrides all four methods, and count the number of times each method executes.

To demonstrate the life cycle of an applet:

1. Create a new empty project named **LifeCycle**. Save the **LifeCycle** project folder in the Chapter.07 folder on your Student Disk. Then add a new class file named **LifeCycle.java** to the LifeCycle project.

2. Above the `public class LifeCycle` header, type the following import statements that you will need for the applet:

```
import java.applet.*;
import java.awt.*;
import java.awt.event.*;
```

3 Position the insertion point to the right of the class header and type `extends Applet implements ActionListener`.

4 Between the class's curly brackets, declare the following six Label objects that you will use to display the names of each of six methods that will execute during the lifetime of the applet:

```
Label messageInit = new Label("init ");
Label messageStart = new Label("start ");
Label messageDisplay = new Label("display ");
Label messageAction = new Label("action ");
Label messageStop = new Label("stop ");
Label messageDestroy = new Label("destroy");
```

5 Declare a Button by typing the following:

```
Button pressButton = new Button("Press");
```

6 Declare six integers that will hold the number of occurrences of each of the six methods by typing the following code on one line:

```
int countInit, countStart, countDisplay, countAction,
countStop, countDestroy;
```

7 Add the following init() method, which adds one to countInit, places the components within the applet, and then calls the display() method:

```
public void init()
{
        ++countInit;
        add(messageInit);
        add(messageStart);
        add(messageDisplay);
        add(messageAction);
        add(messageStop);
        add(messageDestroy);
        add(pressButton);
        pressButton.addActionListener(this);
        display();
}
```

8 Add the following start() method, which adds one to countStart and calls display():

```
public void start()
{
        ++countStart;
        display();
}
```

9 Add the following display() method, which adds one to countDisplay and then displays the name of each of the six methods with the current count and indicates how many times the method has executed:

```
public void display()
{
        ++countDisplay;
        messageInit.setText("init " + countInit);
        messageStart.setText("start " + countStart);
        messageDisplay.setText("display " + countDisplay);
        messageAction.setText("action " + countAction);
        messageStop.setText("stop " + countStop);
        messageDestroy.setText("destroy " + countDestroy);
}
```

10 Add the following stop() and destroy() methods, which each add one to the appropriate counter and call display():

```
public void stop()
{
        ++countStop;
        display();
}
public void destroy()
{
        ++countDestroy;
        display();
}
```

11 When the user clicks pressButton, the following actionPerformed() method will execute; it adds one to countAction and displays it. The method also calls the stop() method. Enter the method:

```
public void actionPerformed(ActionEvent e)
{
        ++countAction;
        display();
}
```

12 Build the project. If necessary, correct any errors and rebuild.

Take a moment to examine the code you created for LifeCycle.java. Each of the methods increments one of the six counters by one, but you never explicitly call any of the methods except display(); each of the other methods will be called automatically. Next, you will create an HTML document so you can test LifeCycle.java.

To create an HTML document to test LifeCycle.java:

1 Add to the project a new Web page named **life.htm**. The Web page opens in the HTML Editor window.

2 In the Source tab of the HTML Editor window, place your insertion point in the blank line following the tag that reads `<P> </P>` and type the opening `<APPLET>` tag that contains the applet's name and dimensions: `<APPLET CODE = "LifeCycle.class" WIDTH = 460 HEIGHT = 200>`.

3 Press the **Enter** key to start a new line and type the applet's closing tag: `</APPLET>`.

4 Rebuild the project, save the life.htm file, and then execute the applet in AppletViewer by typing `jview /a life.htm` at the command line. Figure 7-15 shows the output. When the applet begins, the init() method is called, so one is added to countInit. The init() method calls display(), so one is added to countDisplay. Immediately after the init() method executes, the start() method is executed, and one is added to countStart. The start() method calls display() so one more is added to countDisplay. The first time you see the applet, countInit is 1, countStart is 1, and countDisplay is 2. The methods actionPerformed(), stop(), and destroy() have not yet been executed.

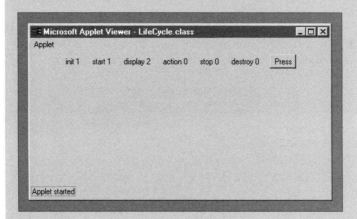

Figure 7-15: LifeCycle applet after startup

5 Select **Stop** from the **Applet** menu in the AppletView window. The Stop command on the Applet menu calls the applet's stop() method. Now select **Start** from the **Applet** menu to call the applet's start() method. The applet now looks like Figure 7-16. The init() method still has been called only once, but when you stopped and restarted the applet, the stop() method executed, then the start() method executed. Therefore, countStop is now 1 and countStart has increased to 2. Additionally, both start() and stop() call display(), so countDisplay() is increased by two, and it now holds the value 4.

> **help**
>
> The Stop command on the Applet menu simulates how the stop() method is called when a user leaves a Web page in a browser window. The Start command on the Applet menu simulates how the start() method is called when a user returns to a Web page in a browser window.

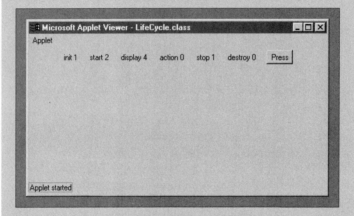

Figure 7-16: LifeCycle applet after selecting the Stop and Start commands

6. Select the **Stop** and **Start commands** from the **Applet** menu again. Now the stop() method has executed twice, the start() method has executed three times, and the display() method has executed a total of six times. See Figure 7-17.

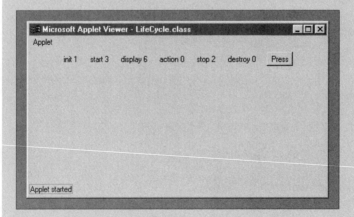

Figure 7-17: LifeCycle applet after being stopped and started twice

7 Click the **Press** button. The count for the actionPerformed() method now is 1, and actionPerformed() calls display(), so countDisplay() is up to 7, as shown in Figure 7-18.

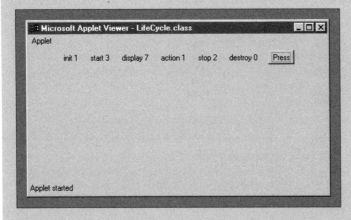

Figure 7-18: LifeCycle applet after you click the Press button

8 Continue to select the **Stop** and **Start commands** and press the button, and note the changes that occur with each activity until you can correctly predict the outcome. Notice that the destroy() method is not executed until you close the applet, and then it is too late to observe an increase in countDestroy.

A Complete Interactive Applet

You are now able to create a fairly complex application or applet. Next, you will create an applet that contains several components, receives user input, makes decisions, uses arrays, performs output, and reacts to the applet life cycle.

The PartyPlanner applet lets its user estimate the cost of an event hosted by Event Handlers Incorporated. Event Handlers uses a sliding fee scale so the per-guest cost decreases as the total number of invited guests increases. Figure 7-19 shows the fee structure.

1 to 24	$27
25 to 49	$25
50 to 99	$22
100 to 199	$19
200 to 499	$17
500 to 999	$14
1,000 and over	$11

Figure 7-19: Cost per guest for events

The applet lets the user enter a number of anticipated guests. The user can press the Enter key or click a Button to perform the fee lookup and event cost calculation. Then the applet displays the cost per person as well as the total cost for the event. The user can continue to request fees for a different number of guests and view the results for any length of time before making another request or leaving the page. If the user leaves the page, however, you want to erase the last number of requested guests and make sure the next user starts fresh with zero guests.

To begin to create an interactive party planner applet:

1 Create a new empty project named **PartyPlanner**. Save the **PartyPlanner** project folder in the Chapter.07 folder on your Student Disk. Then add a new class file named **PartyPlanner.java** to the PartyPlanner project.

2 Above the `public class PartyPlanner` header, type the following import statements that you will need for the applet:

```
import java.applet.*;
import java.awt.*;
import java.awt.event.*;
```

3 Position the insertion point to the right of the class header and type `extends Applet implements ActionListener`.

4 You will need several components: a Label for the company name, a Button the user can click to perform a calculation, a prompt for the Button, a TextField in which the user can enter the number of invited guests, and two more Labels to display output. Add the following code between the class's curly brackets to implement these components:

```
Label companyName = new Label
    ("Event Handlers Incorporated");
Button calcButton = new Button("Calculate");
Label prompt = new Label
    ("Enter the number of guests at your event");
TextField numGuests = new TextField(5);
Label perPersonResult = new Label("Plan with us.");
Label totalResult = new Label("The more the merrier!");
```

5 Additionally, for appearance, create a Font by typing the following:

```
Font bigFont = new Font("Helvetica", Font.ITALIC, 24);
```

6 You can use the init() method to place components within the applet screen and prepare the Button and text-entry field to receive action messages by typing the following:

```
public void init()
{
    companyName.setFont(bigFont);
    add(companyName);
    add(prompt);
    add(numGuests);
    add(calcButton);
    calcButton.addActionListener(this);
    numGuests.addActionListener(this);
    add(perPersonResult);
    add(totalResult);
}
```

7 Add the following start() method, which executes when the applet is first started.

```
public void start()
{
    perPersonResult.setText("Plan with us.");
    numGuests.setText("0");
    totalResult.setText("The more the merrier!");
    invalidate();
    validate();
}
```

You finished the init() and start() methods for the PartyPlanner applet and placed each component in the applet. At this point, the applet doesn't actually do anything; most of the applet's work is contained in the actionPerformed() method, which is the most complicated method in this applet. Next, you will create the actionPerformed() method. You will begin by declaring two parallel arrays—one array will hold guest limits for each of six event rates, and the other array will hold the actual rates.

To complete the PartyPlanner applet:

1 Enter the following method header for actionPerformed() and declare two arrays for guest limits and rates:

```
public void actionPerformed(ActionEvent e)
{
        int[] guestLimit =  { 0, 25, 50,100,200,500,1000};
        int[] ratePerGuest = {27, 25, 22, 19, 17, 14, 11};
}
```

2 Next, add the following variable to hold the number of guests. The user will enter text into a TextField, but you need an integer to perform calculations, so you can use the parseInt() method.

```
int guests = Integer.parseInt(numGuests.getText());
```

You learned about the parseInt() method in Chapter 6.

3 You need two variables that will hold the individual, per-person fee for an event, and the fee for the entire event. Enter the following variables:

```
int individualFee = 0, eventFee = 0;
```

4 Enter the following variables to use as subscripts for the arrays:

```
int x = 0, a = 0;
```

There are a number of ways to search through the guestLimit array to discover the appropriate position of the per-person fee in the ratePerGuest array. One possibility is to use a `for` loop and vary a subscript from five down to zero. If the number of guests is greater than or equal to any value in the guestLimit array, then the corresponding per-person rate in the ratePerGuest array is the correct rate. After finding the correct individual rate, you determine the price for the entire event by multiplying the individual rate by the number of guests. After finding the appropriate individual fee for a given event, you do not want to search through the guestLimit array any longer, so you set the subscript x equal to zero to force an early exit from the for loop.

5 Enter the following for loop:

```
for(x = 6; x >= 0; --x)
    if(guests >= guestLimit[x])
        {
            individualFee = ratePerGuest[x];
            eventFee = guests * individualFee;
            x = 0;
        }
```

6 The only tasks that remain in the actionPerformed() method involve producing output for the user. Enter the following code to accomplish this processing:

```
perPersonResult.setText
        ("$" + individualFee + " per person");
totalResult.setText("Event cost $" + eventFee);
```

7 Add a closing curly bracket for the actionPerformed() method.

8 Add to the project a new Web page named **PartyPlan.htm**. The Web page opens in the HTML Editor window.

9 In the Source tab of the HTML Editor window, place your insertion point in the blank line following the tag that reads <P> </P> and type the opening <APPLET> tag that contains the applet's name and dimensions: <APPLET CODE = "PartyPlanner.class" WIDTH = 320 HEIGHT = 200>.

10 Press the **Enter** key to start a new line and type the applet's closing tag: </APPLET>.

11 Build the project, save the **PartyPlan.htm** file, and then execute the applet in AppletViewer by typing **jview /a partyplan.htm** at the command line. Your output should look similar to Figure 7-1 at the beginning of this chapter. Test the applet with different guest numbers until you are sure that the per-person rates and event rates are correct. For example, if you enter 100 guests, then your output resembles Figure 7-20.

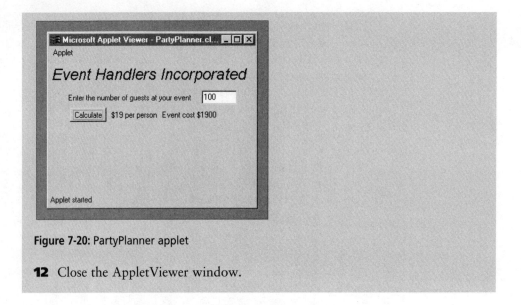

Figure 7-20: PartyPlanner applet

12 Close the AppletViewer window.

Using the setLocation() Method

A serious shortcoming of the objects you have written so far is that you have not been able to choose the location of the Label and Button objects you place within your applets. When you use the add() method to add a component to an applet, it seems to have a mind of its own as to where it is physically placed. Although you need to learn more about the Java programming language before you can change where components are placed initially when you use the add() method, you can use the setLocation() method to change the location of a component at a later time. The **setLocation() method** allows you to place a component at a specific location within the AppletViewer window.

Any applet window consists of a number of horizontal and vertical pixels on the screen. You set the pixel values in the HTML document you write to test the applet. Any component you place on the screen has a horizontal, or **x-axis**, position as well as a vertical, or **y-axis**, position in the window. The upper-left corner of any display is position 0,0. The first, or **x-coordinate**, value increases as you travel from left to right across the window. The second, or **y-coordinate**, value increases as you travel from top to bottom. Figure 7-21 illustrates the screen coordinate positions.

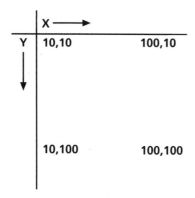

Figure 7-21: Screen coordinate positions

For example, to position a Label object named someLabel at the top-left corner of a window, you write `someLabel.setLocation(0,0);`. If a window is 200 pixels wide and 100 pixels tall, then you can place a Button named pressMe in the approximate center of the window with the statement `pressMe.setLocation(100,50);`.

You can picture a coordinate as an infinitely thin line that lies between the pixels of the output device.

When you use setLocation(), the top-left corner of the component is placed at the specified x- and y-coordinates. If a window is 100 by 100 pixels, then `aButton.setLocation(100,100);` places the Button outside the window, where you cannot see it.

Next, you will create a Label that changes its location with each Button click.

To create a moving Label:

1 Create a new empty project named **MoveLabel**. Save the **MoveLabel** project folder in the Chapter.07 folder on your Student Disk. Then add a new class file named **Move.java** to the MoveLabel project.

2 Above the `public class Move` header, type the following import statements that you will need for the applet:

```
import java.applet.*;
import java.awt.*;
import java.awt.event.*;
```

3 Position the cursor to the right of the class header and type `extends Applet implements ActionListener`.

4 Between the class's curly brackets, declare the following Label and Button, and two integers that will hold the horizontal and vertical coordinates of the Label:

```
Label movingMsg = new Label("Event Handlers Inc.");
Button pressButton = new Button("Press Me");
int xLoc = 20, yLoc =20;
```

5 Enter the following init() method to add the components to the applet screen and prepare the Button to receive messages:

```
public void init()
{
     add(movingMsg);
     add(pressButton);
     pressButton.addActionListener(this);
}
```

6 When the user clicks the Button, the message will move 10 pixels to the right and 10 pixels down. In other words, it will appear to move across the screen on a downward angle. Enter the following actionPerformed method() to do this:

```
public void actionPerformed(ActionEvent e)
{
     movingMsg.setLocation(xLoc+=10, yLoc+=10);
}
```

7 Add to the project a new Web page named **move.htm**. The Web page opens in the HTML Editor window.

8 In the Source tab of the HTML Editor window, place your cursor in the blank line following the tag that reads `<P> </P>` and type the opening `<APPLET>` tag that contains the applet's name and dimensions: `<APPLET CODE = "Move.class" WIDTH = 460 HEIGHT = 300>`.

9 Press the **Enter** key to start a new line and type the applet's closing tag: `</APPLET>`.

10 Build the project and click the **Quick View** tab in the HTML Editor window. Observe how the Label moves each time you click the Press Me button.

Using the setEnabled() Method

You probably have used computer programs in which a component becomes disabled or unusable. For example, a Button might become dim and unresponsive when the programmer no longer wants you to have access to the Button's functionality. You can use the **setEnabled() method** with a component to make it unavailable and, in turn, to make it available again. The setEnabled() method takes an argument of true if you want to enable a component, or false if you want to disable a component.

When you create a component, it is enabled by default.

For example, in the MoveLabel applet, a user can continue to click the Button until the Label moves completely off the screen. If you want to prevent this from happening, you can disable the Button after the Label has advanced as far as you want it to go. Next, you will stop the Label from moving after it reaches a y-coordinate of 280.

To disable the Button:

1 Return to the **Move.java** file in the Text Editor window.

2 Position the insertion point at the end of the statement in the actionPerformed() method, and then press the **Enter** key to start a new line of text. Then add the following statement to disable the Button when the message has moved to a y-coordinate of 280:

```
if(yLoc==280)
        pressButton.setEnabled(false);
```

3 Rebuild and save the project, and then execute the applet in AppletViewer by typing **jview /a move.htm** at the command line. Click the **Press Me** button until the Button is disabled and the Label cannot descend any farther.

Getting Help

Now your Java programs are becoming more sophisticated—each program you write contains several methods and many individual statements. As you continue to learn about programming, many Java applications and applets you write easily could become 20 times larger than the ones you are writing now. There are hundreds of additional Java methods that you have not learned yet, and developers are creating new objects daily for you to use. With all that programming code to write and all those methods to understand, it is easy to get lost. In addition to the Visual J++ help options listed in Chapter 1, there are a variety of Java help sources available on the Internet.

A wealth of material exists at the Microsoft Visual J++ Web site, at http://www.msdn.microsoft.com/visualj/default.asp and the Sun Microsystems Web site, at http://java.sun.com.

Some Java newsgroups on the Web are summarized in Figure 7-22. While you are still a novice programmer, it's a good idea to read the messages that are posted at these newsgroups. Reserve asking questions of your own until you are sure you are not asking a question that has been asked dozens of times before.

Java newsgroups on the Internet
comp.lang.java.advocacy
comp.lang.java.announce
comp.lang.java.api
comp.lang.java.beans
comp.lang.java.gui
comp.lang.java.help
comp.lang.java.misc
comp.lang.java.programmer
comp.lang.java.security
comp.lang.java.setup
comp.lang.java.softwaretools
comp.lang.java.tech
Microsoft.public.java.visualj++

Figure 7-22: Java newsgroups

SUMMARY

- When you write a method that has the same method header as an automatically provided method, you replace or override the original version.
- The start() method executes after the init() method and every time the applet becomes active after it has been inactive. You write your own start() method if there are any actions you want to take when an applet is revisited.

- When a user moves off the page, perhaps by minimizing a window or traveling to a different Web page, the stop() method is invoked.

- The destroy() method is called when the user closes the browser or AppletViewer; this releases any resources the applet may have allocated.

- When you use the add() method to add a component to an applet, you do not determine the physical location of the component. The setLocation() method allows you to place a component at a specific location within an AppletViewer window.

- Any AppletViewer window consists of a number of horizontal and vertical pixels on the screen, called the x-axis positions and y-axis positions, respectively.

- The upper-left corner of any display is position 0,0. The first, or x-coordinate, value increases as you travel from left to right across the window. The second, or y-coordinate, value increases as you travel from top to bottom.

- When you use setLocation(x,y), the top-left corner of the component is placed at the specified x- and y-coordinates.

- You can use the setEnabled() method with a component to make it unavailable and, in turn, to make it available again. The setEnabled() method takes an argument of `true` if you want to enable a component, or `false` if you want to disable a component.

- When you are writing Java programs, you can get help from the Microsoft Visual J++ Web site, the Sun Microsystems Web site, or from Java newsgroups.

QUESTIONS

1. When you write a method that has the same method header as an automatically provided method, you _____ the original version.
   a. destroy
   b. override
   c. call
   d. copy

2. If you do not write an init() method for an applet, then _____.
   a. your program will not compile
   b. your program will compile but not run
   c. you must write a main() method
   d. an automatically provided init() method executes

3. The method that executes immediately after init() is _____.
   a. main()
   b. begin()
   c. start()
   d. stop()

section B

4. The start() method executes _____.
   a. after the init() method
   b. every time the applet becomes active after it has been inactive
   c. both of these
   d. neither of these

5. The method that executes when a user leaves a page is _____.
   a. stop()
   b. destroy()
   c. kill()
   d. finish()

6. The destroy() method is called when the user _____.
   a. closes the browser or AppletViewer window
   b. minimizes the AppletViewer window
   c. leaves the page
   d. shuts down the computer

7. The stop()-and-start() sequence _____ within an applet.
   a. must not occur more than once
   b. might occur any number of times
   c. must never occur
   d. does not usually occur

8. Which of the following statements creates a Label that says "Welcome"?
   a. `Label = new Label("Welcome");`
   b. `Label aLabel = Label("Welcome");`
   c. `aLabel = new Label("Welcome");`
   d. `Label aLabel = new Label("Welcome");`

9. Which of the following statements correctly creates a Font object?
   a. `Font aFont = new Font("TimesRoman", Font.ITALIC, 20);`
   b. `Font aFont = new Font(30, "Helvetica", Font.ITALIC);`
   c. `Font aFont = new Font(Font.BOLD,"Helvetica", 24);`
   d. `Font aFont = new Font(22, Font.BOLD,"TimesRoman");`

10. The method that positions a component within an applet is _____.
    a. position()
    b. setPosition()
    c. location()
    d. setLocation()

11. The y-axis position within a window refers to _____.
    a. horizontal position
    b. vertical position
    c. font size
    d. order of operations

12. The upper-left corner of a display that is 100 × 100 pixels is position _____.
    a. 0,0
    b. 0,100
    c. 100,0
    d. 100,100

13. The upper-right corner of a display that is 100 × 100 pixels is position _____.
    a. 0,0
    b. 0,100
    c. 100,0
    d. 100,100

14. In a window that is 200 × 200 pixels, position 10,190 is nearest to the _____.
    a. top left
    b. top right
    c. bottom left
    d. bottom right

15. You use the setEnabled() method to make a component _____.
    a. available
    b. unavailable
    c. both of these
    d. neither of these

16. Which of the following statements disables a component named someComponent?
    a. `someComponent.setDisabled();`
    b. `someComponent.setDisabled(true);`
    c. `someComponent.setEnabled(false);`
    d. `someComponent.setEnabled(true);`

EXERCISES

For the following exercises, save each program that you create in the Chapter.07 folder on your Student Disk.

1. Create an applet named DoubleInteger that allows the user to enter an integer. When the user presses a Button, the integer is doubled and the answer is displayed.

2. Create an applet named SumIntegers that allows the user to enter two integers into two separate TextFields. When the user presses a Button, the sum of the integers is displayed.

section B

3. a. Create an applet named DivideTwo that allows the user to enter two integers in two separate TextFields. The user can click a Button to divide the first integer by the second integer and display the result.

   b. Modify the DivideTwo applet created in Exercise 3a so that if a user enters zero for the second integer, when the user clicks the Button to divide, the applet displays the message "Division by zero not allowed!"

4. a. Create a payroll applet named CalcPay that allows the user to enter two double values—hours worked and hourly rate. When the user presses a Button, the applet calculates the gross pay.

   b. Modify the payroll applet created in Exercise 4a so that federal withholding tax is subtracted from gross pay based on the following table:

0 to 99.99	10%
100.00 to 299.99	15%
300.00 to 599.99	21%
600.00 and up	28%

5. Create a conversion applet named ConvertMiles that lets the user enter a distance in miles in a TextField, and then converts the miles to kilometers and displays the result in a TextField. Each TextField should have a Label. You can use the formula miles * 1.6 to convert miles to kilometers.

6. Create an applet named CalculateBalance that calculates the current balance in a checking account in a TextField. The user enters the beginning balance, check amount, and deposit amount in separate TextFields with the appropriate Labels. After the applet calculates the current balance, reposition the TextFields and Labels so that the beginning balance appears on the first line, the check and deposit amounts appear on the second line, and the new balance appears on the third line.

7. Create an applet named FamilyRecord that displays two of your family members' names, relationships to yourself, and ages in TextFields when you click a Button. Each TextField should have a Label. After clicking the Button, reposition the TextFields and Labels so that your family members' names appear on the second line, and the family members' relationships to you and ages appear on the third line.

8. Each of the following files in the Chapter.07 folder on your Student Disk has syntax and/or logical errors. Add the files to a new project called FixDebug. Save the FixDebug project under the Chapter.07 folder on your Student Disk. You can test each of these applets with the testDebug.htm file on the Student Disk. Remember to change the Java class file referenced in the HTML file so it matches the DebugSeven applet you are working on.
   a. DebugSeven1.java
   b. DebugSeven2.java
   c. DebugSeven3.java
   d. DebugSeven4.java

CHAPTER 8

Graphics

case ▶ "What are you smiling about?" your mentor, Lynn Greenbrier, asks as she walks by your desk at Event Handlers Incorporated.

"I liked Java programming from the start," you say, "but now that I'm creating applets, I'm *really* having fun."

"If you like what you've done with applets so far," Lynn smiles, "just wait until you add graphics. Java makes working with colors, shapes, pictures, and animation a snap, and graphics add real marketing punch to your applets and Web sites. Let me show you how to use graphics."

Previewing the StopLight Applet

The Chap8StopLight applet works as an interactive advertisement for Event Handlers Incorporated and demonstrates several graphics methods. You can use a completed version of the applet that is saved in the Chapter.08 folder on your Student Disk now.

To run the Chap8StopLight applet:

1 Go to the command-line prompt for the Chapter.08 folder on your Student Disk (A:\Chapter.08\), type **jview /a Chap8Light.htm**, and then press the **Enter** key. It might take a few minutes for the AppletViewer window shown in Figure 8-1 to open.

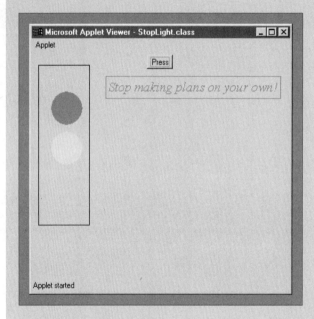

Figure 8-1: Chap8StopLight applet

2 Use the applet by clicking the **Press** button to see the stoplight color and the Event Handlers Incorporated message change. Click the **Press** button as many times as you like.
3 Close the AppletViewer window.

SECTION A
objectives

In this section you will learn:

- About the paint() and repaint() methods
- How to use the drawString() method to draw Strings
- How to use the setFont() and setColor() methods
- How to set an applet's background color
- How to create Graphics objects
- How to draw lines and rectangles
- How to draw ovals

Graphics Basics

The paint() and repaint() Methods

In Chapter 7, you learned that every applet uses four methods: init(), start(), stop(), and destroy(). If you don't write these methods, Java provides you with a "do nothing" copy. You can, however, override any of these automatically supplied methods by writing your own versions.

Actually, a fifth method is used within every applet. The **paint()** method runs when Java displays your applet. You can write your own paint() method to override the automatically supplied one whenever you want to paint graphics, such as shapes, on the screen. As with init(), start(), stop(), and destroy(), if you don't write a paint() method, you get an automatic version from Java. The paint() method executes automatically every time you minimize, maximize, or resize the AppletViewer window or a Web browser window containing an applet.

The paint() method header is `public void paint (Graphics g)`. The header indicates that the method requires a Graphics object argument. However, you don't usually call the paint() method directly. Instead, you call the **repaint()** method, which you can use when a window needs to be updated, such as when it contains new images. The Java system calls the repaint() method when it needs to update a window, or you can call it yourself—in either case, repaint() creates a Graphics object for you. The repaint() method, in turn, calls another method named update(), which then calls paint().

Next you will create a program that demonstrates this series of events using a button and a label. Clicking the button once disables the label and turns it gray. Clicking the button when the label is disabled executes the repaint() method which calls the paint() method. The paint() method then enables the label. The paint() method is also called every time you minimize, maximize, or resize the AppletViewer window or a Web browser window containing an applet. Therefore, if the paint() method is called when the label is disabled, the label will be enabled.

section A

To demonstrate how repaint() and paint() operate using a Button and Label:

1 If necessary, start Visual J++, then create a new empty project named **DemoPaint**. Save the **DemoPaint** project folder in the Chapter.08 folder on your Student Disk. Then add a new class file named **DemoPaint.java** to the project.

2 Above the `public class DemoPaint` header, type the following import statements that you will need for the applet:

```
import java.applet.*;
import java.awt.*;
import java.awt.event.*;
```

3 Add `extends Applet implements ActionListener` to the right of the class header.

4 Between the class's curly brackets, add the following Button and Label:

```
Button enableDisableButton = new Button("Enable/Disable");
Label paintDemoLabel = new Label("Paint Demo");
```

5 Type the following init() method, which adds the Button and Label to the applet:

```
public void init()
{
    add (enableDisableButton);
    add (paintDemoLabel);
    enableDisableButton.addActionListener (this);
}
```

6 Override the paint() method by typing the following code, so the Label is always enabled whenever the paint() method is called. (You first learned about the setEnabled() method in Chapter 7.)

```
public void paint (Graphics g)
{
    paintDemoLabel.setEnabled (true);
}
```

> **help**
>
> Enabling the Label is not actually necessary when the program first launches, since the Label was never disabled. However for this demonstration, adding the setEnabled() method is necessary to ensure that the Label is always enabled whenever the paint() method is called.

7 Type the following actionPerformed() method which uses the isEnabled() function to see if the Label is enabled. If the Label is enabled, it is disabled using the setEnabled() function and the actionPerformed() method ends. If the Label is disabled, the repaint() method is called, which executes the paint() method. The paint() method then enables the Label.

```
public void actionPerformed (ActionEvent e)
{
    if (paintDemoLabel.isEnabled ())
        paintDemoLabel.setEnabled (false);
    else
        repaint ();
}
```

8 Add to the project a new Web page named **testDP.htm**.

9 In the Source tab of the HTML Editor window, place your insertion point in the blank line following the tag that reads `<P> </P>` and type the opening APPLET tag that contains the applet's name and dimensions: `<APPLET CODE = "DemoPaint.class" WIDTH = 100 HEIGHT = 100>`.

10 Press the Enter key to start a new line and type the applet's closing tag: `</APPLET>`.

11 Build and save the project. If necessary, correct any syntax errors and rebuild. Execute the applet in AppletViewer by typing `jview /a testDP.htm` at the command line. When the applet starts, the paint() method executes automatically and enables the Label.

12 Click the Button in the applet. The actionPerformed method uses the isEnabled() method to see if the Label is enabled. Since the Label is enabled, the actionPerformed method disables it, then ends. Click the Button again. This time, when the actionPerformed() method checks to see if the Label is enabled, it calls the repaint() method, since the Label is disabled. The repaint() method then calls the paint() method, which enables the Label.

13 Click the Button again. The Label is disabled. Minimize the AppletViewer window and then restore it. Notice that the paint() method is called and enables the Label. Click the Button again to disable the Label, then resize the window. The Label is enabled again. Click the Button one more time to disable the Label, then maximize the window. With each action, the Label is enabled, demonstrating all the conditions under which the paint() method executes.

14 Close the AppletViewer window.

> **tip**
>
> The repaint() method actually only requests that Java repaint the screen. If a second request to repaint() occurs before Java can carry out the first request, then Java will execute only the last repaint() method.

The drawString() method

The **drawString()** method allows you to draw a String in an applet window. The drawString() method requires three arguments: a String, an x-axis coordinate, and a y-axis coordinate.

You already are familiar with x- and y-axis coordinates because you used them with the setLocation() method for components in Chapter 7. However, there is a minor difference in how you place components using setLocation() and how you place Strings using drawString(). When you use x- and y-coordinates with components, such as Labels, the top-left corner of the component is placed at the coordinate position. When you use x- and y-coordinates with drawString(), the bottom-left corner of the String appears at the coordinates. Figure 8-2 shows the positions of a Label placed at the coordinates 30, 10 and a String placed at the coordinates 10, 30.

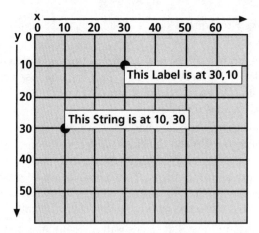

Figure 8-2: Label and String coordinates

The drawString() method is a member of the Graphics class, so you need to use a Graphics object to call it. Recall that the paint() method header shows that the method receives a Graphics object from the update() method. If you use drawString() within paint(), then the Graphics object you name in the header is available to you. For example, if you write a paint() method with the header `public void paint(Graphics brush)`, then you can draw a String within your paint() method by using a statement such as `brush.drawString("Hi",50,80);`.

> **To use drawString() to place a String within an applet:**
>
> **1** Create a new empty project named **DemoGraphics1**. Save the **DemoGraphics1** project folder in the Chapter.08 folder on your Student Disk. Then add a new class file named **DemoGraphics1.java** to the project.
>
> **2** Above the `public class DemoGraphics1` header, type the following import statements that you will need for the applet:
>
> ```
> import java.applet.*;
> import java.awt.*;
> ```
>
> **3** Add **extends Applet** to the right of the class header.
>
> **4** Between the class's curly brackets, declare a String to hold the company name for Event Handlers Incorporated by typing `String companyName = new String("Event Handlers Incorporated");`.
>
> **5** Type the following paint() method that uses a Graphics object to draw the companyName String:
>
> ```
> public void paint(Graphics gr)
> {
>    gr.drawString(companyName,10,100);
> }
> ```
>
> **6** Add to the project a new Web page named **testDG.htm**.
>
> **7** In the Source tab of the HTML Editor window, place your cursor in the blank line following the tag that reads `<P> </P>` and type the opening `<APPLET>` tag that contains the applet's name and dimensions: `<APPLET CODE = "DemoGraphics1.class" WIDTH = 420 HEIGHT = 300>`.
>
> **8** Press the **Enter** key to start a new line and type the applet's closing tag: `</APPLET>`.
>
> **9** Build and save the project, and then execute the applet in AppletViewer. The program's output appears in Figure 8-3.

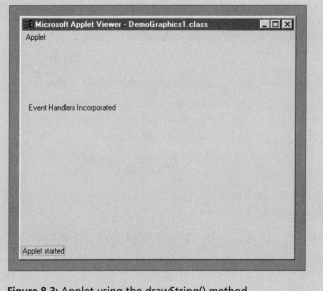

Figure 8-3: Applet using the drawString() method

10 Close the AppletViewer window.

The setFont() and setColor() Graphics Object Methods

You can improve the appearance of Graphics objects by using the setFont() and setColor() Graphics object methods. The setFont() method requires a Font object, which, as you recall, you create with a statement such as `Font someFont = new Font("TimesRoman", Font.BOLD, 16);`. Then you can instruct a Graphics object to use the font by using the font as the argument in a setFont() method. For example, if a Graphics object is named brush, then the font is set to someFont with `brush.setFont(someFont);`.

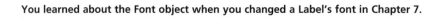

tip

You learned about the Font object when you changed a Label's font in Chapter 7.

You can designate a Graphics color with the setColor() method. The Color class contains 13 constants that appear in Figure 8-4. You can use any of these constants as an argument to the setColor() method. For example, you can instruct a Graphics object named brush to use green paint by using the statement `brush.setColor(green);`. Until you change the color, subsequent graphics output will appear as green.

> **tip**
>
> Java constants usually are written in all uppercase letters, as you learned in Chapter 4. However, unlike other Java constants, color names of the Color class are lowercase.

black	green	pink
blue	lightGray	red
cyan	magenta	white
darkGray	orange	yellow
gray		

Figure 8-4: Color class constants

To add a Font object and some color to your DemoGraphics1 class:

1. Return to the **DemoGraphics1.java** file in the Text Editor window.
2. Just after the companyName declaration, add a Font object by typing the following: `Font bigFont = new Font("Helvetica", Font.ITALIC, 24);`.
3. For the first two statements in the paint() method after the opening curly bracket, type the following statements so the gr object uses the bigFont object and the color magenta:

   ```
   gr.setFont(bigFont);
   gr.setColor(Color.magenta);
   ```

4. Following the existing drawString() method call, type the following lines to change the color and add an additional call to the drawString() method:

   ```
   gr.setColor(Color.orange);
   gr.drawString(companyName,40,140);
   ```

5. Rebuild and save the project, and then execute the applet in AppletViewer. The program's output appears in Figure 8-5. Although the figure is shown in black and white in this book, notice that the Strings on your screen print as magenta and orange text.

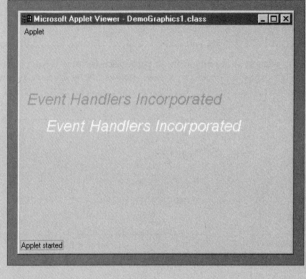

Figure 8-5: DemoGraphics1 applet using font and color

6 Close the AppletViewer window.

You also can create your own Color object with the statement `Color someColor = new Color(r, g, b);`, where *r*, *g*, and *b* are numbers representing the intensity of red, green, and blue you want in your color. The numbers can range from 0 to 255, with 0 being the darkest shade of the color and 255 being the lightest. For example, `color darkPurple = new Color(100, 0, 100);` produces a dark purple color that has red and blue components, but no green. You can create more than 16 million custom colors using this approach.

Some computers cannot display each of the 16 million possible colors. Each computer will display the closest color it can.

You can discover the red, green, or blue components of any existing color with the methods getRed(), getGreen(), and getBlue(). Each of these methods returns an integer. For example, you can discover the amount of red in a magenta color by printing the value of `Color.magenta.getRed();`.

To create a demonstration program that displays several hundred colors:

1 Create a new empty project named **DemoColor**. Save the **DemoColor** project folder in the Chapter.08 folder on your Student Disk. Then add a new class file named **DemoColor.java** to the project.

2. Above the `public class DemoColor` header, type the following import statements that you will need for the applet:

   ```
   import java.applet.*;
   import java.awt.*;
   ```

3. Add `extends Applet` to the right of the class header.
4. Define a small font between the class's curly brackets by typing the following: `Font littleFont = new Font("Helvetica", Font.ITALIC, 6);`.
5. Add the following paint() method with five integer variables. The variables r, g, and b are used to hold red, green, and blue components for custom colors, respectively. The x and y variables are used for the String screen position.

   ```
   public void paint(Graphics gr)
   {
     int r, g , b;
     int x = 0, y = 0;
   ```

6. Set the Graphics object font by typing `gr.setFont(littleFont);`.
7. Create a `for` loop in which the red component will vary from 255 down to 0 in decrements of 20. Within the red `for` loop, vary the intensity of green, and within the green `for` loop, vary the intensity of blue. Although you won't get every possible combination of color components, you will get a wide variety.

   ```
   for(r = 255; r >= 0; r -= 20)
     for(g = 255; g >= 0; g -= 20)
       for(b = 255; b >= 0; b -= 20)
   ```

8. Within the body of the `for` loop, create a new color, set the color, and draw an X. After the X is drawn, increase the x-axis coordinate by 5. When the value of x approaches the horizontal limit of the applet—that is, when it passes 400 or so—increase y and reset x to 0. To accomplish this processing, type the following code:

   ```
   {
     Color variety = new Color(r, g, b);
     gr.setColor(variety);
     gr.drawString("X",x,y);
     x += 5;
       if (x >= 400)
       {
         x = 0;
         y += 10;
       }
   }
   ```

9. Add a closing curly bracket for the paint() method.

> **10** Add to the project a new Web page named **testDC.htm**, and add the tag `<APPLET CODE = "DemoColor.class" WIDTH = 420 HEIGHT = 300>`.
>
> **11** Press the **Enter** key to start a new line and type the applet's closing tag: `</APPLET>`.
>
> **12** Build the project and execute the applet by clicking the **Quick View** tab in the HTML Editor window. You should see an applet filled with hundreds of small Xs in many different colors.

Setting the Background Color

In addition to changing the color of Strings that you display, you can change the background color of your applet. For example, the statement `setBackground (Color.pink);` changes the applet screen color to pink. You do not need a Graphics object to change the applet's background color; it is the applet itself that is changing colors. (You also could write `this.setBackground(Color.pink);` because setBackgound refers to "this" applet.)

Creating Your Own Graphics Object

When you call the paint() method, you can use the automatically created Graphics object, but you also might choose to instantiate your own Graphics objects. For example, you might want to use a Graphics object when some action occurs, such as a mouse event. Because the ActionPerformed() method does not supply you with a Graphics object automatically, you can create your own.

For example, to display a string when the user clicks a Button, you can code an ActionPerformed() method such as the following:

```
public void actionPerformed(ActionEvent e)
{
  Graphics gr = getGraphics();
  gr.drawString("You clicked the button!",50,100);
}
```

This method instantiates a Graphics object named gr. (You can use any legal Java identifier.) The getGraphics() method provides the gr object with Graphics capabilities. Then the gr object can employ any of the Graphics methods you have learned—setFont(), setColor(), and drawString().

> **tip**
>
> Notice that when you create the gr object, you are not calling the Graphics constructor directly. (The name of the graphics constructor is Graphics(), not getGraphics().) You are not allowed to call the Graphics constructor because Graphics() is an abstract class. You will learn about abstract classes in Chapter 10.

Next, you will create a Graphics object named pen.

To write an applet in which you create your own Graphics object:

1 Create a new empty project named **DemoCreateGraphicsObject**. Save the **DemoCreateGraphicsObject** project folder in the Chapter.08 folder on your Student Disk. Then add a new class file named **DemoCreateGraphicsObject.java** to the project.

2 Above the `public class DemoCreateGraphicsObject` header, type the following import statements that you will need for the applet:

```
import java.applet.*;
import java.awt.*;
import java.awt.event.*;
```

3 Add `extends Applet implements ActionListener` to the right of the class header.

4 Type the following code between the class's curly brackets to define a String, a Button, a Font, and two integers to hold x- and y-coordinates:

```
String companyName = new String
   ("Event Handlers Incorporated");
Button moveButton = new Button("Move It");
Font hel12Font = new Font("Helvetica", Font.ITALIC, 12);
int x = 10, y = 50;
```

5 Type the following init() method, which changes the background color, adds the Button to the applet, and prepares the applet to listen for Button events:

```
public void init()
{
   setBackground(Color.yellow);
   add (moveButton);
   moveButton.addActionListener(this);
}
```

6 Within the actionPerformed() method, you can create a Graphics object and use it to draw the String on the screen. Each time a user clicks the Button, the x- and y-coordinates both increase so a copy of the company name appears slightly below and to the right of the previous company name. Type the following code to accomplish this processing:

```
public void actionPerformed(ActionEvent e)
{
   Graphics gr = getGraphics();
   gr.setFont(hel12Font);
   gr.setColor(Color.magenta);
   gr.drawString(companyName,x+=20,y+=20);
}
```

7 Add to the project a new Web page named **testDCGO.htm** and add the tag `<APPLET CODE = "DemoCreateGraphicsObject.class" WIDTH = 420 HEIGHT = 300>`.

8 Press the **Enter** key to start a new line and type the applet's closing tag: `</APPLET>`.

9 Build and save the project, and then execute the applet in AppletViewer by typing `jview /a testDCGO.htm` at the command line. Click the **Move It** button several times to see the String message appear on the screen.

If you run the DemoCreateGraphicsObject applet and click the Button enough times, the "Event Handlers Incorporated" String appears to march off the bottom of the applet. Every time you click the Button, the x- and y-coordinates used by drawString() increase. To prevent the "Event Handlers Incorporated" String from appearing to march off the bottom of the applet, you can check the screen coordinates' values to see whether they exceed the applet's dimensions.

To avoid the error of exceeding the applet viewing area:

1 Return to the **DemoCreateGraphicsObject.java** file in the Text Editor window.

2 Position your cursor to the right of the opening curly bracket in the actionPerformed() method, and then press the **Enter** key to start a new line.

3 Because you add 20 to the x variable each time you draw the String within the applet, you can ensure that the String appears only 12 times by preventing the x-coordinate from exceeding a value of 250. Type the following `if` statement to check the x-coordinate value:

```
if(x < 250)
{
```

4 Position your cursor to the right of the line `gr.drawString(companyName,x+=20,y+=20);`, press the **Enter** key, type the closing curly bracket for the `if` statement, and then press the **Enter** key again.

5 On the new line, type the following `else` statement that disables the Button after the x-coordinate becomes too large:

```
else
    moveButton.setEnabled(false);
```

6 Rebuild and save the project, and then execute the applet in AppletViewer by typing `jview /a testDCGO.htm` at the command line. Now, when you click the Move It button so that the company name moves to x-coordinate 250, the Button is disabled, and the company name no longer violates the limits of the applet size.

Drawing Lines and Rectangles

Just as you can draw Strings using a Graphics object and the drawString() method, Java provides you with several methods for drawing a variety of lines and geometric shapes.

> **tip**
> Any line or shape will be drawn in the current color you set with the setColor() method.

You can use the **drawLine()** method to draw a straight line between any two points on the screen. The drawLine() method takes four arguments—the x- and y-coordinates of the line's starting point, and the x- and y-coordinates of the line's ending point. For example, if you create a Graphics object named pen, then `pen.drawLine(10,10,100,200);` draws a straight line that slants down and to the right, from position 10, 10 to position 100, 200, as shown in Figure 8-6. Because you can start at either end when you draw a line, an identical line is created with `pen.drawLine(100,200,10,10);`.

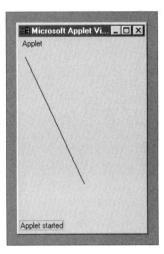

Figure 8-6: Line from position 10, 10 to 100, 200

> **tip**
> It is almost impossible to draw a picture of any complexity without sketching it first on a piece of graph paper to help you determine correct coordinates.

You can use the methods **drawRect()** and **fillRect()**, respectively, to draw the outline of a rectangle or to draw a solid, filled rectangle. Each of these methods requires four arguments. The first two arguments represent the x- and y-coordinates of the upper-left corner of the rectangle. The last two arguments represent the width and height of the rectangle. For example, `drawRect(20,100,200,10);` draws a short, wide rectangle that begins at position 20, 100 and is 200 pixels wide by 10 pixels tall.

For an alternative to the drawRect() method, you can use four calls to drawLine().

The **clearRect()** method also requires four arguments and draws a rectangle. The difference between using the drawRect() and fillRect() methods and using the clearRect() method is that the drawRect() and fillRect() methods use the current drawing color, whereas the clearRect() method uses the current *background* color to draw what appears to be an empty or clear rectangle. For example, the DemoRectangles program shown in Figure 8-7 produces the applet shown in Figure 8-8. The program sets the background color, draws a filled rectangle in a contrasting color, and draws a smaller, clear rectangle (using the background color) within the boundaries of the filled rectangle.

```java
import java.applet.*;
import java.awt.*;
public class DemoRectangles extends Applet
{
  public void paint(Graphics gr)
  {
    gr.setColor(Color.red);
    setBackground(Color.blue);
    gr.fillRect(20,20,120,120);
    gr.clearRect(40,40,50,50);
  }
}
```

Figure 8-7: DemoRectangles program

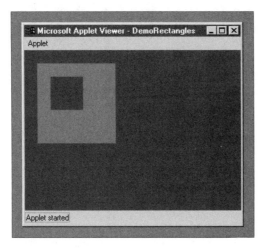

Figure 8-8: Output of the DemoRectangles program

You can create rectangles that have rounded corners when you use the **drawRoundRect()** Graphics method. The drawRoundRect() method requires six arguments. The first four arguments match the four arguments required to draw a rectangle—the x- and y-coordinates of the top-left corner, and the width and height. The two additional arguments represent the arc width and height associated with the rounded corners. If you assign zeros to the arc coordinates, the rectangle will not be rounded at all; instead, the corners will be perfectly square. At the other extreme, if you assign values to the arc coordinates that are at least the width and height of the rectangle, the rectangle is so rounded that it is a circle. The paint() method in Figure 8-9 draws four rectangles with increasingly large corner arcs. Figure 8-10 shows the program's output.

```
public void paint(Graphics gr)
{
  gr.drawRoundRect(20,20,80,80,0,0);
  gr.drawRoundRect(120,20,80,80,10,10);
  gr.drawRoundRect(220,20,80,80,40,40);
  gr.drawRoundRect(320,20,80,80,80,80);
}
```

Figure 8-9: Method that draws rounded rectangles

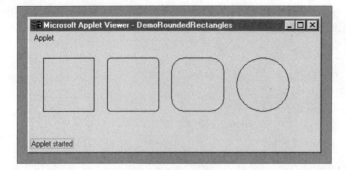

Figure 8-10: Output of the paint() method that draws rounded rectangles

As with the fillRect() method, you can use the **fillRoundRect()** method to create a filled, rounded rectangle.

Drawing Ovals

It is possible to draw an oval using the drawRoundRect() or fillRoundRect() methods, but it is usually easier to use the drawOval() and fillOval() methods. Both the **drawOval()** and **fillOval()** methods draw ovals using the same four arguments that rectangles use. When you supply drawOval() or fillOval() with x- and y-coordinates for the upper-left corner and width and height measurements, you can picture an imaginary rectangle that uses the four arguments. The oval is then placed within the rectangle so it touches the rectangle at the center of each of the rectangle's sides. For example, if you create a Graphics object named tool and draw a rectangle with `tool.drawRect(50,50,100,60);`, and an oval with `tool.drawOval(50,50,100,60);`, then the output will appear as shown in Figure 8-11 with the oval edges just skimming the rectangle sides.

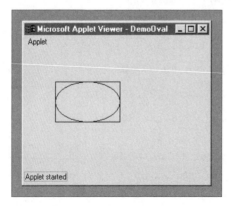

Figure 8-11: Demonstration of the drawOval() method

tip

If you draw a rectangle with identical height and width, you draw a square. If you draw an oval with identical height and width, you draw a circle.

Next, you will add a simple line drawing to the DemoCreateGraphicsObject program. The drawing will appear after the user clicks the Move It button enough times to increase the x-coordinate to 250, which disables the Button.

To add a line drawing to a program:

1 Return to the **DemoCreateGraphicsObject.java** file in the Text Editor window.

2 Position your cursor to the right of the opening curly bracket for the actionPerformed() method, and then press the **Enter** key to start a new line.

3 Type the following to define a Graphics object and set its font and color:

```
Graphics gr = getGraphics();
gr.setFont(hel12Font);
gr.setColor(Color.magenta);
```

4 Replace the current `if...else` structure with the following code that tests the value of x and either draws the company name or disables the Button and draws a logo. When you draw the logo, you set the drawing color to black and draw a simple drawing of the Event Handlers Incorporated logo, which is two overlapping balloons with strings attached:

```
if(x < 250)
{
   gr.drawString(companyName,x+=20,y+=20);
}
else
{
   moveButton.setEnabled(false);
   gr.setColor(Color.black);
   gr.drawOval(50,170,70,70);
   gr.drawLine(85,240,110,300);
   gr.drawOval(100,170,70,70);
   gr.drawLine(135,240,110,300);
}
```

5 Rebuild and save the project, and then execute the applet in AppletViewer. Now, after the company name moves to x-coordinate 250, the Button is disabled and the balloon drawing appears, as shown in Figure 8-12.

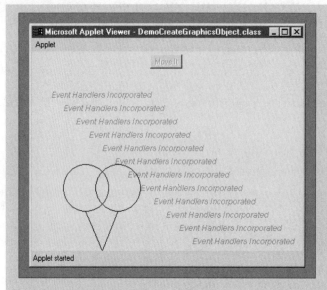

Figure 8-12: Output of the DemoCreateGraphicsObject program with the balloon drawing

6 Close the AppletViewer window.

 # SUMMARY

- The paint() method runs when you display, maximize, minimize, or restore an applet. You can use the paint() method that is supplied automatically by Java, or you can write your own paint() method.

- The paint() method header, `public void paint (Graphics g)`, requires a Graphics object argument.

- You don't usually call the paint() method directly. Instead, you call the repaint() method, which calls the update() method, which calls the paint() method.

- You use the drawString() method to draw a String in an applet. The drawString() method requires three arguments: a String, an x-axis coordinate, and a y-axis coordinate. The x- and y-coordinates represent the bottom-left position of the String.

- The drawString() method is a member of the Graphics class, so you need to use a Graphics object to call it.

- You can instruct a Graphics object to use a font by using the font as the argument in a setFont() method, such as `aGrObject.setFont(aFont);`.

- The setColor() method allows you to designate a Graphics color.

- The Color class contains 13 constants: black, blue, cyan, darkGray, gray, green, lightGray, magenta, orange, pink, red, white, and yellow.

- You can create your own Color object with the statement
  `Color someColor = new Color(r, g, b);`, where r, g, and b are numbers representing the intensity of red, green, and blue you want in your color.

- The methods getRed(), getGreen(), and getBlue() allow you to discover the red, green, or blue components of any existing color. Each method returns an integer.

- You can change the background color of your applet with the setBackground() method.

- You can instantiate your own Graphics objects.

- You can use the drawLine() method to draw a straight line between any two points on the screen. The drawLine() method takes four arguments: the x- and y-coordinates of the line's starting point and the x- and y-coordinates of the line's ending point.

- You can use the drawRect() and fillRect() methods, respectively, to draw the outline of a rectangle or to draw a solid, filled rectangle. Each of these methods requires four arguments. The first two arguments represent the x- and y-coordinates of the upper-left corner of the rectangle. The last two arguments represent the width and height of the rectangle.

- The clearRectangle() method requires four arguments and draws a rectangle using the current background color of the applet to create an empty or clear rectangle.

- You can create rectangles with rounded corners using the drawRoundRect() Graphics method, which requires six arguments. The first four arguments match the four arguments required to draw a rectangle—the x- and y-coordinates of the top-left corner and the width and height. The two additional arguments represent the arc width and height associated with the rounded corners.

- The drawOval() and fillOval() methods draw ovals using four arguments—the x- and y-coordinates for the upper-left corner and the width and height measurements of an imaginary rectangle that surrounds the oval.

QUESTIONS

1. Which of the following methods is not automatically contained in every applet?
   a. destroy()
   b. start()
   c. main()
   d. init()

2. The paint() method executes automatically when you _____ an AppletViewer window.
   a. resize
   b. close
   c. destroy
   d. all of these

section A

3. The method that calls the paint() method for you is _____.
   a. callPaint()
   b. repaint()
   c. requestPaint()
   d. draw()

4. The paint() method header requires a(n) _____ argument.
   a. void
   b. integer
   c. String
   d. Graphics

5. The statement `g.drawString(someString, 50, 100);` places someString's _____ corner at position 50, 100.
   a. top-left
   b. bottom-left
   c. top-right
   d. bottom-right

6. The drawString() method is a member of the _____ class.
   a. Graphics
   b. String
   c. Draw
   d. Applet

7. Which of the following colors is a Color class constant?
   a. brown
   b. CYAN
   c. magenta
   d. RED

8. If you use the setColor() method to change a Graphics object's color to blue, _____ will appear in blue.
   a. only the next graphics output
   b. all graphics output for the remainder of the method
   c. all graphics output for the remainder of the applet
   d. all graphics output until you change the color

9. What do you predict is the value of the expression
   `Color.orange.getRed() > Color.blue.getRed();?`
   a. 0
   b. 255
   c. true
   d. false

10. The correct statement to instantiate a Graphics object named picasso is _____.
    a. `Graphics picasso;`
    b. `Graphics picasso = new Graphics();`
    c. `Graphics picasso = getGraphics();`
    d. `Graphics picasso = getGraphics(new);`

11. If you create a Graphics object named g, then the statement
    g.drawLine(10,200,200,10); draws a line that extends from the
    _____.
    a. top-left of the screen to the top-right
    b. top-left of the screen to the bottom-right
    c. bottom-left of the screen to the top-right
    d. bottom-left of the screen to the bottom-right

12. If you draw two rectangles using the statements g.drawRect(300,400,10,10);
    and g.drawRect(10,10,300,400);, then the first rectangle is _____
    than the second rectangle.
    a. larger and higher
    b. larger and lower
    c. smaller and higher
    d. smaller and lower

13. The statement g.drawRect(200,200,200,5); draws a rectangle that is
    _____.
    a. tall and thin
    b. tall and wide
    c. short and thin
    d. short and wide

14. The statement g.drawRoundRect(100,100,100,100,0,0); draws a shape that
    looks most like a _____.
    a. square
    b. round-edged rectangle
    c. circle
    d. straight line

15. Compared to the drawRect() method, the drawOval() method requires
    _____ arguments.
    a. additional
    b. fewer
    c. the same number of
    d. no

16. If you draw an oval with the same value for width and height, then you draw a(n)
    _____.
    a. circle
    b. square
    c. rounded square
    d. ellipsis

EXERCISES

Save the programs that you create in these exercises in the Chapter.08 folder on your Student Disk. For each applet, create an HTML file to host the applet.

1. Write an applet that displays your first name in every even-numbered font size from 4 through 24. Save the project as FontSizeDemo.

2. Write an applet that displays your name in red the first time the user clicks a Button, and then displays your name larger and in blue the second time the user clicks the Button. Save the project as RedBlue.

3. a. Write an applet that displays a city skyline, similar to the drawing shown in Figure 8-13. Save the project as Skyline.

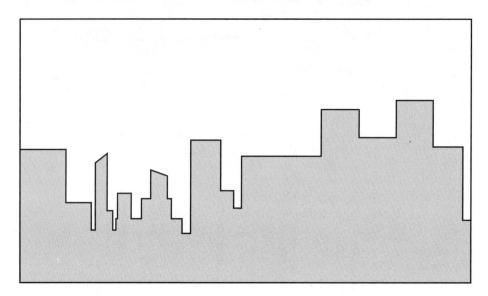

Figure 8-13: Skyline drawing

   b. Add a Button to the Skyline applet. When the user clicks the Button, change the sky color from day to night.
   c. Modify the applet created in Exercise 3b so the sky changes from day to night or night to day with each successive Button click.
   d. Add a moon to the sky for the night view, and a sun for the day view.

4. Using rectangles, rounded rectangles, and ovals, design a modern logo for your personal monogram, and display the logo in an applet. For example, Figure 8-14 shows a simple logo for a person with the initials B.Q. Save the project as Monogram.

Figure 8-14: Monogram example

5. Write an applet that displays a form for creating a phone directory. The form should contain three TextFields and three Labels for first name, last name, and phone number. After the user enters a phone number and presses the Enter key, the program should display the information that was entered. Use the drawString() method to display the information. Use the paint() method to display a heading line for the information display, such as "The information you entered is: ". Save the project as PhoneForm.

6. Write an applet that displays two vertical lines of the same length based on numbers entered by the user. The user enters a beginning point (top) number and an ending point (bottom) number for the first line. The user also enters the number of pixels representing the horizontal gap between the lines. You must calculate the beginning and ending points for the second line based on the numbers entered. There should be three Labels and three TextFields (representing the top, bottom, and gap). When the user presses the Enter key in the third field, display the two lines. Save the project as LineDraw.

7. Write an applet that displays a line graph that plots temperature changes for eight days. Create a TextField and Label for each of eight temperatures that the user enters. Use a prompt above the TextFields telling the user to enter temperatures and to press the Enter key in the eighth TextField when finished. When the user presses the Enter key in the last TextField, display the graph.

To create the graph, draw a horizontal baseline on the screen with the day numbers 1 through 8 displayed at even intervals below the line. With one pixel representing one degree of temperature, draw lines from point to point above the horizontal baseline reflecting the temperature changes from day to day. The graph should appear similar to the drawing shown in Figure 8-15. Save the project as LineGraph.

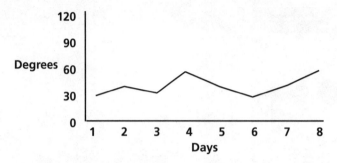

Figure 8-15: LineGraph drawing

8. Write an applet that displays a horizontal bar chart for a company blood drive. The user enters the number of pints of blood donated by employees in each of five departments. There should be a TextField and Label for each department's donor count. When the user presses the Enter key in the last TextField, display the bar chart. To create the chart, create a vertical baseline; then create one horizontal bar for each department. The bar chart should appear similar to the drawing in Figure 8-16. Save the project as BarChart.

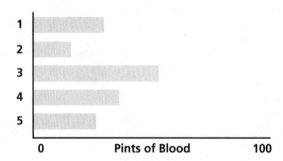

Figure 8-16: BarChart drawing

SECTION B
objectives

In this section you will learn:
- How to draw arcs
- How to create three-dimensional rectangles
- How to create polygons
- How to copy an area
- More about fonts and their methods
- How to create a simple animation

More Graphics Methods

Drawing Arcs

An **arc** is a portion of a circle. In Java, you can draw an arc using the Graphics method **drawArc()**. To use the drawArc() method, you provide six arguments:

- The x-coordinate of the upper-left corner of an imaginary rectangle that represents the bounds of the imaginary circle that contains the arc
- The y-coordinate of the same point
- The width of the imaginary rectangle that represents the bounds of the imaginary circle that contains the arc
- The height of the same imaginary rectangle
- The beginning arc position
- The arc angle

Arc positions and angles are measured in degrees; there are 360 degrees in a circle. The zero-degree position for any arc is at the three o'clock position, as shown in Figure 8-17. The other 359 degree positions increase as you move counterclockwise around an imaginary circle, so that 90 degrees is at the top of the circle in the 12 o'clock position, 180 degrees is opposite the starting position at nine o'clock, and 270 degrees is at the bottom of the circle in the six o'clock position.

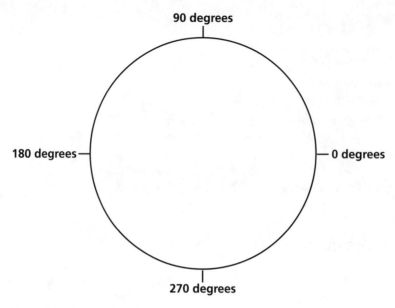

Figure 8-17: Arc positions

The arc angle is the number of degrees over which you want to draw the arc, traveling counterclockwise from the starting position. For example, you could draw a half circle by indicating an arc angle of 180 degrees or a quarter circle by indicating an arc angle of 90 degrees. If you want to travel clockwise from the starting position, you express the degrees as a negative number. Just as when you draw a line, when drawing any arc you can take one of two approaches: either start at point A and travel to point B, or start at point B and travel to point A. For example, to create an arc that looks like the top half of a circle, the statements `g.drawArc(x,y,w,h,0,180);` and `g.drawArc(x,y,w,h,180,-180);` produce identical results. The first statement starts an arc at the three o'clock position and travels 180 degrees counterclockwise to the nine o'clock position. The second statement starts at nine o'clock and travels clockwise to three o'clock.

The fillArc() method creates a solid arc. The arc is drawn and two straight lines are drawn from the arc end points to the center of the imaginary circle whose perimeter the arc occupies. For example, the two statements `gr.fillArc(10,50,100,100,20,320);` and `gr.fillArc(200,50,100,100,340,40);` together produce the output shown in Figure 8-18. Each of the two arcs is in a circle of size 100 by 100. The first almost completes a full circle, starting at position 20 (near two o'clock) and ending 320 degrees around the circle (at position 340, near four o'clock). The second filled arc more closely resembles a pie slice, starting at position 340 and extending 40 degrees to end at position 40.

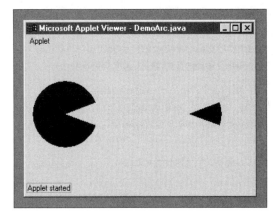

Figure 8-18: Two filled arcs

Creating Three-Dimensional Rectangles

The draw3DRect() method is a minor variation on the drawRect() method. You use the **draw3DRect()** method to draw a rectangle that appears to have shadowing on two of its edges—the effect is one of a rectangle that is slightly raised or slightly lowered. The draw3DRect() method requires a fifth argument in addition to the x- and y-coordinates and width and height required by the drawRect() method. The fifth argument is a Boolean value, which is `true` if you want the raised rectangle effect (darker on the right and bottom) and `false` if you want the lowered rectangle effect (darker on the left and top). There is also a fill3DRect() method for creating filled three-dimensional rectangles.

The three-dimensional methods work well only with lighter drawing colors.

Creating Polygons

When you want to create a shape that is more complex than a rectangle, you can use a sequence of calls to the drawLine() method, or you can use the **drawPolygon()** method to draw complex shapes. The drawPolygon() method requires three arguments: two integer arrays and a single integer.

The first integer array holds a series of x-coordinate positions, and the second array holds a series of corresponding y-coordinate positions. The third integer argument is the number of pairs of points you want to connect. If you don't want to connect all the points represented by the array values, you can assign this third argument integer a value that is smaller than the number of elements in each of the arrays. However, an error occurs if the third argument is a value higher than the available number of coordinate pairs.

For example, examine the code shown in Figure 8-19, which is an applet that has one task: to draw a red, star-shaped polygon. Two parallel arrays are assigned x- and y-coordinates; the paint() method sets the drawing color to red and draws the polygon. The program's output appears in Figure 8-20.

In Chapter 6, you learned that you can use `length` **for the length of an array. Rather than using a constant integer value like 11, it is convenient to use the length of one of the coordinate point arrays, as in** `xPoints.length`.

```
import java.applet.*;
import java.awt.*;
public class Star extends Applet
{
  int xPoints[] = {42, 52, 72, 52, 60, 40,  15, 28,  9, 32, 42};
  int yPoints[] = {38, 62, 68, 80,105, 85, 102, 75, 58, 60, 38};
  public void paint(Graphics gr)
  {
    gr.setColor(Color.red);
    gr.drawPolygon(xPoints, yPoints, xPoints.length);
  }
}
```

Figure 8-19: Star applet

Figure 8-20: Output of the Star applet

You can use the fillPolygon() method to draw a solid shape. The major difference between the drawPolygon() and fillPolygon() methods is that if the beginning and ending points used with the fillPolygon() method are not identical, then the two end points will be connected by a straight line before the polygon is filled with color.

The difference is subtle, but rather than providing the fillPolygon() method with three arguments, you can create a **Polygon object** that defines a polygon, and then pass the constructed object as a single argument to the fillPolygon() method. Note the following statements:

```
Polygon someShape = new Polygon(xPoints, yPoints, size);
fillPolygon(someShape);
```

These statements have the same result as the following:

```
fillPolygon(xPoints, yPoints, size);
```

Additionally, you can instantiate an empty Polygon object (with no points) using the statement `Polygon someFutureShape = new Polygon();`. You use the following statements to add points to the polygon later, using a series of calls to the addPoint() method:

```
someFutureShape.addPoint(100,100);
someFutureShape.addPoint(150,200);
someFutureShape.addPoint(50,250);
```

There is a practical reason for using addPoint() instead of coding the point values: You may want to write a program in which the user enters polygon point values interactively. Whether the user does so from the keyboard or with a mouse, you can continue to add points to the polygon indefinitely.

Copying an Area

After you create a graphics image, you might want to create copies of the image. For example, you might want a company logo to appear several times in an applet. Of course, you can redraw the picture, but you also can use the **copyArea()** method to copy any rectangular area to a new location. The copyArea() method requires six parameters:

- The x- and y-coordinates of the upper-left corner of the area to be copied
- The width and height of the area to be copied
- The horizontal and vertical displacement of the destination of the copy

To demonstrate copying an image:

1 Create a new empty project named **ThreeStars**. Save the **ThreeStars** project folder in the Chapter.08 folder on your Student Disk. Then add a new class file named **ThreeStars.java** to the project.

2 Above the `public class ThreeStars` header, type the following import statements that you will need for the applet:

```
import java.applet.*;
import java.awt.*;
```

3 Add `extends Applet` to the right of the class header.

4 Add the following statements between the class's curly brackets to create a polygon in the shape of a star:

```
int xPoints[] = {42, 52, 72, 52,
                 60, 40, 15, 28, 9, 32, 42};
int yPoints[] = {38, 62, 68, 80,
                 105, 85, 102, 75, 58, 60, 38};
Polygon aStar =
  new Polygon(xPoints, yPoints, xPoints.length);
```

5 Add the following paint() method, which sets a color, draws a star, then draws two additional identical stars:

```
public void paint(Graphics gr)
{
  gr.setColor(Color.red);
  gr.drawPolygon(aStar);
  gr.copyArea(0,0,75,105,125,130);
  gr.copyArea(0,0,75,105,180,70);
}
```

6 Add to the project a new Web page named **testThreeStars.htm** and add the tag `<APPLET CODE = "ThreeStars.class" WIDTH = 420 HEIGHT = 300>`.

7 Press the **Enter** key to start a new line and type the applet's closing tag: `</APPLET>`.

8 Build and save the project, and then execute the applet in AppletViewer. The output should look like Figure 8-21.

Figure 8-21: Output of the ThreeStars applet

9 Close the AppletViewer window.

10 Modify the program to add more stars in any location you choose, rebuild and save the project, and then run the HTML program in AppletViewer to confirm that the stars are copied to your desired locations.

11 Close the AppletViewer window.

Using Font Methods

As you add more components to your applet, positioning becomes increasingly important. In particular, when you draw Strings using different fonts, if you do not place the Strings correctly within your applet, they overlap and become impossible to read. Additionally, even when you define a font such as Font myFont = new Font("TimesRoman",Font.PLAIN,10);, you have no guarantee that the font will be available on every computer that runs your applet. If your user's computer does not have the font loaded, then Java chooses a default replacement font, so you are never completely sure how your output will look. Fortunately, Java provides many useful methods for obtaining information about the fonts you use.

You can discover the fonts that are available on your system by using the **getFontList()** method that is part of a helpful class named the **Toolkit** class. The **getDefaultToolkit()** method provides information about the system in use. One of its methods is the getFontList() method, which returns an array of String objects that are the names of available fonts.

section B

Next, you will write an applet that lists the fonts available on your system.

To write an applet that lists the fonts on your system:

1 Create a new empty project named **FontList**. Save the **FontList** project in the Chapter.08 folder on your Student Disk. Then add a new class file named **FontList.java** to the project.

2 Above the `public class FontList` header, type the following import statements that you will need for the applet:

```
import java.applet.*;
import java.awt.*;
```

3 Add `extends Applet` to the right of the class header.

4 Add the following statement between the class's curly brackets to create two integer variables to hold the x- and y-coordinate positions you will use to draw Strings within the applet: `int x = 10, y = 15;`.

5 Add the following paint() method header and an opening curly bracket. Within the method, declare an array of String objects to which you can assign the font names returned by the getFontList() method.

```
public void paint(Graphics gr)
{
  String availableFonts[] =
     Toolkit.getDefaultToolkit().getFontList();
```

6 Enter the following for loop to the paint() method. This loop will draw each String in the array that was filled using the getFontList() method. You will draw the first String at horizontal position 10 and vertical position 15. You will draw each subsequent String 15 pixels lower within the applet.

```
for(int a = 0; a< availableFonts.length; ++a)
   gr.drawString(availableFonts[a], x, y += 15);
```

7 Type the closing curly bracket for the paint() method.

8 Add to the project a new Web page named **testFontList.htm** and add the tag `<APPLET CODE = "FontList.class" WIDTH = 300 HEIGHT = 250>`.

9 Press the **Enter** key to start a new line and type the applet's closing tag: `</APPLET>`.

10 Build and save the project, and then execute the applet in AppletViewer. Your output should look like Figure 8-22. (Your font list might be different, depending on the fonts that are installed on your computer. If your list is different from the one shown in Figure 8-22, write down on a piece of paper the fonts that you do have, as you will need them in the following steps.)

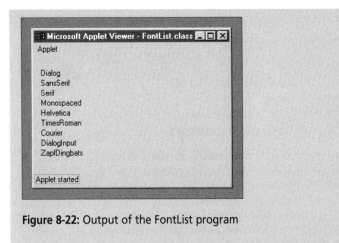

Figure 8-22: Output of the FontList program

11 Close the AppletViewer window.

Typesetters and desktop publishers measure the height of every font in three parts: leading, ascent, and descent. **Leading** is a measure of the amount of whitespace prior to a line of text, or the amount of space between lines. **Ascent** is the height of an uppercase character from a base line to the top of the character. **Descent** measures the size of characters that hang below the baseline, such as the tails on the lowercase letters *g* and *j*. The **height** of a font is the sum of the leading, ascent, and descent. Figure 8-23 shows each of these measurements.

Leading **is pronounced "ledding."**

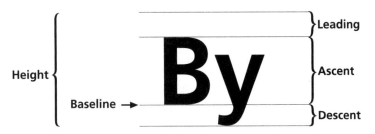

Figure 8-23: Parts of a font's height

You can discover a font's height by using the getFontMetrics() method. The getFontMetrics() method is part of the Graphics class and returns a FontMetrics object. The FontMetrics class contains the following methods that return a font's statistics:

- public int getLeading()
- public int getAscent()
- public int getDescent()
- public int getHeight()

Each of these methods returns an integer value representing the size in points of the requested portion of the Font object. For example, if you define a Font object named myFont and a Graphics object named paintBrush, then you can set the current font for the Graphics object with the statement `paintBrush.setFont(myFont);`. When you code `int heightOfFont = paintBrush.getFontMetrics().getHeight();`, then the heightOfFont variable holds the total height of myFont characters.

Notice the object-dot-method-dot-method construction of the getHeight() statement. Alternatively, if it is clearer to you, you can write two statements. The first statement declares a FontMetrics object: `FontMetrics fmObject = paintBrush.getFontMetrics();`. The second statement assigns a value to heightOfFont: `int heightOfFont = fmObject.getHeight();`.

When you define a Font object, you use point size; one point measures 1/72 of an inch. However, when you use the getFontMetrics() methods, the sizes are returned in pixels.

Next, you will write an applet to demonstrate the FontMetrics() methods. You will create three Font objects and display their metrics.

To demonstrate the FontMetrics methods:

1 Create a new empty project named **DemoFontMetrics**. Save the **DemoFontMetrics** project folder in the Chapter.08 folder on your Student Disk. Then add a new class file named **DemoFontMetrics.java** to the project.

2 Above the `public class DemoFontMetrics` header, type the following import statements that you will need for the applet:

```
import java.applet.*;
import java.awt.*;
```

3. Add **extends Applet** to the right of the class header.
4. Between the class's curly brackets, type the following code to create a String and a few fonts to use for demonstration purposes:

```
String companyName =
   new String("Event Handlers Incorporated");
Font
   courierItalic = new Font("Courier", Font.ITALIC, 16),
   timesPlain = new Font("TimesRoman", Font.PLAIN, 16),
   helvetBold = new Font("Helvetica", Font.BOLD, 16);
```

> If your FontList program showed that you do not have one of these fonts available, then substitute another font that you do have.

5. Add the following code to define four integer variables to hold the four font measurements and two integer variables to hold the current horizontal and vertical output positions within the applet:

```
int ascent, descent, height, leading;
int x = 10, y = 15;
```

6. Within the applet, you will draw Strings for output that you will position 15 pixels apart vertically on the screen. Type the following statement to create a constant to hold this vertical increase value: **static final int INCREASE = 15;**.

7. Add the following statements to start writing a paint() method. Within the method, you set the Font to courierItalic, draw the companyName String to show a working example of the Font, and then call a displayMetrics() method that you will write in Step 8. You will pass the Graphics object to the displayMetrics() method, so the displayMetrics() method can discover the sizes associated with the current Font.

```
public void paint(Graphics gr)
{
   gr.setFont(courierItalic);
   gr.drawString(companyName,x,y);
   displayMetrics(gr);
```

8 Still within the paint() method, perform the same three steps using the timesPlain and the helvetBold fonts. Then type a closing curly bracket at the end of the paint() method.

```
gr.setFont(timesPlain);
gr.drawString(companyName, x,y += 40);
displayMetrics(gr);
gr.setFont(helvetBold);
gr.drawString(companyName, x, y += 40);
displayMetrics(gr);
}
```

9 Next, add the header and opening curly bracket for the displayMetrics() method. The method will receive a Graphics object from the paint() method.

```
public void displayMetrics(Graphics g)
{
```

10 Add the following statements to call the four getFontMetrics() methods to obtain values for the leading, ascent, descent, and height variables:

```
leading = g.getFontMetrics().getLeading();
ascent = g.getFontMetrics().getAscent();
descent = g.getFontMetrics().getDescent();
height = g.getFontMetrics().getHeight();
```

11 Add the following five drawString() statements to display the values. Use the expression y += INCREASE to change the vertical position of each String by the INCREASE constant.

```
g.drawString("Leading is " + leading, x, y += INCREASE);
g.drawString("Ascent is " + ascent, x, y += INCREASE);
g.drawString("Descent is " + descent, x, y += INCREASE);
g.drawString("--------------------", x, y += INCREASE);
g.drawString("Height is " + height, x, y += INCREASE);
```

12 Type the closing curly bracket for the displayMetrics() method.

13 Add to the project a new Web page named **testFontMetrics.htm** and add the tag <APPLET CODE = "DemoFontMetrics.class" WIDTH = 400 HEIGHT = 350>.

14 Press the **Enter** key to start a new line and type the applet's closing tag: </APPLET>.

15 Build and save the project, and then execute the applet in AppletViewer. Your output should look like Figure 8-24. Notice that even though each Font object was constructed with a size of 16, the individual statistics vary for each Font object.

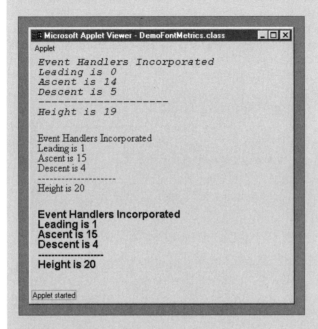

Figure 8-24: Output of the DemoFontMetrics applet

16 Close the AppletViewer window.

A practical use for discovering the height of your font is to space Strings correctly as you print them. For example, instead of placing every String in a series vertically equidistant from the previous String with a statement, such as `g.drawString("Some string", x, y += INCREASE);` (where INCREASE is always the same), you can make the actual increase in the vertical position dependent on the font. If you code `g.drawString("Some string", x, y += g.getFontMetrics().getHeight());`, then you are assured that each String has enough room to display no matter what font is currently in use by the Graphics object.

When you create a String, you know how many characters are in the String. However, you cannot be sure of what font Java will use or substitute, and fonts have different measurements, so it is difficult to know the exact width of the

String in an applet. Fortunately, the FontMetrics() class contains a method named stringWidth() that returns the integer width of a String. The stringWidth() method requires the name of a String as an argument. For example, if you create a String named myString, then you can retrieve the width of myString with `int width = gr.getFontMetrics().stringWidth(myString);`.

Next, you will use the FontMetrics methods to draw a rectangle around a String. Instead of having to guess appropriate pixel positions, you can use the height and width of the String to create a box whose borders are placed symmetrically around the String.

To draw a rectangle around a String:

1 Create a new empty project named **BoxAround**. Save the **BoxAround** project folder in the Chapter.08 folder on your Student Disk. Then add a new class file named **BoxAround.java** to the project.

2 Above the `public class BoxAround` header, type the following import statements that you will need for the applet:

```
import java.applet.*;
import java.awt.*;
```

3 Add **extends Applet** to the right of the header.

4 Enter the following statements between the class's curly brackets to add a String, a Font, and variables to hold the font metrics and x- and y-coordinates:

```
String companyName =
  new String("Event Handlers Incorporated");
Font serifItalic = new Font("Serif", Font.ITALIC, 20);
int leading, ascent, height, width;
int x = 40, y = 60;
```

5 Create the following constant variable that holds a number of pixels indicating the dimensions of the rectangle that you will draw around the String: `static final int BORDER = 5;`.

6 Add the following paint() method, which sets the Font, draws the String, and obtains the font metrics:

```
public void paint(Graphics gr)
{
  gr.setFont(serifItalic);
  gr.drawString(companyName,x,y);
  leading = gr.getFontMetrics().getLeading();
  ascent = gr.getFontMetrics().getAscent();
  height = gr.getFontMetrics().getHeight();
  width = gr.getFontMetrics().stringWidth(companyName);
```

7 Draw a rectangle around the String using the following drawRect() method. See Figure 8-25.

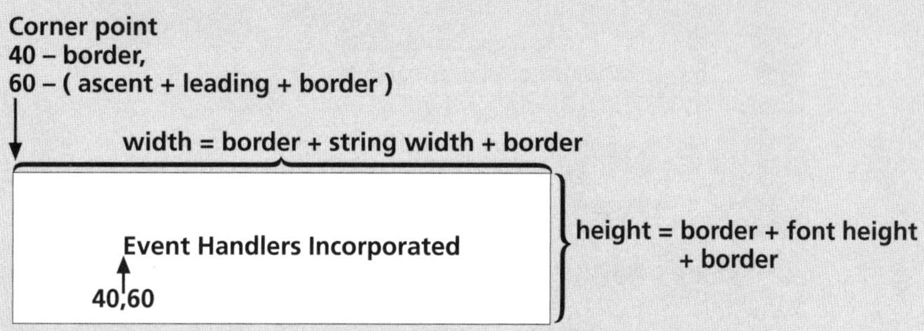

Corner point
40 – border,
60 – (ascent + leading + border)

width = border + string width + border

Event Handlers Incorporated
40, 60

height = border + font height + border

Figure 8-25: Rectangle surrounding a String

The values of the x- and y-coordinates (40, 60) used in the drawString() method indicate the left side of the baseline of the first character in the String. You need to position the upper-left corner of the rectangle so it is five pixels to the left of the String—remember you set the Border constant equal to five pixels. Therefore, the first argument to drawRect() is the x-coordinate minus five, or x - BORDER. The second argument to drawRect() is the y-coordinate of the String minus the ascent of the String, minus the leading of the String, minus five, or y - (ascent + leading + BORDER). The last two arguments to drawRectangle() are the width and the height of the rectangle. The width is the String's width plus five pixels on the left and five pixels on the right. The height of the rectangle is the String's height, plus five pixels above the String and five pixels below the String.

```
gr.drawRect(x - BORDER, y - (ascent + leading + BORDER),
width + 2 * BORDER, height + 2 * BORDER);
```

8 Type the closing curly bracket for the paint() method.

9 Add to the project a new Web page named **testBox.htm** and add the tag `<APPLET CODE = "BoxAround.class" WIDTH = 400 HEIGHT = 120>`.

10 Press the **Enter** key to start a new line and type the applet's closing tag: `</APPLET>`.

11 Build and save the project, and then execute the applet in AppletViewer. Your output should look like Figure 8-26.

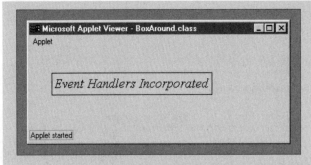

Figure 8-26: Output of the BoxAround program

12 Close the AppletViewer window, and then experiment with changing the contents of the String and the size of the BORDER constant. Confirm that the rectangle is drawn symmetrically around any String object. When you are finished, close the AppletViewer window.

Using Simple Animation

At some point in your life, you may have created simple animation by drawing a series of figures on the pages of a book, and changing each version of the figure slightly from the previous one. When you flip through the pages of the book, the figure appears to move. Movies, whether animated or not, are created in a similar manner—you see a succession of frames of film, and each one contains an image that is modified slightly. Computer animation is achieved in the same fashion—you see a series of images that appear on your screen in rapid succession. You will be able to create fairly sophisticated animation after you have covered Chapter 15. For now, you can use an ActionListener to control drawing different images using the paint() method. Although the product will not be truly animated, you can achieve dynamic results.

Next, you will create an applet for Event Handlers Incorporated that contains a simple graphic of a stoplight, which changes from red to green when the user clicks a Button. In addition, the applet will display different messages when the light is red and green, and a border appears proportionately around each message. Figure 8-27 shows a sketch of the applet.

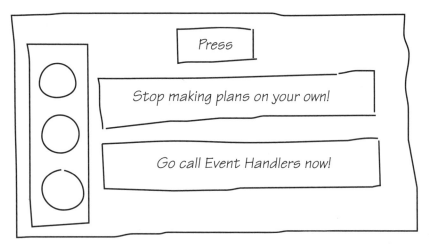

Figure 8-27: Drawing of the StopLight applet

To create the StopLight applet:

1. Create a new empty project named **StopLight**. Save the **StopLight** project folder in the Chapter.08 folder on your Student Disk. Then add a new class file named **StopLight.java** to the project.

2. Above the `public class StopLight` header, type the following import statements that you will need for the applet:

   ```
   import java.applet.*;
   import java.awt.*;
   import java.awt.event.*;
   ```

3. Add `extends Applet implements ActionListener` to the right of the class header.

4. Add the following statements between the class's curly brackets to create a String to hold the messages that will display, a Font in which to display the message, and a Button to click:

   ```
   String msg = new String();
   Font serifItalic = new Font("Serif", Font.ITALIC, 20);
   Button stopStart = new Button("Press");
   ```

5 Enter the following statements to add variables to count the number of Button clicks, measure the font metrics, hold the border size around the String messages, and hold x- and y-coordinate positions for the lights in the stoplight. The red light starts at screen position 30, 60. The yellow light is 60 pixels below, and the green light is 60 additional pixels below the yellow.

```
int buttonCount = 0;
int leading, ascent, descent, height, width;
static final int BORDER = 5;
int redX = 30,  redY = 60,
  yellowX = redX, yellowY = redY + 60,
  greenX = redX, greenY = redY + 120;
```

6 Add the following init() method, which places the Button on the screen and adds the ActionListener:

```
public void init()
{
  add(stopStart);
  stopStart.addActionListener(this);
}
```

7 Within the paint() method, add the following statements to declare x and y variables to hold the coordinates where the String messages will display. The variables redX and greenX hold the stoplight light coordinates, so x and y should each hold a coordinate that represents a position 90 additional pixels to the right.

```
public void paint(Graphics gr)
{
int x, y;
```

8 Set the drawing color to black and draw a rectangle to represent the stoplight by typing the following statements:

```
gr.setColor(Color.black);
gr.drawRect(redX - 20, redY - 40,80,240);
```

9 Add the following statements to set the font for the String message and draw the yellow light for the stoplight. The yellow light will always remain on, so it is not dependent on a Button click. Each of the stoplight lights will have a diameter of 50 pixels.

```
gr.setFont(serifItalic);
gr.setColor(Color.yellow);
gr.fillOval(yellowX,yellowY, 50, 50);
```

10 Use the modulus operator to determine whether the user clicked the Button an even or odd number of times. If odd, then all the "green" or "go" settings should take effect (show the green light and place the "Go" message at a position 90 pixels to the right of the light). Enter the following statements to set the message to the "Go" message, set the x and y variables to the green coordinates, set the color to green, and then draw the green light and green message:

```
if(buttonCount % 2 == 1)
{
  msg = "Go call Event Handlers now!";
  x = greenX + 90;
  y = greenY;
  gr.setColor(Color.green);
  gr.drawString(msg,x,greenY);
  gr.fillOval(greenX, y, 50, 50);
}
```

11 Add the following else clause to the if statement. When the number of Button clicks is even, all of the "stop" and "red" changes take effect.

```
else
{
  msg = "Stop making plans on your own!";
  x = redX + 90;
  y = redY;
  gr.setColor(Color.red);
  gr.drawString(msg, x, redY);
  gr.fillOval(redX, y, 50, 50);
}
```

12 To finish the paint() method, no matter whether the Button click count is even or odd, you need to determine the font metrics and draw an appropriate box around the current message. Add the following statements to your applet, and then type the closing curly bracket for the paint() method.

```
leading = gr.getFontMetrics().getLeading();
ascent = gr.getFontMetrics().getAscent();
descent = gr.getFontMetrics().getDescent();
height = gr.getFontMetrics().getHeight();
width = gr.getFontMetrics().stringWidth(msg);
gr.drawRect(x - BORDER, y - (ascent + leading + BORDER),
  width + 2 * BORDER, height + 2 * BORDER);
}
```

13 At this point, the applet is almost complete. You still need to add the actionPerformed() method that executes when the user clicks the Button. The only tasks performed by the method are to count the number of Button clicks and to call the repaint() method. Add the following method to your applet:

```
public void actionPerformed(ActionEvent e)
{
  ++ buttonCount;
  repaint();
}
```

14 Add to the project a new Web page named **testStopLight.htm** and add the tag `<APPLET CODE = "StopLight.class" WIDTH = 400 HEIGHT = 340>`.

15 Press the **Enter** key to start a new line and type the applet's closing tag: `</APPLET>`.

16 Build and save the project, and then execute the applet in AppletViewer. The output appears in Figure 8-1 at the beginning of this chapter. Click the **Press** button. The new output appears in Figure 8-28. Continue to click the **Press** button and observe the light and message changes.

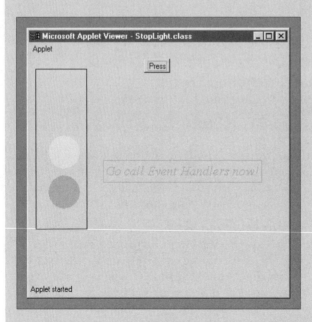

Figure 8-28: Output of the StopLight applet after the user clicks the Button

17 Close the AppletViewer window.

SUMMARY

- An arc is a portion of a circle that you can draw using the Graphics method drawArc(). The drawArc() method requires six arguments: the x-coordinate of the upper-left corner of an imaginary rectangle that represents the bounds of the imaginary circle that contains the arc, the y-coordinate of the same point, the width of the imaginary rectangle that represents the bounds of the imaginary circle that contains the arc, the height of the same point, the beginning arc position, and the arc angle.

- You use the draw3DRect() method to draw a rectangle that appears to have shadowing on two of its edges so the effect is one of a rectangle that is slightly raised or slightly lowered.

- You can use the drawPolygon() method to draw complex shapes. The drawPolygon() method requires three arguments: an integer array that holds a series of x-coordinate positions, another integer array that holds a series of corresponding y-coordinate positions, and an integer argument holding the number of pairs of points you want to connect.

- You can create a Polygon object that defines a polygon, and then pass the constructed object as a single argument to the fillPolygon() method.

- You can add points to a Polygon using the addPoint() method.

- You can use the copyArea() method to copy any rectangular area to a new location.

- You can discover the fonts that are available on your system by using the getFontList() method, which is part of the Toolkit class.

- You can discover the height of a font by using the getFontMetrics() methods, including the getLeading(), getAscent(), getDescent(), and getHeight() methods. Use these methods to display text statistics, no matter what font is currently in use by the Graphics object.

- The FontMetrics() class contains a method named stringWidth() that returns the integer width of a String. The stringWidth() method requires the name of a String as an argument.

- You achieve computer animation by placing a series of images on your screen in rapid succession.

QUESTIONS

1. The drawArc() method requires _____ arguments.
    a. two
    b. four
    c. six
    d. eight

2. The zero-degree position for any arc is at the _____ o'clock position.
   a. 3
   b. 6
   c. 9
   d. 12

3. Which of the following statements creates an arc that is shaped like a smile?
   a. `g.drawArc(x, y, w, h, 0, 0);`
   b. `g.drawArc(x, y, w, h, 0, 180);`
   c. `g.drawArc(x, y, w, h, 180, 0);`
   d. `g.drawArc(x, y, w, h, 180, 180);`

4. The method you use to create a solid arc is _____.
   a. solidArc()
   b. fillArc()
   c. arcSolid()
   d. arcFill()

5. The draw3DRect() method creates rectangles _____.
   a. with three sides
   b. that are cubes
   c. that have shadowing on two edges
   d. that require three arguments

6. The method that draws complex shapes is _____.
   a. drawPolygon()
   b. drawComplex()
   c. drawShape()
   d. drawPicture()

7. The method that draws polygons requires three arguments that consist of _____.
   a. three integers
   b. an array and two integers
   c. two arrays and an integer
   d. three arrays

8. What shape is drawn by the following Java code?

   ```
   int xPoints[] = {40, 80, 20, 40};
   int yPoints[] = {40, 80, 80, 40};
   gr.drawPolygon(xPoints, yPoints, xPoints.length);
   ```

   a. circle
   b. rectangle
   c. triangle
   d. octagon

9. You use the _____ method to copy any rectangular area to a new location.
   a. copyRect()
   b. copyArea()
   c. repeatRect()
   d. repeatArea()

10. The Courier and Serif fonts are available on _____.
    a. no computers
    b. some computers
    c. every computer
    d. every Java-enabled computer

11. The measure of the amount of whitespace prior to a line of text is called _____.
    a. ascent
    b. descent
    c. leading
    d. height

12. The height of an uppercase character from a baseline to the top of the character is _____.
    a. ascent
    b. descent
    c. leading
    d. height

13. Which of the following statements is true for every standard font?
    a. Leading is always greater than ascent.
    b. Descent is always less than or equal to leading.
    c. Height is always greater than or equal to ascent.
    d. Ascent is always less than or equal to descent.

14. To be sure that a vertical series of Strings has enough room to display in an applet, you can code _____.
    a. g.drawString("Some string", x, y +=
       g.getFontMetrics().getHeight());
    b. g.drawString("Some string", x, y +=
       g.getFontMetrics().getLeading());
    c. g.drawString("Some string", x, y +=
       g.getFontMetrics().getAscent());
    d. g.drawString("Some string", x, y +=
       g.getFontMetrics().getDescent());

15. The FontMetrics method named stringWidth() returns _____.
    a. an integer number of characters in a String
    b. an integer number of pixels in the width of a String
    c. a boolean value indicating whether a String has width or is empty
    d. a character value indicating the last character in a String

16. Showing successive images on the screen is called _____.
    a. action-oriented
    b. object-oriented
    c. animation
    d. volatility

EXERCISES

Save the programs that you create in these exercises in the Chapter.08 folder on your Student Disk.

1. a. Write an applet that displays a yellow smiling face on the screen. Save the project as Smile.
   b. Add a Button to the Smile applet so the smile changes to a frown when the user clicks the Button.

2. a. Use polygons and lines to create a graphics image that looks like a fireworks display. Write an applet that displays the fireworks. Save the project as Fireworks.
   b. Add a Button to the Fireworks applet. Do not show the fireworks until the user clicks the Button.

3. a. Write an applet to display your name. Place a box around your name at intervals of 10, 20, 30, and 40 pixels. Save the project as Borders.
   b. Make each of the four borders in the Borders applet display a different color.

4. Write an applet that displays a phrase in every font available on your system. Save the project as MyFonts.

5. Write an applet that displays a graphic of a large cookie. Using arcs, make the cookie appear to have larger and larger bites taken from it each time the user clicks a Button. After four bites, add to the applet a String message containing "Yum!" Save the project as Yum.

6. Write an applet that displays a pie chart representing four categories of investment risk. Supply four labeled TextFields in which the user can enter dollar values for his or her high-risk, medium-risk, low-risk, and no-risk investments. When the user presses the Enter key from within the last TextField, display a pie chart that shows the relative size of each investment category. Use a different color for each slice of the pie. Save the project as PieChart. (*Hint:* To determine the size of any pie slice, you must first determine its percentage of the total. Then use that percentage to determine how many of the 360 available degrees you will allot to that pie slice.)

7. Write an applet that displays a single-line graph of the amount of activity during each hour between 8 a.m. and 4 p.m. The user enters the amounts in TextFields. There should be a Label for each TextField. There should be a baseline at activity 0 and a number at the base designating how that point corresponds to the numbers entered—for example, 9 for amount 1, designating 8 a.m. – 9 a.m.; 10 for amount 2, designating 9 a.m. – 10 a.m.; and so on. Include a prompt above the TextFields indicating what the user needs to do. Save the project as TimeGraph.

8. Each of the following files in the Chapter.08 folder on your Student Disk has syntax and/or logical errors. Add the files to a new project called FixDebug. Save the FixDebug project under the Chapter.08 folder on your Student Disk. You can test each of these applets with the testDebug.htm file on the Student Disk. Remember to change the Java class file referenced in the HTML file so it matches the DebugEight applet you are working on.
   a. DebugEight1.java
   b. DebugEight2.java
   c. DebugEight3.java
   d. DebugEight4.java

CHAPTER 9

Introduction to Inheritance

case ▶ "You look exhausted," Lynn Greenbrier, your mentor at Event Handlers Incorporated, says to you late one Friday afternoon.

"I am," you reply. "Now that I know some Java, I am writing program after program for several departments in the company. It's fun, but it's a lot of work, and the worst thing is that I seem to be doing a lot of the same work over and over."

"What do you mean?" Lynn asks.

"Well, for example, the Event Planning department has asked me to develop several classes that will hold information for every event type handled by Event Handlers. There are weekday and weekend events, events with or without dinners, and events with or without guest speakers. Sure, there are differences between these different types of events, but all events have many things in common—such as an event number and a number of guests."

"I see," Lynn says. "You'd like a way to create a class based on an existing class, just by adding the specific new components the new class needs. You want to avoid rewriting the components that you already created."

"Exactly!" you say. "But, since I can't do that, I guess I'll just have to get back to work."

Lynn says, "You can do exactly that. On Monday morning I'll teach you how to solve these problems using inheritance."

Previewing an Example of Inheritance

Weekend events hosted by Event Handlers Incorporated cost more than weekday events because overtime rates accrue for the staff members who work at the event. Weekend events have all the components of any other event, but they also possess this surcharge. You can use a completed version of the Chap9WeekendEvent project that is saved in the Chapter.09 folder on your Student Disk now.

> **To use the Chap9WeekendEvent project:**
>
> **1** Go to the command prompt for the Chap9WeekendEvent folder in the Chapter.09 folder on your Student Disk, type **jview UseChap9Weekend Event,** and then press the **Enter** key. This program allows you to supply data for a weekend event. The prompts will ask you for an event number, host name, and number of guests. For the host name, you must enter a single word, such as Lee, with no spaces. You can supply any answers you want to the other questions. The data you enter will echo to the screen, and you will see the charge for the event. The charge is calculated at $10 per person, plus a $400 surcharge for the weekend. Figure 9-1 shows a typical program run.

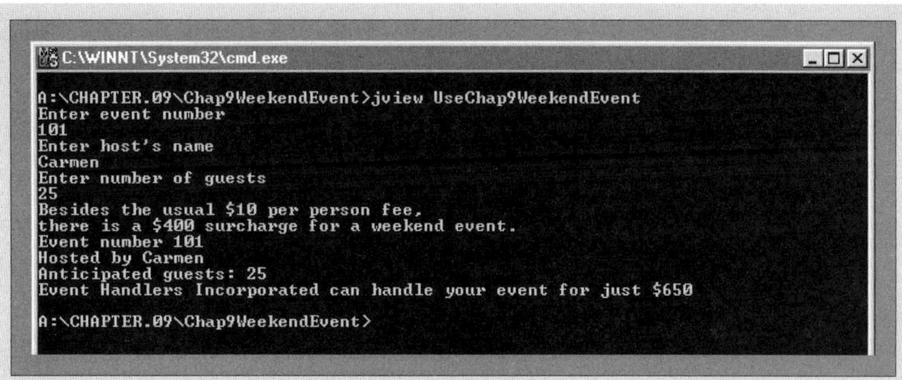

Introduction to Inheritance

```
A:\CHAPTER.09\Chap9WeekendEvent>jview UseChap9WeekendEvent
Enter event number
101
Enter host's name
Carmen
Enter number of guests
25
Besides the usual $10 per person fee,
there is a $400 surcharge for a weekend event.
Event number 101
Hosted by Carmen
Anticipated guests: 25
Event Handlers Incorporated can handle your event for just $650

A:\CHAPTER.09\Chap9WeekendEvent>
```

Figure 9-1: Output of the UseChap9WeekendEvent program

2 Open the **Chap9WeekendEvent** project, then open the **UseChap9Weekend Event.java** file in the Text Editor window, or examine the code shown in Figure 9-2. The program creates a Chap9WeekendEvent object named anEvent and then calls five methods.

```java
public class UseChap9WeekendEvent
{
  public static void main(String[] args) throws Exception
  {
    Chap9WeekendEvent anEvent = new Chap9WeekendEvent();
    anEvent.setEventNum();
    anEvent.setEventHost();
    anEvent.setNumGuests();
    anEvent.computePrice();
    anEvent.printDetails();
  }
}
```

Figure 9-2: UseChap9WeekendEvent.java program

3. Open the **Chap9WeekendEvent.java** file in the Text Editor window, or examine the code shown in Figure 9-3. The class Chap9WeekendEvent does not contain any data fields, and it contains only one method, named computePrice(). However, when you ran the program UseChap9WeekendEvent, you provided input for several data fields. The program called several methods, and displayed several lines of output. The additional fields and methods were available because the Chap9WeekendEvent class inherits its additional components. You will create similar classes in this chapter.

```java
public class Chap9WeekendEvent extends Chap9Event
{
  public void computePrice()
  {
    super.computePrice();
    quotedPrice += 400;
    System.out.println
      ("Besides the usual $10 per person fee,");
    System.out.println
      ("there is a $400 surcharge for a weekend event.");
  }
}
```

Figure 9-3: Chap9WeekendEvent class

SECTION A
objectives

In this section you will learn
- About the concept of inheritance
- About subclasses and superclasses
- How to extend classes
- About polymorphism
- How to override superclass methods

Inheritance

The Inheritance Concept

Inheritance is the principle that you can apply your knowledge of a general category to more specific objects. You are familiar with the concept of inheritance from all sorts of nonprogramming situations.

> You first learned about inheritance in Chapters 2 and 3.

When you use the term *inheritance*, you might think of genetic inheritance. You know from biology that your blood type and eye color are the product of inherited genes; you can say that many of the facts about you—or your data fields—are inherited. Similarly, you often can attribute your behaviors to inheritance; for example, your attitude toward saving money might be the same as your Grandma's, and the odd way that you pull on your ear when you are tired might be the same as what your Uncle Steve does—so your methods are inherited, too.

You also might choose to own plants and animals based on inheritance. You plant impatiens next to your house because they thrive in the shade; you adopt a Doberman pinscher because you need a watchdog. Every individual plant and pet has slightly different characteristics, but within a species, you can count on many consistent inherited attributes and behaviors. Similarly, the classes you create in object-oriented programming languages can inherit data and methods from existing classes. When you create a class by making it inherit data and methods from another class, you are provided with data fields and methods automatically.

From Chapter 2 of this book forward, you have been creating classes and instantiating objects that are members of those classes. For example, consider the simple Employee class shown in Figure 9-4. The class contains two data fields, empNum and empSal, and four methods, a get and set method for each field.

```
public class Employee
{
  private int empNum;
  private double empSal;
  public int getEmpNum()
  {
    return empNum;
  }
  public double getEmpSal()
  {
    return empSal;
  }
  public void setEmpNum(int num)
  {
    empNum = num;
  }
  public void setEmpSal(double sal)
  {
    empSal = sal;
  }
}
```

Figure 9-4: Employee class

After you create the Employee class, you can create specific Employee objects, such as `Employee receptionist = new Employee();` and `Employee deliveryPerson = new Employee();`. These Employee objects can eventually possess different numbers and salaries, but because they are Employee objects, you know that each Employee has *some* number and salary.

Suppose you hire a new Employee named serviceRep. A serviceRep object requires an employee number and a salary, but a serviceRep object also requires a data field to indicate territory served. You can create a new class with a name such as EmployeeWithTerritory, and provide the class with three fields (empNum, empSal, and empTerritory) and six methods (get and set methods for each of the three fields). However, when you create this new class, you are duplicating much of the work that you already have done for the Employee class. The efficient alternative is to create the class EmployeeWithTerritory so it inherits all the attributes and methods of Employee. Then, you can add just the one field and two methods that are additions within EmployeeWithTerritory objects. Figure 9-5 shows a diagram of this relationship.

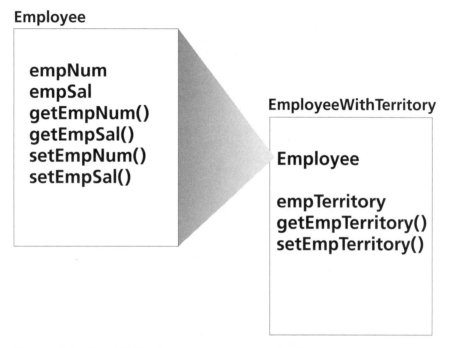

Figure 9-5: EmployeeWithTerritory class inherits from Employee

When you use inheritance to create the EmployeeWithTerritory class, you achieve the following:

- You save time, because the Employee fields and methods already exist.
- You reduce errors, because the Employee methods have already been used and tested.
- You make using the class easier to understand, because you have used the Employee methods on simpler objects and already understand how they work.

The ability to use inheritance in the Java programming language makes programs easier to write, less error-prone, and easier to understand. Imagine that besides creating EmployeeWithTerritory, you also want to create several other specific Employee classes (perhaps EmployeeEarningCommission including a commission rate, or DismissedEmployee including a reason for dismissal). By using inheritance, you can develop each new class correctly and more quickly.

The concept of class inheritance is useful because it makes class code reusable.

A class that is used as a basis for inheritance, such as Employee, is called a **base class**. When you create a class that inherits from a base class (such as EmployeeWithTerritory), it is a **derived class**. When confronted with two classes that inherit from each other, you can tell which class is the base class and which class is the derived class by using the two classes in a sentence with the phrase *is a*. A derived class always "is a" case or instance of the more general base class. For example, a Tree class may be a base class to an Evergreen class. An Evergreen "is a" Tree, so Tree is the base class; however, it is not true for all Trees that "a Tree is an Evergreen." Similarly, an EmployeeWithTerritory "is an" Employee—but not the other way around—so Employee is the base class.

You can use the terms **superclass** and **subclass** as synonyms for *base class* and *derived class*. Thus, Evergreen is a subclass of the Tree superclass. You also can use the terms **parent class** and **child class**. An EmployeeWithTerritory is a child to the Employee parent. Use the pair of terms with which you are most comfortable; all these terms will be used interchangeably in this book.

As an alternative way to discover which of two classes is the base class or subclass, you can try saying the two class names together. When people say their names together, they state the more specific name before the all-encompassing family name, as in "Ginny Kroening." Similarly, with classes, the order that "makes more sense" is the child-parent order. Thus, because "Evergreen Tree" makes more sense than "Tree Evergreen," Evergreen is the child class.

Finally, you usually can distinguish base classes from their subclasses by size. Although it is not required, in general, a subclass is larger than a superclass in the sense that it usually has additional fields and methods. A subclass description might look small, but any subclass contains all of its base class's fields and methods as well as the new, more specific fields and methods you add to a subclass.

Do not think of a subclass as a "subset" of another class. In fact, a subclass is usually larger than its parent.

Extending Classes

You use the keyword **extends** to achieve inheritance within the Java programming language. For example, the class header `public class EmployeeWithTerritory extends Employee` creates a superclass-subclass relationship between both Employee and EmployeeWithTerritory. Each EmployeeWithTerritory automatically receives the data fields and methods of the superclass; you then add new fields and methods to the newly created subclass. Figure 9-6 shows an EmployeeWithTerritory class.

You used the phrase `extends Applet` **throughout Chapters 7 and 8. Every applet that you write is a subclass of the Applet class.**

```
public class EmployeeWithTerritory extends Employee
{
  private int territoryNum;
  public int getTerritoryNum()
  {
    return territoryNum;
  }
  public void setTerritoryNum(int num)
  {
    territoryNum = num;
  }
}
```

Figure 9-6: EmployeeWithTerritory class

When you write a program that instantiates an object using the statement `EmployeeWithTerritory northernRep = new EmployeeWithTerritory();`, then you can use any of the following statements to get field values for northernRep:

- `northernRep.getEmpNum();`
- `northernRep.getEmpSal();`
- `northernRep.getTerritoryNum();`

The northernRep object has access to all three methods—two methods that it inherits from Employee, and one method that belongs to EmployeeWithTerritory.

Similarly, any of the following statements are legal:

- `northernRep.setEmpNum(915);`
- `northernRep.setEmpSal(210.00);`
- `northernRep.setTerritoryNum(5);`

Inheritance is a one-way proposition; a child inherits from a parent, and not the other way around. If a program instantiates an Employee object, as in `Employee aClerk = new Employee;`, then the Employee object does *not* have access to the EmployeeWithTerritory methods. Employee is the parent class, and aClerk is an object of the parent class. It makes sense that a parent class object does not have access to its child's data and methods. When you create the parent class, you will not know how many future subclasses there might be, or what their data or methods might look like. In addition, subclasses are more specific. An Orthodontist class and Periodontist class are children of the Dentist class. You do not expect all members of the general parent class Dentist to have the Orthodontist's braces() method or the Periodontist's deepClean() method. However, Orthodontist objects and Periodontist objects have access to the more general Dentist methods takeXRays() and billPatients().

Next, you will create a working example of inheritance. You will create this example in four parts:

1. First, you will create a general Event class for Event Handlers Incorporated. This Event class will be small—it will hold just one data field and two methods.
2. After you create the general Event class, you will write a program to demonstrate its use.
3. Then you will create a more specific DinnerEvent subclass that inherits the attributes of the Event class.
4. Finally, you will modify the demonstration program to add an example using the DinnerEvent class.

To create the Event class:

1. Create a new empty project named **Event**. Save the **Event** project folder in the Chapter.09 folder on your Student Disk.
2. Add a new class file to the project by selecting **Add Class** from the **Project** menu. The Add Item dialog box appears. In the Add Item dialog box, select **Class** from the **Class** folder, then change the suggested filename to **Event.java** and click the **Open** button. The new class opens in the Text Editor window.
3. The class will host one integer data field—the number of guests expected at the event. Between the class's curly brackets, enter `private int eventGuests;`.
4. Add the following method that displays the number of eventGuests:

```
public void printEventGuests()
{
   System.out.println("Event guests: " + eventGuests);
}
```

5. Next, add a second method that prompts the user for the number of guests and stores the response in the eventGuests field. Begin by typing the following method header, which includes the `throws Exception` clause that handles data entry:

```
public void setEventGuests() throws Exception
{
```

▶ **tip**

You first learned about `throws Exception` in Chapter 5.

Introduction to Inheritance

6. Enter the following code to add an integer variable to hold each character as it is read in from the keyboard and a String variable to which you will add each numeric character the user enters:

```
char inChar;
String guestsString = new String("");
```

7. Prompt the user for the guest number and read in the response using the following code:

```
System.out.print
   ("Enter the number of guests at your event ");
inChar = (char)System.in.read();
```

8. Enter the following while loop. While the user continues to enter digits, add each to a String.

```
while(inChar >= '0' && inChar <= '9')
{
   guestsString = guestsString + inChar;
   inChar = (char)System.in.read();
}
System.in.read();
```

9. When the user finishes entering digits, use the parseInt() method to assign the String value to the eventGuests data field:

```
eventGuests = Integer.parseInt(guestsString);
```

10. Type the closing curly bracket for the setEventGuests() method.

Now that you have created a class, you can use it in an application or applet. A very simple application creates an Event object, sets a value for the data field, and then displays the results.

To write a simple application that uses the Event class:

1. Add a new main class file to the project by selecting **Add Class** from the **Project** menu. The Add Item dialog box appears. In the Add Item dialog box, select **ClassMain** from the **Class** folder, then change the suggested filename to **UseSimpleEvent.java** and click the **Open** button. The new main class opens in the Text Editor window.

> **help**
>
> Be sure to select ClassMain, not Class, from the Add Item dialog box; otherwise, the main() method will not be created.

2. Add `throws Exception` to the right of the main() method.

3 Enter the following code—which declares an Event object, supplies it with a value, and then prints the value—between the main() method's curly brackets:

```
Event anEvent = new Event();
anEvent.setEventGuests();
anEvent.printEventGuests();
```

4 Build the project and execute the program as a console application by typing **jview UseSimpleEvent**, and then enter **100** at the prompt. The program's output appears in Figure 9-7.

```
C:\WINNT\System32\cmd.exe
A:\CHAPTER.09\EVENT>jview UseSimpleEvent
Enter the number of guests at your event 100
Event guests: 100

A:\CHAPTER.09\EVENT>
```

Figure 9-7: Output of the UseSimpleEvent program

Next you will create a new class named DinnerEvent. A DinnerEvent "is a" type of Event at which dinner is served, so DinnerEvent will be a child class of Event.

To create a DinnerEvent class that extends Event:

1 Add a new class file to the project named DinnerEvent.java, and then add **extends Event** to the right of the class header.

2 A DinnerEvent contains a number of guests, but you do not have to define the variable here. The variable already is defined in Event, which is the superclass of this class. You only need to add any variables that are particular to a DinnerEvent. Enter the following code between the curly brackets to add a character to hold the dinner menu choice, which will be *b* or *c* (for *beef* or *chicken*) for each DinnerEvent object: **char dinnerChoice;**.

3 The Event class already contains methods to set and print the number of guests, so DinnerEvent only needs methods to print and set the dinnerChoice variable. Type the printDinnerChoice() method:

```
public void printDinnerChoice()
{
  if(dinnerChoice == 'b')
    System.out.println("Dinner choice is beef");
  else
    System.out.println("Dinner choice is chicken");
}
```

Introduction to Inheritance

4 Enter the following setDinnerChoice() method, which prompts the user for the choice of entrees at the event. For now, to keep this example simple, you will not validate the input character to ensure that it is *b* or *c*; you can add this improvement to the method later. For now, the printDinnerChoice() method will assume that if the choice is not beef, it must be chicken.

```
public void setDinnerChoice() throws Exception
{
  System.out.println("Enter dinner choice");
  System.out.print("b for beef, c for chicken ");
  dinnerChoice = (char)System.in.read();
  System.in.read(); System.in.read();
}
```

Now you can modify the UseSimpleEvent program so that it creates a DinnerEvent as well as a "plain" Event.

To modify the UseSimpleEvent program:

1 Return to the **UseSimpleEvent.java** file in the Text Editor window and save the file, then use the **Save As** command from the **File** menu to save the **UseSimpleEvent.java** file as **UseDinnerEvent.java** in the Event folder in the Chapter.09 folder on your Student Disk. Be sure you have saved the UseSimpleEvent.java file before executing the Save As command.

> The name of the Save As command on the File menu changes to reflect the currently active file. For example, if you select the File menu when the UseSimpleEvent.java file is active, the Save As command is displayed as Save UseSimple.java As.

2 Change the class name from UseSimpleEvent to **UseDinnerEvent**.

3 Position the insertion point at the end of the line that constructs anEvent, and then press the **Enter** key to start a new line. Type the following println() statement so that when you run the program it will be clear to you that you are creating a simple event: `System.out.println("A plain event");`.

4 Position the insertion point at the end of the line that prints the event guests (just before the closing curly brackets), and then press the **Enter** key to start a new line. Add the following two new statements; one constructs a Dinner event, and the other prints a line so that when you run the program you will understand you are creating a DinnerEvent:

```
DinnerEvent aDinnerEvent = new DinnerEvent();
System.out.println("An event with dinner");
```

5 Add the following method calls to set the number of guests and the dinner choice for the DinnerEvent object. Even though the DinnerEvent class does not contain a setEventGuests() method, its parent class (Event) does, so aDinnerEvent can use the setEventGuests() method.

```
aDinnerEvent.setEventGuests();
aDinnerEvent.setDinnerChoice();
```

6 Enter the following code to call the methods that print the entered data:

```
aDinnerEvent.printEventGuests();
aDinnerEvent.printDinnerChoice();
```

7 Rebuild the project and run the **UseDinnerEvent.java** file as a console application. Use the values shown in Figure 9-8. The DinnerEvent object successfully uses the data field and methods of its superclass, as well as its own data field and methods.

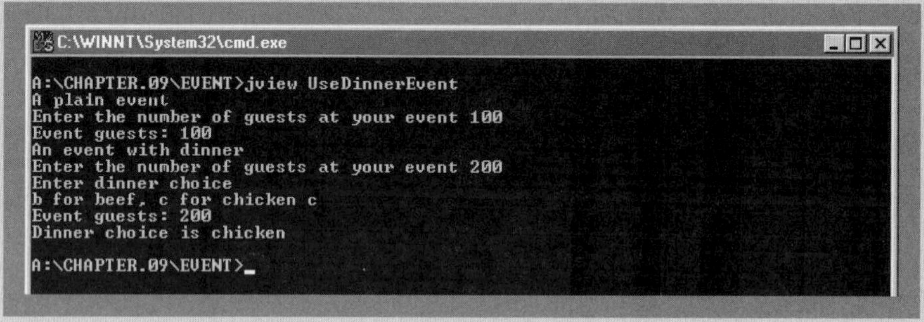

```
A:\CHAPTER.09\EVENT>jview UseDinnerEvent
A plain event
Enter the number of guests at your event 100
Event guests: 100
An event with dinner
Enter the number of guests at your event 200
Enter dinner choice
b for beef, c for chicken c
Event guests: 200
Dinner choice is chicken

A:\CHAPTER.09\EVENT>
```

Figure 9-8: Output of the UseDinnerEvent program

Overriding Superclass Methods

When you create a new subclass by extending an existing class, the new subclass contains data and methods that were defined in the original superclass. Sometimes those superclass data fields and methods are not entirely appropriate for the subclass objects.

When you use the English language, you often use the same method name to indicate diverse meanings. For example, if you think of MusicalInstrument as a class, you can think of play() as a method of that class. If you think of various subclasses such as Guitar and Drum, you know that you carry out the play() method quite differently for each subclass. Using the same method name to indicate different implementations is called **polymorphism**. The word *polymorphism* means "many forms;" there are many forms of action that take place even though you use the same word to describe the action. In other words, there are many forms of the same word depending on the object associated with the word.

For another example, you can create an Employee superclass containing data fields such as firstName, lastName, socialSecurityNumber, dateOfHire, rateOfPay, and so on. The methods contained in the Employee class include the usual set and get methods. If your usual time period for payment to each Employee object is weekly, then your getRateOfPay() method might include a statement such as `System.out.println("Pay is " + rateOfPay + " per week");`.

Imagine your company has a few Employees who are not paid weekly. Maybe a few are paid by the hour, and others are Employees whose work is contracted on a job-to-job basis. Because each Employee type requires different paycheck-calculating procedures, you might want to create subclasses of Employee, such as HourlyEmployee and ContractEmployee.

When you call the getRateOfPay() method for an HourlyEmployee object, you want the display to include the phrase "per hour", as in "Pay is 8.75 per hour". When you call the getRateOfPay() method for a ContractEmployee, you want the display to include "per contract" as in "Pay is 2000 per contract". Each class—the Employee superclass and the two subclasses—requires its own getRateOfPay() method. Fortunately, if you create separate getRateOfPay() methods for each class, then each class's objects will use the appropriate method for that class. Each subclass method overrides any method in the parent class that has the same name and argument list. If you could not override superclass methods, you always could create unique names for each subclass method, such as getRateOfPayForHourly() and getRateOfPayForContractual(), but the classes you create are easier to write and understand if you can use one reasonable name for methods that do essentially the same thing. Because you are attempting to get the rate of pay for each object, getRateOfPay() is a very good method name for all three object types.

tip

You already have overridden methods in your applets. When you write your own init() or start() method within an applet, you are overriding the automatically supplied superclass version you get when you use the phrase `extends Applet`.

tip

If a superclass and its subclasses have methods with the same name but different argument lists, you are overloading methods, and not overriding them. You learned about overloading methods in Chapter 4.

Next, you will create two methods with the same name, printHeader(), with one version in the Event superclass and another in the DinnerEvent subclass. When you call the printHeader() method, the correct version will execute based on the object you use.

To demonstrate that subclass methods override superclass methods with the same name:

1. Return to the **Event.java** file in the Text Editor window and save it, then use the **Save As** command from the **File** menu to save the **Event.java** file as **EventWithHeader.java** in the Event folder in the Chapter.09 folder on your Student Disk. This new class will contain a method that allows you to print a header line of explanatory text with each class object. In addition to providing a descriptive name, changing the class name serves another purpose here. By giving the class a new name, you retain the original class on your disk so you can study the differences later.

2. Change the class name from Event to **EventWithHeader**.

3. Position the insertion point at the end of the line that contains the closing curly bracket for the printEventGuests() method, and then press the **Enter** key to start a new line.

4. Enter the following printHeader() method:

```java
public void printHeader()
{
   System.out.println("Simple event: ");
}
```

5. Return to the **DinnerEvent.java** file in the Text Editor window, save it, and then use the **Save As** command to save the file as **DinnerEventWithHeader.java**.

6. Change the class name from DinnerEvent to **DinnerEventWithHeader** and change the class it extends from Event to **EventWithHeader**.

7. Position the insertion point at the end of the line that contains the closing curly bracket for the printDinnerChoice() method, and then press the **Enter** key to start a new line of text. Then add the following printHeader() method to this class:

```java
public void printHeader()
{
   System.out.println("Dinner event: ");
}
```

You just created a DinnerEventWithHeader class that contains a printHeader() method. Then you extended the class by creating a DinnerEvent subclass containing a method with the same name. Now you will write a program that demonstrates that the correct method executes depending on the object.

To create a program that demonstrates that child class methods override parent class methods with the same name:

1. Add to the project a new main class file named **UseEventsWithHeaders.java**, and then add `throws Exception` to the right of the main() method.

2. Enter the following code between the main() method's curly brackets to create two objects, EventWithHeader and DinnerEventWithHeader:

   ```
   EventWithHeader anEvent = new EventWithHeader();
   DinnerEventWithHeader aDinnerEvent =
      new DinnerEventWithHeader();
   ```

3. Enter the following code to call the three EventWithHeader methods:

   ```
   anEvent.printHeader();
   anEvent.setEventGuests();
   anEvent.printEventGuests();
   ```

4. Enter the following code to call the five DinnerEventWithHeader methods:

   ```
   aDinnerEvent.printHeader();
   aDinnerEvent.setEventGuests();
   aDinnerEvent.setDinnerChoice();
   aDinnerEvent.printEventGuests();
   aDinnerEvent.printDinnerChoice();
   ```

5. Rebuild and save the project and run the **UseEventsWithHeaders.java** file as a console application. Input the values shown in Figure 9-9. For each type of object, the correct method executes.

```
A:\CHAPTER.09\EVENT>jview UseEventsWithHeaders
Simple event:
Enter the number of guests at your event 60
Event guests: 60
Dinner event:
Enter the number of guests at your event 40
Enter dinner choice
b for beef, c for chicken b
Event guests: 40
Dinner choice is beef

A:\CHAPTER.09\EVENT>
```

Figure 9-9: Output of the UseEventsWithHeaders program

6. Save and close the Event project.

SUMMARY

- Inheritance is the principle that you can apply knowledge of a general category to more specific objects.

- The classes you create in object-oriented programming languages can inherit data and methods from existing classes. When you create a class by making it inherit from another class, you are provided with data fields and methods automatically.

- When you extend an existing class, you can add just the fields and methods that are additions within the new class.

- The ability to use inheritance in the Java programming language makes programs easier to write, less error-prone, and easier to understand.

- A class that is used as a basis for inheritance is called a base class, a superclass, or a parent class.

- When you create a class that inherits from a base class, it is a derived class, a subclass, or a child class.

- In general, a subclass is larger than a superclass because you add new, more specific fields and methods to a subclass.

- You use the keyword `extends` to achieve inheritance within the Java programming language.

- Inheritance is a one-way proposition; a child inherits from a parent, but a parent does not inherit from a child.

- If you create separate methods for each subclass of a superclass, then each class's objects will use the appropriate method for that class. Each subclass method overrides the method that has the same name in the parent class. Using the same method name to indicate different implementations is called polymorphism.

QUESTIONS

1. The principle that you can apply knowledge of a general category to more specific objects is called _____.
   a. polymorphism
   b. primogeniture
   c. inheritance
   d. object-oriented programming

2. The primary reason you want to extend classes is to _____.
   a. save duplication of effort
   b. make programs larger
   c. reduce execution time
   d. avoid having to override methods

3. Employing inheritance reduces errors because _____.
   a. the new classes have access to fewer data fields
   b. the new classes have access to fewer methods
   c. you can copy methods that you already created
   d. many of the methods you need already have been used and tested

4. A class that is used as a basis for inheritance is called a _____.
   a. derived class
   b. base class
   c. subclass
   d. species

5. A superclass also can be called a _____.
   a. parent class
   b. subclass
   c. derived class
   d. wonderclass

6. Which of the following choices would most likely describe a parent class/child class relationship?
   a. Rose/Flower
   b. Present/Gift
   c. Green/Yellow
   d. Bird/Sparrow

7. A subclass usually _____ than a superclass.
   a. is simpler
   b. is larger
   c. contains fewer data fields
   d. contains fewer methods

8. The fields and methods in a subclass usually are _____ than those in its superclass.
   a. fewer in number
   b. more specific
   c. more complicated
   d. less prone to error

9. The Java keyword that creates inheritance is _____.
   a. `static`
   b. `enlarge`
   c. `extends`
   d. `inherits`

10. A class named Building has a method named getFloors(). If School is a child class of Building, and GeorgeWashingtonHigh is an object of type School, then which of the following statements is valid?
    a. `Building.getFloors();`
    b. `School.getFloors();`
    c. `GeorgeWashingtonHigh.getFloors();`
    d. All of these statements are valid.

section A

11. School is a child class of Building, BrickHouse is an object of type Building, and GeorgeWashingtonHigh is an object of type School. The School class contains a method named getRoomNum(). Which of the following statements is valid?
    a. `BrickHouse.getRoomNum();`
    b. `GeorgeWashingtonHigh.getRoomNum();`
    c. `School.getRoomNum();`
    d. All of these statements are valid.

12. Which of the following statements is true?
    a. A child class inherits from a parent class.
    b. A parent class inherits from a child class.
    c. Both of these statements are true.
    d. None of these statements are true.

13. Using the same method name to indicate different implementations is called _____.
    a. inheritance
    b. polymorphism
    c. insubordination
    d. implementation hiding

14. When a subclass method has the same name and argument types as a parent class method, the subclass method can _____ the parent class method.
    a. override
    b. overuse
    c. overload
    d. overcompensate

15. If a superclass and subclass have methods with the same name but with different argument lists, you are _____.
    a. overloading methods
    b. overriding a method
    c. creating an error situation
    d. violating the principles of object-oriented programming

EXERCISES

Save the programs that you create in these exercises in the Chapter.09 folder on your Student Disk.

1. Using each pair of class names that follow, choose the name you think is more likely to be the parent class, and then explain your choice.
   a. Bird/Parrot
   b. French/Language
   c. Furniture/Chair

2. Name three possible subclasses for each of the following parent class names:
   a. Food
   b. Movie
   c. Hobby

3. Create a class named Book that contains data fields for title and number of pages. Include get and set methods for these fields. Next create a subclass named Textbook, which contains an additional field that holds a grade level for the Textbook, and additional methods to get and set the grade level field. Write a program that demonstrates using objects of each class.

4. Create a class named Square that contains data fields for height, width, and surfaceArea, and a method named computeSurfaceArea(). Create a child class named Cube. Cube contains an additional data field named depth and a computeSurfaceArea() method that overrides the parent method. Write a program that instantiates a Square object and a Cube object and displays the surface areas of the objects.

5. Create a class named Order that performs order processing of a single item. The superclass has four fields for customer name, customer number, quantity ordered, and unit price. Include set and get methods for each of the fields. This class also needs methods to compute the total price (quantity times unit price) and to display the fields. Create a subclass that overrides computePrice() by adding a shipping and handling charge of $4.00. Write a program that uses these classes.

6. Create a class named Vacation that computes the amount of vacation for an employee. If an employee has worked for more than five years, the total vacation is three weeks annually; otherwise the employee gets two weeks annually. Use a superclass that contains an integer field that holds the number of vacation weeks and get and set methods for the field. Use a superclass object for employees who have earned two weeks of vacation. Use a subclass for extended vacations of three weeks. Obtain the employee information from text fields in an applet. Use text boxes for employee number, employee name, and number of years. Display the number of weeks of vacation after computing the result.

7. Write a superclass for inventory processing. The superclass has fields for quantity in stock, item name, and quantity sold today. Compute the current quantity from this information. Include set and get methods for quantity in stock and item. This class needs methods to compute the current quantity and display the fields. Create a subclass to get the quantity sold today. Write a program to use these classes.

SECTION B
objectives

In this section you will learn
- How to work with superclasses that have constructors
- How to work with superclass constructors that require arguments
- How to access superclass methods
- About information hiding
- Which methods you cannot override

Using Superclasses and Subclasses

Working with Superclasses That Have Constructors

When you create any object, as in `SomeClass anObject = new SomeClass();`, you are calling a class constructor method that has the same name as the class itself. When you instantiate an object that is a member of a subclass, you actually are calling two constructors: the constructor for the base class and the constructor for the extended, derived class. When you create any subclass object, the base class constructor must execute first, and *then* the subclass constructor executes.

In the examples of inheritance you have seen so far in this chapter, each class contained default constructors, so their execution was transparent. However, you should realize that when you create an object using `HourlyEmployee clerk = new HourlyEmployee();` (where HourlyEmployee is a subclass of Employee), both the Employee() and HourlyEmployee() constructors execute.

For example, you can create a class whose constructor does nothing but print a message. Then, when you extend the class, you can create a subclass constructor that prints a different message.

> **To demonstrate that a subclass constructor calls the superclass constructor first:**
>
> **1** Create a new empty project named **DemoConstructors**. Save the **DemoConstructors** project folder in the Chapter.09 folder on your Student Disk.

2 Add to the project a new class file named **ABaseClass.java** and add the following constructor between the class's curly brackets to print a message on the screen:

```
public ABaseClass()
   {
      System.out.println("In base class constructor");
   }
```

3 Add to the project a new class file named **ASubClass.java**, add **extends ABaseClass** to the right of the class header, then between the class's curly brackets add the following constructor that also prints a message on the screen:

```
public ASubClass()
   {
      System.out.println("In subclass constructor");
   }
```

4 Add to the project a new main class file named **DemoConstructors.java** and add `ASubClass child = new ASubClass();` between the main() method's curly brackets to create a child class object.

5 Build the project and then execute the program by running the **DemoConstructors.java** file as a console application. The output appears as shown in Figure 9-10. Even though you create only one subclass object, two separate messages print—one from the superclass constructor and one from the subclass constructor.

```
C:\WINNT\System32\cmd.exe

A:\CHAPTER.09\DemoConstructors>jview DemoConstructors
In base class constructor
In subclass constructor

A:\CHAPTER.09\DemoConstructors>
```

Figure 9-10: Output of the DemoConstructors program

Of course, most constructors perform many more tasks than printing a message to inform you that they exist. When constructors initialize variables, you usually want the base class constructor to take care of initializing the data fields that originate in the base class. The subclass constructor only needs to initialize the data fields that are specific to the subclass.

Next, you will add a constructor to the Event class you created for Event Handlers Incorporated. When you instantiate a subclass DinnerEvent object, the superclass Event constructor will execute.

To add a constructor to the Event class:

1. Open the **Event** project, and then open the **EventWithHeader.java** file in the Text Editor window. Save the **EventWithHeader.java** file as **EventWithConstructor.java**, and then change the class name from EventWithHeader to **EventWithConstructor**.

2. Position your cursor to the right of the statement that declares the eventGuests data field, and then press the **Enter** key to start a new line. Type the following constructor that initializes the number of guests to zero:

```
public EventWithConstructor()
{
   eventGuests = 0;
}
```

3. Open the **DinnerEventWithHeader.java** file in the Text Editor window, save it as **DinnerEventWithConstructor.java**, and then change the class header so that both the class name and the parent class name read as follows:

```
public class DinnerEventWithConstructor
   extends EventWithConstructor
```

4. Add to the project a new main class file named **UseEventsWithConstructors.java** to demonstrate the use of the base class constructor with both a base class object and an extended class object.

5. Enter the following code between the main() method's curly brackets to create definitions of two objects—one is a member of the base class, and the other is a member of the extended class:

```
EventWithConstructor anEvent =
   new EventWithConstructor();
DinnerEventWithConstructor aDinnerEvent =
   new DinnerEventWithConstructor();
```

6. Add the following statements that print a header and the number of guests for the parent class member:

```
anEvent.printHeader();
nEvent.printEventGuests();
```

7. Add statements that print a header and the number of guests for the child class member:

```
aDinnerEvent.printHeader();
aDinnerEvent.printEventGuests();
```

8. Rebuild the project and run the **UseEventsWithConstructors.java** file as a console application. The output is shown in Figure 9-11. The guest number is initialized correctly for objects of both classes.

Introduction to Inheritance

Figure 9-11: Output of the UseEventsWithConstructors program

Using Superclass Constructors That Require Arguments

When you create a class and do not provide a constructor, Java automatically supplies you with one that never requires arguments. When you write your own constructor, you replace the automatically supplied version. Depending on your needs, the constructor you create for a class might require arguments. When you use a class as a superclass, and the class has a constructor that requires arguments, then you must make sure that any subclasses provide the superclass constructor with what it needs.

Don't forget that a class can have many constructors. As soon as you create at least one constructor for a class, you no longer can use an automatic version.

When a superclass constructor requires arguments, you are required to include a constructor for each subclass you create. Your subclass constructor can contain any number of statements, but the first statement within the constructor must call the superclass constructor. Even if you have no other reason for creating a subclass constructor, you must write the subclass constructor so it can call its parent's constructor.

The format of the statement that calls a superclass constructor is `super(list of arguments);`. The keyword **super** always refers to the superclass of the class in which you use it. In addition, except for any comments, the super() statement must be the first statement in the subclass constructor. Not even data field definitions can precede it. For example, suppose that you create an Employee class with a constructor that requires three arguments—a character, a double, and an integer—and you create an HourlyEmployee class that is a subclass of Employee. The following code shows a valid constructor for HourlyEmployee:

```
public HourlyEmployee()
{
  super('P', 12.35, 40);
  // Other statements can go here
}
```

The HourlyEmployee constructor requires no arguments, but it passes three arguments to its superclass constructor. A different HourlyEmployee constructor can require arguments. It could then pass the appropriate arguments on to the superclass constructor. For example:

```
public HourlyEmployee(char dept, double rate, int hours)
{
   super(dept, rate, hours);
   // Other statements can go here
}
```

Although it seems as though you should be able to use the superclass constructor name to call the superclass constructor, Java does not allow you to do so. You must use the keyword name super.

Next, you will modify the Event class so that its constructor requires arguments. Then, to show how the superclass and subclass constructors work, you will create a subclass object that calls its superclass constructor.

To demonstrate how inheritance works when class constructors require arguments:

1 Return to the **EventWithConstructor.java** file in the Text Editor window and save it, and then use the **Save As** command to save the file as **EventWithConstructorArg.java**.

2 Change the class name from EventWithConstructor to **EventWithConstructorArg**, and then change the constructor argument list so it requires an integer argument. In other words, change `public EventWithConstructor()` to `public EventWithConstructorArg(int guests)`.

3 Change the constructor statement that sets eventGuests to zero as follows so that the statement sets the event guests field to the constructor's argument value: `eventGuests = guests;`.

Next, you will add a constructor to the DinnerEvent class so it can call its parent's constructor. The child class constructor will require an integer argument, which it then passes on to the parent class constructor.

To create the child class:

1 Return to the **DinnerEventWithConstructor.java** file in the Text Editor window and save the file, and then use the **Save As** command to save the file as **DinnerEventWithConstructorArg.java**.

2. Change the class header to:

```
public class DinnerEventWithConstructorArg
   extends EventWithConstructorArg
```

3. Position the insertion point after the declaration of the dinnerChoice field, and then press the **Enter** key to start a new line. Create the following constructor that requires an integer argument and passes it on to the superclass constructor:

```
public DinnerEventWithConstructorArg(int guests)
{
   super(guests);
}
```

Now you can create a program to demonstrate creating parent and child class objects when the parent constructor needs an argument.

To create the program:

1. Add to the project a new main class file named **UseEventsWithConstructorArg.java**.
2. Enter the following code between the main() method's curly brackets to create an EventWithConstructorArg object and give it a value for the number of guests:

```
EventWithConstructorArg anEvent =
   new EventWithConstructorArg(45);
```

3. Add the following code to create a DinnerEventWithConstructorArg object. This constructor also requires an integer argument.

```
DinnerEventWithConstructorArg aDinnerEvent =
   new DinnerEventWithConstructorArg(65);
```

4. Add the following statements to print explanations and guest fields for each object:

```
anEvent.printHeader();
anEvent.printEventGuests();
aDinnerEvent.printHeader();
aDinnerEvent.printEventGuests();
```

5. Rebuild the Event project and execute the **UseEventsWithConstructorArg.java** file as a console application. The output appears in Figure 9-12. Each object is correctly initialized because the superclass constructor was correctly called in each case.

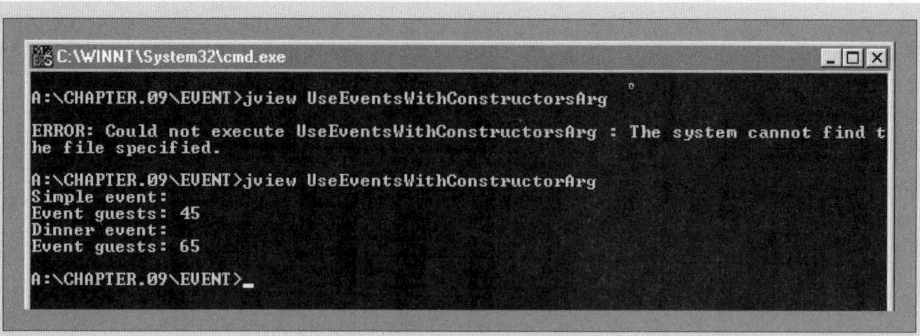

Figure 9-12: Output of the UseEventsWithConstructorArg program

Accessing Superclass Methods

In Section A of this chapter, you learned that a subclass can contain a method with the same name and arguments as a method in its parent class. When the subclass and superclass share a method with the same name and arguments, using the subclass method overrides the parent class method. However, you might want to use the parent class method within a subclass. If so, you can use the keyword **super** to access the parent class method. To demonstrate, you will create a simple subclass that has a method with the same name as a method that is part of its base class.

To access a superclass method from within a subclass:

1 Create a new empty project named **DemoSuper**. Save the **DemoSuper** project folder in the Chapter.09 folder on your Student Disk.

2 Add to the project a new class file named **AParentClass** and add the following variable and method between the class's curly brackets:

```
private int aVal;
   public void printClassName()
   {
      System.out.println("AParentClass");
   }
```

3 Add to the project a new class file named **AChildClass**, and then add **extends AParentClass** to the right of the class header.

4 Add the following method between the class's curly brackets. The method has the same name as the parent's method, but the child can call the parent method without conflict by using the keyword **super**.

```
    public void printClassName()
    {
      System.out.println("I am AChildClass");
      System.out.println("My parent is ");
      super.printClassName();
    }
```

5. Add to the project a new main class file named **DemoSuper.java**.
6. Enter the following code between the main() method's curly brackets to show that the child class can call its parent's method:

```
AChildClass child = new AChildClass();
child.printClassName();
```

7. Build the project and execute the **DemoSuper.java** file as a console application. As the output in Figure 9-13 shows, even though the child and parent classes have methods with the same name, the child class can use the parent class method correctly by employing the keyword super.

Figure 9-13: Output of the DemoSuper program

> **tip**
>
> You can use the keyword this as the opposite of super. For example, if a superclass and its subclass each have a method named someMethod(), then within the subclass, super.someMethod() refers to the superclass version of the method. Both someMethod() and this.someMethod() refer to the subclass version.

Information Hiding

Examine the Student class shown in Figure 9-14. It is constructed in a very typical manner for Java classes. The keyword private precedes each of the data fields, and the keyword public precedes each of the methods. As a matter of fact, the four get and set methods are necessary within the Student class specifically because the data fields are private. Without the public get and set methods, there would be no way to access these private data fields.

```
public class Student
{
  private int idNum;
  private double semesterTuition;
  public int getIdNum()
  {
    return idNum;
  }
  public double getTuition()
  {
    return semesterTuition;
  }
  public void setIdNum(int num)
  {
    idNum = num;
  }
  public void setTuition(double amt)
  {
    semesterTuition = amt;
  }
}
```

Figure 9-14: Student class

When a program is a class user of Student (that is, it instantiates a Student object), then the user cannot alter the data in any private field directly. For example, when you write a main() method that creates a Student as `Student someStudent = new Student();`, you cannot change the Student's idNum with a statement such as `someStudent.idNum = 812;`. The idNum of the someStudent object is not accessible in the main() program that uses the Student object because idNum is private. Only methods that are part of the Student class itself are allowed to alter Student data. To alter a Student's idNum, you must use the public method, setIdNum(), as in `someStudent.setIdNum(812);`.

The concept of keeping data private is known as **information hiding**. When you employ information hiding, you are assured that your data will be altered only by the methods you choose and only in ways that you can control. For example, you might want setIdNum() to check to make sure idNum is within a specific range of values. If a class other than the Student class itself could alter idNum, then idNum could be assigned a value that the Student class couldn't control.

> You first learned about information hiding and using the `public` and `private` keywords in Chapter 3. You may want to review these concepts.

When a class serves as a superclass to other classes you create, your subclasses inherit all the data and methods of the superclass, with one exception: Private members of the parent class are not inherited. If you could use private data outside of its class, the principle of information hiding would be lost. If you intend the Student class data field idNum to be private, then you don't want any outside classes using the field. If a new class could simply extend your Student class and "get to" its data fields without "going through the proper channels," then information hiding would not be operating.

There are occasions when you want to access parent class data from within a subclass. For example, suppose you create two child classes that extend the Student class: PartTimeStudent and FullTimeStudent. If you want the subclass methods to be able to access idNum and semesterTuition, then those data fields cannot be private. However, if you don't want other, non-child classes to access those data fields, then they cannot be public. The solution is to create the fields using the modifier `protected`. Using the keyword `protected` provides you with an intermediate level of security between public and private access. If you create a data field or method that is protected, it can be used within its own class or in any classes extended from that class, but it cannot be used by "outside" classes. In other words, protected members are those that can be used by a class and its descendants.

> Other classes within the same package also can use protected members.

Next, you will use the `protected` access modifier with a superclass data field so that you can access the field within a subclass method.

To create a superclass with a protected field:

1 Open the **Event** project from the Event folder in the Chapter.09 folder on your Student Disk, then open the **EventWithHeader.java** file in the Text Editor window, and then use the **Save As** command to save the file as **EventWithProtectedData.java**. You will use the file that you created before adding constructors just to keep this example simple. Change the class name to **EventWithProtectedData**.

2 Change the modifier on the eventGuests field from `private` to `protected`.

section B

3 Return to the **DinnerEventWithHeader.java** file in the Text Editor window, save it, and then use the **Save As** command to save the file as **DinnerEventWithProtectedData.java**. Change the class name so that it reads as follows:

```
public class DinnerEventWithProtectedData
   extends EventWithProtectedData
```

Assume that Event Handlers Incorporated requires at least 10 guests for an event with dinner, but there is no minimum guest number for other event types. To ensure that DinnerEvents (unlike plain Events) have at least 10 guests, the subclass setEventGuests() method will override the setEventGuests() method in the superclass. The subclass version of the method will call the superclass method, but if the user does not enter a guest number of at least 10, the subclass method will call the superclass method again.

To create the subclass setEventGuests() method:

1 Position the insertion point at the end of the closing curly bracket of the setDinnerChoice() method, press the **Enter** key to start a new line, and then type the following header for the method and the method's opening curly bracket:

```
public void setEventGuests() throws Exception
{
```

2 Call the superclass method with the same name:

```
super.setEventGuests();
```

3 Check the value of the eventGuests data field using the following while loop. Because the field is protected in the base class, you can access the field here in the subclass. While the guest number continues to be too low, issue an error message and call the superclass method.

```
while(eventGuests < 10)
{
   System.out.print("Minimum required for dinner: ");
   System.out.println("10 guests!");
   super.setEventGuests();
}
```

4 Add the closing bracket for the method.

> If eventGuests had not been inherited (that is, if it were still private), you would need to use the `public getEventGuests()` method to access its value.

5. Next create a simple program to test this class. Add to the project a new main class file named **UseProtected.java**, and then add `throws Exception` to the right of the main() method.

6. Create the aDinnerEvent object by entering the following code between the main() method's curly brackets:

```
DinnerEventWithProtectedData aDinnerEvent =
   new DinnerEventWithProtectedData();
```

7. Using the newly created object, print an explanation, set the field values, and then print the field values by entering the following code:

```
aDinnerEvent.printHeader();
aDinnerEvent.setEventGuests();
aDinnerEvent.setDinnerChoice();
aDinnerEvent.printEventGuests();
aDinnerEvent.printDinnerChoice();
```

8. Rebuild the project and execute the **UseProtected.java** file as a console application. When you run the program, make several attempts to set the number of dinner guests to values below 10. The program will continue to prompt you until your guest number meets the required minimum. A sample of the program's output appears in Figure 9-15.

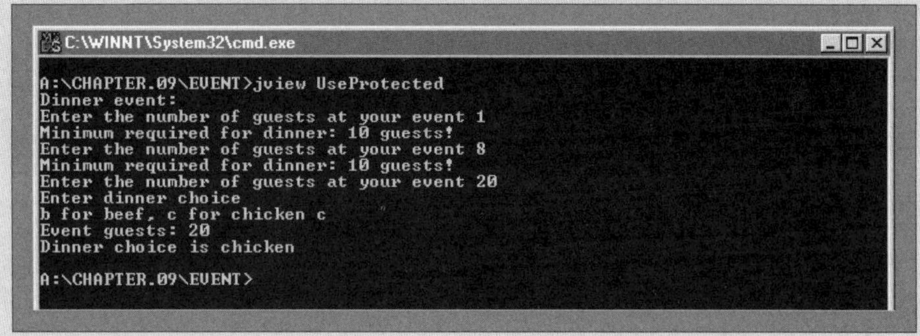

Figure 9-15: Sample output from the UseProtected program

Using Methods That You Cannot Override

There are four types of methods that you cannot override in a subclass:
- `private` methods
- `static` methods
- `final` methods
- Methods within `final` classes

You already know that when you create a private variable in a superclass, the variable is not available for use in a subclass. Similarly, if you create a private method in a superclass, the method is not available for use in any class extended from the superclass. You also know that a subclass can access private variables in the superclass through the use of nonprivate methods. Again, similarly, if a superclass has a nonprivate method that accesses a private method, then a child class can use the inherited nonprivate method to access the noninherited private method.

For example, Figure 9-16 shows a superclass named Super that contains two methods: one method is public and the other method is private.

```
public class Super
{
  public void printPublic()
  {
    System.out.println("This method is public");
    printPrivate();
  }
  private void printPrivate()
  {
    System.out.println("This method is private");
  }
}
```

Figure 9-16: Super method

Figure 9-17 shows a subclass that attempts to extend Super. If you compile the Sub class, you will receive the error message, "Cannot access private member 'void printPrivate()' in class 'Super' from class 'Sub'". The statement that calls printPublic() works correctly because as a public method, printPublic() is inherited by the Sub class. The printPublic() method calls printPrivate(), which is perfectly legal because printPublic() and printPrivate() are methods within the same class. However, within the Sub class, the printPrivate() method is "invisible;" the compiler tells you that it doesn't exist. As a private method, printPrivate() is not inherited.

```
public class Sub extends Super
{
  public void printMessages()
  {
    printPublic();
    printPrivate();   // This statement causes an error
  }
}
```

Figure 9-17: Incorrect Sub class

Additionally, you cannot override a method that is private in a parent class. For example, examine the class in Figure 9-18. This Sub class extends the Super class shown in Figure 9-16 and adds its own printPrivate() method. When a main() program creates a Sub object, as in Sub aSubObject = new Sub();, and calls printPrivate() with aSubObject.printMessages();, then the program will display the message "This method is private" from the Super class, and not "This will never print" from the Sub class method. This result makes sense when you consider that printMessages() is a method that is part of the Super class. The printMessages() method calls the printPrivate() method from its own class. The subclass shown in Figure 9-18 compiles without error, but it is as though the printPrivate() method within the subclass does not exist.

```
public class Sub extends Super
{
  public void printMessages()
  {
    printPublic();
  }
  private void printPrivate()
  {
    System.out.println("This will never print");
  }
}
```

Figure 9-18: Sub class with an invisible method

In addition to private methods, you also cannot override static methods from a parent class. You learned in Chapter 4 that static methods also are called class methods and that they have no objects associated with them. You call a static method using the class name, not an object name. Recall that in Java the keyword `static` implies uniqueness; a static method is unique to the base class and all its descendants.

The main() methods in Java applications always are static.

Methods carrying the access modifier `final` cannot be overridden by subclass methods. In Chapter 4, you learned that you can use the keyword `final` when you want to create a constant, as in `final double TAXRATE = .065;`. You also can use the `final` modifier with methods when you don't want the method to be overridden. You use `static` as a method access modifier when you create *class* methods for which you want to prevent overriding; you use `final` as a method access modifier when you create *instance* methods for which you want to prevent overriding.

You can think of private and static methods as being implicitly final.

You might improve your program's performance by making methods final. Because final methods are guaranteed never to change, the compiler can remove the method calls to final methods, and, in their place, substitute the actual method statements. This process is called **inlining** the code. You are never aware that inlining is taking place; the compiler simply might choose to use this method to save on the overhead of calling a method.

The compiler will choose to inline a final method only if it is a very small method containing only one or two lines of code.

Finally, you can declare a class to be final. When you do so, all of its methods are final no matter what access modifier actually precedes the method name. A final class cannot be a parent.

Java's Math class, which you learned about in Chapter 4, is an example of a final class.

SUMMARY

- When you instantiate an object that is a member of a subclass, you actually are calling two constructors: the constructor for the base class and the constructor for the extended class. The base class constructor executes first, and then the subclass constructor executes.

- When constructors initialize variables, you usually want the base class constructor to take care of initializing the data fields that originate in the base class. The subclass constructor only needs to initialize the data fields that are specific to the subclass.

- When you write your own constructor, you replace an automatically supplied version.

- When a superclass has a constructor that requires arguments, you must make sure that any subclasses provide the superclass constructor with those arguments.

- When a superclass constructor requires arguments, you are required to create a constructor for each subclass you create. The first statement within the constructor must call the superclass constructor.

- The format of the statement that calls a superclass constructor is `super(list of arguments);`. The keyword `super` always refers to the superclass of the class in which you use it.

- You can use the keyword `super` to access the parent class method.

- When a program is a class user, it cannot alter the data in any private field directly. This concept of keeping data private is known as information hiding. Information hiding lets you control how data is used and altered.

- A child class does not inherit private members of a parent class.

- If you create a data field or method that uses the `protected` access modifier, then the field or method can be used within its own class or in any classes extended from that class, but cannot be used by "outside" classes.

- There are four types of methods that you cannot override in a subclass: private methods, static methods, final methods, and methods within final classes.

- If you create a private method in a superclass, the method is not available for use in any class extended from the superclass. If a superclass has a nonprivate method that accesses a private method, then a child class can use the inherited nonprivate method to access the noninherited private method.

- The Java keyword `static` implies uniqueness; a static method is unique to the base class and all its descendants.

- You use `static` as a method access modifier when you create *class* methods for which you want to prevent overriding; you use `final` as a method access modifier when you create *instance* methods for which you want to prevent overriding.

- Because final methods are guaranteed never to change, the compiler can remove the method calls to final methods, and, in their place, substitute the actual method statements. This process is called inlining the code.

- When you declare a class to be final, all of its methods are final no matter what access modifier actually precedes the method name. A final class cannot be a parent.

QUESTIONS

1. When you instantiate an object that is a member of a subclass, the _____ constructor executes first.
   a. subclass
   b. child class
   c. extended class
   d. parent class

2. Usually, a subclass constructor only needs to initialize the data fields that are _____.
   a. specific to the subclass
   b. specific to the superclass
   c. contained in both classes
   d. contained in neither class

3. In Java, the automatically supplied constructor _____ requires arguments.
   a. always
   b. usually
   c. rarely
   d. never

4. When you write your own constructor, you _____ the automatically supplied version.
   a. replace
   b. inherit
   c. augment
   d. promote

5. Which of the following statements is true?
   a. Every superclass must provide arguments for its subclass constructor.
   b. Every subclass must provide arguments for its superclass constructor.
   c. If a superclass constructor requires arguments, then any subclass constructors must provide them.
   d. If a subclass constructor requires arguments, then any superclass constructors must provide them.

6. If a superclass constructor requires arguments, then its subclass _____.
   a. must contain a constructor that requires no arguments
   b. must not contain a constructor
   c. must contain a constructor that requires arguments
   d. must not contain a constructor that requires arguments

7. If a superclass constructor requires arguments, any constructor of its subclasses must call the superclass constructor _____.
   a. as a first statement
   b. as a last statement
   c. at some time
   d. multiple times if multiple arguments are involved

8. The keyword _____ always refers to the superclass of the class in which you use it.
   a. parent
   b. base
   c. super
   d. superclass

9. A child class Motorcycle extends a parent class Vehicle. Each class constructor requires one String argument. The Motorcycle class constructor can call the Vehicle class constructor with the statement _____.
   a. Vehicle("Honda");
   b. Motorcycle("Harley");
   c. super("Suzuki");
   d. None of these answers is correct.

10. A child class Doll extends a parent class Toy. Assume each class has a public void play() method. Which of the following statements calls the play() method that belongs to the Toy class from within the Doll class?
    a. play();
    b. Toy.play();
    c. super.play();
    d. Two of these are correct.

11. A child class Doll extends a parent class Toy. Assume each class has a public void play() method. Which of the following statements calls the play() method that belongs to the Doll class from within the Doll class?
    a. Doll.play();
    b. this.play();
    c. play();
    d. Two of these are correct.

12. In the Java programming language, the concept of keeping data private is known as _____.
    a. polymorphism
    b. information hiding
    c. data deception
    d. concealing fields

13. The members of parent classes that are not inherited are the _____ members.
    a. public
    b. protected
    c. private
    d. friendly

14. Within a subclass, you cannot override _____ methods.
    a. public
    b. private
    c. protected
    d. constructor

15. Within a subclass, you can override _____ methods.
    a. static
    b. protected
    c. final
    d. private

16. Methods that are static methods _____.
    a. also are called class methods
    b. have no objects associated with them
    c. Both of these are correct.
    d. None of these are correct.

17. You call a static method using a(n) _____ name.
    a. class
    b. superclass
    c. object
    d. None of these answers is correct.

18. You use `final` as a method access modifier when you create _____ methods for which you want to prevent overriding.
    a. class
    b. superclass
    c. subclass
    d. instance

19. A compiler can decide to _____ a final method.
    a. duplicate
    b. inline
    c. redline
    d. beeline

20. Which of the following class types can be a parent?
    a. final
    b. static
    c. private
    d. public

EXERCISES

Save the programs that you create in these exercises in the Chapter.09 folder on your Student Disk.

1. a. Create a class named Year that contains a data field that holds the number of days in the year. Include a get method that displays the number of days and a constructor that sets the number of days to 365. Create a subclass named LeapYear. LeapYear's constructor overrides Year's constructor and sets the day field to 366. Write a program that instantiates one object of each class and displays each class's data.

b. Add a method named daysElapsed() to the Year class you created in Exercise 1a. The daysElapsed() method accepts two arguments representing a month and a day; it returns an integer indicating the number of days that have elapsed since January 1 of the year. Create a daysElapsed() method for the LeapYear class that overrides the method in the Year class. Write a program that calculates the days elapsed on March 1 for a Year and for a LeapYear.

2. Create a class named Computer that contains two integer data fields for processor model (for example, 486) and clock speed in megahertz (for example, 166). Include a get method for each field and a constructor that requires a parameter for each field. Create a subclass named MultimediaComputer that contains an additional integer field for the CD-ROM speed. The MultiMedia class also contains a get method for the new data field and a constructor that requires arguments for each of the three data fields. Write a program to demonstrate creating and using an object of each class.

3. Create a class named HotelRoom that includes an integer field for the room number and a double field for the nightly rental rate. Include get methods for these fields and a constructor that requires an integer argument representing the room number. The constructor sets the room rate based on the room number; rooms numbered 299 and below are $69.95 per night, others are $89.95 per night. Create an extended class named Suite whose constructor requires a room number and adds a $40.00 surcharge to the regular hotel room rate based on the room number. Write a program to demonstrate creating and using an object of each class.

4. Create a class named Package with data fields for weight in ounces, shipping method, and shipping cost. The shipping method is a character: *A* for air, *T* for truck, or *M* for mail. The Package class contains a constructor that requires arguments for weight and shipping method. The constructor calls a calculateCost() method that determines the shipping cost based on the following:

Weight (lb)	Shipping Method ($)		
	Air	Truck	Mail
1 to 8	2.00	1.50	.50
9 to 16	3.00	2.35	1.50
17 and over	4.50	3.25	2.15

The Package class also contains a display() method that displays the values in all four fields. Create a subclass named InsuredPackage that adds an insurance cost to the shipping cost based on the following:

Shipping Cost before Insurance ($)	Additional Cost ($)
0 to 1.00	2.45
1.01 to 3.00	3.95
3.01 and over	5.55

section B

Write a program that instantiates at least three objects of each type (Package and InsuredPackage) using a variety of weights and shipping method codes. Display the results for each Package and InsuredPackage.

5. Write a program named CarRental that computes the cost of renting a car for a day, based on the size of the car: economy, medium, or full size. Include a constructor that requires the car size. Add a subclass to add the option of a car phone. Write a program to use these classes.

6. Write a program named CollegeCourse that computes the cost of taking a college course. Include a constructor that requires a course ID number. Add a subclass to compute a lab fee for a course that uses a lab. Write a program to use these classes.

7. Write a program named Discount that computes the price of an item. Include a constructor that requires the quantity, item name, and item number. Add a subclass to provide a discount based on the quantity ordered. Write a program to use these classes.

8. Each of the following files in the Chapter.09 folder on your Student Disk has syntax and/or logical errors. Add the files to a new project called FixDebug. Save the FixDebug project in the Chapter.09 folder on your Student Disk. In each case, fix the problem and run each file as a console application using JVIEW.
    a. DebugNine1.java
    b. DebugNine2.java
    c. DebugNine3.java
    d. DebugNine4.java

CHAPTER 10

Advanced Inheritance Concepts

case ▶ "Inheritance sure makes my programming job easier," you tell Lynn Greenbrier over a frosty lemonade at the Event Handlers Incorporated company picnic.

"You mean your parents knew about object-oriented programming?" Lynn smiles.

"No, you know what I mean!" you smile back. "I'm ready to learn more, though. Can you tell me more about inheritance?"

"Not today," Lynn says. "Go join the potato sack race. But on Monday morning I'll teach you about superclass arrays that can use subclass methods and interfaces. Then you will be an inheritance pro."

Previewing an Example of Using an Abstract Class

Clients at Event Handlers Incorporated can choose many types of entertainment to feature at their events. Even though Event Handlers uses different class types to store different entertainment types, the different entertainment acts need to be stored in a single entertainment database, which can be accomplished through the power of inheritance, abstract classes, and dynamic method binding. You can use a completed version of the EntertainmentSelector program that is saved in the Chapter.10 folder on your Student Disk now.

To use the Chap10EntertainmentSelector class:

1 Go to the command prompt for the Chap10EntertainmentSelector folder in the Chapter.10 folder on your Student Disk, type **jview Chap10EntertainmentSelector**, and then press the **Enter** key. This program allows you to supply data for six entertainment acts that are under contract to Event Handlers Incorporated. When you see the prompt, type **1** for a musical or **2** for a nonmusical weekend event. If you indicated this act is a musical act, the prompt will ask you for an entertainer name and a style of music; if you indicated this act is a non-musical act, the prompt will ask you for an entertainer name and act type. You can supply any answers you want to these questions. After you enter information for six acts, the data you entered will echo to the screen and you will see the charge for each act. Musical acts are paid by the event; non-musical acts are paid by the hour. Then you can select the act you want to perform at your event. The last lines of a typical program run appear in Figure 10-1. You will create a similar program in this chapter.

```
C:\WINNT\System32\cmd.exe
What type of act is this? clown
Please select the type of act you want to enter:
    1 - Musical act
    2 - Any other type of act
1
Enter name of entertainer Garrison Novela
What type of music do they play? classical guitar
Please select the type of act you want to enter:
    1 - Musical act
    2 - Any other type of act
2
Enter name of entertainer Toby Sisselli
What type of act is this? story teller

Our available entertainment selections include:

The Perfect Pitches, featuring barbershop music. Fee is $600 per event
The Crustaceans, featuring rock music. Fee is $600 per event
Dolly Dee, a clown. Fee is $50 per hour
Fingers Mulligan, a clown. Fee is $50 per hour
Garrison Novela, featuring classical guitar music. Fee is $600 per event
Toby Sisselli, a story teller. Fee is $50 per hour

A:\CHAPTER.10\Chap10EntertainmentSelector>
```

Figure 10-1: Output of the Chap10EntertainmentSelector program

SECTION A
objectives

In this section you will learn
- About creating and using abstract classes
- About dynamic method binding
- How to create arrays of subclass objects

Abstract Classes and Dynamic Method Binding

Creating and Using Abstract Classes

Creating new classes is easier after you understand the concept of inheritance. (You learned about inheritance in Chapter 9.) When you use a class as a basis from which to create extended child classes, the child classes are more specific than their parent. When you create a child class, it inherits all the general attributes you need; you must create only the new, more specific attributes. For example, a SalariedEmployee and an HourlyEmployee are more specific than an Employee. They can inherit general attributes, such as an employee number, but add specific attributes, such as pay calculating methods.

Another way to think about a superclass is to notice that it contains the features that are shared by its subclasses. The subclasses are more specific examples of the superclass type; they add additional features to the shared, general features. Conversely, when you examine a subclass, you see that its parent is more general and less specific. Sometimes a parent class is so general that you never intend to create any specific instances of the class. For example, you might never create "just" an Employee; each Employee is more specifically a SalariedEmployee, HourlyEmployee, or ContractEmployee.

A class, such as Employee, that you create only to extend from, but not to instantiate from, is an **abstract class**. An abstract class is one from which concrete objects cannot be created, but from which classes can be inherited. You use the keyword `abstract` when you declare an abstract class.

▶ **tip**

Nonabstract classes from which objects *can* be instantiated are called *concrete classes*.

> **tip**
> In Chapter 9, you learned that you can create final classes if you do not want other classes to be able to extend them. Classes that you declare to be abstract are the opposite; your only purpose in creating them is to enable other classes to extend them.

> **tip**
> In other programming languages, such as C++, abstract classes are known as virtual classes.

Abstract classes are like regular classes because they have data and methods. The difference lies in the fact that you cannot create instances of abstract classes by using the new operator. You create abstract classes simply to provide a superclass from which other objects may inherit.

Usually, abstract classes contain abstract methods. An **abstract method** is a method with no method statements. When you create an abstract method, you provide the keyword `abstract` and the intended method type, name, and arguments, but you do not provide any statements within the method. When you create a subclass that inherits an abstract method from a superclass, you must provide the actions, or implementation, for the inherited method. In other words, you are required to code a subclass method to override the empty superclass method that is inherited.

> **tip**
> If you attempt to instantiate an object from an abstract class, you will receive an error message that you have committed an InstantiationError.

> **tip**
> If you provide an empty method within an abstract class, the method is an abstract method even if you do not explicitly use the keyword `abstract` when defining the method.

For example, suppose you want to create classes to represent different animals, such as Dog and Cow. You can create a generic abstract class named Animal so you can provide generic data fields, such as an animal's name, only once. An Animal is generic, but all specific Animals make a sound. The actual sound differs from Animal to Animal. If you code an empty speak() method in the abstract Animal class, then you require all future Animal subclasses to code a speak() method that is specific to the subclass. Figure 10-2 shows an abstract Animal class containing a data field for the name, a constructor, a getName() method, and an abstract speak() method.

```
public abstract class Animal
{
  private String name;
  public Animal(String nm)
  {
    name = nm;
  }
  public String getName()
  {
    return(name);
  }
  public abstract void speak();
}
```

Figure 10-2: Animal class

The Animal class in Figure 10-2 is declared as abstract. You cannot place a statement such as `Animal myPet = new Animal("Murphy");` within such a program because the program will not execute. Animal is an abstract class, so no Animal objects can exist.

If you declare any method to be an abstract method, then you must declare its class to be abstract as well.

You create an abstract class like Animal so that you can extend it. For example, because a dog is an animal, you can create a Dog class as a child class of Animal. Figure 10-3 shows a Dog class—notice that it extends Animal. The Animal parent class in Figure 10-2 contains a constructor that requires a String holding the Animal's name, so the child Dog class also must contain a constructor that passes a String along to its superclass constructor.

You learned how child class and parent class constructors operate in Chapter 9.

```
public class Dog extends Animal
{
  public Dog(String nm)
  {
    super(nm);
  }
  public void speak()
  {
    System.out.println("Woof");
  }
}
```

Figure 10-3: Dog class

The speak() method within the Dog class is required because the abstract, parent Animal class contains an abstract speak() method. You can code any statements you like within the Dog speak() method, but the speak() method must exist. Remember, you cannot instantiate an Animal object; however, instantiating a Dog object is perfectly legal because Dog is not an abstract class. When you code Dog myPet = new Dog("Murphy");, you create a Dog object. Then when you code myPet.speak();, the correct Dog speak() method executes.

If you do not provide a subclass method to override a superclass abstract method, then you cannot instantiate any subclass objects. In this case, you also must declare the subclass itself to be abstract. Then you can extend the subclass into sub-subclasses in which you write code for the method.

The classes in Figures 10-4 and 10-5 also inherit from the Animal class. When you create a Cow or a Snake object, each Animal will be able to use speak() appropriately.

In Chapter 9, you learned that using the same method name to indicate different implementations is called polymorphism. Using polymorphism, one method name produces different actions for different types of objects.

```
public class Cow extends Animal
{
  public Cow(String nm)
  {
    super(nm);
  }
  public void speak()
  {
    System.out.println("Moo");
  }
}
```

Figure 10-4: Cow class

```
public class Snake extends Animal
{
  public Snake(String nm)
  {
    super(nm);
  }
  public void speak()
  {
    System.out.println("Sss");
  }
}
```

Figure 10-5: Snake class

Next you will create an abstract Entertainment class for Event Handlers Incorporated. The Entertainment class holds data about entertainment acts that customers can hire for their events. The class includes fields for the name of the act and the fee charged for providing the act. Entertainment is an abstract class. You will create two subclasses, MusicalEntertainment and OtherEntertainment. The more specific classes include different methods for calculating the entertainment act's fee (musical acts are paid by the performance; other acts are paid by the hour), as well as different methods for displaying data.

To create an abstract Entertainment class:

1 If necessary, start Visual J++, then create a new empty project named **Entertainment**. Save the **Entertainment** project folder in the Chapter.10 folder on your Student Disk.

2 Add a new class file to the project by selecting **Add Class** from the **Project** menu. The Add Item dialog box appears. In the Add Item dialog box, select **Class** from the **Class** folder, change the suggested filename to **Entertainment.java**, and click the **Open** button. The new class opens in the Text Editor window.

3 Add the word `abstract` to the class header so that it reads `public abstract class Entertainment`.

4 Define the two data fields that hold the entertainer's name and fee as protected rather than private because you will want child classes to be able to access the data fields when the fee is set and when the fields are displayed on the screen. Between the class's curly brackets, define the fields as follows:

```
protected String entertainer;
protected int fee;
```

5 The Entertainment constructor calls two methods. The first method accepts the entertainer's name from the keyboard. The second method sets the entertainer's fee. Because the first method will accept keyboard data entry, you must include the phrase `throws Exception` in the following constructor method header:

```
public Entertainment() throws Exception
{
  setEntertainerName();
  setEntertainmentFee();
}
```

6 Include the following two get methods that return the values for the entertainer's name and the act's fee:

```
public String getEntertainerName()
{
  return entertainer;
}
public double getEntertainmentFee()
{
  return fee;
}
```

Advanced Inheritance Concepts

7 Enter the following setEntertainerName() method, which is similar to other data-entry methods you have coded in previous chapters. It prompts the user for the name of an entertainment act and assigns the characters to the entertainer field.

```
public void setEntertainerName() throws Exception
{
  String inputString = new String();
  char newChar;
  System.out.print("Enter name of entertainer ");
  newChar = (char)System.in.read();
  while(newChar >= 'A' && newChar <= 'z'|| newChar == ' ')
  {
    inputString = inputString + newChar;
    newChar = (char)System.in.read();
  }
  System.in.read();
  entertainer = inputString;
}
```

8 The setEntertainmentFee() method is an abstract method. Each subclass that you eventually create that represents different entertainment types will have a different fee schedule. Type the abstract method definition: **public abstract void setEntertainmentFee();**

You just created an abstract class, but you cannot instantiate any objects from this class. Rather, you must extend this class to be able to create any Entertainment-related objects. Next, you will create a MusicalEntertainment class that extends the Entertainment class. This new class will be concrete; that is, it will enable you to create actual MusicalEntertainment class objects.

To create the MusicalEntertainment class:

1 Add a new class file to the project named **MusicalEntertainment.java**, and then add **extends Entertainment** to the right of the class header.

2 Add the definition of a music type field that is specific to musical entertainment by typing **private String typeOfMusic;** between the class's curly brackets.

3 The MusicalEntertainment constructor must call its parent's constructor. Additionally, it must use the following method that sets the music type in which the entertainer specializes:

```
   public MusicalEntertainment() throws Exception
   {
      super();
      setTypeOfMusic();
   }
```

4 Enter the following setTypeOfMusic() method, which asks for user input:

```
public void setTypeOfMusic() throws Exception
{
   String inputString = new String();
   char newChar;
   System.out.print("What type of music do they play? ");
   newChar = (char)System.in.read();
   while(newChar >= 'A' && newChar <= 'z'|| newChar == ' ')
   {
      inputString = inputString + newChar;
      newChar = (char)System.in.read();
   }
   System.in.read();
   typeOfMusic = inputString;
}
```

5 Event Handlers Incorporated charges a flat rate of $600 per event for musical entertainment. Add the following setEntertainmentFee() method to your program:

```
public void setEntertainmentFee()
{
   fee = 600;
}
```

6 Add the following toString() method that you can use when you want to convert the details of a MusicalEntertainment object into a String so you can easily and efficiently display the contents of the object:

```
public String toString()
{
   return(entertainer + ", featuring " + typeOfMusic +
      " music. Fee is $" + fee + " per event");
}
```

tip

In Chapter 6, you first used the automatically included toString() method that converts objects to Strings. Now, you are overriding that method for this class by writing your own version. You will learn more about the toString() method later in this chapter.

Event Handlers Incorporated classifies all nonmusical entertainment acts—such as clowns, jugglers, and stand-up comics—as OtherEntertainment. The OtherEntertainment class inherits from Entertainment, just as the MusicalEntertainment class does. Whereas the MusicalEntertainment class requires a data field to hold the type of music played by the act, the OtherEntertainment class requires a field for the type of the act. Other differences lie in the content of the prompt within the setTypeOfAct() method and in the handling of fees. Event Handlers Incorporated charges $50 per hour for nonmusical acts, so both the setEntertainmentFee() and toString() methods differ from those in the MusicalEntertainment class.

To create the OtherEntertainment class file:

1 Add a new class file to the project named **OtherEntertainment.java**, and then add **extends Entertainment** to the right of the class header.

2 Type the following String variable between the class's curly brackets to hold the type of the entertainment act (such as comedian): **private String typeOfAct;**.

3 Enter the following code so the OtherEntertainment class constructor calls the parent constructor, then calls its own method to set the act type:

```
public OtherEntertainment() throws Exception
{
  super();
  setTypeOfAct();
}
```

4 Enter the following setTypeOfAct() method:

```
public void setTypeOfAct() throws Exception
{
  String inputString = new String();
  char newChar;
  System.out.print("What type of act is this? ");
  newChar = (char)System.in.read();
  while(newChar >= 'A' && newChar <= 'z' || newChar == ' ')
  {
    inputString = inputString + newChar;
    newChar = (char)System.in.read();
  }
  System.in.read();
  typeOfAct = inputString;
}
```

section A

5 The fee for "other" acts is $50 per hour, so add the following setEntertainmentFee() method:

```
public void setEntertainmentFee()
{
  fee = 50;
}
```

6 Enter the following toString() method:

```
public String toString()
{
  return(entertainer + ", a " + typeOfAct +
    ". Fee is $" +  fee + " per hour");
}
```

Finally, you can create a program that instantiates concrete objects that belong to each of the two child classes.

To create a program that demonstrates using the MusicalEntertainment and OtherEntertainment classes:

1 Add a new main class file to the project by selecting **Add Class** from the **Project** menu. The Add Item dialog box appears. In the Add Item dialog box, select **ClassMain** from the **Class** folder, then change the suggested filename to **DemoEntertainment.java** and click the **Open** button. The new main class opens in the Text Editor window.

> **help**
> Be sure to select ClassMain, not Class, from the Add Item dialog box; otherwise, the main() method will not be created.

2 Add `throws Exception` to the right of the main() method.

3 Between the main() method's curly brackets, enter the following statement that prompts the user to enter a musical act description. Then instantiate a MusicalEntertainment object.

```
System.out.println("Create a musical act description:");
MusicalEntertainment anAct = new MusicalEntertainment();
```

4 Enter the following similar statements for a non-musical act:

```
System.out.println
  ("\nCreate a non-musical act description:");
OtherEntertainment anotherAct = new OtherEntertainment();
```

5 Enter the following lines to display the contents of the two objects:

```
System.out.println("\nDescription of entertainment acts:");
System.out.println(anAct.toString());
System.out.println(anotherAct.toString());
```

6 Build the project and execute the program as a console application by typing **jview DemoEntertainment** at the command line. When the program prompts you to do so, enter the name of a musical act, a type of music, the name of a non-musical act, and the type of act. Figure 10-6 shows a sample program run.

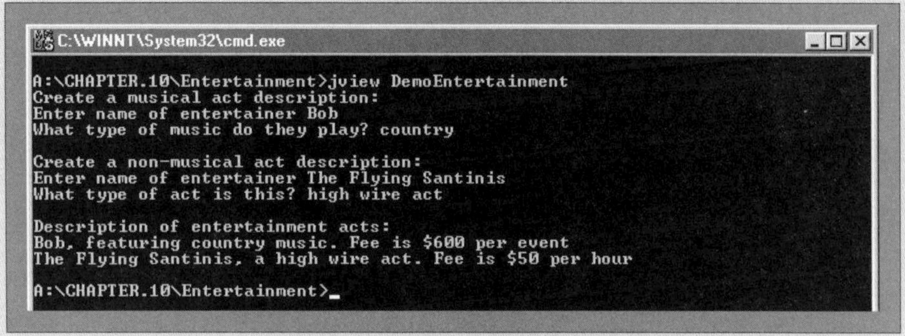

Figure 10-6: Output of the DemoEntertainment program

Using Dynamic Method Binding

When you create a superclass and one or more subclasses, each object of the subclass "is a" superclass object. Every SalariedEmployee "is an" Employee; every Dog "is an" Animal. (The opposite is not true; superclass objects are not members of any of their subclasses. An Employee is *not* a SalariedEmployee; an Animal is *not* a Dog.) Because every subclass object "is a" superclass member, you can convert subclass objects to superclass objects.

When a superclass is abstract, you cannot instantiate objects of the superclass, but whether or not a superclass is abstract, you *can* create a reference to a superclass. A **reference** holds the memory address of a subclass concrete object that "is a" superclass member. When you create a reference, you do not use the keyword new to create a concrete object; you create a variable name to hold the subclass concrete object's memory address.

You have known how to create a reference since Chapter 3. When you code `someClass someObject;`, you are creating a reference. If you later code `someObject = new someClass();`, then you actually set aside memory for someObject.

For example, if you create an Animal class, as in Figure 10-2, and various subclasses, as in Figures 10-3 through 10-5, then you can create a generic Animal reference variable into which you can assign any of the concrete Animal child objects. Figure 10-7 shows an AnimalReference program, and Figure 10-8 shows its output. The variable ref is type Animal. No Animal object is created, but the Dog, Cow, and Snake objects are created. When the Cow object is assigned to the Animal reference, the ref.speak() method call results in "Moo"; when the Dog object is assigned to the Animal reference, the method call results in "Woof".

```java
public class AnimalReference
{
   public static void main(String[] args)
   {
      Animal ref;
      Cow aCow = new Cow("Mabel");
      Dog aDog = new Dog("Rover");
      Snake aSnake = new Snake("Siskal");
      ref = aCow;
      ref.speak();
      ref = aDog;
      ref.speak();
      ref = aSnake;
      ref.speak();
   }
}
```

Figure 10-7: AnimalReference class

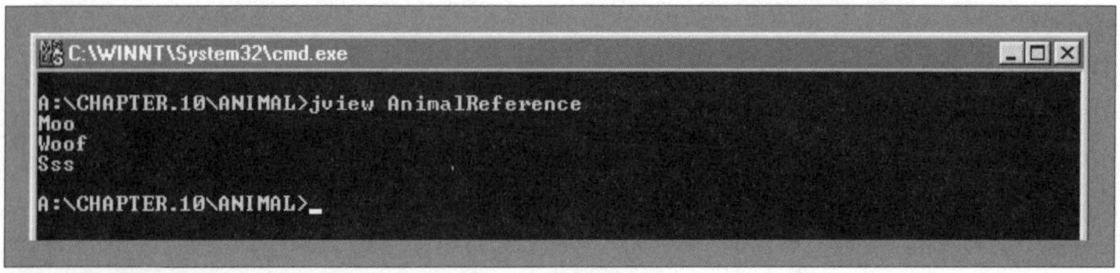

```
C:\WINNT\System32\cmd.exe

A:\CHAPTER.10\ANIMAL>jview AnimalReference
Moo
Woof
Sss

A:\CHAPTER.10\ANIMAL>
```

Figure 10-8: Output of the AnimalReference program

Advanced Inheritance Concepts

> **tip**
> You learned in Chapter 2 that when you assign a variable or constant of one type to a variable of another type, as in `doubleVar = intVar;`, the behavior is called *casting*.

The program in Figure 10-7 demonstrates polymorphic behavior. The same statement `ref.speak();` repeats three times and results in three different outputs. Each reference "knows" the correct way to speak(). This ability of the program to select the correct subclass method is known as **dynamic method binding**. When the program executes, the correct method is attached (or bound) to the program dynamically based on the current, changing context.

> **tip**
> Dynamic method binding is also called *late binding*.

Creating Arrays of Subclass Objects

One reason you might want to create a superclass reference and treat subclass objects as superclass objects is so that you can create an array of different objects that share the same ancestry. For example, even though every Employee object is a SalariedEmployee or an HourlyEmployee subclass object, it can be convenient to create an array of generic Employee objects. As long as every Employee subclass has access to a calculatePay() method, you can manipulate an array of superclass objects invoking the appropriate method for each subclass member. Likewise, an Animal array might contain individual elements that are Dog, Cow, or Snake objects. Again, as long as every Animal subclass has access to a speak() method, you can manipulate an array of superclass objects invoking the appropriate method for each subclass member.

> **tip**
> In Chapter 6, you learned that all elements in a single array must be of the same type.

The statement `Animal[] ref = new Animal[3];` creates an array of three Animal references. The statement reserves enough computer memory for three Animal objects named Animal[0], Animal[1], and Animal[2]. The statement does not actually instantiate Animals; Animals are abstract and cannot be instantiated. The statement simply reserves memory for three Animal object references. If you instantiate three Animal subclass objects, you can place references to those objects in the Animal array, as Figure 10-9 illustrates.

> Recall from Chapter 6 that when you create an array of any type of objects, concrete or abstract, you are not actually constructing those objects. Instead you are creating references to potential objects.

```
public class AnimalArray
{
  public static void main(String[] args)
  {
    Animal[] ref = new Animal[3];
    Cow aCow = new Cow("Mabel");
    Dog aDog = new Dog("Rover");
    Snake aSnake = new Snake("Siskal");
    ref[0] = aCow;
    ref[1] = aDog;
    ref[2] = aSnake;
    for(int x = 0; x < 3; ++x)
      ref[x].speak();
  }
}
```

Figure 10-9: AnimalArray class

Once the objects are in the array, you can manipulate them like any other array objects; for example, you can use a loop and a subscript to get each individual reference to speak(). Figure 10-10 shows the output of the AnimalArray program.

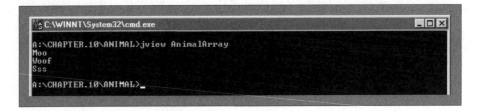

Figure 10-10: Output of the AnimalArray program

Next, you will write a program for Event Handlers Incorporated in which you create an array of Entertainment references. Within the program, you will assign both MusicalEntertainment objects and OtherEntertainment objects to the same array. Then, you can manipulate the different objects by using a `for` loop.

To write a program that uses an Entertainment array:

1. Add to the Entertainment project a new main class file named **EntertainmentDataBase.java**, and then add **throws Exception** to the right of the main() method header.

2. Add the definition of a music type field that is specific to musical entertainment by typing **private String typeOfMusic;** between the class's curly brackets.

3. Create the following array of six Entertainment references and an integer subscript to use with the array between the main() method's curly brackets:

   ```
   Entertainment[] actArray = new Entertainment[6];
   int x;
   ```

4. Enter the following for loop that prompts you to select whether you are going to enter a musical or non-musical entertainment act. Based on user input, instantiate either a MusicalEntertainment or an OtherEntertainment object.

   ```
   for(x = 0; x < actArray.length; ++x)
   {
     char selection;
     System.out.print("Please select the type of ");
     System.out.println("act you want to enter:");
     System.out.println("   1 - Musical act");
     System.out.println("   2 - Any other type of act");
     selection = (char)System.in.read();
     System.in.read(); System.in.read();
     if(selection == '1')
        actArray[x] = new MusicalEntertainment();
     else
        actArray[x] = new OtherEntertainment();
   }
   ```

5. After entering the information for all the acts, display the array contents by typing the following code:

   ```
   System.out.print("\n\nOur available entertainment ");
   System.out.println("selections include:\n");
   for(x = 0; x < actArray.length; ++x)
     System.out.println(actArray[x].toString());
   ```

6. Rebuild and save the project, then execute the program as a console application by typing **jview EntertainmentDataBase** at the command line. Enter some appropriate data, and then compare your results to the output shown in Figure 10-11.

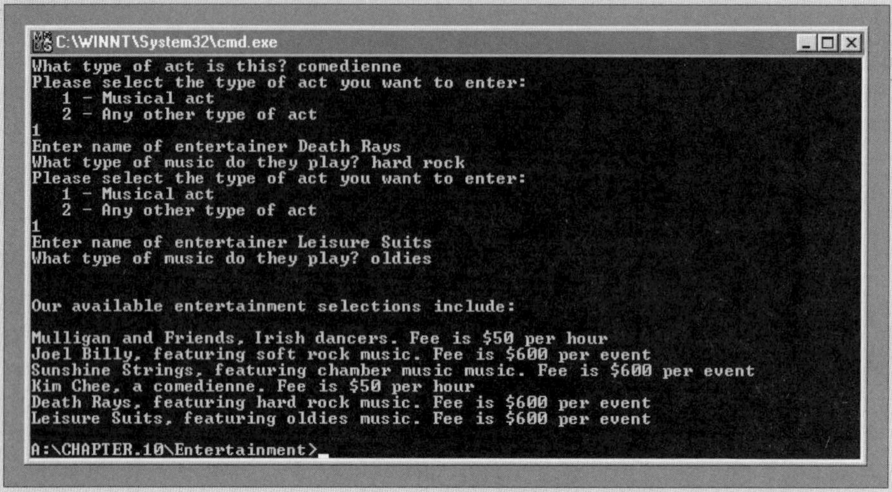

Figure 10-11: Final lines of output of the EntertainmentDataBase program

SUMMARY

- An abstract class is one from which concrete objects cannot be created, but from which classes can be inherited.

- You use the keyword `abstract` when you declare an abstract class.

- You cannot create instances of abstract classes by using the `new` operator. Usually, abstract classes contain abstract methods. An abstract method is a method with no method statements. When you create an abstract method, you provide the keyword `abstract` and the intended method type, name, and arguments, but you do not provide any statements within the method.

- You must code a subclass method to override any abstract superclass method that is inherited.

- When you create a superclass and one or more subclasses, each object of the subclass "is a" superclass object. Because every subclass object "is a" superclass member, you can convert subclass objects to superclass objects.

- You can create a reference to a superclass. When you create a reference, you do not use the keyword `new` to create a concrete object. Instead you create a variable name that holds the memory address of a subclass concrete object that "is a" superclass member.

- The ability of a program to select the correct subclass method is known as dynamic method binding.

- You might want to create a superclass reference and treat subclass objects as superclass objects so you can create an array of different objects that share the same ancestry. You can manipulate an array of superclass objects by invoking the appropriate method for each subclass member.

QUESTIONS

1. Child classes are _____ than their parents.
   a. smaller
   b. more specific
   c. easier to understand
   d. more cryptic

2. If a parent class is so general that you never intend to create any specific instances of it, the class is known in the Java programming language as _____.
   a. theoretical
   b. impractical
   c. virtual
   d. abstract

3. Abstract classes differ from regular classes in that you _____.
   a. must not code any methods within them
   b. must instantiate objects from them
   c. cannot instantiate objects from them
   d. cannot have data fields within them

4. You create instances of abstract classes _____.
   a. automatically when abstract classes are imported into your programs
   b. with the new operator
   c. only when you need them
   d. never

5. Abstract classes can contain _____.
   a. abstract methods
   b. nonabstract methods
   c. both of these
   d. none of these

6. An abstract method is a method with no _____.
   a. method statements
   b. return type
   c. argument list
   d. all of these

7. You write code for an abstract method's implementation _____.
   a. within the subclass
   b. within the superclass
   c. within either class, where it is most convenient
   d. never

8. An abstract class Tree has two subclasses, Evergreen and Deciduous. None of the constructors for these classes requires any arguments. Which of the following statements is legal?
   a. `Tree myTree = new Tree();`
   b. `Evergreen myTree = new Tree();`
   c. `Deciduous myTree = new Deciduous();`
   d. none of these

9. An abstract class Tree has two subclasses, Evergreen and Deciduous. The Tree class contains an abstract method named prune(). Before you can instantiate Evergreen or Deciduous objects, which of the following statements is true?
   a. You must code statements for the prune() method within the Tree class.
   b. You must code statements for the prune() method within both the Evergreen and Deciduous classes.
   c. You must not code statements for the prune() method within either the Evergreen or Deciduous classes.
   d. You may code statements for the prune() method within the Evergreen class or the Deciduous class, but not both.

10. Using the same method name to indicate different implementations is called _____.
    a. overriding
    b. polymorphism
    c. abstraction
    d. inheritance

11. Nonabstract classes are _____.
    a. illegal
    b. concrete
    c. polymorphic
    d. final

12. Which of the following statements is true?
    a. Subclass objects are members of their superclass.
    b. Superclass objects are members of their subclass.
    c. You can convert subclass objects to superclass objects.
    d. Two of these statements are true.

13. When you create a _____, you create a variable name in which you can hold the memory address of an object.
    a. class
    b. superclass
    c. subclass
    d. reference

14. The ability of the program to select the correct subclass method to execute is known as _____ method binding.
    a. polymorphic
    b. dynamic
    c. early
    d. intelligent

15. An abstract class named Game has two subclasses, IndoorGame and OutdoorGame. The Game constructor requires a String argument representing the name of the game. If you declare an array with the statement `Game[] game = new Game[10];`, then which of the following assignments is valid?
    a. `Game[0] = new Game("Chess");`
    b. `Game[1] = new OutdoorGame("Croquet");`
    c. `IndoorGame[2] = new Game("Twister");`
    d. `OutdoorGame[3] = new IndoorGame("Volleyball");`

EXERCISES

As you create projects for each of the following exercises, save them in the Chapter.10 folder on your Student Disk.

1. a. Create an empty project named Bookstore, then create an abstract class named Book that includes a String field for the book's title and a double field for the book's price. Within the Book class, include a constructor that requires the book title and two get methods: one that returns the title and one that returns the price. Also include an abstract method named setPrice(). Create two child classes of Book: Fiction and NonFiction. Within the constructors for the Fiction and NonFiction classes, call setPrice so all Fiction Books cost $24.99 and all NonFiction Books cost $37.99. Finally, write a program that demonstrates that you can create both a Fiction and NonFiction Book and display their fields.

   b. Create a class named BookArray in which you create an array that holds 10 Books, some of which are Fiction and NonFiction. Using a `for` loop, display details about all 10 Books.

2. a. Create an empty project named BankAccounts, then create an abstract class named Account that includes an integer field for the account number and a double field for the account balance. Also include a constructor that requires an account number and sets the balance to 0.0. Include a set method for the balance. Also include two abstract get methods—one for each field. Create two child classes of Account: Checking and Savings. Within the Checking class, the get method displays the String "Checking Account Information", the account number, and the balance. Within the Savings class, add the interest rate, and require the Savings constructor to accept an argument for the value of the interest rate. The Savings get method displays the String "Savings Account Information", the account number, the balance, and the interest rate.

   b. Create a class named AccountArray in which you enter data for a mix of 10 Checking and Savings accounts. Use a `for` loop to display the data.

3. Create an empty project named Automobile, then create an abstract Auto class with fields for the car: make and price. Include get and set methods for these fields; the setPrice() method is abstract. Create two subclasses for individual automobile makers (for example, Ford or Chevy) and include appropriate setPrice() methods in each subclass. Finally, write a program that uses the Auto class and subclasses to display information about different cars.

4. Create a project named Company that includes an abstract class named Division with fields for a company's division name and account number and corresponding get and set methods. Use an abstract constructor in the superclass. Create at least two subclasses for divisions such as Accounting or Human Resources. Write a program that uses the classes and displays information about them.

5. Create a project named UseChildren that uses an abstract Child class and Male and Female subclasses to display the name, gender, and age of two or more children. Use constructors in each of the classes with appropriate arguments. Include get and set methods, at least one of which is abstract.

SECTION B
objectives

In this section you will learn how to:
- Use the Object class and its methods
- Use inheritance to achieve good software design
- Create and use interfaces

Software Design and Interfaces

The Object Class and Its Methods

Every class in Java actually is a subclass, except one: the Object class. When you define a class, if you do not explicitly extend another class, then your class is an extension of the Object class. The Object class includes methods that you can use or override, as you see fit.

> The Object class is defined in the java.lang package, which is imported automatically every time you write a program.

The toString() Method

You already have overridden the Object class toString() method in the steps you used to create the MusicalEntertainment and OtherEntertainment classes. If you do not create a toString() method for a class, then you can use the superclass version of the toString() method. For example, review the Dog class shown in Figure 10-3. Notice that it does not contain a toString() method and that it extends the Animal class. Examine the Animal class shown in Figure 10-2. Notice that it does not define a toString() method either. Yet, when you write the program, shown in Figure 10-12, that prints a Dog object, the program compiles correctly, converts the Dog object to a String, and produces the output shown in Figure 10-13. The output is not very useful, however. It consists of the class name of which the object is an instance, the at sign (@), and a hexadecimal (base 16) number that represents the object. The number, which is expressed as a series of digits and letters, represents a computer memory address that can change every time you run the program, and basically is of no use to you. Usually, it is better to write your own toString() method that displays some or all of the data field values instead of using the automatic toString() method with your classes.

> A good toString() method can be very useful in debugging a program. If you do not understand why a class is behaving as it is, you can print the toString() value and examine its contents.

```
public class DogString
{
   public static void main(String[] args)
   {
      Dog myDog = new Dog("Murphy");
      System.out.println(myDog);
   }
}
```

Figure 10-12: DogString program

```
C:\WINNT\System32\cmd.exe
A:\CHAPTER.10\ANIMAL>jview DogString
Dog@8
A:\CHAPTER.10\ANIMAL>_
```

Figure 10-13: Output of the DogString program

The equals() Method

The Object class also contains an equals() method that takes a single argument, which must be the same type as the type of the invoking method, as in the following example:

`someObject.equals(someOtherObjectOfTheSameType)`

You first used the equals() method to compare String objects in Chapter 6.

The equals() method returns a boolean value indicating whether the objects are equal. The equals() method considers two objects of the same class to be equal only if they have the same memory address; in other words, they are equal only if one is a reference to the other. If you want to consider two objects to be equal only when one is a reference to the other, you can use the Object class equals() method. However, if you want to consider objects to be equal based on their contents, then you must write your own equals() method for your classes.

The program shown in Figure 10-14 instantiates three Dog objects: aBlackLab named Murphy, aCollie named Colleen, and aSchnauzer named Murphy. The Dog class does not override the Object equals() method, so the program in Figure 10-14 produces the output in Figure 10-15. Even though two of the Dog objects have the same name, none of the Dogs are equal because they do not have the same memory address.

```
public class DogCompare
{
  public static void main(String[] args)
  {
    Dog aBlackLab = new Dog("Murphy");
    Dog aCollie = new Dog("Colleen");
    Dog aSchnauzer = new Dog("Murphy");
    System.out.print("The black lab and collie are ");
    if(aBlackLab.equals(aCollie))
      System.out.println("equal");
    else
      System.out.println("not equal");
    System.out.print("The black lab and schnauzer are ");
    if(aBlackLab.equals(aSchnauzer))
      System.out.println("equal");
    else
      System.out.println("not equal");
  }
}
```

Figure 10-14: DogCompare program

Figure 10-15: Output of the DogCompare program when Dog does not override equals()

If your intention is to consider two Dog objects to be equal if the Dogs have the same name, then you can add the equals() method shown in Figure 10-16 to the Dog class.

section B

> You can add the equals() method to the Dog class file anywhere within the file as long as it is not within any other method. The best location is after the closing curly bracket for the Dog class constructor and before the method header for speak(). That way, the equals() method appears in alphabetical order among the methods.

```
boolean equals(Dog anotherDog)
{
  boolean result;
  if(getName().equals(anotherDog.getName()))
    result = true;
  else
    result = false;
  return result;
}
```

Figure 10-16: Dog equals() method

The equals() method in Figure 10-16 returns a boolean value. When you call the method, you use the name of one Dog object, a dot, and the name of another Dog object as an argument within parentheses, as in aBlackLab.equals(aCollie). Therefore, the equals() method header shows that it receives a Dog object, which has the local name anotherDog. When you compare the name of the calling Dog with the argument anotherDog by using the String equals() method, you determine whether the two Dogs are to be considered equal. If you add this equals() method to the Dog class and recompile and run the DogCompare program shown in Figure 10-14, the output, as shown in Figure 10-17, now indicates that two Dog objects with the same name are equal.

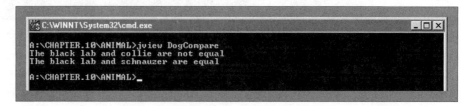

Figure 10-17: Output of the DogCompare program when Dog *does* override equals()

tip

Recall from Chapter 4 that when you use an instance method for a class object, the method receives a `this` reference to the calling object. Therefore, the call to the getName() method retrieves the name for `this` **Dog**. You could replace the expression `getName().equals(anotherDog.getName())` with `this.getName().equals(anotherDog.getName())`.

If there were more fields in the Dog class, you could base equality on a large number of comparisons. Rather than simply comparing names, within the equals() method of the Dog class you could substitute a more detailed comparison, such as the following:

```
if(getName().equals(anotherDog.getName()) &&
   getAge() == anotherDog.getAge() &&
   getGender() == anotherDog.getGender() &&
   getBreed().equals(anotherDog.getBreed())
     result = true;
else
     result = false;
```

This code considers two Dog objects equal only if they have the same name, age, gender, and breed.

Next, you will add an equals() method to Event Handlers Incorporated's Entertainment class. Then you will use the equals() method in the EntertainmentDataBase program to compare each new Entertainment act to every act already residing in the database. Your improved program will not allow two acts to have the same name.

To add an equals() method to the Entertainment class:

1 Open the **Entertainment** project, and then open the **Entertainment.java** file in the Text Editor window.

2 Position your cursor after the closing curly bracket of the Entertainment constructor, and press the **Enter** key to start a new line.

3 Type the equals() method as follows:

```
public boolean equals(Entertainment act)
{
   boolean result;
   if(entertainer.equals(act.entertainer))
      result = true;
   else
      result = false;
   return result;
}
```

section B

Next, you will modify the EntertainmentDataBase program so the user cannot enter Entertainment objects with the same entertainer names.

To modify the EntertainmentDataBase class:

1 Open the **EntertainmentDataBase.java** file in the Text Editor window. Immediately save the file as **EntertainmentNoDuplicates.java**.

> **help**
>
> Be sure you have saved the EntertainmentDataBase.java file before saving it as EntertainmentNoDuplicates.java.

2 Change the class name within the first line of the class file from EntertainmentDataBase to **EntertainmentNoDuplicates**.

3 Position the insertion point at the end of the line that reads actArray[x] = new OtherEntertainment();, and then press the **Enter** key to start a new line.

4 On the new line, add the following for loop that compares the most recently entered actArray element against all previously entered actArray elements. If the new element equals any of the previously entered Entertainment acts, then issue an error message and reduce the subscript by one. Reducing the subscript ensures that the next act you enter will overwrite the duplicate act.

```
for(int y = 0; y < x; ++y)
  if(actArray[x].equals(actArray[y]))
  {
    System.out.println
 ("Sorry, you entered a duplicate act");
    --x;
  }
```

5 Rebuild and save the project, then execute the program as a console application by typing **jview EntertainmentNoDuplicates** at the command line. When you see the prompts, enter any appropriate data. Make sure that you repeat an entertainer's name for several of the prompts. Each time you repeat a name, you will see an error message and you will get another opportunity to enter an act. The program will not end until you enter six acts with unique names.

Using Inheritance to Achieve Good Software Design

When an automobile company designs a new car model, the company does not build every component of the new car from scratch. The company might design a new feature completely from scratch; for example, at some point someone designed the first air bag. Many of a new car's features are simply modifications of existing features. The manufacturer might create a larger gas tank or more comfortable seats, but these new features still possess many of the properties of their predecessors in older models. Most features of new car models are not even modified; instead, existing components, such as air filters and windshield wipers, are included on the new model without any changes.

Similarly, you can create powerful computer programs more easily if many of their components are used either "as-is" or with slight modifications. Inheritance does not enable you to write any programs that you could not write without it; you *could* create every part of a program from scratch. Inheritance simply makes your job easier. Professional programmers constantly create new class libraries for use with Java programs. Having these classes available makes programming large systems more manageable.

You already have used many "as-is" classes, such as String and Applet. In these cases, your programs were easier to write than if you had to invent these classes yourself. Now that you have learned about inheritance, you have gained the ability to modify existing classes as well. When you create a useful, extendable superclass, you and other future programmers gain several advantages:

- Subclass creators save development time because much of the code that is needed for the class already has been written.
- Subclass creators save testing time because the superclass code already has been tested and probably used in a variety of situations. In other words, the superclass code is reliable.
- Programmers who create or use new subclasses already understand how the superclass works, so the time it takes to learn new class features is reduced.
- When you create a new subclass in Java, neither the superclass source code nor the superclass bytecode is changed. The superclass maintains its integrity.

When you think about classes, you need to think about the commonalities among them, and then you can create superclasses from which to inherit. You might be rewarded professionally when you see your own superclasses extended by others in the future.

Creating and Using Interfaces

Many object-oriented programming languages, such as C++, allow a subclass to inherit from more than one parent class. For example, you might create an Employee class that contains data fields pertaining to each employee in your organization. You also might create a Product class that holds information about each product your organization produces. When you create a Patent class for each product for which you hold a patent, you might want to include product information, as well as information about the employee in your company who was responsible for the invention. It would be convenient to inherit fields and methods from both the Product and Employee classes. The capability to inherit from more than one class is called **multiple inheritance**.

Multiple inheritance is a difficult concept, and when programmers use it, they encounter many problems. Programmers have to deal with the fact that variables and methods in the parent classes may have identical names, which creates conflict when the child class uses one of the names. Additionally, you already have learned that a child class constructor must call its parent class constructor. When there are two or more parents, this task becomes more complicated. To which class should super() refer when a child class has multiple parents?

For all of these reasons, multiple inheritance is prohibited in the Java programming language. Java, however, provides an alternative to multiple inheritance, known as an interface. An **interface** looks very much like a class, except all of its methods must be abstract and all of its data (if any) must be static and final. When you create a class that uses an interface, you include the keyword `implements` and the interface name in the class header. This notation requires class objects to include code for all the methods in the interface.

For example, you can create a Working interface to use with the Animal subclasses. For simplicity, give the Working interface a single method named work(). Figure 10-18 shows the Working program.

```
public interface Working
{
   public void work();
}
```

Figure 10-18: Working interface

When any class implements Working, it must also include a work() method. The WorkingDog class in Figure 10-19 extends Dog and implements Working; the class's work() method calls the Dog speak() method, and then produces a line of output.

Advanced Inheritance Concepts

```
public class WorkingDog extends Dog implements Working
{
  public WorkingDog(String nm)
  {
    super(nm);
  }
  public void work()
  {
    speak();
    System.out.println("I can herd cows");
  }
}
```

Figure 10-19: WorkingDog class

When you create a program that instantiates a WorkingDog object, as in Figure 10-20, you can use the work() method. The program output appears in Figure 10-21. You also can create WorkingCow and WorkingHorse classes that implement Working. In addition, if you decide to create a Playing interface, any class that implements Working can implement Playing as well.

```
public class DemoWorkingDog
{
  public static void main(String[] args)
  {
    WorkingDog mySheltie = new WorkingDog("Simon");
    mySheltie.work();
  }
}
```

Figure 10-20: DemoWorkingDog program

Figure 10-21: Output of the DemoWorkingDog program

Abstract classes and interfaces are similar in that you cannot instantiate concrete objects from either one. Abstract classes differ from interfaces in that abstract classes can contain nonabstract methods, but all methods within an interface must be abstract. A class can inherit from only one abstract superclass, but it can implement any number of interfaces.

Beginning programmers sometimes find it difficult to decide when to create an abstract superclass and when to create an interface. You create an abstract class when you want to provide some data or methods that subclasses can inherit, but you want the subclasses to override some specific methods.

For example, suppose you create a CardGame class to use as a base class for different card games. It contains four methods named shuffle(), deal(), listRules(), and keepScore(). The shuffle() method works the same way for every CardGame, so you write the statements for shuffle() within the superclass, and any CardGame objects you create later inherit it. The methods deal(), displayRules(), and keepScore() operate differently for every subclass, so you force CardGame children to contain instructions for those methods by leaving them empty in the superclass. When you write classes named Hearts, Solitaire, and Poker, you extend the CardGame parent class, inherit the shuffle() method, and implement deal(), displayRules(), and keepScore() methods for each specific child.

You create an interface when you know what actions you want to include, but you want every user to define separately the behavior that must occur when the method executes. For example, suppose you create a MusicalInstrument class to use as a base for different musical instrument object classes such as Piano, Violin, and Drum. The parent MusicalInstrument class contains methods like playNote() and outputSound() that apply to every instrument, but you want to implement such methods differently for each type of instrument. By making MusicalInstrument an interface, you require every subclass to code all the methods.

An interface specifies only the messages to which an object can respond; an abstract class can include methods that contain the actual behavior that the object performs when those messages are received.

Additionally, you create an interface when you want a class to implement behavior from more than one parent. A NameThatInstrument card game that requires players to identify instrument sounds they hear by clicking cards, for example, could not inherit from two classes, but it could inherit from CardGame and implement MusicalInstrument.

You used prewritten interfaces earlier in this book. For example, you implemented the ActionListener interface in applets you wrote in Chapters 7 and 8. By implementing ActionListener, you provided your applet the means to respond to ActionEvents. You will use more interfaces in future chapters.

SUMMARY

- A class that you create only to extend from, but not to instantiate from, is abstract.

- You can create powerful computer programs more easily if you use inheritance.

- When you create a useful, extendable superclass, you save development time because much of the code that is needed for the class already has been written. In addition, you save testing time, and because the superclass code is reliable, you reduce the time it takes to learn the new class features. You also maintain superclass integrity.

- The capability to inherit from more than one class is called multiple inheritance. Multiple inheritance is a difficult concept, and it is prohibited in the Java programming language.

- An interface is similar to a class, but all of its methods must be abstract, and all of its data (if any) must be static and final.

- When you create a class that uses an interface, you include the keyword `implements` and the interface name in the class header. This notation requires class objects to include code for all the methods in the interface.

- Abstract classes and interfaces are similar in that you cannot instantiate concrete objects from either.

- Abstract classes differ from interfaces in that abstract classes can contain nonabstract methods, but all methods within an interface must be abstract.

- A class can inherit from only one abstract superclass, but it can implement any number of interfaces.

- You create an abstract class when you want to provide some data or methods that subclasses can inherit, but you want the subclasses to override some specific methods. You also create an abstract class when you want a class to implement behavior from more than one parent.

- You create an interface when you know what actions you want to include, but you want every user to define separately the behavior that must occur when the method executes.

section B

QUESTIONS

1. With the exception of the Object class, every class in Java actually is a(n) _____.
   a. interface
   b. subclass
   c. superclass
   d. abstract class

2. When you define a class, if you do not explicitly extend another class, then your class is an extension of the class named _____.
   a. Master
   b. Super
   c. Object
   d. Class

3. You _____ override the toString() method in any class you create.
   a. cannot
   b. can
   c. must
   d. must implement StringListener to

4. The Object class equals() method takes _____.
   a. no arguments
   b. one argument
   c. two arguments
   d. as many arguments as you need

5. The following statement appears in a Java program:
   if(thing.equals(anotherThing)) x = 1;. You know that _____.
   a. thing is an object of the Object class
   b. anotherThing is the same type as thing
   c. Both of these are correct.
   d. None of these are correct.

6. The equals() method returns a(n) _____ value.
   a. boolean
   b. integer
   c. character
   d. Object class

7. The Object class equals() method considers two objects of the same class to be equal if they have the same _____.
   a. value in all data fields
   b. value in any data field
   c. data type
   d. memory address

8. The value of inheritance is that it makes programming _____.
   a. possible
   b. easier
   c. more worthwhile
   d. original

9. Subclass creators save time because _____.
   a. much of the code that is needed for a class already has been written
   b. subclass code does not need to be tested
   c. subclass statements generally are simpler than superclass statements
   d. they don't waste time calling superclass methods

10. The ability to inherit from more than one parent class is called _____.
    a. abstraction
    b. polymorphism
    c. multiple inheritance
    d. interface implementation

11. Inheritance from more than one parent is prohibited in _____.
    a. Java
    b. C++
    c. Visual Basic
    d. all object-oriented programming languages

12. Within an interface, all _____.
    a. variables must be public
    b. variables must be private
    c. methods must be void
    d. methods must be abstract

13. When you create a class that uses an interface, you include the keyword _____ and the interface's name in the class header.
    a. `interface`
    b. `implements`
    c. `extends`
    d. `listener`

14. You can instantiate concrete objects from an _____.
    a. abstract class
    b. interface
    c. Either a or b.
    d. Neither a nor b.

15. All methods within an _____ must be abstract.
    a. abstract class
    b. interface
    c. Both a and b.
    d. Neither a nor b.

16. In Java, a class can _____.
    a. inherit from only one abstract superclass
    b. implement only one interface
    c. Both a and b.
    d. Neither a nor b.

17. If you know what actions you want to include, but you want every user to define separately the behavior that must occur when the method executes, you should write a(n) _____.

    a. abstract class
    b. interface
    c. final superclass
    d. concrete object

EXERCISES

As you create projects for each of the following exercises, save them in the Chapter.10 folder of your Student Disk.

1. Create a console application project named NewsPaperSubscriber. In the NewsPaperSubscriber class, add fields for a subscriber's street address and the subscription rate. Include get and set methods for the subscriber's street address, and get and set methods for the subscription rate. The set method for the rate is abstract. Include an equals() method that indicates that two Subscribers are equal if they have the same street address. Create child classes named SevenDaySubscriber, WeekdaySubscriber, and WeekendSubscriber. Each child class constructor sets the rate as follows: SevenDaySubscribers pay $4.50 per week, WeekdaySubscribers pay $3.50 per week, and WeekendSubscribers pay $2.00 per week. Each child class should include a toString() method that returns the street address, rate, and service type. Write a program named Subscribers that prompts the user for the subscriber's street address and requested service and creates the appropriate object based on the service type. Do not allow the user to enter more than one subscription type for any given street address.

2. a. Create an interface named Turning, with a single method named turn(). Create a class named Leaf that implements turn() to print "Changing colors". Create a class named Page that implements turn() to print "Going to the next page". Create a class named Pancake that implements turn() to print "Flipping". Write a program named Turners that creates one object of each of these class types and demonstrates the turn() method for each one.

   b. Think of two more objects that use turn(), create classes for them, and then add objects to the Turners program.

3. Create a console application project named Pharmacy that uses an abstract class named Drug and subclasses for two specific drugs to display a drug, its purpose, and the number of times per day it should be taken. Use constructors in each of the classes with appropriate arguments. Include get and set methods, at least one of which is abstract. Prompt the user for the drug to be displayed, and then create the appropriate object.

4. Create a console application project named UseInsurance that uses an abstract Insurance class and Health and Life subclasses to display different types of insurance policies and the cost per month. Use constructors in each of the classes with appropriate arguments. Include get and set methods, at least one of which is abstract. Prompt the user for the type to be displayed, and then create the appropriate object. Also create an interface for a print() method and use this interface with both subclasses.

5. Create a console application project named UseLoan that uses an abstract class named Loan and subclasses to display different types of loans and the cost per month (home, car, and so on). Use constructors in each of the classes with appropriate arguments. Include get and set methods, at least one of which is abstract. Prompt the user for the type to be displayed, and then create the appropriate object. Also create an interface with at least one method that you use with your subclasses.

6. Each of the following files in the Chapter.10 folder on your Student Disk has syntax and/or logical errors. Add the files to a new project called FixDebug. Save the FixDebug project in the Chapter.10 folder on your Student Disk. In each case, fix the problem and run each file as a console application using JVIEW.
   a. DebugTen1.java
   b. DebugTen2.java
   c. DebugTen3.java
   d. DebugTen4.java

CHAPTER 11
Understanding the Abstract Windows Toolkit (AWT)

case ▶ "Learning about inheritance has been interesting," you say to your mentor at Event Handlers Incorporated, Lynn Greenbrier, "and I certainly can see how using inheritance is going to make my programming life easier. But will understanding inheritance help me create fancier applets, such as ones with frames, user lists, and choice boxes?"

"You bet it will," Lynn replies. "One of the reasons I gave you such a thorough grounding in inheritance concepts is so that learning to use Windows-type components will be easier for you. All of the little gadgets such as the choice boxes that you want to put in your applets are relatives, and inheritance makes using all of them possible. More importantly, if you have some knowledge of how inheritance and components work in general, then you will be able to adapt your knowledge to other components."

"I don't have time to show you every component now," Lynn says. "Besides, there are new components that Java developers around the world are developing right this minute."

"In other words, I can use the knowledge you give me about components and I can extend that knowledge to future components. That's just like inheritance," you tell Lynn. "Please explain more."

Previewing the Party Planner Applet for Chapter 11

Event Handlers Incorporated is developing an applet that lets a user determine the price of an event based on several event choices. For some options, such as whether cocktails or dinner will be served, a user can select options in any combination (serve only cocktails, serve only dinner, serve both cocktails and dinner, or serve nothing). For other options, such as the dinner entrée or the entertainment selection, only one choice is allowed. You need a variety of "contraptions" to accommodate these different types of selections. The Chap11PartyPlanner class incorporates several such devices, which you can use now. You will create a similar applet in this chapter.

> **To use the Chap11PartyPlanner class:**
>
> **1** Go to the command prompt for the Chapter.11 folder on your Student Disk, type **jview /a Chap11PartyPlanner.htm** at the command prompt, and then press the **Enter** key. After a few moments, you will see the Party Planner applet shown in Figure 11-1.

Understanding the Abstract Windows Toolkit (AWT)

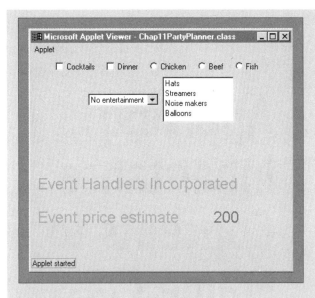

Figure 11-1: Chap11PartyPlanner applet

2. You can use the Party Planner to plan an imaginary event by choosing whether to serve cocktails or dinner (or both or neither). Use the applet and observe that the event's price changes as you make your selections. If you choose to serve dinner, you can select one of three main courses. You also can select from a list of entertainment choices and party favors. The event's price changes as you make each selection.

3. Close the AppletViewer window by clicking the **Close** button ⊠.

SECTION A
objectives

In this section you will learn how to:
- Use the Frame class
- Create a Frame that closes
- Use Adapters
- Use additional Frame class methods
- Use Container class methods

Applying Inheritance Concepts to the Frame Class

Using the Frame Class

Computer programs usually are more user-friendly (and more fun to use) when they contain graphical user interface (GUI) components such as buttons, check boxes, and menus. In Chapter 7, you learned how to add a few GUI components to an applet; in this chapter, you will learn how to add several more.

▶ tip
> You can add GUI components to either applets or applications.

You already know from Chapter 7 that you do not need to create GUI components from scratch; Java's creators packaged the GUI components in the Abstract Windows Toolkit, or AWT, so you can adapt them for your purposes. You insert the import statement `import java.awt;` at the beginning of your Java program files so you can take advantage of the GUI components and their methods, which are stored in the AWT package. Within the AWT package, components such as buttons, check boxes, and labels are defined in the **Component class**.

▶ tip
> Components are also called *widgets*, which stands for *windows gadgets*.

> Java programmers use two pronunciations of *AWT*. You can say the three initials separately (A-W-T), or you can pronounce it as "ought."

When you use components in a Java program, you usually place them in containers. A **container** is a type of component that holds other components so you can treat a group of several components as a single entity. Usually, a container takes the form of a window that you can drag, resize, minimize, maximize, restore, and close. Containers are defined in the **Container class**.

All Java classes are subclasses; they all descend from the Object class. The Component class is a child of the Object class, and the Container class is a child of the Component class. Therefore, every Container object "is a" Component, and every Component Object (including every Container) "is an" Object.

The Container class is also a parent class. Two of its children are the **Panel class** and the **Window class**. You already have used a child class of Panel—the **Applet class** descends from Panel; that is, every Applet "is a" Panel. Similarly, the **Frame class** and **Dialog class** are subclasses of the Window class. Figure 11-2 shows the relationship of Objects, Components, and Containers to some of their children.

> **tip** Recall that the Object class is defined in the java.lang package, which is imported automatically every time you write a Java program.

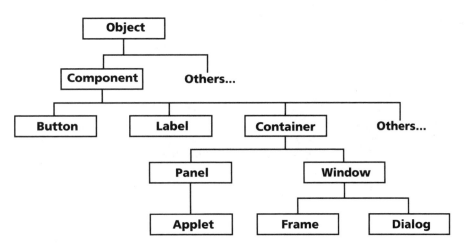

Figure 11-2: Relationships of Object, Component, and Container to some subclasses

The Component class contains many methods that you can use with any Component class descendant. For example, the **setSize() method** allows you to set the physical size of any component. This method requires two integer arguments: the width and height of the component, measured in pixels. The **setVisible() method** makes the component visible or invisible to the user; the method requires a boolean argument of `true` or `false`.

> **tip** You will learn about many more Component class methods later in this chapter.

The Component class is an abstract class. In Chapter 9, you learned that when you create an abstract class you cannot create any concrete instances; instead, you create subclasses from which you create concrete instances. All GUI components, such as the buttons, text fields, and other objects with which the user interacts, are actually subclasses or extensions of the Component class. Likewise, the Container class, which descends from the Component class, is itself an abstract class. Therefore there are no "plain" Containers; every concrete Container object is a member of a subclass of Container. The Window class, which inherits from Container, is not abstract; you can instantiate a Window object. However, Java programmers rarely use Window objects because the Window subclasses, Frame and Dialog, allow you to create more useful objects.

A Frame, then, "is a" Window (as well as a Container, a Component, and an Object). You usually create a Frame so that you can place other objects within it for display. The Frame class has two constructors. The first constructor accepts a String argument that is used as the title for the Frame and is displayed in the Frame's title bar. The second Frame class constructor does not take an argument; Frame objects constructed with the no-argument constructor are untitled. For example, the following two statements construct two Frames: one with the title "Hello", and another Frame with no title:

```
Frame firstFrame = new Frame("Hello");
Frame secondFrame = new Frame();
```

Next, you will create a Frame object that appears on the screen.

To create a Frame object:

1 If necessary, start Visual J++, then create a new console application project named **DemoFrame**. Save the **DemoFrame** project folder in the Chapter.11 folder on your Student Disk.

2 Rename the default Class1.java file as **DemoFrame.java**, then open the file in the Text Editor window.

3 Replace the Class1 class name in the `public class Class1` line with **DemoFrame**.

4 Replace the default comments before the class header with the following statement to import the java.awt classes: `import java.awt.*;`.

5 Replace the `// TODO: Add initialization code here` comment in the main() method with the following code to declare a Frame with a title, set the Frame's size, and make the Frame visible. If you neglect to set a Frame's size, you will see only the title bar of the Frame. If you neglect to make the Frame visible, you will not see anything at all.

```
Frame aFrame = new Frame("This is a frame");
aFrame.setSize(200,100);
aFrame.setVisible(true);
```

Understanding the Abstract Windows Toolkit (AWT)

6 Set the project properties to run the **DemoFrame** file as a console application, then build the project. If necessary, correct any syntax errors and rebuild. Execute the program as a console application by typing `jview DemoFrame` at the command line. The output looks like Figure 11-3.

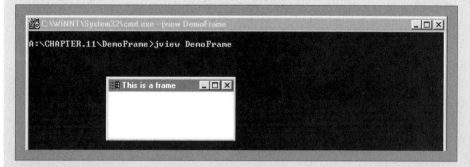

Figure 11-3: Output of the DemoFrame program

The Frame shown in Figure 11-3 resembles frames that you have seen when using different GUI programs. One reason you want to use similar Frame objects in your programs is that users are already familiar with the Frame environment. Users expect to see a title bar at the top of a Frame that contains information (such as "This is a Frame"). Users also expect to see Minimize, Maximize or Restore, and Close buttons in the Frame's upper-right corner. Users usually assume that they can change a Frame's size by dragging its border, or reposition the Frame on their screen by dragging the Frame's title bar to a new location.

To confirm that the Frame you created has Minimize, Maximize, Restore, and dragging capabilities:

1 Click the Frame's **Minimize** button. The Frame minimizes to an icon on the Windows taskbar.

2 Click the Frame's icon on the taskbar. The Frame returns to full size.

3 Click the Frame's **Maximize** button. The Frame fills the screen.

4 Click the Frame's **Restore** button to return the Frame to its original size.

5 Position your mouse pointer on the Frame's title bar, hold down the left mouse button, and then drag the Frame to a new position on your screen. Release the mouse button.

6 You might expect the Close button to function like it does in other programs. Click the **Close** button now. Nothing happens. Although the Frame object you created has many other standard Frame capabilities, it does not possess a method that specifies which action to take when you click it.

> **7** To exit the Frame program, click anywhere in the window that contains your command line, and then press **Ctrl+C** or **Ctrl+Break**. Control returns to the command line and the Frame closes.
>
>
>
> > In Chapter 5, you learned to press Ctrl+C or Ctrl+Break to stop a program that contains an infinite loop.

Creating a Frame That Closes

Your "This is a frame" Frame does not contain a method to specify the action or actions to take when the user clicks the Close button. Java's creators designed Frame objects in this way because closing actions are more varied than actions such as minimizing and restoring. All Frame objects should minimize in the same manner, but closing a Frame might require the program to close a data file, repaint another screen, disable some buttons, change the user's available options, or take some other action. Furthermore, you might write a program for which you do not want to enable the user to close a Frame.

In Chapter 7, you learned that within an event-driven program, a Component on which an event is generated is the *source* of the event, and that an object that is interested in an event is a *listener*. For example, when you want an applet object to be a listener for an action event, you must register the applet as a listener by adding the phrase `implements ActionListener` to your program. Similarly, a class that is a listener for Window events must implement the WindowListener interface. The **WindowListener interface class** provides the following seven Window methods. As with all interfaces, the methods contained in the WindowListener interface are abstract; that is, they all are empty and must be coded within any class that implements the interface.

- windowClosing()
- windowClosed()
- windowDeiconified()
- windowIconified()
- windowOpened()
- windowActivated()
- windowDeactivated()

Each of these seven methods is `public`, has a return type of `void`, and takes a WindowEvent object as an argument. You must include each of these methods in any class that implements WindowListener. However, you are not required to write statements for each of these methods. You must include all of the methods, but you write statements only for the ones you need.

tip

When you compile a class in which you implement WindowListener but fail to code all seven methods, the error message will indicate that your class "must be declared abstract." To satisfy the compiler, you can make your class abstract, and then create a child class that contains implementations of the missing methods. Alternatively, you can just supply your class with implementations of the missing methods.

One of the seven methods inherited through the WindowListener interface is the windowClosing() method. You can write its header as `public void windowClosing(WindowEvent e)`. This method returns nothing and receives a WindowEvent argument, in this case named e.

Within the windowClosing() method, you can code any actions you want to execute when the user closes the Frame. (Don't forget that a Frame "is a" Window.) You can code any Java statements you need within this method, including statements that print messages, draw Graphics objects, or perform mathematical calculations. However, when the user clicks the Close button, he or she usually expects either that the Frame will close or that the program will end.

You already know how to make a Frame appear by passing the setVisible() method a `true` argument. To close a Frame, you pass a `false` argument to setVisible(). If you name the WindowEvent object used within the windowClosing() method e, then you can make the Frame invisible with the statement `e.getWindow().setVisible(false);`.

Instead of just closing the Frame when the user clicks the Close button, you might want the program to end. In this case, the statement you need within the windowClosing() method is `System.exit(0);`. Like println(), the exit() method belongs to the System class. The exit() method's argument is sent to the operating system in which the program is running, and the program ends. By convention, you return a zero to the operating system when a program ends normally, and you return a one when a program ends due to an error. When a user clicks the Close button to end a program, the action constitutes a normal end to a program, so you should use zero as the argument in your exit() statement.

Next, you will create a Frame object that you can close using the Close button. You will need to write instructions for just one of WindowListener's seven methods, the windowClosing() method, but you will need to include empty methods for the other six.

To create a Frame that closes:

1 Create a new empty project named **DemoClosingFrame**. Save the **DemoClosingFrame** project folder in the Chapter.11 folder on your Student Disk.

2 Add a new class file to the project by selecting **Add Class** from the **Project** menu. The Add Item dialog box appears. In the Add Item dialog box, select **Class** from the **Class** folder, then change the suggested filename to **FrameYouCanClose.java** and click the **Open** button. The new class opens in the Text Editor window.

section A

3 Above the class header, type the following import statements that you will need for the program:

```
import java.awt.event.*;
import java.awt.*;
```

4 Add **extends Frame implements WindowListener** to the right of the class header.

5 The constructor for the FrameYouCanClose class can accept a String argument that you pass on to the Frame constructor (because Frame is the parent class of FrameYouCanClose). Additionally, a FrameYouCanClose must be prepared to receive messages. In the same way you add an addActionListener() statement to an applet that employs the mouse, you add an addWindowListener() statement to a Frame that employs the window Close button. To add an addWindowListener() statement, enter the following code between the class's curly brackets:

```
public FrameYouCanClose(String str)
{
  super(str);
  addWindowListener(this);
}
```

> The **this** reference in the statement addWindowListener(this) **refers to** "this" Frame object.

6 To make the program end, type the following windowClosing() method:

```
public void windowClosing(WindowEvent e)
{
  System.exit(0);
}
```

7 Add empty methods for the other six methods required by WindowListener as follows:

```
public void windowClosed(WindowEvent e) {}
public void windowDeiconified(WindowEvent e) {}
public void windowIconified(WindowEvent e) {}
public void windowOpened(WindowEvent e) {}
public void windowActivated(WindowEvent e) {}
public void windowDeactivated(WindowEvent e) {}
```

> You can place the curly brackets in each of the preceding methods on their own lines if you wish. Typing the curly brackets on the same line saves space, but it might be clearer to you to type each bracket on its own line, which accomplishes the same thing.

Next, you will write a main class that uses the FrameYouCanClose class.

To write a main class that uses the FrameYouCanClose class:

1 Add a new main class file to the project by selecting **Add Class** from the **Project** menu. The Add Item dialog box appears. In the Add Item dialog box, select **ClassMain** from the **Class** folder, then change the suggested filename to **DemoClosingFrame.java** and click the **Open** button. The new main class opens in the Text Editor window.

2 Add `import java.awt.*;` above the class header.

3 Between the main() method's curly brackets, instantiate a FrameYouCanClose named aFrame, set its size, and make it visible by entering the following code:

```
FrameYouCanClose aFrame =
  new FrameYouCanClose("This is a frame that closes");
aFrame.setSize(400,100);
aFrame.setVisible(true);
```

4 Build the project and execute the program as a console application by typing **jview DemoClosingFrame** at the command line. Confirm that you still can drag, minimize, restore, and maximize the FrameYouCanClose window, and that you can now click the Close button to close it.

Using an Adapter

The FrameYouCanClose class requires you to write seven methods that the class inherits when you implement WindowListener. Even though you are interested in writing code for only one of the seven methods, you must provide empty methods for the other six because the rules of inheritance force you to code every abstract method that is inherited from classes you implement. Writing six methods you don't need seems like a waste of time, so Java's creators created a shortcut: Instead of implementing the abstract WindowListener class, you can choose to extend (or inherit from) the **WindowAdapter class**, which already has been written to implement the WindowListener class.

Adapter classes implement an abstract class and provide the required methods for all of the abstract class's methods. That way, your class can inherit from the adapter class, and you can override only those methods for which you need special code. Because the inherited methods that were abstract in the original class are not abstract within the adapter class, you don't have to code the methods in a class you extend from an adapter.

Figure 11-4 shows the relationship among WindowListener, WindowAdapter, and a class you create. You always have a choice between implementing WindowListener and providing all seven methods or extending WindowAdapter and providing only the methods that you want to override.

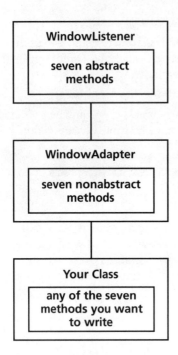

Figure 11-4: Relationship among WindowListener, WindowAdapter, and your class

....

You already have used another Listener class, ActionListener. In addition, Java provides you with a MouseListener, KeyListener, and several other classes. For every Listener class named xxxListener that contains more than one abstract method, Java also provides you with an xxxAdapter class from which your class can inherit, so that you need write only the methods in which you want to code special actions.

....

Next, you will extend the WindowAdapter class so you can use this alternative, shorter program for creating a Frame that you can close using the Close button.

To use the WindowAdapter class:

1. Create a new empty project named **DemoClosingFrame2**. Save the **DemoClosingFrame2** project folder in the Chapter.11 folder on your Student Disk.
2. Add to the project a new class file named **WindowYouCanClose.java**.
3. Add `import java.awt.event.*;` above the class header.
4. Add `extends WindowAdapter` to the right of the class header.
5. Add the following windowClosing() method between the class's curly brackets. This class can contain as many of the seven WindowListener methods as you want; in this case, the windowClosing() method is sufficient, and the only statement you need in windowClosing() is the call to the System.exit() method.

```
public void windowClosing(WindowEvent e)
  {
    System.exit(0);
  }
```

Next, create a FrameYouCanClose2 class, which is similar to the FrameYouCanClose class that you already created, except that it will use a new WindowYouCanClose object.

6. Add to the project a new class file named **FrameYouCanClose2**. Modify the class so that it appears as follows:

```
import java.awt.*;
import java.awt.event.*;
public class FrameYouCanClose2 extends Frame
{
  public FrameYouCanClose2(String str)
  {
    super(str);
    addWindowListener(new WindowYouCanClose());
  }
}
```

tip

You must create the WindowYouCanClose class to extend WindowAdapter, and the FrameYouCanClose2 class to extend Frame. It would be convenient to allow FrameYouCanClose2 to extend both WindowAdapter and Frame, but, as you learned in Chapter 10, Java does not support multiple inheritance.

7 Next, add to the project a new main class file named **DemoClosingFrame2** to demonstrate the FrameYouCanClose2 object. Modify the class so that it appears as follows:

```
import java.awt.*;
public class DemoClosingFrame2
{
  public static void main(String[] args)
  {
    FrameYouCanClose2 aFrame =
      new FrameYouCanClose2("This is a frame that closes");
    aFrame.setSize(400,100);
    aFrame.setVisible(true);
  }
}
```

8 Build the project and execute the program as a console application by typing `jview DemoClosingFrame2` at the command line. You can manipulate this Frame in all the usual ways, including closing it with the Close button.

Using Additional Frame Class Methods

When you extend the Frame class, you inherit several useful methods. Figure 11-5 lists the method header and purpose of several Frame class methods.

Method	Purpose
`void setTitle(String title)`	Sets a Frame's title.
`String getTitle()`	Returns a Frame's title.
`void setResizable(boolean resizable)`	Sets the Frame to be resizable by passing `true` or sets the Frame to be not resizable by passing `false` to the method.
`boolean isResizable()`	Returns `true` or `false` to indicate whether the Frame is resizable.

Figure 11-5: Useful methods of the Frame class

The syntax to use any of these methods consists of a Frame object, a dot, and the method name. For example, if you create a Frame within some other Container such as an applet, then if you construct the Frame with `Frame aFrameInAnApplet = new Frame();`, the statement that sets the Frame's title is `aFrameInAnApplet.setTitle("This is the title");`. Alternatively, if you are using any of these methods within a Frame's class, then the analogous method call to set the title is `this.setTitle("This is the title");`, or more simply, `setTitle("This is the title");`.

Next, you will use several Frame class methods to create a Frame that starts with the ability to be resized, but loses that ability after being minimized.

To create a Frame that you can change from being resizable to having a fixed size:

1. Create a new empty project named **DemoFrameWithFixedSize**. Save the **DemoFrameWithFixedSize** project folder in the Chapter.11 folder on your Student Disk.
2. Add a new class file named **FrameWithFixedSize.java** to the project.
3. Add the following import statements above the class header:

   ```
   import java.awt.event.*;
   import java.awt.*;
   ```

4. Add **extends Frame implements WindowListener** to the right of the class header.
5. Type the following constructor for the FrameWithFixedSize class between the class's curly brackets. To begin, the Frame will be resizable, so set the Frame's title to the String "Size Can Change".

   ```
   public FrameWithFixedSize()
   {
      super("Size Can Change");
      addWindowListener(this);
   }
   ```

6. Add the following windowClosing() method that calls System.exit() when the user clicks the Close button:

   ```
   public void windowClosing(WindowEvent e)
   {
      System.exit(0);
   }
   ```

7 Add the following windowIconified() method that changes the Frame's title and disables the Frame's ability to resize:

```
public void windowIconified(WindowEvent e)
{
  setTitle("Size Can't Change");
  setResizable(false);
}
```

8 Because this class implements WindowListener, you must provide the following methods for the remaining five abstract WindowListener methods:

```
public void windowClosed(WindowEvent e) {}
public void windowDeiconified(WindowEvent e) {}
public void windowOpened(WindowEvent e) {}
public void windowActivated(WindowEvent e) {}
public void windowDeactivated(WindowEvent e) {}
```

9 Add to the project a new main class file named **DemoFrameWithFixedSize.java** that instantiates a FrameWithFixedSize object. Modify the class so that it appears as follows:

```
import java.awt.*;
public class DemoFrameWithFixedSize
{
  public static void main(String[] args)
  {
    FrameWithFixedSize aFrame = new FrameWithFixedSize();
    aFrame.setSize(300,300);
    aFrame.setVisible(true);
  }
}
```

10 Build the project and execute the program as a console application by typing **jview DemoFrameWithFixedSize** at the command line. The Frame object shown in Figure 11-6 opens. As its title bar suggests, you can resize this Frame. Position your mouse pointer on one of the Frame's borders. The pointer changes to a double-headed arrow ↔, which indicates that you can drag the border to make the window larger or smaller.

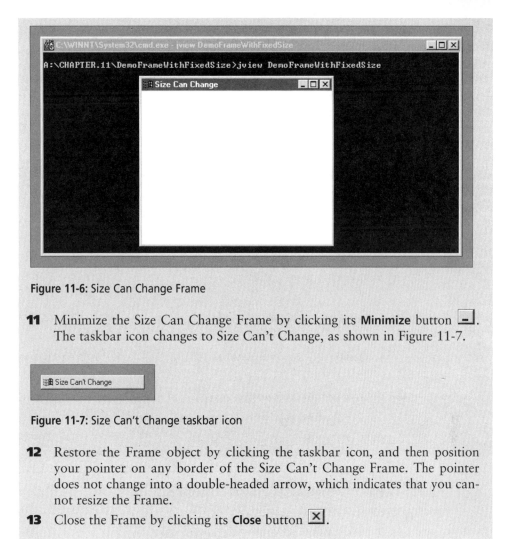

Figure 11-6: Size Can Change Frame

11 Minimize the Size Can Change Frame by clicking its **Minimize** button. The taskbar icon changes to Size Can't Change, as shown in Figure 11-7.

Figure 11-7: Size Can't Change taskbar icon

12 Restore the Frame object by clicking the taskbar icon, and then position your pointer on any border of the Size Can't Change Frame. The pointer does not change into a double-headed arrow, which indicates that you cannot resize the Frame.

13 Close the Frame by clicking its **Close** button.

Using Container Methods

You can see from the partial AWT family tree shown in Figure 11-2 that there are two major types of Container objects: Panels and Windows. You usually create Panels or Windows so they can hold other Component objects such as Buttons and Labels. The basic difference between a Window and a Panel is that a Panel does not have a title bar or the Minimize, Maximize, and Close buttons. Otherwise, Windows and Panels are very close cousins.

tip

The applets that you have created include a title bar and sizing buttons because the AppletViewer program supplied with the Java compiler automatically provides you with a Frame. However, your applets by themselves do not have Frames (unless you decide to declare a Frame object); the applets simply run within the AppletViewer's program window.

As children of the Container class, Windows and Panels share all the common methods provided by their parent, including the methods shown in Figure 11-8.

Method	Purpose
`Component add(Component comp)`	Adds a Component to a Container—for example, `add(someButton);`—to an applet.
`int getComponentCount()`	Returns the number of Components in a Container.
`Component getComponent(int n)`	Returns the nth Component in a Container.
`Component[] getComponents()`	Returns an array of Components in a Container.
`void remove(Component comp)`	Removes the named Component from a Container.
`void removeAll()`	Removes all Components from a Container.

Figure 11-8: Some useful Container class methods

Next, you will create an applet that displays a Frame that contains some Components. This exercise serves two purposes: to show you that you can add Frames to applets just as easily as you can add them to applications and to demonstrate some Container class methods. Within the applet you create, you will add and remove Label Components from a Frame Container based on the number of times the user clicks a Button Component.

To create an applet that displays a Frame:

1. Create a new empty project named **AppletDemoComponents**. Save the **AppletDemoComponents** project folder in the Chapter.11 folder on your Student Disk.
2. Add a new class file named **AppletDemoComponents.java** to the project.
3. Above the class header, type the following import statements that you will need for the applet:

```
import java.applet.*;
import java.awt.*;
import java.awt.event.*;
```

4. Add `extends Applet implements ActionListener` to the right of the class header.
5. Enter the following code between the class's curly brackets so the applet contains a FrameYouCanClose (named fycc for "Frame You Can Close") and a Button that the user can click to display the Frame:

```
private FrameYouCanClose fycc =
   new FrameYouCanClose("Demo Components");
private Button showFrame = new Button("Press Me");
```

6. At different times, the Frame will contain one of three different messages. The user will change the Frame message by clicking the Button object. You also will include a counter so the program can count the number of Button clicks that have occurred. Enter the following code to accomplish these actions:

```
Label msg1 = new Label("Event Handlers Incorporated");
Label msg2 = new Label("Plan with us!");
Label msg3 = new Label
   ("You just relax. We'll manage the fuss.");
int pressCounter = 0;
```

7. Add the following init() method to the applet to add the Button to the applet. The init() method sets the size and adds the ActionListener to the Frame, but it does not yet make the Frame visible.

```
public void init()
{
   add(showFrame);
   fycc.setSize(200,150);
   showFrame.addActionListener(this);
}
```

To review the purpose of each of the applet's methods, refer to Chapter 7.

8 The following actionPerformed() method executes when the user clicks the showFrame Button. If it is the first Button click (if pressCounter is zero), then you want to add the first message (msg1, which reads "Event Handlers Incorporated") to the Frame.

```
public void actionPerformed(ActionEvent e)
{
  if(pressCounter == 0)
    fycc.add(msg1);
```

9 Enter the following code so that if the Button click is not the first click of the showFrame Button, but it is the second click, the program removes msg1 and adds msg2:

```
else if(pressCounter == 1)
{
  fycc.remove(msg1);
  fycc.add(msg2);
}
```

10 Enter the following code so if the Button click is the third Button click, you will remove msg2 and add msg3. Additionally, make the Frame larger to accommodate the longer third message.

```
else if(pressCounter == 2)
{
  fycc.remove(msg2);
  fycc.setSize(400,150);
  fycc.add(msg3);
}
```

11 Enter the following code so that after the first two Button clicks, the message Frame should be visible, but after three Button clicks you can make the Frame invisible:

```
if(pressCounter < 3)
    fycc.setVisible(true);
  else
    fycc.setVisible(false);
```

12 For the fourth Button click, enter the following code to disable the showFrame Button:

```
if(pressCounter == 4)
  showFrame.setEnabled(false);
```

13 Before leaving the actionPerformed() method, enter the following code to add 1 to the pressCounter variable. Then add a closing curly bracket for the method.

```
  ++pressCounter;
}
```

Understanding the Abstract Windows Toolkit (AWT)

14 Add to the project the FrameYouCanClose.java file that you created earlier, by selecting **Add Class** from the **Project** menu. The Add Item dialog box appears. Click the **Existing** tab and locate the FrameYouCanClose.java file in the DemoClosingFrame folder in the Chapter.11 folder on your Student Disk. After locating the file, highlight it, and then click the **Open** button to add it to your project.

Now create an HTML document so you can run the applet.

To run the applet:
1 Add a new Web page named **testComponentApplet.htm** to the project.
2 In the Source tab of the HTML Editor window, place your cursor in the blank line following the tag that reads <P> </P> and type the opening <APPLET> tag that contains the applet's name and dimensions: `<APPLET CODE = "AppletDemoComponents.class" WIDTH = 400 HEIGHT = 300>`.
3 Press the **Enter** key to start a new line and type the applet's closing tag: `</APPLET>`.
4 Build and save the project, and then execute the applet by typing `jview /a testComponentApplet.htm` at the command line. When the AppletViewer window opens, it looks like Figure 11-9.

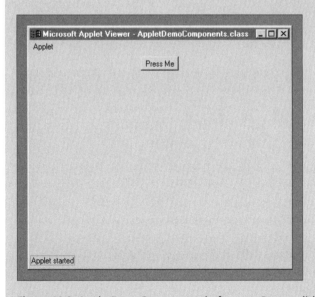

Figure 11-9: AppletDemoComponents before any Button clicks

5 Click the **Press Me** button. A Frame opens with the first message, as shown in Figure 11-10. (You might need to drag the message Frame out of the way to see the button.)

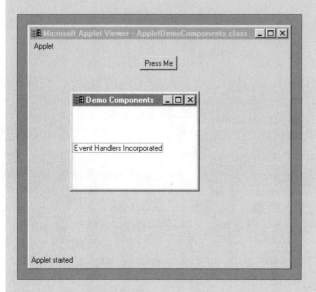

Figure 11-10: AppletDemoComponents after one Button click

6 Click the **Press Me** button again to see the second message, and then click it again to see the final message. When you click the button a fourth time, the Frame disappears; when you click it the fifth time, you disable the button.

7 Close the AppletViewer window by clicking the **Close** button ⨯.

 # SUMMARY

- Java's creators packaged GUI components in the Abstract Windows Toolkit, or AWT, so that you could adapt them for your purposes rather than creating them from scratch.
- Within the AWT package, components are defined in the Component class.
- When you use components in a Java program, you usually place them in containers. A container is a type of Component that holds other Components so you can treat a group of several Components as a single entity. Containers are defined in the Container class.
- All Java classes are subclasses; they all descend from the Object class.

- The Panel class and the Window class descend from the Container class. Every applet is a child of the Panel class.

- The Frame class and the Dialog class are subclasses of the Window class.

- The Component class contains many methods that you can use with any Component class descendant. The setSize() method allows you to set the physical size of any Component. The setVisible() method makes the component visible or invisible to the user.

- The Component class is an abstract class. All of the GUI components, such as buttons, text fields, and other objects with which the user interacts, actually are subclasses or extensions of the Component class.

- The Container class is an abstract class. Every concrete container object is a member of a subclass of Container.

- The Window class, which inherits from Container, is not abstract. Java programmers rarely use Window objects, because the Window subclasses, Frame and Dialog, allow you to create more useful objects.

- You usually create a Frame so you can place other objects within it for display.

- The Frame class has two constructors so you can create a titled or untitled Frame.

- You often create Frames because users are familiar with their operation.

- A class that is a listener for Window events must implement the WindowListener interface. A Frame that closes when the user clicks the Close button must implement WindowListener.

- The WindowListener interface class provides seven abstract Window methods: windowClosing(), windowClosed(), windowDeiconified(), windowIconified(), windowOpened(), windowActivated(), and windowDeactivated().

- When the user clicks the Close button on a Frame, you can code the Frame to lose visibility or to close the program.

- You can use the System.exit() method to end a program. By convention, you return a zero to the operating system when a program ends normally, or a one when a program ends due to an error.

- Adapter classes, such as WindowAdapter, implement an abstract class and provide the required methods for all of the abstract class's methods. This method lets you write methods only for those methods for which you need special code.

- Useful Frame class methods include methods that set and return a Frame's title, and set and return a Frame's resizability. The syntax to use any of these methods consists of a Frame object, a dot, and the method's name.

- The two major types of Container objects are Panels and Windows. As children of the Container class, Windows and Panels share all the common methods provided by their parent, such as those that add a Component to a Container, count Components, get an array of Component names, and remove some or all of the Components from a Container.

QUESTIONS

1. The creators of the Java programming language packaged GUI components in the AWT, or _____.
   a. Abstract Windows Toolkit
   b. Authoring Windows Template
   c. Absolute Widget Tasks
   d. Anonymous Windowing Tool

2. The generic name for the component type that holds other components so you can treat a group of several components as a single entity is _____.
   a. Frame
   b. Window
   c. Container
   d. Receptacle

3. All Java classes are _____.
   a. subclasses
   b. parent classes
   c. Components
   d. Containers

4. Which of the following statements is true?
   a. The Component class descends from the Container class.
   b. The Container class descends from the Frame class.
   c. The Object class descends from the Frame class.
   d. The Component class descends from the Object class.

5. The Container class is a parent to _____.
   a. Component
   b. Object
   c. Window
   d. the AWT

6. The Component class method that allows you to set the physical size of any component is _____.
   a. getSize()
   b. setSize()
   c. getPhysical()
   d. setPhysical()

7. Which of the following classes is abstract?
   a. Button
   b. Frame
   c. Component
   d. Applet

8. Which of the following lines of code instantiates a Container object?
   a. `Container box = new Container();`
   b. `Container = new Container();`
   c. `Container box = new();`
   d. You cannot instantiate a Container object.

9. If you use an argument with a Frame constructor, the argument represents the Frame's _____.
   a. title
   b. size
   c. color
   d. position

10. Within an event-driven program, an object that is interested in an event is a _____.
    a. source
    b. Component
    c. Container
    d. listener

11. The methods contained in the WindowListener interface are _____.
    a. compiled
    b. private
    c. Frames
    d. abstract

12. If you implement the WindowListener interface, you must _____.
    a. write an empty windowClosing() method
    b. write a windowClosing() method that contains instructions
    c. write a windowClosing() method
    d. not write a windowClosing() method

13. If you write a windowClosing() method so that you can override the windowClosing() method within WindowListener, then you must _____.
    a. include the statement `System.exit(0);`
    b. declare the method to be public and void
    c. return a WindowEvent from the method
    d. not code any statements within the method

14. Classes that implement an abstract class and provide the required methods for all of the abstract class's methods are _____ classes.
    a. abstract
    b. void
    c. Adapter
    d. Container

15. The Frame class method isResizable() has a return type of _____.
    a. int
    b. void
    c. public
    d. boolean

section A

16. After a Frame object is constructed, you can set a Frame's title with the method _____.
    a. setTitle()
    b. setLabel()
    c. setFrame()
    d. You cannot set a Frame's title after construction.

17. The two major types of Container objects are _____.
    a. Buttons and Labels
    b. Panels and Windows
    c. Frames and Applets
    d. Applets and Windows

18. Which of the following methods is a Component class method?
    a. setTitle()
    b. windowClosing()
    c. add()
    d. all of these

19. A Frame is _____.
    a. a Container
    b. an Object
    c. both of these
    d. none of these

EXERCISES

Save each of the programs that you create in the exercises in the Chapter.11 folder on your Student Disk.

1. Create a console application project named Rhyme that displays a Frame that contains the words to any well-known nursery rhyme.

2. Create a Frame named EveryMethodFrame that prints an appropriate statement to the command line each time one of the seven WindowAdapter methods executes. Write an applet named DemoEveryMethod that displays the Frame.

3. Create an applet named DemoCountingFrame with a Frame that counts the number of times it has been iconified and displays the total on the screen.

4. Create an applet named RemoveResistance with a Frame that holds five Labels that describe reasons that a customer might not buy your product (for example, "Too expensive"). Every time the user clicks a Button, remove one of the negative reasons.

5. a. Write a program that calculates the weekly salary for an individual based on a regular hourly rate. Allow the user to input the hourly rate, and then pay the user for a 40-hour work week. Use an applet with two Frames. Each Frame should have a text box. Use one Frame for input and one for output showing the total salary for the week.
    b. Write a program that calculates the weekly salary for an individual based on a regular hourly rate, plus a premium for overtime. Allow the user to input the hourly rate, the overtime premium percentage, the regular hours worked, and the overtime hours worked. Use an applet with five Frames. Each Frame should have a text box. Use four Frames for input; the fifth Frame contains the total salary for the week.
6. Write a program that calculates the new balance of a checking account based on the current balance, a check, and/or a deposit. Allow the user to enter the current balance, a check amount, and a deposit amount. Use an applet with four Frames. Each Frame should have a text box. Use three Frames for input; the fourth Frame contains the new balance.
7. Write a program that draws a bar chart based on four input values that represent sales for four divisions of a company. Use a different Frame for each value.

SECTION B
objectives

In this section you will learn how to :
- Use Component methods
- Use a Checkbox
- Use the CheckboxGroup class
- Use a Choice
- Use a List

Using Components

Using Component Methods

Containers, Frames, Windows, Applets, and Panels are also Components, but it is easier to categorize them using the more specific term *Containers* because objects such as Frames visually "contain" other items. Many other Components, which are not Containers, are those objects you think of as controls, such as objects that you can click and drag. The Component class is an abstract class, which means you cannot instantiate a "plain" Component. The Component classes from which you can create non-Container objects are as follows:

- Label
- Button
- Checkbox
- Choice
- List
- TextComponent, which is parent to TextArea and TextField

You have used Components such as Labels and Buttons since Chapter 7, so you already are familiar with a number of Component methods. Figure 11-11 summarizes the major Component methods.

Method	Purpose
`Font getFont()`	Returns the Font used to draw the Component.
`void setFont(Font f)`	Sets the Font used to draw the Component; the lowercase *f* represents the Font object.

Figure 11-11: Component methods

Understanding the Abstract Windows Toolkit (AWT)

Method	Purpose
`void setEnabled(boolean condition)`	Enables the Component to respond to the user, or forbids the Component from responding to the user.
`boolean isEnabled()`	Returns whether the Component can respond to the user.
`void setVisible(boolean condition)`	Makes the Component visible or invisible.
`boolean isVisible()`	Returns whether the Component is visible.
`boolean isShowing()`	Returns whether a Component is set as visible and not obscured by other Components.
`void setSize(int width, int height)`	Sets the Component's size.
`String toString()`	Returns a String describing the Component.
`void setLocation(int x, int y)`	Moves the Component to position x,y within the containing Component.
`void setBackground(Color c)`	Sets the Component's background color to c.
`void setForeground(Color c)`	Sets the Component's foreground color to c.
`repaint()`	Schedules a Component for repainting.

Figure 11-11: Component methods (continued)

tip

You learned about the colors you can use with the setBackground() and setForeground() methods in Chapter 8.

Besides having the general Component methods, Labels and Buttons each have methods that are specific to their class. In Chapter 7, you learned to use getText() and setText() methods with the Label class. You also learned about the getLabel() and setLabel() methods for the Button class. It's easy to get confused with these method names, so try to remember that a Label contains text and a Button wears a Label. The Label class does not have a getLabel() or setLabel() method, and the Button class does not have a getText() or setText() method.

section B

> **To demonstrate using one of the Component methods with a Frame object:**
>
> **1** If necessary, start Visual J++ and open the **AppletDemoComponents** project from the Chapter.11 folder on your Student Disk, then open the **AppletDemoComponents.java** file in the Text Editor window.
>
> **2** Position the insertion point to the right of the `fycc.setSize(200,150);` statement within the init() method, and then press the **Enter** key to start a new line.
>
> **3** Set the fycc Frame's location by typing `fycc.setLocation(100,100);` on the new line.
>
> **4** Rebuild the project and execute the applet by typing `jview /a testComponentApplet.htm` at the command line. The Frame that contains the messages now appears near the middle of the Applet Panel Container, at position 100,100. Click the **Press Me** button three times. Because of the Frame's new position, when the Frame enlarges to accommodate the longer third message, it does not obscure the button.
>
> **5** Close the AppletViewer window.

Using a Checkbox

A **Checkbox** consists of a Label positioned beside a square; you can click the square to display or remove a check mark. Usually you use a Checkbox to allow the user to turn an option on or off. Some Checkbox methods are listed in Figure 11-12.

Method	Purpose
`void setLabel(String label)`	Sets the Label for the Checkbox.
`String getLabel()`	Returns the Checkbox Label.
`void setState(boolean condition)`	Sets the Checkbox state to `true` for checked or `false` for unchecked.
`boolean getState()`	Gets the current state (checked or unchecked) of the Checkbox.

Figure 11-12: Checkbox class methods

When you construct a Checkbox, you can choose whether to assign it a Label. The following statements create two Checkbox objects: one with a Label and one without a Label:

```
Checkbox boxOne = new Checkbox();
Checkbox boxTwo = new Checkbox("Click here please");
```

If you do not initialize a Checkbox with a Label, or if you want to change the Label later, you can use the setLabel() method as in `boxOne.setLabel("Check this box now");`.

You can set the state of a Checkbox with the setState() method; for example, use `boxOne.setState(false);` to ensure that boxOne is unchecked. The getState() method is most useful in boolean expressions, as in `if(boxTwo.getState()) ++votes;`, which adds 1 to a votes variable if boxTwo currently is checked.

Using a Checkbox object requires using a new interface, ItemListener. Whereas ActionListener provides for mouse clicks and requires you to write an actionPerformed() method, ItemListener provides for objects whose states change from `true` to `false` and requires you to write an itemStateChanged() method. When a Checkbox's state is changed from checked to unchecked or from unchecked to checked, the code in the itemStateChanged() method will execute.

Next, you will create an interactive program that Event Handlers Incorporated clients can use to determine an event's price. The base price of an event is $200; serving cocktails adds $300 and serving dinner adds $600. The user can check and uncheck the cocktail and dinner Checkboxes to recalculate the event price.

To write an applet that includes two Checkbox objects:

1 Create a new empty project named **DemoCheckBox**. Save the **DemoCheckBox** project folder in the Chapter.11 folder on your Student Disk.

2 Add a new class file named **DemoCheckBox.java** to the project.

3 Above the class header, type the following import statements that you will need for the program:

```
import java.applet.*;
import java.awt.*;
import java.awt.event.*;
```

4 Add `extends Applet implements ItemListener` to the right of the class header.

5 Between the class's curly brackets, create the following class variables for the company name, a Font, and two Checkboxes. One Checkbox is labeled "Cocktails" and the other is labeled "Dinner".

```
String companyName = new String
("Event Handlers Incorporated");
Font bigFont = new Font("Arial", Font.PLAIN, 24);
Checkbox cocktailBox = new Checkbox("Cocktails");
Checkbox dinnerBox = new Checkbox("Dinner");
```

6 Add the following variables to hold three prices for events with cocktails, events with dinner, and a customer total:

```
int cocktailPrice = 300,
dinnerPrice = 600,
totalPrice = 200;
```

7. Within the applet's init() method, add the following two Checkboxes and register the applet as an ItemListener for each one:

```
public void init()
{
  add(cocktailBox);
  cocktailBox.addItemListener(this);
  add(dinnerBox);
  dinnerBox.addItemListener(this);
}
```

8. Enter the following paint() method for the applet, which sets the Font and colors and draws the Strings:

```
public void paint(Graphics gr)
{
  gr.setFont(bigFont);
  gr.setColor(Color.magenta);
  gr.drawString(companyName,10,100);
  gr.drawString("Event price estimate",10,150);
  gr.setColor(Color.blue);
  gr.drawString(Integer.toString(totalPrice),280,150);
}
```

9. Enter the following itemStateChanged() method, which executes when the user changes the status of one of the two Checkboxes that are registered as ItemListeners. The base price of the event is set at $200. If the cocktail Checkbox is checked, then the program adds the cocktail price ($300) to the event total.

```
public void itemStateChanged(ItemEvent check)
{
  totalPrice = 200;
  if(cocktailBox.getState())
  {
    totalPrice += cocktailPrice;
  }
```

10. Regardless of whether the cocktail Checkbox is checked, if the dinner box is checked, then add the dinner price ($600) to the event's total. Enter the following code:

```
if(dinnerBox.getState())
{
  totalPrice += dinnerPrice;
}
```

11. To end the itemStateChanged() method, call the repaint() method so that the new prices display on the screen, and then add a closing curly bracket as follows:

    **repaint();
    }**

12. Add a new Web page named **testCheckBox.htm** to the project.
13. In the Source tab of the HTML Editor window, place the insertion point in the blank line following the tag that reads <P> </P> and type the opening APPLET tag that contains the applet's name and dimensions: **<APPLET CODE = "DemoCheckBox.class" WIDTH = 400 HEIGHT = 300>**.
14. Press the **Enter** key to start a new line and type the applet's closing tag: **</APPLET>**.
15. Build and save the project, then run the program in AppletViewer by typing **jview /a testCheckBox.htm** at the command line. The output appears as shown in Figure 11-13. Experiment by checking and unchecking the two Checkbox objects. Make sure that the event total is correct whether you select cocktails, dinner, both, or neither.

Figure 11-13: DemoCheckBox applet

16. Close the AppletViewer window.

Using the CheckboxGroup Class

You can use the CheckboxGroup class to group several Checkboxes so a user can select only one Checkbox at a time. When you group Checkbox objects within a CheckboxGroup, all of the other Checkboxes automatically are turned off when the user selects any one Checkbox.

A group of Checkboxes for which a user can select only one at a time also is called a set of radio buttons. (On most car radios, if you push a button to select a station, that station is the only station that you can receive at that time.)

You either can create a CheckboxGroup and then create the individual Checkboxes, or you can create the Checkboxes and then create the CheckboxGroup. When you create a Checkbox, you can assign it to a CheckboxGroup upon construction using the following three-argument constructor:

- The Label for the Checkbox
- The values `true` or `false` to indicate whether you want the individual Checkbox to include a check mark when the applet starts
- The CheckboxGroup name

For example, if you define a CheckboxGroup as `CheckboxGroup favoriteStoogeGroup = new CheckboxGoup("Favorite Among Three Stooges");`, then you can assign an initially unselected Checkbox to the group using the following code:

```
Checkbox larryBox =
   new Checkbox("Larry", false, favoriteStoogeGroup);
```

Alternatively, you can use the following statement to assign a Checkbox to a group after construction using the setCheckboxGroup() method of the Checkbox class:

```
moeBox.setCheckboxGroup(favoriteStoogeGroup);
```

If you assign the `true` state to multiple Checkboxes within a group, each new `true` assignment will negate the previous one.

Figure 11-14 lists the methods you use with the CheckboxGroup class. The user can set one of the Checkboxes within a group to "on" by clicking it with the mouse, or you can set a Checkbox to "on" within your program with a statement such as `favoriteStoogeGroup.setSelectedCheckbox(larryBox);`. You can determine which, if any, of the Checkboxes in a group are selected with the getSelectedCheckbox() method. For example:

```
Checkbox selectedBox =
   favoriteStoogeGroup.getSelectedCheckbox();
```

Understanding the Abstract Windows Toolkit (AWT)

Method	Purpose
`Checkbox getSelectedCheckbox()`	Returns the currently selected Checkbox.
`void setSelectedCheckbox(Checkbox box)`	Selects, or makes `true`, the named box; all others in the group become `false`.

Figure 11-14: CheckboxGroup class methods

> **tip**
>
> Each individual Checkbox object has access to every Checkbox class method regardless of whether the Checkbox is part of a CheckboxGroup.

Next, add a CheckboxGroup to the program that determines the price of an event for Event Handlers Incorporated. If the user wants to serve dinner at an event, the price varies based on the selected menu. Because the user can choose only one entrée (chicken, beef, or fish), it is appropriate to select the entrée using a Checkbox group.

To add a CheckboxGroup to the Event Handlers pricing program:

1 Return to the **DemoCheckBox.java** file in the Text Editor window and save the file as **DemoCheckBoxGroup.java** in the DemoCheckBox folder in the Chapter.11 folder on your Student Disk.

2 Replace the DemoCheckBox class name in the class header with **DemoCheckBoxGroup**.

3 Position the insertion point at the end of the line that declares `totalPrice = 200;`, and then press the **Enter** key to start a new line. The base dinner price currently assumes that the dinner entrée is chicken. Add the following two new variables for the increase in the base dinner price if the selected entrée is either beef or fish: `int beefPrice = 100, fishPrice = 75;`.

4 On the next line, enter the following code to add a CheckboxGroup to hold the three dinner options, and then to add Checkboxes for each of the three entrées. You will initialize each of the three entrée boxes to be unchecked and part of the dinnerGrp group.

```
CheckboxGroup dinnerGrp = new CheckboxGroup();
Checkbox chickenBox = new Checkbox
    ("Chicken", false, dinnerGrp);
Checkbox beefBox = new Checkbox
    ("Beef", false, dinnerGrp);
Checkbox fishBox = new Checkbox
    ("Fish", false, dinnerGrp);
```

5. Within the init() method, position the insertion point to the right of the line that adds the itemListener for the dinnerBox Checkbox (just before the closing curly bracket for the init() method), and then press the **Enter** key to start a new line. Enter the following code to add each of the three dinner selection boxes and to register the applet as a Listener for each Checkbox:

```
add(chickenBox);
chickenBox.addItemListener(this);
add(beefBox);
beefBox.addItemListener(this);
add(fishBox);
fishBox.addItemListener(this);
```

6. Within the itemStateChanged() method, position the insertion point to the right of the statement `totalPrice += dinnerPrice;`, and then press the **Enter** key to start a new line. The statement you located adds $600 to the price of an event when the user checks the dinnerBox. Now, in addition, when the user selects the dinnerBox, the program must determine which dinner entrée the user selected. If the selection is beef or fish, the program should add the appropriate additional price to the event total. If the selection is neither beef nor fish, the program must ensure that the user selected the chickenBox, regardless of whether the user actually selected it. This ensures that a user who has not purposely chosen an entrée can see that the price is based on a chicken entrée. Enter the following code:

```
Checkbox dinnerSelection = dinnerGrp.getSelectedCheckbox();
if(dinnerSelection == beefBox)
   totalPrice += beefPrice;
else if(dinnerSelection == fishBox)
   totalPrice += fishPrice;
else
   chickenBox.setState(true);
```

> **tip**
>
> The expression `if(dinnerSelection == beefBox)` has the same boolean value as `beefBox.getState()`.

7. In the HTML Editor window, return to the **testCheckBox.htm** file that you used to test the DemoCheckBox.java class. Insert the word **Group** in the APPLET CODE statement so that it refers to the DemoCheckBoxGroup class. Save the file as **testCheckBoxGroup.htm** in the DemoCheckBox folder in the Chapter.11 folder on your Student Disk.

8. Rebuild and save the project, then run the applet by typing **jview /a testCheckBoxGroup.htm** at the command line. Check and uncheck each of the available Checkboxes and observe the price changes as you make your selections. Figure 11-15 shows the output when you select a chicken dinner.

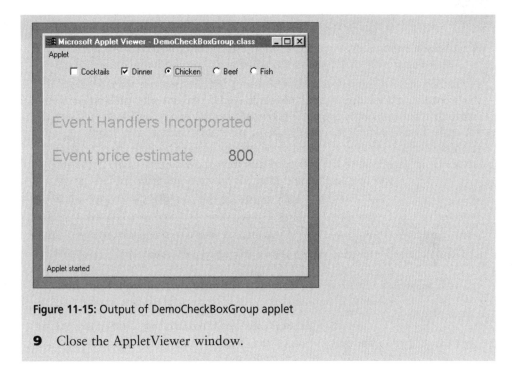

Figure 11-15: Output of DemoCheckBoxGroup applet

9 Close the AppletViewer window.

Using the Choice Class

When you want a user to select an option from a list, you can use a Choice object. A **Choice object** displays an option; clicking the Choice object displays a drop-down menu that contains other options. When the user selects an option from the drop-down menu, the selected item replaces the original item in the display.

In the Windows environment, a Choice is called a *list box*.

You build a Choice by using a constructor with no arguments, and then by adding items to the Choice with the add() method. For example, the following statements create a Choice object with three options:

```
Choice majorChoice = new Choice();
majorChoice.add("English");
majorChoice.add("Math");
majorChoice.add("Sociology");
```

Figure 11-16 lists some of the methods you can use with a Choice object. You choose one of the items in a Choice to be the initially selected item using the select() method, as in `majorChoice.select("Math");`. You can determine the currently selected item with the getSelectedItem() method, as in `String myMajor = majorChoice.getSelectedItem();`.

Method	Purpose
`void add(String item)`	Adds the item to the Choice.
`void select(String item)`	Selects the named item.
`String getSelectedItem()`	Returns the name of the currently selected item.
`int getItemCount()`	Returns the number of items in the Choice.
`String getItem(int index)`	Returns the name of the item at the desired index position.
`void select(int index)`	Selects the item at the index position.
`int getSelectedIndex()`	Returns the position of the currently selected item.

Figure 11-16: Choice class methods

You also can treat the items in a Choice object as an array. For example, you can use the getSelectedIndex() method to determine the list position of the currently selected item. Then you can use the index to access corresponding information. For example, if a Choice named historyChoice has been filled with a list of historical events, such as "Declaration of Independence," "Pearl Harbor," and "Man walks on moon," then after a user chooses one of the items, you can code `int pos = historyChoice.getSelectedIndex();`. Now the variable pos holds the position of the selected item, and you can use the pos variable to access an array of dates so you can display the appropriate one. For example, if `int[] dates = {1776, 1941, 1968};`, then `dates[pos]` holds the year for the selected historical event.

Next, you will create an applet for Event Handlers Incorporated that allows the user to choose the type of entertainment to schedule at an event and display the event price. The entertainment types are no entertainment ($0), a rock band ($725), a pianist ($325), and a clown ($125).

To write an applet with a Choice:

1 Create a new empty project named **DemoChoice**. Save the **DemoChoice** project folder in the Chapter.11 folder on your Student Disk.

2 Add to the project a new class file named **DemoChoice.java**.

3 Above the class header, type the following import statements that you will need for the program:

```
import java.applet.*;
import java.awt.*;
import java.awt.event.*;
```

4. Add **extends Applet implements ItemListener** to the right of the class header.

5. Enter the following code between the class's curly brackets to add the company name and a Font to the applet, and to include a variable to hold the price that the customer will pay for the selected entertainment:

```
String companyName =
   new String("Event Handlers Incorporated");
Font bigFont = new Font("Arial", Font.PLAIN, 24);
int totalPrice = 0;
```

6. Enter the following code to create a Choice object and an array of integers to hold the four prices for the four entertainment types:

```
Choice entertainmentChoice = new Choice();
int[] actPrice = {0,725,325,125};
```

7. Enter the following init() method that adds the Choice object to the applet, registers the applet as an ItemListener for the Choice object, and adds four items to the Choice list:

```
public void init()
{
   add(entertainmentChoice);
   entertainmentChoice.addItemListener(this);
   entertainmentChoice.add("No entertainment");
   entertainmentChoice.add("Rock band');
   entertainmentChoice.add("Pianist");
   entertainmentChoice.add("Clown");
}
```

8. Enter the following paint() method, which sets the applet's appearance and prints the price:

```
public void paint(Graphics gr)
{
   gr.setFont(bigFont);
   gr.setColor(Color.magenta);
   gr.drawString(companyName,10,100);
   gr.drawString("Price for entertainment",10,150);
   gr.setColor(Color.blue);
   gr.drawString(Integer.toString(totalPrice),280,150);
}
```

9 Enter the following itemStateChanged() method, which determines the index of the selected entertainment type and prints the correct price based on the index:

```
public void itemStateChanged(ItemEvent choice)
{
  int actNum = entertainmentChoice.getSelectedIndex();
  totalPrice = actPrice[actNum];
  repaint();
}
```

10 Add a new Web page named **testDemoChoice.htm** to the project.

11 In the Source tab of the HTML Editor window, place the insertion point in the blank line following the tag that reads <P> </P> and type the opening APPLET tag that contains the applet's name and dimensions: **<APPLET CODE = "DemoChoice.class" WIDTH = 400 HEIGHT = 300>**.

12 Press the **Enter** key to start a new line and type the applet's closing tag: **</APPLET>**.

13 Build and save the project, then execute the applet by typing **jview /a testDemoChoice.htm** at the command line. Your applet should look like Figure 11-17.

Figure 11-17: DemoChoice applet

14 Open the Choice object by clicking its list arrow, as shown in Figure 11-18.

Understanding the Abstract Windows Toolkit (AWT)

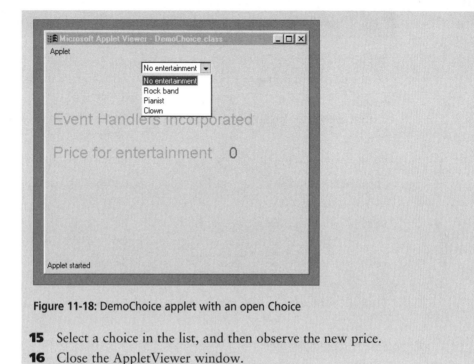

Figure 11-18: DemoChoice applet with an open Choice

15 Select a choice in the list, and then observe the new price.
16 Close the AppletViewer window.

Using a List

With a Choice, only one option is visible on the screen until the user clicks the Choice list arrow to display the menu. When the user selects an item in the menu, only the selected option appears. A **List** is similar to a Choice because you can display an array of options from which to select. However, a List can display multiple items and can also allow the user to make multiple selections. You can construct a List object using one of three constructors:

- List(), which creates a new scrolling list that displays approximately three or four lines. The number of visible lines depends on your system configuration.
- List(int), where int specifies the number of visible lines.
- List(int, boolean), where int specifies the number of visible lines, and a boolean value of true or false determines whether or not a user can make multiple selections.

tip

A vertical scrollbar appears to the right of a List object if the number of choices exceeds the number of visible lines.

Figure 11-19 describes some List class methods.

section B

Method	Purpose
`void add(String item)`	Adds an item to the List.
`void add(String item, int position)`	Adds an item to the indicated position in the List.
`void remove(int position)`	Removes the item at the indicated position.
`void removeAll()`	Removes all items from a List.
`int getItemCount()`	Returns the number of items in the List.
`String getItem(int position)`	Returns the name of the item at the indicated position.
`void select(int position)`	Selects the item at the indicated position.
`void deselect(int position)`	Deselects the item at the indicated position.
`boolean isSelected(int position)`	Determines whether the item at the indicated position is selected.
`String getSelectedItem()`	Returns the name of the selected item.
`int getSelectedIndex()`	Returns the position of the selected item.
`void setMultipleMode(boolean)`	Allows the List to accept multiple selections based on a `true` or `false` argument.
`boolean isMultipleMode()`	Returns whether multiple selections are allowed.
`int[] getSelectedIndexes()`	Returns an array of integers with the positions of all selected items.
`String[] getSelectedItems()`	Returns an array of names of the selected items.

Figure 11-19: List class methods

Next you will create a List from which customers of Event Handlers Incorporated can choose party favor options to purchase for events. First, you will create an applet with a List from which the user can select only a single option, and then you will modify the applet so a user can select as many party favor options as desired.

To write an applet containing a List:

1 Create a new empty project named **DemoList**. Save the **DemoList** project folder in the Chapter.11 folder on your student disk.

2 Add to the project a new class file named **DemoList.java**.

3 Above the class header, type the following import statements that you will need for the program:

```
import java.applet.*;
import java.awt.*;
import java.awt.event.*;
```

4 Add `extends Applet implements ItemListener` to the right of the class header.

5 Enter the following code between the class's curly brackets to include a String, a Font, and a totalPrice variable as you have done with the Checkbox and Choice applets:

```
String companyName = new String
   ("Event Handlers Incorporated");
Font bigFont = new Font("Arial", Font.PLAIN, 24);
int totalPrice = 0;
```

6 Enter the following code to create a List object, as well as an array that will hold prices for four different categories of party favors. Although the List holds only four choices, the List constructor sets the number of visible lines to five to be certain all four choices are visible simultaneously. The List constructor also includes a boolean value of `false`, which disables multiple selections.

```
List partyFavorList = new List(5, false);
int[] favorPrice = {8,10,25,35};
```

7 Enter the following init() method for the DemoList applet, which adds the partyFavor List to the applet, registers the applet as an ItemListener, and adds four party favor items to the List:

```
public void init()
{
  add(partyFavorList);
  partyFavorList.addItemListener(this);
  partyFavorList.add("Hats");
  partyFavorList.add("Streamers");
  partyFavorList.add("Noise makers");
  partyFavorList.add("Balloons");
}
```

8 Enter the following statements to start the paint() method:

```
public void paint(Graphics gr)
{
  gr.setFont(bigFont);
  gr.setColor(Color.magenta);
  gr.drawString(companyName,10,110);
  gr.drawString("Price for favors",10,150);
  gr.setColor(Color.blue);
```

9 Enter the following code that uses the getSelectedIndex() method to determine which option the user has chosen. The corresponding price becomes the totalPrice.

```
int favorNum = partyFavorList.getSelectedIndex();
totalPrice = favorPrice[favorNum];
gr.drawString(Integer.toString(totalPrice),280,150);
```

10 Enter a closing curly bracket for the paint() method.

11 Enter the following itemStateChanged() method, which calls the repaint() method:

```
public void itemStateChanged(ItemEvent check)
{
  repaint();
}
```

12 Add a new Web page named **testDemoList.htm** to the project.

Understanding the Abstract Windows Toolkit (AWT)

13 In the Source tab of the HTML Editor window, place the insertion point in the blank line following the tag that reads <P> </P> and type the opening <APPLET> tag that contains the applet's name and dimensions: **<APPLET CODE = "DemoList.class" WIDTH = 400 HEIGHT = 300>**.

14 Press the **Enter** key to start a new line and type the applet's closing tag: **</APPLET>**.

15 Build and save the project, then test the applet by typing **jview /a testDemoList.htm** at the command line. Make a selection from the party favor List and observe the change in price, as shown in Figure 11-20. Notice that when you make a selection, any previous selection is canceled.

Figure 11-20: DemoList applet

16 Close the AppletViewer window.

The List class provides users with the option of making concurrent multiple selections. For example, the user can choose to have both streamers and balloons at an event. Next, you will modify the DemoList applet so that the List accepts multiple selections.

To create a List that accepts multiple selections:

1 Return to the **DemoList.java** file in the Text Editor window, and then save it as **DemoList2**. Change the class name to **DemoList2**.

2 Enable the partyFavorList to accept multiple selections by changing the boolean value in the List constructor to `true`.

3 Because the user can select several items from the List, you must alter the paint() method to use the getSelectedIndexes() method instead of the getSelectedIndex() method. When getSelectedIndexes() returns an array of numbers representing the selected items, you can use the numbers to access and accumulate the corresponding prices from the favorPrice array. Modify the statement `int favorNum = partyFavorList.getSelectedIndex();` so that it reads `int[] favorNums = partyFavorList.getSelectedIndexes();`.

4 Replace the line `totalPrice = favorPrice[favorNum];` with the following code:

```
totalPrice = 0;
for(int x = 0; x < favorNums.length; ++x)
    totalPrice += favorPrice[favorNums[x]];
```

> The expression `favorPrice[favorNums[x]];` uses one array element (the xth element) of the favorNums array as a subscript to access an element in another array (the favorPrice array). In place of `totalPrice += favorPrice[favorNums[x]];`, you can substitute two statements if doing so makes the logic clearer to you. The two statements are `int selection = favorNums[x];` and `totalPrice += favorPrice[selection];`.

5 Return to the **testDemoList.htm** file in the HTML Editor window. Change the `<APPLET CODE = "DemoList.class" WIDTH = 400 HEIGHT = 300>` statement so that it references **DemoList2.class**. Then save the HTML document as **testDemoList2.htm** in the DemoList folder in the Chapter.11 folder on your Student Disk.

6 Rebuild and save the project, and then test the applet by typing `jview /a testDemoList2.htm` at the command line. As you can see in Figure 11-21, now you can make multiple concurrent selections and see a total price that reflects the multiple selections. Click a List item once to select it, or click a selected item to deselect it.

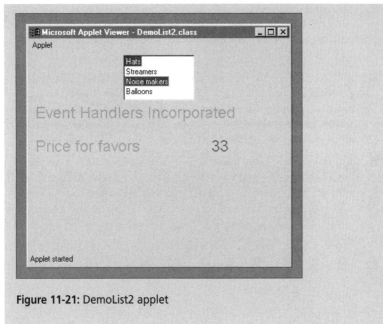

Figure 11-21: DemoList2 applet

7 Close the AppletViewer window.

SUMMARY

- The Component class is an abstract class; non-Container Component objects include Labels, Buttons, Checkboxes, Choices, Lists, and TextComponents.

- The major Component methods include those that get or set a Font size, a location, and colors for the Component, and those that set or determine whether the Component is enabled, visible, enabling, or showing.

- The Label class contains getText() and setText() methods; the Button class contains getLabel() and setLabel() methods.

- A Checkbox consists of a Label positioned beside a square; you can click the square to display or remove a check mark. Checkbox methods include those that set or get the Checkbox's Label, and set or get the Checkbox's state of checked or unchecked.

- The ItemListener interface provides for objects whose state changes from `true` to `false`. Using it requires that you write an itemStateChanged() method.

section B

- You can group several Checkboxes so that only one can be selected at a time, by using the CheckboxGroup class. The methods you use with the CheckboxGroup class include those that set a Checkbox in the group to `true` and that return the currently selected Checkbox.

- A Choice object displays an option; clicking the Choice list arrow displays a menu that contains other options. When the user selects an item in the menu, the selected item replaces the original item in the display. The Choice methods include ones that add an item to the Choice, and ones that select or return an item based on its name or on its position in the menu of Choices.

- A List is similar to a Choice, except that it displays all of the menu options. You can use a List to select multiple items. List class methods include ones that add and remove items, count items, select and deselect items, return the name of items, determine whether an item is selected, and enable the List to accept multiple selections.

QUESTIONS

1. Component classes include all of the following classes except _____.
   a. Object
   b. Label
   c. Choice
   d. Checkbox

2. Component methods include _____.
   a. getName()
   b. setComponent()
   c. isVisible()
   d. deleteComponent()

3. The method that changes the text displayed on a Button is _____.
   a. setText()
   b. setLabel()
   c. setButton()
   d. setName()

4. A Label positioned beside a square that you can click to display or remove a check mark is a _____.
   a. BallotBox
   b. Ballotbox
   c. CheckBox
   d. Checkbox

5. The Checkbox method getState() returns _____.
   a. void
   b. an integer value
   c. a boolean value
   d. a Checkbox object

6. Which of the following statements initializes a Checkbox with the Label "Choose Me"?
   a. Checkbox ChooseMe = new Checkbox();
   b. Checkbox aBox = new ChooseMe();
   c. Checkbox aBox = new Checkbox("Choose Me");
   d. Checkbox aBox = "Choose Me";

7. ItemListener is a(n) _____.
   a. method
   b. Container
   c. Component
   d. interface

8. When you use ItemListener, you must write a method named _____.
   a. itemMethod()
   b. itemStateChanged()
   c. actionPerformed()
   d. listenerActivated()

9. When you group Checkbox objects within a CheckboxGroup, all other Checkboxes automatically are _____ when the user selects a Checkbox.
   a. turned off
   b. turned on
   c. disabled
   d. enabled

10. Which of the following statements is true?
    a. You can create a CheckboxGroup and then create the individual Checkboxes.
    b. You can create Checkboxes and then create their CheckboxGroup.
    c. Both of these are true.
    d. Neither of these is true.

11. Given the statement Checkbox choc = new Checkbox("Chocolate",true,Flavors);, which of the following items is a CheckboxGroup?
    a. choc
    b. Chocolate
    c. Flavors
    d. None of these is a CheckboxGroup.

12. The method getSelectedCheckbox() returns _____.
    a. void
    b. a boolean value
    c. a Checkbox object
    d. a CheckboxGroup object

13. You need to write an applet for students to use to register for classes. Each student must select only one section of English Composition from among 20 numbered section choices. The best Component(s) to use is (are) _____.
    a. 20 Buttons
    b. 20 Checkboxes
    c. one CheckboxGroup
    d. one TextField

14. Clicking a Choice object results in _____.
    a. a check mark appearing on the screen
    b. an item being dimmed
    c. the display of a menu
    d. a Button becoming disabled

15. The Choice constructor takes _____ arguments.
    a. zero
    b. one
    c. two
    d. any number of

16. You _____ of the items in a Choice to be the initially selected item.
    a. must choose one
    b. can choose one
    c. must not choose any
    d. must choose the first

17. If the first item in a Choice named someChoices currently is selected, then the value of someChoices.getSelectedIndex() is _____.
    a. zero
    b. one
    c. true
    d. false

18. The differences between a Choice and a List include the fact that with a List, _____ of the user's options is (are) visible at the same time.
    a. none
    b. one
    c. some
    d. all

19. A user can make multiple selections from a _____.
    a. Choice
    b. List
    c. both of these
    d. none of these

EXERCISES

Save each of the programs that you create in the Chapter.11 folder on your Student Disk.

1. Write an applet named CarOptions for a car dealer. The applet uses a Checkbox so the user can choose as many options as he or she wants on a new car. The options include AM/FM stereo ($200), bucket seats ($300), air conditioning ($600), and sun roof ($1,000). Display a running total of the cost of the selected options.

2. Write an applet named NewHome for a construction company to handle a customer's order to build a new home. Use separate CheckboxGroups to allow the customer to select one of four models (the Aspen, $100,000; the Brittany, $120,000; the Colonial, $180,000; or the Dartmoor, $250,000), the number of bedrooms (two, three, or four; each bedroom adds $10,500), and a garage (no, one-, two-, or three-car; each car adds $7,775). Display the final home price.

3. Create a multiple-choice test question about any topic in this chapter. Write an applet that displays the question and offers the user a Choice of four answers. If the user selects the correct answer, display a congratulatory statement such as "Great!" If the user selects the wrong answer, encourage the user to try again. Name the applet MultipleChoice.

4. Write an applet named Video for a video store. Place the names of 10 of your favorite movies in a List. Let the user select those that he or she wants to rent. Charge $2.00 for most movies and $2.50 for your personal favorite movie. Display the total rental fee.

5. Design an order-form applet named Pizza for a pizzeria. The user makes choices, and the applet displays the price. The user can choose a pizza size of small ($7), medium ($9), large ($11), or extra large ($14), and any number of toppings. There is no additional charge for cheese, but all other toppings add $1 each to the base price. You can choose the toppings that are available, but you must offer at least five different toppings. Your applet can use any appropriate Components.

6. Write a program that allows the user to choose team names that represent opponents in games the user wants to attend. For example, the user might want to select the Packers and Cowboys, but not the Bears. Put at least five team names in a list box, allow the user to select any number, and then display the selected teams.

7. Write a program that allows the user to choose insurance options in Checkboxes. Use a CheckboxGroup for HMO (health maintenance organization) and PPO (preferred provider organization) options; the user can select only one option. Use regular Checkboxes for dental and vision options; the user can select one option, both options, or neither option.

8. Write a program that allows the user to select options for a dormitory room. Use Checkboxes for the options such as private room, Internet connection, cable TV connection, microwave, refrigerator, and so on.

9. Each of the following files in the Chapter.11 folder on your Student Disk has syntax and/or logical errors. Add the files to a new project called FixDebug. Save the FixDebug project under the Chapter.11 folder on your Student Disk. You can test each of these applets with the testDebug.htm file on the Student Disk. Remember to change the Java class file referenced in the HTML file so it matches the DebugEleven applet you are working on.
   a. DebugEleven1.java
   b. DebugEleven2.java
   c. DebugEleven3.java
   d. DebugEleven4.java

CHAPTER 12

Using Layout Managers and the Event Model

case ▶ You have been developing Java applets and applications at Event Handlers Incorporated for several months now. "I've learned so much, yet there's so much more to learn." you say to Lynn Greenbrier one day. "Sometimes I look at an applet I've created and think how far I have come; other times I realize I barely have a start in the Java programming language."

"Go on," Lynn urges. "What do you need to know more about right now?"

"Well, I wish I knew an easier way to place Components accurately within applets," you say. "I'd like to be able to create more complex applets, and the one thing I'm really confused about is handling events. You've tried to teach me about 'registering,' 'listening,' and 'handling,' but I don't yet have the big picture."

"Event handling is a complicated system," Lynn says. "Let's see if I can help you organize it in your mind."

Previewing the Chap12Applet Project

Event Handlers Incorporated is developing an applet that the user can manipulate to uncover an advertising slogan. The user passes the mouse over different regions of the applet surface, individually revealing three colored panels. The user can reveal one-third of the advertising slogan at a time by clicking one of the colored panels. The user also can reposition each slogan segment within its panel area by clicking the mouse in a new position. In this chapter, you will learn about the techniques used to create this applet. Now you can run the finished version of the applet that is saved on your Student Disk.

To run Chap12Applet:

1 Go to the command prompt for the Chap12Applet folder in the Chapter.12 folder on your Student Disk, type **jview /a Chap12Test.htm** at the command prompt, and then press the **Enter** key. After the AppletViewer window opens, you see the prompt, "Roll and click above.", in the lower center of the applet.

2 Roll your mouse across the top half of the applet, revealing each of three colored panels one at a time. When your mouse leaves an area, it goes dark; when your mouse enters a new area, it lights up.

3 When any one of the three colored panels is "on," click the mouse. Depending on the exact position of your mouse, you will see all or part of a slogan segment. If the words within a panel are obscured partially, as shown in Figure 12-1, click the mouse in a new position on the panel; the slogan segment will relocate to that position.

Using Layout Managers and the Event Model

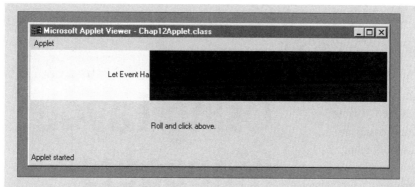

Figure 12-1: Chap12Applet in which the slogan is partially obscured

4 Close the AppletViewer window.

5 You can examine the code used to create the applet by opening the **Chap12Applet** project in Visual J++, then by opening the **Chap12Applet.java** and **Chap12Panel.java** files in the Text Editor window.

SECTION A
objectives

In this section you will learn

- About layout managers
- How to use BorderLayout
- How to use FlowLayout
- How to use GridLayout
- How to use Panels
- About advanced layout managers

Using Layout Managers

When you add more than one or two Components to a Frame, Applet, or any other Container, you can spend a lot of time computing exactly where to place each Component so that the layout is attractive and no Component is obscuring another one, or you can use a layout manager. A **layout manager** is an interface class that aligns your Components so they neither crowd each other nor overlap. For example, one layout manager arranges Components in equally spaced columns and rows; another layout manager centers Components within their Container.

Within the applets you have written, you have been using layout managers without realizing it because every Container (or descendant of the Container class) is associated with an automatic, or default, layout manager. Rather than using the default layout manager, you can explicitly assign an alternative layout manager to any Container you instantiate. Each layout manager defines methods that arrange Components within a Container, and each Component you place within a Container also can be a Container itself, so you actually can assign layout managers within layout managers. The following layout managers are the three most used ones:

- BorderLayout (the default for Window, Frame, and Dialog objects)
- FlowLayout (the default for Panel objects, including applets)
- GridLayout

Using BorderLayout

You can use the BorderLayout class with any Container that has five or fewer Components. (However, any of the Components can be a Container that holds even more Components.) The Components fill the screen in five regions named North, South, East, West, and Center. Figure 12-2 shows five Button objects filling the five regions in an applet.

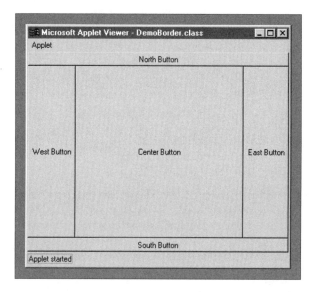

Figure 12-2: Positions using BorderLayout

When you place exactly five Components in a Container and use BorderLayout, each Component fills one entire region, as shown in Figure 12-2. When the program runs, the compiler determines the exact size of each Component based on the Component's contents. When you resize a Container that uses BorderLayout, the regions change in size. If you drag the Container's border to make the Container wider, then the North, South, and Center regions become wider, but the East and West regions do not change. If you increase the Container's height, then the East, West, and Center regions become taller, but the North and South regions do not change.

When you create a Container, you can set its layout manager to BorderLayout with the statement `setLayout(new BorderLayout());`. For example, if you create a Frame with the code `Frame aFrame = new Frame;`, then you can set the aFrame's layout manager with `aFrame.setLayout(new BorderLayout());`.

If you create a class derived from Frame, such as one named FancyFrame, then you can set the layout manager for a particular FancyFrame with a program that uses a FancyFrame object, as follows:

```
FancyFrame aNiceFrame = new FancyFrame();
aNiceFrame.setLayout(new BorderLayout());
```

Alternatively, you can set the layout manager for the new FancyFrame class within the class constructor, as follows:

```
public class FancyFrame extends Frame
{
  public FancyFrame(String str)
  {
    super(str);
    addWindowListener(this);
    setLayout(new BorderLayout());
  }
```

Remember, the statement setLayout(new BorderLayout()); actually means this.setLayout(new BorderLayout()); because this refers to "this" FancyFrame object.

When you use the add() method to add a Component to a Container that uses BorderLayout, you use one of the five area names to specify the region of the Container where the Component should be placed. For example, add(someButton, "South"); places the someButton object in the South region of this Container (whatever the current Container is), and aNiceFrame.add(someCheckbox, "East"); adds someCheckbox to the East region of aNiceFrame.

Next, you will place five Buttons into the five regions of an Applet with BorderLayout. Remember from Chapter 11 that an Applet is a child of the Panel class, which derives from the Container class, so an Applet is a Container and therefore can use a layout manager.

To create an applet that uses BorderLayout:

1 Create a new empty project named **DemoBorder**. Save the **DemoBorder** project folder in the Chapter.12 folder on your Student Disk.

2 Add a new class file to the project by selecting **Add Class** from the **Project** menu. The Add Item dialog box appears. In the Add Item dialog box, select **Class** from the **Class** folder, then change the suggested filename to **DemoBorder.java** and click the **Open** button. The new class opens in the Text Editor window.

3 Above the class header, type the following import statements that you will need for the program:

```
import java.applet.*;
import java.awt.*;
```

4 Add **extends Applet** to the right of the class header.

5 Between the class's curly brackets, enter the following lines to create five Buttons:

```
private Button nb = new Button("North Button");
private Button sb = new Button("South Button");
private Button eb = new Button("East Button");
private Button wb = new Button("West Button");
private Button cb = new Button("Center Button");
```

6 Enter the following code to create the init() method in which you will set the layout manager to BorderLayout:

```
public void init()
{
setLayout(new BorderLayout());
```

7 Next, enter the following code to add the five Buttons to the five regions:

```
add(nb,"North");
add(sb,"South");
add(eb,"East");
add(wb,"West");
add(cb,"Center");
```

8 For this demonstration program, the Buttons are not functional, so there is no need to use the addActionListener() method or to write any other methods. Add a closing curly bracket for the init() method.

9 Add to the project a new Web page named **testBorder.htm**.

10 In the Source tab of the HTML Editor window, place the insertion point in the blank line following the tag that reads <P> </P> and type the opening <APPLET> tag that contains the applet's name and dimensions: **<APPLET CODE = "DemoBorder.class" WIDTH = 400 HEIGHT = 300>**.

11 Press the **Enter** key to start a new line and type the applet's closing tag: **</APPLET>**.

12 Build and save the project, then execute the program in AppletViewer by typing **jview /a testBorder.htm** at the command line to observe the effects of BorderLayout. Your applet should look similar to Figure 12-2, which appears earlier in this chapter.

13 Use the mouse to manipulate the applet borders to make the applet frame wider, narrower, taller, and shorter so you can observe the effect on the sizes of the five regions.

14 Close the AppletViewer window.

section A

When you use BorderLayout with a Container, you are not required to add five Components. If you add fewer Components, any empty Component regions disappear and the remaining Components expand to fill the available space. Next, you will remove a Component from a Container that uses BorderLayout so you can observe the effect.

To create a Container that uses BorderLayout and only four objects:

1 Return to the **DemoBorder.java** file in the Text Editor window and save it as **DemoBorderNoNorth.java**.
2 Change the class name from DemoBorder to **DemoBorderNoNorth**.
3 Comment out the line that declares the North Button (`private Button nb = new Button("North Button");`), by typing two forward slashes (*//*) in front of the line.
4 Within the init() method, comment out the statement that adds the North Button to the applet (`add(nb,"North");`) by typing two forward slashes (*//*) in front of the statement.
5 Return to the **testBorder.htm** file in the HTML Editor window and change the Applet reference from DemoBorder.class to **DemoBorderNoNorth.class**, and then save the file as **testBorderNoNorth.htm**.
6 Rebuild and save the project, then execute the program in AppletViewer by typing `jview /a testBorderNoNorth.htm` at the command line. The output looks like Figure 12-3. Notice that there are only four Components in this Applet and that none has been assigned to the North region. The four Components simply expand their sizes to fit the space.

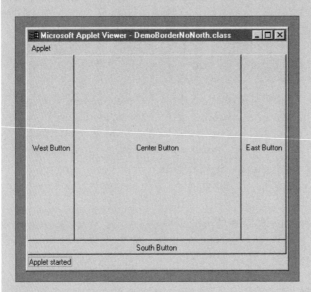

Figure 12-3: DemoBorderNoNorth applet

Close the AppletViewer window.

7 Experiment with removing additional and different Components in the **DemoBorderNoNorth.java** file. Observe the results when you run the applet using AppletViewer.

Using FlowLayout

You can use the FlowLayout class to arrange Components in rows across the width of a Container. Each Component that you add is placed to the right of previously added Components. When there isn't enough room in a row, the next Component wraps around to a new row in much the same way that the words you type wrap to a new line when you use a word processing program.

When you use BorderLayout, the Components you add fill their region. However, when you use FlowLayout, each Component retains its "natural" size; for example, a Button will be large enough to hold its text, but no larger. When you use BorderLayout, if you resize the window, the Components change size accordingly. With FlowLayout, when you resize the window, each Component retains its size, but it might become partially obscured or change position.

To create an applet that demonstrates FlowLayout's appearance:

1 Return to the **DemoBorder.java** file in the Text Editor window and save it as **DemoFlow.java**.

2 Change the class name from DemoBorder to **DemoFlow**.

3 Within the init() method, change the setLayout() statement to `setLayout(new FlowLayout());`.

4 Add to the project a new Web page named **testFlow.htm**.

5 In the Source tab of the HTML Editor window, place the insertion point in the blank line following the tag that reads `<P> </P>` and type the opening `<APPLET>` tag that contains the applet's name and dimensions: `<APPLET CODE = "DemoFlow.class" WIDTH = 350 HEIGHT = 150>`.

6 Press the **Enter** key to start a new line and type the applet's closing tag: `</APPLET>`.

7 Rebuild and save the project, then execute the program in AppletViewer by typing `jview /a testFlow.htm` at the command line. Your output should look like Figure 12-4. (Your output may appear differently, depending on your system configuration.)

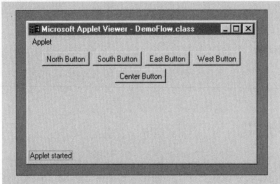

Figure 12-4: DemoFlow applet

8 Experiment with widening and narrowing the AppletViewer window and observe how the Components realign themselves.

9 Close the AppletViewer window.

When you create a FlowLayout object, Components automatically are centered within their assigned Container. Alternatively, you can pass an argument to the constructor indicating whether you want the Components to be left-, right-, or center-aligned. To set the alignment, you use one of three constants that are fields of the FlowLayout class: `FlowLayout.LEFT`, `FlowLayout.RIGHT`, or `FlowLayout.CENTER`. For example, within an applet, the statement `setLayout(new FlowLayout(FlowLayout.LEFT));` ensures that Components will be placed left to right across the applet until the first row is full, at which point a second row will be started at the applet's left edge.

To create an Applet that demonstrates a right FlowLayout:

1 Return to the **DemoFlow.java** file in the Text Editor window and save it as **DemoFlowRight.java**.

2 Change the class name from DemoFlow to **DemoFlowRight**.

3 Within the init() method, change the setLayout() method call to `setLayout(new FlowLayout(FlowLayout.RIGHT));`.

4 Return to the **testFlow.htm** in the HTML Editor window, change the Applet reference to **DemoFlowRight.class**, and then save the file as **testFlowRight.htm**.

5 Rebuild and save the project, then execute the program in AppletViewer by typing `jview /a testFlowRight.htm` at the command line. Compare your output to Figure 12-5. Change the AppletViewer window border and observe the effect on the Components. (Your output may appear differently, depending on your system configuration.)

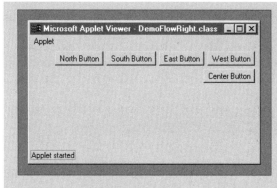

Figure 12-5: DemoFlowRight applet

6 Close the AppletViewer window.

Using GridLayout

If you want to arrange Components into equal rows and columns, you use the **GridLayout class**. When you create a GridLayout object, you indicate the numbers of rows and columns you want, and the Container surface is divided into a grid, much like the screen you see when using a spreadsheet program. For example, the statement `setLayout(new GridLayout(4,5));` establishes a GridLayout with four horizontal rows and five vertical columns.

> You specify rows first, and then columns, which is the same technique you used when specifying two-dimensional arrays in Chapter 6.

As you add new Components to a GridLayout, they are positioned left to right across each row in sequence. You can't skip a position or specify an exact position for a Component. You can specify zero for either the row or column parameter, which will provide an unlimited number of rows or columns.

To demonstrate GridLayout:

1 Open the **DemoBorder.java** file in your text editor, and immediately save the file as **DemoGrid.java**.

2 Change the class name from DemoBorder to **DemoGrid**.

3 Within the init() method, change the setLayout() method call to establish a GridLayout with two rows and three columns: `setLayout(new GridLayout(2,3));`.

4 Return to the **testBorder.htm** file in the HTML Editor window, change the applet reference to **DemoGrid.class**, and then save the file as **testGrid.htm**.

section A

5 Rebuild and save the project, then execute the program in AppletViewer by typing `jview /a testGrid.htm` at the command line. Compare your output to Figure 12-6. The Components are arranged in two rows and three columns. Because there are only five Components, one grid position still is available.

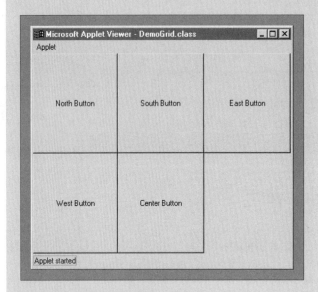

Figure 12-6: DemoGrid applet

6 Close the AppletViewer window.

Using Panels

Using the BorderLayout, FlowLayout, and GridLayout managers provides a limited number of screen arrangements. You can increase the number of possible Component arrangements by using the Panel class. A Panel is similar to a Window in that a Panel is a surface on which you can place Components. But a Panel is *not* a Window; it is a sibling of a Window, as shown in Figure 12-7.

Using Layout Managers and the Event Model

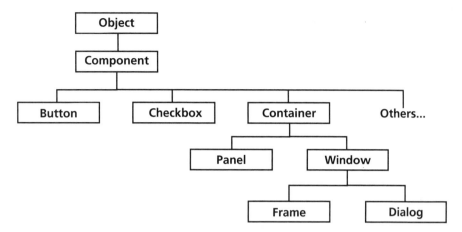

Figure 12-7: Relationship of Panel and Window

A Panel is a Container, which means that it can contain other Components. For example, you can create an applet using BorderLayout and place a Panel in each region. Then within the North Panel, you can place four Buttons using GridLayout, and within the East Panel, you can place three Labels using FlowLayout. By using Panels within Panels, you can create an infinite variety of screen layouts.

Java programmers sometimes refer to Windows and Frames as *top-level* windows. Panels are not top-level; they exist within a Frame or Window.

Every Applet is a Panel. When you create an applet, the AppletViewer window or browser window is the top-level window; your applet is just a Panel displayed in the window.

When you create a Panel object, you can use one of two constructors:

- Panel(), if you want to use the default layout manager, FlowLayout
- Panel(LayoutManager layout), if you want to specify a layout manager

Next, you will create an applet that uses a layout manager and contains a Panel that uses a different layout manager. To begin, you will create one Panel named WesternPanel that holds Buttons indicating the states in which Event Handlers Incorporated does business. Using GridLayout, you will place three Buttons in this Panel to represent three states. When the user clicks a Button, the applet displays the locations of Event Handlers offices in that state. For simplicity, you will activate only one of the three Buttons now.

section A

To create the WesternPanel object:

1 Create a new empty project named **DemoRegion**. Save the **DemoRegion** project folder in the Chapter.12 folder on your Student Disk.

2 Add to the project a new class file named **WesternPanel.java**.

3 Above the class header, type the following import statements that you will need for the program:

```
import java.applet.*;
import java.awt.*;
import java.awt.event.*;
```

4 The WesternPanel class extends Panel and implements ActionListener because the Panel will contain a clickable Button. Add **extends Panel implements ActionListener** to the right of the class header.

5 Enter the following code between the class's curly brackets to create four Components: three Buttons for the three Western states in which Event Handlers operates and a Label:

```
Button wyButton = new Button("Wyoming");
Button coButton = new Button("Colorado");
Button nvButton = new Button("Nevada");
Label infoLabel = new Label("Location Info");
```

6 The following constructor for the WesternPanel sets the layout manager to GridLayout using two rows and two columns. Add the Wyoming Button to the grid, and because you want users to be able to click the Wyoming Button, register the Applet as an ActionListener for this Button. Add the other Buttons and the Label to the grid. For now, these Components are not clickable, so don't use the addActionListener() method with them.

```
public WesternPanel()
{
   setLayout(new GridLayout(2,2));
   add(wyButton);
   wyButton.addActionListener(this);
   add(coButton);
   add(nvButton);
   add(infoLabel);
}
```

Using Layout Managers and the Event Model

7 When the user clicks the Wyoming Button (which is the only active Button), the following actionPerformed() method executes. This method displays the name of the Wyoming location for Event Handlers Incorporated, which is Cody.

```
public void actionPerformed(ActionEvent e)
{
   infoLabel.setText("Cody");
}
```

You just created a Panel with three Buttons and a Label in a GridLayout. Now you will create an applet that uses the WesternPanel in one of the regions of the applet's BorderLayout.

To write an applet that uses the WesternRegion Panel:

1 Add to the project a new class file named **DemoRegion.java**.

2 Above the class header, type the following import statements that you will need for the program:

```
import java.applet.*;
import java.awt.*;
import java.awt.event.*;
```

3 Add **extends Applet** to the right of the class header.

4 Add the following five Panel objects between the class's curly brackets. Four of the Panels will be simple Panel objects; one will be a WesternPanel.

```
Panel np = new Panel();
Panel sp = new Panel();
Panel ep = new Panel();
Panel cp = new Panel();
WesternPanel wp = new WesternPanel();
```

5 Create the following labeled Buttons, one for each of the four non-Western Panels:

```
private Button nb = new Button("North Button");
private Button sb = new Button("South Button");
private Button eb = new Button("East Button");
private Button cb = new Button("Center Button");
```

6 Enter the following init() method, which sets the applet's layout manager to BorderLayout and adds one Component to each of the five BorderLayout regions. The Components for the North, South, East, and Center regions are Buttons. The Component for the Western region is a WesternPanel that contains three Buttons and its own Label.

```
public void init()
{
setLayout(new BorderLayout());
   add(nb,"North");
   add(sb,"South");
   add(eb,"East");
   add(wp,"West");
   add(cb,"Center");
}
```

7 Add to the project a new Web page named **testRegion.htm**.

8 In the Source tab of the HTML Editor window, place the insertion point in the blank line following the tag that reads <P> </P> and type the opening <APPLET> tag that contains the applet's name and dimensions: **<APPLET CODE = "DemoRegion.class" WIDTH = 550 HEIGHT = 150>**.

9 Press the **Enter** key to start a new line and type the applet's closing tag: **</APPLET>**.

10 Build and save the project, then run the applet in AppletViewer by typing **jview /a testRegion.htm** at the command line. Your output should look like Figure 12-8.

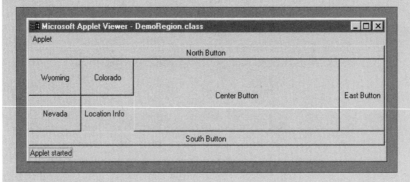

Figure 12-8: DemoRegion applet

11 Click the North, South, Center, and East Buttons. Nothing happens, because you have not activated these Buttons. Similarly, in the West region, click the Colorado and Nevada Buttons; again, no actions result. However, when you click the Wyoming Button, the Label within the Western Panel displays *Cody*, the city name of the Wyoming Event Handlers location.

12 Close the AppletViewer window.

Advanced Layout Managers

As with Components, Java programmers currently are creating new layout managers. You are certain to encounter new and interesting layout managers during your programming career; you even might create your own. Information about more complicated layout managers is available in the Visual J++ documentation. You can also find more information on layout managers at the Web sites and in the newsgroups listed at the end of Chapter 7.

When GridLayout is not sophisticated enough for your purposes, you can use GridBagLayout. The **GridBagLayout class** allows you to add Components to precise locations within the grid, as well as to indicate that specific Components should span multiple rows or columns within the grid. For example, if you want to create a Panel with six Buttons, in which two of the Buttons are twice as wide as the others, you can use GridBagLayout. This class is difficult to use because you must set the position and size for each Component.

The **CardLayout class** allows you to arrange Components as if they are stacked like index or playing cards. Only one Component is visible at a time. You can use methods such as next(), previous(), first(), and last() to display specific cards in the stack.

If you use a `null` layout manager, as in `setLayout(null);`, then you must use the Component class methods setBounds(), setSize(), and setLocation() to position your Components. You would use the null layout manager if you needed a complicated layout design that you could not achieve by using the existing layout managers, or if you wanted to create a new layout manager.

SUMMARY

- A layout manager is an interface class that is part of Java. A layout manager aligns your Components so they neither crowd each other nor overlap.

- Every Container is associated with an automatic, or default, layout manager. Alternatively, you can explicitly assign an alternative layout manager to any Container you instantiate.

- The three most used layout managers are BorderLayout (the default for Window, Frame, and Dialog objects), FlowLayout (the default for Panel objects, which includes applets), and GridLayout.

- You can use the BorderLayout class with any Container that has five or fewer Components. The Components fill the screen in five regions named North, South, East, West, and Center. The compiler determines the exact size of each Component based on the Component's contents.

- When you create a Container, you can set its layout manager using the setLayout() method.

- When you use BorderLayout with a Container and you add fewer than five Components, any empty regions disappear.

- You can use the FlowLayout class to arrange Components in rows across the width of a Container.

- When you use FlowLayout, each Component retains its "natural" size and automatically is centered within its assigned Container.

- You can pass an argument to the FlowLayout constructor to indicate whether you want the Components to be left-, right-, or center-aligned.

- You use the GridLayout class to arrange Components into equal rows and columns. As you add new Components to a GridLayout, they are positioned left to right across each row in sequence.

- A Panel is similar to a Window in that a Panel is a surface on which you can place Components. A Panel is a Container, which means it can contain other Components.

- By using Panels within Panels, you can create an infinite variety of screen layouts.

- When you create a Panel object, you can use one of two constructors: Panel(), if you want to use the default layout manager, FlowLayout; or Panel(LayoutManager layout), if you want to specify a layout manager.

- The GridBagLayout class allows you to add Components to precise locations within the grid, as well as to indicate that specific Components should span multiple rows or columns within the grid.

- The CardLayout class allows you to arrange Components as if they were stacked like index or playing cards. Only one Component is visible at a time.

- If you use a `null` layout manager, as in `setLayout(null);`, then you must use the Component class methods setBounds(), setSize(), and setLocation() to position your Components.

QUESTIONS

1. An interface class that aligns Components so they neither crowd each other nor overlap is a(n) _____ manager.
   a. component
   b. alignment
   c. gridbag
   d. layout

2. Every _____ is associated with a default layout manager.
   a. Object
   b. Component
   c. Container
   d. class

3. The three most used layout managers include all of the following layout managers *except* _____.
   a. BorderLayout
   b. FlowLayout
   c. CurveLayout
   d. GridLayout

4. The default layout manager for applets is _____.
   a. BorderLayout
   b. FlowLayout
   c. CurveLayout
   d. GridLayout

5. At most, you can place _____ Components in a Container that uses BorderLayout.
   a. one
   b. three
   c. five
   d. seven

6. Which of the following areas is a BorderLayout region?
   a. South
   b. Bottom
   c. Under
   d. Region2

7. When you resize a Container that uses BorderLayout, _____.
   a. the Container and the regions both change in size
   b. the Container changes in size, but the regions retain their original sizes
   c. the Container retains its size, but the regions change or might disappear
   d. nothing happens

8. When you create a Frame named myFrame, you can set its layout manager to BorderLayout with the statement _____.
   a. myFrame.setLayout = new BorderLayout();
   b. myFrame.setLayout(new BorderLayout());
   c. setLayout(myFrame = new BorderLayout());
   d. setLayout(BorderLayout(myFrame));

9. If an executing program contains the statement add(aLittleComponent, "East");, then the Container with aLittleComponent must be using _____.
   a. FlowLayout
   b. BorderLayout
   c. RegionLayout
   d. DirectionalLayout

10. You can use the _____ class to arrange Components in rows across the width of a Container.
    a. FlowLayout
    b. BorderLayout
    c. RowLayout
    d. RegionLayout

11. When you use a _____, the Components you add fill their region; they do not retain their "natural" size.
    a. FlowLayout
    b. BorderLayout
    c. FixedLayout
    d. RegionLayout

12. The statement _____ ensures that Components will be placed left to right across the applet surface until the first row is full, at which point a second row will be started at the applet surface's left edge.
    a. setLayout(FlowLayout.LEFT);
    b. setLayout(new FlowLayout(LEFT));
    c. setLayout(new FlowLayout(FlowLayout.LEFT));
    d. setLayout(FlowLayout(FlowLayout.LEFT));

13. You use the _____ class to arrange Components into equal rows and columns.
    a. BorderLayout
    b. FlowLayout
    c. BoxLayout
    d. GridLayout

14. The statement `setLayout(new GridLayout(2,7));` establishes a GridLayout with _____ horizontal row(s).
    a. zero
    b. one
    c. two
    d. seven

15. As you add new Components to a GridLayout, _____.
    a. they are positioned left to right across each row in sequence
    b. you can specify exact positions by skipping some positions
    c. both of these
    d. neither of these

16. A Panel is a _____.
    a. Window
    b. Container
    c. both of these
    d. neither of these

17. The default layout manager for the Panel class is _____.
    a. FlowLayout
    b. GridLayout
    c. BorderLayout
    d. null Layout

18. The _____ class allows you to arrange Components as if they are stacked like index or playing cards.
    a. GameLayout
    b. CardLayout
    c. IndexLayout
    d. StackLayout

19. If you want to invent a new layout manager, you use _____ layout.
    a. Object
    b. void
    c. null
    d. a default

EXERCISES

Save each of the programs that you create in the following exercises in the Chapter.12 folder on your Student Disk.

1. Create a Frame named PoliticalFrame and set the layout to BorderLayout. Place a Button containing the name of a politician in each region (left, center, and right, or West, Center, and East). Each politician's physical position should correspond to your opinion of his or her political stance.

2. Create 16 Buttons, each labeled with a single letter of the alphabet. Create an applet named TwoByTwo that has four panels in a two-by-two grid, and place four of the Buttons within each Panel of the applet.

3. Modify the DemoRegion class you created in this section so the user can choose Northern states instead of Western states. Activate one of the Northern state Buttons. Name the new class DemoNorth.

4. Write a Java application that displays a list of at least 10 items in a store in a Frame. Allow the user to choose any number of items from the list. Display the items that the user chooses.

5. Write a program that displays a list of college courses with days and starting times, for example, "Java, Mon., 5:30 p.m." Allow the user to select any number of courses. Display the courses that the user chooses.

6. Write a program that displays a list of computer terminology (specific hardware items, different operating systems, languages, applications, and so on). Allow the user to choose the items with which he or she has experience. Display the items that the user selects.

SECTION B
objectives

In this lesson you will learn
- More about events and event handling
- How to use the AWTEvent class methods
- How to use event methods from higher in the inheritance hierarchy
- How to handle mouse events

Using Events

Understanding Events and Event Handling

You already have worked with many events in the programs you have written. Beginning in Chapter 7, you learned how to create applets that contain widgets that are controlled by user-initiated events. Now that you understand inheritance and abstract classes, you can take a deeper look at event handling and generalize your knowledge.

Like all Java classes, events are Objects. Specifically, they are Objects that the user initiates, such as keypresses and mouse clicks. Many events that occur have significance only for specific components within a program. For example, you have written programs, as well as used programs written by others, in which pressing the Enter key or double-clicking a specific Component has no effect. Other events have meaning outside your program; for example, clicking the Close button in the AppletViewer window sends a message to the operating system that your computer uses to close the window and stop the program.

The parent class for all event objects is named EventObject, which descends from the Object class. EventObject is the parent of AWTEvent, which in turn is the parent to specific event classes such as ActionEvent and ComponentEvent. Figure 12-9 illustrates these relationships.

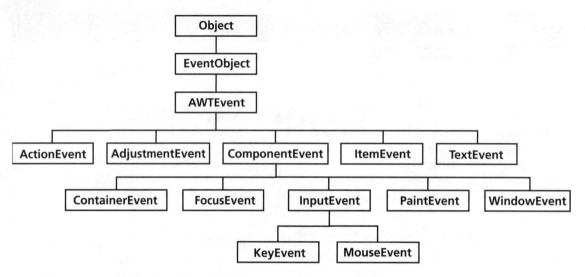

Figure 12-9: Relationships among event classes

The abstract class AWTEvent is contained in the package java.awt.event.

You can see in Figure 12-9 that ComponentEvent is itself a parent to several event classes, including InputEvent, which is parent to KeyEvent and MouseEvent. The family tree for events is fairly deep, but the class names are straightforward and they share basic roles within your programs. For example, ActionEvents pertain to Components, such as Buttons and Checkboxes, that users can click and TextEvents pertain to Components, such as a TextField, into which the user enters text. MouseEvents include determining the location of the mouse and distinguishing between a single- and double-click. Figure 12-10 lists some common user actions and the events that are generated from them.

Because ActionEvents involve the mouse, it is easy to confuse ActionEvents and MouseEvents. If you are interested in ActionEvents, you are interested in changes in a Component; if you are interested in MouseEvents, the focus is on what the user has done manually with the mouse equipment.

Using Layout Managers and the Event Model

User Action	Resulting Event Type
Click a Button	ActionEvent
Move the mouse over a Component	MouseEvent
Click an item in a Choice	ItemEvent
Click an item in a Checkbox	ItemEvent
Change text in a TextField	TextEvent
Open a window	WindowEvent
Iconify a window	WindowEvent
Type a key	KeyEvent

Figure 12-10: Examples of user actions and their resulting event types

When you write programs with GUI interfaces, you are always handling events that originate with the mouse or keys on specific Components or Containers. Just as your telephone notifies you when you have a call, your computer's operating system notifies your program when an AWTEvent occurs, such as when the user clicks the mouse. Just as you can ignore your telephone when you're not expecting or interested in a call, your program can ignore AWTEvents. If you don't care about an event, such as when your program contains a Component on which clicking should have no effect, your program simply ignores the message.

There is no class named Event; the general event class is AWTEvent.

When you care about events—that is, when you *want* to listen for an event—you can implement an appropriate interface for your class, such as ActionListener or WindowListener. For example, `public class someClass implements WindowListener` registers someClass so that it receives notice when any WindowEvent takes place. In this example, someClass becomes known as an event listener; someClass "listens" for events. (You first learned about event listeners in Chapter 7.) Each event class shown in Figure 12-9 has a listener interface associated with it so that for every event class named xxxEvent, there is a listener named xxxListener.

Don't forget that interfaces, such as ActionListener and WindowListener, contain only abstract methods, which means that all interface methods are empty. If you implement a listener, you must provide your own methods for all the methods that are part of the interface. Of course, you might leave the methods empty in your implementation.

tip

Every class xxxEvent has an xxxListener. The MouseEvent class has an additional listener, the MouseMotionListener.

Every xxxListener interface method has return type `void`, and each takes one argument—an object that is an instance of the corresponding xxxEvent class. Thus, the ActionListener interface has a method named actionPerformed(), and its header is `void actionPerformed(ActionEvent e)`. When an action takes place, the actionPerformed() method executes, and e represents an instance of that event. Interface methods, such as actionPerformed(), that are called automatically when an appropriate event occurs are called **event handlers**.

Recall that instead of implementing a listener, you can extend an adapter class, such as WindowAdapter. The adapter classes implement the listener classes and provide empty methods for all the listener methods. When you extend the adapter, you don't have to write all the methods from the original listener. Instead, you need to write only the methods for which you want to provide a specific action.

tip

If a listener has only one method, there is no need for an adapter. For example, the ActionListener class has one method, actionPerformed( ), so there is no ActionAdapter class.

Whether you use a listener or an adapter, you create an event handler when you write code for the listener methods; that is, you are telling your class how to handle the event. After you create the handler, you also must register an instance of the class with the Component that you want the event to affect. For any xxxListener, the method that registers a class instance with a Component is addxxxListener(). The addxxxListener() methods, such as addActionListener() and addItemListener(), all work the same way. They all register a listener with a Component, return `void`, and take an xxxListener object as an argument. For example, if an applet is an ActionListener and contains a Button named pushMe, then within the applet, `pushMe.addActionListener(this);` registers this particular applet as a listener for the pushMe Button. Figure 12-11 lists the events with their listeners and handlers.

Using Layout Managers and the Event Model

Event	Listener	Handler(s)
ActionEvent	ActionListener	actionPerformed(ActionEvent)
ItemEvent	ItemListener	itemStateChanged(ItemEvent)
TextEvent	TextListener	textValueChanged(TextEvent)
AdjustmentEvent	AdjustmentListener	adjustmentValueChanged(AdjustmentEvent)
ContainerEvent	ContainerListener	componentAdded(ContainerEvent)
		ComponentRemoved(ContainerEvent)
ComponentEvent	ComponentListener	componentMoved(ComponentEvent)
		componentHidden(ComponentEvent)
		componentResized(ComponentEvent)
		componentShown(ComponentEvent)
FocusEvent	FocusListener	focusGained(FocusEvent)
		focusLost(FocusEvent)
MouseEvent	MouseListener	mousePressed(MouseEvent)
		mouseReleased(MouseEvent)
		mouseEntered(MouseEvent)
		mouseExited(MouseEvent)
		mouseClicked(MouseEvent)
	MouseMotionListener	mouseDragged(MouseEvent)
		mouseMoved(mouseEvent)
KeyEvent	KeyListener	keyPressed(KeyEvent)
		keyTyped(KeyEvent)
		keyReleased(KeyEvent)
WindowEvent	WindowListener	windowActivated(WindowEvent)
		windowClosing(WindowEvent)
		windowClosed(WindowEvent)
		windowDeiconified(WindowEvent)
		windowIconified(WindowEvent)
		windowOpened(WindowEvent)

Figure 12-11: Events, their listeners, and their handlers

Next, you will create a class that implements KeyListener. You use the KeyListener interface when you are interested in actions the user initiates from the keyboard. The KeyListener interface contains three methods: keyPressed(), keyTyped(), and keyReleased(). For most keyboard applications in which the user must type a keyboard key, it is probably not important whether you take resulting action when a user first presses a key, during the keypress, or upon the key's release; most likely these events occur in quick sequence. However, on those occasions when you don't want to take action while the user holds down the key, you can place the actions in the keyReleased() method.

It is best to use the keyTyped() method when you want to discover what character was typed. When the user presses what is sometimes called an **action key** (that is, a key, such as a function key, that does not generate a character), then keyTyped() does not execute. The methods keyPressed() and keyReleased() provide the only ways to find out about keys that don't generate characters.

Java programmers call keyTyped( ) events "higher level" because they do not depend on the platform or keyboard layout. In contrast, keyPressed( ) and keyReleased( ) events are "lower level" and depend on the platform and keyboard layout.

To create a class that implements KeyListener:

1 Create a new empty project named **KeyFrame**. Save the **KeyFrame** project folder in the Chapter.12 folder on your Student Disk.

2 Add to the project a new class file named **KeyFrame.java**.

3 Above the class header, type the following import statements that you will need for the program:

```
import java.awt.*;
import java.awt.event.*;
```

4 Add **extends Frame implements KeyListener** to the right of the class header.

To keep this example simple, you are not going to implement WindowListener with this Frame. Therefore, you will not be able to close the KeyFrame using the Close button in the upper-right corner of the KeyFrame.

5 Enter the following constructor between the class's curly brackets. The KeyFrame is a Frame, so you can use the Frame method, setTitle(), within the KeyFrame constructor. The following code also registers the Frame as a KeyListener.

```
public KeyFrame()
{
  setTitle("Key Frame");
  addKeyListener(this);
}
```

6 The following keyPressed() method is one of the three abstract methods contained in KeyListener. To prove that this method is activated when the user presses a key, send the simple message "pressed" to the command line.

```
public void keyPressed(KeyEvent e)
{
  System.out.println("pressed");
}
```

7 Similarly, implement the following keyTyped() method to print "typed" at the command prompt:

```
public void keyTyped(KeyEvent e)
{
  System.out.println("typed");
}
```

8 Implement the following keyReleased() method so it prints "released":

```
public void keyReleased(KeyEvent e)
{
  System.out.println("released");
}
```

9 To the project named KeyFrame, add a new main class file named **UseKeyFrame.java** whose only task is to create an instance of the KeyFrame class. Type the following code between the main() method's curly brackets:

```
KeyFrame kFrame = new KeyFrame();
kFrame.setSize(250,50);
kFrame.setVisible(true);
```

10 Build and save the project, then execute the program as a console application by typing **jview UseKeyFrame** at the command line. When the Frame appears on your screen, notice that it does not contain any TextAreas in which you can enter data. Even so, the KeyFrame is a KeyListener; when you type an alphabetic keyboard key, the command line displays three messages: "pressed", "typed", and "released". Figure 12-12 shows these messages. If you type a key that does not generate a character, such as F1 or Alt, you see "pressed" and "released", but not "typed". If you hold down a key, such as the Alt key, you can generate several "pressed" messages before receiving the "released" message.

Figure 12-12: Execution of the UseKeyFrame program

11 You cannot close the KeyFrame using the Close button because you didn't implement WindowListener and provide an implementation of the windowClosing() method. Therefore, you must click the command line and then press **Ctrl+C** to end the program.

Using AWTEvent Class Methods

In addition to the handler methods included with the event listener interfaces, the AWTEvent classes themselves contain methods. You use many of these methods to determine the nature of and the facts about the event in question. For example, the ComponentEvent class contains a getComponent() method that returns the Component that was involved in the event. When you create an application with several Components and use the getComponent() method, the getComponent() method allows you to determine which Component is generating the event. The WindowEvent class contains a similar method, getWindow(), that returns the Window that was the source of the event. Figure 12-13 lists some useful methods for many of the event classes.

All Components have the methods addComponentListener(), addFocusListener(), addMouseListener(), and addMouseMotionListener().

Class	Method	Purpose
EventObject	Object getSource()	Returns the Object involved in the event.
ComponentEvent	Component getComponent()	Returns the Component involved in the event.
WindowEvent	Window getWindow()	Returns the Window involved in the event.
ItemEvent	Object getItem()	Returns the Object that was selected or deselected.
ItemEvent	int getStateChange()	Returns an integer named ItemEvent.SELECTED or ItemEvent.DESELECTED.
InputEvent	int getModifiers()	Returns an integer to indicate which mouse button was clicked.
InputEvent	int getWhen()	Returns a time indicating when the event occurred.
InputEvent	boolean isAltDown()	Returns whether the Alt key was pressed when the event occurred.
InputEvent	boolean isControlDown()	Returns whether the Ctrl key was pressed when the event occurred.

Figure 12-13: Useful event class methods

Class	Method	Purpose
InputEvent	boolean isShiftDown()	Returns whether the Shift key was pressed when the event occurred.
KeyEvent	int getKeyChar()	Returns the Unicode character.
MouseEvent	int getClickCount()	Returns the number of mouse clicks; lets you identify the user's double-clicks.
MouseEvent	int getX()	Returns the x-coordinate of the mouse pointer.
MouseEvent	int getY()	Returns the y-coordinate of the mouse pointer.
MouseEvent	Point getPoint()	Returns the Point object that contains x- and y-coordinates.

Figure 12-13: Useful event class methods (continued)

You can call any of the methods listed in Figure 12-13 by using the object-dot-method format that you use with all class methods. For example, if you have an InputEvent named inEv, and an integer named modInt, then the statement `modInt = inEv.getModifiers();` is valid. You use the getModifiers() method with an InputEvent object, and you can assign the return value to an integer variable. Thus, when you use any of the handler methods from Figure 12-11, such as actionPerformed() or itemStateChanged(), they provide you with an appropriate event object, and you can use the event object within the handler method to obtain information. You simply add a dot and the desired method name from Figure 12-13.

Next, you will modify the KeyFrame class so it uses the getKeyChar() method with the KeyEvent object that is referenced in the keyReleased() handler method.

To use the getKeyChar() method:

1 Return to the **KeyFrame.java** file in the Text Editor window, and then immediately save the file as **KeyFrame2.java**.

2 Change the class name in the class header to **KeyFrame2**.

3 Position the insertion point to the right of the opening curly bracket for the KeyFrame2 class, and then press the **Enter** key to start a new line. Then add a character variable that will hold the key that the user types: `char key;`.

4. Change the constructor name to **KeyFrame2**.
5. Position the insertion point to the right of the println() statement within the keyReleased() method, and then press the **Enter** key to start a new line.

    The header for the keyReleased() method indicates that a KeyEvent named e is an argument to the method. The e object contains information about the event that has occurred. You can use the getKeyChar() method to obtain information about this event. However, you can see in Figure 12-13 that the getKeyChar() method returns an integer, which represents the Unicode value of the typed character. To work with this integer as a character, you must cast the integer before assigning it to the character variable named key.

6. Type **key = (char)e.getKeyChar();**.

> You have been using a similar cast operation to convert input bytes to characters since Chapter 5.

7. Add the following two println() statements to print the character that the user enters and the character that comes next arithmetically:

    ```
    System.out.println("Key is " + key);
    System.out.println("Next key is " + (char)(key + 1));
    ```

8. Return to **UseKeyFrame.java** file in the Text Editor window, and then immediately save the file as **UseKeyFrame2.java**.
9. Change the class header to **public class UseKeyFrame2**. Also change the statement that instantiates a KeyFrame named kFrame, so that it instantiates a KeyFrame2, as follows: **KeyFrame2 kFrame = new KeyFrame2();**.
10. Rebuild and save the project, then execute the program as a console application by typing **jview UseKeyFrame2** at the command line. The program works as it did before and sends messages to the command prompt each time you type a key. However, additional information about the key and its successor also appears because of the getKeyChar() method you are using with the KeyEvent object.
11. Stop execution of the program by clicking the command line and then typing **Ctrl+C**.

Using Event Methods from Higher in the Inheritance Hierarchy

When you use an event such as KeyEvent, you can use any of the event's methods, as when you used getKeyChar() in the last series of steps. Through the power of inheritance, you also can use methods that belong to any class that is a superclass of the event with which you are working. For example, any KeyEvent has access to the InputEvent, ComponentEvent, AWTEvent, EventObject, and Object Event methods as well as the KeyEvent methods.

section B

Next, you will use an ObjectEvent method with an ActionEvent. You can use an ObjectEvent method with an ActionEvent because every ActionEvent is a descendant of ObjectEvent. Therefore, when you create a Component with several Button objects, you can use ObjectEvent's getSource() method to determine the source of the ActionEvent.

To write a class that uses the ObjectEvent method getSource() with an ActionEvent:

1. Create a new empty project named **ButtonFrame**. Save the **ButtonFrame** project folder in the Chapter.12 folder on your Student Disk.
2. Add to the project a new class file named **ButtonFrame.java**.
3. Above the class header, type the following import statements that you will need for the program:

```
import java.awt.*;
import java.awt.event.*;
```

4. Add **extends Frame implements ActionListener** to the right of the class header.
5. Between the class's curly brackets, create the following three Buttons from which the user can choose to change the Frame's background color:

```
Button redButton = new Button("Red");
Button blueButton = new Button("Blue");
Button greenButton = new Button("Green");
```

6. Begin to write the ButtonFrame constructor, set the layout manager to FlowLayout, and set the ButtonFrame title as follows:

```
public ButtonFrame()
{
   setLayout(new FlowLayout());
   setTitle("Button Frame");
```

7. Continue entering the ButtonFrame constructor by registering the ButtonFrame as an ActionListener for each of the three Button objects, and then adding each of the three Buttons to the Frame:

```
redButton.addActionListener(this);
add(redButton);
blueButton.addActionListener(this);
add(blueButton);
greenButton.addActionListener(this);
add(greenButton);
```

8. On the next line, add the closing curly bracket for the constructor.

9. Because ButtonFrame implements ActionListener, you are required to write code for ActionListener's only method, actionPerformed(). The actionPerformed() method provides you with an ActionEvent object with which you can use the EventObject method named getSource().

```java
public void actionPerformed(ActionEvent e)
{
  if(e.getSource() == redButton)
    setBackground(Color.red);
  else if(e.getSource() == blueButton)
    setBackground(Color.blue);
  else setBackground(Color.green);
}
```

10. Add to the project a new main class file named **UseButtonFrame.java**. Between the main() method's curly brackets, enter the following code that creates a ButtonFrame object:

```java
ButtonFrame bFrame = new ButtonFrame();
bFrame.setSize(350,250);
bFrame.setVisible(true);
```

11. Build and save the project, then execute the program as a console application by typing **jview UseButtonFrame** at the command line. Your output should look like Figure 12-14.

Figure 12-14: UseButtonFrame program

12. Click any of the three color Buttons and note the change in the Frame's background color. The Frame listens for action on each of the Buttons, and the single actionPerformed() method executes no matter which Button you click. You achieve different background colors in the Frame because you use the ObjectEvent method getSource() with the ActionEvent generated by each Button click.

> **13** You did not provide the ButtonFrame with a WindowListener interface or appropriate methods, so you must close the Frame by clicking the command line and then pressing **Ctrl+C**.

Using Mouse Events

Even though Java program users sometimes type characters from a keyboard, when you write GUI programs, you probably expect users to spend most of their time operating a mouse. The MouseListener interface provides you with methods named mousePressed(), mouseClicked(), and mouseReleased() that are analogous to the keyboard event methods keyPressed(), keyTyped(), and keyReleased(). With a mouse, however, you are interested in more than its keypresses; you sometimes want to know where a mouse is pointing. The additional interface methods mouseEntered() and mouseExited() inform you when the user has positioned the mouse over a Component (entered) or off a Component (exited). To illustrate, you can create a MouseFrame class that employs these methods. In addition, you can use three of the MouseEvent methods—getX() and getY() return the mouse coordinates, and getClickCount() helps you to distinguish between single- and double-clicks.

> **To write the MouseFrame class:**
> **1** Create a new empty project named **MouseFrame**. Save the **MouseFrame** project folder in the Chapter.12 folder on your Student Disk.
> **2** Add to the project a new class file named **MouseFrame.java**.
> **3** Above the class header, type the following import statements that you will need for the program:
>
> ```
> import java.awt.*;
> import java.awt.event.*;
> ```
>
> **4** Add `extends Frame implements MouseListener` to the right of the class header.
> **5** Create the following three integer variables between the class's curly brackets. Two will hold the x- and y-positions of the mouse; the third will hold the size of a circle you will draw when the user clicks the mouse.
>
> ```
> int x, y;
> int size;
> ```

Using Layout Managers and the Event Model

6 Enter the following MouseFrame constructor, which sets the title and adds the MouseListener:

```
public MouseFrame()
{
  setTitle("Mouse Frame");
  addMouseListener(this);
}
```

7 Enter the following mousePressed() method to get the x- and y-coordinates from the MouseEvent that initiates the mousePressed() method call. The variables x and y will hold the exact position of the mouse location at the time of the event. Additionally, the mousePressed() method repaints the screen.

```
public void mousePressed(MouseEvent e)
{
  x = e.getX();
  y = e.getY();
  repaint();
}
```

You learned about the repaint() method in Chapter 8.

8 Enter the following code. When the user clicks the mouse, set the size variable to 10 or 4, depending on whether the user single- or double-clicks.

```
public void mouseClicked(MouseEvent e)
{
  if(e.getClickCount() == 2)
    size = 10;
  else size = 4;
  repaint();
}
```

9 Enter the following code to change the Frame background color to yellow when the user positions the mouse over the Frame, and then change the background to black when the user places the mouse somewhere else on the screen:

```
public void mouseEntered(MouseEvent e)
{
  setBackground(Color.yellow);
}
public void mouseExited(MouseEvent e)
{
  setBackground(Color.black);
}
```

10 You don't need any special code for the mouseReleased() method, but you must provide the following method because MouseListener is an abstract interface:

```
public void mouseReleased(MouseEvent e)
{
}
```

11 Recall from Chapter 8 that the Graphics method drawOval() requires four arguments; you might envision a rectangle surrounding an oval and provide arguments for the x- and y-coordinates of the upper-left corner and the width and height of the rectangle. The mouseClicked() method sets the value of size to either 4 or 10, depending on the value returned by getClickCount(). To draw a circle with a diameter of either eight or 20 pixels, use `x - size` and `y - size` for the upper-left corner of the rectangle, and use `size * 2` for the width and the height, as follows:

```
public void paint(Graphics g)
{
   g.drawOval(x - size,y - size,size * 2,size * 2);
}
```

12 Add to the project a new main class file named **UseMouseFrame.java**. Between the main() method's curly brackets, enter the following code that establishes a MouseFrame:

```
MouseFrame mFrame = new MouseFrame();
mFrame.setSize(250,150);
mFrame.setVisible(true);
```

13 Build and save the project, then execute the program as a console application by typing **jview UseMouseFrame** at the command line. When the Frame appears on your screen, roll the mouse over the Frame surface so it turns yellow. Roll your mouse off the Frame surface and it turns black. Roll the mouse over the Frame surface and click; a small circle appears at your mouse position. When you click in a new position, the circle relocates. When you double-click, a larger circle appears in the new mouse position, as shown in Figure 12-15.

Using Layout Managers and the Event Model

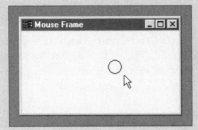

Figure 12-15: UseMouseFrame program

14 After you understand how each MouseListener method contributes to the program's operation, click the command line, and then press **Ctrl+C** to stop the program.

SUMMARY

- Events are Objects that the user initiates, such as keypresses and mouse clicks.

- The parent class for all event objects is named EventObject, which descends from the Object class. EventObject is the parent of AWTEvent, which in turn is the parent to specific event classes such as ActionEvent and ComponentEvent.

- Your computer's operating system notifies your program when an AWTEvent occurs, such as when the user clicks the mouse button.

- When you want to listen for an event, you can implement an appropriate interface for your class, such as ActionListener or WindowListener. The class becomes an event listener. For every event class named xxxEvent, there is a listener named xxxListener.

- Every xxxListener interface method has return type `void`, and each takes one argument—an object that is an instance of the corresponding xxxEvent class.

- Interface methods that are called automatically when an appropriate event occurs are called event handlers.

- As an alternative to implementing a listener, you can extend an adapter class.

- After you create an event handler, you also must register an instance of the class with the Component that you want the event to affect. For any xxxListener, the method that registers a class instance with a Component is addxxxListener().

- The KeyListener interface contains three methods: keyPressed(), keyTyped(), and keyReleased().

- The ComponentEvent class contains a getComponent() method that returns the Component that was involved in the event. The WindowEvent class contains a similar method, getWindow(), that returns the Window that was the source of the event.

section B

- Through the power of inheritance, you can use methods that belong to any class that is a superclass of the event with which you are working.

- The MouseListener interface provides you with methods named mousePressed(), mouseClicked(), and mouseReleased(). The additional interface methods mouseEntered() and mouseExited() inform you when the user positions the mouse over a Component (entered) or off a Component (exited).

QUESTIONS

1. Objects that the user initiates are known as _____.
   a. abstract
   b. final
   c. events
   d. handlers

2. AWTEvent is the child class of _____.
   a. EventObject
   b. Event
   c. ComponentEvent
   d. ItemEvent

3. The immediate parent of KeyEvent and MouseEvent is _____.
   a. ActionEvent
   b. ItemEvent
   c. ComponentEvent
   d. InputEvent

4. When a user clicks a Button, the action generates a(n) _____.
   a. ActionEvent
   b. MouseEvent
   c. ButtonEvent
   d. ClickEvent

5. When you want to listen for an event, you can implement an appropriate _____ for your class.
   a. handler
   b. listener
   c. abstract class
   d. superclass

6. Every xxxListener interface method has return type _____.
   a. xxxEvent
   b. Object
   c. `void`
   d. int

7. Event handlers are _____.
   a. abstract classes
   b. concrete classes
   c. listeners
   d. methods

8. You _____ an adapter.
   a. extend
   b. apply
   c. implement
   d. override

9. What is mouseEntered()?
   a. An event
   b. A handler
   c. A listener
   d. All of these

10. The return type of getComponent() is _____.
    a. Object
    b. Component
    c. int
    d. void

11. The KeyEvent method getKeyChar() returns a(n) _____.
    a. int
    b. char
    c. KeyEvent
    d. AWTEvent

12. The MouseEvent method that allows you to identify double-clicks is _____.
    a. getDouble()
    b. isClickDouble()
    c. getDoubleClick()
    d. getClickCount()

13. You can use methods that belong to any class that is a _____ of the event with which you are working.
    a. superclass
    b. subclass
    c. listener
    d. handler

14. You can use the _____ method to determine the Object where an ActionEvent originates.
    a. getObject()
    b. getEvent()
    c. getOrigin()
    d. getSource()

15. The mousePressed() method is originally defined in the _____.
    a. MouseListener interface
    b. MouseEvent event
    c. MouseObject object
    d. AWTEvent class

16. The mouseEntered() method informs you when the user positions the mouse over a _____.
    a. Frame
    b. Button
    c. Window
    d. Component

EXERCISES

Save each of the programs that you create in the following exercises in the Chapter.12 folder on your Student Disk.

1. Modify the KeyFrame class developed in this chapter so the user can close the Frame by clicking its Close button. Name the new class KeyFrameCanClose. Write a program named UseKeyFrameCanClose to test the class.

2. Create a Frame named FontFrame that holds four Buttons with the names of four different fonts. Draw any String using the font that the user selects. Write a program to instantiate a FontFrame.

3. Create a Frame that uses BorderLayout. Place a Button in the Center region. Each time the user clicks the Button, change the background color in one of the regions.

4. Write a program that lets you determine the integer value returned by the InputEvent method getModifiers() when you press your left, right, or (if you have one) middle mouse button.

5. Create a Frame named MovingLabelFrame. Place a Label on the Frame. When the user clicks the mouse on the Frame's surface, reposition the Label to the new location.

6. Create a Panel named PanelOptions whose constructor accepts two colors and a String. Use the colors for background and foreground to display the String. Create an applet named TeamColors with GridLayout. Display four PanelOptions Panels to display four of your favorite sports teams' names in their team colors.

7. Modify the DemoRegion class you created in Section A of this chapter so that when the user chooses any Western state, an appropriate city name displays. Name the new class DemoWesternStates.

8. Examine the explanation of the getWhen() method in Figure 12-13. The method returns an integer that represents the time; the higher the return value, the more recent the event. Create a Frame named TimeKeeper that displays the time stamp at the command line when the user clicks the mouse on the Frame.

9. Write a program that displays car maintenance services (oil change, tune-up, etc.). Allow the user to select any number of services. If the user clicks the right mouse button, display a message that the user wants service as soon as possible. Display the choices.

10. Write a program that displays types of athletic shoes (for example, running or basketball), and allow the user to select the number of pairs he or she wants for each type (1, 2, or 3). If the user presses the Ctrl key, display a message that the order is doubled. Display the choices.

11. Write a program that displays a choice of foods for breakfast, lunch, and dinner. Use Buttons for each of the foods. When the user clicks a Button, display the name of the food.

12. Each of the following files in the Chapter.12 folder on your Student Disk has syntax and/or logical errors. Add the files to a new project called FixDebug. Save the FixDebug project under the Chapter.12 folder on your Student Disk. You can test each of these applets with the testDebug.htm file on the Student Disk. Remember to change the Java class file referenced in the HTML file so it matches the DebugTwelve applet you are working on.
    a. DebugTwelve1.java
    b. DebugTwelve2.java
    c. DebugTwelve3.java
    d. DebugTwelve4.java

CHAPTER 13

Exception Handling and Debugging

case ▶ When Lynn Greenbrier passes by your desk at Event Handlers Incorporated, she sees a few broken pencils and piles of crumpled paper. "You look upset," she says.

"It's these errors!" you complain.

"Aren't you going overboard?" Lynn asks. "Everyone makes errors when they code programs."

"Oh, I expect typos and compiler errors while I'm developing my programs," you say, "but no matter how well I write my code, the user can still mess everything up by inputting bad data.

The Event Planning department has told me that it has planned events for the 32nd day of the month and for *negative* five people. Even if *my* code is perfect, the user can enter mistakes."

"Then your code isn't perfect yet," Lynn says. "Besides writing programs that can handle ordinary situations, you've got to enable your programs to handle exceptions."

SECTION A
objectives

In this section you will learn:

- About exceptions and the Exception class
- How to `try` code and `throw` and `catch` exceptions
- How to use the Exception getMessage() method
- How to `throw` and `catch` multiple exceptions
- How to use the `finally` block
- About the limitations of traditional methods of error handling

Introduction to Exceptions

Understanding Exceptions

An **exception** is an unexpected or error condition. Anticipating the types of exceptions your program needs to handle and error proofing your code are extremely important programming skills. The programs you write can generate many types of potential exceptions, as in the following examples:

- You issue a command to read a file from a disk, but the file does not exist there.
- You write data to a disk, but the disk is full or unformatted.
- Your program asks for user input, but the user enters invalid data.
- The program attempts to divide a value by zero, access an array with a subscript that is too large, or calculate a value that is too large for the answer's variable type.

These errors are called *exceptions* because, presumably, they are not usual occurrences; they are "exceptional." The object-oriented techniques that manage such errors comprise the group of methods known as **exception handling**.

tip
Providing for exception handling involves an oxymoron: You must expect the unexpected.

Like all other classes in the Java programming language, exceptions are Objects; their class name is Exception. In addition, Java includes two basic classes of errors: Error and Exception. Both of these classes descend from the Throwable class, as shown in Figure 13-1.

section A

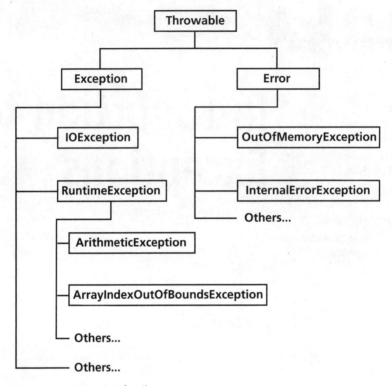

Figure 13-1: Exception family tree

The **Error class** represents serious errors from which your program usually cannot recover. You probably have made these errors in your own programs when you spelled a class name incorrectly or stored a required class in the wrong folder. When a program cannot locate a required class or your system runs out of memory, an Error condition occurs. Of course, a *person* can recover from such errors by moving a file to the correct folder or by physically installing more memory, but it is impossible for a program to recover from these kinds of mistakes.

The **Exception class** comprises less serious errors representing unusual conditions that arise while a program is running and from which the program *can* recover. Some examples of Exception class errors include using an invalid array subscript or performing certain illegal arithmetic operations.

When your code causes an error in a program, whether inadvertently or purposely, you can determine whether the type of Throwable object generated is an Error or an Exception by examining the message that you receive from Java after the error occurs. Next, you will generate an unrecoverable Error.

To cause an unrecoverable Error purposely:

1. Go to the command prompt for the Chapter.13 folder on your Student Disk, type **jview NoSuchClass**, and then press the **Enter** key. Unless you have created a file named NoSuchClass in the current directory, the error message you receive should look like Figure 13-2.

```
A:\CHAPTER.13>jview NoSuchClass
ERROR: Could not execute NoSuchClass : The system cannot find the file specified
.
A:\CHAPTER.13>
```

Figure 13-2: Error message generated by a missing file

When you generate a recoverable Exception, you see a different message. Next you will generate a recoverable Exception.

To cause an Exception purposely:

1. Create a new console application project named **MathError**. Save the **MathError** project folder in the Chapter.13 folder on your Student Disk.
2. Rename the default Class1.java file as **MathError.java**, then open the file in the Text Editor window.
3. Replace the Class1 class name in the `public class Class1` line with **MathError**.
4. Replace the `// TODO: Add initialization code here` comment with the following code that attempts to divide by zero:

   ```
   int num = 13, denom = 0, result;
   result = num / denom;
   ```

> **tip**
>
> You should never write a program that purposely divides a value by zero, but if denom is the result of user input, the situation certainly could occur.

5. Select **MathError Properties** from the **Project** menu. Select the **MathError** file in the **When project runs, load** drop-down list box and set the project to run as a console application. When you are finished, click the **OK** button.

6 Build and save the project, then execute the program as a console application by typing **jview MathError** at the command line. You receive a dialog box stating that an exception has occurred of type java.lang.ArithmeticException, which is a subclass of Exception. The dialog box also prompts you to debug the application. Click the **No** button. The screen displays information describing the nature of the error ("/ by zero"), the method that generated the error (MathError.main), and the filename and line number for the error (MathError.java, line 18; your line number might be different if you include comment lines at the beginning of your program). Your screen should resemble Figure 13-3.

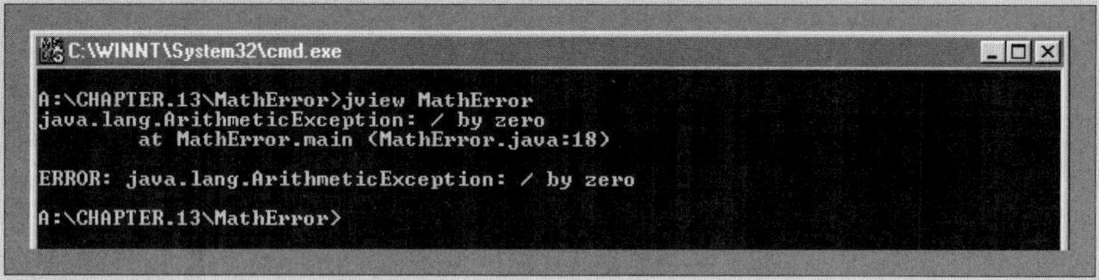

```
A:\CHAPTER.13\MathError>jview MathError
java.lang.ArithmeticException: / by zero
        at MathError.main (MathError.java:18)

ERROR: java.lang.ArithmeticException: / by zero

A:\CHAPTER.13\MathError>
```

Figure 13-3: Exception generated by the MathError class

Just because an Exception occurs, you don't necessarily have to deal with it. In the MathError class, you simply let the offending program terminate. However, the termination of the program is abrupt and unforgiving. When a program divides two numbers (or even performs a less trivial task such as playing a game with the user or balancing a checkbook), the user might be annoyed if the program ends abruptly. If the program is used for air-traffic control or to monitor a patient's vital statistics during surgery, an abrupt conclusion could be disastrous. Object-oriented error-handling techniques provide more elegant solutions than ending the program abruptly.

Programmers had to deal with error conditions long before object-oriented methods were conceived. Probably the most often used error-handling solution has been to terminate the offending program. For example, you can change the main() method of the MathError class to halt the program before dividing by zero, as follows:

```java
public class MathError
{
  public static void main(String[] args)
  {
    int num = 13, denom = 0, result;
    if(denom == 0)
      System.exit(1);
    result = num / denom;
  }
}
```

tip
You first used the System.exit() method in Chapter 11 when you wrote code to close a window. Then, you used zero as the argument because the program was ending normally.

When you use the System.exit() method, the current application ends and control returns to the operating system. The convention is to return one if an error is causing program termination or zero if the program is ending normally. Using this exit() technique circumvents the error message, but exception handling provides a better solution for handling error conditions.

In object-oriented terminology, you "try" a procedure that might not complete correctly. A method that detects an error condition or Exception "throws an Exception," and the block of code that processes the error "catches the Exception."

Trying Code and Catching Exceptions

When you have a piece of code in which something can go wrong, you place the code in a `try` block. A **try block** consists of the following elements:

- The keyword `try`
- An opening curly bracket
- Statements that might cause Exceptions
- A closing curly bracket

You must code at least one `catch` block immediately following a `try` block. Each **catch block** can "catch" one type of Exception. You create a `catch` block by typing the following elements:

- The keyword `catch`
- An opening parenthesis
- An Exception type
- A name for an instance of the Exception type
- A closing parenthesis
- An opening curly bracket
- Statements that take the action you want to use to deal with the error condition
- A closing curly bracket

Additionally, if a method throws an Exception that will be caught, you must use the keyword `throws` followed by an Exception type in the method header. Figure 13-4 shows the general format of a `try...catch` pair.

section A

```
public class someMethod throws someException
{
  try
  {
    // Statements that might cause an Exception
  }
  catch(someException anExceptionInstance)
  {
    // What to do about it
  }
  // Statements here execute even if there was no Exception
}
```

Figure 13-4: General form of a `try...catch` pair

A `catch` block looks a lot like a method named catch() that takes an argument that is some type of Exception. However, it is not a method; it has no return type, and you can't call it directly.

Some programmers refer to a `catch` block as a `catch` *clause*.

In Figure 13-4, someException represents the Exception class or any of its subclasses. If an Exception occurs during execution of the `try` block, then the statements in the `catch` block will execute. If no Exception occurs within the `try` block, then the `catch` block will not execute. Either way, the statements following the `catch` block execute normally. Next, you will alter the MathError class so it catches the division-by-zero Exception.

To catch an ArithmeticException:

1 Select **Save MathError.java As** from the **File** menu and save the file as **MathError2.java**.

2 Change the class name in the class header from MathError to **MathError2**.

3 Position the insertion point at the end of the main() method header (`public static void main(String[] args)`), press the **space bar**, and then type **throws ArithmeticException**.

4. Position the insertion point at the end of the line that declares the three integer variables, and then press the **Enter** key to start a new line.
5. Type `try`, press the **Enter** key, and then type an opening curly bracket.
6. Position the insertion point at the end of the line that performs division (`result = num / denom;`), press the **Enter** key, and then type a closing curly bracket for the `try` block.
7. Press the **Enter** key, and then type a `catch` block that sends a message to the command line, as follows:

```
catch(ArithmeticException error)
{
  System.out.println("Attempt to divide by zero!");
}
```

> **tip**
>
> If you want to send error messages to a different location from "normal" output, you can use System.err instead of System.out. For example, if a program writes a report to a specific disk file, you might want errors to write to a different disk file or to the screen. You will learn more about this technique in Chapter 14.

8. Rebuild and save the project, then execute the MathError2 file as a console application by typing **jview MathError2** at the command line. The output looks like Figure 13-5, which means that the Exception was caught successfully and your error message was printed.

```
C:\WINNT\System32\cmd.exe

A:\CHAPTER.13\MathError>jview MathError2
Attempt to divide by zero!

A:\CHAPTER.13\MathError>
```

Figure 13-5: Output of MathError2

Using the Exception getMessage() Method

When the MathError2 program prints the error message ("Attempt to divide by zero!"), you actually cannot confirm that division by zero was the source of the error. In reality, the `catch` block in the method would catch *any* ArithmeticException generated from within the `try` block in the program. Instead of writing your own message, you can use the getMessage() method that ArithmeticException inherits from the Throwable class. The getMessage() method returns a detailed description of a specific error. To retrieve Java's message about any Throwable Exception named someException, you code `someException.getMessage()`.

section A

To use the getMessage() method with the MathError class:

1 Select **Save MathError2.java As** from the **File** menu and save the file as **MathError3.java**.

2 Change the class name in the class header from MathError2 to **MathError3**.

3 Within the `catch` block, remove the existing println() statement and replace it with `System.out.println("The official message is " + error.getMessage());`.

4 Rebuild and save the project, then execute the MathError3 file as a console application. Figure 13-6 shows the output. Java's analysis of the situation prints instead of your own.

Figure 13-6: Output of MathError3

Of course, you might want to do more in a `catch` block than print an error message; after all, Java did that for you without catching any Exceptions. You might want to add code to correct the error, such as forcing the arithmetic to divide by one rather than by zero. (Dividing by one does not solve the divide-by-zero problem; it is only a way of avoiding the divide-by-zero Exception.)

To add corrective code to the `catch` block of the MathError class:

1 Save the MathError3 file as **MathError4.java** and change the class header to reflect the new class name.

2 Position the insertion point at the end of the println() statement within the `catch` block of the main() method of the class, and then press the **Enter** key to start a new line. Then type the following message to indicate the action you are taking: `System.out.println("Denominator corrected to 1");`. Follow this statement with a recalculation of the result variable by typing the following code on a new line: `result = num / 1;`.

> You can code an `if` statement, such as `if(denom == 0) {System.out.println ("Denominator corrected to 1"); result = num / 1;}`, **to ensure that a denom of zero is indeed the reason for the ArithmeticException. You can achieve the same result by coding** `result = num;` **instead of** `result = num / 1;`.

3. Position the insertion point after the closing curly bracket of the `catch` block, and then press the **Enter** key to start a new line. Add the following println() statement to show the result: `System.out.println("Result is " + result);`.

4. Rebuild and save the project, then execute the MathError4 file as a console application. Figure 13-7 shows the result, which confirms that the `catch` block provides you with a usable result.

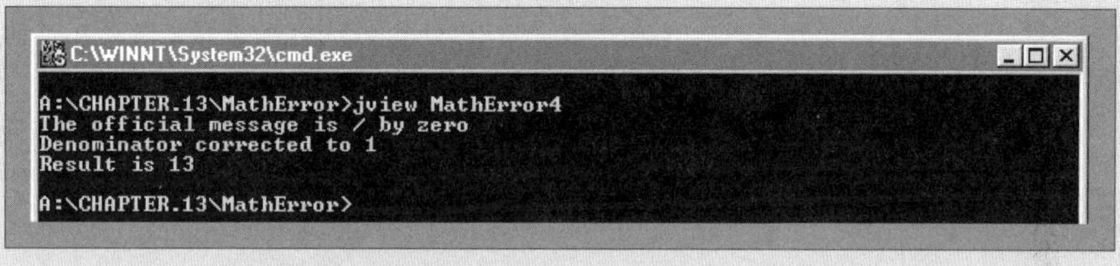

```
A:\CHAPTER.13\MathError>jview MathError4
The official message is / by zero
Denominator corrected to 1
Result is 13

A:\CHAPTER.13\MathError>
```

Figure 13-7: Output of MathError4

Throwing and Catching Multiple Exceptions

You can place as many statements as you need within a `try` block, and you can `catch` as many Exceptions as you want. If you `try` more than one statement, only the first error-generating statement throws an Exception. As soon as the Exception occurs, the logic transfers to the `catch` block, which leaves the rest of the statements in the `try` block unexecuted.

When there are multiple `catch` blocks, they are examined in sequence until a match is found for the Exception that occurred, and then the matching `catch` block executes and each remaining `catch` block is bypassed.

For example, consider the program in Figure 13-8. The main() method in the TwoErrors class throws two types of Exceptions—ArithmeticExceptions and IndexOutOfBoundsExceptions. (An **IndexOutOfBoundsException** is one that occurs when an array subscript is not within the allowed range.)

```
public class TwoErrors
{
   public static void main(String[] args)
      throws ArithmeticException,
      IndexOutOfBoundsException
   {
```

Figure 13-8: TwoErrors class with two `catch` blocks

```java
        int num = 13, denom = 0, result;
        int[] array = {22,33,44};
        try
        {
          result = num / denom;   // First try
          result = array[num];    // Second try
        }
        catch(ArithmeticException error)
        {
          System.out.println("Arithmetic error");
        }
        catch(IndexOutOfBoundsException error)
        {
          System.out.println("Index error");
        }
     }
}
```

Figure 13-8: TwoErrors class with two `catch` blocks (continued)

The TwoErrors class declares three integers and an integer array with three elements. In the main() method, the `try` block executes, and at the first statement within the `try` block, an Exception occurs because the denom in the division problem is zero. The `try` block is abandoned, and the logic transfers to the first `catch` block. Division by zero causes an ArithmeticException, and because the first `catch` block receives an ArithmeticException, the message "Arithmetic error" prints. In this example, the second `try` statement is never attempted, and the second `catch` block is skipped.

If you make one minor change to the class in Figure 13-8, the process changes. You can force the division in the `try` block to succeed by substituting a constant value for the denom variable or reversing the positions of num and denom in the line with the `// First try` comment. With either of these changes, division by zero does not take place. The `// First try` succeeds, and the program proceeds to the `// Second try`. This statement attempts to access element 13 of a three-element array, so it throws an IndexOutOfBoundsException. The `try` block is abandoned, and the first `catch` block is examined and found unsuitable. The program logic proceeds to the second `catch` block whose Exception argument type is a match for the thrown Exception, so the message "Index error" prints.

Sometimes you want to execute the same code no matter which Exception type occurs. For example, within the TwoErrors program in Figure 13-8, each of the two `catch` blocks prints a unique message. Instead, you might want both the ArithmeticException `catch` block and the IndexOutOfBoundsException `catch` block to use the getMessage() method. Because both ArithmeticExceptions and IndexOutOfBoundsExceptions are subclasses of Exception, you can rewrite the TwoErrors class as shown in Figure 13-9.

```java
public class TwoErrors
{
   public static void main(String[] args)
      throws ArithmeticException,
      IndexOutOfBoundsException
   {
      int num = 13, denom = 0, result;
      int[] array = {22,33,44};
      try
      {
         result = num / denom;  // First try
         result = array[num];   // Second try
      }
      catch(Exception error)
      {
         System.out.println("Error is " + error.getMessage());
      }
   }
}
```

Figure 13-9: TwoErrors class with one `catch` block

The `catch` block in Figure 13-9 accepts a more generic Exception argument type than either of the potentially error-causing `try` statements throw, so the generic `catch` block can act as a "catch-all" block. When either an arithmetic or array error occurs, the thrown error is "promoted" to an Exception error in the `catch` block. Through inheritance, ArithmeticExceptions and IndexOutOfBoundsExceptions *are* Exceptions, and an Exception *is* Throwable, so you can use the Throwable class getMessage() method.

When you list multiple `catch` blocks following a `try`, you must be careful that some `catch` blocks don't become unreachable. For example, if the first `catch` block catches an IndexOutOfBoundsException and the second `catch` block catches all other types of Exceptions, then IndexOutOfBoundsException errors will cause the first `catch` to execute and other Exceptions will "fall through" to the more general Exception `catch`. However, if you reverse the sequence of the `catch` blocks, then even IndexOutOfBoundsExceptions will be caught by the Exception `catch`. The IndexOutOfBoundsException `catch` block is unreachable because the Exception `catch` block is in its way, and therefore, the class will not compile.

Using the `finally` Block

When you have actions to perform at the end of a `try...catch` sequence, you can use a `finally` block. The code within a `finally` block executes whether or not the `try` block identifies Exceptions. Usually, you use the `finally` block to perform clean-up tasks that must occur whether or not any errors occurred and whether or not any errors that occurred were caught. Figure 13-10 shows the format of a `try...catch` sequence that uses a `finally` block.

```
public class someMethod throws someException
{
  try
  {
    // Statements that might cause an Exception
  }
  catch(someException anExceptionInstance)
  {
    // What to do about it
  }
  finally
  {
    // Statements here execute even if no Exception occurred
  }
}
```

Figure 13-10: General form of a `try...catch` block with a `finally` block

Compare Figure 13-10 to Figure 13-4 from earlier in this chapter. With the program in Figure 13-4, when the `try` code works without error, control passes to the statements at the end of the method. Additionally, when the `try` code fails and throws an Exception, if the Exception is caught, then the `catch` block executes, and again, control passes to the statements at the end of the method. At first glance, it seems as though the statements at the end of the method always execute. However, there are at least two reasons that the last set of statements might never execute:

- It is possible that an Exception for which you did not plan will occur.
- The `try` or `catch` block might contain a `System.exit();` statement.

Your `try` block might throw an Exception for which you did not provide a `catch`. After all, Exceptions occur all the time without your handling them, as one did in the first MathError program. In case of an unhandled Exception, program execution stops immediately, sending the error to the operating system for handling and abandoning the current method. Likewise, if the `try` contains an exit() statement, execution stops immediately.

When you include a `finally` block, you are assured that the `finally` statements will execute before the method is abandoned—even if the method concludes prematurely. The `finally` block is used most frequently with file input and output, which are covered in Chapter 14. For now, consider part of the logic (in pseudocode) for a typical file-handling program:

```
try
{
  Open the file
  Read the file
  Place the file data in an array
  Calculate an average from the data
  Display the average
}
catch(IOException e)
{
  Issue an error message
}
finally
{
  If the file is open, close it
}
```

If the pseudocode were actually a program, a file would open. If the file does not exist or is empty, an Exception is thrown and the `catch` block handles the error. However, because the program uses an array, it is possible that an uncaught ArrayIndexOutOfBoundsException occurs. In such an event, you still want to close the file. By using the `finally` block, you ensure that the file closes because the code in the `finally` block will execute before control returns to the operating system. The code in the `finally` block executes no matter which of the following outcomes of the `try` block occurs:

- The try ends normally.
- The catch executes.
- An error causes the method to abandon prematurely, which neither finishes the try block nor executes the catch block.

tip

If a try block calls System.exit(), and the finally block calls System.exit(), then the exit() in the finally block is the one that will actually happen. The try block's exit() will be abandoned.

Understanding the Limitations of Traditional Error Handling

Programming errors occurred regularly long before object-oriented programming or the Java programming language was conceived. In a traditional, non-object-oriented, procedural program that performs three methods that depend on each other, the code that provides error checking looks similar to the pseudocode in Figure 13-11.

```
call methodA
if methodA worked
{
  call methodB
  if methodB worked
  {
    call methodC
    if methodC worked
       everything's okay so print finalResult
    else
       set errorCode to 'C'
  }
  else set errorCode to 'B'
}
else set errorCode to 'A'
```

Figure 13-11: Traditional error checking

The program in Figure 13-11 performs methodA, then performs methodB only if methodA is successful. Similarly, methodC executes only when methodA and methodB are successful. When any of the methods fails, the program sets an appropriate errorCode A, B, or C. (Presumably, the errorCode is used later in the program.) The program is difficult to follow, and the point of the program—to print finalResult—is lost in the maze of `if` statements. Additionally, it is easy for you to make coding mistakes within such a program because of the complicated nesting, indenting, and opening and closing of curly brackets.

Compare the same program logic using Java's object-oriented error-handling technique as shown in Figure 13-12. Using the `try...catch` object-oriented method provides the same results as the traditional method provides, but the "real" statements of the program (calling methods A, B, and C, and printing finalResult) are located together, where their logic is easy to follow. The `try` steps usually should work; after all, they are not the "exceptions." It is convenient to see these "usual" steps in one location. The unusual, *exceptional* events are grouped and moved out of the way of the primary action.

```
try
{
   methodA
   methodB
   methodC
   everything's okay so print finalResult
}
catch(methodA's error)
{
   set errorCode to 'A'
}
catch(methodB's error)
{
   set errorCode to 'B'
}
catch(methodC's error)
{
   set errorCode to 'C'
}
```

Figure 13-12: Object-oriented error handling

SUMMARY

- An exception is an unexpected or error condition. The object-oriented techniques to manage such errors comprise the group of methods known as exception handling.

- In Java, there are two basic classes of errors—Error and Exception. Both of these classes descend from the Throwable class.

- The Error class represents serious errors from which your program usually cannot recover.

- The Exception class comprises less serious errors that represent unusual conditions that arise while a program is running and from which the program *can* recover.

- You can determine whether the type of Throwable object generated is an Error or an Exception by examining the message that you receive from Java after the error occurs.

- You can use the System.exit() method to end the current application and return control to the operating system; however, this technique is not object-oriented.

- In object-oriented terminology, you "try" a procedure that might not complete correctly. A method that detects an error condition or Exception "throws an Exception," and the block of code that processes the error "catches the Exception."

- When you have a piece of code in which something can go wrong, you place the code in a `try` block consisting of the keyword `try`, an opening curly bracket, statements that might cause Exceptions, and a closing curly bracket.

- You must code at least one `catch` block immediately following a `try` block. Each `catch` block can catch one type of Exception; within its body, you code statements to handle the error condition.

- If a method throws an Exception, you must use the keyword `throws` followed by an Exception type in the method header.

- For a `try...catch` pair, when an Exception occurs during the execution of the `try` block, the statements in the `catch` block execute.

- Exceptions inherit the getMessage() method from the Throwable class.

- You can place as many statements as you need within a `try` block; only the first error-generating statement throws an Exception.

- You can `catch` as many Exceptions as you want.

- When you use multiple `catch` blocks, they are examined in sequence until a match is found for the Exception that occurred, then the matching `catch` executes.

- You can use a more general Exception class to catch subclass Exceptions.

- When you list multiple `catch` blocks following a `try` block, you must be careful that some `catch` blocks don't become unreachable.

- When you have actions that always must occur at the end of a `try...catch` sequence, you can use a `finally` block.
- In a traditional, non-object-oriented program, error-checking code is complex. In contrast, object-oriented exception handling allows you to isolate error-handling code.

QUESTIONS

1. In object-oriented programming terminology, an unexpected or error condition is a(n) _____.
   a. anomaly
   b. exception
   c. aberration
   d. deviation

2. All Java Exceptions are _____.
   a. Errors
   b. RuntimeExceptions
   c. Throwables
   d. Omissions

3. Which of the following statements is true?
   a. Errors are more serious than Exceptions.
   b. Exceptions are more serious than Errors.
   c. Errors and Exceptions are equally serious.
   d. Exceptions and Errors are the same thing.

4. The default Exception error message provides _____ a default Error message.
   a. more information than
   b. less information than
   c. the same amount of information as
   d. less useful information than

5. When an Exception occurs, you _____ handle it.
   a. cannot
   b. are required to
   c. can
   d. can but never want to

6. When you use the System.exit() method, _____
   a. the current application ends
   b. control returns to the operating system
   c. both a and b
   d. neither a nor b

section A

7. In object-oriented terminology, you _____ a procedure that might not complete correctly.
   a. try
   b. catch
   c. handle
   d. encapsulate

8. A method that detects an error condition or Exception _____ an Exception.
   a. tries
   b. catches
   c. handles
   d. encapsulates

9. A try block includes all of the following elements except _____.
   a. the keyword try
   b. the keyword catch
   c. curly brackets
   d. statements that might cause Exceptions

10. You _____ one catch block immediately following a try block.
    a. can code up to
    b. must code at least
    c. must code exactly
    d. never code just

11. If a method _____, you write throws followed by an Exception type in the method header.
    a. throws an Exception
    b. catches an Exception
    c. either throws or catches an Exception
    d. throws an Exception that will be caught

12. Objects of type _____ can use the getMessage() method.
    a. Throwable
    b. Exception
    c. ArithmeticException
    d. All of these are correct.

13. You _____ within a try block.
    a. must place only a single statement
    b. can place any number of statements
    c. must place at least two statements
    d. must place a catch block

14. You can place _____ within a try block.
    a. a variable declaration
    b. an assignment statement
    c. a method call
    d. Any of these is correct.

15. If you try more than one statement, _____ error-generating statement throws an Exception.
    a. only the first
    b. only the last
    c. only the most serious
    d. each

16. When a try block generates an Exception and you use multiple catch blocks, _____.
    a. they all execute
    b. only the first one executes
    c. only the first matching one executes
    d. only the last matching one executes

17. The catch block that begins catch (Exception e) can catch Exceptions of type _____.
    a. IOException
    b. ArithmeticException
    c. both of these
    d. neither of these

18. The catch block that begins catch (Exception e) can catch Exceptions of type _____.
    a. Throwable
    b. Error
    c. both of these
    d. neither of these

19. The code within a finally block executes when the try block _____.
    a. identifies one or more Exceptions
    b. does not identify any Exceptions
    c. either a or b
    d. neither a nor b

20. The finally block is used most frequently for _____.
    a. constructing objects
    b. printing error messages
    c. closing files
    d. providing for System.exit()

21. An advantage to using a try...catch block is that exceptional events are _____.
    a. eliminated
    b. reduced
    c. integrated with "regular" events
    d. isolated from "regular" events

EXERCISES

Save the programs that you create in the exercises in the Chapter.13 folder on your Student Disk.

1. Write a program named GoTooFar in which you declare an array of five integers and store five values in the array. Initialize a subscript to zero. Write a `try` block in which you access each element of the array, subsequently increasing the subscript by one. Create a `catch` block that catches the eventual ArrayIndexOutOfBoundsException, and then print to the screen the message, "Now you've gone too far."

2. The Integer.parseInt() method requires an integer argument. Write a program in which you try to parse a String. Catch the NumberFormatExceptionError that is thrown, and then display an appropriate error message.

3. Write a program that prompts the user to enter a number. Subtract 60 from the number, and then declare an array using the calculated size. If you attempt to declare an array whose computed size is negative, the program should throw an Exception. Use a `catch` block to catch the Exception if there is one, and then display the associated message.

4. Write a program that declares an object of a class, but do not construct it. Call a method with the object to see whether doing so produces an Exception. Use a `catch` block to catch the Exception if there is one, and then display the associated message.

5. Write an applet that declares a reference to a component, but does not construct it. (For example, `Button myButton`, not `Button myButton = new Button("This is my Button");`.) Add the component to the applet to see whether an Exception is produced. Use a `catch` block to catch the Exception if there is one, and then display the associated message.

SECTION B
objectives

In this lesson you will learn:

- How to specify the Exceptions a method can throw
- How to handle the same Exception uniquely with each `catch`
- How to create your own Exception subclasses
- How to debug Visual J++ programs
- How to trace program execution
- How to trace variables with debug windows
- How to trace exceptions through the call stack

Advanced Exception Concepts and Debugging

Specifying the Exceptions a Method Can Throw

When you write a method that might throw an Exception, you can type the clause `throws xxxException` after the method header to indicate the type of Exception that might be thrown. Every Java method you write has the potential to throw an Exception. Some Exceptions, such as an InternalErrorException, can occur anywhere at any time. However, for most Java methods that you write, you do not use a `throws` clause. For example, you have used a `throws` clause only a few times in all the programs you have written while working through this book. Most of the time, you let Java handle the Exception by shutting down the program. Your programs would become unwieldy if you were required to provide for every possible error, including equipment failures, memory problems, and so on. Most exceptions never have to be explicitly thrown or caught.

> Specifically, you never have to throw Error or RuntimeException exceptions explicitly. Most of the errors you have received when you have made mistakes in your Java programs are RuntimeExceptions.

One "exception" to the rule of not throwing Exceptions involves the IOException. You learned in Chapter 5 that you must include a `throws` clause in the method header of programs that allow keyboard input, and in this section you will discover that you must include a `throws` clause in programs that use file input. However, even when you are not *required* to handle an Exception, you might choose to do so. When your method will throw an Exception that you want to handle, you must include the `throws` clause in the method header.

Java also requires that you throw an InterruptedException, which you use when working with threads. You will learn about threads in Chapter 15.

When a method you write throws an Exception, the method itself can catch the Exception, although it is not required to do so. There are many times when you won't want a method to handle its own Exception. With many methods, you want the method to check for errors, but you do not want to require a method to handle an error if it finds one. The calling program might need to handle the error differently depending on its purpose. For example, one program that divides values might need to terminate if division by zero occurs. A different program might want the user to reenter the data to be used. The method that contains the division statement can throw the error; the calling program can assume the responsibility for handling the error detected by the method.

You know a method can throw without catching because you have written methods that use keyboard input. With those methods, you threw an Exception, but you did not provide a `catch` block.

Java requires that you use the `throws` clause in the header of a method that might throw an Exception so programs that use your methods are notified of the Exception potential. When you use any method, you must know three pieces of information to use the method to its full potential:

- The type and number of arguments the method requires
- The method's return type
- The type and number of Exceptions the method throws

To use a method, you must first know what types of arguments the method requires that you send it. You *can* call a method without knowing its return type, but if you do so, you can't benefit from any value that the method returns. (Additionally, if you use a method without knowing its return type, you probably don't really understand the purpose of the method.) Similarly, you can't make wise decisions about what to do in case of an error if you don't know what types of Exceptions a method might throw. A method's header, including its name, arguments, and `throws` clause, is called the method's **signature**.

Next, you will create a class that contains two methods that throw Exceptions but don't catch them. The PickMenu class allows Event Handlers Incorporated customers to choose a dinner menu selection as part of their event planning process. Before you create PickMenu, you will create the Menu class that lists dinner choices for customers and allows them to make a selection.

To create the Menu class:

1. Create a new empty project named **PlanMenu**. Save the **PlanMenu** project folder in the Chapter.13 folder on your Student Disk.

2. Add a new class file to the project by selecting **Add Class** from the **Project** menu. The Add Item dialog box appears. In the Add Item dialog box, select **Class** from the **Class** folder, then change the suggested filename to **Menu.java** and click the **Open** button. The new class opens in the Text Editor window.

3. Between the class's curly brackets, type the following String array for three entrée choices:

   ```
   String[] entreeChoice = {"Rosemary Chicken",
     "Beef Wellington", "Maine Lobster"};
   ```

4. Add the displayMenu() method, which lists each entrée option with a corresponding number the customer can type to make a selection. Even though the entreeChoice subscripts are 0, 1, and 2, most users would expect to type 1, 2, or 3, so you will print (x + 1) rather than x in the println() method.

   ```
   public void displayMenu()
   {
     System.out.println
       ("Type your selection, then press Enter.");
     for(int x = 0; x < entreeChoice.length; ++x)
       System.out.println
         ("Type " + (x + 1) + " for " + entreeChoice[x]);
   }
   ```

5. Create the following getSelection() method, which requires an integer argument and returns the name of one of the selected menu items. Because the user enters a value that is one higher than the actual subscript, you need to subtract one from x when accessing the array.

   ```
   public String getSelection (int x)
   {
     return (entreeChoice[x - 1]);
   }
   ```

Next, you can create the PickMenu class, which lets the customer choose from the available dinner entrée options. The PickMenu class declares a Menu, an integer that holds the user's numeric menu choice, and a String named guestChoice that holds the name of the entrée that the customer selects.

To enable the PickMenu class to operate with different kinds of Menus in the future, you pass a Menu to PickMenu's constructor. This technique provides two advantages. First, when the menu options change, you can alter the contents of the Menu.java file without changing any of the code in any programs that use Menu.

Second, you can extend Menu, perhaps to VegetarianMenu, LowSaltMenu, or KosherMenu, and still use the existing PickMenu class. When you pass any Menu or Menu subclass into the PickMenu constructor, the correct customer options will display.

To create the PickMenu class:

1. Add a new class file named **PickMenu** to the PlanMenu project.
2. Between the class's curly brackets, add three data fields: a Menu, and both a number and a String that reflect the customer's choice:

```
Menu briefMenu;
int choice;
String guestChoice = new String();
```

3. Enter the following PickMenu constructor, which receives an argument representing a Menu. The constructor assigns this Menu argument to the local Menu, and then calls the setChoice() method, which will prompt the user to select from the available menu. The PickMenu() constructor method must throw an Exception because it calls the setGuestChoice() method, which uses keyboard input. Any method that uses keyboard input or calls a method that uses keyboard input must throw the potential Exception.

```
public PickMenu(Menu theMenu) throws Exception
{
   briefMenu = theMenu;
   setGuestChoice();
}
```

> **tip**
>
> In Chapter 9, you encountered a similar situation in which you had to throw an Exception in a method that did not directly perform input. You created an Event class whose set method threw an Exception. When you wrote a UseSimpleEvent.java program that instantiated an Event, the main() method of UseSimpleEvent was required to throw the Exception that the Event class method could generate.

4. The following setGuestChoice() method displays the menu and reads keyboard data entry, so the method throws an Exception. Start the method by declaring a character and String for input:

```
public void setGuestChoice() throws Exception
{
   char newChar;
   String inputString = new String();
```

5 Add the following data-entry procedure, which is similar to others that you have written:

```
System.out.println("Choose from the following menu:");
briefMenu.displayMenu();
newChar = (char)System.in.read();
while(newChar >= '0' && newChar <= '9')
{
   inputString = inputString + newChar;
   newChar = (char)System.in.read();
}
System.in.read();
```

6 Add the following code to convert the entered String to an integer, and then use it as an argument to the getSelection() method that you wrote in the Menu class. Because briefMenu is a Menu, it has access to the getSelection() method. When you pass an integer to the getSelection() method, it returns one of the Strings in the menu. Here, you assign the returned String to the guestChoice field. Finally, you end the setGuestChoice() method with a closing curly bracket.

```
choice = Integer.parseInt(inputString);
guestChoice = briefMenu.getSelection(choice);
}
```

7 The following getGuestChoice() method is simpler; it returns the String that represents the customer's menu selection:

```
public String getGuestChoice()
{
   return(guestChoice);
}
```

You created a Menu class that simply holds a list of food items, displays itself, and allows you to retrieve a specific item. You also created a PickMenu class that has fields that hold a user's specific selection from a given menu and methods to get and set values for those fields. The PickMenu class contains two methods that throw Exceptions, but no methods that contain any way to catch those Exceptions. Next, you can write a program that uses the PickMenu class. This program can catch Exceptions that PickMenu throws.

To write the PlanMenu class:

1. Add a new main class file named **PlanMenu** to the PlanMenu project.

2. Between the main() method's curly brackets, construct the following Menu named briefMenu, and also declare a PickMenu object that you name entree. You do not want to construct a PickMenu object yet because you want to be able to catch the Exception that the PickMenu constructor might throw. Therefore, you want to wait and construct the PickMenu object within a `try` block. For now, you will just declare entree and assign it `null`. Additionally, declare a String that will hold the customer's menu selection.

```
Menu briefMenu = new Menu();
PickMenu entree = null;
String guestChoice = new String();
```

3. Immediately following the `String guestChoice = new String();` line, write the following `try` block that constructs a PickMenu item. If the construction is a success, the next statement assigns a selection to the entree object. Because entree is a PickMenu object, it has access to the getGuestChoice() method in the PickMenu class, and you can assign the method's returned value to the guestChoice String.

```
try
{
   PickMenu selection = new PickMenu(briefMenu);
   entree = selection;
   guestChoice = entree.getGuestChoice();
}
```

4. The `catch` block must immediately follow the `try` block. When the `try` block fails, guestChoice will not have a valid value, so recover from the Exception by assigning a value to guestChoice within the following `catch` block:

```
catch(Exception error)
{
   guestChoice = "an invalid selection";
}
```

5. Use the following code to print the customer's choice at the end of the PlanMenu program:

```
System.out.println("You chose " + guestChoice);
```

6. Select **PlanMenu Properties** from the **Project** menu. Select the **PlanMenu** file in the **When project runs, load** drop-down list box and set the project to run as a console application. When you are finished, click the **OK** button.

Exception Handling and Debugging

7 Build and save the project, then execute the PlanMenu file as a console application. Choose an entrée selection by typing its number from the menu and compare your results to Figure 13-13.

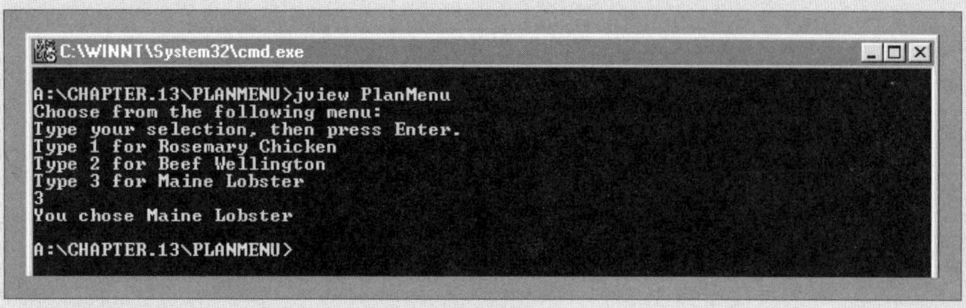

```
A:\CHAPTER.13\PLANMENU>jview PlanMenu
Choose from the following menu:
Type your selection, then press Enter.
Type 1 for Rosemary Chicken
Type 2 for Beef Wellington
Type 3 for Maine Lobster
3
You chose Maine Lobster

A:\CHAPTER.13\PLANMENU>
```

Figure 13-13: Sample run of the PlanMenu program

The PlanMenu program works well when you enter a valid menu selection. One way that you can force an Exception to take place is to enter an invalid menu selection at the prompt.

8 Run the PlanMenu program again and, type **4**, **A**, or any other invalid value at the prompt. Entering 4 produces an ArrayIndexOutOfBoundsException, and entering A produces a NumberFormatException. If the program lacked the `try...catch` pair, either entry would halt the program. However, because the setGuestChoice() method in the PickValue class throws either type of Exception and the PlanMenu program catches it, guestChoice takes on the value "an invalid selection" and the program ends smoothly, as shown in Figure 13-14.

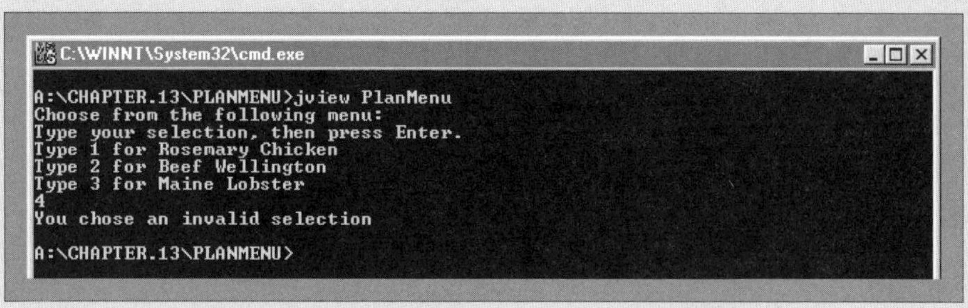

```
A:\CHAPTER.13\PLANMENU>jview PlanMenu
Choose from the following menu:
Type your selection, then press Enter.
Type 1 for Rosemary Chicken
Type 2 for Beef Wellington
Type 3 for Maine Lobster
4
You chose an invalid selection

A:\CHAPTER.13\PLANMENU>
```

Figure 13-14: Exceptional run of the PlanMenu program

Handling Exceptions Uniquely with Each `catch`

An advantage of using object-oriented exception-handling techniques is the ability to deal with Exceptions appropriately as you make conscious decisions about how to handle them. When methods from other classes throw Exceptions, they don't have to catch them; instead, your calling program can catch them, and then you can decide what you want to do. You can make your reaction to Exceptions specific for your current purposes. For example, the PickMenu class you created throws Exceptions. When you write new programs that use the PickMenu class, you can decide to handle error conditions differently within each program you write.

Next, you will extend the Menu class to create a new class named VegetarianMenu. Subsequently, when you write a program that uses PickMenu with the VegetarianMenu, you can deal with any Exception differently than you did when you wrote the PlanMenu program.

To create the VegetarianMenu class:

1 Add to the PlanMenu project a new class file named **VegetarianMenu**.

2 Add **extends Menu** to the right of the class header.

3 Between the class's curly brackets, provide new menu choices for the VegetarianMenu as follows:

```
String[] vegEntreeChoice = {"Spinach Lasagna",
   "Cheese Enchiladas", "Fruit Plate"};
```

4 Add the following constructor that calls the superclass constructor and then assigns each vegetarian selection to the Menu superclass entreeChoice array:

```
public VegetarianMenu()
{
   super();
   for(int x = 0; x < vegEntreeChoice.length; ++x)
      entreeChoice[x] = vegEntreeChoice[x];
}
```

Now write a program that uses VegetarianMenu. You could write any program, but for demonstration purposes, you simply can modify PlanMenu.java.

5 Return to the **PlanMenu.java** file in the Text Editor window, and then immediately save it as **PlanVegetarianMenu.java**.

6 Change the class name in the header to **PlanVegetarianMenu**.

7 Change the first statement within the main() method as follows so it declares a VegetarianMenu instead of a Menu: **VegetarianMenu briefMenu = new VegetarianMenu();**

8 Change the println() statement in the catch block as follows so it is specific to this program that uses the VegetarianMenu: **guestChoice = "an invalid vegetarian selection";**

9 Rebuild and save the project, then run the PlanVegetarianMenu file as a console application. When you see the vegetarian menu, enter a valid selection and confirm that the program works correctly. Then, run the program again and enter an invalid selection. The error message, shown in Figure 13-15, identifies your invalid entry as "an invalid *vegetarian* selection".

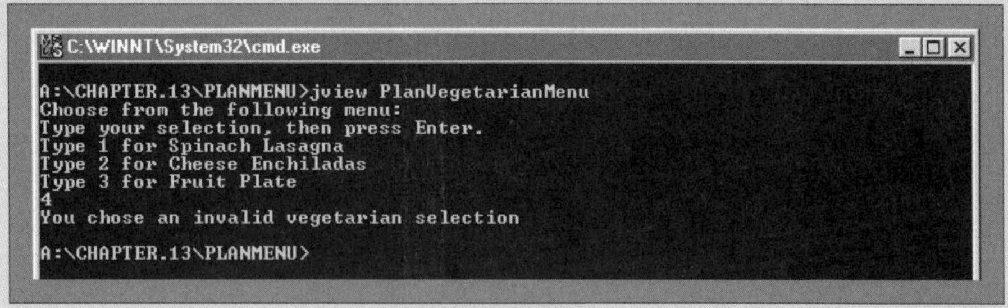

Figure 13-15: Exceptional run of the PlanVegetarianMenu program

Remember that you did not change the PickMenu class. Your new PlanVegetarianMenu program uses the PickMenu class that you wrote and compiled before a VegetarianMenu ever existed. However, because PickMenu throws uncaught Exceptions, you can handle those Exceptions as you see fit in any new programs in which you catch them.

Creating Your Own Exceptions

Java provides over 30 categories of Exceptions that you can throw in your programs. However, Java's creators could not predict every condition that might be an Exception in your programs. For example, you might want to declare an Exception when your bank balance is negative or when an outside party attempts to access your e-mail account. Most organizations have specific rules for defining what constitutes exceptional data: for example, an employee number must not exceed three digits, or an hourly salary must not be less than the legal minimum wage. You can handle these potential error situations with `if` statements, or you can create your own Exceptions.

To create your own Exception that you can throw, you must extend a subclass of Throwable. Recall from Figure 13-1 that Throwable has two subclasses, Exception and Error, which are used to distinguish between recoverable and nonrecoverable errors. Because you always want to create your own Exceptions for recoverable errors, you should extend your Exceptions from the Exception class. Although you can extend any existing Exception subclass, such as ArithmeticException or NullPointerException, usually you want to extend Exception.

> **tip**
> When you create an Exception, it's conventional to end its name with *Exception*.

Next, you will create a PartyException class for Event Handlers Incorporated to demonstrate how to create your own Exception. The PartyException class has just one method—a constructor. You can include data fields and other methods within the PartyException class if you want. For example, you might want the PartyException class to contain a customized toString() method that you can use to display party details. To keep this example simple, however, you will include only the constructor. The constructor will take a String argument representing the name of the party, such as the "Jones" party. You will pass this String along to the Exception superclass so you can use the String within superclass methods such as getMessage().

To write your own Exception:

1 Create a new empty project named **ThrowParty**. Save the **ThrowParty** project folder in the Chapter.13 folder on your Student Disk.

2 Add to the project a new class file named **PartyException**.

3 Add `extends Exception` to the right of the class header.

4 Enter the following constructor between the class's curly brackets:

```
Public PartyException(String s)
{
   super(s);
}
```

Next, you can create a Party class that holds information about any party hosted by Event Handlers Incorporated. The Party class holds two fields—the name of the party host and the number of guests—and it contains a constructor that requires values for both fields. Event Handlers does not host parties with fewer than 10 guests. Therefore, you want to test the guest number in the constructor, and throw a PartyException when the guest number is less than 10. The PartyException class constructor requires a String argument, so pass the name of the party host to the Exception. That way, you can use the host's name in error messages generated by the Exception class.

> **tip**
> You can throw any type of Exception at any time, not just Exceptions of your own creation. For example, within any program, you can code `throw(new RuntimeException());`. Of course, you would not want to do so without good reason; Java handles RuntimeExceptions for you by stopping the program. Because you cannot anticipate every possible error, Java's automatic action is often the best course of action.

To create the Party class:

1. Add to the ThrowParty project a new class file named **Party**.
2. Enter the following code between the class's curly brackets:

```
String host = new String();
int guests;
public Party(String hst, int gst) throws PartyException
{
   host = hst;
   guests = gst;
   if(gst < 10)
      throw(new PartyException(hst));
}
```

Now you can write a program that instantiates a few Party objects. When you run the program, you can observe which objects generate PartyExceptions.

To write the ThrowParty program:

1. Add a new main class file named **ThrowParty** to the ThrowParty project.
2. Between the main() method's curly brackets, enter the following code that constructs three Party objects in a `try` block:

```
try
{
   Party first = new Party("Jones",15);
   Party second = new Party("Lewis",5);
   Party third = new Party("Newman",10);
}
```

3. Enter the following code to catch any PartyExceptions and use the Exception class getMessage() method to display a message:

```
catch(PartyException error)
{
   System.out.println("Party Error: "
   + error.getMessage());
}
```

4. Select **ThrowParty Properties** from the **Project** menu. Select the **ThrowParty** file in the **When project runs, load** drop-down list box and set the project to run as a console application. When you are finished, click the **OK** button.

5. Build and save the project, then run the ThrowParty file as a console application. Compare your results to Figure 13-16. The Party objects with 10 or more guests execute successfully, but the Party object with too few guests generated a PartyException.

Figure 13-16: Output of the ThrowParty program

You should not create an excessive number of special Exception types for your classes, especially if the Java development environment already contains an Exception that will catch the error. Extra Exception types add a level of complexity for other programmers who will use your classes. However, when appropriate, specialized Exception classes provide an elegant way for you to handle error situations. They enable you to separate your error code from the usual, nonexceptional sequence of events.

Understanding Debugging

When you write a program using Java, Visual Basic, C++, or any other programming language, you will invariably encounter errors in your code. Three types of errors can occur in a Java program: syntax errors, logic errors, and run-time errors.

Syntax or **compiler errors** occur when you enter code that the compiler does not recognize. Syntax errors include invalid statements, missing punctuation, and incorrectly typed keywords. As you recall from Chapter 2, dynamic syntax checking in the Text Editor window automatically underlines certain types of invalid syntax with a squiggly red line and adds a SmartEditor error to the Task List. For example, if you enter the statement `System.out.println("Hello World")`, the statement `Expected ';'` appears in the Task List since the statement is missing an ending semicolon. If you enter the keyword `public` using uppercase letters, a SmartEditor error automatically appears since Java does not recognize the word `PUBLIC` as a keyword. (Remember, Java is case-sensitive.) Similarly, SmartEditor errors appear if your code does not have matching numbers of opening and closing curly brackets.

Other types of syntax errors are "caught" only when you build or rebuild the project. For example, if you were to enter the statement `System.out.prinln("Hello World");` (*println* is misspelled), a SmartEditor error does not automatically appear until you build the project. After you build the project, a SmartEditor error that reads `'prinln' is not a method in class 'PrintStream'(J0235)` appears in the Task List.

If the compiler encounters a problem while a program is executing, that problem is called a **run-time error**. The exceptions you have worked with in this chapter have all been run-time errors. Run-time errors are generated only during program execution and do not create SmartEditor errors in the Text Editor window. A dividing-by-zero error is a typical run-time error. For example, the following statements compile properly when you use the Build command, but cause a run-time error when the program executes since you are attempting to divide by zero:

```
int num = 13, denom = 0, result;
result = num / denom;
```

In this case, the program raises an exception of type java.langArithmeticException when it executes.

Logic errors are problems in the design of a program that prevent it from running as you anticipate. The logic behind any program involves executing the various statements and procedures in the correct order to produce the desired results. For example, when you do the laundry, you normally wash, dry, iron, then fold. If a laundry program irons, folds, dries, then washes, you have a logic error and the program executes incorrectly. Examples of logic errors in a computer program include multiplying two values when you mean to divide them or producing output prior to obtaining the appropriate input. Logic errors are not usually associated with syntax errors. A program can be syntactically correct and still not function properly because of design problems.

Any error in a computer program that causes it to function incorrectly is called a bug. Logic, syntax, and run-time errors are examples of bugs. **Debugging** describes the act of tracing and resolving errors in a computer program. Legend has it that the term *debugging* was first coined by Grace Murray Hopper, a mathematician who was instrumental in developing the COBOL programming language. As the story from the 1940s goes, a moth short-circuited a primitive computer that Hopper was using. Removing the moth from the computer *debugged* the system and resolved the problem. Today, a *bug* refers to any sort of problem in the design and operation of a computer program.

Do not confuse bugs with computer viruses. Bugs are errors within a computer program that occur because of syntax errors, design flaws, or run-time errors. Viruses are self-contained programs designed to "infect" a computer system and cause mischievous or malicious damage. Actually, virus programs themselves can contain bugs if they contain syntax errors or do not perform (or damage) as their creators envisioned.

Through your work in this chapter, you now know how to handle run-time errors in your programs using exception handling. Anticipating the types of exceptions your program needs to handle and bulletproofing your code are extremely important programming skills. You have also learned to use dynamic syntax checking and SmartEditor errors in the Task List to help you correct syntax errors in your code. Next you will learn how to use the tools available in Visual J++'s internal debugger to trace logic errors in your programs.

As you work with the Visual J++ debugging tools, keep in mind that debugging is not an exact science—every program you write is different and requires different methods of debugging. In addition, the Visual J++ debugging tools only help you find bugs, not correct them. Your own logical and analytical skills are the best debugging resources you have. For example, even though you may use one of the J++ debugging tools to find a bug, you must use your own logical and analytical skills to correct the error.

To customize various debugging features, select Options from the Tools menu, then select the Text Editor or Debugger categories in the Options dialog box.

Tracing Program Execution with the Visual J++ Debugger

Up to this point, you have resolved logical errors by examining each line of a program in the Text Editor window. Examining your code is usually the first step to take when you have a logical error. However, it can be very difficult to spot an error by simply examining code. For instance, examine the following code:

```
boolean vegMenu;
int mealPrice = 10;
vegMenu = false;
if(vegMenu == true);
      mealPrice = 8;
System.out.println(mealPrice);
```

The mealPrice integer is initially assigned a value of 10, and the vegMenu boolean variable is set to `false`. The `if` statement evaluates the vegMenu variable to see whether it is set to `true`. Since it is not set to `true`, the next line should be skipped and the `System.out.println(mealPrice);` statement should print a value of 10. However, the line `if(vegMenu == true);` contains an ending semicolon which marks the end of the `if` statement. Therefore, the line `mealPrice = 8` is another statement in the program that always executes, regardless of whether the `if` statement evaluates to `true` or `false`. The code is syntactically correct, but does not function as you anticipated. As you can see from this example, it is easy to overlook very minor logic errors in your code.

Logic errors can be even more difficult to spot when you are creating a large program that includes multiple classes and methods. For instance, you may have a main class that instantiates objects from several other classes. Each instantiated object may then call methods from its parent class. Attempting to trace the logic and flow of such a program in the Text Editor window can be difficult. The Visual J++ Debug menu provides several tools that help you trace each line of code, creating a much more efficient method of resolving logic errors.

Using Step Commands

The Step Into, Step Over, and Step Out commands on the Debug menu allow you to enter break mode. **Break mode** temporarily suspends, or pauses, program execution. When you use the Step Into command, a program executes an individual line of code and then pauses until you instruct the debugger to continue. This feature gives you an opportunity to evaluate a program's flow and structure as it is being executed.

As you step into a class, the debugger stops at each line within every procedure that a program calls. When stepping through a program to trace a logical error, it is convenient to be able to skip procedures that you know are functioning correctly. The Step Over command allows you to skip procedure calls. The program still executes procedures that you step over, but it appears as if a single statement executes.

The Step Out command executes all remaining code in the current procedure. If the current procedure was called from another procedure, all remaining code in the current procedure is executed and the debugger stops at the next statement in the calling procedure.

When a program enters break mode, program execution is not stopped—it is only suspended. To resume program execution after entering break mode, select Continue from the Debug menu. The Continue command ends the debugging session and executes the rest of the program normally. You can also end a debugging session and halt program execution by selecting the End command from the Debug menu.

You can enter break mode during program execution by selecting Break from the Debug menu or by pressing Ctrl+Break.

Although you can make changes to code while in break mode, they will not take effect while the program is executing. You must end program execution (using the Continue or End commands), rebuild the project, and then start the program again.

You can also trace program execution with the Run To Cursor command on the Debug menu. When you select the Run To Cursor command, the program runs normally until it reaches the statement where your cursor is located. You can then use the Step Into, Step Over, and Step Out commands to continue tracing program execution. The Run To Cursor command is useful if you are sure that your program is functioning correctly up to a certain point in the code.

Next, you will practice tracing program execution using the Step Into, Step Over, Step Out, and Run To Cursor commands.

To practice tracing program execution:

1. Open the **PlanMenu** project from the Chapter.13 folder on your Student Disk, then open the **PlanMenu.java** file in the Text Editor window.

2. Place the insertion point anywhere in the line that reads `String guestChoice = new String();` and select **Run To Cursor** from the **Debug** menu. The program starts running. You briefly see a command window, then program execution enters break mode and a yellow arrow in the margin of the Text Editor window points to the next statement to be processed, as shown in Figure 13-17.

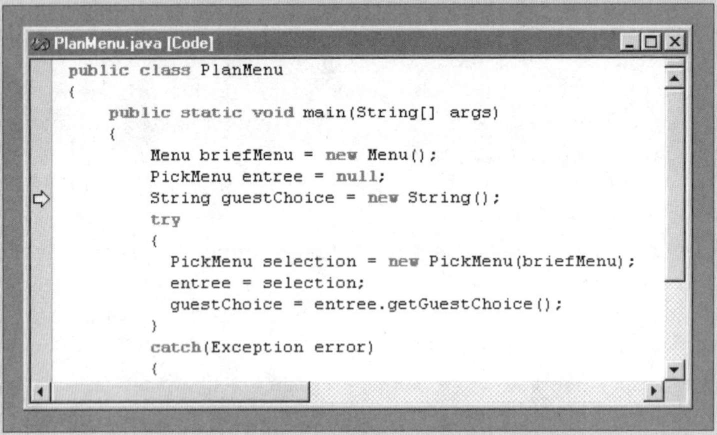

Figure 13-17: PlanMenu program in break mode

help — The debugger executes all statements before the line that your cursor is in when you select the Run To Cursor command; the statement in the line containing your cursor is the next statement to be processed.

3. Select **Step Into** from the **Debug** menu. The debugger processes the current statement and moves the yellow arrow to the next line which contains the statement `PickMenu selection = new PickMenu(briefMenu);`. This statement instantiates a new PickMenu object.

tip — Most of the commands on the Debug menu can also be executed using keyboard shortcuts or buttons on the Debug toolbar. Each command's keyboard shortcut is listed to the right of the command on the Debug menu. To display a ToolTip for a specific Debug toolbar button, hold your pointer over the desired button.

4. Select the **Step Into** command one more time. This time, control is transferred to the constructor in the PickMenu class.

Exception Handling and Debugging   657

5 Now select the **Step Out** command from the **Debug** menu. The rest of the statements in the PickMenu class execute normally and a command window appears that prompts you to make a menu selection.

6 Make a selection in the command window and press the **Enter** key. The debugger pauses at the statement following the line that instantiates the PickMenu object (`entree = selection;`).

7 Select the **Step Into** command to process the `entree = selection;` statement. The line `guestChoice = entree.getGuestChoice();`, is highlighted.

8 This time, select the **Step Over** command from the **Debug** menu. The debugger executes the `guestChoice = entree.getGuestChoice();` statement and highlights the next line. If you had selected the Step Into command, program execution would have transferred to the getGuestChoice() method in the PickMenu class.

9 Select **Continue** from the **Debug** menu.

> After you select the Continue command, the command window displays a prompt that states the type of entrée you ordered, and then quickly closes. As you recall from Chapter 2, when a program that creates system output is executed using JVIEW from *within* the IDE (as you did here when you used the tracing tools), the command window closes immediately after completing its task.

> The Debug menu contains two additional commands that you can use in break mode to assist in tracing program execution: Set Next Statement and Show Next Statement. When you are stepping through a program, you use the Set Next Statement command to change which statement should be executed next. You use the Show Next Statement command to highlight the next statement to be executed.

> You can select how the debugger handles Java exceptions using the Java Exceptions dialog box. The Java Exceptions dialog box displays a hierarchical list of all Java exceptions. For each individual exception, you can select whether the debugger will enter break mode, continue and break only if the exception is not handled, or use the break setting from the exception's superclass. To access the Java Exceptions dialog box, select Java Exceptions from the Debug menu.

Tracing Program Execution with Breakpoints

Another method of tracing program execution in Visual J++ involves inserting breakpoints into code. A **breakpoint** is a position within a code file at which program execution enters break mode. Once a program is paused at a breakpoint, you can use the Step Into, Step Over, Step Out, and Run To Cursor commands to trace program execution, or you can use the Continue command to complete program execution or run to the next breakpoint. Multiple breakpoints provide a convenient way to pause program execution at key positions in your code where you think there may be a bug.

Next, you will practice using breakpoints.

To practice using breakpoints:

1 Return to the **PlanMenu.java** file in the Text Editor window.

2 Position the insertion point anywhere in the line that reads `Menu briefMenu = new Menu();` and select **Insert Breakpoint** from the **Debug** menu. A red circle appears in the margin of the Text Editor window next to the line containing the breakpoint.

You can also insert a breakpoint by clicking once in the left margin, next to the line where you want to insert a breakpoint.

3 Add another breakpoint in the line that reads `PickMenu selection = new PickMenu(briefMenu);`. Figure 3-18 shows how the Text Editor window appears with the two breakpoints.

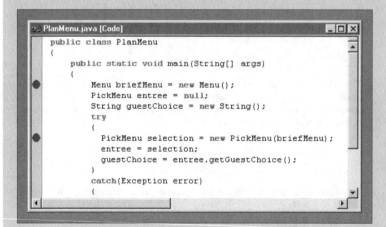

Figure 3-18: Breakpoints in the Text Editor window

4 Select **Start** from the **Debug** menu. The program starts running and opens a command window, then pauses at the first breakpoint. A yellow arrow appears in the margin of the Text Editor window on top of the red circle that marks the breakpoint.

5 Select **Continue** from the **Debug** menu. The statements between the two breakpoints execute, then program execution pauses at the second breakpoint.

6 Select **End** from the **Debug** menu to cancel program execution. At this point, you can continue program execution, set additional breakpoints, or use any of the other debug commands.

To remove breakpoints from a file:

1 Place the insertion point anywhere in the line containing the first breakpoint and select **Remove Breakpoint** from the **Debug** menu. The red circle in the margin of the Text Editor window is removed.

> Instead of removing a breakpoint, you can disable it by placing the insertion point in the line containing the breakpoint and selecting Disable Breakpoint from the Debug menu. A disabled breakpoint appears as a white circle in the left margin of the Text Editor window. To activate a disabled breakpoint, place the insertion point in the line containing the breakpoint and select Enable Breakpoint from the Debug menu.

2 Repeat Step 1 to remove the second breakpoint in the file.

> You can remove all breakpoints in a project by selecting Clear All Breakpoints from the Debug menu.

> You can add, enable, disable, and remove breakpoints using the Breakpoints dialog box. To access the Breakpoints dialog box, select Breakpoints from the Debug menu. You can also use the Breakpoints dialog box to set the conditions for which a program should pause at a breakpoint. For example, you can set a breakpoint to occur only when the contents of a variable match a specific value.

Tracing Variables and Expressions with Debug Windows

As you trace program execution using step commands and breakpoints, you may also need to trace how variables and expressions change during the course of program execution. For example, you may have a line that reads `resultNum = firstNum / secondNum`. You know this line is causing a divide-by-zero error, but you do not know exactly when secondNum is being changed to a zero value. The ability to trace program execution and locate the exact location where secondNum is being changed to a zero value allows you to pinpoint the cause of the logic problem. When your program is in break mode, Visual J++ displays several debug windows—Autos, Locals, Watch, and Immediate—that help you trace and analyze variables and expressions.

> Any error or exception messages that are generated while you are debugging an application are printed to the Output window. To display the Output window, point to Other Windows on the View menu, then click Output Window. You can also display the Output window by pressing Ctrl+Alt+O. You first learned about the Output window in Chapter 2.

Using the Autos Window

If you are stepping through a program and execute a statement that declares int sampleVariable = 1;, sampleVariable comes into scope. When you reach the end of a block in which a variable is declared, the variable goes out of scope. (You learned about scope in Chapter 4.) The Autos window displays variables within the current scope.

Variables displayed in the Autos window with a plus sign next to them represent classes. For example, an object instantiated from a class will have a plus sign next to it in the Autos window. Clicking a plus sign displays variable information for that class. The Autos window contains three columns: Name, Value, and Type.

Display the Autos window by pointing to Debug Windows on the View menu and clicking Autos. An example of the Autos window is shown in Figure 13-19.

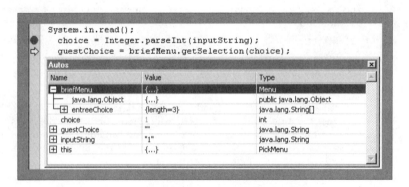

Figure 13-19: Example of the Autos window

The Autos window helps you see how different values affect program execution. As you step through code in break mode, you can change the value of a variable in the Autos window by clicking once on the value in the Value column, entering a new value, and pressing Enter. Changing a value when in break mode changes the value only for the current instance of program execution.

Using the Locals Window

The Locals window displays all variables within the currently executing method. If a variable within the current method has not yet been initialized, the variable's value will read `Error: variable is not in scope`. Like the Autos window, the Locals window contains three columns: Name, Value, and Type.

Display the Locals window by pointing to Debug Windows on the View menu and then clicking Locals. An example of the Locals window is shown in Figure 3-20.

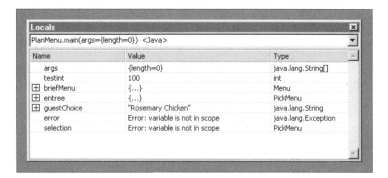

Figure 3-20: Example of the Locals window

At the top of the Locals window is a drop-down list box containing a list of all the methods from which the current method was called. To display a method's variables, select the method in the drop-down list box.

The Locals window helps you see how different values in the currently executing method affect program execution. You change the value of a variable in the Locals window by clicking once on the value in the Value column, entering a new value, and pressing Enter.

Using the Watch Window

The Watch window is used for monitoring and changing specific variables that you enter. Unlike the Autos window, which shows variables for the current and previous lines, or the Locals window, which shows variables for the current method, the Watch window shows information on variables that you specifically enter. For example, you can enter the name of a variable into the Watch window and monitor how the variable changes during the course of program execution. You can also enter expressions in the Watch window and observe how their values change as the program executes. For example, if you place the expression `sampleVariable * 2` in the Watch window, its value changes as sampleVariable changes. Like the Autos and Locals windows, the Watch window contains three columns: Name, Value, and Type.

Display the Watch window by pointing to Debug Windows on the View menu and then clicking Watch. An example of the Watch window is shown in Figure 3-21.

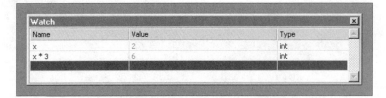

Figure 3-21: Example of the Watch window

You enter variable names and expressions directly into a row in the Watch window, or you drag a variable or expression onto the Watch window from the Text Editor window, the Autos window, or the Locals window.

Using the Immediate Window

The Immediate window also allows you to view and change values. Unlike the Autos, Locals, and Watch windows, the Immediate window does not contain Name, Value, and Type columns. Instead, it appears as a blank window into which you can type variable names or expressions. You can also drag variables and expressions from the Text Editor window into the Immediate window. Once you have entered a variable or expression into the Immediate window, pressing the Enter key prints the variable's or expression's value on the next line. You can assign a new value to a variable by typing the variable name followed by an equal sign and the new value.

Display the Immediate window by pointing to Debug Windows on the View menu and then clicking Immediate. An example of the Immediate window is shown in Figure 3-22.

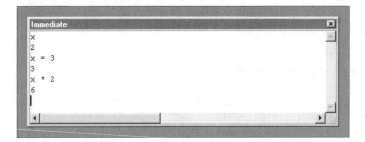

Figure 3-22: Example of the Immediate window

After pressing the Enter key to display the value of a variable or expression, you can redisplay the value by placing the insertion point in the line containing the variable or expression in the Immediate window and pressing the Enter key again.

With other programs that are part of Visual Studio, such as Visual Basic and Visual C++, you can enter complex commands into the Immediate window. In Visual J++, the Immediate window is used primarily for displaying and changing values. It is often easier to monitor and change values in Visual J++ using the Watch window.

> **tip**
>
> In addition to the using the debug windows to learn the value of a variable, in break mode you can learn the value of a variable by holding your mouse over the variable to display a ToolTip.

Combining Debug Windows

When you display the Autos, Locals, Watch, and Immediate windows, you may find it necessary to reposition each window to see it properly on your screen. If you drag one window on top of another window, the two windows will combine into a single window with tabs at the bottom representing each individual window. To separate an individual window from a combined window, place the insertion point on the window's tab, hold down your left mouse button, then drag to a new position.

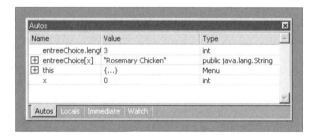

Figure 13-23: Example of combined debug windows

Next, you will practice tracing variables.

> **To practice tracing variables:**
>
> **1** Return to the **PlanMenu.java** file in the Text Editor window and add a breakpoint to the line that reads `PickMenu entree = null;`.
>
> **2** Open the **PickMenu.java** file in the Text Editor window and add a breakpoint to the line that reads `choice = Integer.parseInt(inputString);`.
>
> **3** Display the Watch window by pointing at **Debug Windows** on the **View** menu and then selecting **Watch**.
>
> **4** Highlight the word *choice* in the `choice = Integer.parseInt(inputString);` line, then hold down your left mouse button and drag onto the Watch window. The word *choice* appears in the Name column of the Watch window. The choice variable is an integer that contains a number representing an entrée selection.

5 Execute the program by selecting **Start** from the **Debug** menu. The program starts, then enters break mode at the first breakpoint.

6 Observe the value of the choice variable in the Watch window. The variable has not yet come into scope, so the value should read `Error: symbol "choice" not found`.

> **help** It may be necessary to redisplay the Watch window after starting the program.

7 Display the Autos window by pointing at **Debug Windows** on the **View** menu and then selecting **Autos**, or by clicking the **Autos** tab in the combined debug window. The Autos window appears, displaying a single entry, briefMenu, which is an object instantiated from the Menu class. Since the object was instantiated in the previous line, it is within the current scope. Expand briefMenu in the Autos window by clicking the plus sign. Beneath briefMenu, you should see the entreeChoice array, which was declared when the briefMenu object was instantiated from the Menu class. Clicking the plus sign next to the entreeChoice array displays the three elements it contains: Rosemary Chicken, Beef Wellington, and Maine Lobster.

8 Display the Locals window by pointing at **Debug Windows** on the **View** menu and then selecting **Locals**. The Locals window appears, displaying the variables that are local to the main() method of the PlanMenu class. Click the arrow next to the drop-down list box at the top of the Locals window. Only one entry should appear in the list, `PlanMenu.main(args={length=0}) <Java>`, which represents the main() method of the PlanMenu class. If you were stepping through a method that had been called by the main() method, then an entry for that called method would also be visible in the drop-down list box.

9 Select **Continue** from the **Debug** menu. When you are prompted to choose from the menu, select the first choice, **Rosemary Chicken**, and press **Enter**. The program continues, then stops at the second breakpoint in the PickMenu class.

10 Observe the value of the choice variable in the Watch window. The value is now zero since it was declared at the start of the PickMenu class, but no value was assigned to it.

11 Click the arrow next to the drop-down list box at the top of the Locals window. Three entries are now visible: the main() method entry from the PlanMenu class, an entry for the PickMenu constructor that was called by the main() method of the PlanMenu class, and the setGuestChoice method of the PickMenu class, which was called by the PickMenu class constructor.

12 Select **Step Into** from the **Debug** menu. Now look at the value of the choice variable in the Watch window. It has changed to 1, which represents the Rosemary Chicken selection you made in Step 9. Click once in the box containing the value of 1 and type 3, which represents the Maine Lobster selection, then press **Enter**. You can use the same procedure to change the value of a variable in the Locals window and the Autos window.

Exception Handling and Debugging

13 You can also change the value of a variable in the Immediate window. Point to **Debug Windows** on the **View** menu, then select **Immediate**. In the Immediate window, type **choice = 3**, then press **Enter**.

You can also display each of the debug windows using keyboard shortcuts or buttons on the Debug toolbar. Each window's keyboard shortcut is listed to the right of the window name on the Debug submenu of the View menu. To display a description, or ToolTip, for a specific debug window, hold your pointer over the desired button on the Debug toolbar.

14 Select **Step Over** from the **Debug** menu to assign the appropriate string ("Maine Lobster") to the guestChoice string, based on the choice variable. To confirm that the entrée selection has been changed to Maine Lobster, hold your mouse over the guestChoice variable in the line that reads `guestChoice = briefMenu.getSelection(choice);`. A ToolTip containing the name of the variable and its value displays, as shown in Figure 13-24.

```
    System.in.read();
    choice = Integer.parseInt(inputString);
    guestChoice = briefMenu.getSelection(choice);
  }       guestChoice = "Maine Lobster"
  public String getGuestChoice()
```

Figure 13-24: ToolTip displaying a variable name and value

15 Select **End** from the **Debug** menu. Then remove the breakpoints from the PlanMenu.java and PickMenu.java files.

Another debug window, the Threads window, is used for debugging multithreaded applications. You will learn about multithreading in Chapter 15.

Tracing Exceptions through the Call Stack

When one method calls another, the computer's operating system must keep track of where the called method came from, and program control must return to the calling method when the called method is complete. For example, if methodA calls methodB, the operating system has to "remember" to return to methodA when methodB ends. Similarly, if methodB calls methodC, then while methodC is executing, the computer needs to "remember" that it is going to return to methodB and, eventually, to methodA. The memory location where the computer stores the list of locations to which the system must return is known as the **call stack**. The earliest method call is stored at the bottom of the call stack whereas subsequent calls are "stacked" on top.

When a method throws an Exception, and if the method does not catch the Exception, then the Exception is thrown to the next method "up" the call stack, or in other words, to the method that called the offending method. If methodA calls methodB, and methodB calls methodC, and methodC throws an Exception, then Java looks first for a catch block in methodC. If none exists, then Java looks for a catch block in methodB. If methodB does not have a catch block, then Java looks to methodA. This system has great advantages because it allows your methods to handle Exceptions more appropriately. However, when a program uses several classes, it has the disadvantage of making it very difficult for the programmer to locate the original source of an Exception.

You already have used the Throwable method getMessage() to obtain information about an Exception. Another useful Exception method is the printStackTrace() method. When you catch an Exception, you can call printStackTrace() to display a list of methods in the call stack so you can determine the location of the Exception.

To use the printStackTrace() method:

1 In the PlanMenu project, open the **PlanMenu.java** file in the Text Editor window, then immediately save the file as **PlanMenuWithStackTrace.java**.

2 Change the class header in order to match the new class name (PlanMenuWithStackTrace).

3 Position the insertion point within the catch block after the opening curly bracket and before the statement guestChoice = "an invalid selection";, and then press the **Enter** key to start a new line.

4 Type the following two new statements to identify and print the stack trace:

```
System.out.println("Stack Trace");
error.printStackTrace();
```

5 Rebuild and save the project, then execute the PlanMenuWithStackTrace file as a console application. After the menu appears, enter an invalid selection. For example, if you enter 4, your screen looks like Figure 13-25. If you read the list that follows the "Stack Trace" heading, you see that an ArrayIndexOutOfBoundsException occurred in the method Menu.getSelection(). That method was called by the PickMenu.setGuestChoice() method, which in turn was initiated by the PickMenu constructor. The PickMenu constructor was called from the PlanMenuWithStackTrace.main() method. You see the line number as additional information within each method where the Exception occurred (your line numbers might be different). Using printStackTrace() can be a useful debugging tool.

Exception Handling and Debugging

```
C:\WINNT\System32\cmd.exe

A:\CHAPTER.13\PLANMENU>jview PlanMenuWithStackTrace
Choose from the following menu:
Type your selection, then press Enter.
Type 1 for Rosemary Chicken
Type 2 for Beef Wellington
Type 3 for Maine Lobster
4
Stack Trace
java.lang.ArrayIndexOutOfBoundsException
        at Menu.getSelection (Menu.java:14)
        at PickMenu.setGuestChoice (PickMenu.java:25)
        at PickMenu.<init> (PickMenu.java:10)
        at PlanMenuWithStackTrace.main (PlanMenuWithStackTrace.java:10)
You chose an invalid selection

A:\CHAPTER.13\PLANMENU>
```

Figure 13-25: Exceptional run of the PlanMenuWithStackTrace program

6 Run the PlanMenuWithStackTrace program again and enter **A** for the user selection. You can see from the stack trace that this time the Exception does not originate in the Menu.getSelection() method. This program stops at the parseInt() method before the program attempts getSelection().

Often, you do not want to place a printStackTrace() method call in a finished program. Your program user has no interest in the cryptic messages that print. However, while you are developing a program, printStackTrace() can be a very useful tool for diagnosing your program's problems.

SUMMARY

- You can use the clause `throws xxxException` after the method header to indicate the type of Exception that might be thrown.

- Most Java methods that you write do not use a `throws` clause; most exceptions never have to be explicitly thrown or caught.

- When a method you write throws an Exception, the method can, but is not required to, catch the Exception.

- It is good style to let a calling program assume responsibility for handling an error detected by a called method.

- A method's header, including its return type, name, arguments, and `throws` phrase, constitutes the method's signature.

- An advantage of using object-oriented exception-handling techniques lies in your ability to make your reaction to Exceptions specific for your current purposes.

- You can create your own Exceptions by extending the Exception class.

section B

- Three types of errors can occur in a Java program: syntax errors, logic errors, and run-time errors.

- Syntax or compiler errors occur when you enter code that is not recognized by the compiler.

- If the compiler encounters a problem while a program is being executed, it is called a run-time error.

- Logic errors refer to problems with the design of a program that prevent it from running as you anticipate.

- Debugging is the act of tracing and resolving errors in a computer program.

- The Visual J++ debugging tools only help you find bugs, not resolve them. The best resources you have to assist in finding and resolving bugs are your own logical and analytical skills.

- Break mode is the temporary suspension of program execution.

- Stepping into a program executes an individual line of code and then pauses until you instruct the debugger to continue.

- Stepping over a statement that calls a procedure from another class executes the call as if it were a single statement. Procedures that you step over are still executed, but it appears as if a single statement were executed.

- Stepping out of a procedure executes all remaining code in the current procedure.

- A breakpoint is a position within a code file where program execution enters break mode.

- As you trace program execution using step commands and breakpoints, you can also trace how variables and expressions change during the course of program execution using the Autos window, Locals window, Watch window, and Immediate window. You trace how variables and expressions change during program execution to debug logic errors.

- The Autos window displays variables within the current scope.

- The Locals window displays all variables within the currently executing method.

- You use the Watch window to monitor specific variables.

- You use the Immediate window to view and change values.

- You can change the value of variables in the Autos, Locals, Watch, and Immediate windows.

- The memory location where the computer stores the list of locations to which the system must return after method calls is known as the call stack.

- When a method throws an Exception and if the method does not catch the Exception, the Exception is thrown to the next method "up" the call stack.

- The printStackTrace() method displays a list of methods in the call stack.

QUESTIONS

1. When you write a method that might throw an xxxException, you can use the clause _____ after the method header to indicate the type of Exception that might be thrown.
   a. `throws xxxException`
   b. `catches xxxException`
   c. `tries xxxException`
   d. `uses xxxException`

2. Which methods can throw an Exception?
   a. Methods with a `throws` clause
   b. Methods with a `catch` block
   c. Methods with both a `throws` clause and a `catch` block
   d. Any method

3. You must always throw a(n) _____.
   a. Error
   b. Exception
   c. RuntimeException
   d. IOException

4. You must always catch _____.
   a. an IOException
   b. any thrown Exception
   c. any unthrown Exception
   d. You are not required to catch anything.

5. A method can _____.
   a. check for errors but not handle them
   b. handle errors but not check for them
   c. either of these
   d. neither of these

6. When you use any method, you must know three pieces of information to use the method to its full potential, except for _____.
   a. the method's return type
   b. the type of arguments the method requires
   c. the number of statements within the method
   d. the type of Exceptions the method throws

7. A method's header also is called its _____.
   a. prototype
   b. Exception
   c. signature
   d. endorsement

section B

8. The memory location where the computer stores the list of locations to which the system must return is known as the _____.
   a. registry
   b. call stack
   c. chronicle
   d. archive

9. Java provides you with _____ categories of Exceptions that you can throw in your programs.
   a. two
   b. over 30
   c. over 250
   d. several thousand

10. To create your own Exception that you can throw, you *must* extend a subclass of _____.
    a. Object
    b. Throwable
    c. Exception
    d. Error

11. To create your own Exception that you can throw, you *usually* extend a subclass of _____.
    a. Object
    b. Throwable
    c. Exception
    d. Error

12. To create your own Exception that you can throw, you are *allowed* to extend _____.
    a. ArrayIndexOutOfBoundsException
    b. Object
    c. AWTEvent
    d. any of these

13. A divide-by-zero error is an example of a _____ error.
    a. syntax
    b. run-time
    c. logical
    d. compiler

14. The act of tracing and resolving errors in a computer program is called _____.
    a. logical analysis
    b. exception handling
    c. debugging
    d. decompiling

15. The temporary suspension of program execution is called _____
    a. break mode
    b. halting
    c. interrupting
    d. selective compiling

16. _____ a program executes an individual line of code and then pauses until you instruct the debugger to continue.
    a. Stepping out of
    b. Stepping over
    c. Stepping into
    d. Stepping across

17. A position within a code file where program execution enters break mode is called a _____.
    a. logical error
    b. syntax error
    c. breakpoint
    d. trace command

18. The debug window that shows variables *only* for the currently executing method is called the _____ window.
    a. Watch
    b. Autos
    c. Immediate
    d. Locals

19. You can get a list of the methods through which an Exception has traveled by using the _____ method.
    a. getMessage()
    b. callStack()
    c. getPath()
    d. printStackTrace()

20. The printStackTrace() method is most useful for _____.
    a. diagnosing your program's problems
    b. telling the user how to fix a problem
    c. communicating with other methods about the problem
    d. all of these

EXERCISES

Save the programs that you create in the exercises in the Chapter.13 folder on your Student Disk.

1. Write a program named SqrtError that throws and catches an ArithmeticException. Declare a variable and assign it a value. Test the variable, and if it is negative, throw an ArithmeticException. Otherwise, use the Math.sqrt() method to determine the square root.

section B

2. Create an EmployeeException class whose constructor receives a String that consists of an employee's ID and pay rate. Create an Employee class with two fields, IDNum and hourlyWage. The Employee constructor requires values for both fields. Upon construction, throw an EmployeeException if the hourlyWage is less than 6.00 or over 50.00. Write a program that establishes at least three Employees with hourlyWages that are above, below, and within the allowed range.

3. a. Create an IceCreamConeException class whose constructor receives a String that consists of an ice cream cone's flavor and number of scoops. Create an IceCreamCone class with two fields—iceCreamFlavor and scoops. The IceCreamCone constructor calls two data-entry methods—getFlavor() and getScoops(). The getScoops() method throws an IceCreamConeException when the scoop quantity exceeds three. Write a program that establishes several IceCreamCone objects and handles the Exception.
   b. Modify the IceCreamCone getFlavor() method to ensure that the user enters a valid flavor. Allow at least four flavors of your choice. If the user's entry does not match a valid flavor, throw an IceCreamConeException.

4. Write a program that displays a student ID number and asks the user to enter a numeric test score for the student. Create a ScoreException class, and throw a ScoreException for that class if the user does not enter a valid score (less than or equal to 100 and greater than or equal to 0). Catch the ScoreException and then display an appropriate message.

5. Write a program that displays a student ID number and asks the user to enter a test letter grade for the student. Create an Exception class named GradeException, and throw a GradeException if the user does not enter a valid letter grade. Catch the GradeException and then display an appropriate message.

6. Write an applet that prompts the user for an ID number and an age. Create an Exception class and throw an Exception of that class if the ID is not in the range of valid ID numbers (zero through 899), or if the age is not in the range of valid ages (0 through 89). Catch the Exception and then display an appropriate message.

7. Each of the following files in the Chapter.13 folder on your Student Disk has syntax and/or logical errors. Add the files to a new project called FixDebug. Save the FixDebug project in the Chapter.13 folder on your Student Disk. In each case, fix the problem using the debugging skills and tools you learned in this chapter and run each file as a console application.
   a. DebugThirteen1.java
   b. DebugThirteen2.java
   c. DebugThirteen3.java
   d. DebugThirteen4.java

CHAPTER 14

File Input and Output

case ▶ "Haven't I seen you spending a lot of time at the keyboard lately?" asks Lynn Greenbrier one day at Event Handlers Incorporated.

"I'm afraid so," you answer. "I'm trying to write a program that displays a month's scheduled events, one at a time. Every time I run it, I have to enter the data for every event—the host's name, the number of guests, and so on."

"You're typing all the data over and over again?" Lynn asks in disbelief. "It's time for me to show you how to save data to a file."

Previewing a Program That Uses File Data

Event Handlers Incorporated stores a record of each scheduled event in a disk file. Any employee in the company can view the scheduled events on-screen. You will create a similar program in this chapter; however, you can use a completed version of the Chap14ReadFile program that is saved in the Chapter.14 folder on your Student Disk now.

To use the Chap14ReadFile class:

1 Go to the command prompt for the Chap14ReadFile folder in the Chapter.14 folder on your Student Disk, type **jview Chap14ReadFile**, and then press the **Enter** key. This program lets you view previously stored data about events, one event at a time.

2 Click the **View Event** button. The data for the Curfman event displays and shows that the event is scheduled for the first day of the month with 100 guests, as shown in Figure 14-1.

Figure 14-1: Chap14ReadFile program

3 Click the **View Event** button again to view the data for nine additional events. Click the **Close** button ⊠ to exit the program at any time, or the program will exit automatically when you reach the end of the stored data file.

SECTION A
objectives

In this section you will learn:
- How to use the File class
- About file organization and streams
- How to use streams
- How to write to a file
- How to read data from a file

Introduction to the File Class

Using the File Class

Computer users use the term *file* to describe the objects that they store on permanent storage devices, such as floppy disks. Some files are **data files** that contain facts and figures, such as employee numbers, names, and salaries. Other files are **program files** that store software instructions. Yet other files can store graphics, text, or operating-system instructions. Although their contents vary, files have many common characteristics: Each file occupies a section of disk (or other storage device) space, has a name, and has a specific time of creation. You can use the **File class** to gather file information. The File class does not provide any opening, processing, or closing capabilities for files. Rather, you use the File class to obtain information about a file, such as its size, its last modification date, and whether it exists or is open.

You must include the statement `import java.io.*` in any program that uses the File class. The java.io package contains all the classes you use in file processing. The File class is a direct descendant of the Object class. You can create a File object using a constructor that includes a filename, such as `File someData = new File("data.txt");`, where data.txt is a file on the default disk drive. You also can specify a path for the file, as in `File someData = new File("A:\\Chapter.14\\data.txt")`, in which the argument to the constructor contains a disk drive and path. Figure 14-2 lists some useful File class methods.

The *io* in java.io stands for *i*nput/output.

Recall that the back slash (\) is used as part of an escape sequence in Java. You must type *two* back slashes to indicate a single back slash to the operating system. You learned about the escape sequence in Chapter 2.

section A

Method	Purpose
`boolean canRead()`	Returns `true` if a file is readable.
`boolean canWrite()`	Returns `true` if a file is writeable.
`boolean exists()`	Returns `true` if a file exists.
`String getName()`	Returns the file's name.
`String getPath()`	Returns the file's path.
`String getParent()`	Returns the name of the folder in which to find the file.
`long length()`	Returns the file's size.
`long lastModified()`	Returns the time the file was last modified. This time depends on the system and should be used only to compare it to other files' times, and not as an absolute time.

Figure 14-2: File class methods

Next, you will write a class that examines a file and prints appropriate messages concerning its status.

To create a class that uses a File object:

1. If necessary, start Visual J++, then create a new console application project named **CheckFile**. Save the **CheckFile** project folder in the Chapter.14 folder on your Student Disk.
2. Rename the default Class1.java file as **CheckFile.java**, then open the file in the Text Editor window.
3. Replace the default comments before the class header with the following statement to import the file classes: `import java.io.*;`.
4. Replace the Class1 class name in the `public class Class1` line with **CheckFile**.
5. Replace the `// TODO: Add initialization code here` comment in the main() method with the following line to create a File object that represents a disk file named data.txt: `File f = new File("data.txt");`.
6. Press the **Enter** key and type the following `if` statements to test for the file's existence. If the file exists, print its name and size, and then test whether the file can be read or written.

   ```
   if(f.exists())
   {
   ```

```
      System.out.println(f.getName() + " exists");
      System.out.println
        ("The file is " + f.length() + " bytes long");
      if(f.canRead())
        System.out.println(" ok to read");
      if(f.canWrite())
        System.out.println(" ok to write");
    }
```

7 Enter the following `else` clause to print a message if the file does not exist:

```
else
  System.out.println("File does not exist");
```

8 Add a new text file to the project by selecting **Add Item** from the **Project** menu. The Add Item dialog box appears. In the Add Item dialog box, select **Text** from the **Other** folder, then change the suggested filename to **data.txt** and click the **Open** button. The new text file is added to the list of files in the CheckFile project.

9 Open the data.txt file in the Text Editor window and then type the alphabet: **abcdefghijklmnopqrstuvwxyz**.

10 Set the project properties to run the **CheckFile** file as a console application, then build and save the project. If necessary, correct any syntax errors and rebuild. Execute the program as a console application by typing `jview CheckFile` at the command line. The output appears in Figure 14-3.

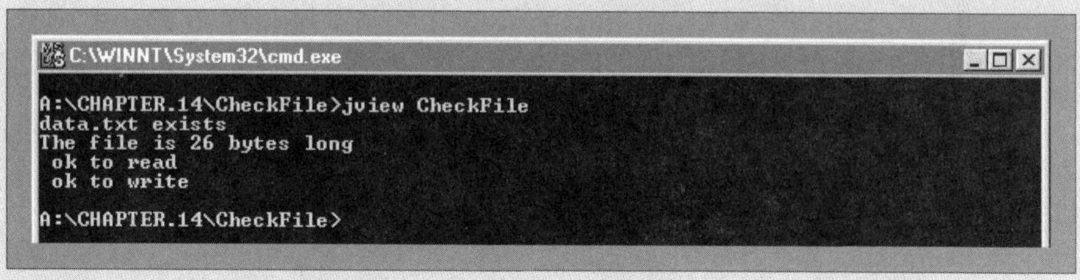

```
C:\WINNT\System32\cmd.exe

A:\CHAPTER.14\CheckFile>jview CheckFile
data.txt exists
The file is 26 bytes long
 ok to read
 ok to write

A:\CHAPTER.14\CheckFile>
```

Figure 14-3: Output of the CheckFile program

help

> If you added comments to the beginning of your data.txt file, then your program will count the total number of characters in the file, including the comments.

Next, you will change the program to test for a file that does not exist.

To check for a nonexistent file:

1. Return to the **CheckFile.java** file in the Text Editor window and save the file as **CheckFile2.java**.
2. Change the class name to **CheckFile2**.
3. Change the filename you use in the File constructor as follows so that it refers to a nonexistent file: `File f = new File("nodata.txt");`.
4. Rebuild and save the project, then run CheckFile2 as a console application. Unless you have a file named nodata.txt in the CheckFile project directory, the output looks like Figure 14-4.

```
C:\WINNT\System32\cmd.exe
A:\CHAPTER.14\CheckFile>jview CheckFile2
File does not exist

A:\CHAPTER.14\CheckFile>
```

Figure 14-4: Output of the CheckFile2 program

In the preceding steps, the program found the file named data.txt because the file was physically located in the current directory from which you were working. You can check the status of files in other directories by using a File constructor with two String arguments. The first String represents a path to the filename and the second String represents the filename. For example, `File myFile = new File("\\com\\eventhandlers","data.txt");` refers to a file located in the eventhandlers folder within the com folder in the root directory.

Next you will create a second data file so that you can compare its size and time stamp with the data.txt file.

To create a data2.txt file and a program to compare this file to data.txt:

1. Select **Add Item** from the **Project** menu to add a new text file named **data2.txt** to the project. Open the data2.txt file in the Text Editor window and then type the first 10 letters of the alphabet: **abcdefghij**.
2. Add to the project a new main class file named **CheckTwoFiles.java**.
3. Add `import java.io.*;` before the class header.
4. Between the main() method's curly brackets, enter the following code to declare two file objects:

   ```
   File f1 = new File("data.txt");
   File f2 = new File("data2.txt");
   ```

5 If both files exist, the following code compares their creation times and prints the filename with the more recent time stamp:

```
if(f1.exists() && f2.exists())
{
  System.out.println("The more recent file is ");
  if(f1.lastModified() > f2.lastModified())
    System.out.println(f1.getName());
  else
    System.out.println(f2.getName());
```

6 Enter the following code to compare the length of the files and print the name of the longer file:

```
System.out.println("The longer file is ");
if(f1.length() > f2.length())
  System.out.println(f1.getName());
else
  System.out.println(f2.getName());
```

7 Add a closing curly bracket for the if statement.

8 Rebuild and save the project, then run the CheckTwoFiles program as a console application. The output appears in Figure 14-5. The data2.txt file was created after the data.txt file, so it is more recent, but it has fewer characters.

```
C:\WINNT\System32\cmd.exe
A:\CHAPTER.14\CheckFile>jview CheckTwoFiles
The more recent file is
data2.txt
The longer file is
data.txt
A:\CHAPTER.14\CheckFile>
```

Figure 14-5: Output of the CheckTwoFiles program

Data File Organization and Streams

Most businesses generate and use large quantities of data every day. You can store data in variables within a program, but this type of storage is temporary. When the program ends, the variables no longer exist and the data is lost. Variables are stored in the computer's main or primary memory, which is called **RAM** (**random access memory**). When you need to retain data for any significant amount of time, you must save the data on a permanent, secondary storage device such as a floppy disk, hard drive, or compact disc (CD).

> Most computers do not yet contain compact disc drives that let you write data to the discs, because such devices are expensive. If your CD drive allows reading of data, but not writing, then it is a CD-ROM drive—that is, a compact disc with read-only memory.

> You can erase data from files, so some programmers prefer the term *persistent* to *permanent*. In other words, you can remove data so it is not permanent, but the data remains in the file even when the computer loses power, so, unlike RAM, the data tends to persist or persevere.

Data used by businesses is stored in a data hierarchy, as shown in Figure 14-6. The smallest, useful piece of data that is of interest to most people is the character. A **character** is any one of the letters, numbers, or other special symbols, such as punctuation marks, which you can read and to which you can assign meaning. Characters are made up of bits (the zeros and ones that represent computer circuitry), but people who use data are not concerned with whether the internal representation for an *A* is 01000001 or 10111110.

> Java uses Unicode to represent its characters. You first learned about Unicode in Chapter 3.

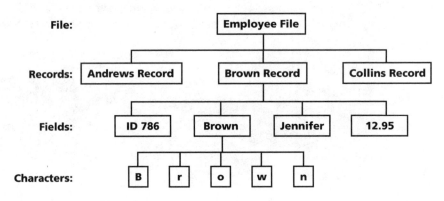

Figure 14-6: Data hierarchy

When businesses use data, they group characters into fields. A **field** is a group of characters that has some meaning. For example, the characters *T*, *o*, and *m* might represent your first name. Data items such as last name, Social Security number, zip code, and salary are data fields.

Fields are grouped together to form **records**. An individual's name, Social Security number, zip code, and salary represent that individual's record. When programming in Java, you have created many classes, such as an Employee class or a Student class, that represent records. These classes contain individual variables that represent data fields. A business's data records usually represent a person, item, sales transaction, or some other concrete object or event.

Records are grouped to create files. **Files** consist of related records, such as a company's personnel file that contains one record for each company employee. Some files have only a few records; perhaps your professor maintains a file of 25 records for your class, with one record for each student. Other files contain thousands of records. For example, a large insurance company maintains a file of policyholders, and a mail-order catalog company maintains a file of available items.

Before a program can use a data file, the program must **open** the file. Similarly, when you are finished using a file, the program should **close** the file. If you fail to close an input file, there usually are not any serious consequences; the data still exists in the file. If you fail to close an output file, however, the data may not be accessible later. You should always close every file you open, and you should close the file as soon as you no longer need it. When you leave a file open for no reason, you use computer resources, and your computer's performance suffers. Additionally, another program might be waiting to use the file.

People view files as a series of records with each record containing data fields, but Java views files as a series of bytes. When you perform an input operation in a program, you can picture bytes flowing into your program from an input device through a **stream**, which functions as a pipeline or channel. When you perform an output operation, some bytes flow out of your program through another stream to an output device, as shown in Figure 14-7. A stream is an object, and as do all objects, streams have data and methods. The methods allow you to perform actions such as opening, closing, and flushing the stream.

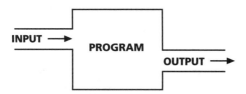

Figure 14-7: File stream

Most streams flow in only one direction; each stream is either an input or output stream. You might open several streams at once within your program. For example, three streams are required by a program that reads a data disk (one input stream), checks the data for invalid values, and then writes some records to a file of valid records and writes others to a file of invalid records (two output streams).

Random access files use streams that flow in two directions. You will use a random access file in Section B of this chapter.

Using Streams

A partial family tree of the Stream classes appears in Figure 14-8. InputStream and OutputStream are subclasses of Object. They are abstract classes that contain methods for performing input and output. As abstract classes, these methods must be overridden in their child classes. FileInputStream and FileOutputStream provide the capability to read from and write to disk files. The class FilterOutputStream descends from OutputStream. In turn, FilterOutputStream is parent to PrintStream. You use PrintStream for handling output to the standard output device, which usually is the monitor. The System class declares an object of type PrintStream. This object is System.out, which you have used extensively throughout this book, and it is used most often with the println() method.

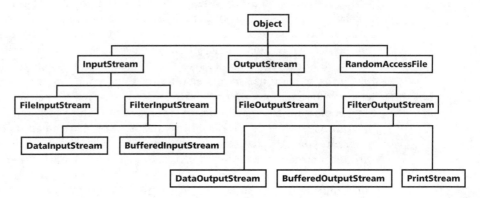

Figure 14-8: Partial family tree for Stream classes

The System class defines an additional object, System.err. The output from System.err and System.out can go to the same device; in fact, the output from both often goes to the command line on the monitor. The difference is that System.err usually is reserved for error messages, and System.out is reserved for valid output. You can direct either System.err or System.out to a new location, such as a disk file, if you want to keep a log of the error messages generated by a program separate from the other standard output.

The InputStream class is parent to FilterInputStream, which is parent to BufferedInputStream. The object System.in is a BufferedInputStream object. The System.in object captures keyboard input; you have used this object with its read() method. A **buffer** is a small memory location that you use to hold data temporarily. The BufferedInputStream class allows keyboard data to be held until the user presses the Enter key. That way, the user can backspace over typed characters to change the data before the program stores it, which allows the operating system—instead of your program—to handle the complicated tasks of deleting characters as the user backspaces and replacing the deleted characters with new ones.

> Using a buffer for input or output improves program performance. Input and output operations are relatively slow compared to computer processor speeds. Holding input or output until there is a "batch" makes programs run faster.

You can create your own InputStream and OutputStream objects and assign System.in and System.out to them respectively. Then you can use the InputStream method read() to read in one character at a time. The read() method returns an integer that represents the Unicode value of the typed character; the method returns a value of -1 when it encounters an end-of-file condition, known as EOF. Next, you will create InputStream and OutputStream objects so you can read from the keyboard and write to the screen.

> You also can identify EOF by throwing an EOFException. You will use this technique in Section B of this chapter.

To create a program that reads from the keyboard and writes to the screen:

1 Create a new console application project named **ReadKBWrite**. Save the **ReadKBWrite** project folder in the Chapter.14 folder on your Student Disk.

2 Rename the default Class1.java file as **ReadKBWriteScreen.java**, then open the file in the Text Editor window.

3 Replace the default comments before the class header with the following statement to import the file classes: `import java.io.*;`.

4 Replace the Class1 class name in the `public class Class1` line with **ReadKBWriteScreen**.

5 Add `throws IOException` to the right of the main() method header. The main() method throws an IOException because you will perform input and output operations.

6 Replace the `// TODO: Add initialization code here` comment in the main() method with the following code to declare InputStream and OutputStream objects, as well as an integer to hold each character the user types:

```
InputStream istream;
OutputStream ostream;
int c;
```

7 Enter the following code to assign the System.in object to istream, and the System.out object to ostream:

```
istream = System.in;
ostream = System.out;
```

8 Use the following `try` block to read from the file. If an IOException occurs, you can print an appropriate message. Within the `try` block, execute a loop that reads from the keyboard until the end-of-file condition occurs (the read() method returns -1). While there is not an end-of-file condition, send the character to the ostream object.

> **tip**
>
> You learned about `try` blocks in Chapter 13.

```
try
{
   while((c = istream.read()) != -1)
   {
     ostream.write(c);
   }
}
```

9 Use the following `catch` block to handle any IOException:

```
catch(IOException e)
{
   System.out.println("Error: " + e.getMessage());
}
```

10 Regardless of whether an IOException occurs, you want to close the streams. Use the following `finally` block to ensure that the streams are closed:

```
finally
{
   istream.close();
   ostream.close();
}
```

11 Set the project properties to run the **ReadKBWriteScreen** file as a console application, build and save the project, then execute the program as a console application. At the command line, type any series of characters and then press the **Enter** key. Every time you type a character, a buffer holds it until you press the Enter key, at which time the stored characters echo to the screen. *Do not try to end the program yet.*

The `while` loop in the ReadKBWriteScreen program continues until the read() method returns -1. However, you cannot end the program by typing *-1*. Typing a minus sign (-) and a one (*1*) results in two additional characters being sent to the buffer. Instead, you must type Ctrl+Z, which the operating system recognizes as the end of the file.

To end the ReadKBWriteScreen program:

1 At the command line, type **Ctrl+Z**. The program ends.

> Do *not* press Ctrl+C to end the program. Doing so breaks out of the program before its completion and does not properly close the files.

Writing to a File

Instead of assigning files to the standard input and output devices, you also can assign a file to the InputStream or OutputStream. For example, you can read data from the keyboard and store it permanently on a disk. To read data from the keyboard and store it permanently on a disk, you can construct a FileOutputStream object and assign it to the OutputStream. If you want to change a program's output device, you don't have to make any changes to the program other than assigning a new object to the OutputStream; the rest of the program's logic remains the same. Java lets you assign a file to a stream object so that screen output and file output work in exactly the same manner.

You can associate a File object with the output stream in one of two ways:

- You can pass the filename to the constructor of the FileOutputStream class.
- You can create a File object by passing the filename to the File constructor. Then you can pass the File object to the constructor of the FileOutputStream class.

The second method has some benefits—if you create a File object, you can use the File class methods such as exists() and lastModified() to retrieve file information.

> Because applets are designed for distribution over the Internet, you are not allowed to use an applet to write to files on a client's workstation. Applets that write to a client's file could destroy a client's existing data.

To create a program that writes keyboard data to a file:

1 Return to the **ReadKBWriteScreen.java** file in the Text Editor window and save it as **ReadKBWriteFile.java**.

2 Change the class header to `public class ReadKBWriteFile`.

3 Position the insertion point at the end of the line that defines the ostream object (`OutputStream ostream;`), and then press the **Enter** key to start a new line. On the new line, define a file object as follows:

```
File outFile = new File("datafile.txt");
```

> **4** Replace the statement that assigns System.out to the ostream object with the statement `ostream = new FileOutputStream(outFile);`.
>
> **5** Rebuild and save the project, then execute the **ReadKBWriteFile** file as a console application. At the command line, type **This is my output file**, and then press the **Enter** key. After you press the Enter key, the characters will not display on the screen; instead, they are output to a file named datafile.txt that is written in the current directory.
>
> **6** Type **Ctrl+Z** to stop the program.
>
> **7** Open the **datafile.txt** file, which is located in the ReadKBWrite project folder, in the Text Editor window. The characters are an exact copy of the ones you entered at the keyboard.

You could enter any number of characters to the output stream before ending the program and they would be saved in the output file. If you run the ReadKBWriteFile program again, the program will overwrite the existing datafile.txt file with your new data.

Reading from a File

The process you use to read data from a file is similar to the one you use to write data to a file. You can assign a File object to the input stream.

> **To read data from a file:**
>
> **1** Open the **ReadKBWriteScreen.java** file you created earlier in this chapter, and then immediately save the file as **ReadFileWriteScreen.java**.
>
> **2** Change the class header to `public class ReadFileWriteScreen`.
>
> **3** Position the insertion point to the right of the statement that declares the OutputStream object named ostream, and then press the **Enter** key to start a new line. On the new line, enter the following code to create a File object to refer to the datafile.txt file you created:
>
> ```
> File inFile = new File("datafile.txt");
> ```
>
> **4** Change the statement that assigns the System.in object to istream, so that you can use the File object for input instead of the keyboard, by typing the following:
>
> ```
> istream = new FileInputStream(inFile);
> ```
>
> **5** Rebuild and save the project, then run the ReadFileWriteScreen as a console application. The data you stored in the datafile.txt file (`This is my output file`) displays on the screen, and the program ends.

SUMMARY

- Files are objects that you store on permanent storage devices, such as floppy disks.

- You can use the File class to gather file information. File methods include canRead(), canWrite(), exists(), getName(), getPath(), getParent(), length(), and lastModified().

- You can create a File object using a constructor that includes a filename and optional path. You also can use a File constructor with two String arguments: a path name and the filename.

- Data used by businesses is stored in a data hierarchy that includes files, records, fields, and characters. A field is a group of characters that has some meaning, such as last name, Social Security number, zip code, or salary. Fields are grouped together to form records. An individual's name, Social Security number, zip code, and salary represent that individual's record. Files consist of related records, such as a company's personnel file, which contains one record for each company employee.

- Before a program can use a data file, the program must open the file. Similarly, when you are finished using a file, the program should close the file. You should always close every file you open, and you should always do so as soon as you no longer need the file.

- Java views a file as a series of bytes.

- A stream is an object through which input and output data flow.

- InputStream and OutputStream are subclasses of Object. They are abstract classes that contain methods for performing input and output.

- FileInputStream and FileOutputStream provide the capability to read from and write to disk files.

- The class FilterOutputStream descends from OutputStream. In turn, FilterOutputStream is parent to PrintStream. You use PrintStream for handling output to the standard output device, which usually is the monitor.

- The System class defines System.out and System.err for output. System.err usually is reserved for error messages, and System.out is reserved for valid output.

- The InputStream class is parent to FilterInputStream, which is parent to BufferedInputStream. The object System.in is a BufferedInputStream object that captures keyboard input.

- A buffer is a small memory location that is used to hold data temporarily.

- The BufferedInputStream class allows keyboard data to be held until the user presses the Enter key, which allows the operating system to handle the complicated task of deleting characters as the user backspaces and deletes characters.

- You can create your own InputStream and OutputStream objects and assign System.in and System.out to them respectively. Then you can use the InputStream method read() to read in one character at a time.

- The read() method returns an integer that represents the Unicode value of the typed character; the method returns a value of -1 when it encounters an end-of-file condition, known as EOF.
- To assign a file to a stream object, you can construct a FileOutputStream object and assign it to the OutputStream. You can associate a File object with the output stream by passing a filename to the constructor of the FileOutputStream class. Alternatively, you can create a File object by passing the filename to the File constructor. Then you can pass the File object to the constructor of the FileOutputStream class.
- To read data from a file, you can assign a File object to the input stream.

QUESTIONS

1. Files always _____.
    a. hold software instructions
    b. occupy a section of storage space
    c. remain open during the execution of a program
    d. all of these

2. The File class enables you to _____.
    a. open a file
    b. close a file
    c. determine a file's size
    d. all of these

3. The _____ package contains all the classes you use in file processing.
    a. java.file
    b. java.io
    c. java.lang
    d. java.process

4. The statement `File aFile = new File("myFile");` creates a file _____.
    a. on the disk in drive A
    b. on the hard drive (drive C)
    c. in the Temp folder on drive C
    d. in the current project folder

5. The File method canWrite() returns a(n) _____ value.
    a. integer
    b. boolean
    c. Object
    d. void

6. Data used by businesses is stored in a data hierarchy that includes the following items, from largest to smallest:
   a. file, field, record, character
   b. record, file, field, character
   c. file, record, field, character
   d. record, field, file, character

7. A group of characters that has meaning is a _____.
   a. file
   b. record
   c. field
   d. byte

8. Files consist of related _____.
   a. records
   b. fields
   c. data segments
   d. archives

9. Before a program can use a data file, the program must _____ the file.
   a. create
   b. open
   c. store
   d. close

10. When you perform an input operation in a Java program, you use a _____.
    a. pipeline
    b. channel
    c. moderator
    d. stream

11. Most streams flow _____.
    a. in
    b. out
    c. either in or out, but only in one direction
    d. both in and out concurrently

12. InputStream and OutputStream are _____.
    a. subclasses of Object
    b. abstract classes
    c. used for performing input and output
    d. all of these

13. The output from System.err and System.out _____ goes to the same device.
    a. never
    b. seldom
    c. usually
    d. always

14. A small memory location that is used to hold data temporarily is a _____.
    a. stream
    b. buffer
    c. stack
    d. channel

15. The read() method returns a value of -1 when it encounters a(n) _____.
    a. input error
    b. integer
    c. end-of-file condition
    d. negative value

16. You can associate a File object with the output stream by passing a _____ to the constructor of the FileOutputStream class.
    a. filename
    b. File object
    c. either of these
    d. neither of these

EXERCISES

Save the projects that you create in the exercises in the Chapter.14 folder on your Student Disk.

1. Create a file using any word processing program or text editor. Write a program named FileStatistics that displays the file's name, parent, size, and time of last modification.

2. Create two files using any word processing program or text editor. Write a program named SameFolder that determines whether the two files are located in the same folder.

3. Write a program that determines which, if any, of the following files are stored on your computer: autoexec.bat, biology.101, command.com, and windows.exe.

4. Write a program that allows the user to display the contents of any file with a .java extension. Prompt the user to enter the filename; then have the program display the first 20 lines of the file and pause. When the user presses the Enter key, display the next 20 lines.

5. Write a program that allows the user to display the contents of .java files starting at the first closing curly bracket (}). Prompt the user to enter the filename, and then have the program display the first 20 lines following the first closing bracket and pause. When the user presses the Enter key, display the next 20 lines.

6. Write a program that allows the user to create a file of employee names and phone extensions. Prompt the user to enter the filename, and then prompt the user to enter the names and extension numbers. The user should press Ctrl+Z after entering all of the data. The program then displays the data from the file just created.

SECTION B
objectives

In this section you will learn how to:
- Write formatted file data
- Read formatted file data
- Use random access files

Advanced File Techniques

Writing Formatted File Data

Usually, you do not want to read data files as a series of characters. For example, you might have a data file that contains personnel records that include an employee ID number, name, and salary for each employee in your organization. Rather than reading a series of bytes, it is more useful to be able to read such a file in groups of bytes that constitute an integer, a String, and a double. You can use the DataInputStream and DataOutputStream classes to create formatted input and output.

DataOutputStream objects enable you to write binary data to an OutputStream. Much of the data you write with DataOutputStream objects is not readable in the Text Editor window; instead the data is formatted correctly for its type, and you can read the data later with a DataInputStream object.

The DataOutput interface is implemented by DataOutputStream. The DataOutput interface includes methods such as writeBoolean(), writeChar(), writeDouble(), writeFloat(), and writeInt(). Each method writes data in the correct format for the data type its name indicates. You can use the method writeUTF() to write Unicode format strings.

> Sources are divided on the meaning of the acronym *UTF*. The most popular interpretations include Unicode Transformation Format, Unicode Transfer Format, and Unicode Text Format.

When you create a DataOutputStream, you can assign a FileOutputStream object to it so that your data is stored in a file. Using DataOutputStream with a FileOutputStream allows you to use the writeXXX() method that is appropriate for the data you want to write. You connect a DataOutputStream to a FileOutputStream using a method known as **chaining** the stream objects. That is, if you define a DataOutputStream object with a statement such as `DataOutputStream out;`, then when you call the DataOutputStream constructor, you pass a FileOutputStream object to it (for example, `out = new DataOutputStream(new FileOutputStream("someFile"));`).

section B

In the next series of steps, you will create a full-blown project for Event Handlers Incorporated that uses a GUI interface to capture data about an event from a user, and writes that data to an output file using the DataOutput interface. The data required includes the host's name, the date, and the number of guests. For simplicity, this program accepts event dates for the current month only, so the date field is an integer. Figure 14-9 shows a preliminary sketch of the user's interface.

Figure 14-9: Sketch of the user's interface

To create a Frame for data entry:

1. Create a new empty project named **CreateEventFile**. Save the **CreateEventFile** project folder in the Chapter.14 folder on your Student Disk.
2. Add a new class file named **CreateEventFile.java** to the project.
3. Above the class header, type the following import statements that you will need for the program:

   ```
   import java.io.*;
   import java.awt.*;
   import java.awt.event.*;
   ```

4. To the right of the class header, add **extends Frame implements ActionListener, Window Listener**. CreateEventFile is a Frame that reacts to a mouse click when you click an object within the Frame and when you click the Frame's Close button. Therefore, you must implement both ActionListener and WindowListener.
5. Between the class's curly brackets, enter the following code to create a Label for the company name and a Font object to use with the company name:

   ```
   private Label companyName =
      new Label("Event Handlers Incorporated");
   Font bigFont = new Font("Helvetica", Font.ITALIC, 24);
   ```

6 Enter the following code to create a label that tells the user to enter data and to create TextFields for the host, date, and guests. Because a host's name is usually several characters long, the field for the host's name should be wider than that of the fields for the date and number of guests.

```
private Label prompt =
   new Label("Enter this month's events");
private TextField host = new TextField(10);
private TextField date = new TextField(4);
private TextField guests = new TextField(4);
```

7 Enter the following code to create a Label for each of the TextFields and to include a Button object that the user can click when a data record is complete and ready to be written to the data file:

```
private Label hLabel = new Label("Host");
private Label dLabel = new Label("Date");
private Label gLabel = new Label("Guests");
private Button enterDataButton =
   new Button("Enter data");
```

8 When you write the user's data to an output file, you will use the DataOutputStream class, so create a DataOutputStream object as follows: `DataOutputStream ostream;`.

Next, you will add the CreateEventFile's constructor to the class. The constructor calls its parent's constructor, which is the Frame class constructor, and passes to it a title to use for the Frame. The constructor also attempts to open an events.txt file for output. If the open fails, the constructor's `catch` block handles the Exception; otherwise you add all the TextField, Label, and Button Components to the Frame.

To write the CreateEventFile class constructor:

1 In the CreateEventFile.java file, press the **Enter** key to start a new line below the statement that declares the DataOutputStream object, and then type the following constructor header and opening curly bracket and call the superclass constructor:

```
public CreateEventFile()
{
   super("Create Event File");
```

2 Add the following `try...catch` block to create the file:

```
try
{
```

```
      ostream = new
      DataOutputStream(new FileOutputStream("events.txt"));
   }
   catch(IOException e)
   {
      System.err.println("File not opened");
      System.exit(1);
   }
```

> **tip**
> Notice the use of the System.err object to display an error message. Alternatively, you can display the message on System.out.

3. After the file is open, use the following code to set the Frame's size, choose a layout manager, and add all the necessary Components to the Frame:

```
setSize(400,200);
setLayout(new FlowLayout());
companyName.setFont(bigFont);
add(companyName);
add(prompt);
add(hLabel);
add(host);
add(dLabel);
add(date);
add(gLabel);
add(guests);
add(enterDataButton);
```

4. To finish the Frame constructor, enter the following code to register the Frame as a listener for the Button, make the Frame visible, and make the Frame a WindowListener so you can use the Close button. Finally, add a closing curly bracket for the constructor.

```
enterDataButton.addActionListener(this);
setVisible(true);
addWindowListener(this);
}
```

When the user sees the Frame, he or she can enter data in each of the available TextFields. When the user completes a record for a single event, he or she clicks the Button, which causes the actionPerformed() method to execute. This method must retrieve the text from each of the TextFields and write it to a data file in the correct format.

To add the actionPerformed() method to the CreateEventFile program:

1. Within the CreateEventFile.java file, press the **Enter** key to start a new line below the constructor method, and then type the following header for the actionPerformed method, which contains an integer variable that holds the number of guests:

   ```
   public void actionPerformed(ActionEvent e1)
   {
      int numGuests;
   ```

2. Include the data retrieval and the subsequent file writing in a `try` block so that you can handle any I/O errors that occur. You will use the parseInt() method to convert the TextField guest number to a usable integer, but you will accept the host and date fields as simple text. You can use the appropriate DataOutputStream methods to write formatted data to the output file.

tip

You first learned about parseInt() and the Integer class in Chapter 6.

   ```
   try
   {
      numGuests = Integer.parseInt(guests.getText());
      ostream.writeUTF(host.getText());
      ostream.writeUTF(date.getText());
      ostream.writeInt(numGuests);
   ```

3. Continue the `try` block by removing the data from each TextField after it is written to the file. Then end the `try` block.

   ```
   host.setText("");
   date.setText("");
   guests.setText("");
   }
   ```

4. There are two types of Exceptions that you might want to deal with in this application. Because the host name and date fields are text, the user can enter any type of data. However, the guest field must be an integer. When you use the parseInt() method with data that cannot be converted to an integer (such as alphabetic letters), a NumberFormatException error occurs. In this case, you can write an error message to the standard error device explaining the problem as follows:

   ```
   catch(NumberFormatException e2)
   {
      System.err.println("Invalid number of guests");
   }
   ```

5 A more serious Exception occurs when the program cannot write the output file, so you should catch the IOException, print an error message, and exit using the following code:

```
catch(IOException e3)
{
  System.err.println("Error writing file");
  System.exit(1);
}
```

6 Add a closing curly bracket for the actionPerformed() method.

The CreateEventFile class is a Frame that implements WindowListener. When the user is finished entering event data, he or she will click the Frame's Close button. When the user closes the Frame, you want to close the data file to which you have been writing the event records and then exit the program. You perform these tasks within the windowClosing() method. Additionally, because you are implementing WindowListener, you must include the six other window action methods.

To write the necessary window methods:

1 Within the CreateEventFile.java file, press the **Enter** key to start a new line after the closing curly bracket of the actionPerformed() method, and then add the following windowClosing() method. This method attempts to close the file and catches the possible Exception. If an Exception occurs, exit the program with the standard error code (the value 1); otherwise, exit the program with the standard "normal" exit code (the value 0).

```
public void windowClosing(WindowEvent e)
{
  try
  {
    ostream.close();
  }
  catch(IOException e4)
  {
    System.err.println("File not closed");
    System.exit(1);
  }
  System.exit(0);
}
```

2 Next, add the following other six window methods as empty, do-nothing versions:

```
public void windowClosed(WindowEvent e) {}
```

```
public void windowDeiconified(WindowEvent e) {}
public void windowIconified(WindowEvent e) {}
public void windowOpened(WindowEvent e) {}
public void windowActivated(WindowEvent e) {}
public void windowDeactivated(WindowEvent e) {}
```

Next, you will create a program that uses the CreateEventFile Frame. The program's only task is to instantiate a CreateEventFile Frame object.

To write a program that uses a CreateEventFile Frame:

1. Add a new main class file named **EventFile.java** to the project.
2. Between the main() method's curly brackets, type **CreateEventFile cef = new CreateEventFile();**.
3. Set the project properties to run the **EventFile** file as a console application.
4. Build and save the project, then execute the **EventFile** file as a console application. The program looks like Figure 14-10.

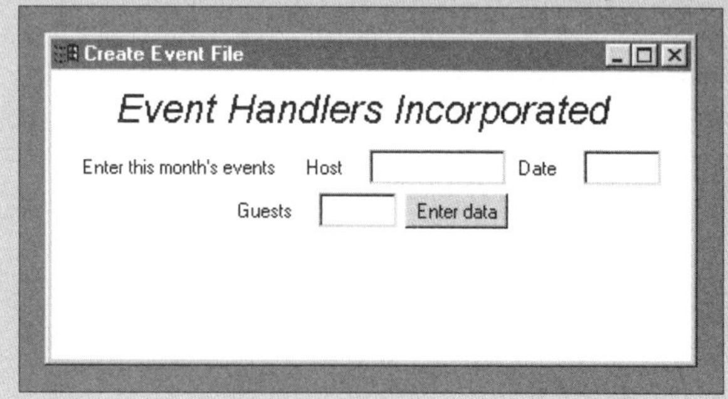

Figure 14-10: User interface for the EventFile program

5. Type sample data into the TextFields in the Frame. For example, an event might consist of host **Albertson**, on the **12th**, with **100** guests. After entering the data into the three data fields, click the **Enter data** button. The program sends your data to the file and clears the fields. Now you can enter a second record, and then click the **Enter data** button again. Repeat this process until you have entered five data records.
6. Click the **Close** button ⊠ in the CreateEventFile Frame to close it.
7. Examine the files listed in Project Explorer. Confirm that your program created the events.txt data file in the CreateEventFile folder in the Chapter.14 folder on your Student Disk. You will write a program to read the file in the next series of steps.

Reading Formatted File Data

DataInputStream objects enable you to read binary data from an InputStream. The DataInput interface is implemented by DataInputStream. The DataInput interface includes methods such as readByte(), readChar(), readDouble(), readFloat(), readInt(), and readUTF(). In the same way that the writeXXX() methods of DataOutput correctly format data you write to a file, each DataInput readXXX() method correctly reads the type of data indicated in its name.

When you want to create a DataInputStream object that reads from a file, you use the same chaining technique you used for output files. In other words, if you define a DataInputStream object as `DataInputStream in;`, then you can associate it with a file when you call its constructor, as in `in = new DataInputStream(FileInputStream("someFile"));`.

When you read data from a file, you need to determine when the end of the file has been reached. In Section A of this chapter, you learned that you can determine EOF by checking for a return value of -1 from the read() method. Alternatively, if you attempt each file read() from within a `try` block, you can catch an EOFException. When you catch an EOFException, it means you have reached the end of the file and you should take appropriate action, such as closing the file.

tip

Most Exceptions represent error conditions. An EOFException is more truly an "exception" in that most read() method calls do not result in EOF; only the last read() for a file does.

Next, you will create a Frame in which employees of Event Handlers Incorporated can view each individual record stored in the events.txt file. The user interface will look like the interface used in the CreateEventFile Frame, but the user will not enter data within this Frame. Instead, the user will click a Button to see each succeeding record in the event.txt file.

To create a Frame for viewing file data:

1 Add a new class file named **ReadEventFile.java** to the CreateEventFile project.

2 Above the class header, type the following import statements that you will need for the program:

```
import java.io.*;
import java.awt.*;
import java.awt.event.*;
```

3 Add `extends Frame implements ActionListener, WindowListener` to the right of the class header.

4 Between the class's curly brackets, enter the following code to declare all of the Labels, TextFields, and associated values that will appear in the Frame. The text of the prompt and Button have changed, but these statements are basically the same as the statements in the CreateEventFile.java file.

```java
private Label companyName =
  new Label("Event Handlers Incorporated");
Font bigFont = new Font("Helvetica", Font.ITALIC, 24);
private Label prompt =
  new Label("View this month's events");
private TextField host = new TextField(10);
private TextField date = new TextField(4);
private TextField guests = new TextField(4);
private Button viewEventButton =
  new Button("View Event");
private Label hLabel = new Label("Host");
private Label dLabel = new Label("Date");
private Label gLabel = new Label("Guests");
```

5 Enter the following code to declare a DataInputStream object. Then, write the ReadEventFile constructor method that uses a try...catch block to open a file. Notice that you can chain the DataInputStream object and a FileInputStream object using the same technique you used for output.

```java
DataInputStream istream;
public ReadEventFile()
{
  super("Read Event File");
  try
  {
    istream = new DataInputStream (new FileInputStream
    ("A:\\Chapter.14\\CreateEventFile\\events.txt") );
  }
  catch(IOException e)
  {
    System.err.println("File not opened");
    System.exit(1);
  }
```

6 After successfully opening the file, set the Frame size, layout manager, and font for the Frame as follows:

```java
setSize(375,200);
setLayout(new FlowLayout());
companyName.setFont(bigFont);
```

7 Add the Frame's Components as follows:

```
add(companyName);
add(prompt);
add(hLabel);
add(host);
add(dLabel);
add(date);
add(gLabel);
add(guests);
add(viewEventButton);
```

8 Enter the following code to ensure that the Frame listens for Window and Button messages and to make the Frame visible:

```
addWindowListener(this);
viewEventButton.addActionListener(this);
setVisible(true);
```

9 Add the closing curly bracket for the ReadEventFile constructor.

10 Type the beginning of the following actionPerformed() method. This method declares variables for the file field data, and then uses a `try` block to call the appropriate readXXX() method for each field. Each data field then displays in the correct TextField.

```
public void actionPerformed(ActionEvent e1)
{
  String theHost, theDate;
  int numGuests;
  try
  {
    theHost = istream.readUTF();
    theDate = istream.readUTF();
    numGuests = istream.readInt();
    host.setText(theHost);
    date.setText(theDate);
    guests.setText(String.valueOf(numGuests));
  }
```

11 Code the following two `catch` blocks for the `try` block that reads the data fields. The first `catch` block catches the EOFException and calls a closeFile() method. The second `catch` block catches IOExceptions and exits the program if there is a problem with the file.

```
catch(EOFException e2)
{
  closeFile();
}
```

```
      catch(IOException e3)
      {
        System.err.println("Error reading file");
        System.exit(1);
      }
```

12 Add the closing curly bracket for the actionPerformed() method.

13 Write the following closeFile() method that closes the DataInputStream object and exits the program:

```
public void closeFile()
{
  try
  {
    istream.close();
    System.exit(0);
  }
  catch(IOException e)
  {
    System.err.println("Error closing file");
    System.exit(1);
  }
}
```

14 You must include the seven methods in the WindowAdapter interface. The only method you need to code for this Frame is the windowClosing() method. If the user closes the Frame to exit the program before reading through all the file records and encountering EOF, then you should make sure the file closes.

```
public void windowClosing(WindowEvent e)
{
  try
  {
    istream.close();
  }
  catch(IOException e4)
  {
    System.err.println("File already closed");
    System.exit(1);
  }
  System.exit(0);
}
public void windowClosed(WindowEvent e) {}
public void windowDeiconified(WindowEvent e) {}
public void windowIconified(WindowEvent e) {}
public void windowOpened(WindowEvent e) {}
```

section B

```
public void windowActivated(WindowEvent e) {}
public void windowDeactivated(WindowEvent e) {}
```

Next you will write a short host program that creates a ReadEventFile Frame so Event Handlers employees can examine the existing file of scheduled events.

To write a program that creates a Frame and displays file data:

1 Add a new main class file named **EventFile2.java** to the CreateEventFile project.
2 Above the class header, type the following import statement that you will need for the program: `import java.io.*;`.
3 Between the main() method's curly brackets, add the following code to instantiate a ReadEventFile object: `ReadEventFile ref = new ReadEventFile();`.
4 Rebuild and save the project, then execute the program as a console application by typing `jview EventFile2` at the command line. After the application starts, click the **View Event** button. Figure 14-11 shows the interface with the first record from the events.txt data file displayed. Click the **View Event** button again to see the second record. Continue clicking the **View Event** button until you reach the end of the file; when you do, the Frame closes and the program ends.

Figure 14-11: Output of the EventFile2 program

Creating Random Access Files

The files you wrote to and read from in this chapter are **sequential access files**, which means that you accessed the records in sequential order from beginning to end. For example, if you wrote an Event record with host name *Adams*, and then you created an Event record with host name *Brown*, when you retrieve the records you see that they remain in the original data-entry order. Businesses store data in sequential order when they use the records for **batch processing**. For example, when a company produces paychecks, the records for the pay period are gathered together in a batch and the checks are calculated and printed in sequence.

For many applications, sequential access is inefficient. These applications, known as **real-time applications**, require that a record be accessed immediately while a client is waiting. For example, if a customer telephones a department store with a question about a monthly bill, the customer service representative does not need to access every customer account in sequence. With tens of thousands of account records to read, it would take too long to access the customer's record. Instead, customer service representatives require **random access files**, which are files in which records can be located in any order. Because they enable you to locate a particular record directly (without reading all of the preceding records), random access files also are called **direct access files**. You can use the RandomAccessFile class to create your own random access files.

The RandomAccessFile class contains the same read(), write(), and close() methods as InputStream and OutputStream, but it also contains a seek() method that lets you select a beginning position within a file before you read or write data. For example, if you declare a RandomAccessFile object named myFile, then the statement `myFile.seek(200);` selects the 200th position within the file. The 200th position represents the 201st byte because, as with Java arrays, the numbering of file positions begins at zero. The next read() or write() method will operate from the newly selected starting point. For example, if you store records that are 50 bytes long, you can access the *n*th record using the statement `myFile.seek((n-1) * 50);`.

When you declare a RandomAccessFile object, you include a filename as you do with other file objects. You also include *r* or *rw* within double quotation marks as a second argument to indicate that the file is open for reading only ("r") or for both reading and writing ("rw"). For example, `RandomAccessFile myFile = new RandomAccessFile("C:\\Temp\\someData.txt","rw");` opens the someData.txt file so that either the read() or write() method can be used on the file. This feature is particularly useful in random access processing. For example, consider a business with 20,000 customer accounts. When the customer who has the 14,607th record in the file acquires a new telephone number, it is convenient to access the 14,607th record directly, read() it to confirm it represents the correct customer, and then write() the new telephone number to the file.

To see how the seek() method works:

1 Create a new console application project named **AccessRandomly**. Save the **AccessRandomly** project folder in the Chapter.14 folder on your Student Disk.

2. Rename the default Class1.java file as **AccessRandomly.java**, then open the file in the Text Editor window.
3. Replace the default comments before the class header with the following statement to import the file classes: `import java.io.*;`.
4. Replace the Class1 class name in the `public class Class1` line with **AccessRandomly**.
5. Add `throws IOException` to the right of the main() method header.
6. Replace the `// TODO: Add initialization code here` comment with the following code to declare an OutputStream object for output, an integer to hold data temporarily, and a new RandomAccessFile. You will use the data file for reading only, so you include "r" as the second argument in the RandomAccessFile constructor.

```
OutputStream ostream;
int c;
RandomAccessFile inFile =
   new RandomAccessFile("datafile.txt","r");
```

7. Enter the following code to assign ostream to the standard output device. Then `try` accessing the seventh file position, which is represented by the number six. Read this position, and then display its contents.

```
ostream = System.out;
try
{
   inFile.seek(6);
   c = inFile.read();
   ostream.write(c);
}
```

8. Add the following `catch` clause for the file and then close the files:

```
catch(IOException e)
{
   System.out.println("Error: " + e.getMessage());
}
finally
{
   inFile.close();
   ostream.close();
}
```

9. Use the **Add Item** command on the **Project** menu to add a new text file to the AccessRandomly project named datafile.txt. Open the datafile.txt file in the Text Editor window and type **This is my random access file**, then save and close the file.

10. Set the project properties to run the **AccessRandomly** file as a console application, then build and save the program. Execute the program as a console application by typing **jview AccessRandomly** at the command line. The output is the seventh character in the file, as shown in Figure 14-12.

Figure 14-12: Output of the AccessRandomly program

When you access a file randomly, you do not read all the data that precedes the data you are seeking. Accessing data randomly is one of the major features that makes large data systems worth maintaining.

SUMMARY

- You can use the DataInputStream and DataOutputStream classes to create formatted input and output.

- The DataOutput interface includes methods such as writeBoolean(), writeChar(), writeDouble(), writeFloat(), and writeInt(). Each method writes data in the correct format for the data type its name indicates. You can use the method writeUTF() to write Unicode format strings.

- When you create a DataOutputStream, you can assign a FileOutputStream object to it so you can use the writeXXX() method that is appropriate for the data you want to write. You connect a DataOutputStream to a FileOutputStream using a method known as chaining the stream objects.

- DataInputStream objects enable you to read binary data from an InputStream. The DataInput interface includes methods such as readByte(), readChar(), readDouble(), readFloat(), readInt(), and readUTF(). Each DataInput readXXX() method correctly reads the type of data indicated in its name.

- When you want to create a DataInputStream object that reads from a file, you use the same chaining technique you used for output files.

- If you attempt each file read() from within a `try` block, you can catch an EOFException and take appropriate action, such as closing the file.

- Businesses store data in sequential order when they use the records for batch processing.

- Real-time applications require that a record be accessed immediately while a client is waiting.

section B

- Random access files, or direct access files, are files in which records can be located in any order.

- The RandomAccessFile class contains the same read(), write(), and close() methods as InputStream and OutputStream, but it also contains a seek() method that lets you select a beginning position within a file before you read or write.

- When you declare a RandomAccessFile object, you include a filename as you do with other file objects. You also include "r" or "rw" as a second argument to indicate that the file is open for reading only, or for both reading and writing.

QUESTIONS

1. You use DataInputStream and DataOutputStream classes to be able to _____.
   a. recognize EOF
   b. format input and output
   c. use Strings within files
   d. use binary data within files

2. The method that outputs integer data to a file is _____.
   a. writeInt()
   b. outInt()
   c. writeInteger()
   d. outInteger()

3. You connect a DataOutputStream to a FileOutputStream by using a method known as _____.
   a. sequencing
   b. iteration
   c. piggy-backing
   d. chaining

4. DataInputStream objects enable you to _____ binary data from an InputStream.
   a. read
   b. write
   c. delete
   d. override

5. The DataInput interface includes methods such as _____.
   a. inByte() and inChar()
   b. read() and write()
   c. readInt() and readUTF()
   d. open() and close()

6. When you catch a(n) _____, it means you have reached the end of the file.
   a. IOException
   b. EOFException
   c. NumberFormatException
   d. DataEntryException

7. When you access records in the order in which they are physically stored on an input device, you are using _____ access methods.
   a. direct
   b. random
   c. transaction
   d. sequential

8. Businesses store data in sequential order when they use the records for _____ processing.
   a. batch
   b. bunch
   c. transaction-oriented
   d. random

9. Which of the following applications is most likely to use sequential file processing?
   a. A program that schedules airline reservations
   b. A credit card company's end-of-month billing program
   c. A college registration program
   d. A program that checks a customer's credit card balance before a transaction

10. Applications that require that a record be accessed immediately while a client is waiting require _____.
    a. batch processing
    b. sequential access
    c. off-line processing
    d. random access

11. The method that the RandomAccessFile class contains that does not exist in the InputStream class is _____.
    a. read()
    b. close()
    c. seek()
    d. delete()

12. You can open a RandomAccessFile object for _____.
    a. reading
    b. writing
    c. both of these
    d. neither of these

EXERCISES

Save the projects that you create in the exercises in the Chapter.14 folder on your Student Disk.

1. a. Write a program for a mail-order company. Name the class MailOrderWrite. The program uses a data-entry screen in which the user types an item number and a quantity. Write each record to a file.
   b. Write a program named MailOrderRead that reads the data file created in Exercise 1a and displays one record at a time on the screen.

2. a. Write a program for a mail-order company. Name the class MailOrderWrite2. The program uses a data-entry screen in which the user types an item number and a quantity. The valid item numbers and prices are as follows:

Item Number	Price ($)
101	4.59
103	29.95
107	36.50
125	49.99

When the user enters an item number, check the number to make sure that it is valid. If it is valid, write a record that includes item number, quantity, price each, and total price.
   b. Write a program named MailOrderRead2 that reads the data file created in Exercise 2a and displays one record at a time on the screen.

3. a. Write a program that allows a user to enter an integer representing a file position. Access the requested position within a file and display the character there. Name the program SeekPosition.
   b. Modify the program created in Exercise 3a so that you display the next five characters after the requested position. Name the program Seek2.

4. Write a program that creates a frame with text fields for order processing. Include frames for item description, item number, and item cost. Write each complete record to a file. Write the item number as an integer.

5. Write a program that creates a frame with text fields for payroll information. Include text fields for employee number, hourly rate, regular hours worked, and overtime hours worked. Write each completed record to a file. Write the employee number to the file as an integer.

6. Write a program that creates a frame with text fields for course information. Include text fields for the course ID, course title, and number of students enrolled. Write each completed record to a file. Write the number of students to the file as an integer.

7. Each of the following files in the Chapter.14 folder on your Student Disk has syntax and/or logical errors. Add the files to a new project called FixDebug. Save the FixDebug project in the Chapter.14 folder on your Student Disk. In each case, fix the problem and run each file as a console application using JVIEW.
   a. DebugFourteen1.java
   b. DebugFourteen2.java
   c. DebugFourteen3.java
   d. DebugFourteen4.java

CHAPTER 15

Multi-threading and Animation

case ▶ "I thought I had learned a lot about Java," you tell Lynn Greenbrier during your six-month performance review at Event Handlers Incorporated. "I've learned to write applets and applications, extend classes, and write data files. But there's something missing. I want to create applets for Event Handlers in which figures move. I want programs in which different activities take place on the screen at the same time, just like these dynamic Web sites I've seen that promote other companies."

chapter 15

"You can put all those ideas together with animation, and you almost know enough to create animation now," Lynn explains. "You know about applets, exceptions, inheritance, and graphics. Let me tell you a little about threads, and then you can get started on animation."

Previewing a Program That Displays Animation

Event Handlers Incorporated wants an animated stick figure to appear on its Web site. The figure appears to be using the Event Handlers company name as a yo-yo. You will create a similar program in this chapter, but you can use a completed version of the Chap15Animation applet that is saved in the Chapter.15 folder on your Student Disk now.

To use the Chap15Animation class:

1   Go to the command prompt for the Chapter.15 folder on your Student Disk, type **jview /a Chap15Animation.htm** at the command prompt, and then press the **Enter** key. You will see a moving figure as shown in Figure 15-1.

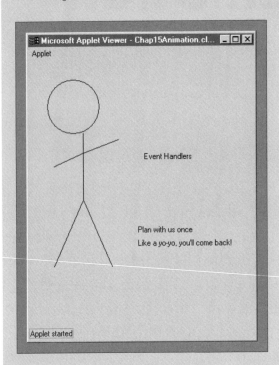

Figure 15-1: Chap15Animation applet

2   When you are finished viewing the applet, click the AppletViewer's **Close** button ⊠.

SECTION A
objectives

In this section you will learn:
- About the concept of multithreading
- How to use the Thread class
- About a thread's life cycle
- How to use the sleep() method
- How to set thread priority
- How to use the Runnable interface

Introduction to Multithreading

The Concept of Multithreading

A **Thread** is the flow of execution of one set of program statements. When you execute a program statement by statement, from beginning to end, you are **following a Thread**. Each of the programs you have written so far while working through this book has had a single thread. This means that at any one time, Java is executing a single program statement.

Single-thread programs contain statements that execute in very rapid sequence, but only one statement executes at a time. When a computer contains a single central processing unit (CPU, or processor), it can execute only one computer instruction at a time, regardless of its processor speed. When you use a computer with multiple CPUs, the computer can execute multiple instructions simultaneously.

The Java programming language allows you to **launch**, or start, multiple Threads, no matter which type of processor you use. Using multiple Threads of execution is known as **multithreading**. If you use a computer system that contains more than one CPU, multiple threads can execute simultaneously. Figure 15-2 illustrates how multithreading executes in a multiprocessor system.

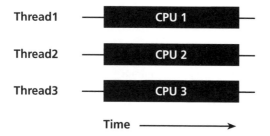

Figure 15-2: Executing multiple threads in a multiprocessor system

If you use a computer with a single processor, the multiple threads share the CPUs time, as shown in Figure 15-3. The CPU devotes a small amount of time to one task, and then devotes a small amount of time to another task. The CPU never actually performs two tasks at the same instant. Instead, it performs a piece of one task, and then a piece of another task. The CPU performs so quickly that each of the tasks seems to be executing uninterrupted.

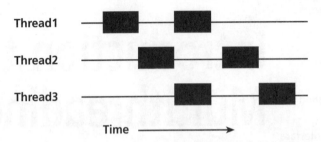

Figure 15-3: Executing multiple threads in a single-processor system

Perhaps you have seen an expert chess player (called a chess master) who participates in chess games with several opponents at once. The chess master makes a move on the first playing board, and then moves to the second board against a second opponent, while the first opponent analyzes his next move. The master can move to the third board, make a move, and return to the first board before the first opponent is even ready to respond. To the first chess player, it seems as though the expert player is devoting all of her time to him. Because the expert is so fast, she can play other opponents in the first opponent's "down time." Executing multiple threads on a single CPU works in a similar way. The CPU transfers its attention from thread to thread so quickly that the tasks don't even "miss" the CPU's attention.

You use multithreading to make your programs perform better. Multithreaded programs often run faster, but more importantly, they are more user-friendly. With a multithreaded program, the user can continue to click buttons while your program is reading a data file. With multithreading, an animated figure can display on one part of the screen while the user makes menu selections on another part of the screen. When you use the Internet, multithreading becomes very important. For example, you can begin to read a long text file or listen to an audio file while it is still downloading.

> Programmers sometimes use the term *execution context* to describe a thread. They also refer to a thread as a *lightweight process* because it is not a full-blown program. Rather, a thread must run within the context of a full, "heavyweight" program.

Using the Thread Class

You can create threads by extending the **Thread class**, which is defined in the java.lang package. To create a thread, you define a class that extends the Thread class. The Thread class contains a method named run(). You override the run() method to tell the system how to execute the Thread. For example, you can write the HelloThread class shown in Figure 15-4, which prints a "Hello" message to the screen 10 times. The HelloThread class contains a single method—the run() method—which prints a space, "Hello", and another space 10 times.

```
class HelloThread extends Thread
{
  public void run()
  {
    for(int x = 0; x < 10; ++x)
    System.out.print(" Hello ");
  }
}
```

Figure 15-4: HelloThread class

When you create a class that extends Thread, you inherit the start() method. You use the **start() method** with an instantiated Thread object; it tells the system to start execution of the thread. For example, you can write a program that instantiates and starts a HelloThread object, as shown in Figure 15-5.

```
class DemoHelloThread
{
  public static void main(String[] args)
  {
    HelloThread hello = new HelloThread();
    hello.start();
  }
}
```

Figure 15-5: DemoHelloThread class

The DemoHelloThread class instantiates a HelloThread object named hello. When you use the start() method with the hello object, the run() method within the HelloThread class executes. The output appears in Figure 15-6; the "Hello" message prints 10 times.

```
C:\WINNT\System32\cmd.exe
A:\CHAPTER.15\DemoThreads>jview DemoHelloThread
 Hello  Hello  Hello  Hello  Hello  Hello  Hello  Hello  Hello  Hello
A:\CHAPTER.15\DemoThreads>
```

Figure 15-6: Output of the DemoHelloThread program

You can achieve multithreading by starting more than one Thread object. For example, if you create a GoodbyeThread (see Figure 15-7), and a DemoHelloGoodbyeThreads class with a main() method (see Figure 15-8), then the output appears as shown in Figure 15-9.

```
class GoodbyeThread extends Thread
{
  public void run()
  {
    for(int x = 0; x < 10; ++x)
      System.out.print(" Goodbye ");
  }
}
```

Figure 15-7: GoodbyeThread class

```
class DemoHelloGoodbyeThreads
{
  public static void main(String[] args)
  {
    HelloThread hello = new HelloThread();
    GoodbyeThread goodbye = new GoodbyeThread();
    hello.start();
    goodbye.start();
  }
}
```

Figure 15-8: DemoHelloGoodbyeThreads class

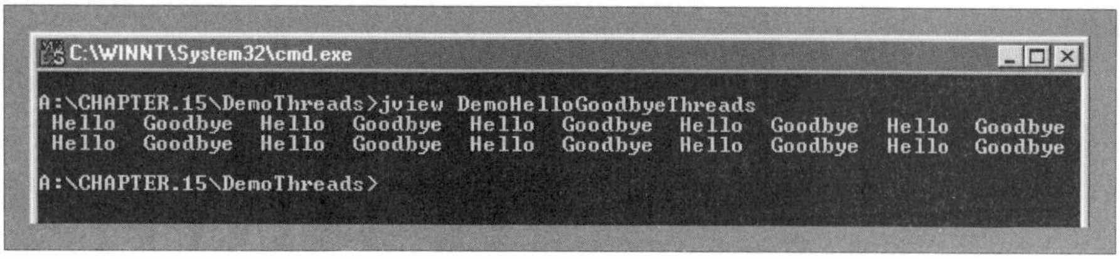

Figure 15-9: Output of the DemoHelloGoodbyeThreads program

If you run the DemoHelloGoodbyeThreads program, your output might not appear exactly like Figure 15-9. In fact, if you run your program multiple times, your output might look like Figure 15-10. In four subsequent runs of the program, the output can vary. Depending on available resources, the operating system might alternate between "Hello" and "Goodbye", or execute several repetitions of the HelloThread in a row, followed by several repetitions of the GoodbyeThread. Each thread completes its 10 repetitions, but you have no guarantee as to the exact pattern of execution.

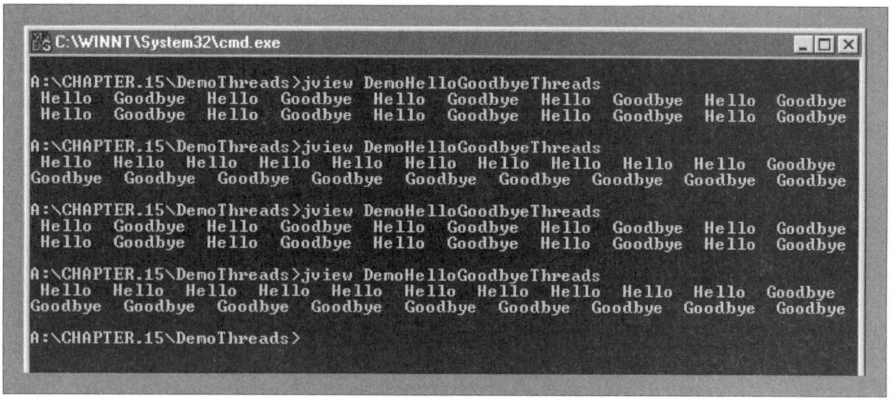

Figure 15-10: Multiple runs of the DemoHelloGoodbyeThreads program

Understanding a Thread's Life Cycle

A thread can be in one of five states during its life: new, ready, running, inactive, or finished. When you create a thread, it is in the **new** state; the only method you can use with a new thread is the method to start it. When you call the thread's start() method, the thread enters the **ready state**. A ready thread is **runnable**, which means that it can run. However, a runnable thread might not be in the **running state** because the CPU might be busy elsewhere. Just as your runnable automobile cannot pass through an intersection until the traffic officer waves you on, a runnable thread cannot actually run until the CPU allocates some time to it.

section A

If you call a Thread method that the thread's present state does not allow, Java throws an IllegalThreadStateException. For example, you cannot call the stop() method for a thread that is new and has not been started.

When a thread begins to execute, it is in the running state. A thread runs until it becomes inactive or finishes. A thread enters the **inactive state** when you call the Thread sleep() or suspend() method, or it might become inactive if it must wait for another thread to finish and for the CPU to have available time. When a thread completes the execution of its run() method, it is in the **finished** or **dead state**. A Thread can also enter the finished state before its run() method completes if you call the Thread stop() method. You can use the isAlive() method to determine whether a thread is currently alive, which means that it has started but has not stopped. The isAlive() method returns `false` if a thread is new or finished; otherwise it returns `true`. Figure 15-11 summarizes several useful methods of the Thread class.

Method	Description
start()	Starts the thread, causing the run() method to execute.
stop()	Stops the thread.
suspend()	Suspends the thread until you use the resume() method.
resume()	Resumes the thread you suspended.
isAlive()	Returns `true` or `false` to indicate whether the thread is currently running.
setPriority()	Lets you set a priority from 1 to 10 for the thread by passing an integer.

Figure 15-11: Thread class methods

You will learn about thread priority in the next section.

Next you will extend the Thread class so it repeats a character on the screen. Then you will create three Thread objects to observe how they execute concurrently.

To create a class that extends Thread:

1 If necessary, start Visual J++, then create a new empty project named **DemoThreads**. Save the **DemoThreads** project folder in the Chapter.15 folder on your Student Disk.

2 Add a new class file named **ShowThread.java** to the project.

3 Add **extends Thread** to the right of the class header.

4 Between the class's curly brackets, enter the following two data members: a character that you will display on the screen, and an integer that holds the number of repetitions for display.

```
private char oneChar;
private int rep = 100;
```

5 Create the following constructor for the ShowThread class. The constructor accepts a character and assigns it to the oneChar variable.

```
public ShowThread(char printChar)
{
   oneChar = printChar;
}
```

6 Enter the following run() method, which prints the character as many times as the rep value specifies:

```
public void run()
{
   for(int x = 0; x < rep; ++x)
   System.out.print(oneChar);
}
```

Next you will write a DemoThreads class containing a main() method that declares and uses three ShowThread objects.

To write the DemoThreads class:

1 Add to the project a new main class file named **DemoThreads.java**.

2 Enter the following statements between the main() method's curly brackets:

```
ShowThread showA = new ShowThread('A');
ShowThread showB = new ShowThread('B');
ShowThread showC = new ShowThread('C');
showA.start();
showB.start();
showC.start();
```

3 Set the project properties to run the **DemoThreads** file as a console application, then build and save the project. If necessary, correct any syntax errors and rebuild. Execute the program as a console application by typing **jview DemoThreads** at the command line. The output appears similar to Figure 15-12, although the sequence of the execution of your ShowThread objects might vary.

Figure 15-12: Output of the DemoThreads program

4 Run the program several more times and examine the output for changes in the sequence of execution.
5 Return to the **ShowThread.java** file in Text Editor window and change the value in the rep variable definition so that it is `private int rep = 500;`.
6 Rebuild, save, and execute the project. Observe any differences in your output.

Using the sleep() Method

One very interesting and useful member of the Thread class is the sleep() method. You use the sleep() method to pause a thread for a specified number of milliseconds. Writing `sleep(500);` within a Thread class's run() method causes the execution to "rest" for 500 milliseconds, or half a second. For example, you may have a Java application that displays a picture of an open eye. Periodically, the eye "closes," then after a certain amount of time, reopens. You accomplish this type of timing using the sleep() method.

When you use the sleep() method, you must catch an InterruptedException, which is the type of Exception thrown when a program stops running before its natural end. When you use the sleep() method, you intend for your program to be interrupted, so you usually catch the Exception and take no action.

To demonstrate using the sleep() method:

1 Create a new empty project named **DemoSleepThread**. Save the **DemoSleepThread** project folder in the Chapter.15 folder on your Student Disk.
2 Add a new class file named **SleepThread.java** to the project.
3 Above the class header, type the following import statement that you will need for the program: `import java.awt.*;`.
4 Add `extends Thread` to the right of the class header.

5 Between the class's curly brackets, enter the following lines of the run() method, which uses a loop to print 100 integers:

```
public void run()
{
   for(int x = 0; x < 100; ++x)
   {
      System.out.print(x + " ");
```

6 Within the for loop, add the following try block. You will test the loop counter variable. When its value is 25, pause for three seconds; when it is 75, pause for five seconds. Then end the try block and catch the InterruptedException.

```
try
{
 if(x == 25)
    sleep(3000);
 if(x == 75)
    sleep(5000);
}
catch(InterruptedException e){}
```

7 Add two closing curly brackets: one for the for loop and one for the run() method.

8 Add to the project a new main class file named **DemoSleepThread.java**.

9 Between the main() method's curly brackets, enter the following statements to create a SleepThread object and demonstrate its use:

```
SleepThread sThread = new SleepThread();
sThread.start();
```

10 Set the project properties to run the **DemoSleepThread** file as a console application, then build and save the project. Execute the program as a console application by typing `jview DemoSleepThread` at the command line. When the program runs, 25 integers display, and then you must wait during a three-second sleep. When the program resumes, 50 more integers display, and then you must wait during a five-second sleep. When the program completes, all 100 integers (0 through 99) appear on the screen.

Thread Priority

Every Java thread has a **priority**, or rank, in terms of preferential access to the operating system's resources. Each Thread object's priority is represented by an integer in the range of 1 to 10. If you do not assign a priority to a Thread object, it assumes a default priority of 5. You can change a thread's priority by using the setPriority() method, or you can determine a thread's priority with the getPriority() method. If you extend a thread from an existing thread, the child thread assumes its parent's priority.

There are many circumstances in which you may want to specify the priority of a thread. Consider a Java application containing two threads: one thread that uses the sleep() method to create an animation, and another thread that responds to user input. You always want a thread that responds to user input to have a higher priority than a Thread that displays a visual effect such as animation.

The Thread class contains three constants—MIN_PRIORITY, NORM_PRIORITY, and MAX_PRIORITY—which represent 1, 5, and 10 respectively. When you set a thread's priority, you can use an integer, as in myThread.setPriority(10);, or you can use one of the three constants, as in myThread.setPriority(Thread.MAX_PRIORITY);. You also can use an arithmetic expression, such as yourThread.setPriority(Thread.MAX_PRIORITY - 2);.

If you use the priority constants with your Thread objects, then your threads will have the appropriate relative priority even if the developers of Java decide to change the priority numbers in the future.

When you run a Java program, the runnable thread with the highest priority runs first. If several threads have the same priority, they run in rotation. Lower-priority threads can run only when higher-priority threads are not runnable (such as when they are finished, suspended, or asleep).

In general, when ThreadA has higher priority than ThreadB, ThreadA will be running and ThreadB will be waiting. However, sometimes Java will choose to run ThreadB to avoid starvation. **Starvation** occurs when a thread cannot make any progress because of the priorities of other threads.

The ultimate form of starvation is called deadlock. *Deadlock* **occurs when two threads must wait for each other to do something before either can progress.**

Next you will set the priorities of some threads to observe the effects.

To demonstrate thread priorities:

1 Open the **DemoThreads** project, then open the **DemoThreads.java** file in the Text Editor window. Save the DemoThreads.java file as **DemoThreadsPriority.java**.

2 Change the class header to `class DemoThreadsPriority`.

3 Position the insertion point to the right of the line with the third showThread declaration (showC), and then press the **Enter** key to start a new line.

4. Type the following lines to set the showB thread's priority to 1 and the showC thread's priority to 10:

```
showB.setPriority(Thread.MIN_PRIORITY);
showC.setPriority(Thread.MAX_PRIORITY);
```

5. Rebuild and save the project, and run the DemoThreadsPriority file as a console application by typing **jview DemoThreadsPriority** at the command line. The output looks similar to Figure 15-13. Notice that the highest priority thread (showC) finishes first and the lowest priority thread (showB) finishes last.

Figure 15-13: Output of the DemoThreadsPriority program

Using the Runnable Interface

You can create a thread subclass by inheriting from the Thread class, but this approach won't work if you want your thread subclass to inherit from another class as well. For example, if you want to create an applet that can run as a thread, you cannot inherit from both Applet and Thread. Java will not let you inherit from two classes, so you must implement an interface. You can implement the **Runnable interface** as an alternative to inheriting from the Thread class.

▶ tip

You learned about implementing interfaces in Chapter 10.

For example, you can write an applet that acts as a timer, by counting and displaying seconds as they pass. You declare an integer variable—for example, `int secs = 0;`. The applet's paint() method contains a statement that adds one to

section A

the secs variable (++secs;) and displays the current count of seconds—for example, gr.drawString("Time: " + secs, x, y);.

To let the applet run indefinitely, you can create an infinite loop that repaints the screen every 1,000 milliseconds (or every second) as follows:

```
while(true)
{
  repaint();
  try
  {
    clock.sleep(1000);
  }
  catch(InterruptedException e)
}
```

The problem with this approach is that while the infinite while loop is running, the CPU is occupied and cannot perform any other actions, such as carrying out the repaint() method. Instead of displaying a counter, the applet appears to freeze the screen.

The solution is to place the while loop in a thread that can share time with the operating system's default thread in which the applet runs.

To create an applet that implements the Runnable interface:

1 Create a new empty project named **TimerApplet**. Save the **TimerApplet** project folder in the Chapter.15 folder on your Student Disk.

2 Add a new class file named **TimerApplet** to the project.

3 Above the class header, type the following import statements that you will need for the program:

```
import java.applet.*;
import java.awt.*;
```

4 Add **extends Applet implements Runnable** to the right of the class header.

5 Between the class's curly brackets, create String messages, a Font object, and an integer to count the seconds as follows:

```
private String msg1 = new String("Time is passing");
private String msg2 = new String("Plan your event today");
private Font bigFont = new Font("Arial", Font.ITALIC, 24);
private int secs;
```

6. On the next line, declare a Thread object named clock as follows: `private Thread clock;`. The value of this object is `null` because you have not yet called the Thread constructor.

7. When the applet is initialized, the clock thread will have the value `null`, so instantiate a Thread with the following code. The run() method of the TimerApplet will execute when the thread is created because the `this` in `clock = new Thread(this);` refers to "this" applet.

```
public void init()
{
  if(clock == null)
  {
    clock = new Thread(this);
    clock.start();
  }
}
```

8. The applet contains the following run() method because the applet implements Runnable. You place the infinite loop that calls repaint() every second within the run() method as follows.

```
public void run()
{
  while(true)
  {
    repaint();
    try
    {
      clock.sleep(1000);
    }
    catch(InterruptedException e)
    {
    }
  }
}
```

9. Add the following stop() method, which suspends the clock thread. The start() method resumes it.

```
public void stop()
{
  clock.suspend();
}
public void start()
{
  clock.resume();
}
```

10 Stop the clock in the applet's destroy() method as follows:

```
public void destroy()
{
  clock.stop();
}
```

11 Enter the following TimerApplet's paint() method, which adds one to the seconds counter and displays the messages on the screen:

```
public void paint(Graphics gr)
{
  ++secs;
  gr.setFont(bigFont);
  gr.setColor(Color.magenta);
  gr.drawString(msg1,10,100);
  gr.drawString("Time: " + secs, 10, 130);
  gr.drawString(msg2,10,150);
}
```

12 Add to the project a new Web page named **testTimer.htm**.

13 In the Source tab of the HTML Editor window, place the insertion point in the blank line following the tag that reads <P> </P> and type the opening <APPLET> tag that contains the applet's name and dimensions: **<APPLET CODE = "TimerApplet.class" WIDTH = 350 HEIGHT = 200>**.

14 Press the **Enter** key to start a new line and type the applet's closing tag: **</APPLET>**.

15 Build and save the project, then execute the program in AppletViewer by typing **jview /a testTimer.htm** at the command line. The output appears similar to Figure 15-14. As you watch the timer, the time value changes every second.

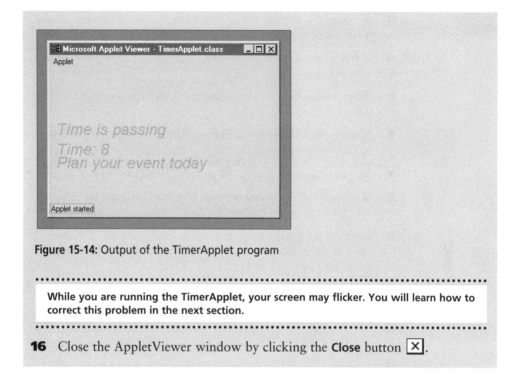

Figure 15-14: Output of the TimerApplet program

> ▶ **tip**
> While you are running the TimerApplet, your screen may flicker. You will learn how to correct this problem in the next section.

16 Close the AppletViewer window by clicking the **Close** button ☒.

The TimerApplet that you created uses the default system thread, and your timer uses its own Thread. You could not have created this applet without using the power of multithreading.

SUMMARY

- A thread is the flow of execution of one set of program statements. When you execute a program statement by statement, from beginning to end, you are following a thread.

- The Java programming language allows you to launch, or start, multiple threads, whether the computer you are using has a single or multiple CPUs. Using multiple threads of execution is known as multithreading. You use multithreading to make your programs perform better.

- You can create threads by extending the Thread class, which is defined in the java.lang package. The Thread class contains a method named run() that you override to tell the system how to execute the thread.

- You use the start() method with an instantiated Thread object to tell the system to start execution of the thread.

- You can achieve multithreading by starting more than one Thread object.

- A thread can exist in one of five states during its life: new, ready, running, inactive, or finished.

- A ready thread is runnable—that is, capable of being run—but it might not be running at the moment.

- When a thread begins to execute, it is in the running state. A thread runs until it becomes inactive or finishes.

- You can use the isAlive() method to determine whether a thread is currently alive—that is, started but not stopped.

- You use the sleep() method to pause a thread for a specified number of milliseconds.

- When you use the sleep() method, you must catch an InterruptedException, which is the type of Exception thrown when a program stops running before its natural end.

- Every thread in Java has a priority, or rank, in terms of preferential access to the operating system's resources. Each Thread object's priority is represented by an integer in the range of 1 to 10; 5 is the default.

- You can change a thread's priority by using the setPriority() method, or determine a thread's priority with the getPriority() method.

- The Thread class contains three constants—MIN_PRIORITY, NORM_PRIORITY, and MAX_PRIORITY—which represent 1, 5, and 10 respectively.

- When you run a Java program, the runnable thread with the highest priority runs first. If several threads have the same priority, they run in rotation.

- Starvation occurs when a thread cannot make any progress because of the priorities of other threads.

- You can implement the Runnable interface as an alternative to inheriting from the Thread class.

QUESTIONS

1. A thread is the _____ one set of program statements.
   a. amount of memory occupied by
   b. flow of execution of
   c. machine language code for
   d. area of memory occupied by

2. Within single-thread programs, statements execute _____.
   a. one at a time
   b. simultaneously
   c. simultaneously, if they are different threads
   d. simultaneously, if they are in the same thread

3. Starting a thread also is called _____.
   a. initializing
   b. unraveling
   c. propelling
   d. launching

4. If you use a computer with a single processor, the CPU _____ performs two tasks at the same instant.
   a. always
   b. sometimes
   c. sometimes, if you declare threads,
   d. never

5. You can create threads by _____ the Thread class.
   a. making a copy of
   b. instantiating
   c. extending
   d. overriding

6. You override the _____ method to tell the system how to execute a thread.
   a. thread()
   b. execute()
   c. run()
   d. start()

7. When you create a Thread object, you use the _____ method to start execution of the thread.
   a. thread()
   b. execute()
   c. run()
   d. start()

8. You achieve _____ by starting more than one Thread object.
   a. polythreading
   b. bithreading
   c. abstract threading
   d. multithreading

9. Which of the following states is *not* possible for a thread?
   a. ready
   b. finished
   c. altered
   d. new

10. A ready thread is always _____.
    a. runnable
    b. running
    c. both of these
    d. neither of these

section A

11. When you call a thread's suspend() or sleep() method, it _____.
    a. becomes runnable
    b. throws an Exception
    c. becomes inactive
    d. reinitializes

12. The isAlive() method returns `false` if a thread is _____.
    a. new
    b. finished
    c. either a or b
    d. neither a nor b

13. A thread's rank in terms of preferential access to the operating system's resources is its _____.
    a. priority
    b. prerogative
    c. supremacy
    d. license

14. If you do not assign a priority to a Thread object, it assumes a priority of _____ by default.
    a. 0 (zero)
    b. 1
    c. 5
    d. 10

15. Which of the following threads would most likely run first?
    a. A finished thread with priority 10
    b. A suspended thread with priority 5
    c. A runnable thread with priority NORM_PRIORITY
    d. A runnable thread with priority 2

16. Java sometimes will choose to run a low-priority thread to avoid _____.
    a. construction
    b. death
    c. starvation
    d. sedation

17. You can use the Runnable _____ to inherit Thread methods.
    a. interface
    b. method
    c. mode
    d. formula

18. When you define a thread as `private Thread someThread;`, the value of someThread is _____.
    a. zero
    b. `null`
    c. `false`
    d. unknown

E X E R C I S E S

Save each of the programs that you create in the exercises in the Chapter.15 folder on your Student Disk.

1. a. Create a Thread class whose constructor accepts any String you pass it. The run() method displays the String 100 times. Write a program that instantiates three threads to which you pass your first name and the first names of two friends. Start the threads and observe which thread wins the race.

    b. Set different priorities for the three Thread objects you created in Exercise 1a, and then run the program again.

2. Create two classes that extend Thread—LovesMe and LovesMeNot. Each thread displays the phrase its name implies 100 times. Write a program to start the two threads; the final message is the answer to your question!

3. Create a class named RaceHorse that extends Thread. Each RaceHorse has a name and a run() method that displays the name 500 times. The last RaceHorse to finish is the loser.

4. Write a program that creates five threads, each of which displays a different character. Give two threads the minimum priority, two threads the maximum priority, and one thread the default priority.

5. Write an applet that creates a thread that displays a character repeatedly. The character moves down the window in a diagonal line from the left side. When it reaches the bottom, the character moves up the window toward the right side in a diagonal line. The character changes color when it goes up the window.

SECTION B

objectives

In this section you will learn how to:

- Create an animated figure
- Reduce flickering
- Use predrawn animated Image objects
- Use Java's garbage collection feature
- Use animation in a Web browser page

Animation

Creating an Animated Figure

Cartoonists create animated films by drawing a sequence of frames or cells. These individual drawings are shown to the audience in rapid sequence to give the illusion of natural movement. You create computer animation using the same techniques. If you display computer images as fast as your CPU can process them, you might not be able to see anything. Most computer animation employs the Thread class sleep() method to pause for short periods of time between animation cells, so the human brain has time to absorb each image's content.

Artists often spend a great deal of time creating the exact images they want to use in an animation sequence. As a much simpler example, Event Handlers Incorporated wants you to create a stick figure whose arm moves up and down. The only difference between creating a stick figure and a more complex graphic image is in the amount of time and degree of artistic talent you have.

You begin to create computer animation by using graph paper to create a sketch of a figure, as in Figure 15-15.

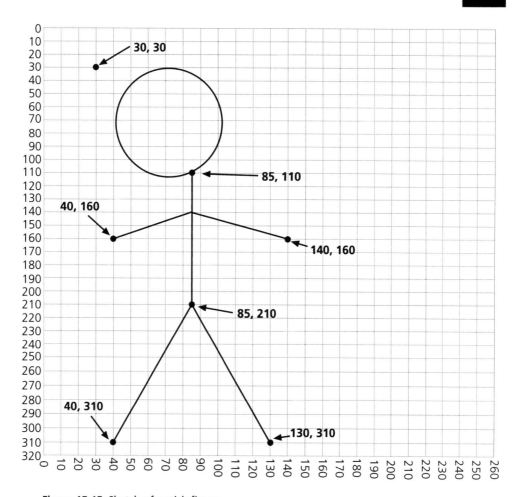

Figure 15-15: Sketch of a stick figure

To create the illusion that this figure's arm moves, you create a second sketch in which the arm is slightly raised from its position in the first sketch. The arm in the third drawing is slightly higher, and so on. Figure 15-16 shows four potential arm positions for the stick figure.

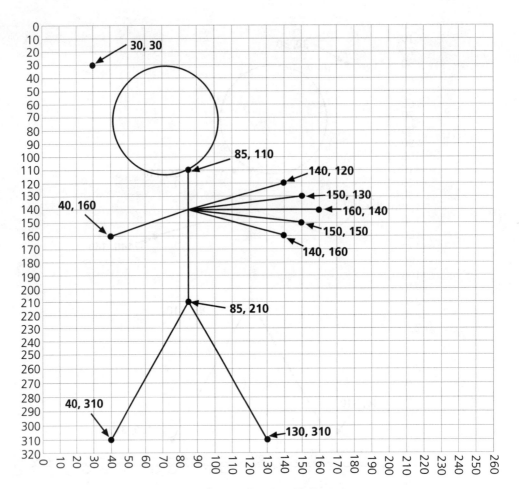

Figure 15-16: Sketch of four arm positions for the stick figure

Each time you draw the stick figure on the screen, the arm will appear slightly higher, giving the viewer the illusion of movement. The head, body, and legs of the stick figure never change. You can draw the stick figure's body using constant values for the drawing coordinates, but you need variables to store the horizontal and vertical positions of the end of the moving arm. One efficient approach is to use parallel arrays to store the x- and y-coordinates for the end position of each of the arm positions, as in the following example:

```
int[] horiz = {140, 150, 160, 150, 140};
int[] vert =  {160, 150, 140, 130, 120};
```

Each time you redraw the stick figure, you can increase a subscript and use the next horizontal and vertical coordinate pair to indicate the end of the figure's arm. When you have used all five arm coordinates, you can reduce the subscript to a value of zero, and then begin again.

To create an animated stick figure for Event Handlers Incorporated:

1 Create a new empty project named **AnimatedFigure**. Save the **AnimatedFigure** project folder in the Chapter.15 folder on your Student Disk.

2 Add a new class file named **AnimatedFigure** to the project.

3 Above the class header, type the following import statements that you will need for the program:

```
import java.applet.*;
import java.awt.*;
```

4 Add **extends Applet** to the right of the class header.

5 Between the class's curly brackets, create the following index with the horizontal and vertical position arrays, as well as the arrays themselves, which are loaded with values taken from the preliminary sketches:

```
private int index = 0;
int[] horiz = {140,150,160,150,140};
int[] vert =  {160,150,140,130,120};
```

6 Add the following variable to store the sleep time. If you want to speed up or slow down the figure later, it will be convenient to change the value in this variable. For now, set the sleep time to 100 milliseconds as follows: **private int sleep = 100;**.

7 In the start() method of the applet, ensure that the index begins with value zero using the following code:

```
public void start()
{
   index = 0;
}
```

8 Within the paint() method, add the following code to draw the figure's head, body, and two legs, using the sketch in Figure 15–15 as a reference for the coordinates:

```
public void paint(Graphics gr)
{
   gr.drawOval(30,30,80,80);
   gr.drawLine(85,110,85,210);
   gr.drawLine(85,210,40,310);
   gr.drawLine(85,210,130,310);
```

9 You can create the figure's left arm by using the coordinates in the sketch. The right arm always starts at the same position on the body, but the hand end of the arm might be in any one of four positions taken from the horizontal and vertical arrays.

section B

```
gr.drawLine(85,140,40,160);
gr.drawLine(85,140,horiz[index],vert[index]);
```

10 After drawing the right arm, use the following code to increase the index so the program will use the next set of horizontal and vertical arm positions the next time the paint() method executes. When the index exceeds the array length, reset the index to zero.

```
++index;
if(index == horiz.length)
   index = 0;
```

11 Add the following `try` block to sleep for the designated amount of time and catch any Exception thrown by the Thread class:

```
try
{
   Thread.sleep(sleep);
}
catch(InterruptedException e)
{
}
```

12 The last step in the paint() method is to call the following repaint() method, which calls paint(), to start the method again, draw the figure with a new arm position, update the index, and sleep. Add a closing curly bracket for the paint() method.

```
   repaint();
}
```

13 Add to the project a new Web page named **testAnim.htm**.

14 In the Source tab of the HTML Editor window, place the insertion point in the blank line following the tag that reads <P> </P> and type the opening <APPLET> tag that contains the applet's name and dimensions: `<APPLET CODE = "AnimatedFigure.class" WIDTH = 350 HEIGHT = 400>`.

15 Press the **Enter** key to start a new line and type the applet's closing tag: `</APPLET>`.

16 Build and save the project, then execute the program in AppletViewer by typing `jview /a testAnim.htm` at the command line. The output appears similar to Figure 15-17; a stick figure's arm waves up and down.

Figure 15-17: Output of the AnimatedFigure applet

17 Close the AppletViewer window.

Next, you will add some text to the applet. Event Handlers Incorporated wants the company name to move up and down on the screen, as though the stick figure is using the name as a yo-yo. Additional text appears in a fixed position in the applet.

To add text to the applet:

1 Return to the **AnimatedFigure.java** file in the Text Editor window, and then immediately save the file as **AnimatedFigure2.java**.

2 Change the class name to **AnimatedFigure2**.

3 Within the paint() method, position the insertion point at the end of the last drawLine() method call (the statement that draws the moving arm), and then press the **Enter** key to start a new line.

4 To draw the "Event Handlers" name as though it is moving along with the stick figure's arm, indicate the name's vertical position as 30 pixels below the arm's current vertical position as follows:
`gr.drawString("Event Handlers",180, vert[index] + 30);`.

section B

5 Add the following text lines at lower positions on the next two lines:

```
gr.drawString("Plan with us once",170,260);
gr.drawString("Like a yo-yo, you'll come back!",170,280);
```

6 Return to the **testAnim.htm** file in the Text Editor window. Change the APPLET CODE reference to **"AnimatedFigure2.class"**, and then save the HTML document as **testAnim2.htm**.

7 Rebuild and save the program, then execute the program in AppletViewer by typing **jview /a testAnim2.htm** at the command line. The output looks like Figure 15-18. The stick figure appears to use the Event Handlers company name as a yo-yo.

Figure 15-18: Output of the AnimatedFigure2 applet

8 Close the AppletViewer window.

Reducing Flickering

When you create an applet with animation, your screen might flicker. To understand why your screen flickers, you must recall the applet life cycle that you learned about in Chapter 7.

The faster your processor speed is, the less flickering you will see.

When you change a drawing in an applet, such as when you reposition the stick figure's arm and the moving text String, you call the repaint() method to repaint the applet surface. The repaint() method calls the update() method, which clears the viewing area, and then calls the paint() method, which contains the instructions for drawing the figure and String in their new positions. If the repaint() method did not call update() to clear the screen, then all previous versions of the applet would remain visible, and after the first five passes through the paint() method you would see all five of the figure's arms and all five messages, as shown in Figure 15-19.

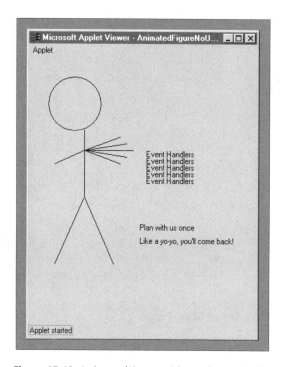

Figure 15-19: AnimatedFigure without the update() method

Your program must clear the screen so only one version of the arm and message appears at a time, but clearing the screen takes enough time that your eye detects it and causes the screen to flicker. One way to reduce or eliminate flickering is to override the applet's update() method so that the viewing area is *not* cleared. After all, every time you call update() to clear the screen, the head, body, legs, and left arm of the stick figure and two messages are immediately redrawn in the same positions from which they were just cleared. It is more efficient to draw the unchanging parts of the screen just once when the applet starts, and then constantly redraw only those portions of the screen that actually change.

The trick for "erasing" a portion of a drawing on the screen is to use the Applet's background color to redraw the portion of the screen that you want to erase. When you create graphics using the background color, the graphics seem to disappear. In other words, to appear to move the stick figure's arm, you draw over its "old" arm in the background color (white), and then draw the new arm position in the previous drawing color (black).

For example, if the applet background color is white and the drawing color is black, one way to draw over the "old" arm line is to save the arm coordinates in variables each time you draw an arm in black. Then you update the index that points to the array of arm-coordinate positions. Before you draw the next black arm using the new index, you draw the "old" arm in white using the old coordinates.

To reduce flickering in the AnimatedFigure2 applet:

1 Return to the **AnimatedFigure2.java** file in the Text Editor window, and then immediately save the file as **AnimatedFigure3.java**.

2 Change the class name from AnimatedFigure2 to **AnimatedFigure3**.

3 Position the insertion point at the end of the statement that declares the vert array, and then press the **Enter** key to start a new line. Create the following two new integer variables that will hold the previous arm coordinates. Initialize these variables to the first pair of coordinates. Then create a variable to indicate whether the paint() method is on its first or a subsequent execution.

```
int oldx = horiz[0],oldy = vert[0];
boolean firstTime = true;
```

4 Position the insertion point to the right of the closing curly bracket for the start() method, and then press the **Enter** key to start a new line. Type the following code to override the applet's automatic update() method. The update() method calls paint(), passing along the Graphics object received from the repaint() method.

```
public void update(Graphics gr)
{
   paint(gr);
}
```

5 Delete the current paint() method statements up to, but not including, the statement ++index;. Begin the following replacement paint() method by drawing the head, body, legs, left arm, and constant text only if this is the first pass through the paint() method. Conclude the if block by setting the firstTime variable to `false`.

```
public void paint(Graphics gr)
{
   if(firstTime)
   {
```

```
gr.drawOval(30,30,80,80);
gr.drawLine(85,110,85,210);
gr.drawLine(85,210,40,310);
gr.drawLine(85,210,130,310);
gr.drawLine(85,140,40,160);
gr.drawString("Plan with us once",170,260);
gr.drawString
   ("Like a yo-yo, you'll come back!",170,280);
firstTime = false;
}
```

6 Continue adding the following paint() method statements that execute every time the paint() method executes. First, set the drawing color to the background color, and redraw the arms and moving String in the background color to make them invisible:

```
gr.setColor(getBackground());
gr.drawLine(85,140,oldx, oldy);
gr.drawString("Event Handlers",180, oldy + 30);
```

7 Add the following code to change the drawing color back to the usual drawing color (black), and then to draw the new arm and the new moving message in their new positions:

```
gr.setColor(getForeground());
gr.drawLine(85,140,horiz[index],vert[index]);
gr.drawString("Event Handlers",180, vert[index] + 30);
```

8 Before increasing the index for the next execution of the paint() method, use the following code to save the current arm coordinates by storing them in the oldx and oldy variables:

```
oldx = horiz[index];
oldy = vert[index];
```

9 Return to the **testAnim2.htm** file in the Text Editor window. Change the APPLET CODE reference to **"AnimatedFigure3.class"**, and then save the HTML document as **testAnim3.htm**.

10 Rebuild and save the program, then execute the program in AppletViewer by typing **jview /a testAnim3.htm** at the command line. When the applet runs, you will not see any flickering.

11 Minimize the AppletViewer window, and then restore it. You can see only the moving arm and message. Close the AppletViewer window.

The flickering disappears in the AnimatedFigure3 applet because the update() method no longer redraws the entire screen. However, a problem occurs when you minimize, restore, or move the applet—the figure is no longer visible—and only the moving arm and message remain. When you start the applet, firstTime equals true, the figure is drawn, and firstTime is set to `false`. When you minimize the applet, it is still running. When you restore the applet, the applet is redrawn, but because the applet is still running, firstTime already is set to `false`. The head and other body parts are drawn only when firstTime is `true`, so the applet now shows a disembodied arm.

To correct the applet problem:

1 Return to the **AnimatedFigure3.java** file in the Text Editor window, and immediately save the file as **AnimatedFigure4.java**.

2 Change the class name to **AnimatedFigure4**.

3 Within the update() method, position your cursor after the method's opening curly bracket, and then press the **Enter** key to start a new line.

4 Add the statement `firstTime = true;`. Now, every time the applet restarts, it will redraw the head and body.

5 Return to the **testAnim3.htm** file in the Text Editor window. Change the `APPLET CODE` reference to `"AnimatedFigure4.class"`, and then save the HTML document as **testAnim4.htm**.

6 Rebuild and save the project, then execute the program in AppletViewer by typing `jview /a testAnim4.htm` at the command line. The applet runs the same as before. Minimize the AppletViewer window and then restore it. The entire figure and complete set of messages are visible.

7 Close the AppletViewer window.

Using Images

If your artistic talent is limited to drawing stick figures, you can use a variety of more sophisticated predrawn animated images within your applets. The Applet method **getImage()** loads a stored image into an applet. The getImage() method requires two arguments: a URL object and the name of an image file. **URL** is an acronym for **Uniform Resource Locator**, which is the standard form for an Internet address; it is also the name for a Java class that holds Internet address objects. The method that returns a URL object is **getDocumentBase()**. You can require your applet to retrieve an image from the Internet by providing its address as an argument to getDocumentBase(), but because Internet addresses can change and sites can shut down, it is safer to use the getDocumentBase() method with no argument, which tells getDocumentBase() to access an image that you have stored in the same folder as the HTML file that controls the applet.

For example, you can declare an Image object and assign an image to it from the current folder with a statement such as `Image myImage = getImage(getDocumentBase(),"someFile");`. Image files usually are stored in one of two formats:

- Graphics Interchange Format (with the file extension .gif)
- Joint Photographic Experts Group (with the file extension .jpeg or .jpg)

tip

When you call getImage(), an image is loaded in a separate thread of execution, which allows the program to continue while the image loads.

Usually, you use getImage() in an applet's init() method, and drawImage() in an Applet's paint() method. The drawImage() method requires the following four arguments:

- The name of the image
- The x-coordinate where you want the image to display within the applet
- The y-coordinate where you want the image to display within the applet
- The ImageObserver

The **ImageObserver** is an interface that updates images as they load. Within your applets, the ImageObserver will be the applet itself, so you will use `this` as the ImageObserver.

Next, you will load a predrawn animated .gif file into an applet and execute it. The .gif file includes 16 frames that display a falling egg that Event Handlers Incorporated is using in an advertising slogan to give Event Handlers a "crack" at planning the customer's next party.

To demonstrate loading a predrawn animated image into an applet:

1. Create a new empty project named **LoadImage**. Save the **LoadImage** project folder in the Chapter.15 folder on your Student Disk.
2. Add a new class file named **LoadImage.java** to the project.
3. Above the class header, type the following import statements that you will need for the program:

   ```
   import java.applet.*;
   import java.awt.*;
   ```

4. Add **extends Applet** to the right of the class header.
5. Declare an Image object between the class's curly brackets that will represent the falling egg as follows: `private Image egg;`.
6. The Chapter.15 folder on your Student Disk contains an animated .gif file named egg.gif. Use Windows Explorer to copy the egg.gif file into the LoadImage project folder in the Chapter.15 folder on your Student Disk.
7. Enter the following init() method, which loads the egg.gif file in the applet:

   ```
   public void init()
   {
      egg = getImage(getDocumentBase(),"egg.gif");
   }
   ```

section B

8 Enter the following paint() method, which draws the egg Image at location 1,1 within the applet, and also draws two Strings:

```
public void paint(Graphics g)
{
  g.drawImage(egg,1,1,this);
  g.drawString
    ("Planning your next party?",100,50);
  g.drawString
    ("Give Event Handlers a crack at it.",100,300);
}
```

9 Add to the project a new Web page named **testImage.htm**.

10 In the Source tab of the HTML Editor window, place the insertion point in the blank line following the tag that reads <P> </P> and type the opening <APPLET> tag that contains the applet's name and dimensions: <APPLET CODE = "LoadImage.class" WIDTH = 300 HEIGHT = 350>.

11 Press the **Enter** key to start a new line and type the applet's closing tag: </APPLET>.

12 Build and save the project, then execute the program in AppletViewer by typing **jview /a testImage.htm** at the command line. The animation shows an egg that falls and cracks open at the bottom of the applet viewing area. See Figure 15-20.

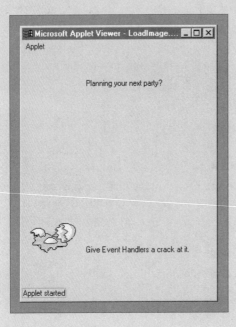

Figure 15-20: LoadImage applet

> **13** Close the AppletViewer window.

Many animated images are available on the Web in the form of shareware or public domain files. Use a search engine to search for keywords such as *gif files*, *jpeg files*, *jpg files*, and *animation* to find sources of these types of images.

> The egg file is available at www.mediabuilder.com. Note that not all images on the Internet are free; many are protected by copyright and you must purchase them to use them. Be sure to check with the creator of any images before you use them in your programs.

Garbage Collection

The Java programming language supports a garbage collection feature that you seldom find in other programming languages. The **garbage collector** provides for the automatic clean-up of unnecessarily reserved memory.

With many programming languages, when you allocate memory from the memory that is available (often known as the **heap**), you must purposely deallocate it or your system's performance begins to slow down as less memory is available. The Java garbage collector automatically sweeps through memory looking for unneeded objects and destroys them. Out-of-scope objects or objects with `null` references are available for garbage collection. Partially constructed objects that throw an Exception during construction also are available for collection.

> You first learned about garbage collection in Chapter 6.

Garbage collection works by running as a very low-priority thread. Typically, this thread runs only if available memory is very low. That is, all other threads must be delayed by memory limitations before the garbage collector gets the opportunity to run.

You cannot prevent the garbage collector from running, but you can request that it run by using the statement `System.gc();`. For example, suppose you write a program that counts seconds and uses a string named `counter` to hold the values "one", "two", and so on. When you assign "two" to `counter`, the memory that holds the character string "one" becomes garbage. Instead of allowing the useless strings to accumulate in memory, you might want to use the `System.gc();` statement. Using this statement does not force the garbage collector to run; it is a request to the system to schedule the garbage collector. The garbage collector will actually run when all other threads are delayed.

Putting Your Animation in a Browser Page

If you browse the Internet, you probably have seen examples of animation on Web pages. Web page creators use animation to attract your attention and to make their pages interesting. Next, you will create an applet that displays a moving word. As a stand-alone applet, it is interesting, but using the applet becomes much more interesting when you run several versions of it in a Web browser at the same time.

Each version of the applet displays the single string "Party" at x- and y-coordinates. After each display, you use the Thread class sleep() method to pause. Then you "erase" the string by drawing it in the background color and redraw it in a new position. The new position is three pixels to the right and down from the previous string, so the illusion is that the string is moving down and to the right. When the string reaches the right edge of the viewing area, you begin to subtract three pixels from the horizontal and vertical coordinates, so the string appears to reverse course and move up and to the left.

To create the first applet that will run in the browser:

1 Create a new empty project named **BouncingParty**. Save the **BouncingParty** project folder in the Chapter.15 folder on your Student Disk.

2 Add a new class file named **BouncingParty1** to the project.

3 Above the class header, type the following import statements that you will need for the program:

```
import java.applet.*;
import java.awt.*;
```

4 Add **extends Applet** to the right of the class header.

5 Between the class's curly brackets, establish variables for the step value increase for each drawString() and for the x- and y-coordinates as follows:

```
private int step = 3;
private int x = 10, y = 10;
```

6 Also establish variables for the maximum screen positions, the previous screen positions, and the sleep interval as follows:

```
int oldx, oldy;
private int sleep = 20;
```

7 Type the following update() method that calls the paint() method so Java doesn't call its own update() method, which would clear the viewing area and increase flickering:

```
public void update(Graphics gr)
{
   paint(gr);
}
```

8 Begin the following paint() method, which draws "Party" in the background color at the previous x- and y-coordinates, and then draws the string in the foreground color at the new coordinates:

```
public void paint(Graphics gr)
{
   gr.setColor(getBackground());
   gr.drawString("Party", oldx, oldy);
   gr.setColor(getForeground());
   gr.drawString("Party", x, y);
```

9 Save the x and y values in the oldx and oldy variables. Then increase x and y by the step value as follows:

```
oldx = x;
oldy = y;
x += step;
y += step;
```

10 When the string approaches the edge of the applet viewing area, you want to reverse the direction of movement. You can reverse the direction of movement by changing the step value to its negative equivalent as follows:

```
if(x < 10 || x > 90)
{
   step = -step;
}
```

11 Enter the following code to sleep for the specified time, and then repaint the screen:

```
try
{
   Thread.sleep(sleep);
}
catch(InterruptedException e)
{
}
repaint();
```

12 Add the closing curly bracket for the paint() method.

> **13** Add to the project a new Web page named **testParty.htm**.
> **14** In the Source tab of the HTML Editor window, place the insertion point in the blank line following the tag that reads `<P> </P>` and type the opening `<APPLET>` tag that contains the applet's name and dimensions: `<APPLET CODE = "BouncingParty1.class" WIDTH = 120 HEIGHT = 120>`.
> **15** Press the **Enter** key to start a new line and type the applet's closing tag: `</APPLET>`.
> **16** Build and save the project, then execute the program in AppletViewer by typing `jview /a testParty.htm` at the command line. The word "Party" moves up and down the screen. Close the AppletViewer window.

The simple BouncingParty1 applet is interesting, but it won't hold your attention for very long. If you create several similar applets and run them at the same time, the output will be more interesting. Next, you will create two more applets that display a moving "Party" message. You will alter each applet so that the displayed string starts in a slightly different position within each applet.

> **To create applets in which the moving string starts in a different position:**
> **1** Return to the **BouncingParty1.java** applet in the Text Editor window, and then immediately save the applet as **BouncingParty2.java**.
> **2** Change the class name to **BouncingParty2**.
> **3** Change the beginning x and y variable values from 10 to **40** so the statement becomes `private int x = 40, y = 40;`.
> **4** Save the **BouncingParty2.java** file, then save it as **BouncingParty3.java**.
> **5** Change the class name to **BouncingParty3**.
> **6** Change the values for both the x and y variables to **70**.

You now have three similar applets that each display a moving "Party" string. Next, you will incorporate these three applets into an HTML document and view it in a Web browser. To make the HTML document more interesting, you will add two headings to the document.

You first learned about HTML in Chapter 7.

HTML provides six levels of headings named H1 through H6. H1 headings are the largest, and H6 headings are the smallest. Just as with the `<APPLET>` and `</APPLET>` tags you have been using in your HTML documents, the heading tags come in pairs. You place text you want to display between a pair such as `<H1>` and `</H1>`.

HTML document authors seldom use H6 headings; they are very small.

To create an HTML document to use with your browser to view the three applets:

1. Add to the project a new Web page named **testParties.htm**.
2. In the Source tab of the HTML Editor window, place the insertion point in the blank line following the tag that reads <P> </P> and enter the following HTML code, which consists of a large heading, three applets, and another heading:

   ```
   <H1>We keep your party moving</H1>
   <APPLET CODE = "BouncingParty1.class"
      WIDTH = 120 HEIGHT = 120>
   </APPLET>
   <APPLET CODE = "BouncingParty2.class"
      WIDTH = 120 HEIGHT = 120>
   </APPLET>
   <APPLET CODE = "BouncingParty3.class"
      WIDTH = 120 HEIGHT = 120>
   </APPLET>
   <H1>at Event Handlers Incorporated</H1>
   ```

3. Rebuild and save the project, then click the **Quick View** tab in the HTML Editor window. The three applets run within the HTML document as shown in Figure 15-21.

Figure 15-21: Three applets running in Quick View

4. Experiment with modifying the step variable value and the sleep time in the BouncingParty applets and observe the results in Quick View.

SUMMARY

- You create computer animation by displaying images in rapid sequence.

- Most computer animation employs the Thread class sleep() method to pause for short periods of time between animation cells, so the viewer has time to absorb each image's content.

- When you change a drawing in an applet, you call the repaint() method to repaint the applet surface. The repaint() method calls the update() method. The update() method clears the viewing area and calls the paint() method, which contains the drawing instructions.

- Clearing the screen takes enough time that your eye detects it and the screen flickers. One way to reduce or eliminate flickering is to override the applet's update() method so that the viewing area is *not* cleared.

- To "erase" a portion of a drawing on the screen, you use the applet's background color to redraw the portion of the screen that you want to erase.

- The Applet method getImage() loads a stored image into an applet. The getImage() method requires two arguments: a URL object and the name of an image file.

- *URL* is an acronym for Uniform Resource Locator, which is the standard form for an Internet address; it is also the name for a Java class that holds Internet address objects.

- Image files are usually stored in Graphics Interchange Format (with file extension .gif) or Joint Photographic Experts Group (with file extension .jpeg or .jpg).

- The drawImage() method requires four arguments: the name of the image, the x- and y-coordinates where you want the image to display within the applet, and the ImageObserver.

- Garbage collection runs as a low-priority thread and provides for the automatic clean-up of unnecessarily reserved memory.

- Web page creators use animation to attract your attention and to make their pages interesting.

QUESTIONS

1. Most computer animation employs the Thread class _____ method to pause for short periods of time between animation cells.
    a. wait()
    b. pause()
    c. sleep()
    d. delay()

2. You usually create animation by using _____.
   a. a single image
   b. a series of images
   c. the Animation class
   d. the Draw object

3. An applet's repaint() method automatically calls the _____ method.
   a. redraw()
   b. update()
   c. drawString()
   d. revision()

4. The applet method that automatically clears the viewing area is _____.
   a. clear()
   b. redraw()
   c. update()
   d. view()

5. You would see all versions of an animated drawing at the same time if you did not call an applet's _____ method.
   a. clear()
   b. paint()
   c. draw()
   d. update()

6. A way to reduce screen flickering is to _____.
   a. redraw the entire image with each call to the paint() method
   b. redraw only those portions of the screen that actually change
   c. call the paint() method directly instead of repaint()
   d. call the clear() method

7. You erase an image from the screen by redrawing a previously drawn image in the _____ color.
   a. same
   b. foreground
   c. background
   d. lightest

8. To create the illusion that an object moves up and to the left, you would _____.
   a. increase its x-coordinate and decrease its y-coordinate
   b. decrease its x-coordinate and increase its y-coordinate
   c. increase both its x- and y-coordinates
   d. decrease both its x- and y-coordinates

9. The Applet method getImage() _____.
   a. allows you to draw an image on the screen
   b. loads a stored image into an applet
   c. produces a copy of a displayed image
   d. returns the name of an image when you point to it with your mouse

10. The standard form for an Internet address is known as its _____.
    a. WWW
    b. ISP
    c. URL
    d. GIF

11. The _____ provides for the automatic clean-up of unnecessarily reserved memory.
    a. Java VM
    b. clean-up() method
    c. garbage collector
    d. internal Java release function

EXERCISES

Save each of the programs that you create in the exercises in the Chapter.15 folder on your Student Disk.

1. a. Write an applet that displays a stick figure doing jumping jacks. Name the applet Jumping.

    b. Add text to the Jumping applet so it serves as an advertisement for a health club.

2. a. Write an applet that displays a figure that walks from left to right across the screen. When the figure nears the right side of the screen, start the figure at the left again. Name the applet Walking.

    b. Write an HTML document that displays three walking figures. Add text describing a fund-raising walk-a-thon.

3. Write an applet that shows a bouncing ball. The ball reverses direction when it nears the edge of the viewing area. Name the applet Pong.

4. Locate a public domain animated .gif file on the Web, and then include the file in an applet.

5. Write an applet that creates a straight line that constantly rotates in a circle.

6. Write an applet that simulates a marquee by displaying a string of characters one at a time from right to left across the screen. When the string message is fully displayed, start the message again.

7. Write an applet that displays a digital clock that displays the hour, minute, and second, and then updates the time every second.

8. Each of the following files in the Chapter.15 folder on your Student Disk has syntax and/or logical errors. Add the files to a new project called FixDebug. Save the FixDebug project in the Chapter.15 folder on your Student Disk. You can use the testDebug3.htm and testDebug4.htm files in the Chapter.15 folder on your Student Disk to test the applets in DebugFifteen3.java and DebugFifteen4.java respectively.
    a. DebugFifteen1.java
    b. DebugFifteen2.java
    c. DebugFifteen3.java
    d. DebugFifteen4.java

CHAPTER 16

Windows Applications and Packaging

case ▶ "I love using Java," you say to Lynn Greenbrier, your mentor at Event Handlers Incorporated. "But a few weeks ago, the marketing department came to me with a bunch of new programming requests from corporate clients."

"Tell me more," says Lynn.

"These clients don't want to use the Internet to supply us with event information," you say. "They all use Windows 95, 98, or NT, and they want a stand-alone application they can use for event planning. I wrote a Java program, but it doesn't look like a real Windows application. I had to re-create many of the standard Windows features, and the program ran very slowly. So, while I love Java, I'm feeling a bit frustrated."

section A

Lynn Greenbrier smiles and says, "I've got just the thing to solve your problems. Visual J++ has tools you can use to access Windows operating system functionality. Those tools will let you use Java to write real Windows applications. To start, let me tell you about Windows Foundation Classes."

Previewing the Windows Party Planner Application

In this chapter, you will use Java to create a Windows application that is similar to the Party Planner Applet you created in Chapter 11. You will create a Windows-based Party Planner program so you can see the differences between programs created with the Abstract Windows Tool Kit (AWT) and programs created as Windows applications. Like the applet in Chapter 11, the Event Handlers Incorporated Windows application lets a user determine the price of an event based on several event choices. Users can select some options in any combination (serve only cocktails, serve only dinner, serve both cocktails and dinner, or serve nothing). For other options, such as the entrée to serve for dinner or the entertainment selection, only one choice is allowed. You need check boxes, lists, and radio buttons to accommodate these different types of selections. The Chap16PartyPlanner application incorporates several such devices, which you can use now. You will create a similar application in this chapter.

To preview the Windows Party Planner application:

1 Using Windows Explorer, go the Chapter.16 folder on your Student Disk and run the **WindowsPartyPlanner.exe** file. After a few moments, you will see the Windows Party Planner window shown in Figure 16-1.

Figure 16-1: Windows Party Planner application

2. You can use the Windows Party Planner application to plan an imaginary event by choosing whether to serve cocktails or dinner (or both or neither). Use the program now and observe how the event's price changes as you make selections. If you choose to serve dinner, you can select one of three main courses. You also can select from a list of entertainment choices and party favors. The event's price changes as you make each selection.

3. Close the application by clicking the **Exit** button.

SECTION A
objectives

In this section you will learn:
- About Windows architecture and the Win32 API
- How to use J/Direct
- About native applications and architecturally neutral applications
- About Windows Foundation Classes (WFCs) for Java
- How to create Windows applications using WFCs
- About WFC forms
- About WFC controls

J/Direct and Windows Foundation Classes for Java

Windows Architecture and the Win32 API

In this chapter, you will learn how to use Visual J++ and the Java programming language to create Windows applications. Using the Java programming language to create Windows applications allows you to use your knowledge of Java to harness the features of Windows operating systems such as prebuilt dialog boxes, buttons, and other Windows elements. To create Windows applications with Java, you first need to understand how Windows operating systems are designed.

There are two types of Windows operating systems: 16-bit and 32-bit. The older Windows 3.1 operating system is **16-bit**. Current **32-bit** Windows operating systems are Windows NT, Windows 95, Windows 98, and Windows CE. The term **bit** refers to the width of a computer microprocessor's data bus. You can think of the data bus as the number of roads leading into a microprocessor. The wider the data bus, the more information can be sent simultaneously to the microprocessor.

> Visual J++ is a 32-bit application designed for 32-bit Windows operating systems.

The actual speed with which information is processed also depends on several other factors, including the microprocessor architecture (80386, i486, Pentium, and so on) and the megahertz at which the microprocessor operates. The 80386 and i486 microprocessors have 32-bits wide data buses, whereas the Pentium family of microprocessors has 64-bits wide data buses. The ability to take advantage of data bus width depends on the operating system or application that is accessing the microprocessor. For example, Windows 3.1 can operate on 80386, i486, and Pentium microprocessors, but can use only 16 bits of each data bus, even though the 80386 and i486 microprocessors are 32-bits wide and the Pentium chip is 64-bits wide.

All 32-bit Windows operating systems share a common application programming interface known as the Win32 API. An **application programming interface (API)** is a library of methods and attributes that allows programmers to access the features and functionality of an application or operating system. Windows operating systems are actually complex applications written in the C and C++ programming languages. The Win32 API allows you to access and use standard Windows GUI features such as the Open and Save dialog boxes, and controls such as buttons, scrollbars, and list boxes in new applications that you write. You have already worked with similar GUI components in the AWT.

Using the common functionality available in the Win32 API helps to maintain a consistent look for Windows-based applications. In the same manner that the AWT saves time when writing Java applications, the Win32 API minimizes development time for Windows applications, since you use preexisting components without having to create them from scratch. Win32 API functions are grouped in the following categories:

- Window Management
- Window Controls
- Shell Features
- Graphics Device Interface
- System Services
- International Features
- Network Services

APIs represent a more advanced form of object-oriented programming. Just as methods and attributes of an individual object are exposed through inheritance or an interface, libraries of methods and attributes are exposed through an API.

Using J/Direct to Access the Win32 API

Many programming languages, including Visual Basic and Visual C++, directly access the functionality in the Win32 API. The Java programming language, however, does not directly access Win32 API functions—such as standard Windows GUI features. Visual J++ has a special utility called J/Direct that allows you to access the Win32 API. **J/Direct** translates the Win32 API syntax into a format that can be used with Java. With J/Direct, you can place calls to the Win32 API directly into your code.

To use J/Direct to call Win32 API functions, you include the following:

- A Win32 API function method declaration
- Special comments that contain a directive to locate a dynamic-link library (DLL) for the Win32 API function

The code in Figure 16-2 calls the Win32 API MessageBox function, which displays a simple Windows dialog box. The dialog box generated by the program in Figure 16-2 is shown in Figure 16-3.

```
public class MessageBoxApp
{
    public static void main(String args[])
    {
        MessageBox(0, "This is a message box.",
            "Message Box Title", 0);
    }
    /**
    * @dll.import("USER32", auto)
    */
    public static native int MessageBox(int hWnd, String lpText,
        String lpCaption, int uType);
```

Figure 16-2: MessageBoxApp using J/Direct to call the Win32 MessageBox function

Figure 16-3: Output of the Win32 MessageBoxApp

The last statement in the code in Figure 16-2 is the MessageBox method declaration. The MessageBox method declaration includes the **native modifier**, which informs Java that the method is implemented in another programming language—in this case, the programming language is the Win32 API. Unlike most methods with which you have worked, the MessageBox method declaration ends in a semicolon, rather than being followed by curly brackets containing the method's statements. Since the method is implemented outside Java, you do not need to create the method body.

By convention, you add J/Direct calls to the end of a class file.

Dynamic-link libraries contain the methods and other components in the Win32 API, and are files with an extension of .dll. When you use a J/Direct call in a Java program, the program locates the specific DLL containing the object you are calling by using a directive. A **directive** tells the compiler in which DLL a method is located. Immediately above the MessageBox method declaration in Figure 16-2 are comments containing the directive for the MessageBox function. (You first learned about comments in Chapter 2.) As you know, the compiler ignores text placed within comments. Unlike other types of text that are placed within comments, directives are not ignored by the compiler. You usually place directives immediately above a J/Direct call. There are three types of directives: @dll.import for declaring functions, @dll.struct for declaring structures, and @dll.structmap for declaring fixed-size

Strings and arrays embedded in structures. The @dll.import directive in Figure 16-2 instructs the compiler to look for the MessageBox function in USER32.DLL.

Structures are used in the C/C++ programming languages and are similar to classes.

The MessageBox function is available in two versions: ANSI or Unicode. The auto modifier in the @dll.import directive instructs the compiler to use the optimal version of the MessageBox function, ANSI or Unicode, depending on the version of Windows being used.

If you know the correct syntax for J/Direct calls and directives that you want to include in your Java application, then you can type them directly into a Java file. However, the syntax for J/Direct calls and directives is unique for the specific API function being called. An easier method of including J/Direct calls in your code is to use the Visual J++ J/Direct Call Builder dialog box. The J/Direct Call Builder dialog box inserts the appropriate syntax and directives for the J/Direct calls you want to use in your program. Figure 16-4 displays an example of the J/Direct Call Builder dialog box.

Figure 16-4: J/Direct Call Builder dialog box

The J/Direct Call Builder dialog box contains several options to assist you in locating a J/Direct call. The default option in the Source drop-down list box is WIN32.TXT, which lists methods, structures, and constants contained in standard Win32 API DLLs. You can click the Methods check box, Structs check box, or Constants check box to filter the visible elements. The Target text box displays the class to which the selected J/Direct call will be added. By default, a class named Win32 will be added to your project to contain J/Direct calls. Using a separate class to contain J/Direct calls is good practice, particularly if you have multiple classes in your project, all of which may need to access J/Direct calls.

Next you will create a Java console application project and use the J/Direct Call Builder to add J/Direct calls to the program. In the following exercise, do not worry about the syntax for the arguments in the MessageBox and MessageBeep Win32 API calls. Win32 API programming is a complex topic and beyond the scope of this text. The only purpose of the exercise is to show how a Java

section A

application can use Win32 API calls with J/Direct. Later in this section, you will learn an easier method for working with J/Direct calls in Visual J++.

To create a Java console application with J/Direct calls:

1. If necessary, start Visual J++, then create a new console application project named **Win32Example**. Save the **Win32Example** project folder in the Chapter.16 folder on your Student Disk.
2. Rename the default Class1.java file as **Win32Example.java**, then open the file in the Text Editor window.
3. Replace the Class1 class name in the `public class Class1` line with **Win32Example**.
4. Point to **Other Windows** on the **View** menu, then select **J/Direct Call Builder**.
5. Although placing J/Direct calls in a separate class is good programming practice, for this exercise you will add the J/Direct calls to the Win32Example class. Click the **ellipsis (...)** next to the Target text box. The Select class dialog box displays, as shown in Figure 16-5.

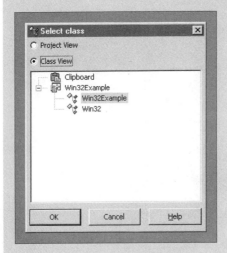

Figure 16-5: Select class dialog box

6. In the Select class dialog box, click the **Win32Example** class, and then select the **OK** button. The Select class dialog box closes, and the J/Direct Call Builder dialog box redisplays with the Win32Example class visible in the Target text box.

> **help**
>
> The text in the Target text box will read "Win32Example\Win32Example." The text to the left of the backward slash (\) represents the name of the project and the text to the right of the backward slash represents the class. In this case, both the project and class are named "Win32Example."

Windows Applications and Packaging

7 Place your cursor in the **Find** text box and begin typing **MessageBox**. The list of J/Direct calls scrolls to match the typed text. When you see MessageBox in the list, click it, then click the **Copy To Target** button. The MessageBox J/Direct call and directive are added to the bottom of the class file.

8 Repeat Step 7 to add the MessageBeep call to the Win32Example class.

9 Close the J/Direct Call Builder dialog box by clicking the **Close** button ⊠.

10 In the main() method, replace the `// TODO: Add initialization code here` comment with the following code, which creates two Strings and adds the Win32API MessageBox() and MessageBeep() functions:

```
String messageBoxTitle = "Event Planners";
String messageBoxText = "Thank you for planning with us!";
MessageBox(0, messageBoxText, messageBoxTitle, 0);
MessageBeep(0);
```

11 In the Win32Example properties window, deselect the **Launch as a console application** check box to run the Win32Example file using WJVIEW. You are selecting WJVIEW since the application will not require a separate console application window, as is created with JVIEW.

12 Build and save the project, then execute the program by selecting **Start** from the **Debug** menu. A dialog box appears as shown in Figure 16-6.

Figure 16-6: Output of the Win32Example program

13 Click the **OK** button. You should hear an audible beep after the dialog box closes.

Native Applications versus Architecturally Neutral Applications

The programs you have created in previous chapters have been true Java applications or applets. Recall from Chapter 1 that Java programs are architecturally neutral. You can use the Java programming language to write a program that will run on any platform for which there is a Java Virtual Machine (VM). The Win32Example program, however, can run only on a 32-bit Windows platform. Adding J/Direct calls to the Win32Example program removes its architectural neutrality—it is no longer a true Java program since it can run only on 32-bit Windows platforms. While you are giving up architectural neutrality, you are gaining the ability to use your Java programming skills to create Windows applications.

Throughout this book, you have imported Java packages into the applications and applets you created. As you learned in Chapter 4, packages are related groups of classes and class members that are grouped together into a single library. Examples of the packages you have used include the java.applet package for working with applets, and the java.awt (Abstract Windows Toolkit) package, which contains commonly used components such as labels, menus, and buttons. Many Java packages contain classes that are available only if you explicitly import a package into your program. For example, to include the java.awt package in a program, you must include the statement `import java.awt.*` before the declaration of a class header.

The packages that comprise the Java programming language are considered to be part of the Java API, very similar to the way internal Windows functions and features are part of the Win32 API. If you create a program using only the standard Java packages that are part of the original Java API developed by Sun Microsystems, then the program will run on any platform for which there is a Java VM. Packages that are part of the Java API are listed in Figure 16-7.

java.applet	java.math
java.awt	java.net
java.awt.datatransfer	java.security
java.awt.event	java.security.acl
java.awt.image	java.security.interfaces
java.beans	java.sql
java.io	java.text
java.lang	java.util
java.lang.reflect	java.util.zip

Figure 16-7: Java API Packages

In contrast to Java API packages, the Java VM cannot use components that exist within an individual operating system. You must rely on the internal capabilities of the Java programming language and the packages listed in Figure 16-7. For example, in a true Java application, to create a dialog box that opens files, you must use the components in the java.awt package to build the dialog box. The final result may resemble a Windows Open dialog box, but it will not be a *true* Windows dialog box. A true Windows Open dialog box is part of the Win32 API.

True Java applications do not run as fast as applications that are native to a specific operating system. This difference in speeds is a result of the Java VM. While the Java VM allows Java applications to be architecturally neutral, it adds an additional layer that an application must pass through to run. The flowchart in Figure 16-8 shows the additional Java VM layer through which an application must pass to work with a particular operating system. Figure 16-9 shows the direct access to an operating system that a native application has.

Figure 16-8: Java VM program execution

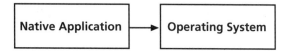

Figure 16-9: Native program execution

J/Direct allows you to include native Win32 API calls within a Java application. These J/Direct calls bypass the Java VM and directly access the Windows operating system, similar to the way native programs access an operating system. Since they can run only on 32-bit Windows platforms, programs that use J/Direct are no longer true Java programs. The trade-off is that J/Direct programs execute faster since they bypass the additional Java VM layer.

Windows Foundation Classes for Java

Creating Windows applications requires a thorough knowledge of Win32 API programming. Although J/Direct helps you access the Win32 API features, using it is complex and requires familiarity with the Win32 API. To make the task of creating Windows applications with Visual J++ easier, Microsoft created Windows Foundation Classes for Java. **Windows Foundation Classes (WFCs)** are packages of J/Direct calls that are translated into the Java programming language. You still access the same functions that you access with J/Direct calls, but the complicated J/Direct calls and directives are unnecessary. Instead, you import a WFC package into a class and work with the package's components, similar to how you work with Java API packages. WFCs allow you to access the Win32 API directly and eliminate the need to understand Win32 API programming. The WFC packages are listed in Figure 16-10.

For experienced C++ programmers, WFCs are comparable to Microsoft Foundation Classes (MFCs), which provide a C++ language API that accesses the Windows native C-language API.

Package	Description
com.ms.wfc.app	Contains classes for application and Thread control and access to the Clipboard and Registry.
com.ms.wfc.core	Provides core WFC functionality; this package should be included in every WFC program.

Figure 16-10: WFC packages

Package	Description
com.ms.wfc.data	Contains data access classes using the ActiveX Data Objects (ADO) object model. Also contains classes that use ADO to access databases.
com.ms.wfc.html	Contains Java classes for accessing Dynamic HTML (DHTML).
com.ms.wfc.io	Provides classes for working with file input and output.
com.ms.wfc.ui	Contains user interface classes for controls such as buttons and labels.
com.ms.wfc.util	Contains miscellaneous utility classes.

Figure 16-10: WFC packages (continued)

Java programs using WFCs must include the following:

- The `import com.ms.wfc.core.*;` statement
- Import statements for other packages you want to use in your program
- Classes that are extended from parent classes in the WFC packages
- Calls to the specific methods and functions within the imported WFC packages

Figure 16-11 shows a modified version of the MessageBoxApp program from Figure 16-2 that uses WFCs instead of a J/Direct call to call the Win32 API MessageBox function. The program in Figure 16-11 creates the same dialog box as the program in Figure 16-2, but does not require the J/Direct call and directive. Instead, it imports the required com.ms.wfc.core package, which contains the MessageBox class, and uses the show() method of the MessageBox class to display the dialog box.

```
import com.ms.wfc.core.*;
import com.ms.wfc.ui.*;
class MessageBoxApp
{
      public static void main(String args[])
      {
            MessageBox.show("This is a message box",
                  "Message Box Title", MessageBox.OK);
      }
}
```

Figure 16-11: MessageBoxApp calling the Win32 MessageBox function with WFCs

The MessageBox class contains three constructors: the text to be displayed in the MessageBox, the dialog box title, and the dialog box style. The MessageBox.OK field determines the style of the dialog box; it displays a simple dialog box containing an OK button. You can create a MessageBox without the title and style constructors by typing `MessageBox.show("Text String");`. The title bar of a MessageBox created without the title constructor is blank. The style of a MessageBox created without the style constructor defaults to the MessageBox.OK field. The show() method is the only method available in the MessageBox class.

> The MessageBox Fields topic in Visual J++ on-line help lists other style fields that can be used with the MessageBox class.

Next you will modify the Win32Example program so that it uses both a WFC package and J/Direct call.

To modify the Win32Example program so that it uses both a WFC package and a J/Direct call:

1 Return to the Win32Example.java file in the Text Editor window and save the file as **Win32Example2.java**.

2 Replace the Win32Example class name in the `public class Win32Example` header with **Win32Example2**.

3 Replace the default comments above the class header with the following import statements:

```
import com.ms.wfc.core.*;
import com.ms.wfc.ui.*;
import java.awt.*;
```

4 Delete the comments containing the directive and J/Direct MessageBox call located at the bottom of the class file.

5 Replace the statement that reads `MessageBox(0, messageBoxText, messageBoxTitle, 0);` with **`MessageBox.show(messageBoxText, messageBoxTitle, MessageBox.OK);`**.

6 Set the project properties to run the **Win32Example2** file instead of the Win32Example file. Rebuild and save the project, then run the program by selecting **Start** from the **Debug** menu. The WFC package generates the MessageBox. A J/Direct call creates the audible beep that sounds when you click the **OK** button.

Programs created in Visual J++ can include any combination of Java API packages, WFC packages, and J/Direct calls. Remember that whenever you call the Win32 API using WFC packages and J/Direct calls, your application can run only on 32-bit Windows platforms. If you know your application will run only in Windows, using the Win32 API is an appropriate and useful programming technique. However, if you plan to distribute your program widely and intend for it to run on multiple platforms as a true Java application or applet, you should avoid using the Win32 API. In any case, the Win32 API is not a replacement for the core Java programming language—it is only a supplement that allows Java programs to take advantage of Windows operating systems.

Using the Visual J++ Application Wizard

You can create Windows applications by including J/Direct calls, importing a WFC package into a class file, and adding the appropriate classes and methods from the package to your code. Windows applications, however, usually include a form, which is a standard element of most Windows applications. A form contains a title bar, Minimize button, Maximize button, Close button, and control menu. You use forms to display information and receive input from the user. You could manually add a form to a project, then add the appropriate code to manipulate the form, but doing so can be a time-consuming process. In addition, Windows applications with forms require some special code to function properly. An easier way to create a form-based Windows application is to use the Application Wizard. The **Application Wizard** is a tool in Visual J++ that walks you through the process of creating a Windows application project.

> Forms were first discussed in Chapter 1. You will learn more about forms in Section B of this chapter.

When you run the Application Wizard, you are presented with several screens from which you select options for your Windows application project. The first screen you see is the Introduction screen, which allows you to load a profile containing settings from a previous Application Wizard session. Figure 16-12 displays an example of the Introduction screen.

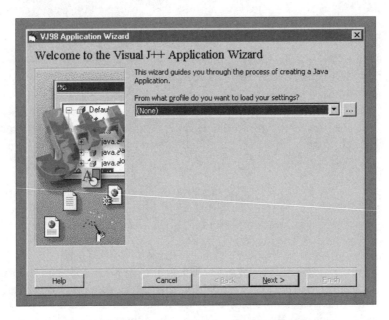

Figure 16-12: Introduction screen of the Application Wizard

The next screen in the Application Wizard is the Application Features screen which contains four elements that can be added to a program: Menu, Edit, Tool Bar, and Status Bar. The Menu option adds a predefined menu to the form. The Edit option fills the form with an editable text box, similar to a page in a word-processing program. The Tool Bar option adds predefined toolbar buttons to the form. The Status Bar option adds a status bar to the bottom of the form. Figure 16-13 displays an example of the Application Features screen.

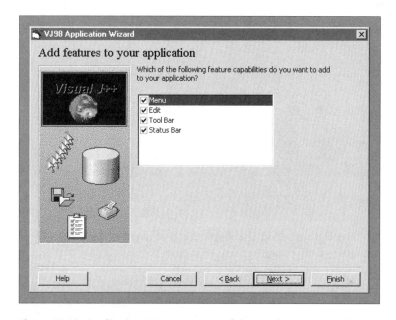

Figure 16-13: Application Features screen of the Application Wizard

If you are using Visual J++ Professional or Enterprise edition, the second screen in the Application Wizard is the Application Type screen. The Application Type screen allows you to choose Form Based Application or Form Based Application with Data. The Form Based Application with Data option creates a Windows-based application that reads data from an external database file.

Following the Application Features screen in the Application Wizard is the Commenting Style screen. The Commenting Style screen determines the types of comments the Application Wizard will generate for your program. The three available options are JavaDoc comments, TODO comments, and Sample Functionality comments. Figure 16-14 displays an example of the Commenting Style screen.

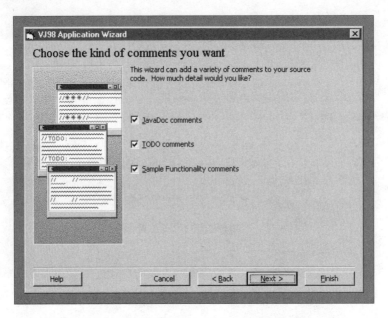

Figure 16-14: Commenting Style screen of the Application Wizard

The last screen in the Application Wizard is the Summary screen, which saves the settings for the current Application Wizard session and allows you to view and save a report of the current settings. Figure 16-15 displays an example of the Summary screen.

Figure 16-15: Summary screen of the Application Wizard

Windows Applications and Packaging

> **tip**
>
> If you are using Visual J++ Professional or Enterprise edition, the Packaging Options screen appears before the Summary screen. The Packaging Options screen allows you to choose the type of package that will be created when you build your application.

Next you will use the Application Wizard to create a Windows application project.

To create a Windows application project using the Application Wizard:

1. Select **New Project** from the **File** menu. The New Project dialog box appears. Click the **Applications** folder on the **New** tab, then click **Application Wizard**. Replace the suggested project name in the Name text box with **WindowsPartyPlanner**, change the location of the project folder to the Chapter.16 folder on your Student Disk if necessary, and then click the **Open** button. The Introduction screen of the Application Wizard displays.

2. Since this is your first time using the Application Wizard, you should not have any stored profiles. Click the **Next** button to continue. The Application Features screen of the Application Wizard displays.

3. Deselect all four options in the Application Features screen: Menu, Edit, Tool Bar, and Status Bar. Click the **Next** button. The Commenting Style screen of the Application Wizard displays.

> **help**
>
> Any of the options in the Application Wizard can be removed or added once you create the project.

4. Deselect all three options in the Commenting Style screen: JavaDoc comments, TODO comments, and Sample Functionality comments. Click the **Next** button. The Summary screen of the Application Wizard displays.

5. Click the **Finish** button to create the project. The Application Wizard builds the new project and opens the WindowsPartyPlanner form. Your form should resemble Figure 16-16.

section A

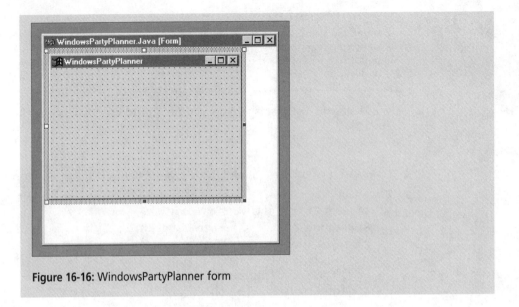

Figure 16-16: WindowsPartyPlanner form

You can quickly create a form-based Windows application by selecting Windows Application from the Applications folder in the New Project dialog box. The skeleton of a form-based Windows application is created containing JavaDoc comments, TODO comments, and Sample Functionality comments.

WFC Forms

You create Java Windows applications using WFC form files. **WFC form files** are very similar to standard Java files: They have an extension of .java, they contain Java code, and you can edit them using the Text Editor window. However, you can also work with a WFC form in the Forms Designer window. You use the **Forms Designer window** to create and edit the visual aspects of a WFC form. Although you are using a graphical interface to create the visual aspects of the application, all of the visual elements in the Forms Designer window, including the form itself, are represented by Java code. For example, the form displayed in the Forms Designer window in Figure 16-17 is actually generated by the code displayed in the Text Editor window in Figure 16-18.

Windows Applications and Packaging

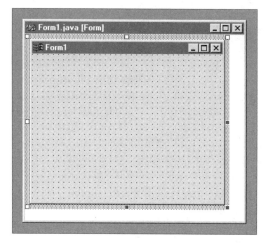

Figure 16-17: WFC form in the Forms Designer window

```
import com.ms.wfc.app.*;
import com.ms.wfc.core.*;
import com.ms.wfc.ui.*;
import com.ms.wfc.html.*;
public class Form1 extends Form
{
    public Form1()
    {
        initForm();
    }
    public void dispose()
    {
        super.dispose();
        components.dispose();
    }

    /**
     * NOTE: The following code is required by the Visual J++
     * designer.  It can be modified using the form editor.
```

Figure 16-18: WFC form in the Text Editor window

To display the code in a WFC application:

1. Activate the Forms Designer window.
2. Select **Code** from the **View** menu. The form's code displays in the Text Editor window.
3. Redisplay the Forms Designer window by selecting **Designer** from the **View** menu.

> **tip**
> You can also view the Code window by pressing F7 and the Designer window by pressing Shift+F7.

As you learned in Chapter 4, the package that is implicitly (or automatically) imported into every standard Java program is named java.lang. The classes it contains are fundamental classes of Java. The package that contains the fundamental classes for WFC applications is com.ms.wfc.core. This class must be explicitly imported into every WFC application. In other words, you must use the `import com.ms.wfc.core;` statement at the beginning of a WFC class file.

> **tip**
> When you create a WFC program using the Application Wizard or the Windows Application option in the New Project dialog box, Visual J++ automatically includes the necessary import statements for WFC packages.

Extending the Form class of the com.ms.wfc.ui package into a subclass creates the form you see in the Forms Designer window. The Form class in WFCs is similar to the Frame class in the AWT. Like the AWT Frame class, the WFC Form class extends the Component class. Specific components in WFCs, such as labels, buttons, and check boxes, are contained in the Control class. Since Forms are usually created to hold other components, the Form class also extends the Control class. Therefore, a Form is a Component as well as a Control.

> **tip**
> You will learn more about the Control class later in this section.

When you extend the Frame class, you inherit several useful methods. Figure 16-19 lists the method header and purpose of several WFC Form class methods.

Method	Purpose
`void add( Control control )`	Adds a control to the form.
`void close()`	Closes the form.
`Control getActiveControl()`	Returns the control that has the focus.
`int getBorderStyle()`	Returns the form's border style in the form of an integer representing a border style constant.
`void setActiveControl( Control value )`	Sets the focus to a specified control.
`void setBorderStyle( int borderStyle )`	Sets the form's border style using an integer representing a border style constant.
`void setVisible( boolean value )`	Sets a form's visible property to `true` or `false`.

Figure 16-19: Useful methods of the WFC Form class

Standard Java console applications are executed using statements in a main() method, whereas Java applets rely on the init(), start(), stop(), destroy(), and paint() methods. WFC applications also use a main() method, but they must be executed using the run() method of the Application class found in the com.ms.wfc.app package. The Application.run() method is placed in the main() method of a WFC class with a single argument containing the keyword new and the name of the WFC class. For example, if you have a WFC class named sampleWFCClass, then you must write the main() method as follows:

```
public static void main(String args[])
{
        Application.run(new sampleWFCClass());
}
```

When a WFC application is started, the Application.run method is executed, which runs any statements in the main class body, then calls the class constructor. The class constructor then calls the initForm() method. The **initForm()** method is used to set the properties of the form and initialize any components it contains. Any additional constructor code is placed after the call to the initForm() method. You cannot use the initForm() method to remove components or to reset properties; you use the method only for setting default values.

When you close a WFC application using the Close button ⊠ in the form's title bar, any statements in the main() method following the initForm() method are executed, then the Application.exit method of the com.ms.wfc.app package is called. You can also quit a WFC application by calling the Application.exit method from anywhere in the code. The Form class contains an automatically created method named dispose() which is called when the Application.exit method is executed to release any of the Form's resources. The dispose() method is similar to the destroy() method that is called in an applet when a user closes the browser or AppletViewer. (You learned about the destroy() method in Chapter 7.)

WFC applications usually override the dispose() method to remove any components (such as buttons or labels) that the Form creates. For example, when you use the Application Wizard or the Windows Application option in the New Project dialog box to create a new WFC program, Visual J++ automatically creates a Container named components in the class body to contain the Form's components. A dispose() method is also added as follows:

```
public void dispose()
{
        super.dispose();
        components.dispose();
}
```

The `super.dispose();` statement is added to call the base dispose() method to clean up the application's system-level resources. The `components.dispose();` statement then disposes of the components Container.

Any statements following the Application.run() method in the main() method are called after the dispose() method.

Figure 16-20 shows the life cycle of a WFC application.

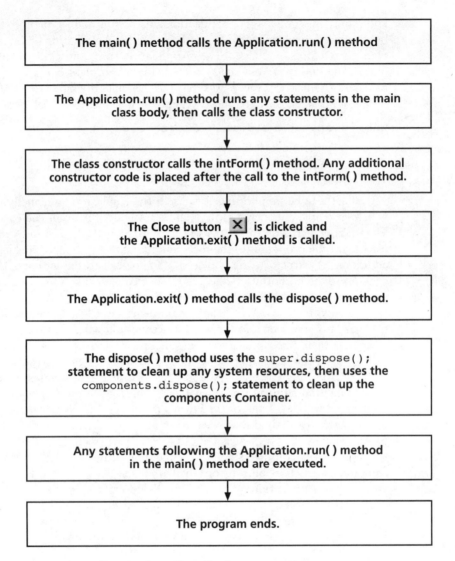

Figure 16-20: Life cycle of a WFC application

Next you will change properties for the WindowsPartyPlanner program and examine the code behind the Forms Designer window.

Windows Applications and Packaging

To change properties for the WindowsPartyPlanner program and examine the code behind the Forms Designer window:

1. Return to the Forms Designer window in the WindowsPartyPlanner program. If necessary, display the Properties window by selecting **Properties Window** from the **View** menu. Locate and click the text box for the text property in the Properties window. The text property for a form represents the text that appears in the form's title bar. Change the present value to **Event Handlers Incorporated**. The new text appears in the form's title bar.

> You first learned about the Properties window in Chapter 1.

2. Locate and click the **backColor** property in the Properties window. The property in the Settings list for the backColor property should be a gray box followed by the word "Control". The Control color property represents a constant in the Color class. (The Color class is a member of the com.ms.wfc.ui package.) Click the drop-down arrow next to the Settings box. The list displays, containing a System tab and a Palette tab. The System tab contains additional constants available in the Color class. Click the **Palette** tab and select a light blue. The background of the form changes to the selected color.

3. Locate the **size** property in the Properties window and click the **Plus** box to expand the property. Beneath the size property are the x and y properties. Change the x property to **350** and the y property to **300**.

> You can also resize a form with your mouse by dragging one of the sizing handles located at the form's corners and sides.

4. Locate and click the **borderStyle** property in the Properties window. Click the drop-down arrow next to the Settings box and select **Fixed Dialog**. The Fixed Dialog border prevents users from resizing the form when the application is running.

5. Locate and click the **startPosition** property in the Properties window. The startPosition property determines where the form is initially placed on your screen. Change the default option of Windows Default Location to **Center Screen**.

6. Build the project as you would any Java program by selecting **Build** from the **Build** menu.

7. Select **Code** from the **View** menu to examine the form's code. The first lines of code in the class are the required WFC import statements. The class header extends the Form class. The first two methods in the class are the class constructor and the dispose() method. Following the dispose() method is a gray box containing code that includes the initForm() method.

The code in the gray box is automatically generated by Visual J++ for the visual aspects of the form. Within the initForm() method, you should recognize several methods including the setText() method, which sets the form's title bar to "Event Handlers Incorporated," and the setBorderStyle() method, which sets the form's border style to Fixed Dialog. The last method in the class is the main() method, which contains a single statement, `Application.run(new WindowsPartyPlanner());`, to start the application.

> If you view the code for a WFC class while its associated Forms Designer window is open, the code that is being controlled by the Forms Designer window is marked in gray. You cannot edit this code while the WFC file's Forms Designer window is open. To edit code that is automatically generated by Visual J++, close the WFC file's associated Forms Designer window. It is easier to allow Visual J++ to handle code generation for the initForm() method.

Next you will execute the WindowsPartyPlanner class.

To execute the WindowsPartyPlanner class:

1. Select **Start** from the **Debug** menu. The form appears in the center of your screen. The title bar should read "Event Handlers Incorporated" and the background color of the form should appear as the color you selected in the preceding steps.

> You execute WFC applications with JVIEW or WJVIEW, just as you would execute standard Java applications. However, since the WindowsPartyPlanner program is a Windows application, running the program does not require a separate command line, as does a console application. Visual J++ automatically selects WJVIEW as the default program in the Properties dialog box for the WindowsPartyPlanner project; you don't need to set the program properties manually.

2. Close the form by clicking the **Close** button ⊠ in the title bar. The Close button automatically calls the Application.exit() method and the program ends.

So far, the WindowsPartyPlanner program consists of only a form with a title bar. Next you will use the Toolbox to add WFC controls to the form.

WFC Controls

You already know from Chapter 11 that Java's creators packaged GUI components in the Abstract Windows Toolkit so you can adapt them for your purposes. You insert the import statement `import java.awt;` at the beginning of your Java program files so you can take advantage of the GUI components and their methods, which are stored in the AWT package. Within the AWT package, components such as buttons, check boxes, and labels descend from the Component class. In WFC programming, components descend from the Control class of the com.ms.wfc.ui package.

You have already used a child class of the Control class—the MessageBox class descends from Control. Every MessageBox "is a" Control.

The WFC Control class descends from the WFC Component class. Like the AWT Component class, the WFC Component class contains several methods that you can use with any of its descendants, such as components that extend the WFC Control class. For example, the getChildOf() method is used to determine whether the current component is the child of a specified component. However, many of the methods contained in the AWT Component class, such as the setSize() and setVisible() methods, are not available in the WFC Component class. Instead, they are located in the WFC Control class.

Components in the AWT package are usually placed in containers. A container is a type of component that holds other components so you can treat a group of several components as a single entity. In the AWT, the Container class descends from the Component class. Child classes of the AWT Container class include the Panel class, Window class, and Frame class. These classes are containers as well as components. In standard Java programming, the Container class is a physical component that contains other programs. For example, in the AWT, the Frame class, which is a Container, contains other components such as Buttons and Labels.

In standard Java packages, the Container and Component classes are part of the java.awt package. The Container and Component classes in WFCs are part of the com.ms.wfc.core package.

In WFC programming, the Control class (which contains many of the same components as the AWT Component class) does not descend from the Container class. Instead, the Control class descends directly from the Component class. Therefore, components in the Control class are not containers as they are in the AWT Component class. The Container class in WFC is used to organize other components logically, rather than physically, as is the Container class in the AWT. For example, a Frame created with the AWT "is a" Container since it can contain other components such as Buttons and Labels. In WFCs, a Form (which is also a Control) is not a container, although components are placed on it. Instead, a new Container is declared in the body of a Form's code to contain the Form's components using the statement `Container components = new Container();`.

When you use the Application Wizard or the Windows Application option in the New Project dialog box, the statement `Container components = new Container();` is automatically created for you and should not be modified.

The Toolbox in the Forms Designer window contains various WFC controls that you can add to your form. Next you will use the Toolbox to add WFC controls to the WindowsPartyPlanner program. In Section B, you will add the code that is necessary to make the WFC controls function.

> **tip**
>
> You first learned about the Toolbox in Chapter 1.

To use the Toolbox to add WFC controls to the WindowsPartyPlanner program:

1 Return to the WindowsPartyPlanner form in the Forms Designer window.

2 If necessary, select **Toolbox** from the **View** menu, and then click the **WFC Controls** button.

3 First you will add a Cocktails CheckBox and a Dinner CheckBox. To add the first CheckBox, click once on the **CheckBox** control in the WFC Controls tab, and then click once on the form in the approximate location where you want to place the check box. (Refer to Figure 16-1 to see where to place each control for the WindowsPartyPlanner.)

> **help**
>
> To learn the function of each control on the WFC Controls tab of the Toolbox, hold your mouse over a control to display its ToolTip.

> **tip**
>
> You can move any control after you have added it to a form by selecting the control, holding down the left mouse button, and dragging the control to the desired location.

4 After you add the CheckBox to the form, click the CheckBox to display its properties in the Properties window. Change the CheckBox's name property to **cocktailBox**, and its Text property to **Cocktails**. The name property is the name of the control, and the text property is the text that is displayed as the control's label or default value.

5 Add to the form a second CheckBox that you will name dinnerBox. Then change the CheckBox's name property to **dinnerBox**, and its text property to **Dinner**.

6 Use the ComboBox control to add a ComboBox to the form directly beneath cocktailBox. Change the ComboBox's name property to **entertainmentChoice** and its text property to **No Entertainment**.

> **tip**
>
> A WFC ComboBox is similar to the AWT Choice component, which you learned about in Chapter 11.

7 You can add more items to the ComboBox using the items property box. The items property box contains the items that will appear in the ComboBox at run time. Click once in the items property box for entertainmentChoice. Notice that the items property default setting is (Strings). Click the **ellipsis (...)** button that appears to the right of the items property default setting (Strings).

The String List Editor dialog box appears. Enter the following additional four items into the dialog box, then select the **OK** button:

```
No Entertainment
Rock Band
Pianist
Clown
```

8 Use the ListBox control to add a ListBox to the form directly beneath the entertainmentChoice control. The selectionMode property of ListBox determines what type of selections users can make: None, One, Multi Simple, or Multi Extended. A selectionMode property of None sets the properties so that users cannot make a selection. A selectionMode property of One lets users select only one choice and allows them to select a different item if they change their mind. Multi Simple allows users to select multiple items. Multi Extended is similar to Multi Simple, but allows users to use their Shift, Ctrl, and arrow keys to make selections. Change the ListBox's name property to **partyFavorList**, and change the selectionMode to **One**.

> **tip**
> A WFC ListBox is similar to the AWT List component, which you learned about in Chapter 11.

9 Use the items property to open the String List Editor dialog box for partyFavorList, enter the following four items into the dialog box, then select the **OK** button:

```
Hats
Streamers
Noise Makers
Balloons
```

10 Beneath the dinnerBox control, use the GroupBox control to add a GroupBox. To add a GroupBox, click once on the **GroupBox** icon in the WFC Controls tab. Then point your mouse at the approximate location where you want the upper-left corner of the GroupBox to appear on the form, click and hold your left mouse button, and drag until the GroupBox reaches the desired size. You can resize a GroupBox after creating it using one of the sizing handles located at its corners and sides. Change the GroupBox's name property to **dinnerGrp** and change its text property to **Entree**.

> **tip**
> A GroupBox is the equivalent of the AWT CheckboxGroup, which you learned about in Chapter 11.

11 Within dinnerGrp, add three RadioButtons named chickenButton, beefButton, and fishButton. Make sure that each RadioButton and its associated text is contained within the boundaries of dinnerGrp. If part of a RadioButton is outside the boundaries of a GroupBox, then it is not considered to be part of the group.

To add each RadioButton, click once on the **RadioButton** control in the WFC Controls tab. Then click once on the form in the approximate location where you want to place the RadioButton.

12. Change the name property of the first RadioButton to **chickenButton** and its text property to **Chicken**. Change the name property of the second RadioButton to **beefButton** and its text property to **Beef**. Change the name property of the third RadioButton to **fishButton** and its text property to **Fish**.

13. Set chickenButton as the default RadioButton in the group by changing its checked property to `true`.

> Only one RadioButton within a Groupbox can have its check property set to `true`. All other RadioButtons must be set to `false`.

14. Below the partyFavor list and the dinnerGrp GroupBox, use the Label control to add a Label to the form. Click once on the Label control in the WFC Controls tab. Then click once on the form in the approximate location where you want to place the Label. Change the Label's name property to **companyLabel** and its text property to **Event Handlers Incorporated**. Use the font property to change the Label's font to MS Sans Serif, its size to 14 points, and its style to bold.

15. Add another Label to the form. Change the Label's name property to **priceLabel** and its text property to **Event price estimate**. Use the font property to change the Label's font to MS Sans Serif, its size to 14 points, and its style to bold.

16. To the right of the priceLabel, add a final Label to the form. Change the Label's name property to **totalPriceLabel** and its text property to **200**. Set the Label's font properties to MS Sans Serif, 14 points, and bold.

17. Add a Button to the bottom of the form. Click once on the **Button** control in the WFC Controls tab. Then click once on the form in the approximate location where you want to place the Button. Change the Button's name property to **buttonExit** and its text property to **Exit**.

18. Build and save the project, then run the program by selecting **Start** from the **Debug** menu. Your program should appear similar to Figure 16-1. You should be able to select all the options on the form. However, you still need to write code to generate the event price.

19. Close the form by clicking the **Close** button in the title bar.

Remember that although Visual J++ automatically generates the code that builds the controls you added, you can write the code manually when the Forms Designer window is closed. The controls you just created require a fairly long segment of code. For example, you created a GroupBox containing three

CheckBoxes, and modified several properties for each control. The code required to create and set properties for the GroupBox and its CheckBoxes is as follows:

```
GroupBox dinnerGrp = new GroupBox();
RadioButton chickenButton = new RadioButton();
RadioButton beefButton = new RadioButton();
RadioButton fishButton = new RadioButton();

dinnerGrp.setLocation(new Point(184, 48));
dinnerGrp.setSize(new Point(136, 112));
dinnerGrp.setTabIndex(0);
dinnerGrp.setTabStop(false);
dinnerGrp.setText("Entree");

chickenButton.setLocation(new Point(16, 16));
chickenButton.setSize(new Point(100, 23));
chickenButton.setTabIndex(0);
chickenButton.setText("Chicken");
chickenButton.setChecked(true);

beefButton.setLocation(new Point(16, 40));
beefButton.setSize(new Point(100, 23));
beefButton.setTabIndex(1);
beefButton.setText("Beef");
beefButton.setChecked(false);

fishButton.setLocation(new Point(16, 64));
fishButton.setSize(new Point(100, 23));
fishButton.setTabIndex(2);
fishButton.setText("Fish");
fishButton.setChecked(false);

dinnerGrp.setNewControls(new Control[] {
      fishButton,
      beefButton,
      chickenButton});
```

You should understand the purpose of each of these statements, even though you can have Visual J++ generate them automatically.

In Section B, you will learn about events in WFC programs and write the code to finish the WindowsEventPlanner application.

SUMMARY

- There are two types of Windows operating systems: 16-bit and 32-bit. The older Windows 3.1 operating system is 16-bit. Current 32-bit Windows operating systems are Windows NT, Windows 95, Windows 98, and Windows CE.
- Visual J++ is a 32-bit application designed for 32-bit Windows operating systems. The term *bit* refers to the width of a microprocessor's data bus.

- An application programming interface (API) is a library of methods and attributes that provide access to the features and functionality of an application or operating system. All 32-bit Windows operating systems share a common API called the Win32 API.
- Using the common functionality available in the Win32 API helps to maintain a consistent look for Windows-based applications.
- J/Direct translates the Win32 API syntax into a format that can be used with Java.
- Methods and other components in the Win32 API are contained in dynamic-link libraries (DLLs). DLLs are files with an extension of .dll.
- A directive tells the compiler in which DLL to find a method. There are three types of directives: @dll.import for declaring functions, @dll.struct for declaring structures, and @dll.structmap for declaring fixed-size strings and arrays embedded in structures.
- If you know the correct syntax for J/Direct calls and directives that you want to include in your Java application, then you can code them directly into a Java file. You can also insert J/Direct calls and directives into your code using the Visual J++ J/Direct Call Builder.
- Adding J/Direct calls removes a Java program's architectural neutrality—the program is no longer a true Java program since it can run only on Windows platforms. However, J/Direct allows you to use your Java programming skills to create Windows applications.
- Although programs you create that use only Java API packages will run on any platform for which there is a Java VM, the Java VM cannot use components that exist within an individual operating system.
- True Java applications will not run as fast as applications that are native to a specific operating system. This difference in speeds is a result of the Java VM. Although the Java VM allows Java applications to be architecturally neutral, it adds an extra translation layer that an application must pass through to run.
- Windows Foundation Classes (WFCs) for Java are packages of J/Direct calls that are translated into the Java programming language.
- The MessageBox class contains three constructors: the text to be displayed in the MessageBox, the dialog box title, and the dialog box style.
- Programs created in Visual J++ can include any combination of Java API packages, WFC packages, and J/Direct calls.
- If your application will run only in Windows, there is no reason not to use the Win32 API. However, if your program will be widely distributed on multiple platforms as a true Java application or applet, then you should avoid using the Win32 API.
- The Application Wizard is a tool in Visual J++ that walks you through the process of creating a Windows application project.
- WFC form files are very similar to standard Java files: They have an extension of .java, contain Java code, and can be edited using the Text Editor window.
- The package that contains the fundamental classes for WFC applications is com.ms.wfc.core. This class must be explicitly imported into every WFC application.
- The Form class in WFCs is similar to the Frame class in the AWT.
- WFC applications use a main() method, similar to Java applications, but must be executed using the run() method of the Application class found in the com.ms.wfc.app package.
- The Application.run() method is placed in the main() method of a WFC class with a single argument containing the keyword **new** and the name of the WFC class.
- The initForm() method is used to set the properties of the form and any components it contains. Any additional constructor code is placed after the call to the initForm() method.

- When you close a WFC application using the Close button ⊠, the Application.exit method of the com.ms.wfc.app package is called.
- You can also quit a WFC application by calling the Application.exit method from anywhere in the code.
- The dispose() method is similar to the destroy() method that is called in an applet when using a Web browser or AppletViewer.
- With WFC programming, components descend from the Control class of the com.ms.wfc.ui package.
- The WFC Control class descends from the WFC Component class. Like the AWT Component class, the WFC Component class contains several methods that you can use with any of its descendants, such as components that extend the WFC Control class.
- Many of the methods contained in the AWT Component class, such as the setSize() and setVisible() methods, are not available in the WFC Component class. Instead, they are located in the WFC Control class.
- In WFC programming, the Control class does not descend from the Container class. Instead, the Control class descends directly from the Component class. Therefore, components in the Control class are not containers as they are in the AWT Component class.
- The Container class in WFC logically organizes other components, whereas the Container class in the AWT physically organizes components.

QUESTIONS

1. The term *bit* refers to _____.
    a. the amount of memory in your computer
    b. the width of a computer microprocessor's data bus
    c. code statements in a WFC application
    d. the size of a computer's hard drive

2. _____ is a 16-bit Windows operating system.
    a. Windows NT
    b. Windows 95
    c. Windows 3.1
    d. Windows 98

3. A library of methods and attributes that provide programmatic access to an application or operating system is called _____.
    a. an application programming interface (API)
    b. a Windows Foundation Class (WFC) program
    c. a dynamic link library (DLL)
    d. the Abstract Windows Toolkit (AWT)

4. You can directly access the Win32 API in Visual J++ by using _____.
    a. standard Java statements
    b. the Sun JDK
    c. J/Direct calls
    d. the java.awt package

section A

5. A simple Win32 API dialog box that displays a message and an OK button is created with _____.
   a. the initform() function
   b. the System.out.print() method
   c. the MessageBox function
   d. the Beep function

6. The declaration that informs Java that a method is implemented in another programming language is called the _____ modifier.
   a. `external`
   b. `final`
   c. `public`
   d. `native`

7. A _____ tells the compiler in which DLL a method will be found.
   a. parameter
   b. // TODO comment
   c. constructor
   d. directive

8. You can type J/Direct calls directly into a file or insert them using _____.
   a. Object Browser
   b. J/Direct Call Builder
   c. the Properties window
   d. the Open dialog box

9. Java programs containing J/Direct calls or that import WFC packages can run _____.
   a. on any platform for which there is a Java VM
   b. on Windows NT but not on Windows 95
   c. on Windows 95 and Windows 98, but not on Windows NT
   d. on any 32-bit Windows platform

10. Windows Foundation Classes (WFCs) are _____.
    a. special Java packages that make Java programs architecturally neutral
    b. part of the java.awt package
    c. packages of standard Java calls that are used in true Java applications
    d. packages of J/Direct calls that are translated into the Java programming language

11. The package that should be imported into every WFC application is _____.
    a. com.ms.wfc.app
    b. com.ms.wfc.core
    c. com.ms.wfc.data
    d. com.ms.wfc.html

12. Programs created in Visual J++ can include _____.
    a. Java API packages, but not WFC packages or J/Direct calls
    b. WFC packages and J/Direct calls, but not Java API packages
    c. only Java API packages
    d. any combination of Java API packages, WFC packages, and J/Direct calls

13. Your program should include calls to the Win32 API when _____.
    a. you are planning on distributing your program on a wide range of platforms
    b. your program will run only on 32-bit Windows platforms

c. your program will never run on 32-bit Windows platforms
d. you want your program to be architecturally neutral

14. The Win32 API is _____.
    a. the most recent version of Java
    b. part of every Java program
    c. a replacement for the Java programming language
    d. intended only as a supplement to the Java programming language

15. The Application Wizard walks you through the process of creating _____.
    a. a console application project
    b. a Windows application project
    c. an Applet
    d. a program's graphical user interface (GUI)

16. You create and edit the visual aspects of a WFC application using the _____.
    a. Object Browser window
    b. Win32 API
    c. Forms Designer window
    d. Class Outline window

17. You create a form in a WFC application by extending the Form class of the _____ package into a subclass.
    a. com.ms.wfc.core
    b. com.ms.wfc.data
    c. com.ms.wfc.app
    d. com.ms.wfc.ui

18. To execute a WFC application, you must include the _____ method in a program's main() method.
    a. Application.run()
    b. Show()
    c. DisplayForm()
    d. MessageBox()

19. A form's properties and components are initialized using the _____.
    a. Form constructor
    b. initForm() method
    c. main() method
    d. Application.run() method

20. A form is closed when _____.
    a. the program receives a close notification from the Win32 API
    b. the last statement in the main() method is executed
    c. the Application.exit() method is called
    d. the Application.close() method is called

21. The _____ method removes any of the components created by a WFC application.
    a. remove()
    b. dispose()
    c. kill()
    d. quit()

22. Specific components in WFCs, such as labels, buttons, and check boxes, are contained in the _____ class.
    a. Form
    b. Control
    c. Component
    d. Container
23. Controls in WFC applications descend from _____.
    a. both the Component class and Container class
    b. the Component class but not the Container class
    c. the Container class but not the Component class
    d. neither the Container class nor the Component class

E X E R C I S E S

Save each of the programs that you create in the exercises in the Chapter.16 folder on your Student Disk.

1. Write a Java Windows application that prompts users to select which invitation they would like displayed: Birthday, Graduation, or Anniversary. Add three Strings to the program for each invitation type. The Birthday invitation should read "Please join us for our son's birthday." The Graduation invitation should read "We are celebrating our daughter's graduation from college." The Anniversary greeting should read "You are cordially invited to attend our 25th wedding anniversary." Add J/Direct calls to the program that call the MessageBox and the Beep functions. Display a MessageBox containing the selected invitation, and then call the Beep function after the user presses the OK button. Name the project SelectAnInvitation.

2. Write a WFC application project that displays a form containing the words to any well-known song. Name the project Song.

3. Create a WFC application project named EmploymentApplication. Include Edit boxes for a name, address, and city. Create a ComboBox that allows users to select a single state. Fill the state ComboBox with the abbreviations of at least five states in your area. Create a ListBox that allows users to select a range containing their years of experience: 0-1, 1-3, 3-5, 5-10, or 10+. Allow the user to select only one entry at a time. Add a GroupBox for the type of employment the user is seeking. Include five RadioButtons in the GroupBox: Management, Clerical, Industrial, Technical, and Construction. At the bottom of the form, add three CheckBoxes: Willing to Relocate, Available for Overtime, and Available for Travel.

4. Windows applications usually contain an About box that displays legal and other information about the program. Use a WFC application to create an About box for the WindowsPartyPlanner application you created in this section. Look in the About boxes for other Windows applications on your computer for ideas of the type of information to include in your About box. You can display the About box for most Windows applications by selecting About from the Help menu. Experiment with fonts and the different controls available in the Toolbox.

5. Review some of the applets and applications you have created in previous chapters. Try to simulate the same designs in a WFC program. Do you find creating visual interfaces easier with the AWT or in WFC programs?

SECTION B
objectives

In this section you will learn:
- About WFC Events
- How to create and use packages
- How to use Visual J++ packaging to distribute programs

WFC Events and Packaging

WFC Events

In standard Java programming, you tell your program to listen for an event by implementing an event interface such as ActionListener. You have worked with event interfaces, such as ActionListener, since Chapter 7, so you know that the ActionListener interface listens for ActionEvents, which are the types of events that occur when a user clicks a Button. To implement ActionListener, you

- Import java.awt.event.*
- Add `implements Action Listener` to the right of the class header
- Add the addActionListener() method to each item, such as a Button, that responds to ActionEvents
- Add an actionPerformed(ActionEvent e) method to the class

When you work with Event objects, such as ActionEvent, you create only a single method to handle *all* instances of a specific event type. Whereas you may have two or more buttons in a class that are registered as ActionListeners, a class can contain only one actionPerformed(ActionEvent e) method.

Instead of accessing internal Java events contained in the java.awt.event package, components in WFC applications access standard Windows events that are available as methods in the Control class. You do not need to import a different package or implement an event interface. A variety of different Windows events are available for different types of controls. Figure 16-21 lists some common Windows events that are automatically available to a Button in a WFC application.

Event	Occurs When
Click	The Button is clicked
Enter	The Button gains focus
Leave	The Button loses focus

Figure 16-21: Common Windows events available to a Button

Event	Occurs When
MouseDown	The Button is clicked and the mouse is not released
MouseUp	The Button is clicked and the mouse is released after being held down

Figure 16-21: Common Windows events available to a Button (continued)

> Unlike the single actionPerformed(Event e) method in standard Java applications, each control in a WFC program can have its own Click method.

You register AWT components to listen for events using the add<event>Listener() method, where <event> represents the specific type of event. For example, the addActionListener() method registers a component to listen for ActionEvents. You register WFC controls for events using the addOn<event>() method. The addOn<event>() method accepts a single parameter known as a delegate. A **delegate** is a wrapper class that is used for passing one method to another method.

> You first encountered wrapper classes in Chapter 6, where you learned that a wrapper is a class or object that is "wrapped" around a simpler thing.

> Delegates are similar in function to pointers found in other programming languages such as C, C++, and Pascal.

WFC delegate classes are comparable to AWT event interfaces. For example, the generic EventHandler delegate handles roughly the same events as the AWT ActionListener interface. Other delegates include the MouseEventHandler delegate, which handles mouse events in the same manner as the AWT MouseListener class, and the KeyEventHandler delegate, which processes keypresses, similar to the AWT KeyListener class.

When you register a component in a WFC application, you essentially "delegate" the responsibility of the event to another method, known as an event handler. An **event handler** is a method created to run in response to a particular event. The following code adds a new EventHandler to a Button named myButton and passes the event to an event handler method called myButton_Click():

```
Button myButton = new Button();
myButton.addOnClick(new EventHandler(this.myButton_Click));
```

An event handler receives two items from a delegate: a reference to the component that initiated the event, and the event object itself. Any method that you intend to use as an event handler must include arguments to access these two items. For example, the following code shows a typical click event handler for a button:

```
private void myButton_click(Object source, Event e)
{
        // Add statements here
}
```

When you work with events in WFC applications, Visual J++ automatically creates an event's delegate and event handler method for you. You can also create a new event handler method from scratch. When Visual J++ automatically creates an event handler method for you, the name of the event handler method is associated with the name of the component for which it was created. For example, the default name of the event handler for myButton is myButton_click. If you intend to use a single, automatically created event handler method with multiple controls, you may want to rename the event handler with a more logical name. When you create a new method from scratch that will be used as an event handler, be sure to include the `Object source, Event e` arguments in the method's header.

Next you will add functionality to the WindowsPartyPlanner application. To do so, you will add events that will calculate the price of the event based on the items that users select. You will also enable the Exit button so that clicking it ends the application.

To add events to the WindowsPartyPlanner application:

1 If necessary, open the WindowsPartyPlanner project from the Chapter.16 folder on your Student Disk, then open the WindowsPartyPlanner.java file in the Forms Designer window.

2 Click the **Exit** button in the Forms Designer window, then click the **Events button** in the Properties window. A list of events that are available for a WFC Button appears. Double-click anywhere on the line for the Click event. Visual J++ switches to code view and automatically generates an event handler skeleton for the Exit button's Click event.

3 Locate the buttonExit_click() method and add `Application.exit();` between the method's curly brackets. This statement allows you to call the internal Application.exit() method.

> You can also create a default event handler skeleton for a control by double-clicking it in the Forms Designer window. The default event depends on the control. For example, a Button control's default event is the Click event, while a GroupBox control's default event is the Enter event.

4 In the Code window, locate the WindowsPartyPlanner class. Immediately following the class's opening curly brackets, add the following variables for the event prices:

```
int cocktailPrice = 300, dinnerPrice = 600;
int beefPrice = 100, fishPrice = 75;
int[] actPrice = {0, 725, 325, 125};
int[] favorPrice = {8,10,25,35};
```

5 Locate the class's main method, and enter the following eventOptionsChanged() method immediately after the main() method. The eventOptionsChanged method will update the event price whenever an option is changed in the form. All of the form controls that can change the event's pricing will call the eventOptionsChanged() method as a delegate.

```
public void eventOptionsChanged(Object source, Event e)
{
        int totalPrice = 200;
        if(cocktailBox.getCheckState() == 1)
                totalPrice += cocktailPrice;
        if(dinnerBox.getCheckState() == 1)
        {
                totalPrice += dinnerPrice;
                if(beefButton.getChecked())
                   totalPrice += beefPrice;
                else if(fishButton.getChecked())
                        totalPrice += fishPrice;
                else
                        chickenButton.setChecked(true);
        }
        int actNum = entertainmentChoice.getSelectedIndex();
        if(actNum != -1)
                totalPrice += actPrice[actNum];
        int[] favorNums = partyFavorList.getSelectedIndices();
        for(int x = 0; x < favorNums.length; ++x)
           totalPrice += favorPrice[favorNums[x]];
        totalPriceLabel.setText(Integer.toString(totalPrice));
}
```

6 Save the project so the eventOptionsChanged() method is available to the controls in the Forms Design window.

> **help**
>
> From working with similar code based on the AWT, you should recognize the methods in the preceding code. However, some of the method names differ slightly from their counterparts in the AWT.

7 Return to the Forms Designer window, click the **Cocktails** CheckBox, then click the drop-down arrow to the right of the Click event's Settings box in the Properties window. A list displays containing the two valid event handler methods: buttonExit_Click and eventOptionsChanged(). Click the **eventOptionsChanged()** method. Visual J++ automatically places the insertion point in the eventOptionsChanged() method in the Code window. Scroll to the gray-screened code that is being generated by Visual J++ until you find the statement that reads `cocktailBox.addOnClick(new EventHandler(this.eventOptionsChanged));`. Notice that the delegate calls the eventOptionsChanged() method. This statement is the only code necessary to call the eventOptionsChanged() method as a Click event for the Cocktails CheckBox.

8 Repeat Step 6 to add a selectedIndexChanged event that calls the eventOptionsChanged() method for the Dinner Checkbox, the PartyFavor ListBox, and each of the three entrée Radio Buttons.

9 Add a selectedIndexChanged event for the Entertainment Choice ComboBox that also calls the eventOptionsChange() method.

10 Rebuild and save the project. If necessary, correct any syntax errors and rebuild again. Execute the program by selecting **Start** from the **Debug** menu, and test each of the components.

Creating and Using Packages

Just as Java's creators have provided you with packages, such as java.util and java.awt, you can create your own packages. When you create your own classes, you can place these classes in packages so that you or other programmers can easily import related classes into new programs.

> Creating packages encourages others to reuse software because packages make it convenient to import many related classes at once.

When you create classes for others to use, most often you do not want to provide users with your .java files, which contain your source code. You expend significant effort in developing workable code for your programs. If you provide your source code to people, other programmers will be able to copy your programs, make minor changes, and market the new product themselves, profiting from your effort. Instead of providing users with your .java files, you provide users with the .class compiled files, which allow users to run the program you have developed. Similarly, when other programmers use classes you have developed, they need only the completed compiled code in the .class files to import into their programs. You place the .class files in a package so other programmers can import them.

To place the compiled code into a package, you include the `package` statement at the beginning of your class file, outside the class definition. The statement `package com.course.animals;` indicates that the compiled file should be placed in a folder named com.course.animals. The statement includes the keyword `package` followed by the path of the folder that should contain the .class file. In this case, the `package` statement indicates that the compiled file will be stored in the animals subfolder inside the course subfolder inside the com subfolder (or com\course\animals). The path name can contain as many levels as you want.

The package statement, import statements, and comments are the only statements that appear outside class definitions in Java program files.

Building a project creates the new package. If the Animal class file in a project named myProject contains the statement `package com.course.animals;`, then the Animal.class file will be placed in the myProject\com\course\animals folder. If any of the subfolders do not exist within the myProject project folder, Visual J++ will create them. You can then move the com folder to the root of a drive. For example, moving the com folder to the root of the C drive creates a directory structure of c:\com\course\animals. If you then package compiled files for Dog.java, Cow.java, and so on, future programs only need to use the statement `import com.course.animals.*` to be able to use all the related classes. Alternatively, you can list each class separately, as in `import com.course.Dog;` and `import com.course.Cow;`. Usually, if you want to use only one or two classes in a package, you use separate import statements for each class. If you want to use many classes in a package, it is easier to import the entire package, even if you do not use some of the classes.

You cannot import more than one package in one statement; for example, `import com.*` **does not work.**

Before you import a custom package into a project, you must use the Project Properties dialog box to specify where Visual J++ should look for the package. You use the Classpath tab in the Project Properties dialog box to specify the location of packages that your project will import. An example of the Classpath tab of the Project Properties dialog box is displayed in Figure 16-22.

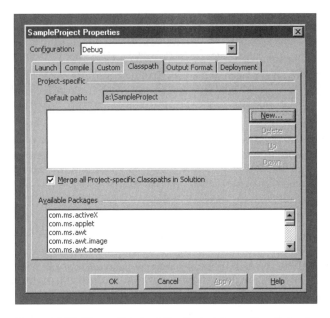

Figure 16-22: Classpath tab of the Project Properties dialog box

The Available Packages list at the bottom of the dialog box displays the default Java packages that are installed on your system. If you scroll through the list, you will recognize several of the packages, including the com.ms.wfc.ui and the java.awt packages. The Default path text box displays the path of the current project folder. Immediately below the Default path text box is a list of project-specific packages that are required by the current project.

Because the Java programming language is used extensively on the Internet, it is important to give every package a unique name. Sun Microsystems, the creator of the Java programming language, has defined a convention for naming packages. Under this convention, you use your Internet domain name in reverse order. For example, if your domain name is course.com, then you begin all of your package names with `com.course`. Then you organize your packages into subfolders in the course directory. Using this convention ensures that your package names will not conflict with those of any other Java code providers.

Using Visual J++ Packaging to Distribute Programs

The most common way to distribute (or *deploy*) a Java applet is to include it on a Web page using the `<APPLET>` tag. For someone to use the program you created, they need only use a Web browser to access the Web page containing your applet. In contrast, you distribute standard Java applications (not WFCs) on floppy disk, CD-ROM, or a network drive. Additionally, when someone wants to use a Java application (as opposed to a Java applet) that you wrote, he or she must also have a copy of JVIEW or WJVIEW. You also distribute WFC applications on floppy

section B

disk, CD-ROM, or a network drive, and people who want to use the application must also have a copy of JVIEW or WJVIEW.

▶ tip

The JVIEW program that comes with your version of Visual J++ is freely distributable to your users. You can download JVIEW from http://www.microsoft.com/java/.

Distributing a Java applet or application consisting of a single class file is fairly simple, especially if the program accesses only internal Java packages. However, distributing programs consisting of multiple classes that import packages other than the internal Java packages can be much trickier. You now know how to create and import Java packages. To make distribution easier, Visual J++ also enables you to compile your project in several types of **output formats,** or packages. The Standard edition of Visual J++ allows you to create Microsoft Cabinet (CAB) files or Windows executable (EXE) files. A **CAB file** is a Microsoft format that contains compressed files and a security feature called digital signature that is used with ActiveX controls and Web browsers. A **Windows EXE file** is a standard file that starts applications on Windows platforms. Whenever you select a program to run using the Windows Start menu, you are usually launching a Windows EXE file. You use the Visual J++ Properties dialog box to select a project's output format.

The Professional and Enterprise editions of Visual J++ also allow you to create COM DLL, Setup, and ZIP package types.

So far, you have used the Properties dialog box to select which file to load when running your program and whether to run the program as a console application. You have also used the Properties dialog box to add new class paths to your project so that you can import custom packages. You can also use the Properties dialog box to select your project's build configuration. A **build configuration** contains the options that the compiler uses when you build your project. There are two types of build configurations: debug and release. A debug build includes full debugging information that allows you to catch release-build errors and check for memory errors, for example. A release build is the version of your application that you will release to users.

Next you will create a release build of the WindowsPartyPlanner project as a Windows EXE package.

> **To create a release build of the WindowsPartyPlanner project as a Windows EXE package:**
>
> **1** If necessary, open the **WindowsPartyPlanner** project from the Chapter.16 folder on your Student Disk.
>
> **2** After opening the project, select **WindowsPartyPlanner Properties** from the **Project** menu. The WindowPartyPlanner Properties dialog box displays.

3. At the very top of the dialog box is the Configuration drop-down list box. It contains three entries: Release, Debug, and All Configurations. Select **Release** from the **Configuration** drop-down list box.

> The All Configurations option allows you to apply properties to both release and debug property sets simultaneously.

4. Click the **Compile** tab, which is used for changing compiler settings. The default option for release configurations removes settings that create debug information and selects the Optimize compiled code check box, which helps Java applications run faster. Click the Output Directory text box and type **A:\Chapter.16\OutputDirectory,** where A: is the drive containing your Student Disk. The Output Directory is where Visual J++ places the necessary files to run an application.

5. Click the **Output Format** tab. Make sure the **Enable Packaging** check box is selected, then select **Windows EXE** from the **Packaging type** drop-down list box. In the File name text box, change the drive, directory, and filename to A:\Chapter.16\OutputDirectory\WindowsPartyPlanner.exe.

6. Select the **Advanced** button. The Advanced...Properties dialog box displays. The EXE/DLL Options tab in the Advanced...Properties dialog box is used for setting version information which can be viewed in Windows by users of your application. An example of the EXE/DLL Options tab is displayed in Figure 16-23.

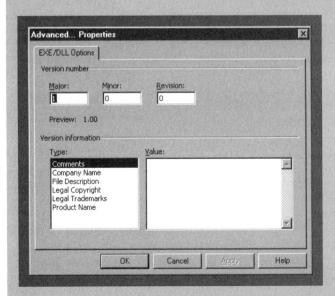

Figure 16-23: EXE/DLL Options tab

help
> The Advanced...Properties dialog box is shared by the COM DLL output format, which is a package type that is available only in the Professional and Enterprise editions of Visual J++.

7 Select the **Major** text box, and change the version number to **2**. You set the version number to 2 instead of 1 since your program is actually the second version of the PartyPlanner application—you created the first version in Chapter 10.

8 Select **Comments** in the **Type** list, then select the **Value** box and type **This is my first Windows application!**

9 Select **Company Name** in the **Type** list, then select the **Value** box and type **Event Handlers Incorporated**.

10 Select **Product Name** in the **Type** list, then select the **Value** box and type **Windows Party Planner**.

11 Click the **OK** button to close the Advanced...Properties dialog box.

12 You use the Package Contents section of the Output Format to select the files that will be packaged with your application. The default option includes class files and other types of files your application may require, such as graphics and sound files. The drop-down list box contains several other combinations of file types you can select. Instead of using default file types, select the **These outputs** button, which allows you to select the individual files you want to include with your program. The two files listed are WindowsPartyPlanner.Java and WindowsPartyPlanner.class. Since you do not want to give users access to your source code, deselect **WindowsPartyPlanner.java**, then click the **OK** button to close the WindowsPartyPlanner Properties dialog box.

13 On the **Build** menu, point to **Build Configuration** and click **Release**. This command instructs Visual J++ to create a release version of the application the next time you build the project.

14 Build the project. When the project is finished building, open Windows Explorer and click the OutputDirectory folder in the Chapter.16 folder on your Student Disk. You should see two files: WindowsPartyPlanner.exe and WindowsPartyPlanner.class. Right click once on the **WindowsParty Planner.exe** file and select **Properties** from the shortcut menu. The WindowsPartyPlanner.exe Properties dialog box displays. Click the **Version** tab, and then click each of the entries in the **Item name** list. You should see the information from Steps 7, 8, 9, and 10 that you entered. Some of the entries are created automatically, such as the Language item. Click **OK** to close the WindowsPartyPlanner.exe Properties dialog box.

15 Execute the WindowsPartyPlanner.exe file by double-clicking **Windows PartyPlanner.exe**. The Windows Party Planner should run the same as when you ran it from within Visual J++.

S U M M A R Y

- Components in WFC applications can access standard Windows events that are available as methods in the Control class.
- Unlike the single actionPerformed(Event e) method in standard Java applications, each control in a WFC program can have its own Click method.
- A delegate is a wrapper class that is used for passing one method to another method.
- WFC delegate classes are comparable to AWT event interfaces.
- When you register a component in a WFC application, you "delegate" the responsibility for the event to an event handler method.
- An event handler is a method created to run in response to a particular event. An event handler receives two arguments from a delegate: a reference to the component that initiated the event, and the event object itself.
- In WFC applications, Visual J++ automatically creates an event's delegate and event handler method for you.
- When you create a number of classes that inherit from each other, you can place these classes in a package.
- When you create classes for others to use, you most often do not want to provide users with your source code in .java files. Rather, you provide users with compiled .class files.
- You place .class files in a package so other programmers can import them.
- To place compiled code in a specific folder, you include the **package** statement at the beginning of your .class file.
- Package statements, import statements, and comments are the only statements that appear outside class definitions in Java program files.
- Because the Java programming language is used extensively on the Internet, it is important to give every package a unique name. The convention for naming packages involves using your Internet domain name in reverse order.
- The JVIEW program that comes with Visual J++ is freely distributable to users of your programs.
- Visual J++ enables you to compile your project in several types of packages, or output formats, to make distribution easier. A CAB file is a Microsoft format that contains compressed files. A Windows EXE file is a standard file that starts applications on Windows platforms.
- Visual J++ has two types of build configurations: debug and release. A debug build includes information that assists in the debugging process. A release build is the version that is distributed to your program's users and does not contain debugging information.

Q U E S T I O N S

1. WFC controls are registered for events using the _____ method.
   a. registerEvent()
   b. add<event>Listener()
   c. addOn<event>()
   d. <event>Register()

2. A wrapper class that is used for passing one method to another method is called a _____.
   a. parameter
   b. constructor
   c. function
   d. delegate
3. Which is the correct syntax to add a delegate to a component named myButton?
   a. `myButton.addOnClick(new EventHandler());`
   b. `myButton.addOnClick(new EventHandler(Click));`
   c. `myButton.addOnClick(new EventHandler(this.myButton_Click));`
   d. `myButton. (new EventHandler(this.myButton_Click));`
4. The WFC delegate that is most similar to the AWT ActionListener interface is _____.
   a. EventHandler
   b. MouseEventHandler
   c. KeyEventHandler
   d. KeyListener
5. A(n) _____ is a method created to run in response to a particular event.
   a. event controller
   b. response function
   c. control routine
   d. event handler
6. An event handler receives two arguments from a delegate: a reference to the component that initiated the event, and the _____.
   a. type of Windows platform
   b. Java version number
   c. event object itself
   d. name of the application
7. Which is the correct syntax for the header of a click event handler for a component named myButton?
   a. `private void myButton_click(Event e)`
   b. `private void myButton_click(Object source)`
   c. `private void myButton_click(Object source, Event e)`
   d. `private void myButton_click()`
8. You place class groups in _____ so you or other programmers can easily import them into new programs.
   a. abstract classes
   b. interfaces
   c. packages
   d. bundles
9. The files you usually place in packages are files with the extension _____.
   a. .doc
   b. .class
   c. .java
   d. .javac

10. You include a(n) _____ statement at the beginning of a class file to place the compiled class code into the indicated folder.
    a. build
    b. bundle
    c. export
    d. package

11. The location of custom packages that are imported into a Java file must be specified in the _____ tab of the Project Properties dialog box.
    a. Classpath
    b. Launch
    c. Compiler
    d. Custom Build Rules

12. If your Internet domain name is mycompany.com, then your package names should begin with _____.
    a. mycompanycom
    b. commycompany
    c. com.mycompany
    d. mycompany.com

13. The Standard edition of Visual J++ can package files as Windows EXE and _____ package types.
    a. Setup
    b. COM DLL
    c. ZIP
    d. CAB

14. Visual J++ projects have two types of build configurations: debug and _____.
    a. final
    b. release
    c. completion
    d. non-debug

EXERCISES

Save each of the programs that you create in the exercises in the Chapter.16 folder on your Student Disk.

1. Create a WFC program named ButtonEvents and add a button to the program's form. Add an event handler for at least three of the button's events. Use a MessageBox to display the name of the event each time it is executed.

2. Create a WFC program named SharedEvents. Add three buttons to the program: Button1, Button2, and Button3. Also add a label. Add to each button a delegate that calls a single event handler method. Each time you click a button, display the button's name in the label.

3. a. Create a WFC program that calculates the weekly salary for an individual based on a regular hourly rate. Allow the user to input the hourly rate and then pay the user for a 40-hour week. Use two forms. Each form should have a text box. Use one form for input and one for output showing the total salary for the week. On the input form, include a button that displays the output form, and on the output form, include a button that displays the input form.

   b. Write a WFC program that calculates the weekly salary for an individual based on a regular hourly rate, plus a premium percent for overtime. Allow the user to input the hourly rate, the overtime premium percent, the regular hours worked, and the overtime hours worked.

4. Write a WFC program that calculates the new balance of a checking account based on the current balance, a check, or a deposit. Allow the user to enter the current balance, a check amount, and a deposit amount.

5. Create a Java class file named stringPackage and declare a String named packageString. Assign the text "You have imported a package!" to packageString. Write a public method named getPackageString that returns packageString. Export the class to a package named com.stringPackage. Create a WFC application that imports the stringPackage. Add to the WFC program's main form a button that calls the getPackageString method in the stringPackage class.

Index

16-bit Windows operating system, 756
32-bit Windows operating system, 756

A

aBackspaceChar variable, 94
ABaseClass.java file, 465
abstract classes, 404, 487–497, 528, 681–682
   abstract methods, 489
   empty methods, 488
   example, 486
   instantiating concrete objects, 516
   instantiating objects, 488
   interfaces, 516
   nonabstract methods, 516
abstract keyword, 488, 492
abstract methods, 488
   abstract classes, 489
   overriding, 490
access modifiers, 59–60, 106, 183
AccessRandomly class, 703–704
AccessRandomly.java file, 704
accumulating, 251–253
AChildClass class, 470
action keys, 602
ActionEvent class, 597, 599, 601
ActionEvents class, 360, 598

ActionListener class, 534
ActionListener interface, 360, 434, 436, 517, 541, 599–601, 608, 787
actionPerformed() method, 360, 362–363, 376–377, 379, 382–383, 386, 397, 404, 405–406, 438, 542, 589, 600, 606, 609, 694–696, 700, 787
actions and event types, 599
actual parameters, 116
adapter classes, 533–536, 600
Add Class command, 111, 131, 143, 146, 172, 185, 220, 349, 452–453, 492, 496, 531, 533, 543, 580, 643
Add Item command, 37–38, 275, 677–678, 704
Add Item dialog box, 36–37, 111, 131, 143, 146, 172, 185, 220, 347, 349, 452–453, 492, 496, 531, 533, 543, 580, 677
Add Member Variable dialog box, 141
add() method, 348, 384, 559–560, 564, 580, 772
Add Method command, 132, 142–143
Add Method dialog box, 132–134
Add Project dialog box, 39
Add Web Page command, 347

addActionListener() method, 360, 532, 588, 600, 787–788
addComponentListener() method, 605
addFocusListener() method, 605
addItemListener() method, 600
addition (+) operator, 88
addMouseListener() method, 605
addMouseMotionListener() method, 605
addOnevent() method, 788
addPoint() method, 423
addTextListener() method, 360
AdjustmentEvent event, 601
AdjustmentListener interface, 601
Adobe PageMill, 342
advanced layout managers, 591
Advanced...Properties dialog box, 795–796
Alive() method, 718
alternative if, 215
aName string, 300
AND (&&) operator, 229–234
anEvent Event object, 221
anEvent object, 445
Animal array, 499
Animal class, 488–490, 507
   reserving memory for objects, 499
AnimalArray class, 500
AnimalReference class, 498

Index

animated figure, 732–738
    arm positions, 733–734
AnimatedFigure applet, 735–737
    adding text, 737–738
AnimatedFigure2 applet, 737–738
    reducing flickering, 740–741
AnimatedFigure2.java file, 737
AnimatedFigure3 class, 740–741
AnimatedFigure3.java file, 742
AnimatedFigure4 class, 742
animation, 434–438, 712
    animated figure, 732–738
    images, 742–745
    pausing cells, 732
    reducing flickering, 738–742
    Web pages, 746–749
anotherEmpMethod() method, 160
anotherName string, 300
anotherNumber variable, 157
aNumber variable, 157
AParentClass class, 470
API (application programming interface), 757
append() method, 328–329
AppleDemoComponents.java file, 541
Applet class, 348–349, 373, 450, 513, 527
<APPLET> tag, 340–341, 377, 397, 399
</APPLET> tag, 397, 399
AppletDemoComponents project, 541, 552
    running, 543–544
AppletDemoComponents.java file, 552
applets, 337, 340
    accepting event messages, 360
    adding button and label, 396–397
    automatically creating, 351
    avoiding exceeding viewing area, 406
    background color, 404
    BorderLayout class, 580–581
    Buttons, 356–359
    components, 348
    compromising security, 352
    containing list, 565–567
    dimensions, 397
    displaying, 395
    displaying code, 347
    displaying frame, 541–543
    distributing, 793–796
    drawing string in window, 398–400
    from empty file, 351
    expecting events, 360
    frames, 540
    height and width, 347
    hiding/viewing components, 387
    inheritance from Applet class, 348–349
    initialization tasks, 349
    labels, 348–354
    layout managers, 578
    life cycle, 373–379
    loading predrawn animated image into, 743–744
    main() method, 59
    methods, 349, 772–773
    moving, 347
    name, 397
    output, 363–365
    as panels, 587
    placing components at specific location, 384–387
    placing string within, 399–400
    regions, 578–579
    resizing, 347
    responding to events, 360–362
    sizing button, 540
    as subclass, 450
    TextFields, 356–359
    title bar, 540
    with two checkboxes, 553–555
    updating, 353
    writing, 348–354
    x- and y-coordinate, 384
AppletViewer, 336–337, 353–354, 395, 540
    minimizing and restoring window, 397
Application class, 773
Application Wizard, 766–770
Application.exit() method, 789
applications, 111, 337
    native *versus* architecturally neutral, 761–763
Applications folder command, 15
architecturally neutral applications, 7, 761–763
arcs, 419–420
arguments, 54–55, 112
    listing separately, 116
    order, 116
    passing, 55

Index

sending to constructors, 168–172
arithmetic
    operators, 87–88
    statements, 87–89
    unlike operands, 93
ArithmeticException class, 626–630, 649
ArrayIndexOutOfBounds Exception exception, 633, 666
arrays, 268–269
    Choice objects, 560
    comparing string to block element, 301–302
    declaring, 269–272
    element, 270
    Employee objects, 499
    Event object, 275–276
    initializing, 272–273
    length field, 290–291
    literal constants, 281
    for loop, 273–274
    methods, 275
    more common items, 279
    multidimensional, 327
    naming, 272
    number of elements in, 290–291
    of objects, 274–278
    one-dimensional, 324
    parallel, 279, 284, 734
    passing by reference, 286
    passing to methods, 284–289
    reserving memory locations, 270
    searching for exact match, 278–283
    searching for range match, 283–284
    single-dimensional, 324
    sorting objects, 319–322
    sorting primitive elements, 313–314
    square brackets, 270
    storing strings, 322–323
    strings, 297
    subclass objects, 499–502
    subscripts, 270, 273–274
    symbolic constants, 281
    two-dimensional, 324–327
    variable names, 281
    variables, 269–270
ascent, 427
assemblers, 4
assignment operator (=), 83
asterisk (*) wildcard symbol, 191
ASubClass.java file, 465
attributes, 5–6, 340, 346
Autos window, 660, 664
aValue variable, 159
aWorker.getEmpNum() method, 180
AWT (Abstract Windows Toolkit), 348, 526
AWT package, 776–771
AWTEvent class, 597–599
    methods, 604–607

B

<B> tag, 338
b variable, 403
BackColor property, 33, 775
background color, 408
    applets, 404
backslash (\) escape sequence, 69, 95
Backspace (\b) escape sequence, 95
Bank Balance program, 256–257
bankBal variable, 257
BankLoan class, 117
base, 16, 95
base class, 450
batch processing, 703
bigFont object, 355, 401
billPatients() method, 452
binary operators, 251
block comments, 69
block scope, 160–162
blocks, 156–163
<BODY> tag, 346
boolean data type, 90–91
boolean expressions, 214, 237–238
boolean primitive type, 82
boolean variables, 90–91
BorderLayout class, 578–583
borderStyle property, 32, 775
BouncingParty project, 746
BouncingParty1 applet, 746–748
BouncingParty1 class, 746–748
BouncingParty2, 748
BouncingParty2.java file, 748
BoxAround project, 432

 tag, 339
braces() method, 452
break; statement, 280
break keyword, 234–235
Break mode, 655
breakpoints, 657–659
briefMenu variable, 664
bubble sort, 314–315

Index

bubbleSort() method, 316–317, 319–321
BufferedInputStream class, 682
buffers, 682
bugs, 653
Build command, 72, 85, 104
    Ctrl+Shift+B key combination, 72
build configuration, 794
Build Configuration command, 796
Button class, 550–551
Button control, 780
buttonExit_click() method, 789
ButtonFrame constructor, 608
ButtonFrame project, 608
ButtonFrame.java file, 608
buttons, 356–359
    Windows events, 787–788
byte data type, 84
byte primitive type, 82
bytecode, 7

C

CAB (Cabinet) files, 794
calculateAge() method, 118–119
calculatePay() method, 499
calculateRaise() method, 117
call stack, 666
canRead() method, 676
canWrite() method, 676
CardGame class, 516
CardLayout class, 591
Carriage return (\r) escape sequence, 95
Cascade command, 17
case keyword, 234–235
case structure example, 235
case-sensitivity, 67
casting, 499
catch blocks, 625–627, 646, 684, 700
    multiple exceptions, 629–632
    uniquely handling exceptions, 647–649
    unreachable, 632
catch keyword, 625
CD-ROM drives, 680
chaining stream objects, 691
changeSalary() method, 136
Chap3Events Properties command, 104
Chap3EventSite.java file, 104
Chap3Events.vjp project, 104
Chap3SetupSite.java file, 104
Chap5ChooseManager.java file, 204
Chap5Event project, 204
Chap6Events program, 268
Chap8StopLight applet, 394
Chap9WeekendEvent class, 446
Chap9WeekendEvent project, 444
Chap10EntertainmentSelector class, 486
Chap11PartyPlanner class, 524–525
Chap12Applet project, 576–577
Chap12Applet.java file, 577
Chap12Panel.java file, 577
Chap14ReadFile class, 674
Chap15Animation class, 712
char data type, 94–96
char primitive type, 82
character strings, 94
characters, 94–96, 680
    deleting, 682
charAt() method, 303
check boxes, 552–555
Checkbox class, 550, 552–555
    assigning to CheckboxGroup class, 556
    methods, 552
CheckBox control, 778
checkboxes, grouping, 556–559
CheckboxGroup class, 556–559, 779
    methods, 556–557
CheckFile class, 676–677
CheckFile project, 676
CheckFile2 program, 678
CheckFile.java file, 676
CheckTwoFiles.java file, 678
child classes, 450–451, 487
    methods overriding parent class methods, 459
Choice class, 550, 559–563
Choice component, 778
Choice objects, 559–563
    arrays, 560
    methods, 559–560
ChooseManager program, 217, 250
    improving, 233–234, 250–251
    modifying, 221
    previewing with Event class, 204
    switch structure decision making, 236–237
ChooseManager Properties command, 217
ChooseManager.java file, 217, 233, 250

Index

class client, 125
.class files, 72, 337, 341, 791
class keyword, 59
class members, 126–127
class methods, 180, 478
    Math class, 187
    navigating to, 127
    this reference, 181
class objects, 125
Class Outline
    adding instance method to EventSite class, 132
    adding setSiteNumber() method to EventSite class, 133
    class members, 127
    classes, 127
    commands, 128
    Ctrl+Alt+T key combination, 126
    displaying, 126
    EventSite class node, 132
    icons, 128
    inserting variables and methods in alphabetical order, 141
    javadoc comments, 69, 127
    Javadoc pane, 126
    manually adding code, 128
    member variables, 140–141
    Method icon, 127
    methods, 140–141
    navigating to classes or class members, 126
    packages, 127
    Private Access icon, 127
    SetUpSite class object, 127
    updates to, 126
class user, 125

class variables, 181–183
Class1 class, 66
Class1.java file, 65
class-dot-object-dot-method format, 55
classes, 5, 56, 124–125
    abstract, 404, 486–497, 528
    access modifiers, 129
    base, 450
    basic, 187
    blocks, 156–163
    calling another class method, 109
    child, 450–451, 487
    Class Outline, 127
    concrete, 487
    constructors, 467
    creation of, 129–131
    data, 129
    derived, 450
    extended access, 129
    extending, 450–456
    fields, 130, 133, 137–138
    filenames and, 67
    final, 478, 488
    friendly access, 129
    getSource() method, 608–610
    growing large, 180
    header, 129
    implementing KeyListener interface, 602–604
    import statement, 190–191
    information hiding, 471–475
    inheritance, 124, 447–450
    instance methods, 180
    instance variables, 125, 130

instances, 5, 124, 135
is-a relationships, 124
manually listing members, 62
member variables, 125
members, 61
methods, 129–130, 180–181
naming, 56–58, 129
nonabstract, 487
versus objects, 124
optional, 187
organizing, 137
overriding variables, 159–160
parent, 450–451
preventing instantiation, 188
prewritten, 186
protected members, 473
public, 129
related groups navigating to, 126
same method in different, 109
static methods, 180
unique identifier, 138
variables, 181–182
virtual, 488
wrappers, 307
Clear All Breakpoints command, 659
clear rectangles, 408
clearRect() method, 408
Click event, 787, 789
Close All command, 42
Close button, 20
close() method, 703, 772
closeFile() method, 700–701

Index

closing
    data files, 681
    frames, 530–533
code, reusable, 448–449
Code command, 771
Code window (F7) function key, 772
color
    background, 404, 408
    computer display of, 402
    DemoGraphic1 class, 401
    displaying several hundred, 402–404
    graphics, 400–401
    lines, 407
Color class, 775
    color names, 401
Color objects, user-created, 402
COM (Component Object Model), 195
COM DLL files, 794
combining debug windows, 663
ComboBox control, 778
com.course.animals folder, 792
coming into scope, 157
commands, 20–21
comment tokens, 68
commenting out statements, 68
comments, 68–69, 140
    Windows programs, 767
commissions, 231, 233
com.ms.wfc.app package, 763, 773
com.ms.wfc.core package, 763–764, 772
com.ms.wfc.data package, 764
com.ms.wfc.html package, 764
com.ms.wfc.io package, 764

com.ms.wfc.ui package, 764, 775, 777, 793
com.ms.wfc.util package, 764
compact disc drives, 680
companyName String, 399
compareTo() method, 301, 322
comparing
    files, 678
    objects for equality, 508–512
    strings, 299–303
comparison operators, 90
compiler errors, 27–28, 652
compilers, 4
compiling programs, 72
Complete Word command, 62
Component add() method, 540
Component class, 526, 528, 550, 772, 777
ComponentEvent class, 597–598, 601, 604–605
ComponentListener interface, 601
components, 348, 526–527, 776–777
    aligned to grid, 585–586
    aligning, 578, 584–585
    automatically centering in container, 584
    changing, 598
    check boxes, 552–555
    as child of component, 777
    determining size, 579
    horizontal placement, 583–585
    methods, 550–552, 605
    precise location within grid, 591
    setting size, 527
    stacking, 591

    as subclasses, 528
compound statements, 217–221
computePrice() method, 446
concrete classes, 487
conditional operator, 237
conditions, 229–230
console applications, 337
    methods, 772
console window, 70
constant variable, 183
constants, 82–83, 183–186, 401
    initializing with value, 184
    prewritten, 187
    type casting, 93–94
constructor methods, 135, 145–147
constructors, 145–147, 489
    adding to Event class, 466–467
    altering, 170–172
    Buttons, 358
    Date class, 191
    naming, 145
    overloading, 172–174
    requiring arguments, 467–470
    sending arguments to, 168–172
    StringBuffer class, 328
    superclasses, 464–467
    tasks, 465
    TextField objects, 356–357
Container class, 527, 777
Container object, 528
    BorderLayout class and only four objects, 582
    ContainerEvent event, 601
    ContainerListener interface, 601

Index

containers, 527, 550, 777
    methods, 539–544
    resizing, 579
Contents command, 35
context-sensitive help, 36–34
Continue command, 655, 657–658, 664
ContractEmployee class, 457
Control class, 772, 777
Control color property, 775
control menu, 20
controls, 26
copyArea() method, 423
copying graphics area, 423–425
countDisplay() method, 377
counted loops, 254
counting, 251
Cow class, 488, 491
CreateEventFile class, 696
    constructor, 693–694
CreateEventFile program, 692
    adding actionPerformed() method, 695–696
    window methods, 696–697
CreateEventFile.java file, 692
curly brackets ({}), 68
custom Graphics objects, 404–406
Customize command, 22
Customize Toolbox command, 27
customizing
    toolbars, 22
    Toolbox, 343

D

data
    arithmetic statements, 87–89
    boolean data type, 90–91
    char data type, 94–96
    characters, 680
    constants, 82–83
    fields, 680
    floating-point data types, 91–92
    numeric type conversion, 93–94
    primitive types, 82
    records, 680
    saving, 679–680
    variables, 82–83
    writing formatted, 691–698
data files, 675, 679–681
data types, 84
data2.txt file comparing to data.txt file, 678–679
datafile.txt file, 686
DataInput interface, 698
DataInputStream class, 691
DataOutput interface, 691
DataOutputStream class, 691
data.txt file, 675, 677
    comparing data2.txt file to, 678–679
Date class, 190–194
Date object, 191
dates, 165, 191–193
deadlock, 722
deal() method, 516
debug build, 794
Debug toolbar, 656
debug windows, 659–665
Debug Windows command, 663–664
debugging, 507, 652–654
    Autos window, 660
    combining debug windows, 663
    customizing features, 654
    ending session, 655
    error or exception messages, 660
    exception handling, 657
    Immediate window, 662
    Locals window, 661
    Step commands, 655–657
    tracing exceptions through call stack, 665–667
    tracing program execution, 654–659
    tracing variables and expressions, 659–665
    tracing variables example, 663–665
    Watch window, 661–662
declaring objects, 134–136
deepClean() method, 452
Default Debug layout, 19
Default Design layout, 19
Default Full Screen layout, 19
default keyword, 234–235, 251
default window layouts, 19
Define Window Layout dialog box, 19–20
definite loops, 254
delegates, 788–789
deleting
    characters, 682
    Window layouts, 20
DemoArray program, 271–274
DemoArray.java file, 271
DemoBlock class, 161–162
DemoBlock project, 161–162
DemoBlock Properties command, 162
DemoBlock.java file, 161
DemoBorder project, 580
DemoBorder.java file, 580

Index

DemoBorderNoNorth applet, 582–583
DemoBorderNoNorth class, 582
DemoBorderNoNorth.java file, 582
DemoCheckBox applet, 553–555
DemoCheckBoxGroup applet, 557–559
DemoCheckBoxGroup.java file, 557
DemoCheckBox.java file, 553, 557
DemoChoice applet, 560
  open Choice, 560–563
DemoChoice.java file, 560
DemoClassVar program, 185–186
DemoClosingFrame project, 531
DemoClosingFrame2 class, 536
DemoClosingFrame2 project, 535
DemoClosingFrame.java file, 533
DemoColor project, 402
DemoColor.java file, 402
DemoConstruct.java file, 172
DemoConstructors program, 464–465
DemoCreateGraphicsObject applet, 406
DemoCreateGraphicsObject class, 405
DemoCreateGraphicsObject program, 405, 411–412
DemoCreateGraphicsObject.java file, 411
DemoDate program, 192–194

DemoDate Properties command, 194
DemoDate.java file, 193
DemoEntertainment program, 496–497
DemoFlow applet, 583–584
DemoFlow class, 583
DemoFlow.java file, 583
DemoFlowRight applet, 584–585
DemoFlowRight class, 584
DemoFlowRight.java file, 584
DemoFontMetrics project, 428
DemoFrame class, 528
DemoFrame project, 528
DemoFrame.java file, 528
DemoFrameWithFixedSize class, 538
DemoFrameWithFixedSize project, 537
DemoFrameWithFixedSize.java file, 538
DemoGraphics1 class, 401–402
DemoGraphics1 project, 399
DemoGraphics1.java file, 399, 401
DemoGrid applet, 585–586
DemoGrid class, 585
DemoGrid.java file, 585
DemoHelloGoodbyeThreads class, 716
DemoHelloGoodbyeThreads program, 716–717
DemoHelloThread class, 715
DemoIncrement project, 252–253
DemoIncrement Properties command, 252
DemoIncrement.java files, 252
DemoInput class, 206

DemoInput program, 205–207
DemoList applet, 565–567
DemoList2 applet, 568–569
DemoList2 class, 568
DemoList.java file, 565
DemoMath project, 189–190
DemoMath Properties command, 189
DemoMath.java file, 189
demoMethod() method, 162
DemoOverload project, 165–166
DemoOverload Properties command, 166
DemoOverload.java file, 165
DemoPaint project, 396
DemoRectangles program, 408
DemoRegion applet, 588–591
DemoRegion.java file, 589
DemoSleepThread project, 720
DemoStringBuffer program, 329
DemoStringBuffer.java file, 329
DemoSuper program, 470–471
DemoThreads class, 719–720
DemoThreads project, 718
DemoThreads.java file, 719
DemoThreadsPriority class, 722–723
DemoThreadsPriority.java file, 722
DemoVariables class, 85
DemoVariables program, 85–86
  arithmetic statements, 88–89
  boolean variables, 91
  combining method arguments, 87
  escape sequence, 96
  floating-point variables, 92

Index

DemoVariables Properties command, 85
DemoWorkingDog program, 515
Dentist class, 451
deprecation error, 194
deptName array, 297
derived class, 450
descent, 427
deselect() method, 564
Design toolbar, 343
Design view, 342
Designer window (Shift+F7) key combination, 772
designers, 25–26
destroy() method, 349, 373–374, 376–377, 379, 395, 726, 772–773
development environments, 8
dialog boxes, 21
Dialog class, 527–528
DinnerEvent class, 454–455, 457
    adding constructor, 468–469
DinnerEvents class, 474
DinnerEventWithConstructorArg.java file, 468
DinnerEventWithConstructor.java file, 466, 468
DinnerEventWithHeader class, 458–459
DinnerEventWithHeader.java file, 458, 466, 474
DinnerEventWithProtectedData.java file, 474
direct access files, 703
directive, 758
Disable Breakpoint command, 659

disabling breakpoints, 659
disk files, reading and writing, 682
DismissedEmployee class, 449
display() method, 375–378
displayMenu() method, 643
displayMetrics() method, 429–430
displayRules() method, 516
dispose() method, 773, 775
distributing programs, 793–796
dividing by zero, 623
division (/) operator, 88
@dll.import directive, 758–759
@dll.struct directive, 758–759
@dll.structmap directive, 758–759
do keyword, 257
Dockable command, 18
dockable toolbars, 23
dockable windows, 17–18
Document Outline window, 126
documenting programs, 68–70, 144
Dog class, 55, 488–490, 507, 509, 514
    detailed comparison, 511
    equals() method, 510
    speak() method, 490
Dog objects, comparing for equality, 508–509
DogCompare program, 509
DogString program, 508
Double class, 307
double data type, 91–92, 167
double primitive type, 82
Double quotation mark (\") escape sequence, 95

doubleValue() method, 307
doubleValue variable, 167
Double.valueOf() method, 307
do...while loop, 256–257
draw3DRect() method, 421
drawArc() method, 419–420
drawImage() method, 743
drawing
    flowcharts, 211–212
    lines and rectangles, 407–410
    ovals, 410–412
drawLine() method, 407–408, 421
drawOval() method, 410, 612
drawPolygon() method, 421–423
drawRect() method, 408, 433
drawRoundRect() method, 409–410
drawString() method, 398–401, 404, 406, 433, 746
Drum class, 456, 516
dual-alternative if, 216
dynamic method binding, 497–499
dynamic syntax checking, 62

E

E constant, 187
Edit Parameter List dialog box, 134
egg.gif file, 743
elements, 270
else clause, 406, 677
emp array, 275

Index

Employee class, 129–130, 168, 172, 270, 274, 319–320, 447–448, 450, 457, 464, 467, 487, 680
  comments, 140
  fields, 130, 137–139, 169
  instance variables, 130
  methods, 138–139
  overriding variable, 160
  shell, 129
  static ID number field, 182
  symbolic constant COMPANY_ID, 184
  values for data fields, 145
Employee() method, 135, 145, 169
Employee objects, 320–321, 448, 451
  arrays, 499
EmployeeEarningCommission class, 449
EmployeeWithTerritory class, 448–451
empMethod() method, 160
empty body, 247
encapsulation, 6
End command, 659
End of File (Ctrl+Z) key combination, 684–685
endsWith() method, 303
Enter event, 787
Entertainment class
  abstract, 491–493
  equals() method, 511
Entertainment project, 492, 511
EntertainmentDataBase class, 512
EntertainmentDataBase program, 501–502

EntertainmentDataBase.java file, 501, 512
Entertainment.java file, 492, 511
EntertainmentNoDuplicates class, 512
EntertainmentNoDuplicates.java file, 512
entreeChoice array, 648, 664
EOF (end-of-file condition), 683
EOFException exception, 683, 698, 700
equal to (==) operator, 90, 214
equals() method, 300, 508–512
equalsIgnoreCase() method, 300
erasing data from files, 680
Error class, 621, 622, 649
Error exception, 641
error handling, 634–635
Error Help command, 63
error messages
  displaying, 694
  output to command line, 682
errors
  sending messages, 627
  serious, 622
  terminating program, 624
  unrecoverable, 623
ErrorTip, 63
escape sequence, 94–96, 675
EvenInt program, 258, 260–261
EvenInt Properties command, 258
EvenInt.java file, 258–259
Event class, 220, 452–453, 457
  adding constructor, 466–467
  adding method, 288

  application that uses, 453–454
  extending, 454–455
  previewing Choose Manager class, 204
event handlers, 600, 788–789
  default skeleton, 789
event handling, 597–604
Event objects, 597
  arrays and, 275–276
Event project, 452, 473
EventArray program, 275–276
  adding method call and method, 288–289
  array length field, 291
  event pricing with parallel arrays, 281–282
  event types and manager names array, 298
  forcing valid Event objects, 282–283
  interactive, 277–278
EventArray.java file, 276, 298
eventCode array, 298
event-driven programming, 359–362
EventFile class, 697
EventFile2 program, 702
EventFile2.java file, 702
Event.java file, 275, 458
EventObject class, 597, 605
eventOptionsChanged() method, 790–791
events, 359–362, 444, 597–604
  GUI interfaces, 599
  inherited methods, 607–610
  listener for class, 599
  listening for, 599
  mouse, 610–613

Index

as objects, 597
source of, 530
types, 599
WFC programs, 787–791
Events button, 789
Events project, 109, 118, 126, 130
Events Properties command, 110
EventSite class, 136, 170–171
    class variable, 185
    constructors, 146–147
    data fields, 141–143
    instance methods, 132–133
    methods, 141–143
    overloading constructor, 173–174
    setSiteNumber() method, 133–134
    testing, 143–145
EventSite project, 170, 185
EventSite Properties command, 172
EventSite.java file, 131–132, 146, 170
EventWithConstructorArg class, 468
EventWithConstructorArg.java file, 468
EventWithConstructor.java file, 466, 468
EventWithHeader class, 458–459
EventWithHeader.java file, 458, 466, 473
EventWithProtectedData class, 473
EventWithProtectedData.java file, 473
Evergreen class, 450

Exception class, 621, 649, 651
exception handling, 621
    debugging, 657
Exception superclass, 650
exceptions, 206, 621–625
    catch block, 625–627
    finally block, 632–634
    MathError class, 624
    purposely causing, 623–624
    specifying which one method can throw, 641–647
    throwing and catching multiple, 629–632
    tracing through call stack, 665–667
    try block, 625–627
    types, 621
    uniquely handled by catch block, 647–649
    user-created, 649–652
EXE (Windows executable) files, 794
executing applets, 338
execution context, 714
exists() method, 676, 685
Exit command (Alt+F4) key combination, 46
exit() method, 531
exiting Visual J++, 20, 46
expressions
    tracing with debug windows, 659–665
    viewing value, 662
extended, 129
extending classes, 450–456
extends keyword, 348, 450

F

FancyFrame class, 579–580
fields, 125, 130, 680
    access modifiers, 130
    Employee class, 137–139
    EventSite class, 141–143
    friendly, 130
    private, 130
File class, 675–679
    methods, 676
FileInputStream class, 682
filenames and class names, 67
FileOutputStream class, 682, 685
files, 675–679, 681
    adding to project, 37–38
    buffers, 682
    closing, 42–43
    comparing, 678
    creation of, 44–46
    erasing data from, 680
    new, 42
    not part of project, 25
    opening, 44–46, 65–66
    output to command line, 682
    output to monitor, 682
    printing status message, 676–677
    random access, 702–705
    reading formatted data from, 698–702
    reading from, 686
    saving, 41
    sequential access, 702
    as series of bytes, 681
    streams, 681
    testing for nonexistent, 678

Index

writing formatted data, 691–698
writing to, 685–686
fill3DRect() method, 421
fillArc() method, 420
filled
    ovals, 410
    polygons, 423
    rectangles, 408
    rounded rectangles, 410
    three-dimensional rectangles, 421
fillOval() method, 410
fillPolygon() method, 423
fillRect() method, 408
fillRoundRect() method, 410
FilterInputStream class, 682
FilterOutputStream class, 682
final access modifier, 478
final classes, 478, 488
final keyword, 183–184
final methods, 478
finally block, 632–634, 684
FindState project, 301–302
FindState.java file, 301
FindStudent program, 326–327
FindStudent.java file, 326
First class, 56, 105
    main () method, 59
    nameAndAddress() method, 108
first() method, 591
First program, 107
firstInit variable, 209
firstName variable, 94
firstState string object, 302
firstTime variable, 740, 742
Fixed Dialog border, 775
fixed-size frames, 537–539

float data type, 91–92
float primitive type, 82
floating toolbars, 23
floating windows, 17–18
floating-point data types, 91–92
floating-point numbers, 91–92
flow charts, 211–212
FlowLayout class, 578–585, 608
FocusEvent event, 601
FocusListener interface, 601
folders, expanding and collapsing, 24
following a thread, 713
Font object, 354
Font objects, 400, 428
    adding to DemoGraphics1 class, 401
font property, 32
FontList project, 426
FontMetrics class, 428
fonts, 354–356
    ascent, 427
    descent, 427
    height, 427–428
    leading, 427
    listing system, 425
    methods, 425–434
    setting current, 428
for loops, 254–256, 258, 273–274, 276–277, 281–283, 291, 316, 403, 426, 500–501, 512, 721
    breaking out early, 280
    nesting, 257–261
    pausing program execution, 256
    printing integers, 255
    searching array with, 278–279

    variables, 255
Form class, 772
Form feed (\f) escape sequence, 95
form files, 23
Form1 properties, 30
formal parameters, 116
forms, 25
    background color, 33
    changing color, 775
    preventing resizing, 775
    properties, 30
    resizing, 775
    setting properties, 773
    WFC Controls, 26, 777–778
Forms Designer, 25–26
    code, 775–776
    Exit button, 789
    Shift+F7 key combination, 26
    WFC controls, 777
    WFC form, 771
    window, 770–771
forward slash (/), 69
fragments, 343
Frame class, 527–528, 777
    inheritance, 526–530
    methods, 536–539
Frame objects, 529
    closing actions, 530–533
    component methods with, 552
    creation of, 528–529
frames, 528, 587
    adding components, 700
    applets, 540
    buttons, 529
    Close button, 529

Index

closing, 530–533
for data entry, 692–693
fixed-size, 537–539
Maximize button, 529
Minimize button, 529
resizing, 529
Restore button, 529
title bar, 529
viewing file data, 698–702
visibility, 528, 531
FrameWithFixedSize class, 537
FrameWithFixedSize.java file, 537
FrameYouCanClose class, 531–532
empty methods, 533
FrameYouCanClose2 class, 535
FrameYouCanClose.java file, 531, 543
friendly fields, 130
Full Screen command, 19
full-screen windows, 19
FullTimeStudent class, 473
fundamental classes, 187

G

g variable, 403
garbage collection, 745
garbage collector, 299, 745
gathering information, 675
General tools, 26
getActiveControl() method, 772
getAscent() method, 428
getBlue() method, 402
getBorderStyle() method, 772
getChildOf() method, 777
getClickCount() method, 310, 606, 612

getComponent() method, 604–605
getComponentCount() method, 540
getComponents() method, 540
getDate() method, 125
getDay() method, 192
getDefaultToolkit() method, 425
getDescent() method, 428
getDocumentBase() method, 742
getEmpNum() method, 131, 181, 451
getEmpSal() method, 321, 451
getEventGuests() method, 474
getFont() method, 550
getFontList() method, 425–426
getFontMetrics() method, 428, 430
getGraphics() method, 404
getGreen() method, 402
getGuestChoice() method, 645–646, 657
getHeight() method, 428
getImage() method, 742–743
getItem() method, 560, 564, 605
getItemCount() method, 560, 564
getKeyChar() method, 606–607
getLabel() method, 358, 551–552
getLeading() method, 428
getManagerName() method, 143
getMessage() method, 627–629, 631, 650–651, 666
  MathError class, 628
getModifiers() method, 605–606
getMonth() method, 192
getName() method, 488, 511, 676

getParent() method, 676
getPath() method, 676
getPoint() method, 606
getRateOfPay() method, 457
getRateOfPayForContractual() method, 457
getRateOfPayForHourly() method, 457
getRed() method, 402
getSelectedCheckbox() method, 556
getSelectedIndex() method, 560, 564, 566
getSelectedIndexes() method, 564, 568
getSelectedItem() method, 559–560, 564
getSelection() method, 643, 645
getSiteNumber() method, 132–133, 136
getSource() method, 605, 608–610
getState() method, 552–553
getStateChange() method, 605
getTerritoryNum() method, 451
getText() method, 357, 362, 551
getTime() method, 125, 191, 194
getTitle() method, 536
getUsageFee() method, 142–143
getWhen() method, 605
getWindow() method, 605
getX() method, 606, 610
getY() method, 606, 610
getYear() method, 192
.gif file extension, 743
GIF (Graphics Interchange Format), 743
Go To Definition command, 127

Index

going out of scope, 157
GoodbyeThread class, 716
gr object, 404
graphic files, 23
graphics, 395
    animation, 434–438
    arcs, 419–420
    color, 400–401
    copying an area, 423–425
    drawing string in applet window, 398–400
    fonts, 400
    lines and rectangles, 407–410
    ovals, 410–412
    painting on-screen, 395
    polygons, 421–423
    three-dimensional rectangles, 421
Graphics class, 398, 404, 428
Graphics objects, 398–399, 403, 430
    custom, 404–406
    defining, 411
    improving appearance, 400–404
    setting font and color, 411
greater than (>) operator, 90, 214
greater than or equal to (>=) operator, 90, 214
Greet applet, 347, 349–350
    adding TextField and Button, 358–359
    changing label font, 354–356
    Enter key, 362
    greeting, 361–362
    personalGreeting Label, 363
    redrawing AppletViewer window, 364
    removing components, 364–365
    without Test.htm file, 354
Greet properties command, 350
Greet.java file, 349, 355, 361
GridBagLayout class, 291
GridLayout class, 578–583, 585–586
GroupBox control, 779
grouping checkboxes, 556–559
guestChoice string, 643, 646
guestLimit array, 382–383
GUI components, 526
GUI interfaces and events, 599
Guitar class, 456

H

<H1>...</H1> tag, 748
HACK comment token, 68
heap, 745
Hearts class, 516
height, 427–428
heightOfFont variable, 428
Hello class, 67, 77
Hello project folder, 37
Hello Properties dialog box, 71, 74
Hello solution, 40
Hello.class file, 71
Hello.java file, 65, 71
    running with WJVIEW, 74–75
Hello.java file, comments, 70
HelloThread class, 715
Hello_World solution, 41–43
help
    bookmarks, 34–36
    context-sensitive, 36–37
    dialog boxes, 36–37
    displaying topics, 34
    hyperlinks, 36
    InfoViewer, 34
    Internet, 37
    key words, 34
    programming terms, 36–37
    searching for work or phrase, 34
    table of contents format, 34
    ToolTips, 34
    topics, 34
hexadecimal, 95
high-level programming, 3–4
historyChoice class, 560
Hopper, Grace Murray, 653
HourlyEmployee class, 129, 457, 464, 487
    constructor, 467–468
.htm extension, 337
HTML documents
    appearance, 343
    blank lines, 339–340
    boldface, 338
    creation of, 342–347
    formatting text, 343
    headings, 748
    identifying, 338
    inserting HTML tags, 344–345
    navigating through elements, 345–346
    nonbreaking space code ( ), 340
    objects, 343
    tables, 345
    tags, 338
HTML Editor
    basic HTML template, 345

Index

changing options, 342
commands, 344
Design toolbar, 343
Design view, 342–343
Format menu, 344
HTML document creation, 342–347
HTML menu, 344
HTML toolbar, 343
keyboard shortcuts, 344
Quick View, 342
Source tab, 347
Source view, 342–343
Table menu, 344
Toolbox, 343
HTML editors, 342
.html extension, 337
HTML files, 23, 25
HTML (HyperText Markup Language), 337
fragments, 343
on-line documentation, 338
HTML Outline window, 345–346
HTML toolbar, 21, 343
HTML tools, 26
<HTML>...</HTML> tag, 338

I

i variable, 298
i486 microprocessors, 756
IDE (Integrated Development Environment)
designers, 25–26
main window, 20–23
managing windows, 17–20
menu bar, 20–21
Project Explorer, 23–25
Properties window, 30–33
Task List, 27–29
toolbars, 21–23
Toolbox, 26–27
IExplore.exe file, 350
if statements, 212–215, 278, 282, 649, 654, 676
compound statements, 217–221
else clause, 437
multiple dependent statements, 218
nested, 222
single dependent statement, 218
if...else statements, 215–217, 232
indentation, 216
multiple dependent statements, 219
nested, 222
illegal methods, 168
images
animation, 742–745
file formats, 742–743
public domain files, 745
shareware, 745
Immediate window, 662, 665
immutable objects, 299
implementation hiding, 112–113
implements ActionListener phrase, 530
implements keyword, 514
import statement, 190–191
in object, 205
INCREASE constant, 430
indefinite loops, 248

Index command, 35
indexOf() method, 303, 305
IndexOutOfBoundsException exception, 629–630, 632
infinite loops, 246
information hiding, 130, 471–475
InfoViewer
bookmarks, 35–36
Contents tab, 34
context-sensitive help, 36–37
Favorites tab, 34, 36
hyperlinks, 36
Index tab, 34
Search tab, 34
table of contents window, 34
Toolbox topic, 35
topic window, 34
inheritance, 5, 124, 184, 447–450
abstract classes, 487–497
constructors requiring arguments, 468
direction of, 451
event methods, 607–610
example, 444–446
extending classes, 450–456
Frame class, 526–530
from two classes, 723–727
good software design, 513
multiple, 535
overriding superclass methods, 456–459
init() method, 349, 363, 373–374, 377, 381, 386, 395–396, 405, 436, 457, 541, 558, 561, 566, 581–582, 590, 743, 772

Index

initForm() method, 773, 775–776
inlining code, 478
InputEvent class, 598, 605–606
InputStream class, 681–683
Insert Breakpoint command, 658
Insert() method, 328–329
Insert Table command, 345
Insert Table dialog box, 345
inside block, 156
instance methods, 132–133, 180, 478
instance variables, 125, 130
InstantiationError error, 488
int data type, 84–86
int primitive type, 82
int variables, 84–86
Integer class, 306
Integer.parseInt() method, 308
integers, 84–86, 88, 167
Integrated Development Environment, 15
IntelliSense technology, 61–63
interactive programs, 205
interfaces, 6–7, 514–517
InternalErrorException exception, 641
Internet help, 37
interpreters, 4, 7
InterruptedException exception, 642, 720
intValue variable, 167
invalid syntax, 652
invalidate() method, 364
Inventory class, 125
IOException exception, 641, 683–684, 696, 700
is-a relationships, 124, 450

isAltDown() method, 605
isControlDown() method, 605
isEnabled() function, 397
isEnabled() method, 551
isMultipleMode() method, 564
isResizable() method, 536
isSelected() method, 564
isShiftDown() method, 606
isShowing() method, 551
isVisible() method, 551
ItemEvent class, 599, 601, 605
ItemListener interface, 553, 601
itemOrdered variable, 278
itemStateChanged() method, 553–554, 558, 562, 566, 606
iteration, 245

J

J++ IDE (Integrated Development Environment), 15–33
Java API, 762
Java console application with J/Direct calls, 760–761
Java Exceptions command, 657
Java Exceptions dialog box, 657
.java file extension, 23, 66, 337, 770, 791
Java files, 23
    modifying output, 76
    renaming, 66
    where to input code, 67
Java programming language
    architecturally neutral, 7
    case-sensitivity, 55
    compiling code, 72
    development environments, 8

help sources, 387–388
newsgroups, 388
Java programming structure
    access modifiers, 59
    arguments, 54–55
    classes, 56
    classes and curly brackets ({}), 59
    literal strings, 54
    main() method, 59–60
    methods, 54–55
    naming classes, 56–58
    naming conventions, 58
    passing arguments, 55
    programs, 54–60
    reserved keywords, 56–57
    statements ending with semicolon, 54
    Unicode, 56
    white space, 59
Java VM (Virtual Machine), 7, 761
java.applet package, 348, 762
java.awt package, 348, 762, 793
    importing classes, 528
java.awt.event package, 360, 598, 787
javadoc, 69
javadoc comments, 69–70, 126–127, 142, 767, 769
java.io package, 675
java.lang package, 187, 256, 303, 306, 507, 527, 772
java.util package, 190
java.util.Date class, 191
J/Direct, 763
    accessing Win32 API, 757–761

Index

Call Builder dialog box, 759–760
calls and directives, 759
JDK (Java Development Kit), 8
  javadoc, 69
  programs, 61
.jpeg file extension, 743
JPEG (Joint Photographic Experts Group), 743
.jpg file extension, 743
JVC (Microsoft Compiler for Java), 72
JVIEW, 70–73, 793, 794
jview command, 337
jview Hello command, 77

K

keepScore() method, 516
keyboard
  focus, 357–358
  writing to screen from, 683–684
keyboard input, 205–210
  capturing, 682
KeyEvent class, 598, 606
KeyEvent event, 599, 601
KeyEventHandler delegate, 788
KeyFrame class, 603
  getKeyChar() method, 606–607
KeyFrame project, 602
KeyFrame2 class, 606–607
KeyFrame2.java file, 606
KeyFrame.java file, 602
KeyListener interface, 534, 601, 788
  class implementing, 602–604

keyPressed() method, 602–603
keyReleased() method, 602–603, 606–607
keyTyped() method, 602–603
keyboard, 348

L

Label class, 348, 550, 551
Label control, 780
labels, 348–354
languages, 3
last() method, 591
lastInit variable, 209
lastModified() method, 676, 685
late binding, 499
layout managers, 578
  advanced, 591
  BorderLayout class, 578–583
  FlowLayout class, 583–585
  GridLayout class, 585–586
leading, 427
Leave event, 787
length() method, 297, 676
less than (<) operator, 90, 214
less than or equal to (<=) operator, 90, 214
libraries of classes, 126, 186
LifeCycle program, 374–379
LifeCycle.java file, 374
life.htm file, 377
lightweight process, 714
line comments, 68
lines
  color, 407
  drawing, 407–410
List class, 550, 563–569
  methods, 563

List component, 779
List Members command (Ctrl+J) key combination, 62
List objects, 563–569
ListBox control, 779
listener object, 359
listeners, 359, 530
  for event classes, 599
listRules() method, 516
lists
  concurrent multiple selections, 567–569
  selecting option from, 559–563
  vertical scrollbar, 563–569
literal constant integer, 84
literal constants, 82, 183, 281
literal strings, 54, 85, 297
LoadImage applet, 743–744
LoadImage.java file, 743
local variable, 114
Locals window, 661, 664
logic errors, 116, 652–654
long data type, 84
long primitive type, 82
loopCount variable, 246–248
LoopingBankBal program, 249
loops
  body, 245–246
  control variables, 246–247
  counted, 254
  decrementing variable, 247–248
  definite, 254
  depending on arithmetic, 248
  empty body, 247
  executing at least once, 256–257

Index

executing twice, 247–248
incrementing variable, 247
indefinite, 248
infinite, 246
nesting, 257–261
testing condition, 254–256

M

machine language, 3
main() method, 59–60, 106, 109, 478, 772–773, 776
  using FrameYouCanClose class, 533
managerName array, 298
Math class, 187–190, 196, 478
Math.abs() method, 187
mathematical constants, 183
MathError class, 623–624
  adding corrective code to catch block, 628–629
  catching division-by-zero Exception, 626–627
  exception, 624
  getMessage() method, 628
MathError Properties command, 623
MathError2 class, 626
MathError2.java file, 626
MathError3 class, 628
MathError3.java file, 628
MathError4 class, 628–629
MathError4.java file, 628
MathError.java file, 623
Math.max() method, 187
matrix, 324
Maximize button, 20
MAX_PRIORITY constant, 722
mealPrice integer, 654

member variables, 125, 140–141
members, 61
memory, allocating and deallocating, 745
menu bar, 20–21
Menu class, 642–643
Menu.java file, 643
menus, 20–21
MessageBeep call, 761
MessageBox call, 761
MessageBox class, 764–765, 777
MessageBox function, 758–759
MessageBoxApp class, 758
  calling Win32 MessageBox function with WFCs, 764
  methodGetsArray() method, 286
  methodGetsOneInt() method, 285–286
methods, 6, 105
  abstract, 488
  access modifiers, 106
  actual parameters, 116
  adding and deleting parameters, 134
  alphabetical order, 138, 144
  ambiguity, 166–168
  applets, 349, 772–773
  arguments, 54–55, 112, 116
  arrays, 275
  assigning value, 117–118
  blocks, 156–163
  boolean type, 117
  calling from another class, 111
  Choice object, 559–560
  class objects, 125
  Class Outline, 140–141

class type, 117
compiler unable to select version, 167–168
components, 550–552, 605
console applications, 772
containers, 539
declaring, 106, 113
declaring variables, 158
displaying variables, 661
double type, 117
dynamically binding, 497–499
event handlers, 600
existing in black box, 113
final, 478
final modifier, 478
fonts, 425–434
formal parameters, 116
frame class, 536–539
header, 59–60
illegal, 168
instance, 478
method header, 59–60
multiple-argument, 115–116
names, 55
with no arguments, 105–111
order of arguments, 116
out object, 55
overloading, 163–166, 457
overriding, 373, 456–459
passing array to, 284–289
placement, 107
prewritten, 187
prewritten imported, 190–194
private, 130, 476–477
public, 106, 130

Index

receiving arguments and returning value, 118
requirements, 106
return type, 117
returning message, 125
returning value, 117–119, 125
reusable, 106
same in different classes, 109
signature, 642
single-argument, 112–115
specifying which exception to throw, 641–647
static, 478
static modifier, 131
this reference, 511
throwing exception, 625
throwing without catching, 642
throws clause, 641–642
used from anywhere in class, 106
variables, 116
void type, 117
you cannot override, 475–478
methodWithRedeclarations() method, 159
methodWithTwoBlocks() method, 156–158
microprocessor architecture, 756
Microsoft FrontPage, 342
Microsoft on the Web command, 37
Microsoft Visual J++ Web site, 388
Microsoft Word, 342
middleInit variable, 209
Minimize button, 20
MIN_PRIORITY constant, 722
modifying programs, 76–77
modulus (%) operator, 88, 258, 437
moneyAmount variable, 114
monitors, 341
mouse
   events, 610–613
   manual actions, 598
mouseClicked() method, 610, 612
MouseDown event, 788
mouseEntered() method, 610
MouseEvent class, 598–599, 601, 606
MouseEventHandler delegate, 788
mouseExited() method, 610
MouseFrame class, 610–613
MouseFrame project, 610
MouseFrame.java file, 610
MouseListener class, 534, 788
MouseListener interface, 601, 610–611
MouseMotionListener interface, 601
mousePressed() method, 610–611
mouseReleased() method, 610, 612
MouseUp event, 788
move.htm file, 386
Move.java file, 385
MoveLabel applet, 385–387
moving windows, 18
multidimensional arrays, 327
multiple inheritance, 514, 535
multiple-argument methods, 115–116
multithreading, 713–714, 716
MusicalEntertainment class, 491, 493–496, 501
MusicalEntertainment.java file, 493
MusicalInstrument class, 456, 516
myAge variable, 83
myFont object, 428
myNewSalary variable, 117

N

nameAndAddress() method, 106–109, 117
named shortcuts, 27
NameThatInstrument class, 516
naming projects, 15
native applications, 761–763
native modifier, 758
nested blocks, 156, 159
nested if statements, 222, 234, 236
nested if...else statements, 222, 232, 234
nested loops, 257–261
New File command, 44
   Ctrl+Shift+N key combination, 45
New File dialog box, 44–45
new keyword, 270, 297
new operator, 135
New Project command, 65, 347, 769
   Ctrl+N key combination, 15, 65
New Project dialog box, 14–15, 65, 347, 351, 769, 772
new projects, 14–17
Newline or line feed (\n) escape sequence, 95

Index

next() method, 591
nodata.txt file, 678
nonabstract classes, 487
nonbreaking space code ( ), 340
nonprinting characters, 94
NORM_PRIORITY constant, 722
NoSuchClass class, 623
not equal to (!=) operator, 90, 214
NOT operator, 237–238
null layout manager, 591
NullPointerException class, 649
NumberFormatException exception, 695
numeric type conversion, 93–94
Numinput program, 307–308
Numinput.java file, 307

O

Object Browser, 195–196
Object class, 527, 597, 675, 681
    methods, 507–513
object methods, 180–181
object-oriented programming, 4–7, 112
    versus procedural programming, 5
objects, 5, 30, 124
    accessing methods of, 136
    allocating memory, 135
    appearance, 30
    arrays of, 274–278
    available properties, 32
    behavioral aspects, 30
    versus classes, 124
    comparing for equality, 508–512
    converting to string, 507–508
    correct data fields, 180–181
    creation of, 135
    declaring, 134–136
    displaying all properties, 33
    encapsulation, 6
    identifier, 135
    immutable, 299
    inheritance, 5
    instantiating, 135
    interfaces, 6
    managing, 30–33
    manually listing members, 62
    naming, 135
    new operator, 135
    predictable attributes, 125–126
    type, 135
oneChar variable, 719
one-dimensional array, 324
oneSite object, 135–136
oneWorker object, 270
on-line help system, 34–37
    HTML (HyperText Markup Language), 338
Open (Ctrl+O) key combination, 44
Open File command, 45
Open File dialog box, 45–46
Open Project command, 43
Open Project dialog box, 43–44
opening data files, 681
operands, 93
operations, 4
operators
    precedence, 89, 238–239
    unary, 189
optional classes, 187
Options command, 61, 63, 342
Options dialog box, 63, 68, 75, 342
OR operator, 229–234
organizing classes, 137–144
Orthodontist class, 451–452
Other Windows command, 28, 74, 126, 195, 346, 760
OtherEntertainment class, 491, 495–496, 501
OtherEntertainment.java file, 495
out object, 55, 205
output formats, 794
Output window (Ctrl+Alt+O) key combination, 75
outputSound() method, 516
OutputStream class, 681, 683
outside block, 156
ovals
    drawing, 410–412
    filled, 410
oven Temperature variable, 82
overloadDate() method, 165–166
overloading, 163–166
    constructors, 172–174
    EventSite constructor, 173–174
    methods, 163–166
    overloadDate() method, 165–166
overloading methods, 457
overriding methods, 373, 456–459
overriding variables, 159–160

P

<p> tag, 339
package keyword, 792
package statement, 792
packages, 126, 183, 186, 762, 794
    Class Outline, 127
    importing, 792
    J/Direct calls, 763
    managing, 126
    naming, 793
    representing all classes, 191
    versus solutions, 126
    user-created, 791–793
    viewing, 195–196
paint() method, 395–399, 401, 403, 409, 422, 424, 426, 429–430, 432, 434, 437, 554, 561, 566, 568, 723, 726, 735–736, 739–741, 747, 773
paintBrush object, 428
painting on-screen graphics, 395
Panel class, 527, 586–591, 777
panels, 539, 586–591
parallel arrays, 279, 284, 734
Parameter Info command, 62
Parameter Info (Ctrl+Shift+I) key combination, 62
parent class, 450–451
    accessing data from, 473
    child class methods overriding, 459
    general, 487
    private members, 473
parseInt() method, 306, 382, 453, 695
parsing strings, 307
PartTimeStudent class, 473

Party class, 124–125, 650–651
PartyException class, 650
PartyPlanner applet, 336, 379–384, 524–525
PartyPlanner.java file, 380
PassArray program, 287
PassArrayElement program, 285
passing arguments, 55
passing references, 181
pausing threads, 720
Payroll class, 125
Pentium family of microprocessors, 756
Periodontist class, 451–452
personalGreeting Label, 363
PI constant, 187, 196
Piano class, 516
PickMenu class, 642–645
PickMenu.java file, 644, 663
pixels (picture elements), 341
PlanMenu class, 646–647, 664
PlanMenu program, 643, 656
PlanMenu Properties command, 646
PlanMenu.java file, 648, 656, 658
PlanMenuWithStackTrace program, 667–668
PlanMenuWithStackTrace.java file, 666
PlanVegetarianMenu class, 648
PlanVegetarianMenu program, 648–649
PlanVegetarianMenu.java file, 648
platforms, 7
play() method, 456
Playing interface, 515
playNote() method, 516

Poker class, 516
Polygon object, 423
polygons, 423
polymorphic behavior, 499
polymorphism, 456–459, 490
porting, 7
pos variable, 560
postfix -- decrement operator, 253
postfix ++ increment operators, 251–253
postfix ++ shortcut operator, 251
precedence, 238–239
predictRaise() method, 113–114
predictRaiseGivenIncrease() method, 115–116
prefix -- decrement operator, 253
prefix ++ increment operators, 251–253
prefix ++ shortcut operator, 251
pressCounter variable, 542
previous() method, 591
prewritten
    classes, 186–187
    imported methods, 190–194
    interfaces, 517
    methods, 187
primary key, 138
primitive types, 82, 303
print() method, 55, 85, 217, 297, 329
printClassName() method, 471
printDinnerChoice() method, 454–455, 459
printEventGuests() method, 452, 459
printHeader() method, 457–459

printing, 55–56
println() method, 55, 85, 110, 113, 136, 161, 205, 216, 258, 297, 317, 455, 607, 648, 682
printMessages() method, 477
printPrivate() method, 476–477
printPublic() method, 476
printStackTrace() method, 666–667
PrintStream class, 682
private access, 130
private fields, 130
private keyword, 471, 473
private members, 473
private methods, 130, 476–477
private variables, 476
procedural programming, 4, 352
  versus object-oriented programming, 5
procedures, 4
program files, 675
programs, 3
  as-is components, 513
  boolean values, 213
  Break mode, 655
  class names and filenames, 67
  comments, 68–70
  compiling, 72
  curly brackets ({}), 68
  debugging, 507
  distributing, 793–796
  documenting, 68–70, 144
  dynamic syntax checking, 62
  executing from command line, 77
  interactive, 205
  invalid syntax, 652
  Java interpreters, 70
  Java programming structure, 54–60
  JDK (Java Development Kit), 61
  logic, 4
  making decisions, 212–215
  modifying, 76–77
  modifying components, 513
  multithreading, 713–714
  pausing, 256, 260–261
  placement of methods, 107
  preventing from running as anticipated, 653
  problems during execution, 653
  procedural, 359
  recompiling, 72
  running, 70–75
  run-time values, 205
  single-thread, 713
  Statement Completion, 61–62
  statements ending with semicolon, 54
  stepping through, 655–657
  storing user response, 213
  syntax coloring, 61
  syntax errors, 62–63
  tasks defined in Task List, 66
  Text Editor window, 61–65
  that use file data, 674
  tracing execution, 654–659
  tracing variables and expressions, 659–665
  user interface, 697
  using WFCs (Windows Foundation Classes), 764
  Word Completion, 62
  writing first, 65–67
Programs menu, 14
Project Explorer
  buttons, 25
  context-sensitive help, 36
  Ctrl+Alt+J key combination, 24
  displaying, 23–24
  displaying contents of Hello solution, 23
  Forms Designer window, 26
  Package View button, 25
  Solution 'Hello' icon, 40
  Solution icon, 39
project files, 25
Project Properties dialog box, 792
projects, 16
  adding files, 37–38
  adding to solutions, 38–39
  automatically saving, 75
  build configuration, 794
  changes reflected in solutions, 16
  closing, 42–43
  directory-based, 23
  existing, 15
  files, 23
  naming, 15
  new, 14–17
  opening, 43–44
  recently opened, 15
  renaming, 40
  saving, 41
prompt, 206
properties, 30–33
  tags, 346
Properties command, 31, 71–72

Properties dialog box, 71
Properties window, 25, 30–33, 346, 775, 789
Properties Window command, 347
protected keyword, 473
protected members, 473
pseudocode, 211
public classes, 129
public keyword, 129, 471, 473, 652
public methods, 130

Q

Quick View, 342, 352–353

R

r variable, 403
radio buttons, 556
RadioButton control, 780
RadioButtons class, 779–780
raiseRates() method, 289
RAM (random access memory), 679
random access files, 702–705
    streams, 681
RandomAccessFile class, 703
ratePerGuest array, 383
read() method, 205, 209–210, 682–683, 698, 703
readByte() method, 698
readChar() method, 698
readDouble() method, 698
ReadEventFile.java file, 698
ReadFileWriteScreen.java file, 686

readFloat() method, 698
reading from files, 686
readInt() method, 698
ReadKBWrite project, 683–684
ReadKBWriteFile class, 685–686
ReadKBWriteFile.java file, 685
ReadKBWriteScreen class, 683
ReadKBWriteScreen.java file, 683
readUTF() method, 698
real-time applications, 703
Rebuild command, 72, 74, 77, 85–86
recently opened projects, 15
recompiling programs, 72
records, 680
    batch processing, 703
rectangles
    clear, 408
    drawing, 407–410
    drawing around strings, 432–434
    filled, 408
    filled, rounded, 410
    round-cornered, 409
    three-dimensional, 421
references, 497–499
    passing, 181
Refresh command, 347, 355, 359
release build, 794
Remove Breakpoint command, 659
remove() method, 364, 540, 564
removeAll() method, 540, 564
removing breakpoints, 659
Rename command, 40
renaming
    class files, 72
    Java files, 66

projects, 40
solutions, 40
Window layouts, 20
repaint() method, 395–398, 438, 551, 555, 566, 724–725, 739–740
replace() method, 303
requestFocus() method, 357–358
reserved keywords, 56–57
resizing
    applets, 347
    containers, 579
    forms, 775
    frames, 529
    windows, 18
resume() method, 718
reusable code, 448–449
reusable methods, 106
round-cornered rectangles, 409
run() method, 714–715, 718–719, 721, 725, 773
Run To Cursor command, 655–657
Runnable interface, 723–727
running programs, 70–75
run-time errors, 652–653
RuntimeException exception, 641

S

SalariedEmployee class, 129, 487
salesFigure array, 270
Sample Functionality comments, 767, 769
Save All command, 41
Save As command, 42, 455, 458, 468, 473–474

Index

Save command, 41
    Ctrl+S key combination, 41
Save dialog box, 42
Save icon, 41
Save Java file command, 45
saving data, 679–680
scientific notation, 91
scope, 162
screen
    printing line of output to, 55
    redrawing with background color, 740
    reducing animation flickering, 738–742
    writing from keyboard, 683–684
Script Outline window, 346
scripting languages, 346
Search command, 35
searching arrays, 278–283
secondState string object, 302
SecretPhrase program, 305–306
SecretPhrase.java file, 305
seek() method, 703–705
Select class dialog box, 760
select() method, 559–560, 564
selectedIndexChanged event, 791
selectionMode property, 779
sequential access files, 702
serious errors, 622
serviceRep object, 448
Set Next Statement command, 657
setActiveControl() method, 772
setBackground() method, 551
setBorderStyle() method, 772, 776
setBounds() method, 591
setCharAt() method, 328
setCheckboxGroup() method, 556
setChoice() method, 644
setColor() method, 400–404, 407
setDate() method, 125
setDay() method, 192
setDinnerChoice() method, 459
setEditable() method, 357
setEmpNum() method, 133, 169
setEnabled() method, 387, 551, 396–397
setEntertainerName() method, 492–493
setEntertainmentFee() method, 492–496
setEventGuests() method, 453, 456, 459, 474–475
setEventMinRate() method, 288–289
setFont() method, 354–355, 400–404, 550
setForeground() method, 551
setGuestChoice() method, 644–645
setIdNum() method, 472–473
setLabel() method, 358, 551–553
setLayout() method, 583–585
setLocation() method, 384–386, 398, 551, 591
setManagerName() method, 143
setMonth() method, 192
setMultipleMode() method, 564
setPriority() method, 718, 722
setResizable() method, 536
setSelectedCheckbox() method, 557
setSiteNumber() method, 133–134, 136
setSize() method, 527, 551, 591, 777
setState() method, 552–553
setText() method, 348, 357, 551, 776
setTime() method, 125
setTitle() method, 536
setTypeOfAct() method, 495
setTypeOfMusic() method, 494
Setup files, 794
SetUpSite class, 109–110, 118, 127
SetUpSite file, 110
SetUpSite() method, 136
SetUpSite program, 119
    syntax error, 110
    viewing, 104
SetUpSite.java file, 118, 126, 136
setVisible() method, 527, 531, 551, 772, 777
setYear() method, 192
shapes
    coordinates, 407
    lines, 407–410
    rectangles, 407–410
short data type, 84
short primitive type, 82
shortcut arithmetic operators, 251–253
show() method, 764–765
Show Next Statement command, 657
Show Tasks command, 28, 33
ShowThread class, 719
ShowThread.java file, 718
shuffle() method, 516
signature, 642

Index

significant digits, 91
simpleInterest() method, 163–164, 168
simpleInterestrateUsingDouble() method, 164
simpleInterestRateUsingInt() method, 164
simpMeth() method, 167
Single quotation mark (\') escape sequence, 95
single-alternative if, 215
single-argument methods, 112–115
single-argument operator, 189
single-dimensional array, 324
single-thread programs, 713
sleep() method, 256, 720–722, 732, 746
SleepThread.java file, 720
.sln extension, 41
SmartEditor error, 62, 652
Snake class, 491
solid arcs, 420
Solitaire class, 516
solutions, 16
    adding projects, 38–39
    closing, 42–43
    name of current, 20
    opening, 43–44
    versus packages, 126
    renaming, 40
    saving, 41
someException exception, 627
someMethod() method, 471
someNumbers array, 325
someNums array, 315
someVar variable, 158
SortCharArray program, 316–319

sorting
    arrays of objects, 319
    ascending order, 313–319
    bubble sort, 314–315
    descending order, 313–319
    primitive array elements, 313–319
    strings, 322–323
    temporary variable, 313–314
sortStrings() method, 322
SortStrings program, 322–323
SortStrings.java file, 322
source code, compiling into bytecode, 71
source object, 359
Source view, 342
speak() method, 488, 490, 499, 514
specially marked code comments, 27
square() method, 112
Standard toolbar, 21, 41
    Add Item button, 38
    Load/Save Window UI dropdown list box, 20
    New Project button, 65
    Project Explorer button, 24
    Properties Window button, 31
    Save All button, 41
    Task List button, 29
    Toolbox button, 27
Star applet, 422
Start button, 14
Start command, 73–74, 377–378, 658, 664, 761, 776, 791
    F5 function key, 73–74, 350
Start menu, 14

start() method, 349, 373–375, 377–378, 381, 395, 457, 715, 725, 735, 740, 772
startPosition property, 775
startsWith() method, 303
startTime variable, 193
Statement Completion, 61–62, 67
statementOfPhilosophy() method, 109, 127
statements
    commenting out, 68
    ending with semicolon, 54
states, 5
static class variables, 182
static keyword, 60, 106, 180, 478
static methods, 180, 478
static modifier, 131
status bar, 20
Step commands, 655–657
Step Into command, 655–657, 664
Step Out command, 655, 657
Step Over command, 655, 657, 665
stick figure. *See* animated figure
stop command, 377, 378
stop() method, 349, 373–373, 376–378, 395, 718, 725, 772
Stop Program
    Ctrl+Break key combination, 530
    Ctrl+C key combination, 530
StopLight applet, 394, 435–438
StopLight project, 435
streams, 679–685
    random access files, 681
String array, 643

String class, 60, 297, 299–300, 513
string constants, 94
String data type, 142, 297
String List Editor dialog box, 779
String objects, 297
String variable name, 299
StringBuffer class, 328–330
strings, 94, 268
    adding characters at specific locations, 328
    altering one character, 328
    appending, 328
    arrays, 297
    beginning and ending, 303
    comparing, 299–303
    comparing to each array element, 301–302
    concatenation, 304
    converting object to, 507–508
    converting primitive type to, 303
    converting to numbers, 306–308
    declaring, 297–299
    displaying, 297
    drawing rectangles around, 432–434
    equivalent, 300
    exact width of, 431–432
    ignoring case when comparing, 300
    immutable, 299, 328
    length, 297
    lowercase, 303
    parsing, 307
    position of character, 303
    printing, 56
    replacing characters in, 303
    returning zero, 301
    sorting, 322–323
    spacing correctly, 431
    specific character in, 303
    substrings, 304
    Unicode values, 301
    uppercase, 303
stringWidth() method, 432
Student class, 471–473, 680
Sub class, 476–477
sub variable, 273
subclass objects
    arrays, 499–502
    converting to superclass objects, 497
subclasses, 450, 451, 487, 513, 528
    accessing parent class data from, 473
    accessing superclass methods, 470–471
    coding methods, 488
    constructor calling superclass constructor first, 464–465
    constructors, 467
    methods you cannot override, 475–478
    setEventGuests() method, 474–475
    size of, 450
    specificity, 451
subscripts, 270
substring() method, 304
subtraction (-) operator, 88
Sun Microsystems Web site, 388
Super class, 476–477
super keyword, 467–468, 470
superclass objects, 497
superclasses, 487
    abstract classes as, 488
    accessing methods, 470–471
    constructors, 464–467
    constructors requiring arguments, 467–470
    overriding methods, 456–459
    private members, 473
    private method, 476–477
    private variable, 476
    protected field, 473–474
    reference to, 497–498
    size of, 450
suspend() method, 718
switch keyword, 234–235
switch statement, 234–237
switching Window layouts, 20
symbolic constants, 82, 183–184
    arrays, 281
syntax errors, 62–63, 72, 116, 652
    online help, 63
system, information about, 425
System class, 55, 126, 205, 531, 682
    members, 62
System.exit() method, 625

T

Tab (\t) escape sequence, 95
TabChar variable, 94
Table tool, 345
tables, 345
tags, 338
    attributes, 340, 346

Index

listing of, 339
properties, 346
takeXRays() method, 452
Task List
　adding tasks, 28–29
　buttons, 28
　columns, 28
　comments, 68
　compiler errors, 72, 77
　Ctrl+Alt+K key combination, 29
　keyboard shortcuts, 29
　SmartEditor error, 62, 652
　tasks defined in, 66
tasks, 28
temp variable, 314, 321
tenMult array, 272
testAnim2.htm Web page, 738
testAnim3.htm Web page, 741
testAnim.htm Web page, 736
testBorderNoNorth.htm file, 582
testBox.htm Web page, 433
testCheckBoxGroup.htm file, 558
testCheckBox.htm Web page, 555, 558
testComponentApplet.htm Web page, 543
TestConstructor class, 147
TestConstructor.java file, 146
testDCGO.htm Web page, 406
testDC.htm Web page, 404
testDemoChoice.htm Web page, 562
testDemoList2.htm Web page, 568
testDemoList.htm Web page, 566
testDG.htm Web page, 399
testDP.htm Web page, 397
TestExpandedClass class, 143–144
TestExpandedClass.java file, 143
TestFile.java file, 45–46
testFlow.htm Web page, 583
testFontList.htm Web page, 426
testFontMetrics.htm Web page, 430
testGrid.htm Web page, 585
Test.htm Web page, 347, 350–351
　AppletViewer, 353–354
　Quick View, 352
　updating, 355, 359, 362
testImage.htm Web page, 744
testing
　LifeCycle program, 377–379
　for nonexistent files, 678
testParties.htm Web page, 749
testParty.htm Web page, 748
testRegion.htm Web page, 590
TestStatement.java file, 111
testStopLight.htm Web page, 438
testThreeStars.htm Web site, 424
testTimer.htm Web page, 726
Text Editor window, 350, 770–771
　breakpoints, 658
　changing options, 61
　dynamic syntax checking, 62, 66
　Find and Replace command, 290
　keyboard shortcuts, 63–65
　Statement Completion, 61–62, 67
　syntax coloring, 61
　Task List, 27
　WFC form, 771
　Word Completion, 62
text editors, 61, 342
TextComponent class, 550
TextEvent event, 599, 601
TextEvents class, 598
TextFields, 356–359
TextListener interface, 601
this keyword, 471
this reference, 180–183, 348, 511
Thread class, 256, 714–717, 722, 732
　extending, 718–719
　methods, 718
threads, 713
　creation of, 714–717
　dead state, 718
　deadlock, 722
　finished state, 718
　garbage collection, 745
　inactive state, 718
　life cycle, 717–720
　new state, 717
　pausing, 720
　priority, 721–723
　ready state, 717
　runnable, 717
　running state, 717–718
　starting execution, 715
　starvation, 722
three-dimensional rectangles, 421
ThreeStars project, 424

Index

Throwable class, 621, 649
throwing the exception, 206
ThrowParty program, 650–652
ThrowParty Properties command, 651
throws clause, 641–642
throws Exception clause, 452–453, 459, 475, 496, 501
throws Exception phrase, 492
throws IOException clause, 704
throws keyword, 625
Tile Horizontally command, 17
Tile Vertically command, 17
time, 191–192
TimerApplet program, 724–727
title bar, 18, 20, 46
TODO comment token, 68
TODO comments, 767, 769
toLowerCase() method, 303
toolbars
    context-sensitivity, 21
    customizing, 22
    describing button functions, 34
    displaying/hiding, 21–22
    dockable, 23
    drop-down list, 21
    floating, 23
    ToolTips, 34
Toolbars command, 22
Toolbars submenu, 22
Toolbox, 26–27
    Ctrl+Alt+X key combination, 27
    customizing, 343
    ToolTips, 27, 34
Toolbox command, 778
Toolkit class, 425
ToolTips, 27, 34

Topics Found dialog box, 37
toString() method, 303–304, 494–496, 507–508, 551, 650
totalPrice variable, 565
toUpperCase() method, 303
tracing
    exceptions through call stack, 665–667
    variables and expressions, 659–665
tracing program execution
    breakpoints, 657–659
    exercise, 656–657
    Step commands, 655
Tree class, 450
true Java application, 762
try block, 625–627, 646, 683, 695, 721, 736
    multiple exceptions, 629–632
try keyword, 625
try...catch block, 693–694
    with finally block, 632
twoDeclarations() method, 158
two-dimensional arrays, 324–327
TwoErrors class, 629–631

U

unary operators, 189, 251
undefined variable or class name message, 109
UNDONE comment token, 68
Unicode, 56, 317, 680
Unicode Web site, 95
unifying type, 93
unique identifier, 138
unrecoverable error, 623

update() method, 395, 398, 739–740, 742, 747
updating windows, 395
URLs (Uniform Resource Locators), 742
U.S. Naval Observatory Web site, 193
usageFee variable, 142
UseButtonFrame program, 608–610
UseButtonFrame.java file, 609
UseChap9WeekendEvent.java program, 445
UseDinnerEvent class, 455
UseDinnerEvent program, 455
UseEventsWithConstructorArg program, 468–469
UseEventsWithConstructorArg.java file, 469
UseEventsWithConstructors.java file, 466
UseEventsWithHeaders program, 459
UseEventsWithHeaders.java file, 459
UseKeyFrame program, 602–604
UseKeyFrame2.java file, 607
UseKeyFrame.java file, 603
UseMouseFrame program, 610–613
UseMouseFrame.java file, 612
UseProtected program, 475
UseProtected.java file, 475
user interface, 6
user-created
    exceptions, 649–652
    packages, 791–793
UserInitials program, 207–210
UserInitials Properties command, 208

UserInitials.java file, 207
UseSimpleEvent program, 454
    modifying, 455–456
UseSimpleEvent.java file, 453

V

valA variable, 313–314
valB variable, 313–314
validate() method, 364
validValues array, 279
values, 91
variables, 4, 82–83, 183
    access modifiers, 183
    accumulating, 251–253
    assigning, 83
    assigning new value, 662
    within block, 157
    changing, 661–662
    changing values, 660
    counting, 251
    data types, 84
    declaring, 83, 85–86, 157
    declaring and displaying, 85
    increasing by one, 251–252
    initializing, 83
    int data type, 84–86
    for loop, 255
    monitoring, 661–662
    names, 281
    naming, 83
    nested blocks, 159
    out of scope, 660
    overriding, 159–160
    reassigning value, 159
    reference types, 272
    scope, 157
    storing, 679

testing against series of integer or character values, 234
    tracing with debug windows, 659–665
    type casting, 93–94
VegetarianMenu class, 648–649
vegMenu variable, 654
View Designer command, 26
Violin class, 516
virtual classes, 488
viruses, 653
visible frames, 528
Visual Basic layout, 20
Visual InterDev, 16
Visual J++, 8–9
    debugger, 654–659
    design time, 20
    exiting, 20, 46
    help, 33–37
    IDE (Integrated Development Environment), 16–33
    minimizing and maximizing main window, 20
    new projects, 14–17
    solutions, 16
    starting session, 15
Visual Studio, 16, 34
.vjp extension, 41
void keyword, 60

W

warnings, 27
Watch window, 661–662, 664
Web browsers
    executing applets, 338
    ignoring tags, 339

rendering HTML documents, 342
    window, 395
Web pages, 337
    animation, 746–749
    HTML tools, 26
weekend event, 444
WesternPanel object, 588–589
WesternPanel.java file, 588
WFC applications, 773
    distributing, 793–794
    events, 787–791
    executing, 776
    life cycle, 773–774
WFC controls, 26, 776–781
WFC delegate classes, 788
WFC Form class, 772
WFC form files, 770–776
WFC forms, 770–771
WFCs (Windows Foundation Classes), 763–765
while keyword, 245
while loops, 245–251, 254, 306, 453, 474, 684
    bank balance program, 256
    infinite, 724
    loop control variable, 246
    nesting, 257–261
    printing integers, 254
    searching array with, 280
    testing loop control variable, 246
white space, 59
widgets, 526
wildcard symbol, 191
Win32 API, 756–757
    accessing with J/Direct, 757–761
    DLLs (dynamic-link libraries), 758

Index

Windows Open dialog box, 762
Win32 API MessageBeep() function, 761
Win32 API MessageBox() function, 757–758, 761
Win32Example class, 760
Win32Example program, 760–761
    both WFC package and J/Direct call, 765
Win32Example2.java file, 765
Win32Example.java file, 760
Window class, 527–528, 777
window layouts, 19–20
Window menu, 18
Window objects, 528
windowActivated() method, 530, 532, 538, 697
WindowAdapter class, 533–535
windowClosed() method, 530, 532, 538, 696
windowClosing() method, 530–532, 535, 537, 696, 701
windowDeactivated() method, 530, 532, 538, 697
windowDeiconified() method, 530, 532, 538, 697
WindowEvent class, 599, 601, 605
windowIconified() method, 530, 532, 538
WindowListener class, 534, 538
    methods, 530531
WindowListener interface, 599, 601, 696
windowOpened() method, 530, 532, 538, 697
WindowPartyPlanner Properties dialog box, 794–795

windows, 539, 587
    attributes, 5–6
    automatically arranging, 17
    default layout, 19
    dockable, 17–18
    floating, 17–18
    full-screen, 19
    gadgets, 526
    layouts, 19
    moving, 18
    resizing, 18
    title bar, 18
    updating, 395
Windows 3.1, 756
Windows 95, 756
Windows 98, 756
Windows architecture, 756–757
Windows CE, 7556
Windows dialog box, 757–758
Windows NT, 756
Windows Open dialog box, 762
Windows Party Planner application, 754–755
Windows programs
    Application Wizard, 766–770
    comments, 767
    displaying code, 771
    editable text box, 767
    elements, 767
    forms, 766
    menus, 767
    package type, 769
    reading data from external database, 767
    status bar, 767
    toolbar buttons, 767
    WFC form files, 770–776

windowsIconified() method, 697
WindowsPartyPlanner class, 790, 796
    executing, 776
WindowsPartyPlanner form, 769–770
WindowsPartyPlanner program
    adding events, 789–791
    adding WFC controls, 778–780
    changing properties, 775–776
    release build, 794–796
WindowsPartyPlanner Properties command, 794
WindowsPartyPlanner.exe file, 796
WindowsPartyPlanner.exe Properties dialog box, 796
WindowsPartyPlanner.Java file, 796
WindowYouCanClose class, 535
WindowYouCanClose.java file, 535
WJVIEW, 70, 74–75, 793–794
Word Completion, 62
WordPerfect, 342
work() method, 514–515
Working interface, 514–515
WorkingCow class, 515
WorkingDog class, 514–515
WorkingHorse class, 515
wrapper classes, 788
wrappers, 307
write() method, 703
writeBoolean() method, 691
writeChar() method, 691

writeDouble() method, 691
writeFloat() method, 691
writeInt() method, 691
writeUTF() method, 691
writing
    to files, 685–686
    first program, 65–67
    formatted data, 691–698

X

x-axis, 384
x-coordinate, 384

Y

y-axis, 384
y-coordinate, 384
yourAge variable, 83

Z

ZIP package type, 794

END-USER LICENSE AGREEMENT FOR MICROSOFT SOFTWARE
Microsoft Visual J++, 90-Day Trial Edition

END-USER LICENSE AGREEMENT FOR MICROSOFT SOFTWARE IMPORTANT- READ CAREFULLY: This Microsoft End-User License Agreement ("EULA") is a legal agreement between you (either an individual or a single entity) and Microsoft Corporation for the Microsoft software product identified above, which includes computer software and may include associated media, printed materials, and "online" or electronic documentation ("SOFTWARE PRODUCT"). The SOFTWARE PRODUCT also includes any updates and supplements to the original SOFTWARE PRODUCT provided to you by Microsoft. By installing, copying, downloading, accessing or otherwise using the SOFTWARE PRODUCT, you agree to be bound by the terms of this EULA. If you do not agree to the terms of this EULA, do not install, copy, or otherwise use the SOFTWARE PRODUCT.

SOFTWARE PRODUCT LICENSE

The SOFTWARE PRODUCT is protected by copyright laws and international copyright treaties, as well as other intellectual property laws and treaties. The SOFTWARE PRODUCT is licensed, not sold.

1. **GRANT OF LICENSE.** This EULA grants you the following rights:

    1.1 License Grant. Microsoft grants to you as an individual, a personal nonexclusive license to make and use copies of the SOFTWARE PRODUCT for the sole purposes of evaluating and learning how to use the SOFTWARE PRODUCT, as may be instructed in accompanying publications or documentation. You may install the software on an unlimited number of computers provided that you are the only individual using the SOFTWARE PRODUCT.

    1.2 Academic Use. You must be a "Qualified Educational User" to use the SOFTWARE PRODUCT in the manner described in this section. To determine whether you are a Qualified Educational User, please contact the Microsoft Sales Information Center/One Microsoft Way/Redmond, WA 98052-6399 or the Microsoft subsidiary serving your country. If you are a Qualified Educational User, you may either: (i) exercise the rights granted in Section 1.1, OR (ii) if you intend to use the SOFTWARE PRODUCT solely for instructional purposes in connection with a class or other educational program, this EULA grants you the following alternative license models:

    (A) Per Computer Model. For every valid license you have acquired for the SOFTWARE PRODUCT, you may install a single copy of the SOFTWARE PRODUCT on a single computer for access and use by an unlimited number of student end users at your educational institution, provided that all such end users comply with all other terms of this EULA, OR

    (B) Per License Model. If you have multiple licenses for the SOFTWARE PRODUCT, then at any time you may have as many copies of the SOFTWARE PRODUCT in use as you have licenses, provided that such use is limited to student or faculty end users at your educational institution and provided that all such end users comply with all other terms of this EULA. For purposes of this subsection, the SOFTWARE PRODUCT is "in use" on a computer when it is loaded into the temporary memory (i.e., RAM) or installed into the permanent memory (e.g., hard disk, CD ROM, or other storage device) of that computer, except that a copy installed on a network server for the sole purpose of distribution to other computers is not "in use". If the anticipated number of users of the SOFTWARE PRODUCT will exceed the number of applicable licenses, then you must have a reasonable mechanism or process in place to ensure that the number of persons using the SOFTWARE PRODUCT concurrently does not exceed the number of licenses.

2. **DESCRIPTION OF OTHER RIGHTS AND LIMITATIONS.**

    (Limitations on Reverse Engineering, Decompilation, and Disassembly. You may not reverse engineer, decompile, or disassemble the SOFTWARE PRODUCT, except and only to the extent that such activity is expressly permitted by applicable law notwithstanding this limitation.

    (Separation of Components. The SOFTWARE PRODUCT is licensed as a single product. Its component parts may not be separated for use on more than one computer.

    (Rental. You may not rent, lease or lend the SOFTWARE PRODUCT.

    * Trademarks. This EULA does not grant you any rights in connection with any trademarks or service marks of Microsoft.

    (Software Transfer. The initial user of the SOFTWARE PRODUCT may make a one-time permanent transfer of this EULA and SOFTWARE PRODUCT only directly to an end user. This transfer must include all of the SOFTWARE PRODUCT (including all component parts, the media and printed materials, any upgrades, this EULA, and, if applicable, the Certificate of Authenticity). Such transfer may not be by way of consignment or any other indirect transfer. The transferee of such one-time transfer must agree to comply with the terms of this EULA, including the obligation not to further transfer this EULA and SOFTWARE PRODUCT.

    (No Support. Microsoft shall have no obligation to provide any product support for the SOFTWARE PRODUCT.

    (Termination. Without prejudice to any other rights, Microsoft may terminate this EULA if you fail to comply with the terms and conditions of this EULA. In such event, you must destroy all copies of the SOFTWARE PRODUCT and all of its component parts.

3. **COPYRIGHT.** All title and intellectual property rights in and to the SOFTWARE PRODUCT (including but not limited to any images, photographs, animations, video, audio, music, text, and "applets" incorporated into the SOFTWARE PRODUCT), the accompanying printed materials, and any copies of the SOFTWARE PRODUCT are owned by Microsoft or its suppliers. All title and intellectual property rights in and to the content which may be accessed through use of the SOFTWARE PRODUCT is the property of the respective content owner and may be protected by applicable copyright or other intellectual property laws and treaties. This EULA grants you no rights to use such content. All rights not expressly granted are reserved by Microsoft.

4. **BACKUP COPY.** After installation of one copy of the SOFTWARE PRODUCT pursuant to this EULA, you may keep the original media on which the SOFTWARE PRODUCT was provided by Microsoft solely for backup or archival purposes. If the original media is required to use the SOFTWARE PRODUCT on the COMPUTER, you may make one copy of the SOFTWARE PRODUCT solely for backup or archival purposes. Except as expressly provided in this EULA, you may not otherwise make copies of the SOFTWARE PRODUCT or the printed materials accompanying the SOFTWARE PRODUCT.

5. **U.S. GOVERNMENT RESTRICTED RIGHTS.** The SOFTWARE PRODUCT and documentation are provided with RESTRICTED RIGHTS. Use, duplication, or disclosure by the Government is subject to restrictions as set forth in subparagraph (c)(1)(ii) of the Rights in Technical Data and Computer Software clause at DFARS 252.227-7013 or subparagraphs (c)(1) and (2) of the Commercial Computer Software-Restricted Rights at 48 CFR 52.227-19, as applicable. Manufacturer is Microsoft Corporation/One Microsoft Way/Redmond, WA 98052-6399.

6. **EXPORT RESTRICTIONS.** You agree that you will not export or re-export the SOFTWARE PRODUCT, any part thereof, or any process or service that is the direct product of the SOFTWARE PRODUCT (the foregoing collectively referred to as the "Restricted Components"), to any country, person, entity or end user subject to U.S. export restrictions. You specifically agree not to export or re-export any of the Restricted Components (i) to any country to which the U.S. has embargoed or restricted the export of goods or services, which currently include, but are not necessarily limited to Cuba, Iran, Iraq, Libya, North Korea, Sudan and Syria, or to any national of any such country, wherever located, who intends to transmit or transport the Restricted Components back to such country; (ii) to any end-user who you know or have reason to know will utilize the Restricted Components in the design, development or production of nuclear, chemical or biological weapons; or (iii) to any end-user who has been prohibited from participating in U.S. export transactions by any federal agency of the U.S. government. You warrant and represent that neither the BXA nor any other U.S. federal agency has suspended, revoked, or denied your export privileges.

7. **NOTE ON JAVA SUPPORT.** THE SOFTWARE PRODUCT MAY CONTAIN SUPPORT FOR PROGRAMS WRITTEN IN JAVA. JAVA TECHNOLOGY IS NOT FAULT TOLERANT AND IS NOT DESIGNED, MANUFACTURED, OR INTENDED FOR USE OR RESALE AS ON-LINE CONTROL EQUIPMENT IN HAZARDOUS ENVIRONMENTS REQUIRING FAIL-SAFE PERFORMANCE, SUCH AS IN THE OPERATION OF NUCLEAR FACILITIES, AIRCRAFT NAVIGATION OR COMMUNICATION SYSTEMS, AIR TRAFFIC CONTROL, DIRECT LIFE SUPPORT MACHINES, OR WEAPONS SYSTEMS, IN WHICH THE FAILURE OF JAVA TECHNOLOGY COULD LEAD DIRECTLY TO DEATH, PERSONAL INJURY, OR SEVERE PHYSICAL OR ENVIRONMENTAL DAMAGE.

MISCELLANEOUS

If you acquired this product in the United States, this EULA is governed by the laws of the State of Washington. If you acquired this product in Canada, this EULA is governed by the laws of the Province of Ontario, Canada. Each of the parties hereto irrevocably attorns to the jurisdiction of the courts of the Province of Ontario and further agrees to commence any litigation which may arise hereunder in the courts located in the Judicial District of York, Province of Ontario. If this product was acquired outside the United States, then local law may apply. Should you have any questions concerning this EULA, or if you desire to contact Microsoft for any reason, please contact Microsoft, or write: Microsoft Sales Information Center/One Microsoft Way/Redmond, WA 98052-6399.

LIMITED WARRANTY

LIMITED WARRANTY. Microsoft warrants that (a) the SOFTWARE PRODUCT will perform substantially in accordance with the accompanying written materials for a period of ninety (90) days from the date of receipt, and (b) any Support Services provided by Microsoft shall be substantially as described in applicable written materials provided to you by Microsoft, and Microsoft support engineers will make commercially reasonable efforts to solve any problem. To the extent allowed by applicable law, implied warranties on the SOFTWARE PRODUCT, if any, are limited to ninety (90) days. Some states/jurisdictions do not allow limitations on duration of an implied warranty, so the above limitation may not apply to you.

CUSTOMER REMEDIES. Microsoft's and its suppliers' entire liability and your exclusive remedy shall be, at Microsoft's option, either (a) return of the price paid, or (b) repair or replacement of the SOFTWARE PRODUCT that does not meet Microsoft's Limited Warranty and that is returned to Microsoft with a copy of your receipt. This Limited Warranty is void if failure of the SOFTWARE PRODUCT has resulted from accident, abuse, or misapplication. Any replacement SOFTWARE PRODUCT will be warranted for the remainder of the original warranty period or thirty (30) days, whichever is longer. Outside the United States, neither these remedies nor any product support services offered by Microsoft are available without proof of purchase from an authorized international source.

NO OTHER WARRANTIES. TO THE MAXIMUM EXTENT PERMITTED BY APPLICABLE LAW, MICROSOFT AND ITS SUPPLIERS DISCLAIM ALL OTHER WARRANTIES AND CONDITIONS, EITHER EXPRESS OR IMPLIED, INCLUDING, BUT NOT LIMITED TO, IMPLIED WARRANTIES OR CONDITIONS OF MERCHANTABILITY, FITNESS FOR A PARTICULAR PURPOSE, TITLE AND NON-INFRINGEMENT, WITH REGARD TO THE SOFTWARE PRODUCT, AND THE PROVISION OF OR FAILURE TO PROVIDE SUPPORT SERVICES. THIS LIMITED WARRANTY GIVES YOU SPECIFIC LEGAL RIGHTS. YOU MAY HAVE OTHERS, WHICH VARY FROM STATE/JURISDICTION TO STATE/JURISDICTION.

LIMITATION OF LIABILITY. TO THE MAXIMUM EXTENT PERMITTED BY APPLICABLE LAW, IN NO EVENT SHALL MICROSOFT OR ITS SUPPLIERS BE LIABLE FOR ANY SPECIAL, INCIDENTAL, INDIRECT, OR CONSEQUENTIAL DAMAGES WHATSOEVER (INCLUDING, WITHOUT LIMITATION, DAMAGES FOR LOSS OF BUSINESS PROFITS, BUSINESS INTERRUPTION, LOSS OF BUSINESS INFORMATION, OR ANY OTHER PECUNIARY LOSS) ARISING OUT OF THE USE OF OR INABILITY TO USE THE SOFTWARE PRODUCT OR THE FAILURE TO PROVIDE SUPPORT SERVICES, EVEN IF MICROSOFT HAS BEEN ADVISED OF THE POSSIBILITY OF SUCH DAMAGES. IN ANY CASE, MICROSOFT'S ENTIRE LIABILITY UNDER ANY PROVISION OF THIS EULA SHALL BE LIMITED TO THE GREATER OF THE AMOUNT ACTUALLY PAID BY YOU FOR THE SOFTWARE PRODUCT OR U.S.$5.00; PROVIDED, HOWEVER, IF YOU HAVE ENTERED INTO A MICROSOFT SUPPORT SERVICES AGREEMENT, MICROSOFT'S ENTIRE LIABILITY REGARDING SUPPORT SERVICES SHALL BE GOVERNED BY THE TERMS OF THAT AGREEMENT. BECAUSE SOME STATES/JURISDICTIONS DO NOT ALLOW THE EXCLUSION OR LIMITATION OF LIABILITY, THE ABOVE LIMITATION MAY NOT APPLY TO YOU.